Real-Time Rendering

Real-Time Rendering

Tomas Möller
Eric Haines

A K Peters
Natick, Massachusetts

Editorial, Sales, and Customer Service Office

A K Peters, Ltd.
63 South Avenue
Natick, MA 01760

Cover images: Top left column (cars at night): Courtesy of Digital Illusions CE AB. Top right column (cars at daylight): Courtesy of Nya Perspektiv AB.
Top row (castle images): Courtesy of Agata and Andrzej Wojaczek (agand@clo.com), Advanced Graphics Applications Inc.
Bottom row (checkerboard images): Courtesy of J.L. Mitchell and E. Hart, ATI Technologies Inc.
Back cover: Courtesy of Digital Illusions CE AB and Matrox Graphics Inc.

Library of Congress Cataloging-in-Publication Data

Möller, Tomas, 1971-
   Real-time rendering / Tomas Möller, Eric Haines.
       p.   cm.
   Includes bibliographical references.
    ISBN 1-56881-101-2
    1. Computer graphics. 2. Real-time data processing. I. Haines, Eric, 1958- . II. Title.
   T385.M635   1999   99-29006
    006.6'773--dc21   CIP

Printed in the United States of America
03 02 01 00   10 9 8 7 6 5 4 3

Dedicated to Eva Akenine
T.M.

Dedicated to Cathy Haines
E.H.

Contents

Preface   **xiii**

1   Introduction   **1**
  1.1   Contents Overview   2
  1.2   Notation and Definitions   3
     1.2.1   Mathematical Notation   3
     1.2.2   Geometrical Definitions   5

2   The Graphics Rendering Pipeline   **7**
  2.1   Architecture   8
  2.2   The Application Stage 10
  2.3   The Geometry Stage 11
     2.3.1   Model and View Transform 12
     2.3.2   Lighting and Shading 13
     2.3.3   Projection 14
     2.3.4   Clipping 16
     2.3.5   Screen Mapping 16
  2.4   The Rasterizer Stage 17
  2.5   Through the Pipeline 20

3   Transforms   **23**
  3.1   Basic Transforms 25
     3.1.1   Translation Matrix 25
     3.1.2   Rotation Matrices 26
     3.1.3   Scaling Matrix 27
     3.1.4   Shearing Matrices 29
     3.1.5   Concatenation of Transforms 31
     3.1.6   The Rigid-Body Transform 33
     3.1.7   Normal Transform 34
     3.1.8   Computation of Inverses 35
  3.2   Special Matrix Transforms and Operations 36
     3.2.1   The Euler Transform 36

	3.2.2	Extracting Parameters from the Euler Transform	38
	3.2.3	Matrix Decomposition	40
	3.2.4	Rotation About an Arbitrary Axis	41
3.3	Quaternions		42
	3.3.1	Mathematical Background	43
	3.3.2	Quaternion Transforms	45
3.4	Interpolation		52
3.5	Projections		57
	3.5.1	Orthographic Projection	57
	3.5.2	Perspective Projection	60

4 Visual Appearance — **65**

4.1	Light Sources		65
4.2	Material		67
4.3	Lighting and Shading		68
	4.3.1	Diffuse Component	71
	4.3.2	Specular Component	73
	4.3.3	Ambient Component	77
	4.3.4	Lighting Equation	78
4.4	Aliasing and Antialiasing		81
4.5	Transparency, Alpha, and Compositing		85
4.6	Fog		89
4.7	Gamma Correction		93

5 Texturing — **99**

5.1	Generalized Texturing		100
5.2	Image Texturing		106
	5.2.1	Magnification	107
	5.2.2	Minification	108
5.3	Texture Caching and Compression		117
5.4	Multipass Rendering		119
5.5	Multitexturing		121
5.6	Texture Animation		122
5.7	Texturing Methods		123
	5.7.1	Alpha Mapping	123
	5.7.2	Light Mapping	124
	5.7.3	Gloss Mapping	125
	5.7.4	Environment Mapping	127
	5.7.5	Bump Mapping	136
	5.7.6	Other Texturing Techniques	143

6 Special Effects **145**
   6.1 The Rendering Spectrum 146
   6.2 Image-Based Rendering 147
      6.2.1 Lens Flare and Bloom 150
      6.2.2 Billboarding 152
      6.2.3 Full-Screen Billboarding 155
      6.2.4 Particle Systems 156
      6.2.5 Fixed-View Effects 157
   6.3 Motion Blur 158
   6.4 Depth of Field 159
   6.5 Reflections 160
      6.5.1 Planar Reflections 161
      6.5.2 Glossy Effects 165
      6.5.3 Reflections from Curved Reflectors 166
   6.6 Shadows 167
      6.6.1 Planar Shadows 167
      6.6.2 Shadows on Curved Surfaces 175
   6.7 Lines 183
      6.7.1 Edge Highlighting 184
      6.7.2 Polygon Edge Rendering 184
      6.7.3 Hidden-Line Rendering 185
      6.7.4 Haloing 186
   6.8 Height-Field and Volume Rendering 186

7 Speed-Up Techniques **191**
   7.1 Culling Techniques 191
      7.1.1 Backface and Clustered Culling 192
      7.1.2 Hierarchical View-Frustum Culling 194
      7.1.3 Portal Culling 200
      7.1.4 Detail Culling 203
      7.1.5 Occlusion Culling 204
   7.2 Impostors 218
      7.2.1 Nailboards 221
      7.2.2 Hierarchical Image Caching 222
      7.2.3 Related Work 224
   7.3 Levels of Detail 224
      7.3.1 Discrete Geometry LODs 225
      7.3.2 Alpha LODs 226
      7.3.3 Geomorph LODs 227
      7.3.4 LOD Management 228
   7.4 Triangle Strips, Fans, and Meshes 231

7.4.1   Strips 232
7.4.2   Fans 235
7.4.3   Creating Strips 236
7.4.4   Polygon Meshes 240

8   Pipeline Optimization   **241**
8.1   Locating the Bottleneck 242
      8.1.1   Testing the Application Stage 243
      8.1.2   Testing the Geometry Stage 243
      8.1.3   Testing the Rasterizer Stage 244
8.2   Optimization 244
      8.2.1   Application Stage 244
      8.2.2   Geometry Stage 248
      8.2.3   Rasterizer Stage 250
      8.2.4   Overall Optimization 252
8.3   Balancing the Graphics Pipeline 254
8.4   Host and Accelerator 258
8.5   Multiprocessing 260
      8.5.1   Multiprocessor Pipelining 260
      8.5.2   Parallel Processing 264

9   Polygonal Techniques   **267**
9.1   Sources of Three-Dimensional Data 268
9.2   Tessellation 269
      9.2.1   Shading Problems 271
      9.2.2   Edge Cracking and T-Vertices 274
9.3   Consolidation 275
9.4   Simplification 281

10   Intersection Test Methods   **289**
10.1   Definitions 291
10.2   Rules of Thumb 295
10.3   Ray/Sphere Intersection 295
       10.3.1   Mathematical Solution 296
       10.3.2   Optimized Solution 297
10.4   Ray/Box Intersection 299
       10.4.1   Slabs Method 299
       10.4.2   Woo's Method 302
10.5   Ray/Triangle Intersection 303
       10.5.1   Intersection Algorithm 303
       10.5.2   Implementation 305

10.6 Ray/Polygon Intersection 306
    10.6.1 The Crossings Test 307
10.7 Plane/Box Intersection Detection 310
    10.7.1 AABB 311
    10.7.2 OBB 312
10.8 Triangle/Triangle Intersection 313
    10.8.1 Interval Overlap Method 314
    10.8.2 ERIT's Method 317
    10.8.3 Performance Comparison 318
10.9 Cube/Polygon Intersection 319
    10.9.1 General Algorithm 319
10.10 BV/BV Intersection Tests 322
    10.10.1 Sphere/Box Intersection 323
    10.10.2 AABB/AABB Intersection 324
    10.10.3 k-DOP/k-DOP Intersection 324
    10.10.4 OBB/OBB Intersection 325
10.11 View Frustrum Intersection 330
    10.11.1 Frustum/Sphere Intersection 332
    10.11.2 Frustum/Box Intersection 335
10.12 Line/Line Intersection Tests 336
    10.12.1 Two Dimensions 336
    10.12.2 Three Dimensions 338
10.13 Intersection Between Three Planes 339

11 Collision Detection   **341**
11.1 Collision Detection with Rays 343
11.2 General Hierarchical Collision Detection 344
    11.2.1 Hierarchy Building 345
    11.2.2 Collision Testing between Hierarchies 347
    11.2.3 Cost Function 348
11.3 OBBTree 349
11.4 k-DOPTree 354
11.5 A Multiple Objects CD System 357
    11.5.1 The First-Level CD 358
    11.5.2 Summary 360

12 Graphics Hardware   **363**
12.1 Buffers and Buffering 363
    12.1.1 A Simple Display System 363
    12.1.2 The Color Buffer 365
    12.1.3 Z-buffering and W-buffering 368

12.1.4 Single, Double, and Triple Buffering 370
12.1.5 Stereo Buffers 372
12.1.6 Stencil and Accumulation Buffering 373
12.1.7 Memory 374
12.2 Architecture 375
12.2.1 General 375
12.2.2 Case Study: Neon 378
12.2.3 Case Study: VISUALIZE fx 380
12.2.4 Case Study: InfiniteReality 383
12.2.5 Other Architectures 386

13 The Future   **389**
13.1 Everything Else 389
13.2 You 391

A Some Linear Algebra   **395**
A.1 The Euclidean Space 396
A.2 Geometrical Interpretation 398
A.3 Matrices 403
A.3.1 Definitions and Operations 403
A.3.2 Change of Base 410
A.4 Homogeneous Notation 411
A.5 Geometry 412
A.5.1 Lines 412
A.5.2 Planes 414
A.5.3 Convex Hull 415
A.5.4 Miscellaneous 416

B Trigonometry   **419**
B.1 Definitions 419
B.2 Trigonometric Laws and Formulae 421

References   **427**

Index   **463**

Preface

The title *Real-Time Rendering* pretty much sums it up. This book is about algorithms which create synthetic images fast enough that the viewer can interact with a virtual environment. We have focused on three-dimensional rendering and, to a limited extent, user interaction. Modeling, animation, and many other areas are important to the process of making a real-time application, but these topics are beyond the scope of this book.

This field is rapidly evolving and so it is a moving target. Graphics accelerators for the consumer market are currently doubling in speed every six months. Graphics libraries appear, evolve, and often die out. For these reasons we have avoided describing specific APIs, chipsets, buses, memory architectures, etc., except where it serves the goal of informing you, the reader, about some general concept. We have endeavored to describe algorithms that, by their popularity or lasting value, are likely to be used for some time to come.

We expect you to have some basic understanding of computer graphics before reading this book. The equivalent of a semester course in graphics should be sufficient, though we cannot guarantee we will not sometimes lose you along the way. Some of the later chapters in particular are meant for implementors of various complex algorithms. If some section does pass you by, skim on through. One of the most valuable services we feel we can provide is to at least let you realize what you do not yet know, and to know where to look for it later.

This book does not exist in a vacuum; we make a point of referencing relevant material wherever possible, as well as providing a summary of further reading and resources at the end of most chapters. We also spent much time searching for reference locations on the web; many current papers are available there for free. The days are coming to an end when only those living near a good research library could learn about various algorithms.

Because web resources are notoriously transient and because the field is evolving so rapidly, we maintain a web site related to this book at http://www.realtimerendering.com/. The site contains links to tutorials, demonstration programs, code samples, software libraries, and much more.

Our true goal and guiding light while writing this book was simple. We wanted to write a book that we wished we had owned when we had started out, a book that was both unified yet crammed with details not found in introductory texts. We hope that you will find this book, our view of the world, of some use in your travels.

Acknowledgements

Many people helped in making this book. Some of the greatest contributions were made by those who reviewed parts of it. The reviewers willingly gave the benefit of their expertise, helping to significantly improve both content and style. We wish to thank (in alphabetical order) Thomas Barregren, Michael Cohen, Walt Donovan, Angus Dorbie, Michael Garland, Stefan Gottschalk, Ned Greene, Ming C. Lin, Jason L. Mitchell, Liang Peng, Keith Rule, Ken Shoemake, John Stone, Phil Taylor, Ben Trumbore, Jorrit Tyberghein, and Nick Wilt. We cannot thank you enough.

Many other people contributed their time and labor to this project. Some let us use images, others provided models, still others pointed out important resources or connected us with people who could help. In addition to the people listed above, we wish to acknowledge the help of Tony Barkans, Daniel Baum, Nelson Beebe, Curtis Beeson, Tor Berg, David Blythe, Chas. Boyd, Don Brittain, Ian Bullard, Javier Castellar, Satyan Coorg, Jason Della Rocca, Paul Diefenbach, Alyssa Donovan, Dave Eberly, Kells Elmquist, Stuart Feldman, Fred Fisher, Tom Forsyth, Marty Franz, Thomas Funkhouser, Andrew Glassner, Bruce Gooch, Larry Gritz, Robert Grzeszczuk, Paul Haeberli, Evan Hart, Paul Heckbert, Chris Hecker, Joachim Helenklaken, Hugues Hoppe, John Jack, Mark Kilgard, David Kirk, James Klosowski, Subodh Kumar, André LaMothe, Jeff Lander, Jens Larsson, Jed Lengyel, Fredrik Liliegren, David Luebke, Thomas Lundqvist, Tom McReynolds, Stan Melax, Don Mitchell, André Möller, Steve Molnar, Scott R. Nelson, Hubert Nguyen, Doug Rogers, Holly Rushmeier, Gernot Schaufler, Jonas Skeppstedt, Stephen Spencer, Per Stenström, Jacob Ström, Filippo Tampieri, Gary Tarolli, Ken Turkowski, Turner Whitted, Agata and Andrzej Wojaczek, Andrew Woo, Steve Worley, Brian Yen, Hans-Philip Zachau, Gabriel Zachmann, and Al Zimmerman. We also wish to thank the journal *ACM Transactions on Graphics* for providing a stable web site for this book.

Alice and Klaus Peters and the staff at A K Peters, particularly Carolyn Artin and Sarah Gillis, have been instrumental in making this book a reality. To all of you, thanks.

Finally, our deepest thanks go to our families and friends for providing support throughout this incredible, sometimes grueling, often exhilarating process.

Tomas Möller
Eric Haines
March, 1999

Chapter 1
Introduction

Real-time rendering is concerned with making images rapidly on the computer. It is the most highly interactive area of computer graphics. An image appears on the screen, the viewer acts or reacts, and this feedback affects what is generated next. This cycle of reaction and rendering happens at a rapid enough rate that the viewer does not see individual images but rather becomes immersed in a dynamic process.

The rate at which images are displayed is measured in frames per second (fps) or Hertz (Hz). At one frame per second, there is little sense of interactivity; the user is painfully aware of the arrival of each new image. At around 6 fps, a sense of interactivity starts to grow. An application displaying at 15 fps is certainly real-time; the user focuses on action and reaction. There is a useful limit, however: from about 72 fps and up, differences in the display rate are effectively indetectable.

However, there is more to real-time rendering than interactivity. If this was the only criterion, any application that rapidly responded to user commands and drew anything on the screen would qualify. Rendering in real-time usually means three-dimensional rendering.

Interactivity and some sense of connection to three-dimensional space are sufficient conditions for real-time rendering, but a third element is rapidly becoming part of its definition: graphics acceleration hardware. While hardware dedicated to three-dimensional graphics has been available on professional workstations for many years, it is only relatively recently that the use of such accelerators at the consumer level has become possible. With the recent rapid advances in this market, add-on three-dimensional graphics accelerators are becoming as standard for home computers as a pair of speakers. While it is not absolutely required for real-time rendering, graphics accelerator hardware is becoming an important component of more and more real-time applications. Two excellent examples of the results of real-time rendering made possible by hardware acceleration are shown in Plate I and Plate II (following p. 194).

1

1.1   Contents Overview

What follows is a brief overview of the chapters ahead.

Chapter 2, The Graphics Rendering Pipeline. This chapter deals with the heart of real-time rendering, the mechanism that takes a scene description and converts it into something we can see.

Chapter 3, Transforms. The basic tools to manipulate position, scaling, orientation, etc, of objects and the viewer are transforms.

Chapter 4, Visual Appearance. This chapter covers the definition of materials and lights and their use in achieving a realistic surface appearance. Also covered are other appearance-related topics, such as providing higher image quality through antialiasing and gamma correction.

Chapter 5, Texturing. One of the most powerful hardware-accelerated tools for real-time rendering is the ability to display data such as images on surfaces. This chapter discusses the mechanics of this technique, called texturing, and presents a wide variety of methods for applying it.

Chapter 6, Special Effects. There is more to rendering than creating surfaces, materials, and textures. This chapter presents techniques and tricks beyond the basics.

Chapter 7, Speed-Up Techniques. After you make it go, make it go fast. Various forms of culling, model representation, and geometry consolidation are covered here.

Chapter 8, Pipeline Optimization. Once an application is running and uses efficient algorithms, it can be made even faster using various optimization techniques. Finding the bottleneck and deciding what to do about it are the topics covered here.

Chapter 9, Polygonal Techniques. Geometric data comes from a wide range of sources, and sometimes requires modification in order to be rendered rapidly and well. This chapter discusses polygonal data and ways to clean it up and simplify it.

Chapter 10, Intersection Test Methods. Intersection testing is important for rendering, user interaction, and collision detection. In-depth coverage is provided here for a wide range of the most efficient algorithms for common geometric intersection tests.

Chapter 11, Collision Detection. Finding out whether two objects touch each other is a key element of many real-time applications. This chapter presents some efficient algorithms in this rapidly evolving field.

Chapter 12, Graphics Hardware. While graphics-hardware-accelerated algorithms have been discussed in the previous chapters, this chapter focuses on components such as color depth, frame buffers, and basic architecture types.

Case studies of a few representative graphics accelerators are provided.

Chapter 13, The Future. Take a guess (we do).

We have included appendices on linear algebra and trigonometry.

1.2 Notation and Definitions

First, we shall explain the mathematical notation used in this book. For a more thorough explanation of many of the terms used in this section, see Appendix A.

1.2.1 Mathematical Notation

Table 1 summarizes most of the mathematical notation we will use. Some of the concepts will be described at some length here.

Type	Notation	Examples
angle	lower-case Greek	$\alpha_i, \phi, \rho, \eta, \gamma_{242}, \theta$
scalar	lower-case italic	a, b, t, u_k, v, w_{ij}
vector or point	lower-case bold	$\mathbf{a}, \mathbf{u}, \mathbf{v}_s \; \mathbf{h}(\rho), \mathbf{h}_z$
matrix	capital bold	$\mathbf{T}(t), \mathbf{X}, \mathbf{R}_x(\rho)$
plane	π: a vector + a scalar	$\pi : \mathbf{n} \cdot \mathbf{x} + d,$ $\pi_1 : \mathbf{n}_1 \cdot \mathbf{x} + d_1$
triangle	$\triangle$ 3 points	$\triangle \mathbf{v}_0 \mathbf{v}_1 \mathbf{v}_2, \triangle \mathbf{cba}$
line segment	two points	$\mathbf{uv}, \mathbf{a}_i \mathbf{b}_j$
geometric entity	capital italic	A_{OBB}, T, B_{AABB}

Table 1. Summary of the notation used in this book.

The angles and the scalars are taken from $\mathbb{R}$, i.e., they are real numbers. Vectors and points are denoted by bold lower-case letters, and the components are accessed as

$$\mathbf{v} = \begin{pmatrix} v_x \\ v_y \\ v_z \end{pmatrix},$$

that is, in column vector format, which is commonly used in the computer graphics world. For example, the following books use this sort of vector and matrix notation: *Computer Graphics— Principles and Practice* [108], *Introduction to*

Computer Graphics [109], and *Interactive Computer Graphics—A top-down approach with OpenGL* [11]. At some places in the text we use (v_x, v_y, v_z) instead of the formally more correct $(v_x \ v_y \ v_z)^T$, since the former is easier to read.

In homogeneous coordinates (see Appendix section A.4), a coordinate is represented by $\mathbf{v} = (v_x \ v_y \ v_z \ v_w)^T$, where a vector is $\mathbf{v} = (v_x \ v_y \ v_z \ 0)^T$ and a point is $\mathbf{v} = (v_x \ v_y \ v_z \ 1)^T$. Sometimes we use only 3-element vectors and points, but we try to avoid any ambiguity as to which type is being used at any point. For matrix manipulations it is extremely advantageous to have the same notation for vectors as for points (see chapter 3 on transforms and appendix section A.4 on homogeneous notation). In some algorithms it will be convenient to use numeric indices instead of x, y, and z, for example $\mathbf{v} = (v_0 \ v_1 \ v_2)^T$. All of these rules for vectors and points also hold for 2-element vectors; in that case, we simply skip the last component of a 3-element vector.

The matrix deserves a bit more explanation. The common sizes that will be used are 2×2, 3×3, and 4×4. We will review the manner of accessing a 3×3 matrix $\mathbf{M}$, and it is simple to extend this process to the other sizes. The (scalar) elements of $\mathbf{M}$ are denoted m_{ij}, $0 \le (i,j) \le 2$, where i denotes the row and j the column, as in Equation 1.1.

$$\mathbf{M} = \begin{pmatrix} m_{00} & m_{01} & m_{02} \\ m_{10} & m_{11} & m_{12} \\ m_{20} & m_{21} & m_{22} \end{pmatrix} \tag{1.1}$$

The following notation, shown in Equation 1.2 for a 3×3 matrix, is used to isolate vectors from the matrix $\mathbf{M}$: $\mathbf{m}_{,j}$ represents the jth column vector and $\mathbf{m}_{i,}$ represents the ith row vector (in column vector form). As with vectors and points, indexing the column vectors can also be done with x, y, z, and sometimes w, if that is more convenient.

$$\mathbf{M} = \begin{pmatrix} \mathbf{m}_{,0} & \mathbf{m}_{,1} & \mathbf{m}_{,2} \end{pmatrix} = \begin{pmatrix} \mathbf{m}_x & \mathbf{m}_y & \mathbf{m}_z \end{pmatrix} = \begin{pmatrix} \mathbf{m}_{0,}^T \\ \mathbf{m}_{1,}^T \\ \mathbf{m}_{2,}^T \end{pmatrix} \tag{1.2}$$

A plane is denoted $\pi : \mathbf{n} \cdot \mathbf{x} + d$ and contains its mathematical formula, the plane normal $\mathbf{n}$ and the scalar d. π is the common mathematical notation for a plane. The plane π is said to divide the space into a *positive half-space*, where $\mathbf{n} \cdot \mathbf{x} + d > 0$, and a *negative half-space*, where $\mathbf{n} \cdot \mathbf{x} + d < 0$. All other points are said to lie in the plane.

A triangle can be defined by three points $\mathbf{v}_0$, $\mathbf{v}_1$, and $\mathbf{v}_2$ and is denoted by $\triangle \mathbf{v}_0 \mathbf{v}_1 \mathbf{v}_2$.

Table 1.2 presents a few additional mathematical operators and their notation. The dot, cross, determinant, and length operators are covered in Appendix A.

	Operator	Description
1:	$\cdot$	dot product
2:	$\times$	cross product
3:	$\mathbf{v}^T$	transpose of the vector $\mathbf{v}$
4:	$\otimes$	piecewise vector multiplication
5:	$\perp$	the unary, perp dot product operator
6:	$\|\cdot\|$	determinant of a matrix
7:	$\|\cdot\|$	absolute value of a scalar
8:	$\|\cdot\|$	length (or norm) of argument

Table 1.2. Notation for some mathematical operators.

The transpose operator turns a column vector into a row vector and vice versa. Thus a column vector can be written in compressed form in a block of text as $\mathbf{v} = (v_x \ v_y \ v_z)^T$. Operator 4 requires further explanation: $\mathbf{u} \otimes \mathbf{v}$ denotes the vector $(u_x v_x \ u_y v_y \ u_z v_z)^T$, i.e., component i of vector $\mathbf{u}$ and component i of vector $\mathbf{v}$ are multiplied and stored in component i of a new vector. In this text this operator is used exclusively for color vector manipulations. Operator 5, introduced in *Graphics Gems IV* [184], is a unary operator on a two-dimensional vector. Letting this operator work on a vector $\mathbf{v} = (v_x \ v_y)^T$ gives a vector that is perpendicular to $\mathbf{v}$, i.e., $\mathbf{v}^{\perp} = (-v_y \ v_x)^T$. Note also that we use $|a|$ to denote the absolute value of the scalar a, while $|\mathbf{A}|$ means the determinant of the matrix $\mathbf{A}$. Sometimes, we also use $|\mathbf{A}| = |\mathbf{a} \ \mathbf{b} \ \mathbf{c}| = \det(\mathbf{a}, \mathbf{b}, \mathbf{c})$, where $\mathbf{a}$, $\mathbf{b}$, and $\mathbf{c}$ are column vectors of the matrix $\mathbf{A}$.

Further on, we call the common planes $x = 0$, $y = 0$, and $z = 0$ the *coordinate planes* or *axis-aligned planes*. The axes $\mathbf{e}_x = (1 \ 0 \ 0)^T$, $\mathbf{e}_y = (0 \ 1 \ 0)^T$, and $\mathbf{e}_z = (0 \ 0 \ 1)^T$ are called *main axes* or *main directions* and sometimes the x-axis, y-axis and z-axis. This set of axes is often called the *standard basis*. Unless otherwise noted, we will use orthonormal bases (consisting of mutually perpendicular unit vectors; see Appendix section A.3.1).

We use a right-hand coordinate system (see Appendix section A.2) since this is the standard system for three-dimensional geometry in the field of computer graphics.

Colors are represented by a three-element vector, such as $(red, green, blue)$, where each element has the range $[0, 1]$.

1.2.2 Geometrical Definitions

The rendering primitives (also called drawing primitives) used by most graphics hardware are points, lines, and triangles.[1]

---

[1]The only exceptions we know of are Pixel-Planes [112], which could draw spheres, and the NVIDIA NV1 chip, which could draw ellipsoids.

Throughout this book, we will refer to a collection of geometric entities as either a *model* or an *object*. A *scene* is a collection of models comprising everything that is included in the environment to be rendered. A scene can also include material descriptions, lighting, and viewing specifications.

Examples of objects are a car, a building, and even a line. In practice, an object often consists of a set of drawing primitives, but this may not always be the case; an object may have a higher kind of geometrical representation, such as Bézier curves or surfaces, Non-Uniform Rational B-Splines (NURBS), subdivision surfaces, etc. Also, objects can consist of other objects, e.g., we call a car model's door an object or a subset of the car.

Further Reading and Resources

The most important resource we can refer you to is the website for this book, `http://www.realtimerendering.com/`. It contains links to the latest information and websites relevant to each chapter. The field of real-time rendering is changing with real-time speed. In the book we have attempted to focus on concepts that are fundamental and techniques that are unlikely to go out of style. On the website we have the opportunity to present information that is relevant to today's software developer and the ability to remain up-to-date.

Chapter 2
The Graphics Rendering Pipeline

"A chain is no stronger than its weakest link"
–Anonymous

This chapter is concerned with presenting the core of real-time graphics, namely, the *graphics rendering pipeline*, hereafter referred to as the rendering pipeline or simply the pipeline. The main function of the pipeline is to generate, or *render*, a two-dimensional image, given a virtual camera, three-dimensional objects, light sources, lighting models, textures, and more. The rendering pipeline is thus the underlying tool for real-time rendering. The process of using the pipeline is depicted in Figure 2.1. The locations and shapes of the objects in the image are determined by their geometry, the placement of the camera in the environment and the characteristics of that environment. The appearance of the objects is affected by material properties, light sources, textures, and lighting models.

The different stages of the rendering pipeline will be discussed and explained here, with focus on the function and not on the implementation. This is because some of the implementation will be dealt with in later chapters, but also because some stages are taken as givens. For example, what is important to someone using lines are characteristics such as vertex data formats, colors and pattern types, and whether, say, depth cueing is available, not whether lines are implemented via Bresenham's line drawing algorithm [48] or via a symmetric double-step algorithm [387]. Often these stages are implemented in hardware, which makes it impossible to optimize or improve on the implementation. Details of basic draw and fill algorithms are covered in depth in books such as Rogers's [300]. What we can optimize is how and when we use the given implementations.

The goal of this chapter is thus to provide a detailed understanding of the function of the rendering of images, while omitting discussion of implementation issues.

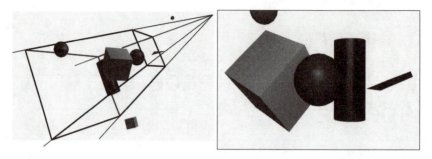

Figure 2.1. In the left image, a virtual camera is located at the tip of the pyramid (where four lines converge). Only the primitives inside the view volume are rendered. For an image that is rendered in perspective (as is the case here), the view volume is a frustum, i.e., a truncated pyramid with a rectangular base. The right image shows what the camera "sees." Note the bottommost cube in the left image is not in the rendering to the right because it is located outside the view frustum. Also, the triangle in the left image is clipped against the smaller (*hither*) plane of the frustum, which results in a quadrilateral.

2.1   Architecture

In our world, pipelines appear in many different forms, from oil pipelines to factory assembly lines to ski lifts. They also appear in graphics rendering.

A pipeline consists of several stages [180]. In the case of the oil pipeline, oil cannot move from the first stage of the pipeline to the second until the oil already in that second stage has moved on to the third stage, and so forth. This implies that the speed of the pipeline is determined by its slowest pipeline stage, no matter how fast the other stages may be.

Ideally, a non-pipelined construction that is divided into n pipelined stages should give a speed-up of a factor of n, which is the reason to use it. For example, a ski chairlift containing only one chair is inefficient; adding more chairs creates a proportional speed-up in the number of skiers brought up the hill. The pipeline stages execute in parallel, but they are stalled until the slowest stage has finished its task. For example, if the steering wheel attachment stage on a car assembly line takes three minutes and every other stage takes two minutes, the best rate that can be achieved is one car made every three minutes; the other stages must be idle for one minute while the steering wheel attachment is completed. For this particular pipeline, the steering wheel stage is the *bottleneck*, since it determines the speed of the entire production.

This kind of pipeline construction is also found in the context of real-time computer graphics. A coarse division of the real-time rendering pipeline into three *conceptual stages* is shown in Figure 2.2. The stages are called *application*, *geometry*, and *rasterizer*. This structure is the core—the engine of the

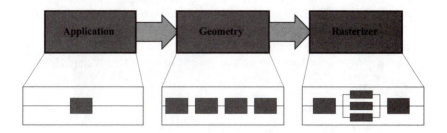

Figure 2.2. The basic construction of the rendering pipeline, consisting of three stages: application, geometry, and the rasterizer. Each of these stages may be a pipeline in itself, as illustrated below the geometry stage, or a stage may be (partly) parallelized as shown below the rasterizer stage. In this illustration, the application stage is a single process, but this stage could also be pipelined or parallelized.

rendering pipeline —which is used in real-time computer graphics applications, and is thus an essential base for the discussion in the subsequent chapters. This pipeline is also found in the majority of computer graphics systems. Each of these stages is usually a pipeline in itself, which means that it consists of several substages. We differentiate between the *conceptual stages* (application, geometry, and rasterizer), functional stages, and pipeline stages. A functional stage has a certain task to perform, but does not specify the way that task is executed in the pipeline. A pipeline stage, on the other hand, is executed simultaneously with all the other pipeline stages. A pipeline stage may also be parallelized in order to meet high performance needs. For example, the geometry stage may be divided into five functional stages, but it is the implementation of a graphics system that determines its division into pipeline stages. A given implementation may combine two functional stages into one pipeline stage, while it divides another, more time-consuming, functional stage into several pipeline stages, or even parallelizes it.

It is the slowest of the pipeline stages that determines the *rendering speed*, the update speed of the images. This speed may be expressed in frames per second (fps), that is, the number of rendered images per second, or in Hz (which is simply the notation for $1/second$, i.e., the frequency). Since we are dealing with a pipeline, it does not suffice to add up the time it takes for all the data we want to render to pass through the entire pipeline. This, of course, is a consequence of the pipeline construction, which allows the stages to execute in parallel. If we could locate the bottleneck, i.e., the slowest stage of the pipeline, and measure how much time it takes data to pass through that stage, then we could compute the rendering speed. Assume, for example, that the bottleneck stage takes 20 ms (milliseconds) to execute, then the rendering speed would be $1/0.020 = 50$ Hz. However, this is only true if the output device can update at this particular speed; otherwise, the true output rate will be slower. In other pipelining contexts, the term *throughput* is used instead of rendering speed.

EXAMPLE: RENDERING SPEED Assume that our output device's maximum update frequency is 60 Hz, and that the bottleneck of the rendering pipeline has been found. Timings show that this stage takes 62.5 ms to execute. The rendering speed is then computed as follows. First, ignore the output device, which gives us a maximum rendering speed of $1/0.0625 = 16$ Hz. Second, adjust this value to the frequency of the output device: 60 Hz implies that rendering speed can be 60 Hz, $60/2 = 30$ Hz, $60/3 = 20$ Hz, $60/4 = 15$ Hz, $60/5 = 12$ Hz, and so forth. This means that we can expect the rendering speed to be 15 Hz, since this is the maximum speed the output device can manage that is less than 16 Hz. □

As the name implies, the application stage is driven by the application and is therefore implemented in software. This stage may, for example, contain collision detection, speed-up techniques, animations, force feedback, etc. The next step, implemented either in software or in hardware, depending on the architecture, is the geometry stage, which deals with transforms, projections, lighting, etc. That is, this stage computes what is to be drawn, how it should be drawn, and where it should be drawn. Finally, the rasterizer stage draws (renders) an image with use of the data that the previous stage generated. This last stage is most often implemented in hardware, but software implementations exist. These stages and their internal pipelines will be discussed in the next three sections.

2.2   The Application Stage

The developer has full control over what happens in the application stage, since it always executes in software. Therefore, the developer can change the implementation in order to change performance. In the other stages it is harder to change the implementation, since parts or all of those stages are built upon hardware. However, it is still possible to affect the time consumed by the geometry and the rasterizer stages, by, for example, decreasing the number of triangles to be rendered during the application stage.

At the end of the application stage, the geometry to be rendered is fed to the next stage in the rendering pipeline. These are the rendering primitives, i.e., points, lines, and triangles, that might eventually end up on the screen (or whatever output device is being used). This is the most important task of the application stage.

A consequence of the software-based implementation of this stage is that it is not divided into substages, as are the geometry and the rasterizer stages.[1] However, this stage could be executed in parallel on several processors in order to increase performance. In CPU design, this would be called a *superscalar* construction, since it is able to execute several things at the same time in the same stage. In Section 8.5, two different methods for utilizing multiple processors will be presented.

One process commonly implemented in this stage is collision detection. After a collision is detected between two objects, a response may be generated and sent back to the colliding objects as well as to a force feedback device. The application stage is also the place to take care of input from other sources, such as the keyboard, the mouse, a virtual reality (VR) helmet, etc. Depending on this input, several different kinds of actions may be taken. Other processes implemented in this stage include texture animation, animations via transforms, geometry morphing, or any kind of calculations that are not performed in any other stages. Speed-up techniques, such as hierarchical-view frustum culling, among others (see Chapter 7), are also implemented here.

2.3 The Geometry Stage

The geometry stage is responsible for the majority of the per-polygon operations or per-vertex operations.[2] This stage is further divided into the functional stages shown in Figure 2.3. Note again that, depending on the implementation, these functional stages may or may not be equivalent to pipeline stages. In some cases,

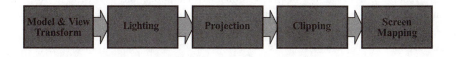

Figure 2.3. The geometry stage subdivided into a pipeline of functional stages.

---

[1]Of course, since it probably executes on a pipelined CPU, you could say that the application stage is further subdivided into several pipeline stages, but this is not relevant here.

[2]An example in which the geometry stage is not involved is vertex morphing (where vertices are moved over time), which takes place in the application stage.

a number of consecutive functional stages form a single pipeline stage (which runs in parallel with the other pipeline stages). In other cases, a functional stage may be subdivided into several smaller pipeline stages.

For example, at one extreme, all stages in the entire rendering pipeline may run in software, and then you could say that your entire pipeline consists of one pipeline stage. At the other extreme, each functional stage could be subdivided into several smaller pipeline stages, and each such pipeline stage could execute on a designated floating point processor.

Also note that the geometry stage performs a very demanding task. With a single light source, each vertex requires approximately 100 individual precision floating point operations [5].

2.3.1 Model and View Transform

On its way to the screen, a model is transformed into several different *spaces* or *coordinate systems*. Originally, a model resides in its own *model space*, which simply means that it has not been transformed at all. Each model can be associated with a *model transform* so that it can be positioned and oriented. It is possible to have several model transforms associated with the same model. This allows several copies (called *instances*) of the same model to have different locations, orientations, and sizes in the same scene, without requiring replication of the basic geometry.

It is the vertices and the normals of the model that are transformed by the model transform. The coordinates of an object are called *model coordinates*, and after the model transform has been applied to these coordinates, the model is said to be located in *world coordinates* or in *world space*. The world space is unique, and after the models have been transformed with their respective model transforms, all models exist in this same space.

As mentioned previously, only the models that the camera (or observer) sees are rendered. The camera has a location in world space and a direction, which are used to place and aim the camera. To facilitate projection and clipping, the camera and all the models are transformed with the *view transform*. The purpose of the view transform is to place the camera at the origin and aim it, to make it look in the direction of the negative z-axis,[3] with the y-axis pointing upwards and the x-axis pointing to the right. The actual position and direction after the view transform has been applied is dependent on the underlying Application Program Interface (API). The space thus delineated is called the *camera space* or more

---

[3]We will be using the $-z$ axis convention; some texts prefer looking down the $+z$ axis. The difference is mostly semantic, as transform between one and the other is simple.

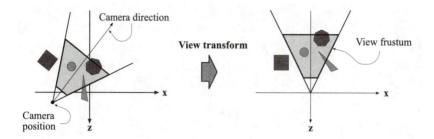

Figure 2.4. In the left illustration, the camera is located and oriented as the user wants it to be. The view transform relocates the camera at the origin looking along the negative z-axis, as shown on the right. This is done to make the clipping and projection operations simpler and faster. The light gray area is the view volume. Here perspective viewing is assumed, since the view volume is a frustum. Similar techniques apply to any kind of projection.

commonly the *eye space*. An example of the way in which the view transform affects the camera and the models is shown in Figure 2.4. Both the model transform and the view transform are implemented as 4×4 matrices, which is the topic of Chapter 3. For efficiency reasons these are usually concatenated into one matrix before transforming the models. If they are concatenated in this way, however, the world space is not available—one moves directly to eye space.

2.3.2   Lighting and Shading

In order to lend models a more realistic appearance, the scene can be equipped with one or more light sources. One may choose whether or not the lights affect the appearance of the geometry. The geometric models may also have a color associated with each vertex, or a texture (an image) "glued onto" them. Figure 2.5 gives an example. Notice how a texture gives the surface a three-dimensional effect without lighting, but solid colors are unconvincing.

For those models that are to be affected by light sources, a *lighting* equation is used to compute a color at each vertex of the model. This equation approximates the real-world interaction between photons and surfaces. In the real world, photons are emitted from light sources and are reflected or absorbed by surfaces. In real-time graphics, not much time can be spent on simulating this phenomenon. For example, true reflections and shadows normally are not part of this equation. Also, models are normally represented graphically by triangles, as these are the geometric primitives used by most graphics hardware. The color at each vertex of the surface is computed using the location of the light sources and their properties, the position and the normal of the vertex, and the properties of the

Figure 2.5. A scene without lighting is on the left, a lit scene on the right.

material belonging to the vertex. Then the colors at the vertices of a triangle are interpolated over the triangle when rendering to the screen. This interpolation technique is called *Gouraud shading* [138]. The lighting equation and shading are treated in more detail in Chapter 4.

Normally, lighting is calculated in world space, but if the light sources are transformed with the view transform, the same lighting effect is obtained in eye space. This is because the relative relationships between light sources, the camera, and the models are preserved if all entities that are included in the lighting calculations are transformed to the same space, namely the eye space.

2.3.3   Projection

After lighting, rendering systems perform *projection*, which transforms the view volume into a unit cube with its extreme points at $(-1 \quad -1 \quad -1)^T$ and $(1 \quad 1 \quad 1)^T$.[4] The unit cube is called the *canonical view volume*. There are essentially two projections methods, namely *orthographic* (also called *parallel* [5]) and *perspective* projection. See Figure 2.6.

The view volume of orthographic viewing is normally a rectangular box, and the orthographic projection transforms this view volume into the unit cube. The main characteristic of orthographic projection is that parallel lines remain parallel after the transform. This transformation is a combination of a translation and a scaling.

---

[4]Different volumes can be used, for example $0 \leq z \leq 1$. Blinn has an interesting article [41] on using other intervals.

[5]Actually, orthographic is just one type of parallel projection. There is also an oblique parallel projection method [162], which is much less common.

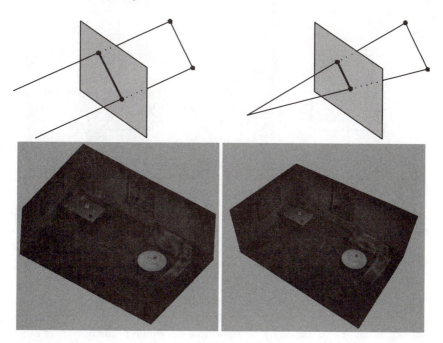

Figure 2.6. On the left is an orthographic, or parallel, projection; on the right is a perspective projection.

The perspective projection is a bit more complex. In this type of projection, the farther away an object lies from the camera, the smaller it appears after projection. In addition, parallel lines may converge at the horizon. The perspective transform thus mimics the way we perceive objects' size. Geometrically, the view volume, called a *frustum*, is a truncated pyramid with rectangular base. The frustum is transformed into the unit cube as well. Both orthographic and perspective transforms can be constructed with 4×4 matrices (see Chapter 3), and after either transform the models are said to be in *normalized device coordinates*.

Although these transformations transform one volume into another, they are called projections because after display the z-coordinate is not stored in the image generated.[6] In this way the models are projected from three to two dimensions.

---

[6] Rather, the z-coordinate is stored in a Z-buffer. See section 2.4.

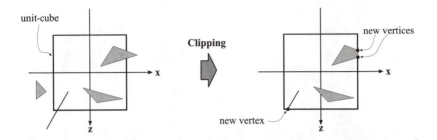

Figure 2.7. After the projection transform, only the primitives inside the unit cube (which correspond to primitives inside the view frustum) are desired for continued processing. Therefore, the primitives outside the unit cube are discarded, primitives totally inside are kept, and primitives intersecting with the unit cube are clipped against the unit cube, and thus new vertices are generated and old ones are discarded.

2.3.4   Clipping

Only the primitives wholly or partially inside the view volume need to be passed on to the rasterizer stage, which then draws them on the screen. A primitive that lies totally inside the view volume will be passed on to the next stage as is. Primitives totally outside the view volume are not passed on further, since they are not rendered. It is the primitives that are partially inside the view volume that require *clipping*. For example, a line that has one vertex outside and one inside the view volume should be clipped against the view volume, so that the vertex that is outside is replaced by a new vertex that is located at the intersection between the line and the view volume. Due to the projection transformation, the transformed primitives are clipped against the unit cube. The advantage of performing the view transformation and projection before clipping is that it makes the clipping problem consistent; primitives are always clipped against the unit cube. The clipping process is depicted in Figure 2.7.

2.3.5   Screen Mapping

Only the (clipped) primitives inside the view volume are passed on to the screen mapping stage, and the coordinates are still three-dimensional when entering this stage. The x- and y-coordinates of each primitive are transformed to form *screen coordinates*. Screen coordinates together with the z-coordinates are also called *window coordinates*. Assume that the scene should be rendered into a window with the minimum corner at (x_1, y_1) and the maximum corner at (x_2, y_2), where $x_1 < x_2$ and $y_1 < y_2$. Then the screen mapping is a translation followed by a

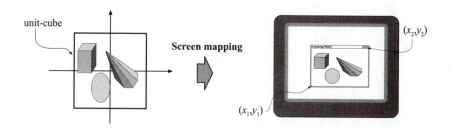

Figure 2.8. The primitives lie in the unit cube after the projection transform, and the screen mapping procedure takes care of finding the coordinates on the screen.

scaling operation. The z-coordinate is not affected by this mapping. The new x- and y-coordinates are said to be screen coordinates. These, along with the z-coordinate ($-1 \leq z \leq 1$), are passed on to the rasterizer stage. The screen mapping process is depicted in Figure 2.8.

2.4 The Rasterizer Stage

Given the transformed and projected vertices, colors, and texture coordinates (all from the geometry stage), the goal of the rasterizer stage is to assign correct colors to the pixels[7] to render an image correctly. This process is called *rasterization* or *scan conversion*, which is thus the conversion from two-dimensional vertices in screen space—with a z-value (depth-value), a color, and possibly a texture coordinate associated with each vertex—into pixels on the screen.[8] Unlike the geometry stage, which handles per-polygon operations, the rasterizer stage handles per-pixel operations. The information for each pixel is located in the *color buffer*, which is a rectangular array of colors (a red, a green, and a blue component for each color). For high-performance graphics, it is critical that the rasterizer stage be implemented in hardware. Akeley and Jermoluk [4] and Rogers [300] offer more information on scan conversion.

---

[7]Short for *picture elements*.

[8]Pipeline diagrams sometimes depict this stage in two parts. The first is called *triangle setup*, in which the various differentials and other data for the triangle's surface are computed, and the second part is called rasterization, in which the pixels are checked and filled.

To avoid allowing the human viewer to see the primitives as they are being rasterized and sent to the screen, *double buffering* is used. This means that the rendering of a scene takes place off screen, in a *back buffer*. Once the scene has been rendered in the back buffer, the contents of the back buffer are swapped with the contents of the *front buffer* which was previously displayed on the screen. The swapping occurs when the electron gun of the monitor cannot disturb the display.

This stage is also responsible for resolving visibility. This means that when the whole scene has been rendered, the color buffer should contain the colors of the primitives in the scene which are visible from the point of view of the camera. For most graphics hardware this is done with the Z-buffer (also called *depth buffer*) algorithm [53].[9] A Z-buffer is the same size and shape as the color buffer, and for each pixel it stores the z-value from the camera to the currently closest primitive. This means that when a primitive is being rendered to a certain pixel, the z-value on that primitive at that pixel is being computed and compared to the contents of the Z-buffer at the same pixel. If the new z-value is smaller than the z-value in the Z-buffer, then the primitive that is being rendered is closer to the camera than the primitive that was previously closest to the camera at that pixel. Therefore, the z-value and the color of that pixel are updated with the z-value and color from the primitive that is being drawn. If the computed z-value is greater than the z-value in the Z-buffer, then the color buffer and the Z-buffer are left untouched. The Z-buffer algorithm is very simple, has $O(n)$ convergence (where n is the number of primitives being rendered), and works for any drawing primitive for which a z-value can be computed for each (relevant) pixel. Also note that this algorithm allows the primitives to be rendered in any order, which is another reason for its popularity. However, partially transparent primitives cannot be rendered in just any order. They must be rendered after all opaque primitives, and in back-to-front order. For more information on different buffers and buffering, see Section 12.1.

Texturing is a technique used to increase the level of realism in a rendered three-dimensional world, and it is treated in more detail in Chapter 5. Simply put, texturing an object means "gluing" an image onto that object. This process is depicted in Figure 2.9. The image may be one-, two- or three-dimensional, but two-dimensional images are certainly the most common. The target object can be a set of connected triangles, but may be a set of lines, quadrilaterals, spheres, cylinders, parametric surfaces, etc.

We have mentioned that the color buffer is used to store colors and that the Z-buffer stores z-values for each pixel. However, there are other buffers

---

[9]In case a Z-buffer is not available, a BSP tree can be used to render a scene in back-to-front order. See Section 7.1.2 for information about BSP trees.

Figure 2.9. A cow model without textures is shown on the left. The two textures in the middle are "glued" onto the cow, and the result is shown on the right. The top texture is for the eyes, while the bottom texture is for the body of the cow. *(Cow model is reused courtesy of Jens Larsson.)*

that can be used to create some different combinations of images. The *alpha channel* is associated with the color buffer and stores a related opacity value for each pixel. The *stencil buffer* is part of OpenGL, and usually contains from one to eight bits per pixel. Primitives can be rendered into the stencil buffer using various functions, and the buffer's contents can then be used to control the rendering into the color buffer and Z-buffer. As an example, assume that a filled circle has been drawn into the stencil buffer. This can be combined with an operator that only allows rendering of subsequent primitives into the color buffer where the circle is present. The stencil buffer is a powerful tool for generating special effects.

The *frame buffer* generally consists of all the buffers on a system, but it is sometimes used to mean just the color buffer and Z-buffer as a set. In 1990, Haeberli and Akeley [147] presented another complement to the frame buffer called the *accumulation buffer*. In this buffer, images can be accumulated using a set of operators. For example, a set of images showing an object in motion can be accumulated and averaged in order to generate motion blur. Other effects that can be generated include depth of field, antialiasing, soft shadows, etc.

When the primitives have reached and passed the rasterizer stage, those that are visible from the point of view of the camera are displayed on screen. These primitives are rendered using an appropriate shading model, and they appear textured if textures were applied to them.

2.5   Through the Pipeline

Points, lines, and triangles are the rendering primitives from which a model or an object is built. Here we will follow a model through the entire graphics rendering pipeline, consisting of the three major stages: application, geometry, and the rasterizer. In this example, the model includes both lines and triangles, and some of the triangles are textured by a two-dimensional image. Moreover, the model is being lit by one light source, and the scene should be rendered with perspective into a window on screen.

Application

Here, the user can interact with the models in the scene if the application allows that. Assume that the user has selected a subset of the scene, and moves it (using the mouse). The application stage must then see to it that the model transform for that subset of the models is updated to accommodate for that translation. Also, the camera might move along a predefined path, and the camera parameters, such as position and view direction, must therefore be updated. At the end of the application stage, the primitives of the model are fed to the next major stage in the pipeline— the geometry stage.

Geometry

The view transform has been computed in the previous stage, and there it was also concatenated with the model transform for a certain model. After all vertices and normals of the model have been transformed with this matrix, the models are in eye space. Then lighting at the vertices is computed using material properties, textures, and light source properties, followed by projection-transforming the model into a unit cube, and all primitives outside the cube are discarded. All primitives intersecting the unit cube are clipped against the cube in order to obtain a set of primitives that lies totally inside the unit cube. The vertices then are mapped into the window on the screen. After all these per-polygon operations have been performed, the resulting data is passed on to the rasterizer—the final major stage in the pipeline.

Rasterizer

In this stage, all primitives are rasterized, i.e., converted into pixels in the window. Those primitives that have been associated with a texture are rendered with that texture (image) applied to them. Visibility is resolved via the Z-buffer algorithm.

Summary

The rest of this book builds upon the graphics pipeline structure. The place in this pipeline where software leaves off and acceleration hardware takes over is constantly shifting. Trade-offs in price, speed, and quality are some of the major factors in this equation. We will focus on providing methods to increase speed and improve image quality, while also describing the features and limitations of hardware acceleration algorithms and graphics APIs. We will not be able to cover every topic in depth, so our goal is to introduce concepts and terminology, give a sense of how and when various methods can be applied, and provide pointers to the best places to go for more in-depth information.

Further Reading and Resources

Blinn's book *A Trip Down the Graphics Pipeline* [43] is a great resource for learning about the subtleties of the rendering pipeline as well as implementation tips and tricks.

Chapter 3
Transforms

"What if angry vectors veer
Round your sleeping head, and form.
There's never need to fear
Violence of the poor world's abstract storm."
–Robert Penn Warren

For the computer graphics practitioner, it is extremely important to master transforms. With them, you can position, reshape, and animate objects, lights, and
cameras, can ensure that all computations are carried out in the same coordinate
system, and can project objects onto a plane in different ways. These are only a
few of the operations that can be performed with transforms, but they are sufficient to demonstrate the importance of the transform's role in real-time graphics,
or, for that matter, any kind of computer graphics.

This chapter will begin with the most essential, basic transforms, in the form
of 4×4 matrices. These are indeed *very* basic, and this section could be seen as
a "reference manual" for simple transforms. More specialized matrices are then
described, followed by a discussion and description of quaternions, a powerful
transform tool. Then, interpolators are described, and the chapter ends with
projection matrices. Most of these transforms, their notations, functions, and
properties are summarized in Table 3.1. Again we use homogeneous notation,
denoting points and vectors in the same way (using bold lower-case letters). A
vector is represented as $\mathbf{v} = (v_x \ v_y \ v_z \ 0)^T$ and a point as $\mathbf{v} = (v_x \ v_y \ v_z \ 1)^T$.
Throughout the chapter we will make extensive use of the terminology and
homogeneous notation explained in Appendix A. You may wish to review this
appendix now.

Transforms are a basic tool for manipulating geometry. Even though most
graphics Application Programmer Interfaces (APIs) include a matrix class which
implements most or all of the transforms discussed in this chapter, it is still
important to understand how transforms behave and interact.

23

Notation	Name	Characteristics
$\mathbf{T}(\mathbf{t})$	translation matrix	Moves a point. Affine.
$\mathbf{R}_x(\rho)$	rotation matrix	Rotates ρ radians around the x-axis. Similar notation for the y- and z-axes. Orthogonal & affine.
$\mathbf{R}$	rotation matrix	Any rotation matrix. Orthogonal & affine.
$\mathbf{S}(\mathbf{s})$	scaling matrix	Scales along all x-, y-, and z-axes according to s. Affine.
$\mathbf{H}_{ij}(s)$	shear matrix	Shears component i by a factor s, with respect to component j. $i, j \in \{x, y, z\}$. Affine.
$\mathbf{E}(h, p, r)$	Euler transform	Orientation matrix given by the Euler angles head (yaw), pitch, roll. Orthogonal & affine.
$\mathbf{P}_o(s)$	orthographic projection	Parallel projects onto some plane or to a volume.
$\mathbf{P}_p(s)$	perspective projection	Projects with perspective onto a plane or to a volume.
$\mathtt{slerp}(\hat{\mathbf{q}}, \hat{\mathbf{r}}, t)$	slerp transform	Creates an interpolated quaternion with respect to the quaternions $\hat{\mathbf{q}}$ and $\hat{\mathbf{r}}$, and the parameter t.

Table 3.1. Summary of most of the transforms discussed in this chapter.

It is worthwhile to understand the real matrices behind the function calls. Knowing what the matrix does after such a function call is a start, but understanding the properties of the matrix itself will take you further. For example, such an understanding enables you to discern when you are dealing with an orthogonal matrix, whose inverse is its transpose (see page 410), making for faster matrix inversions. Knowledge like this can lead to accelerated code.

3.1 Basic Transforms

This section describes the most basic transforms, such as translation, rotation, scaling, shearing, transform concatenation, the rigid-body transform, normal transform (which is not so normal), and computation of inverses. For the experienced reader this can be used as a reference manual for simple transforms, and for the novice it can serve as an introduction to the subject. This material is necessary background for the rest of this chapter and for other chapters in this book.

All translation, rotation, scaling, reflection, and shearing matrices are affine. The main characteristic of an affine matrix is that it preserves the parallelism of lines, but not necessarily lengths and angles. An affine transform may also be any sequence of concatenations of individual affine transforms. We start with the simplest of transforms—the translation.

3.1.1 Translation Matrix

A translation is one of the most simple transforms, and it is represented by a translation matrix, $\mathbf{T}$. This matrix translates an entity by a vector $\mathbf{t} = (t_x \ t_y \ t_z)^T$. $\mathbf{T}$ is given below by Equation 3.1.

$$\mathbf{T}(\mathbf{t}) = \mathbf{T}(t_x, t_y, t_z) = \begin{pmatrix} 1 & 0 & 0 & t_x \\ 0 & 1 & 0 & t_y \\ 0 & 0 & 1 & t_z \\ 0 & 0 & 0 & 1 \end{pmatrix} \quad (3.1)$$

An example of the effect of the translation transform is shown in Figure 3.1. It

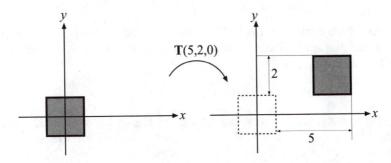

Figure 3.1. The square on the left is transformed with a translation matrix $\mathbf{T}(5, 2, 0)$, whereby the square is moved 5 distance units to the right and 2 upwards.

is easily shown that the multiplication of a point $\mathbf{p} = (p_x \ p_y \ p_z \ 1)^T$ with $\mathbf{T(t)}$ yields a new point $\mathbf{p}' = (p_x + t_x \ p_y + t_y \ p_z + t_z \ 1)^T$, which is clearly a translation. Notice that a vector $\mathbf{v} = (v_x \ v_y \ v_z \ 0)^T$ is left unaffected by a multiplication by $\mathbf{T}$, as it should be. In contrast, both points and vectors are affected by the rest of the affine transforms. The inverse of a translation matrix is $\mathbf{T}^{-1}(\mathbf{t}) = \mathbf{T}(-\mathbf{t})$, that is, the vector $\mathbf{t}$ is negated.

3.1.2   Rotation Matrices

A more elaborate set of transforms is represented by the rotation matrices, $\mathbf{R}_x(\phi)$, $\mathbf{R}_y(\phi)$, and $\mathbf{R}_z(\phi)$, which rotate an entity ϕ radians around the x-, y-, and z-axes respectively. They are given by Equations 3.2–3.4.

$$\mathbf{R}_x(\phi) = \begin{pmatrix} 1 & 0 & 0 & 0 \\ 0 & \cos\phi & -\sin\phi & 0 \\ 0 & \sin\phi & \cos\phi & 0 \\ 0 & 0 & 0 & 1 \end{pmatrix} \tag{3.2}$$

$$\mathbf{R}_y(\phi) = \begin{pmatrix} \cos\phi & 0 & \sin\phi & 0 \\ 0 & 1 & 0 & 0 \\ -\sin\phi & 0 & \cos\phi & 0 \\ 0 & 0 & 0 & 1 \end{pmatrix} \tag{3.3}$$

$$\mathbf{R}_z(\phi) = \begin{pmatrix} \cos\phi & -\sin\phi & 0 & 0 \\ \sin\phi & \cos\phi & 0 & 0 \\ 0 & 0 & 1 & 0 \\ 0 & 0 & 0 & 1 \end{pmatrix} \tag{3.4}$$

For every 3×3 rotation matrix,[1] $\mathbf{R}$, that rotates ϕ radians around any axis, the sum of the diagonal elements is constant independent of the axis. This sum, called the *trace* [226], is:

$$\mathrm{tr}(\mathbf{R}) = 1 + 2\cos\phi \tag{3.5}$$

The effect of a rotation matrix may be seen in Figure 3.5 on page 32. What characterizes a rotation matrix, $\mathbf{R}_i(\phi)$, besides the fact that it rotates ϕ radians around axis i, is that it leaves all points on the rotation axis, i, unchanged. Note that $\mathbf{R}$ will also be used to denote a rotation matrix around any axis. All

---

[1] If the bottom row and rightmost column is deleted from a 4×4 matrix, a 3×3 matrix is obtained.

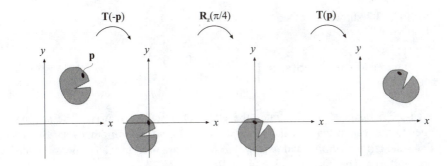

Figure 3.2. Example of rotation around a specific point **p**.

rotation matrices are orthogonal (easily verified using the definition of orthogonal matrices given on page 410 in Appendix A), which means that $\mathbf{R}^{-1} = \mathbf{R}^T$. This also holds for concatenations of any number of these transforms. But there is also an additional way to obtain the inverse, $\mathbf{R}_i^{-1}(\phi) = \mathbf{R}_i(-\phi)$, that is, rotate in the opposite direction around the same axis.

EXAMPLE: ROTATION AROUND A POINT Assume that we want to rotate an object by ϕ radians around a certain point, **p**, around the z-axis. What is the transform? This scenario is depicted in Figure 3.2. Since a rotation around a point is characterized by the fact that the point itself is unaffected by the rotation, the transform starts by translating the object so that **p** coincides with the origin, which is done with $\mathbf{T}(-\mathbf{p})$. Thereafter follows the actual rotation: $\mathbf{R}_z(\phi)$. Finally, the object has to be translated back to its original position using $\mathbf{T}(\mathbf{p})$. The resulting transform, $\mathbf{X}$, is then given by:

$$\mathbf{X} = \mathbf{T}(\mathbf{p})\mathbf{R}_z(\phi)\mathbf{T}(-\mathbf{p}). \qquad (3.6)$$

$\square$

3.1.3 Scaling Matrix

A scaling matrix, $\mathbf{S}(\mathbf{s}) = \mathbf{S}(s_x, s_y, s_z)$, scales an entity with factors s_x, s_y, and s_z along the x-, y-, and z-directions respectively. This means that a scaling matrix can be used to enlarge or diminish an object. Setting any of the components of **s** to 1 naturally avoids a change in scaling in that direction. Also, the larger the s_i ($i \in \{x, y, z\}$), the larger the scaled entity gets in that direction.

Equation 3.7 shows **S**.

$$\mathbf{S}(\mathbf{s}) = \begin{pmatrix} s_x & 0 & 0 & 0 \\ 0 & s_y & 0 & 0 \\ 0 & 0 & s_z & 0 \\ 0 & 0 & 0 & 1 \end{pmatrix} \tag{3.7}$$

Figure 3.5 on page 32 illustrates the effect of a scaling matrix. The scaling operation is called *uniform* if $s_x = s_y = s_z$ and *non-uniform* otherwise. Sometimes the terms *isotropic* and *anisotropic* scaling are used instead of uniform and non-uniform. The inverse is $\mathbf{S}^{-1}(\mathbf{s}) = \mathbf{S}(1/s_x, 1/s_y, 1/s_z)$.

Using homogeneous coordinates, another valid way to create a uniform scaling matrix is by manipulating matrix element at position $(3,3)$, i.e., the element at the lower right corner. This value affects the w-component of the homogeneous coordinate, and so scales every coordinate transformed by the matrix. For example, to scale uniformly by a factor of 5, the elements at $(0,0)$, $(1,1)$, and $(2,2)$ in the scaling matrix can be reset from 1 to 5, or the element at $(3,3)$ can be reset from 1 to $1/5$. This is shown below.

$$\mathbf{S} = \begin{pmatrix} 5 & 0 & 0 & 0 \\ 0 & 5 & 0 & 0 \\ 0 & 0 & 5 & 0 \\ 0 & 0 & 0 & 1 \end{pmatrix} = \begin{pmatrix} 1 & 0 & 0 & 0 \\ 0 & 1 & 0 & 0 \\ 0 & 0 & 1 & 0 \\ 0 & 0 & 0 & 1/5 \end{pmatrix} \tag{3.8}$$

However, in practice many systems that theoretically support 4×4 matrices actually support only 3×4 matrices (i.e., three rows and four columns) for modeling transforms, with the bottom row always assumed to be $(0,0,0,1)$. In such cases modifying the element at position $(3,3)$ will have no effect on the object being scaled. Setting the element at the lower right (position $(3,3)$) to generate a uniform scaling may be inefficient, since it involves divides in the homogenization process; if the element is 1, no divides are necessary. Of course, if the system always does this division without testing for 1, then there is no extra cost.

A negative value on one or three of the components of s gives a *reflection matrix*, also called a *mirror matrix*.[2] If only two scale factors are -1, then we will rotate π radians. Reflection matrices usually require special treatment when detected. For example, a triangle with vertices in a counter-clockwise order will get a clockwise order when transformed by a reflection matrix. This order change can cause incorrect lighting and backface culling to occur. To detect whether a given matrix reflects in some manner, compute the determinant of the upper left 3×3 elements of the matrix. If the value is negative, the matrix is reflective.

---

[2]According to some definitions of a reflection matrix, the negative component(s) must equal -1.

EXAMPLE: SCALING IN A CERTAIN DIRECTION The scaling matrix $\mathbf{S}$ only scales along the x-, y-, and z-axes. If scaling should be performed in other directions, a compound transform is needed. Assume that scaling should be done along the axes of the orthonormal, right-oriented vectors $\mathbf{f}^x$, $\mathbf{f}^y$, and $\mathbf{f}^z$. First, construct the matrix $\mathbf{F}$ as below.

$$\mathbf{F} = \begin{pmatrix} \mathbf{f}^x & \mathbf{f}^y & \mathbf{f}^z & \mathbf{0} \\ 0 & 0 & 0 & 1 \end{pmatrix} \tag{3.9}$$

The idea is to make the coordinate system given by the three axes coincide with the standard axes, then use the standard scaling matrix, and then transform back. The first step is carried out by multiplying with the transpose, i.e., the inverse, of $\mathbf{F}$. Then the actual scaling is done, followed by a transform back. The transform is shown in Equation 3.10.

$$\mathbf{X} = \mathbf{F}\mathbf{S}(\mathbf{s})\mathbf{F}^T \tag{3.10}$$

$\square$

3.1.4 Shearing Matrices

Another class of transforms is the shearing matrices. These can, for example, be used in games to distort an entire scene in order to create a psychedelic effect or to create fuzzy reflections by jittering (see Section 6.5.2). There are six basic shearing matrices,[3] and they are denoted $\mathbf{H}_{xy}(s)$, $\mathbf{H}_{xz}(s)$, $\mathbf{H}_{yx}(s)$, $\mathbf{H}_{yz}(s)$, $\mathbf{H}_{zx}(s)$, and $\mathbf{H}_{zy}(s)$. The first subscript is used to denote which coordinate is being changed by the shear matrix, while the second subscript indicates the coordinate which does the shearing. An example of a shear matrix, $\mathbf{H}_{xz}(s)$, is shown in Equation 3.11. Observe that the subscript can be used to find the position of the parameter s in the matrix below; the x (whose numeric index is 0) identifies row zero, and the z (whose numeric index is 2) identifies column two, and so the s is located there:

$$\mathbf{H}_{xz}(s) = \begin{pmatrix} 1 & 0 & s & 0 \\ 0 & 1 & 0 & 0 \\ 0 & 0 & 1 & 0 \\ 0 & 0 & 0 & 1 \end{pmatrix} \tag{3.11}$$

The effect of multiplying this matrix with a point $\mathbf{p}$ yields a point: $(p_x + sp_z \quad p_y \quad p_z)^T$. Graphically, this is shown for the unit square in Figure 3.3. The inverse of $\mathbf{H}_{ij}(s)$ (shearing the ith coordinate with respect to the jth coor-

---

[3] Actually, there are *only* six shearing matrices, because we shear in planes orthogonal to the main axes. However, a general shear matrix can shear orthogonally to any plane.

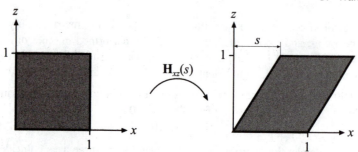

Figure 3.3. The effect of shearing the unit square with $\mathbf{H}_{xz}(s)$. Both the y- and z-values are unaffected by the transform, while the x-value is the sum of the old x-value and s multiplied by the z-value, causing the square to be tilted.

dinate, where $i \neq j$), is generated by shearing in the opposite direction, that is, $\mathbf{H}_{ij}^{-1}(s) = \mathbf{H}_{ij}(-s)$.

Some computer graphics texts [108, 109] use a slightly different kind of shear matrix:

$$\mathbf{H}'_{xy}(s, t) = \begin{pmatrix} 1 & 0 & s & 0 \\ 0 & 1 & t & 0 \\ 0 & 0 & 1 & 0 \\ 0 & 0 & 0 & 1 \end{pmatrix} \qquad (3.12)$$

Here, however, both subscripts are used to denote that these coordinates are to be sheared by the third coordinate. The connection between these two different kinds of descriptions is $\mathbf{H}'_{ij}(s, t) = \mathbf{H}_{ik}(s)\mathbf{H}_{jk}(t)$, where k is used as an index to the third coordinate. The right matrix to use is a matter of taste and API support.

Finally, it should be noted that since the determinant of any shear matrix $|\mathbf{H}| = 1$, this is a volume preserving transformation.

EXAMPLE: ROTATION AS THREE SHEARS Here it will be shown that a rotation can be written as the concatenation of three shearing matrices. For simplicity, the derivation will be done in two dimensions. The three-dimensional version is obtained by taking the two-dimensional result and extending it to a 4×4 matrix, by filling the appropriate positions with ones and zeros.

Start by multiplying three shear matrices, where the first and third shear the x-coordinate with respect to the y-coordinate. The second matrix shears the y-coordinate with respect to the x-coordinate. The resulting matrix $\mathbf{X} = \mathbf{H}_{xy}(c)\mathbf{H}_{yx}(b)\mathbf{H}_{xy}(a)$ is shown below.

$$\mathbf{X} = \begin{pmatrix} 1 & c \\ 0 & 1 \end{pmatrix} \begin{pmatrix} 1 & 0 \\ b & 1 \end{pmatrix} \begin{pmatrix} 1 & a \\ 0 & 1 \end{pmatrix} = \begin{pmatrix} 1 + bc & abc + a + c \\ b & 1 + ab \end{pmatrix} \tag{3.13}$$

In order to make this behave as a rotation, the following matrix equation is obtained.

$$\begin{pmatrix} 1 + bc & abc + a + c \\ b & 1 + ab \end{pmatrix} = \begin{pmatrix} \cos\phi & -\sin\phi \\ \sin\phi & \cos\phi \end{pmatrix} \tag{3.14}$$

This trivially gets $b = \sin\phi$, and since $\cos\phi = 1 + bc = 1 + ab$, we find that $a = c$. Using these results and the fact that $b = -(abc + a + c)$, we obtain a second-degree equation whose solution is $a = c = (-1 \pm \cos\phi)/\sin\phi$. This equation is unstable when $\sin\phi$ is near zero, i.e., when ϕ is near zero. The half-angle relation (see page 426) says $\tan(\phi/2) = (1 - \cos\phi)/\sin\phi$, and so we can instead use $a = c = -\tan(\phi/2)$ [281].

Since a solution to a, b, and c exists, it has been verified that a rotation can indeed be written as the multiplication of three shearing matrices. Setting $\phi = \pi/6$ yields the three shears shown in Figure 3.4. □

3.1.5 Concatenation of Transforms

Due to the non-commutativity of the multiplication operation on matrices, the order in which the matrices occur matters. Concatenation of transforms is therefore said to be order-dependent.

As an example of order dependency, consider two matrices, $\mathbf{S}$ and $\mathbf{R}$. $\mathbf{S}((2 \ \ 0.5 \ \ 1)^T)$ scales the x-component by a factor two and the y-component by

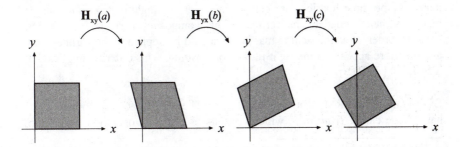

Figure 3.4. Rotating a unit-square $\pi/6$ radians by shearing three times. The parameters are $a = c = \sqrt{3} - 2$ and $b = 1/2$.

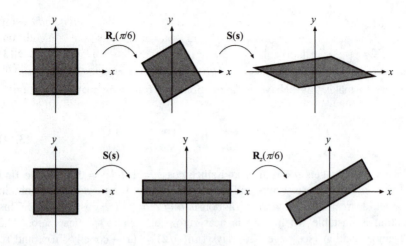

Figure 3.5. This illustrates the order dependency when multiplying matrices. In the top row, the rotation matrix $\mathbf{R}_z(\pi/6)$ is applied followed by a scaling, $\mathbf{S}(\mathbf{s})$, where $\mathbf{s} = \begin{pmatrix} 2 & 0.5 & 1 \end{pmatrix}^T$. The composite matrix is then $\mathbf{S}(\mathbf{s})\mathbf{R}_z(\pi/6)$. In the bottom row, the matrices are applied in the reverse order, yielding $\mathbf{R}_z(\pi/6)\mathbf{S}(\mathbf{s})$. The results are clearly different. It generally holds that $\mathbf{MN} \neq \mathbf{NM}$, for arbitrary matrices $\mathbf{M}$ and $\mathbf{N}$.

a factor 0.5. $\mathbf{R}_z(\pi/6)$ rotates $\pi/6$ radians counterclockwise around the z-axis (which points outwards from the paper). These matrices can be multiplied in two ways, with the results being totally different. The two cases are shown in Figure 3.5.

The obvious reason to concatenate a sequence of matrices into a single one is to gain efficiency. For example, imagine that you have an object which has several thousand vertices, and that this object must be scaled, rotated, and finally translated. Now, instead of multiplying all vertices with each of the three matrices, the three matrices are concatenated into a single matrix. This single matrix is then applied to the vertices. This composite matrix is $\mathbf{C} = \mathbf{TRS}$. Note the order here: the scaling matrix, $\mathbf{S}$, should be applied to the vertices first, and therefore appears to the right in the composition. This ordering implies that $\mathbf{TRSp} = (\mathbf{T}(\mathbf{R}(\mathbf{Sp})))$.[4]

EXAMPLE: THE VRML TRANSFORM NODE   The VRML 97 file format [362] has a node called *Transform*, which consists of a scaling operation, a rotation,

---

[4]Another valid notational scheme sometimes seen in computer graphics uses matrices with translation vectors in the bottom row. In this scheme, the order of matrices would be reversed, i.e., the order of application would read from left to right. Vectors and matrices in this notation are said to be in *row-major* form since the vectors are rows. In this book we use *column-major* form.

and a translation. The transform begins by translating to the *center point* using
$\mathbf{T}(-\mathbf{c})$. The scaling, $\mathbf{S}$, and rotation, $\mathbf{R}$, are done around this point. In addition,
a separate scaling rotation $\mathbf{R}_s^T$ occurs before the scaling and is undone after
the scaling, to allow specification of non-uniform scaling in any basis. The
transform ends by translating from the center point back to the origin using
$\mathbf{T}(\mathbf{c})$, then finally performing the translation desired, $\mathbf{T}(\mathbf{t})$. Using these steps,
the concatenation is:

$$\mathbf{X} = \mathbf{T}(\mathbf{t})\mathbf{T}(\mathbf{c})\mathbf{R}\mathbf{R}_s\mathbf{S}\mathbf{R}_s^T\mathbf{T}(-\mathbf{c}) \qquad (3.15)$$

$\square$

3.1.6 The Rigid-Body Transform

When a person grabs a solid object, say a pen from a table, and moves it to
another location, perhaps to her shirt pocket, only the object's orientation and
location change, while the shape of the object generally is not affected. Such
a transform, consisting of concatenations of only translations and rotations, is
called a *rigid-body transform* and has the characteristic of preserving lengths
and angles.

Any rigid-body matrix, $\mathbf{X}$, can be written as the concatenation of a translation
matrix, $\mathbf{T}(\mathbf{t})$, and a rotation matrix, $\mathbf{R}$. Thus, $\mathbf{X}$ has the appearance of the matrix
in Equation 3.16.

$$\mathbf{X} = \mathbf{T}(\mathbf{t})\mathbf{R} = \begin{pmatrix} r_{00} & r_{01} & r_{02} & t_x \\ r_{10} & r_{11} & r_{12} & t_y \\ r_{20} & r_{21} & r_{22} & t_z \\ 0 & 0 & 0 & 1 \end{pmatrix} \qquad (3.16)$$

The inverse of $\mathbf{X}$ is computed as $\mathbf{X}^{-1} = (\mathbf{T}(\mathbf{t})\mathbf{R})^{-1} = \mathbf{R}^{-1}\mathbf{T}(\mathbf{t})^{-1} = \mathbf{R}^T\mathbf{T}(-\mathbf{t})$. Thus, to compute the inverse, the upper left 3×3 matrix of $\mathbf{R}$
is transposed, and the translation values of $\mathbf{T}$ change sign. These two new ma-
trices are multiplied together to obtain the inverse. Another way to compute the
inverse of $\mathbf{X}$ is to consider $\mathbf{R}$ (making $\mathbf{R}$ appear as 3×3 matrix) and $\mathbf{X}$ in the
following notation.

$$\bar{\mathbf{R}} = \begin{pmatrix} \mathbf{r}_{,0} & \mathbf{r}_{,1} & \mathbf{r}_{,2} \end{pmatrix} = \begin{pmatrix} \mathbf{r}_{0,}^T \\ \mathbf{r}_{1,}^T \\ \mathbf{r}_{2,}^T \end{pmatrix}$$

$$\Longrightarrow$$

$$\mathbf{X} = \begin{pmatrix} \bar{\mathbf{R}} & \mathbf{t} \\ \mathbf{0}^T & 1 \end{pmatrix}$$

(3.17)

Here, $\mathbf{0}$ is a 3×1 column vector filled with zeros. Some simple calculations yield the inverse in the expression shown in Equation 3.18.

$$\mathbf{X}^{-1} = \begin{pmatrix} \mathbf{r}_0, & \mathbf{r}_1, & \mathbf{r}_2, & -\bar{\mathbf{R}}^T \mathbf{t} \\ 0 & 0 & 0 & 1 \end{pmatrix}$$

(3.18)

3.1.7 Normal Transform

A single matrix can be used to consistently transform points, lines, polygons, and other geometry. The same matrix can also transform vectors following along these lines or on the surfaces of polygons. However, this matrix cannot always be used to transform one important geometric property, the surface normal (and also the vertex lighting normal). Normals must be transformed by the transpose of the inverse of the matrix used to transform geometry [158] (see Turkowski's gem [355] for a proof and applications in backface culling and shading). So, if the matrix used to transform geometry is called $\mathbf{M}$, then we must use the matrix, $\mathbf{N}$, below to transform the normals of this geometry.

$$\mathbf{N} = (\mathbf{M}^{-1})^T$$

(3.19)

Figure 3.6 shows what can happen if the proper transform is not used.

In practice, we do not have to compute the inverse if we know the matrix is orthogonal, i.e., that it was formed from only rotations. In this case, the matrix itself can be used to transform normals, since the inverse of an orthogonal matrix is its transpose. Two matrix transposes cancel out, giving the original rotation matrix. Furthermore, translations do not affect vector direction, so any number of translations can be performed without affecting the normal. After transformation we can also avoid the step of renormalizing the normals (i.e., making their lengths 1 again). This is because length is preserved by a matrix formed with just

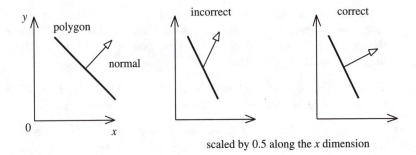

Figure 3.6. On the left is the original geometry, a polygon and its normal shown from the side. The middle illustration shows what happens if the model is scaled along the x-axis by 0.5 and the normal uses the same matrix. The right figure shows the proper transform of the normal.

rotations and translations (see Section 3.1.6 on rigid-body transforms). Finally, if a matrix formed by rotations and translations also has only uniform scalings (including uniform reflection matrices) used in forming it, such scalings affect only the length of the transformed normal, not its direction. If such scalings are used, then the normals do have to be renormalized. To summarize, if the object is transformed by a matrix consisting of a series of rotations, translations, and uniform scalings, the normal can be safely transformed by this same matrix.

Even if it turns out that the full inverse must be computed, only the transpose of the *adjoint* (see Section A.3.1) of the matrix's upper left 3×3 is needed. The adjoint of the matrix is similar to the inverse, except that the matrix computed is not divided by the original matrix's determinant. The adjoint is faster to compute than the inverse. We do not need to divide by the determinant, since we know we generally have to normalize the transformed normal anyway.

It is worth repeating that normal transforms are not an issue in systems where after transformation the surface normal is derived from the triangle (e.g., using the cross product of the triangle's edges). However, it is often the case that triangle vertices contain normal information for lighting, and so normal transformation must be addressed.

3.1.8 Computation of Inverses

Inverses are needed in many cases, for example when changing back and forth between coordinate systems. Depending on the available information about a transform, one of the following three methods of computing the inverse of a matrix can be used.

- If the matrix is a single transform or a sequence of simple transforms with given parameters, then the matrix can be computed easily by "inverting the parameters" and the matrix order. For example, if $\mathbf{M} = \mathbf{T}(\mathbf{t})\mathbf{R}(\phi)$, then $\mathbf{M}^{-1} = \mathbf{R}(-\phi)\mathbf{T}(-\mathbf{t})$.

- If the matrix is known to be orthogonal, then $\mathbf{M}^{-1} = \mathbf{M}^T$, i.e., the transpose is the inverse. Any sequence of rotations is orthogonal.

- If nothing in particular is known, then Cramer's rule or Gaussian elimination must be used to compute the inverse (see Section A.3.1).[5]

The purpose of the inverse computation can also be taken into account when optimizing. For example, if the inverse is to be used for transforming vectors, then only the 3×3 upper left part of the matrix normally needs to be inverted (see the previous section).

3.2   Special Matrix Transforms and Operations

In this section, a number of matrix transforms and operations that are essential to real-time graphics will be introduced and derived. First, we present the Euler transform (along with its extraction of parameters), which is an intuitive way to describe orientations. Then we touch upon retrieving a set of basic transforms from a single matrix. Finally, a method is derived that rotates an entity around an arbitrary axis.

3.2.1   The Euler Transform

This transform is an intuitive way to construct a matrix to orient yourself (i.e., the camera) or other entity in a certain direction. Its name comes from the great Swiss mathematician Leonard Euler (1707–1783).

First, some kind of default view direction must be established. Most often it lies along the negative z-axis with the head oriented along the y-axis, as depicted in Figure 3.7. The Euler transform is the multiplication of three matrices, namely the rotations shown in the figure. More formally, the transform, denoted $\mathbf{E}$, is given by Equation 3.20.[6]

$$\mathbf{E}(h, p, r) = \mathbf{R}_z(r)\mathbf{R}_x(p)\mathbf{R}_y(h) \qquad (3.20)$$

---

[5]Singular value decomposition (SVD) can also be used to compute inverses. Consult, for example, Golub and Van Loan's book [129] on this.

[6]Actually, the order of the matrices can be chosen in 24 different ways [331], but we choose this one because it is commonly used.

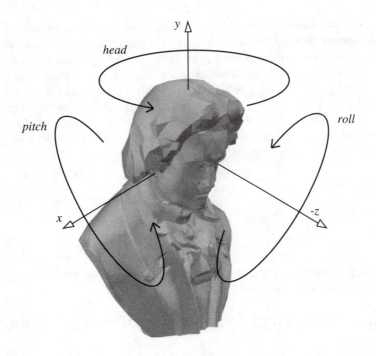

Figure 3.7. Depicting the way, in terms of the Euler transform, you turn your *head*, *pitch*, and *roll*. The default view direction is shown, looking along the negative z-axis with the head oriented along the y-axis.

Since $\mathbf{E}$ is a concatenation of rotations it is also clearly orthogonal. Therefore its inverse can be expressed as $\mathbf{E}^{-1} = \mathbf{E}^T = (\mathbf{R}_z \mathbf{R}_x \mathbf{R}_y)^T = \mathbf{R}_y^T \mathbf{R}_x^T \mathbf{R}_z^T$, although it is of course easier to use the transpose of $\mathbf{E}$ directly.

The Euler angles h, p, and r represent how much the head, pitch, and roll should rotate around their respective axes and in which order.[7] This transform is intuitive and therefore easy to discuss in layperson's language. For example, changing the head angle makes the viewer shake his head "no," changing the pitch makes him nod, and rolling makes him tilt his head. Rather than talking about rotations around the x-, y-, and z-axes, we talk about altering the head, pitch, and roll. Note that this transform can orient not only the camera but also any object or entity as well.

When you use Euler transforms, something called *gimbal lock* may occur [328, 367]. This happens when rotations are made so that one degree of freedom

---

[7]Sometimes the angles are all called "rolls," e.g., our "head" is the "y-roll" and our "pitch" is the "x-roll". Also, "head" is sometimes known as "yaw," for example in flight simulation.

is lost. For example, start with $h = 0$, i.e., we do not rotate around the y-axis. This should then be followed by a rotation around the x-axis. Say we rotate $\pi/2$ radians ($90°$) around the x-axis. Finally, we would like to rotate around the world z-axis, but due to our previous rotation, our rotation matrix around the z-axis at this point would actually be a rotation around the y-axis. The conclusion is that we have lost one degree of freedom—we cannot rotate around the world z-axis. Quaternions (see Section 3.3) do not have this defect.

Another way to see that one degree of freedom is lost is to set $p = \pi/2$ and examine what happens to the Euler matrix $\mathbf{E}(h, p, r)$:

$$\mathbf{E}(h, \pi/2, r) = \begin{pmatrix} \cos r \cos h - \sin r \sin h & 0 & \cos r \sin h + \sin r \cos h \\ \sin r \cos h + \cos r \sin h & 0 & \sin r \sin h - \cos r \cos h \\ 0 & 1 & 0 \end{pmatrix}$$

$$= \begin{pmatrix} \cos(r+h) & 0 & \sin(r+h) \\ \sin(r+h) & 0 & -\cos(r+h) \\ 0 & 1 & 0 \end{pmatrix}$$

Since the matrix is only dependent on one angle $(r + h)$, we conclude that one degree of freedom has been lost.

3.2.2   Extracting Parameters from the Euler Transform

In some situations it is useful to have a procedure that extracts the Euler parameters, h, p, and r, from an orthogonal matrix. This procedure is shown in Equation 3.21.[8]

$$\mathbf{F} = \begin{pmatrix} f_{00} & f_{01} & f_{02} \\ f_{10} & f_{11} & f_{12} \\ f_{20} & f_{21} & f_{22} \end{pmatrix} = \mathbf{R}_z(r)\mathbf{R}_x(p)\mathbf{R}_y(h) = \mathbf{E}(h, p, r) \qquad (3.21)$$

Concatenating the three rotation matrices in Equation 3.21 yields:

$$\mathbf{F} = \begin{pmatrix} \cos r \cos h - \sin r \sin p \sin h & -\sin r \cos p & \cos r \sin h + \sin r \sin p \cos h \\ \sin r \cos h + \cos r \sin p \sin h & \cos r \cos p & \sin r \sin h - \cos r \sin p \cos h \\ -\cos p \sin h & \sin p & \cos p \cos h \end{pmatrix}$$

$$(3.22)$$

From this it is apparent that the pitch parameter is given by $\sin p = f_{21}$. Also, dividing f_{01} by f_{11}, and similarly dividing f_{20} by f_{22}, gives rise to the

---

[8]The 4×4 matrices have been abandoned for 3×3 matrices, since the latter provide all the necessary information for a rotation matrix; i.e., the rest of the 4×4 matrix always contains zeros and a one in the lower right position.

following extraction equations for the head and roll parameters.

$$\frac{f_{01}}{f_{11}} = \frac{-\sin r}{\cos r} = -\tan r$$

$$\frac{f_{20}}{f_{22}} = \frac{-\sin h}{\cos h} = -\tan h$$

(3.23)

Thus, the Euler parameters h (head), p (pitch), and r (roll) are extracted from a matrix $\mathbf{F}$ using the C-math function atan2(y,x)[9] as in Equation 3.24.

$$h = \text{atan2}(-f_{20}, f_{22})$$
$$p = \arcsin(f_{21})$$
$$r = \text{atan2}(-f_{01}, f_{11})$$

(3.24)

However, there is a special case we need to handle. It occurs when $\cos p = 0$, because then $f_{01} = f_{11} = 0$, and so the atan2 function cannot be used. That $\cos p = 0$ implies that $\sin p = \pm 1$, and so $\mathbf{F}$ simplifies to:

$$\mathbf{F} = \begin{pmatrix} \cos(r \pm h) & 0 & \sin(r \pm h) \\ \sin(r \pm h) & 0 & -\cos(r \pm h) \\ 0 & \pm 1 & 0 \end{pmatrix}$$

(3.25)

The remaining parameters are then obtained by arbitrarily setting $h = 0$ [352], and then $\sin r / \cos r = \tan r = f_{10}/f_{00}$, which gives $r = \text{atan2}(f_{10}, f_{00})$.

Note that from the definition of arcsin (see Section B.1), $-\pi/2 \le p \le \pi/2$, which means that if $\mathbf{F}$ was created with a value of p outside this interval, the original parameter cannot be extracted. That h, p, and r are not unique means that more than one set of the Euler parameters can be used to yield the same transform. More about Euler angle conversion can be found in Shoemake's 1994 article [331]. The simple method outlined above can result in problems with numerical instability, which is avoidable at some cost in speed [284, 332].

EXAMPLE: CONSTRAINING A TRANSFORM Imagine you are holding a wrench snapped to a screw bolt and to get the screw bolt in place you have to rotate the wrench around the x-axis. Now assume that your input device (mouse, VR-gloves, space-ball, etc.) gives you an orthogonal transform for the movement of the wrench. The problem that we encounter is that you do not want to apply that transform to the wrench, which supposedly should only rotate around the

---

[9]The function atan2(y,x) is a extension of the mathematical function $\arctan(x)$. The main differences between them are that $-\frac{\pi}{2} < \arctan(x) < \frac{\pi}{2}$, that $0 \le \text{atan2}(y, x) < 2\pi$, and that an extra argument has been added to the latter function. This extra argument avoids division by zero, i.e., $x = y/x$ except when $x = 0$.

x-axis. So to restrict the input transform, called $\mathbf{P}$, to a rotation around the x-axis, simply extract the Euler angles, h, p, and r, using the method described in this section, and then create a new matrix $\mathbf{R}_x(p)$. This is then the sought-after transform that will rotate the wrench around the x-axis (if $\mathbf{P}$ now contains such a movement). □

3.2.3   Matrix Decomposition

Up to this point we have been working under the assumption that we know the origin and history of the transformation matrix we are using. This is often not the case: for example, nothing more than a concatenated matrix may be associated with some transformed object. The task of retrieving various transforms from a concatenated matrix is called *matrix decomposition*.

There are many reasons to retrieve a set of transformations. Uses include:

- Extracting just the scaling factors for an object.

- Finding transforms needed by a particular system. For example, VRML [362] uses a *Transform* node (see Section 3.1.5) and does not allow the use of an arbitrary 4×4 matrix.

- Determining whether a model has undergone only rigid-body transforms.

- Interpolating between keyframes in an animation where only the matrix for the object is available.

- Removing shears from a rotation matrix.

We have already presented two decompositions, those of deriving the translation and rotation matrix for a rigid-body transformation (Section 3.1.6) and deriving the Euler angles from an orthogonal matrix (Section 3.2.2).

As we have seen, it is trivial to retrieve the translation matrix, as we simply need the elements in the last column of the 4×4 matrix. We can also determine if a reflection has occurred by checking whether the determinant of the matrix is negative. To separate out the rotation, scaling, and shears takes more determined effort.

Fortunately, there are a number of articles on this topic, as well as code available online. Thomas [352] and Goldman [126, 127] each present somewhat different methods for various classes of transformations. Shoemake [330] improves upon their techniques for affine matrices, as his algorithm is independent of frame of reference and attempts to decompose the matrix in order to obtain rigid-body transforms.

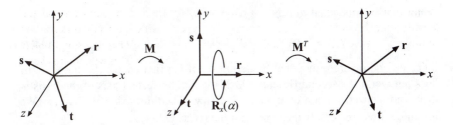

Figure 3.8. Rotation about an arbitrary axis, **r**, is accomplished by finding an orthonormal basis formed by **r**, **s**, and **t**. We then align this basis with the standard basis so that **r** is aligned with the x-axis. The rotation around the x-axis is performed there, and finally we transform back.

3.2.4   Rotation About an Arbitrary Axis

Sometimes it is convenient to have a procedure that rotates an entity by some angle around an arbitrary axis. Assume that the rotation axis, **r**, is normalized and that a transform should be created that rotates α radians around **r**.

To do this, first find two more arbitrary axes of unit length that are mutually orthogonal with themselves and with **r**, i.e., orthonormal. These should form a basis.[10] The idea is to change bases (Section A.3.2) from the standard basis to this new basis, and then rotate α radians around, say, the x-axis (which then should correspond to **r**) and finally transform back to the standard basis [76]. This procedure is illustrated in Figure 3.8.

The first step is to compute the orthonormal axes of the basis. The first axis is **r**, i.e., the one we want to rotate around. We now concentrate on finding the second axis, **s**— knowing that the third axis, **t**, will be the cross product of the first and the second axis, $\mathbf{t} = \mathbf{r} \times \mathbf{s}$. If we take an arbitrary vector **v** and compute the cross product between **r** and **v**, we get a vector that is orthogonal to **r**, which is what we wanted. This is not always true, because **v** might be parallel to **r**, in which case $\mathbf{s} = \mathbf{r} \times \mathbf{v} = (0, 0, 0)^T$.

To solve this problem, we use the following approach. We first compute:

$$\mathbf{v} = \mathbf{r} \times \mathbf{e}_x = \mathbf{r} \times (1, 0, 0)^T = (0, r_z, -r_y)^T \qquad (3.26)$$

If $\mathbf{v} \cdot \mathbf{v} < \epsilon$, where epsilon is a small number[11], then we know $\mathbf{e}_x$ was parallel or very close to parallel to **r** and we made a bad choice. If so, we try with another

---

[10]An example of a basis is the standard basis, which has the axes: $\mathbf{e}_x = (1, 0, 0)$, $\mathbf{e}_y = (0, 1, 0)$, and $\mathbf{e}_z = (0, 0, 1)$.

[11]For floating-point precision 0.0001 works fine.

vector that is orthogonal to $\mathbf{e}_x$:

$$\mathbf{v} = \mathbf{r} \times \mathbf{e}_y = \mathbf{r} \times (0,1,0)^T = (-r_z, 0, r_x)^T \tag{3.27}$$

Since $\mathbf{e}_x$ and $\mathbf{e}_y$ are orthogonal by definition, if the first choice (Equation 3.26) does not work, the second (Equation 3.27) will. The second axis of the basis is then a normalized version of $\mathbf{v}$, i.e., $\mathbf{s} = \frac{1}{||\mathbf{v}||}\mathbf{v}$. The third axis is $\mathbf{t} = \mathbf{r} \times \mathbf{s}$. We use these three vectors as the rows in a matrix as below.

$$\mathbf{M} = \begin{pmatrix} \mathbf{r}^T \\ \mathbf{s}^T \\ \mathbf{t}^T \end{pmatrix} \tag{3.28}$$

This matrix transforms the vector $\mathbf{r}$ into the x-axis ($\mathbf{e}_x$), $\mathbf{s}$ into the y-axis, and $\mathbf{t}$ into the z-axis. So the final transform for rotating α radians around the normalized vector $\mathbf{r}$ is then:

$$\mathbf{X} = \mathbf{M}^T \mathbf{R}_x(\alpha) \mathbf{M} \tag{3.29}$$

In words, this means that first we transform so that $\mathbf{r}$ is the x-axis (using $\mathbf{M}$), then we rotate α radians around this x-axis (using $\mathbf{R}_x(\alpha)$), and then we transform back using the inverse of $\mathbf{M}$, which in this case is $\mathbf{M}^T$ because $\mathbf{M}$ is orthogonal.

Another method for rotating around an arbitrary, normalized axis $\mathbf{r}$ by ϕ radians has been presented by Goldman [125]. Here, we simply present his transform:

$$\mathbf{R} =$$

$$\begin{pmatrix} \cos\phi + (1-\cos\phi)r_x^2 & (1-\cos\phi)r_x r_y - r_z\sin\phi & (1-\cos\phi)r_x r_z + r_y\sin\phi \\ (1-\cos\phi)r_x r_y + r_z\sin\phi & \cos\phi + (1-\cos\phi)r_y^2 & (1-\cos\phi)r_y r_z - r_x\sin\phi \\ (1-\cos\phi)r_x r_z - r_y\sin\phi & (1-\cos\phi)r_y r_z + r_x\sin\phi & \cos\phi + (1-\cos\phi)r_z^2 \end{pmatrix} \tag{3.30}$$

In Section 3.3.2 we present yet another method for solving this problem, using quaternions. Also in that section are more efficient algorithms for related problems, such as rotation from one vector to another.

3.3 Quaternions

Although quaternions were invented back in 1843 by Sir William Rowan Hamilton as an extension to the complex numbers, it was not until 1985 that Shoemake [328] introduced them to the field of computer graphics. Quaternions are a powerful tool for constructing transforms with compelling features, and in some ways they are superior to both Euler angles and matrices, especially when it comes to rotations and orientations.

A quaternion has four components, so we choose to represent them as vectors, but to differentiate them we put a hat on them: $\hat{q}$. We begin with some mathematical background on quaternions, which is then used to construct interesting and useful transforms.

3.3.1 Mathematical Background

We start with the definition of a quaternion.

Definition. A quaternion $\hat{q}$ can be defined in the following ways, all equivalent.

$$\hat{q} = (\mathbf{q}_v, q_w) = (q_x, q_y, q_z, q_w) = iq_x + jq_y + kq_z + q_w,$$

$$i^2 = j^2 = k^2 = -1, \ jk = -kj = i, \ ki = -ik = j, \ ij = -ji = k$$

(3.31)

The vector $\mathbf{q}_v = (q_x \ q_y \ q_z)$ is called the imaginary part and q_w is called the real part of the quaternion $\hat{q}$, while i, j, and k are called imaginary units. □

For the imaginary part, $\mathbf{q}_v$, we can use all the normal vector operations, such as addition, scaling, dot product, cross product, and more. Using the definition of the quaternion, the multiplication operation between two quaternions, $\hat{q}$ and $\hat{r}$, is derived as shown below. Note that the multiplication of the imaginary units is non-commutative.

Multiplication :
$$\begin{aligned}
\hat{q}\hat{r} &= (iq_x + jq_y + kq_z + q_w)(ir_x + jr_y + kr_z + r_w) = \\
&\quad i(q_y r_z - q_z r_y + r_w q_x + q_w r_x) + \\
&\quad j(q_z r_x - q_x r_z + r_w q_y + q_w r_y) + \\
&\quad k(q_x r_y - q_y r_x + r_w q_z + q_w r_z) + \\
&\quad q_w r_w - q_x r_x - q_y r_y - q_z r_z = \\
&= (\mathbf{q}_v \times \mathbf{r}_v + r_w \mathbf{q}_v + q_w \mathbf{r}_v, \ q_w r_w - \mathbf{q}_v \cdot \mathbf{r}_v)
\end{aligned}$$

(3.32)

As can be seen in the above equation, we use both the cross product and the dot product to compute the multiplication of two quaternions.[12] Along with the

---

[12]In fact, the quaternion multiplication is the origin of both the dot product and the cross product.

definition of the quaternion, the definitions of addition, conjugate, norm, and an identity are needed:

Addition : $\hat{q} + \hat{r} = (\mathbf{q}_v, q_w) + (\mathbf{r}_v, r_w) = (\mathbf{q}_v + \mathbf{r}_v, q_w + r_w)$

Conjugate : $\hat{q}^* = (\mathbf{q}_v, q_w)^* = (-\mathbf{q}_v, q_w)$

Norm : $n(\hat{q}) = \hat{q}\hat{q}^* = \hat{q}^*\hat{q} = \mathbf{q}_v \cdot \mathbf{q}_v + q_w^2 = q_x^2 + q_y^2 + q_z^2 + q_w^2$

Identity : $\hat{i} = (\mathbf{0} \ \ 1)$

$$(3.33)$$

When $n(\hat{q}) = \hat{q}\hat{q}^*$ is simplified (result shown above), the imaginary parts cancel out and only a real part remains. The norm is sometimes denoted $||\hat{q}||^2 = n(\hat{q})$ [240]. A consequence of the above is that a multiplicative inverse, denoted by $\hat{q}^{-1}$, can be derived. The equation $\hat{q}^{-1}\hat{q} = \hat{q}\hat{q}^{-1} = 1$ must hold for the inverse (as is common for a multiplicative inverse). We derive a formula from the definition of the norm:

$$n(\hat{q}) = \hat{q}\hat{q}^* \qquad\qquad (3.34)$$
$$\Longleftrightarrow \qquad\qquad (3.35)$$
$$\frac{\hat{q}\hat{q}^*}{n(\hat{q})} = 1 \qquad\qquad (3.36)$$

This gives the multiplicative inverse as shown below.

Inverse : $\hat{q}^{-1} = \dfrac{1}{n(\hat{q})}\hat{q}^* \qquad\qquad (3.37)$

The formula for the inverse uses scalar multiplication, which is an operation derived from the multiplication seen in Equation 3.32: $s\hat{q} = (0, \ s)(\mathbf{q}_v, \ q_w) = (s\mathbf{q}_v, \ sq_w)$, and $\hat{q}s = (\mathbf{q}_v, \ q_w)(0, \ s) = (s\mathbf{q}_v, \ sq_w)$, which means that scalar multiplication is commutative: $s\hat{q} = \hat{q}s = (s\mathbf{q}_v, \ sq_w)$.

The following collection of rules are simple to derive from the definitions.

Conjugate rules : $(\hat{q}^*)^* = \hat{q}$

$$(\hat{q} + \hat{r})^* = \hat{q}^* + \hat{r}^* \qquad\qquad (3.38)$$

$$(\hat{q}\hat{r})^* = \hat{r}^*\hat{q}^*$$

Norm rules : $n(\hat{q}^*) = n(\hat{q})$

$$(3.39)$$

$$n(\hat{q}\hat{r}) = n(\hat{q})n(\hat{r})$$

Laws of Multiplication :

Linearity : $\hat{\mathbf{p}}(s\hat{\mathbf{q}} + t\hat{\mathbf{r}}) = s\hat{\mathbf{p}}\hat{\mathbf{q}} + t\hat{\mathbf{p}}\hat{\mathbf{r}}$

$$(s\hat{\mathbf{p}} + t\hat{\mathbf{q}})\hat{\mathbf{r}} = s\hat{\mathbf{p}}\hat{\mathbf{r}} + t\hat{\mathbf{q}}\hat{\mathbf{r}} \qquad (3.40)$$

Associativity : $\hat{\mathbf{p}}(\hat{\mathbf{q}}\hat{\mathbf{r}}) = (\hat{\mathbf{p}}\hat{\mathbf{q}})\hat{\mathbf{r}}$

A unit quaternion, $\hat{\mathbf{q}} = (\mathbf{q}_v, \ q_w)$, is such that $n(\hat{\mathbf{q}}) = 1$. From this it follows that $\hat{\mathbf{q}}$ may be written as

$$\hat{\mathbf{q}} = (\sin \phi \mathbf{u}_q, \ \cos \phi) \qquad (3.41)$$

for some three-dimensional vector $\mathbf{u}_q$, such that $||\mathbf{u}_q|| = 1$, because

$$n(\hat{\mathbf{q}}) = n(\sin \phi \mathbf{u}_q, \ \cos \phi) = \sin^2 \phi (\mathbf{u}_q \cdot \mathbf{u}_q) + \cos^2 \phi = \sin^2 \phi + \cos^2 \phi = 1 \qquad (3.42)$$

if and only if $\mathbf{u}_q \cdot \mathbf{u}_q = 1 = ||\mathbf{u}_q||^2$. As will be seen in the next section, unit quaternions are perfectly suited for creating rotations and orientations in a most efficient way.

3.3.2 Quaternion Transforms

We will now study a subclass of the quaternion set, namely those of unit length, called *unit quaternions*. The most important fact about unit quaternions is that they can represent any three-dimensional rotation, and that this representation is extremely compact and simple.

Now we will describe what makes unit quaternions so useful for rotations and orientations. First, put the four coordinates of a vector $\mathbf{p} = \begin{pmatrix} p_x & p_y & p_z & p_w \end{pmatrix}^T$ into the components of a quaternion $\hat{\mathbf{p}}$, and assume that we have a unit quaternion $\hat{\mathbf{q}} = (\sin \phi \mathbf{u}_q, \ \cos \phi)$. Then

$$\hat{\mathbf{q}}\hat{\mathbf{p}}\hat{\mathbf{q}}^{-1} \qquad (3.43)$$

rotates $\hat{\mathbf{p}}$ (and thus the point $\mathbf{p}$) around the axis $\mathbf{u}_q$ by an angle 2ϕ. Note that since $\hat{\mathbf{q}}$ is a unit quaternion, $\hat{\mathbf{q}}^{-1} = \hat{\mathbf{q}}^*$. This rotation, which clearly can be used to rotate around any axis, is illustrated in Figure 3.9.

Any non-zero real multiple of $\hat{\mathbf{q}}$ also represent the same transform, which means that $\hat{\mathbf{q}}$ and $-\hat{\mathbf{q}}$ represents the same rotation. That is, negating the axis, $\mathbf{u}_q$, and the real part, q_w, creates a quaternion which rotates exactly as the original

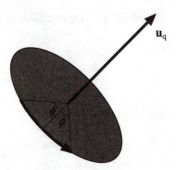

Figure 3.9. Illustration of the rotation transform represented by a unit quaternion, $\hat{q} = (\sin\phi \mathbf{u}_q, \cos\phi)$. The transform rotates 2ϕ radians around the axis $\mathbf{u}_q$.

quaternion does. It also means that the extraction of a quaternion from a matrix can return either $\hat{q}$ or $-\hat{q}$.

One reason for using (unit) quaternions instead of matrices is that their multiplication is much more economical than multiplication of matrices, thanks to the more optimal, more compact, less redundant representation of the quaternion. Given two unit quaternions, $\hat{q}$ and $\hat{r}$, the concatenation of first applying $\hat{q}$ and then $\hat{r}$ to a quaternion, $\hat{p}$ (which can be interpreted as a point $\mathbf{p}$), is given by Equation 3.44.

$$\hat{r}(\hat{q}\hat{p}\hat{q}^*)\hat{r}^* = (\hat{r}\hat{q})\hat{p}(\hat{r}\hat{q})^* = \hat{c}\hat{p}\hat{c}^* \tag{3.44}$$

Here, $\hat{c} = \hat{r}\hat{q}$ is the unit quaternion representing the concatenation of the unit quaternions $\hat{q}$ and $\hat{r}$.

Matrix Conversion

Since some systems have matrix multiplication implemented in hardware, we need conversion methods for transforming a quaternion into a matrix and vice versa. A quaternion, $\hat{q}$, can be converted into a matrix $\mathbf{M}^q$, as expressed in Equation 3.45 [328, 329].

$$\mathbf{M}^q = \begin{pmatrix} 1 - s(q_y^2 + q_z^2) & s(q_x q_y - q_w q_z) & s(q_x q_z + q_w q_y) & 0 \\ s(q_x q_y + q_w q_z) & 1 - s(q_x^2 + q_z^2) & s(q_y q_z - q_w q_x) & 0 \\ s(q_x q_z - q_w q_y) & s(q_y q_z + q_w q_x) & 1 - s(q_x^2 + q_y^2) & 0 \\ 0 & 0 & 0 & 1 \end{pmatrix} \tag{3.45}$$

Here, the scalar is $s = 2/n(\hat{\mathbf{q}})$. For unit quaternions, this simplifies to:

$$\mathbf{M}^q = \begin{pmatrix} 1 - 2(q_y^2 + q_z^2) & 2(q_x q_y - q_w q_z) & 2(q_x q_z + q_w q_y) & 0 \\ 2(q_x q_y + q_w q_z) & 1 - 2(q_x^2 + q_z^2) & 2(q_y q_z - q_w q_x) & 0 \\ 2(q_x q_z - q_w q_y) & 2(q_y q_z + q_w q_x) & 1 - 2(q_x^2 + q_y^2) & 0 \\ 0 & 0 & 0 & 1 \end{pmatrix} \quad (3.46)$$

Once the quaternion is constructed, *no* trigonometric functions need to be computed, so the conversion process is efficient in practice.

The reverse conversion, from an orthogonal matrix, $\mathbf{M}^q$, into a unit quaternion, $\hat{\mathbf{q}}$, is a bit more involved. Key to this process are the following differences made from the matrix in Equation 3.46.

$$\begin{aligned} m_{21}^q - m_{12}^q &= 4q_w q_x \\ m_{02}^q - m_{20}^q &= 4q_w q_y \\ m_{10}^q - m_{01}^q &= 4q_w q_z \end{aligned} \quad (3.47)$$

The implication of these equations is that if q_w is known, the values of the vector $\mathbf{v}_q$ can be computed, and thus $\hat{\mathbf{q}}$ derived. The trace, $\mathrm{tr}(\mathbf{M})$, of a matrix, $\mathbf{M}$, is simply the sum of the diagonal elements of the matrix. The trace of $\mathbf{M}^q$ is calculated by:

$$\mathrm{tr}(\mathbf{M}^q) = 4 - 2s(q_x^2 + q_y^2 + q_z^2) =$$

$$= 4\left(1 - \frac{q_x^2 + q_y^2 + q_z^2}{q_x^2 + q_y^2 + q_z^2 + q_w^2}\right) = \quad (3.48)$$

$$= \frac{4q_w^2}{q_x^2 + q_y^2 + q_z^2 + q_w^2} = \frac{4q_w^2}{n(\hat{\mathbf{q}})}$$

This result yields the following conversion for a unit quaternion:

$$q_w = \frac{1}{2}\sqrt{\mathrm{tr}(\mathbf{M}^q)}$$

$$q_x = \frac{m_{21}^q - m_{12}^q}{4q_w}$$

$$q_y = \frac{m_{02}^q - m_{20}^q}{4q_w} \quad (3.49)$$

$$q_z = \frac{m_{10}^q - m_{01}^q}{4q_w}$$

To have a numerically stable routine [329], divisions by small numbers should be avoided. Therefore, first, set $t = q_w^2 - q_x^2 - q_y^2 - q_z^2$, from which it follows that

$$
\begin{aligned}
m_{00} &= t + 2q_x^2 \\
m_{11} &= t + 2q_y^2 \\
m_{22} &= t + 2q_z^2 \\
u = m_{00} + m_{11} + m_{22} &= t + 2q_w^2
\end{aligned}
\tag{3.50}
$$

which in turn implies that the largest of m_{00}, m_{11}, m_{22}, and u determine which of q_x, q_y, q_z, and q_w is largest. If q_w is largest, then Equation 3.49 is used to derive the quaternion. Otherwise, we note that the following holds:

$$
\begin{aligned}
4q_x^2 &= +m_{00} - m_{11} - m_{22} + m_{33} \\
4q_y^2 &= -m_{00} + m_{11} - m_{22} + m_{33} \\
4q_z^2 &= -m_{00} - m_{11} + m_{22} + m_{33} \\
4q_w^2 &= \mathrm{tr}(\mathbf{M}^q)
\end{aligned}
\tag{3.51}
$$

The appropriate equation of the ones above is then used to compute the largest of q_x, q_y, and q_z, after which Equation 3.47 is used to calculate the remaining components of $\hat{\mathbf{q}}$. Luckily, there is code for this—see the *Further Reading and Resources* at the end of this chapter.

Spherical Linear Interpolation

Spherical linear interpolation is an operation that, given two unit quaternions, $\hat{\mathbf{q}}$ and $\hat{\mathbf{r}}$, and a parameter $t \in [0, 1]$, computes an interpolated quaternion. This is useful for animating objects, for example. It is not as useful for interpolating camera orientations, as the camera's "up" vector can become tilted during the interpolation, usually a disturbing effect [108].

The algebraic form of this operation is expressed by the composite quaternion, $\hat{\mathbf{s}}$, below.

$$
\hat{\mathbf{s}}(\hat{\mathbf{q}}, \hat{\mathbf{r}}, t) = (\hat{\mathbf{r}}\hat{\mathbf{q}}^{-1})^t \hat{\mathbf{q}}
\tag{3.52}
$$

However, for software implementations, the following form, where `slerp` stands for spherical linear interpolation, is much more appropriate.

$$
\hat{\mathbf{s}}(\hat{\mathbf{q}}, \hat{\mathbf{r}}, t) = \mathtt{slerp}(\hat{\mathbf{q}}, \hat{\mathbf{r}}, t) = \frac{\sin(\phi(1-t))}{\sin \phi}\hat{\mathbf{q}} + \frac{\sin(\phi t)}{\sin \phi}\hat{\mathbf{r}}
\tag{3.53}
$$

In the above equation, $\cos \phi = q_x r_x + q_y r_y + q_z r_z + q_w r_w$ [79]. For $t \in [0, 1]$, the `slerp` function computes (unique[13]) interpolated quaternions that together

---

[13]If and only if $\hat{\mathbf{q}}$ and $\hat{\mathbf{r}}$ are not opposite.

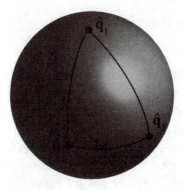

Figure 3.10. Unit quaternions are represented as points on the unit sphere. The function `slerp` is used to interpolate between the quaternions, and the interpolated path is a great arc on the sphere. Note that interpolating from $\hat{q}_1$ to $\hat{q}_2$ and interpolating from $\hat{q}_1$ to $\hat{q}_3$ to $\hat{q}_2$ are not the same thing, even though they arrive at the same orientation.

constitute the shortest arc on a four-dimensional unit sphere from $\hat{q}$ ($t = 0$) to $\hat{r}$ ($t = 1$). The arc is located on the circle that is formed from the intersection between the plane given by $\hat{q}$, $\hat{r}$, and the origin, and the four-dimensional unit sphere. This is shown in Figure 3.10. The computed rotation quaternion rotates around a fixed axis at constant speed. A curve such as this, that has constant speed and minimal acceleration, is called a *geodesic* curve [85].

The `slerp` function is perfectly suited for interpolating between two orientations. This procedure is not as simple with the Euler transform, because when several Euler angles need to be interpolated, gimbal lock (see Section 3.2.1) can occur.

Euler Quaternions

Now we will use quaternions to create an Euler transform [328]. First, recall that the Euler transform (Section 3.2.1) is the concatenation of three rotation matrices:

$$\mathbf{E}(h, p, r) = \mathbf{R}_z(r)\mathbf{R}_x(p)\mathbf{R}_y(h) \tag{3.54}$$

These rotations matrices can be expressed as unit quaternions as:

$$\begin{aligned}
\hat{q}_{head} &= ((0, \sin h, 0), \ \cos h) \\
\hat{q}_{pitch} &= ((\sin p, 0, 0), \ \cos p) \\
\hat{q}_{roll} &= ((0, 0, \sin r), \ \cos r)
\end{aligned} \tag{3.55}$$

where we put extra parentheses around the imaginary part of the quaternions. The quaternion that represents the entire Euler transform is then the concatenation of the three quaternions, as shown below.

$$\hat{e} = \hat{q}_{head}\hat{q}_{pitch}\hat{q}_{roll} \qquad (3.56)$$

The $\hat{e}$ quaternion can then be used to transform vectors and points, or it can be converted into a matrix and then used.

Rotation from One Vector to Another

A transform that is used frequently is the one that, given two unit vectors s and t, creates a matrix that rotates s into t. The mathematics of quaternions simplifies this procedure greatly. First the unit rotation axis, called u for simplicity, is computed as $u = (s \times t)/||s \times t||$. Second, $s \cdot t = \cos(2\phi)$ and $||s \times t|| = \sin(2\phi)$, where 2ϕ is the angle between s and t. The quaternion that represent the rotation from s to t is then $\hat{q} = (\sin\phi u, \cos\phi)$, where $\cos\phi$ and $\sin\phi$ can be obtained using the half-angle relations (see page 426). This quaternion can then be converted to a matrix, if needed.

There is also an efficient way to create the matrix that represents a rotation from s to t, another transform that is often needed. Here the vector u and the scalars $\sin(2\phi)$ and $\cos(2\phi)$ are as above. We start with a derivation of the upper left component of the matrix in Equation 3.46, which is $m_{00}^q = 1 - 2(q_y^2 + q_z^2)$. For a unit quaternion, $\hat{q} = (\sin\phi u, \cos\phi)$, we simplify, extend, and simplify again:

$$
\begin{aligned}
m_{00}^q &= 1 - 2(q_y^2 + q_z^2) = 1 - 2(u_y^2 + u_z^2)\sin^2\phi = \\
&= 1 - 2(u_x^2 + u_y^2 + u_z^2)\sin^2\phi + 2u_x^2\sin^2\phi = \\
&= 1 - 2\sin^2\phi + 2u_x^2\sin^2\phi = \\
&= \cos(2\phi) + (1 - \cos(2\phi))u_x^2
\end{aligned}
\qquad (3.57)
$$

In the first line we make use of the fact that $q_i = u_i\sin\phi$, if $i \in \{x, y, z\}$, which is the definition of our unit quaternion. Then, in the second line, we add the term $2u_x^2\sin^2\phi$ and also subtract it. In the third line we use the fact that $||u||^2 = u_x^2 + u_y^2 + u_z^2 = 1$ for unit quaternions. Finally, we use the fact that $1 - 2\sin^2(2\phi) = \cos(2\phi)$. This means that we can compute the upper left component of the matrix using $\cos(2\phi)$ and u, which we had already computed. Similar computations can be made for the other two components in the diagonal of the matrix.

Now, let us focus on another non-diagonal element of the matrix, say, m_{10}^q, to the middle left, and simplify in the same manner as for the diagonal element simplified above.

$$
\begin{aligned}
m_{10}^q &= 2(q_x q_y + q_w q_z) = 2u_x u_y \sin^2\phi + 2u_z \cos\phi\sin\phi = \\
&= (1 - \cos(2\phi))u_x u_y + u_z \sin(2\phi)
\end{aligned}
\qquad (3.58)
$$

Again, we end up with a formula that only uses the components we have already computed. The first line uses our definition of the quaternion, and the second uses $1 - 2\sin^2\phi = \cos(2\phi)$ and $2\sin\phi\cos\phi = \sin(2\phi)$. Similar computations can be made for the other non-diagonal elements in the matrix.

So using the above simplifications, the matrix that represents a rotation from the unit vector **s** to the unit vector **t** is denoted $\mathbf{R}(\mathbf{s}, \mathbf{t})$; it is shown below.

$$\mathbf{R}(\mathbf{s}, \mathbf{t}) = \begin{pmatrix} e + fu_x^2 & fu_xu_y - gu_z & fu_xu_z + gu_y & 0 \\ fu_xu_y + gu_z & e + fu_y^2 & fu_yu_z - gu_x & 0 \\ fu_xu_z - gu_y & fu_yu_z + gu_x & e + fu_z^2 & 0 \\ 0 & 0 & 0 & 1 \end{pmatrix} \tag{3.59}$$

Here, $e = \cos(2\phi) = \mathbf{s} \cdot \mathbf{t}$, $f = 1 - e$, $g = \sin(2\phi) = \|\mathbf{s} \times \mathbf{t}\|$, and $\mathbf{u} = (\mathbf{s} \times \mathbf{t})/\|\mathbf{s} \times \mathbf{t}\|$. Notice how all expensive trigonometric functions are avoided, making for a fast implementation. We still need to compute a square root when computing $\|\mathbf{s} \times \mathbf{t}\|$, but this can also be avoided. To avoid it, we start with the following variable: $\mathbf{v} = \mathbf{s} \times \mathbf{t}$. This means that the normalized version would be:

$$\mathbf{u} = \frac{1}{\|\mathbf{s} \times \mathbf{t}\|}\mathbf{v} = \frac{1}{\sin(2\phi)}\mathbf{v} = \left(\frac{v_x}{\sin(2\phi)}, \frac{v_y}{\sin(2\phi)}, \frac{v_z}{\sin(2\phi)}\right)^T \tag{3.60}$$

Now, let us see what this means for the diagonal elements of the matrix in Equation 3.64. Again, we simplify only the upper left element.

$$\begin{aligned} m_{00}^q &= e + fu_x^2 = \cos(2\phi) + (1 - \cos(2\phi))u_x^2 = \\ &= \cos(2\phi) + (1 - \cos(2\phi))\frac{v_x^2}{\sin^2(2\phi)} = \\ &= e + hv_x^2 \end{aligned} \tag{3.61}$$

Here we set $h = (1 - \cos(2\phi))/\sin^2(2\phi)$. Since in it the $\sin(2\phi)$ term is squared, we can avoid the square root for all diagonal elements. This can also be done for the non-diagonal elements as shown next.

$$\begin{aligned} m_{10}^q &= fu_xu_y + gu_z = (1 - \cos(2\phi))\frac{v_xv_y}{\sin^2(2\phi)} + \sin(2\phi)\frac{v_z}{\sin(2\phi)} = \\ &= (1 - \cos(2\phi))\frac{v_xv_y}{\sin^2(2\phi)} + v_z \end{aligned} \tag{3.62}$$

And again we see that the square root has disappeared. To summarize, we use the following intermediate calculations:

$$\mathbf{v} = \mathbf{s} \times \mathbf{t}$$
$$e = \cos(2\phi) = \mathbf{s} \cdot \mathbf{t}$$
$$h = \frac{1 - \cos(2\phi)}{\sin^2(2\phi)} = \frac{1 - e}{\mathbf{v} \cdot \mathbf{v}}$$

(3.63)

This gives the following rotation matrix, which is inexpensive to compute (in comparison to using the quaternion-to-matrix conversion directly):

$$\mathbf{R}(\mathbf{s}, \mathbf{t}) = \begin{pmatrix} e + hv_x^2 & hv_xv_y - v_z & hv_xv_z + v_y & 0 \\ hv_xv_y + v_z & e + hv_y^2 & hv_yv_z - v_x & 0 \\ hv_xv_z - v_y & hv_yv_z + v_x & e + hv_z^2 & 0 \\ 0 & 0 & 0 & 1 \end{pmatrix}$$

(3.64)

Note that care must be taken when $\mathbf{s}$ and $\mathbf{t}$ are parallel or near parallel, because then $||\mathbf{s} \times \mathbf{t}|| \approx 0$. If $\phi \approx 0$ then we can return the identity matrix. However, if $2\phi \approx \pi$ then we can rotate π radians around *any* axis. This axis can be found as the cross product between $\mathbf{s}$ and any other vector that is not parallel to $\mathbf{s}$ (see Section 3.2.4).

EXAMPLE: POSITIONING AND ORIENTING A CAMERA   Assume that the default position for a virtual camera (or viewpoint) is $(0 \ \ 0 \ \ 0)^T$ and the default view direction $\mathbf{v}$ is along the negative z-axis, i.e., $\mathbf{v} = (0 \ \ 0 \ \ -1)^T$. Now, the goal is to create a transform that moves the camera to a new position $\mathbf{p}$, looking in a new direction $\mathbf{w}$. Start by orienting the camera, which can be done by rotating the default view direction into the destination view direction. $\mathbf{R}(\mathbf{v}, \mathbf{w})$ takes care of this. The positioning is simply done by translating to $\mathbf{p}$, which yields the resulting transform $\mathbf{X} = \mathbf{T}(\mathbf{p})\mathbf{R}(\mathbf{v}, \mathbf{w})$. In practice, after the first rotation another vector-vector rotation will most likely be desired to rotate the view's up direction to some desired orientation.   □

3.4   Interpolation

In this section we will take a brief look at interpolation. Interpolation is used in many different contexts and is performed using a great many different methods. For real-time graphics, interpolation is often used to move (using transforms) the viewer along a predefined path. This may involve changing both the position and the orientation.

Say there are two points and you want the camera to move from the first point to the second in a certain amount of time, independent of the performance of the underlying hardware. As an example, assume that the camera should move from one point to the other in one second, and that the rendering of one frame takes 50 ms. This means that we will be able to render 20 frames during that second. Therefore, we want to move the camera to 20 different locations during this second so that the camera appears to be moving from the first point to the second. On a faster computer one frame might only take 25 ms, which would be equal to 40 frames per second, and so we would want to move the camera to 40 different locations. This is all possible with interpolation techniques.

The simplest kind of interpolation is *linear interpolation*. Using linear interpolation, the path from one point to another is a straight line (shown at the left in Figure 3.11). Assume that the two points of a path are called $\mathbf{p}_0$ and $\mathbf{p}_1$. Linearly interpolating between these two points is done using the following formula, where $t \in [0, 1]$.

$$\mathbf{p}(t) = \mathbf{p}_0 + t(\mathbf{p}_1 - \mathbf{p}_0) \tag{3.65}$$

For this formula, $\mathbf{p}(0) = \mathbf{p}_0$ and $\mathbf{p}(1) = \mathbf{p}_1$. So if we would like to move the camera from $\mathbf{p}_0$ to $\mathbf{p}_1$ linearly in 20 steps during one second, then we would use $t_i = \frac{1}{20-1}i$, where i is the frame number (starting from 0).

When you are interpolating between only two points, linear interpolation may suffice, but for more points it often does not. For example, when several points are interpolated, the sudden changes at the points (also called joints) that connect two segments become unacceptable. This is shown at the right of Figure 3.11.

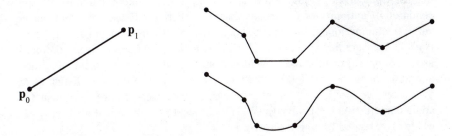

Figure 3.11. Linear interpolation between two points is the path on a straight line (left). This may work fine when only two points are involved, but when more points are on the path, this is not acceptable. For seven points, linear interpolation is shown at the upper right, and Hermite interpolation is shown at the lower right. What is most objectionable about using linear interpolation are the discontinuous changes (sudden jerks) at the joints between the linear segments.

A better solution is to use splines. Here we will briefly present Hermite interpolation, which uses a type of spline. This is a smooth interpolating function with much better qualities than linear interpolation. We begin with two points, $\mathbf{p}_0$ and $\mathbf{p}_1$, which have tangent vectors $\mathbf{m}_0$ and $\mathbf{m}_1$, respectively. The Hermite interpolant, $\mathbf{p}(t)$, where $t \in [0, 1]$, is:

$$\mathbf{p}(t) = (2t^3 - 3t^2 + 1)\mathbf{p}_0 + (t^3 - 2t^2 + t)\mathbf{m}_0 + (t^3 - t^2)\mathbf{m}_1 + (-2t^3 + 3t^2)\mathbf{p}_1$$

$$(3.66)$$

We also call $\mathbf{p}(t)$ a Hermite curve segment. This is a cubic interpolant, since t^3 is the highest exponent in the above formula, and the following hold:

$$\mathbf{p}(0) = \mathbf{p}_0$$
$$\mathbf{p}(1) = \mathbf{p}_1$$
$$\frac{d\mathbf{p}}{dt}(0) = \mathbf{m}_0 \qquad\qquad (3.67)$$
$$\frac{d\mathbf{p}}{dt}(1) = \mathbf{m}_1$$

See Figure 3.12 for some examples. All these examples interpolate the same points, but have different tangents. Note also that different lengths of the tangents give different results; longer tangents have a greater impact on the overall shape.

Next, we will discuss how to use Hermite interpolation to interpolate a set of more than two points. But first we will introduce the continuity measure. For curves in general, we use the C^n notation to differentiate between different kinds of continuity at the joints. This means that all the n:th first derivatives should be continuous and non-zero all over the curve. Continuity of C^0 means that the segment should join at the same point, so linear interpolation fulfills this condition. Continuity of C^1 means that if we derive once at any point on the curve (including joints), the result should also be continuous, and so on. There is also a measure that is denoted G^n. Let us look at G^1 (geometrical) continuity as an example. For this, the tangent vectors from the curve segments that meet at a joint should be parallel, but they do not need to be of the same length as do the tangent vectors in C^1. In other words, G^1 is a weaker continuity than C^1, and a curve that is C^1 is always G^1. The concept of geometrical continuity can easily be extended to higher dimensions.

At the left in Figure 3.13, we show C^0, G^1, and C^1 continuity between two Hermite curve segments. As can be seen in this figure, for C^1 continuity the tangent vectors at a joint should be parallel and have equal length. In order to interpolate several points with Hermite curve segments between them, we must compute tangents for each joint. Since two curve segments are joined at one

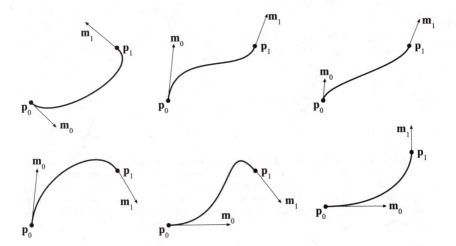

Figure 3.12. Hermite interpolation. A curve is defined by two points, p_0 and p_1, and a tangent, m_0 and m_1, at each point.

point, each curve can have its own tangent at the joint. However, these tangents should be parallel and of equal length for C^1 continuity, which is preferable to C^0 and G^1.

Here we will present one way to compute such tangents. Assume that we have n points, $\mathbf{p}_0, \ldots, \mathbf{p}_{n-1}$, which should be interpolated with $n-1$ Hermite curve segments. We assume that there is only one tangent at each point, and we start to look at the "inner" tangents, $\mathbf{m}_1, \ldots, \mathbf{m}_{n-2}$. A tangent at $\mathbf{p}_i$ can be computed as a combination of the two chords [211]: $\mathbf{p}_i - \mathbf{p}_{i-1}$, and $\mathbf{p}_{i+1} - \mathbf{p}_i$, as shown at the left in Figure 3.14. First, a tension parameter, a, is introduced. This controls how sharp the curve is going to be at the joint. The tangent is computed as:

$$\mathbf{m}_i = \frac{1-a}{2}((\mathbf{p}_i - \mathbf{p}_{i-1}) + \mathbf{p}_{i+1} - \mathbf{p}_i) \qquad (3.68)$$

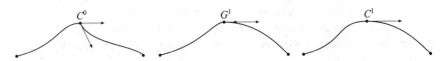

Figure 3.13. Left: the upper curve has non-parallel tangents at the joints and so has only C^0 continuity; the middle curve has parallel tangent vectors but different lengths and so has G^1; and the rightmost curve has parallel tangent vectors with same length and so has C^1 continuity.

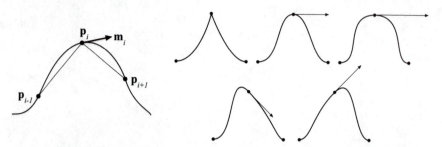

Figure 3.14. One method of computing the tangents is to use a combination of the chords (left). The upper row at the right shows three curves with different tension parameters (a). The left curve has $a \approx 1$, which means high tension; the middle curve has $a \approx 0$, which is default tension; and the right curve has $a \approx -1$, which is low tension. The bottom row of two curves at the right shows different bias parameters. The curve on the left has a negative bias, and the right curve has a positive bias.

The top row at the right in Figure 3.14 shows different tension parameters. The default value is $a = 0$; higher values give sharper bends (if $a > 1$ there will be a loop at the joint), and negative values give more slackened joints. Second, a bias parameter, b, is introduced. If we ignore the tension ($a = 0$) for a while, then the tangent is computed as below.

$$\mathbf{m}_i = \frac{1+b}{2}(\mathbf{p}_i - \mathbf{p}_{i-1}) + \frac{1-b}{2}(\mathbf{p}_{i+1} - \mathbf{p}_i) \qquad (3.69)$$

The default value is $b = 0$. A positive bias gives a bend that is more directed toward the chord $\mathbf{p}_i - \mathbf{p}_{i-1}$, and a negative bias gives a bend that is more directed toward the other chord: $\mathbf{p}_{i+1} - \mathbf{p}_i$. This is shown in the bottom column on the right in Figure 3.14. Combining the tension and the bias gives:

$$\mathbf{m}_i = \frac{(1-a)(1+b)}{2}(\mathbf{p}_i - \mathbf{p}_{i-1}) + \frac{(1-a)(1-b)}{2}(\mathbf{p}_{i+1} - \mathbf{p}_i) \qquad (3.70)$$

The user can either set the tension and bias parameters or let them have their default values. Note that each point can in fact have its own unique parameters. The tangents at the first and the last points can also be computed with these formulae; one of the chords is simply set to a length of zero.

Yet another parameter that controls the continuity can be incorporated into the tangent equation; see Kochanek and Bartels's paper [211] or the 1990 book by Foley et al. [108].

Orientations also have to be interpolated. Spherical linear interpolation (slerp) can be used between two points. For cases in which several points are involved and more than C^0 continuity is required, the reader is directed to

Shoemake [328], Pletinckx [289], or Schlag's gem [316]. For more references to spline interpolation, see the *Further Reading and Resources* at the end of this chapter.

3.5 Projections

Before one can actually render a scene, all relevant objects in the scene must be projected onto some kind of plane or into some kind of simple volume. After that, clipping and rendering are performed.

The transforms seen so far in this chapter have left the fourth component, the w-component, unaffected. That is, points and vectors have retained their types after the transform. Also, the bottom row in the 4×4 matrices has always been $(0\ 0\ 0\ 1)$. *Perspective projection matrices* are exceptions to both of these properties: the bottom row contains vector and point manipulating numbers, and, the homogenization process is often needed (i.e., w is often not 1, so a division by w is needed to obtain the point). *Orthographic projection*, which is dealt with first in this section, is a simpler kind of projection that is also commonly used.

In this section, it is assumed that the viewer is looking along the negative z-axis, with the y-axis pointing up and the x-axis to the right. This is a right-handed coordinate system. Some texts use a left-handed systems in which the viewer looks along the positive z-axis. Both systems are valid; this book uses right-handed modeling and viewing of coordinate systems for reasons of consistency.

3.5.1 Orthographic Projection

A characteristic of an orthographic projection is that parallel lines remain parallel after the projection. Matrix $\mathbf{P}_o$, shown below, is a simple orthographic projection matrix that leaves the x- and y-components of a point unchanged, while setting the z-component to zero, i.e., it orthographically projects onto the plane $z = 0$.

$$\mathbf{P}_o = \begin{pmatrix} 1 & 0 & 0 & 0 \\ 0 & 1 & 0 & 0 \\ 0 & 0 & 0 & 0 \\ 0 & 0 & 0 & 1 \end{pmatrix} \tag{3.71}$$

The effect of this projection is illustrated in Figure 3.15. Clearly, $\mathbf{P}_o$ is non-invertible, since its determinant $|\mathbf{P}_o| = 0$. In other words, the transform drops from three to two dimensions, and there is no way to retrieve the dropped dimension. A problem with using this kind of orthographic projection for viewing

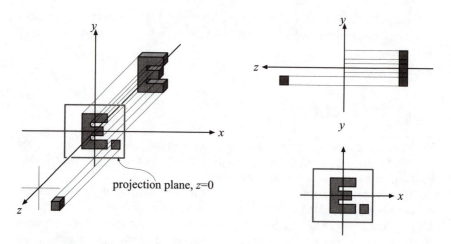

projection plane, $z=0$

Figure 3.15. Three different views of the simple orthographic projection generated by Equation 3.71. This projection can be seen as the viewer is looking along the negative z-axis, which means that the projection simply skips (or sets to zero) the z-coordinate while keeping the x- and y-coordinates. Note that objects on both sides of $z = 0$ are projected onto the projection plane.

is that it projects both points with positive and points with negative z-values onto the projection plane. It is usually useful to restrict the z-values (and the x- and y-values) to a certain interval, from, say n (near plane) to f (far plane).[14] This is the purpose of the next transformation.

A more common matrix for performing orthographic projection is expressed in terms of the six-tuple, (n, f, l, r, b, t), denoting the near, far, left, right, bottom, and top planes. This matrix essentially scales and translates the AABB (axis-aligned bounding box; see the definition in Section 10.1) formed by these planes into an axis-aligned cube. The minimum corner of the AABB is $(l, b, n)^T$ and the maximum corner is $(r, t, f)^T$. The axis-aligned cube has a minimum corner of $(-1, -1, -1)^T$ and a maximum corner of $(1, 1, 1)^T$. This cube is called the *canonical view volume*, and the coordinates in this volume are called *normalized device coordinates*.[15] The procedure is shown in Figure 3.16. The reason for transforming into the canonical view volume is that clipping is more efficiently performed there, especially in the case of a hardware implementation.

After the transformation into the canonical view volume, vertices of the geometry to be rendered are clipped against this cube. The geometry not outside the

---

[14]The near plane is also called the *front plane* or *hither*; the far plane is also the *back plane* or *yon*.

[15]Some APIs use other canonical volumes, such as an AABB from $(-1, -1, 0)^T$ to $(1, 1, 1)^T$.

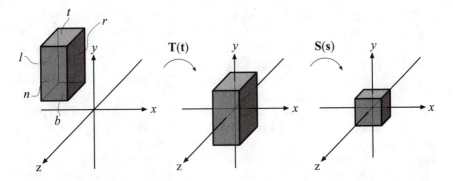

Figure 3.16. Transforming an axis-aligned box on the canonical view volume. The box on the left is first translated, making its center coincide with the origin. Then it is scaled to get the size of the canonical view volume, shown at the right.

cube is finally rendered by dropping the z-coordinate and mapping the remaining unit square to the screen. This orthographic transform is shown here:

$$\mathbf{P}_o = \mathbf{S(s)T(t)} = \begin{pmatrix} \dfrac{2}{r-l} & 0 & 0 & 0 \\ 0 & \dfrac{2}{t-b} & 0 & 0 \\ 0 & 0 & \dfrac{2}{f-n} & 0 \\ 0 & 0 & 0 & 1 \end{pmatrix} \begin{pmatrix} 1 & 0 & 0 & -\dfrac{l+r}{2} \\ 0 & 1 & 0 & -\dfrac{t+b}{2} \\ 0 & 0 & 1 & -\dfrac{f+n}{2} \\ 0 & 0 & 0 & 1 \end{pmatrix} =$$

$$\begin{pmatrix} \dfrac{2}{r-l} & 0 & 0 & -\dfrac{r+l}{r-l} \\ 0 & \dfrac{2}{t-b} & 0 & -\dfrac{t+b}{t-b} \\ 0 & 0 & \dfrac{2}{f-n} & -\dfrac{f+n}{f-n} \\ 0 & 0 & 0 & 1 \end{pmatrix}$$

(3.72)

As suggested by the above equation, $\mathbf{P}_o$ can be written as the concatenation of a translation, $\mathbf{T(t)}$, followed by a scaling matrix, $\mathbf{S(s)}$, where $\mathbf{s} = (2/(r-l), 2/(t-b), 2/(f-n))^T$ and $\mathbf{t} = (-(r+l)/2, -(t+b)/2, -(f+n)/2)^T$. This matrix is invertible[16], i.e., $\mathbf{P}_o^{-1} = \mathbf{T(-t)S}((r-l)/2, (t-b)/2, (f-n)/2)$.

---

[16]If and only if $n \neq f$, $l \neq r$, and $t \neq b$; otherwise no inverse exist.

This gives a clean derivation and an equation that transforms directly from world space to another related space, but in fact the resulting transform is *not* what is commonly used. In computer graphics, a left-hand coordinate system is used in projection—i.e., for the screen, the x-axis goes to the right, y-axis goes up, and the z-axis goes into the screen. For example, to get the orthographic projection used in OpenGL [276], multiply by $S(1, 1, -1)$ before transforming into the canonical view volume. The resulting matrix becomes $P'_o = S(s)T(t)S(1, 1, -1)$. All this does is negate element $(2, 2)$ of the matrix and make it $-2/(f - n)$. The major reason for switching to a left-handed coordinate system is that then the z-axis points inwards, making Z-buffering more intuitive, as objects farther away have higher z values. Also, switching makes the far plane value greater than the near plane value.

Some systems also map the z-depths to the range $[0, 1]$ instead of $[-1, 1]$. This can be accomplished by a simple scaling and translation matrix applied after the orthographic matrix, i.e.:

$$\mathbf{M}_{st} = \begin{pmatrix} 1 & 0 & 0 & 0 \\ 0 & 1 & 0 & 0 \\ 0 & 0 & 0.5 & 0.5 \\ 0 & 0 & 0 & 1 \end{pmatrix} \tag{3.73}$$

3.5.2 Perspective Projection

A much more interesting transform than orthographic projection is perspective projection, which is used in the majority of computer graphics applications. Here, parallel lines are generally not parallel after projection; rather, they may converge to a single point at their extreme.

First, we shall present an instructive derivation for a perspective projection matrix that projects onto a plane $z = -d$, $d > 0$. We derive from world space to simplify understanding of how the world-to-view conversion proceeds, and where the switch from right-handed world coordinates to left-handed view coordinates takes place. This derivation is followed by the more conventional matrices used in, for example, OpenGL [276].

Assume that the camera (viewpoint) is located at the origin, and that we want to project a point, $\mathbf{p}$, onto the plane $z = -d$, $d > 0$, yielding a new point $\mathbf{q} = (q_x \quad q_y \quad -d)^T$. This scenario is depicted in Figure 3.17. From the similar

projection plane, $z = -d$

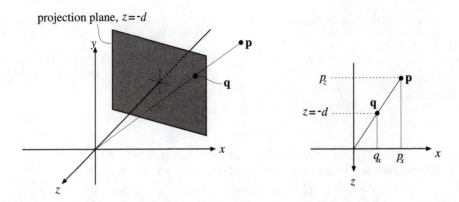

Figure 3.17. The notation used for deriving a perspective projection matrix. The point **p** is projected onto the plane $z = -d$, $d > 0$, which yields the projected point **q**. The projection is performed from the perspective of the camera's location, which in this case is the origin. The similar triangle used in the derivation is shown for the x-component at the right.

triangles shown in this figure, the following derivation, for the x-component of **q**, is obtained:

$$\frac{q_x}{p_x} = \frac{-d}{p_z}$$

$$\Longleftrightarrow \tag{3.74}$$

$$q_x = -d\frac{p_x}{p_z}$$

The expressions for the other components of **q** are $q_y = -dp_y/p_z$ (obtained similarly to q_x), and $q_z = -d$. Together with the above formula, these give us the perspective projection matrix, $\mathbf{P}_p$, as shown here:

$$\mathbf{P}_p = \begin{pmatrix} 1 & 0 & 0 & 0 \\ 0 & 1 & 0 & 0 \\ 0 & 0 & 1 & 0 \\ 0 & 0 & -1/d & 0 \end{pmatrix} \tag{3.75}$$

That this matrix yields the correct perspective projection is confirmed by the simple verification of Equation 3.76.

$$\mathbf{q} = \mathbf{P}_p\mathbf{p} = \begin{pmatrix} 1 & 0 & 0 & 0 \\ 0 & 1 & 0 & 0 \\ 0 & 0 & 1 & 0 \\ 0 & 0 & -1/d & 0 \end{pmatrix} \begin{pmatrix} p_x \\ p_y \\ p_z \\ 1 \end{pmatrix} = \begin{pmatrix} p_x \\ p_y \\ p_z \\ -p_z/d \end{pmatrix} \Leftrightarrow \begin{pmatrix} -dp_x/p_z \\ -dp_y/p_z \\ -d \\ 1 \end{pmatrix}$$

(3.76)

The last step comes from the fact that the whole vector is divided by the w-component (in this case $-p_z/d$), in order to get a 1 in the last position.

As with the orthographic transformation, there is also a perspective transform that, rather than actually projecting onto a plane (which is non-invertible), transforms the view frustum into the canonical view volume described previously. Here the view frustum is assumed to start at $z = n$ and end at $z = f$. The rectangle at $z = n$ has the minimum corner at (l, b, n) and the maximum corner at (r, t, n). This is shown in Figure 3.18.

The parameters (l, r, b, t, n, f) determine the field of view of the camera. The greater the field of view, the more the camera "sees." The horizontal field of view is determined by the angle between the left and the right planes of the frustum. In the same manner, the vertical field of view is determined by the angle between the top and the bottom planes. Asymmetric frustums can be created by $r \neq -l$ or $t \neq -b$. Asymmetric frustums are, for example, used for stereo viewing (see Section 12.1.5) and in CAVEs [74]. The perspective transform matrix that transforms the frustum into a unit cube is given by Equation 3.77.

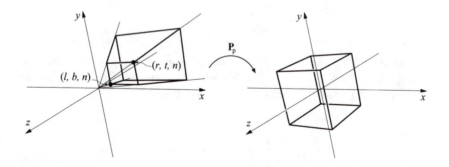

Figure 3.18. The matrix $\mathbf{P}_p$ transforms the view frustum into the unit cube, which is called the canonical view volume.

$$P_p = \begin{pmatrix} \dfrac{2n}{r-l} & 0 & -\dfrac{r+l}{r-l} & 0 \\ 0 & \dfrac{2n}{t-b} & -\dfrac{t+b}{t-b} & 0 \\ 0 & 0 & \dfrac{f+n}{f-n} & -\dfrac{2fn}{f-n} \\ 0 & 0 & 1 & 0 \end{pmatrix} \tag{3.77}$$

After applying this transform to a point, we will get another point $q = (q_x, q_y, q_z, q_w)^T$. The w-component, q_w, of this point will (most often) be non-zero and not equal to one. To get the projected point, p, we need to divide by q_w: $p = (q_x/q_w, q_y/q_w, q_z/q_w, 1)^T$. The matrix P_p always sees to it that $z = f$ maps to $+1$ and $z = n$ maps to -1. As in the orthographic case, after the perspective transform, clipping and rendering are performed.

To get the perspective transform used in OpenGL, first multiply with $S((1 \; 1 \; -1)^T)$, for the same reasons as for the orthographic transform. This simply negates the values in the third column of Equation 3.77. After this mirroring transform has been applied, the near and far values are entered as positive values, with $0 < n' < f'$, as they would traditionally be presented to the user. However, they still represent distances along the world's negative z-axis, which is the direction of view. For reference purposes, here is the OpenGL equation:

$$P_{OpenGL} = \begin{pmatrix} \dfrac{2n}{r-l} & 0 & \dfrac{r+l}{r-l} & 0 \\ 0 & \dfrac{2n}{t-b} & \dfrac{t+b}{t-b} & 0 \\ 0 & 0 & -\dfrac{f'+n'}{f'-n'} & -\dfrac{2f'n'}{f'-n'} \\ 0 & 0 & -1 & 0 \end{pmatrix} \tag{3.78}$$

Some APIs (e.g., DirectX) map the near plane to $z = 0$ (instead of $z = -1$) and the far plane to $z = 1$, which gives a slightly different matrix. Transforming to this form is done the same way as it was for orthographic matrices, by applying the matrix in Equation 3.73 last. Here is that form:

$$P_{[0,1]} = \begin{pmatrix} \dfrac{2n}{r-l} & 0 & \dfrac{r+l}{r-l} & 0 \\ 0 & \dfrac{2n}{t-b} & \dfrac{t+b}{t-b} & 0 \\ 0 & 0 & -\dfrac{f'}{f'-n'} & -\dfrac{f'n'}{f'-n'} \\ 0 & 0 & -1 & 0 \end{pmatrix} \tag{3.79}$$

Further Reading and Resources

One of the best books for building up one's intuition about matrices in a painless fashion is Farin and Hansford's *The Geometry Toolbox* [105]. Another useful reference is Rogers's *Mathematical Elements for Computer Graphics* [299]. For a different perspective, many computer graphics texts, such as Watt and Watt's [367], Hearn and Baker's [162], and the two books by Foley et al. [108, 109], also cover matrix basics. The *Graphics Gems* series [17, 117, 166, 208, 282] presents various transform-related algorithms and has code available online for many of these. Golub and Van Loan's *Matrix Computations* [129] is the place to start for a serious study of matrix techniques. See http://www.realtimerendering.com/ for code for many different transforms, including quaternions.

For spline interpolation, we refer the interested reader to Watt and Watt [367] or Rogers's [299]. For more in-depth coverage see Farin's [104] thorough treatment.

Chapter 4
Visual Appearance

"Light makes right."
–Andrew Glassner

When you render images of three-dimensional models, the models should not only look good geometrically, they should also have a realistic visual appearance. This is usually accomplished via a combination of techniques, such as associating a material with each surface, applying various kinds of light sources, adding textures, using fog, transparency, and antialiasing techniques, compositing, and more. We will deal with many of these methods in this chapter, with texture treated in the next, and special effects in the chapter following that.

4.1 Light Sources

Humans can see an object because photons bounce off (or are emitted from) the surface of the object and reach the eyes of the viewer. These photons may come from other objects or from *light sources*. In this context, there are three different types of light sources—*directional lights*, *point lights*, and *spot lights*, which are illustrated in Figure 4.1. The ways in which the parameters of the different types of light sources interact with the properties of a surface are described in Section 4.3.

A directional light is considered to be positioned infinitely far away from the objects that are being lit. An example of such a light is the sun. Point and spot lights are called *positional lights* because they each have a location in space. A positional light can be thought of as a single point that emits photons. In contrast, real light sources have an area or volume, and so cast shadows with soft edges (see Section 6.6). Positional and directional light sources cast shadows with sharp edges. In Figure 4.2, the three different light source types illuminate a square.

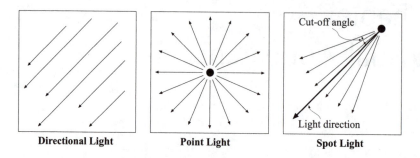

Directional Light   **Point Light**   **Spot Light**

Figure 4.1. Three different types of light sources. A directional light is positioned infinitely far away, and the light rays from such a light source are therefore parallel when they arrive at an object. A point light has a position in space and sends light rays uniformly in every direction from that position. A spot light is like a point light but it emits light only within the volume of a cone, defined by a cut-off angle and a light direction. An example of a spot light is a flashlight's beam.

All three light source types have intensity parameters in common. Each light source normally has an intensity and sometimes a color to it. Color is normally described as a set of red, green, and blue values (a.k.a., *RGB*). In theory this vector could be made arbitrarily long; see Hall's 1989 book [156] for more on color representation. A light can be further subdivided and have an ambient, diffuse, and specular intensity (these terms will be defined later on). These qualities are summarized in Table 4.1, where the s is short for *source*, in order to avoid confusion with the light vector, l, used later on. This kind of division is not physically accurate, but it gives the user of a real-time graphics application more control over scene appearance. This table shows the common light source

Figure 4.2. Here a square, subdivided into $100 \times 100 \times 2$ triangles, is lit by a directional light source (left), a point light source (middle), and a spot light (right).

Notation	Description
s_{amb}	Ambient intensity color
s_{diff}	Diffuse intensity color
s_{spec}	Specular intensity color
s_{pos}	Light source position (four elements)

Table 4.1. Table of common light source parameters for directional, point, and spot lights.

parameters for the light sources in OpenGL [276]. Some graphics APIs describe the intensities with fewer parameters.

A spot light has a few more parameters. First, it has a direction vector, which is where the spot light points. This parameter is denoted s_{dir}. It also has a *cut-off angle*, s_{cut}, which is half the angle of the spot light cone. Then, to control attenuation within the cone, it has a *spot exponent*, s_{exp}, which can be used to concentrate the light distribution in the center of the cone, and let it fall off exponentially from the center. The light direction and the cut-off angle parameters are shown at the right in Figure 4.1. Other parameters are possible for spot light control; for example, the edge of the spot light's effect can be softened so it does not drop off so sharply.

In the real world a light drops off with the square of the distance from it. In the computer graphics world the norm is that lights do not drop off with distance. Such lights are generally easier to control (because there is no need to worry about the effect of distance), and their effects may be computed more quickly. Directional light sources have no drop-off effects by definition, since they are infinitely far away. However, positional light sources sometimes allow control of their intensity based on distance. For example, OpenGL has three parameters, l_c, l_l, and l_q, that are used to control the attenuation which is proportional to some function of the distance from the light source. These parameters are described in more detail in Section 4.3.4.

4.2 Material

In real-time systems a material consists of a number of material parameters, namely ambient, diffuse, specular, shininess, and emissive. The color of a surface with a material is determined by these parameters, the parameters of the light sources that illuminate the surface, and a lighting model. This interaction is explained in the next section. The best way to get to know what these parameters actually do is to experiment with them in an interactive setting. See

Notation	Description
$\mathbf{m}_{amb}$	Ambient material color
$\mathbf{m}_{diff}$	Diffuse material color
$\mathbf{m}_{spec}$	Specular material color
m_{shi}	Shininess parameter
$\mathbf{m}_{emi}$	Emissive material color

Table 4.2. Table of material constants.

the *Further Reading and Resources* section at the end of this chapter for some online programs that allow such experimentation.

4.3   Lighting and Shading

Lighting is the term that is used to designate the interaction between material and light sources, as well as their interaction with the geometry of the object to be rendered. As will be seen in the subsequent sections in this chapter, lighting can also be used with colors, textures, and transparency. All these elements are combined into a visual appearance on the screen.

Shading is the process of performing lighting computations and determining pixels' colors from them. There are three main types of shading: flat, Gouraud, and Phong. These correspond to computing the light per polygon, per vertex, and per pixel. In flat shading, a color is computed for a triangle and the triangle is filled with that color. In Gouraud shading [138], the lighting at each vertex of a triangle is determined, and these lighting samples (i.e., computed colors) are interpolated over the surface of the triangle. In Phong shading [286], the shading normals stored at the vertices are used to interpolate the shading normal at each pixel in the triangle. This normal is then used to compute the lighting's effect on that pixel. The effect of these three methods on the same lighting and materials is shown in Figure 4.3.

Flat shading runs fast and is simple to implement. While it does not give a smooth look to curved surfaces as Gouraud shading does, this can be an advantage; sometimes the user wants to see the underlying facets making up the model. Most graphics hardware implement Gouraud shading because of its speed and much improved quality. It is about as fast as flat shading, because the effect of lighting is computed only at the triangle vertices. A problem with this technique is that the shading is highly dependent on the level of detail of the objects that are rendered. This problem is illustrated in Figure 4.4. Problems

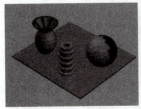

Figure 4.3. The same scene is shown with flat, Gouraud, and Phong shading, respectively (the flat shaded image has no specular highlighting component computed).

with Gouraud shading include missing highlights, failure to capture spot-light effects, and Mach banding [120, 156] (see Figure 4.3). As we will discuss in Section 5.7.2, these limitations can be partially overcome by using textures to represent lighting effects. Phong shading avoids these problems by interpolating the surface normal and computing the lighting at each pixel. Because per-pixel lighting is more complex and much more costly than per-vertex lighting, Phong shading is currently uncommon in commercial graphics hardware. This situation is likely to change.

Gouraud shading can achieve essentially the same shading result as Phong shading by subdividing a surface into triangles smaller than a pixel. This algorithm would be quite slow in practice, but it is a way in which Gouraud shading hardware can be coerced into acting more like a Phong shader. The concept of subdividing a surface into tiny fragments, rendering each of these, and then blending the results is powerful (though rarely used in real-time systems). For example, it is the basis of Pixar's RenderMan system [65], which is used in film production.

The illumination at the vertices (or at all pixels for Phong shading) is computed using a *lighting model*. For real-time graphics purposes, all of these models are very similar, and each can be divided into three major parts, namely the *diffuse*, the *specular*, and the *ambient* components. These parts and their sum are illustrated in Figure 4.11.

It should be mentioned that this sort of lighting model is not based on much physical theory, but the result is still fairly good. Ultimately, the lighting model should simulate exactly the way photons interact with the physical environment (i.e., the surfaces in the scene), but because of the complexity of such a simulation it is infeasible for real-time purposes. Radiosity [59, 121, 333] and global illumination [121, 327] techniques are rendering methods that can render extremely realistic images (at the cost of time).

Now we will review each lighting model component and then see how these are combined into a lighting equation. For good or ill, graphics accelerators and

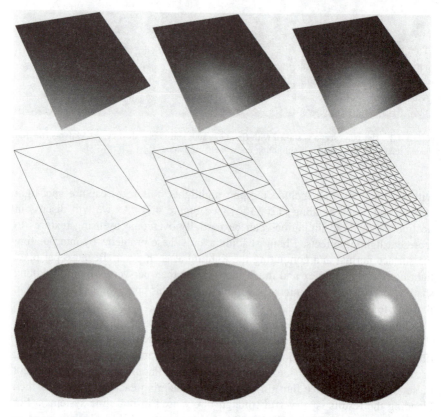

Figure 4.4. Shading is affected by the drawing primitives' size and location. The top row shows three squares with 2, 18, and 288 triangles. The middle row shows the wire frames of those shapes. The image at the right, with the highest triangle density, has the best shading. The bottom row shows how the quality of shading (and the silhouette quality) of approximations of spheres increases with the number of triangles. The spheres contain (left to right) 256, 1024, and 16, 384 triangles.

APIs seem to use the type of lighting model we will describe.[1] There are also more accurate models describing the interaction of light and material, such as Cook-Torrance's model [62, 63], He's model [161], and Oren and Nayar's model [279]. Lastra et al. have done research on implementing different illumination models as part of a hardware accelerator [222]. Still, it is unlikely that these will have any direct influence on commercial graphics hardware in the near future.

---

[1]It is often possible for application writers to substitute a different model and simply send down their own color per vertex. However, if per-pixel shading is available in hardware, this option becomes difficult, if not impossible.

However, this does not mean that the parameters in the equations we will present need to be exposed directly to the user as they stand. For example, Strauss [345] discusses more intuitive user controls for setting material values.

A different class of lighting models is the type used for non-photorealistic rendering (NPR). One idea behind NPR is "amplification through simplification" [243]; by simplifying and stripping out clutter, one can amply the effect of information relevant to the presentation. An example of accentuating the edges of objects is shown in Figure 6.19 on page 175 [132]. Another concept is that different styles of rendering have their own mood, meaning, and vocabulary (just as varying the font gives a different feel to the text). For example, the thick-edged, simple filled-cell cartoon style is well accepted; its lighting model is trivial, usually consisting of either simple filled regions or two levels of brightness for a color, lit and shadowed. Different lighting models are useful for technical illustration [94, 131, 132], sketching [241, 305, 377, 378], or painting effects [148]. An overview of early NPR research can be found in Lansdown and Schofield's survey article [221].

4.3.1 Diffuse Component

This part of the lighting model is the one with most connection to physical reality and the interaction between photons and surfaces. This is because it is based on a law of physics called Lambert's law, which states that for ideally diffuse (totally matte) surfaces, the reflected light is determined by the cosine between the surface normal n and the light vector l. The light vector goes from the surface point p to the light source. See Figure 4.5.

Specifically, the effect of the light is

$$i_{diff} = n \cdot l = \cos \phi \qquad (4.1)$$

where both n and l are normalized. Note that diffuse lighting is zero if the angle $\phi > \pi/2$, i.e., the surface faces away from the light.

The right side of Figure 4.5 shows a geometric interpretation of Lambert's Law. First, the light rays are shown hitting the surface perpendicularly. These rays are a distance l apart. The intensity of the light is related to this distance; the intensity decreases as l becomes greater. On the far right the light rays are shown coming from a different direction. They make an angle ϕ with the normal of the plane. The distance between the light rays where they hit the surface is $l/\cos\phi$. Since the intensity is inversely proportional to this distance, this means that the diffuse lighting must be proportional to $\cos \phi$.

When a photon arrives at a diffuse surface, it is momentarily absorbed in that surface. Depending on the color of the photons from the light source and the

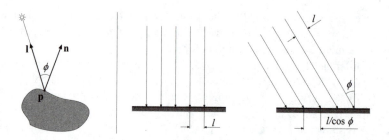

Figure 4.5. The diagram on the left shows the geometry for diffuse lighting. The illustration on the right shows light hitting a surface straight on and at an angle.

color of the material, the photons may be totally absorbed or they may be sent away in an arbitrary reflection direction. Valid reflection directions are those that make an angle with the normal that is less than $\pi/2$ radians (i.e., those above the surface plane, not through it). For diffuse reflection, the probability for the new reflection direction is then equal for every direction. This means that the diffuse component of the lighting equation is independent of the camera's position and direction. In other words, the diffuse component is *view independent*; the surface being lit looks the same from any angle. This can be seen in the equation itself, as the viewer's location does not play a part in it.

To make use of the diffuse color of the light source, s_{diff}, and the diffuse color of the material, m_{diff}, Equation 4.1 is redefined into Equation 4.2, where i_{diff} is the color of the diffuse contribution.

$$i_{diff} = (\mathbf{n} \cdot \mathbf{l})\mathbf{m}_{diff} \otimes s_{diff} \tag{4.2}$$

Remember that the $\otimes$ operator performs componentwise multiplication (see Section 1.2). Incorporating the fact that the diffuse lighting is zero if the angle between $\mathbf{n}$ and $\mathbf{l}$ is greater than $\pi/2$ radians gives Equation 4.3.

$$i_{diff} = \max((\mathbf{n} \cdot \mathbf{l}), 0)\mathbf{m}_{diff} \otimes s_{diff} \tag{4.3}$$

EXAMPLE: DIFFUSE COMPONENT The color vector $\mathbf{m}_{diff} \otimes s_{diff}$ of Equation 4.2 is used to express the fact that photons from the light source will only be diffusely reflected if the material is of the same color as the photons. For example, if a light sends out the diffuse light $s_{diff} = (1.0, 1.0, 1.0)$, which represents white light, and the material of an object has the diffuse parameter $m_{diff} = (1.0, 0.0, 0.0)$, which represents red, then $\mathbf{m}_{diff} \otimes s_{diff} = (1.0, 0.0, 0.0)$, which means that the diffuse component can be at most $(1.0, 0.0, 0.0)$. If, instead, the color of the light source is red and the color of the material is white, the result will be the same.

Assume that we have a blue light source, $s_{diff} = (0.0, 0.0, 1.0)$, and a red material, $m_{diff} = (1.0, 0.0, 0.0)$; then $m_{diff} \otimes s_{diff} = (0.0, 0.0, 0.0)$. This means that a red surface cannot reflect blue light.

In conclusion, $m_{diff} \otimes s_{diff}$ describes the fact that a surface can only diffusely reflect photons of the same color as the surface. The other photons are absorbed by the surface. $\qquad\square$

4.3.2 Specular Component

While the purpose of the diffuse component is to catch the behavior of matte surfaces, the purpose of the specular component is to make a surface look shiny by making highlights appear. Highlights help the viewer determine the direction and/or locations of light sources. The effect of using highlights is shown in Figure 4.6. A popular model used in hardware graphics to simulate the effects of highlights is expressed in Equation 4.4, where $\mathbf{v}$ is the vector from the point $\mathbf{p}$ to be shaded to the viewer, and $\mathbf{r}$ is the reflection of light vector $\mathbf{l}$ around the normal $\mathbf{n}$.

$$i_{spec} = (\mathbf{r} \cdot \mathbf{v})^{m_{shi}} = (\cos \rho)^{m_{shi}} \qquad (4.4)$$

This is called the *Phong lighting equation* [286] (not to be confused with Phong shading, which has to do with interpolating normals and lighting per pixel). It is used to describe the fact that some incident photons tend to bounce off in the reflection direction $\mathbf{r}$. In practice, Equation 4.4 means that the specular contribution gets stronger the more closely aligned the reflection vector $\mathbf{r}$ is with the view vector $\mathbf{v}$. The geometry of the specular component is depicted on the left in Figure 4.7.

Figure 4.6. Left: object without specular component, i.e., without highlights. Right: object with highlights.

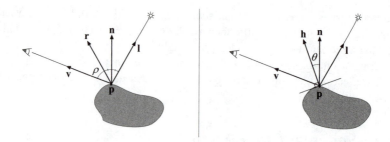

Figure 4.7. This figure shows the geometry for the two different specular lighting equations described in the text. In the left illustration, the light vector **l** is reflected around **n**, which yields the reflection vector **r**. The formula for the specular attenuation factor is then $(\mathbf{r} \cdot \mathbf{v})^{m_{shi}}$, which is dependent on the view vector **v** from the point **p** to the viewer. The right figure shows the geometry for another specular lighting equation. There, the half vector is $\mathbf{h} = (\mathbf{l} + \mathbf{v})/\|\mathbf{l} + \mathbf{v}\|$, and the specular attenuation factor is instead $(\mathbf{n} \cdot \mathbf{h})^{m_{shi}}$, which is also dependent on **v**. OpenGL and Direct3D use the specular lighting equation shown on the right.

The light vector, **l**, is reflected around the normal, **n**, which yields the reflection vector **r**. This is calculated by

$$\mathbf{r} = 2(\mathbf{n} \cdot \mathbf{l})\mathbf{n} - \mathbf{l} \tag{4.5}$$

where **l** and **n** are assumed to be normalized, and therefore **r** is normalized too. If $\mathbf{n} \cdot \mathbf{l} < 0$ then the surface faces away from the light and a highlight normally is not computed. The reflection vector geometry is shown in Figure 4.8.

Turning back to Equation 4.4, we see that this term is at maximum when **r** and **v** are equal, which means that if we look at a surface and the reflection vector of a light source points directly back at us, then the specular component is maximized, and thus produces a highlight there. As the angle between the viewer and the reflection direction increases, the specular component drops off. While the diffuse term is view-independent, the specular term is highly view-dependent, since the highlights change position on the surface if the viewer moves. A popular variation of Equation 4.4 was first presented by Blinn [37]:

$$i_{spec} = (\mathbf{n} \cdot \mathbf{h})^{m_{shi}} = (\cos \theta)^{m_{shi}} \tag{4.6}$$

where **h** is the normalized half vector between **l** and **v**:

$$\mathbf{h} = \frac{\mathbf{l} + \mathbf{v}}{\|\mathbf{l} + \mathbf{v}\|} \tag{4.7}$$

This geometry is depicted in the right part of Figure 4.7. The rationale behind Equation 4.6 is that **h** is the normal of the plane through the point **p** that reflects the light from the light source (which comes from direction l) perfectly into the eye of the viewer, i.e., the camera. So the term $\mathbf{n} \cdot \mathbf{h}$ is maximized when the normal $\mathbf{n}$ at $\mathbf{p}$ coincides with the half-vector $\mathbf{h}$. The factor $\mathbf{n} \cdot \mathbf{h}$ decreases when the angle between $\mathbf{n}$ and $\mathbf{h}$ increases. One reason to use this equation is so that the underlying API does not need to compute a reflection vector, and so can be faster. If a directional light and an orthographic (parallel) view is used (or if a non-local viewer is used—see Section 8.2.2), then the light direction and view direction are both constants, and $\mathbf{h}$ is then constant for the entire scene.

The relationship between these two kinds of specular lighting is shown below [106].

$$(\mathbf{r} \cdot \mathbf{v})^{m_{shi}} \approx (\mathbf{n} \cdot \mathbf{h})^{4m_{shi}} \tag{4.8}$$

As with the diffuse case, to make this equation take into account the material parameters of the surface at $\mathbf{p}$ as well as the light source parameters, the specular attenuation factor from Equation 4.6 is multiplied with the color vector $\mathbf{m}_{spec} \otimes \mathbf{s}_{spec}$, which describes the photons from a light source that could be specularly reflected off a surface with the material parameter $\mathbf{m}_{spec}$. In this way, Equation 4.9 is obtained. OpenGL and Direct3D implementations use this formula.

$$\mathbf{i}_{spec} = (\mathbf{n} \cdot \mathbf{h})^{m_{shi}} \mathbf{m}_{spec} \otimes \mathbf{s}_{spec} \tag{4.9}$$

Also, as with the diffuse contribution, if the angle between $\mathbf{n}$ and $\mathbf{h}$ is greater than $\pi/2$, then the specular contribution should be zero. This is expressed in the equation below.

$$\mathbf{i}_{spec} = \max((\mathbf{n} \cdot \mathbf{h}), 0)^{m_{shi}} \mathbf{m}_{spec} \otimes \mathbf{s}_{spec} \tag{4.10}$$

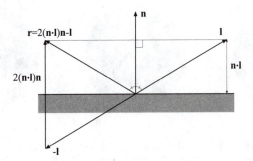

Figure 4.8. This figure shows how the reflection vector $\mathbf{r}$ can be computed using simple linear algebra. The light vector $\mathbf{l}$ is reflected around the normal $\mathbf{n}$ in order to generate $\mathbf{r}$. First, $\mathbf{l}$ is projected onto $\mathbf{n}$, and we get a scaled version of the normal: $(\mathbf{n} \cdot \mathbf{l})\mathbf{n}$. Then $\mathbf{l}$ is negated, and if we add two times the projection vector, the reflection vector is obtained: $\mathbf{r} = 2(\mathbf{n} \cdot \mathbf{l})\mathbf{n} - \mathbf{l}$.

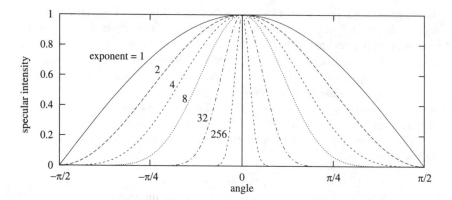

Figure 4.9. The shininess parameter, m_{shi}, raises the dot product of two vectors to a power. The dot product is the cosine of the angle between these two vectors, so for $m_{shi} = 1$ a cosine curve is produced. As m_{shi} increases, the curve is pulled in, making for a tighter highlight and a shinier impression.

The parameter m_{shi} describes the *shininess* of the surface—the greater m_{shi}, the more "shiny" the surface appears. Figure 4.9 shows how increasing m_{shi} has the effect of narrowing the area in which the highlight is rendered.

Using m_{shi} to raise the contribution to a power is just one way of controlling the way in which reflected intensity drops off. Phong's illumination model has little physical validity; it just looks reasonable under most circumstances. See Figure 4.10 for an example of a situation in which the Phong model looks unrealistic when per-pixel shading is used [384].

Figure 4.10. When the shininess component, m_{shi}, is low and the light is beyond the object, Phong highlighting can produce artifacts as the shading algorithm improves. Here the shininess is about 7, and $\mathbf{n} \cdot \mathbf{h}$ Phong/Blinn highlighting is used, with two light sources. On the left is a Gouraud shaded sphere with little tessellation. In the middle the Gouraud shaded sphere is highly tessellated. On the right the sphere is per-pixel shaded, and an unnatural line where the light drops to zero is most visible.

It is perfectly reasonable to use other specular highlight functions. For example, Schlick [318] gives an alternate approximation to Phong's equation which is normally faster to compute. Using the terminology from Equation 4.4:

$$t = (\cos \rho)$$

$$\mathbf{i}_{spec} = \frac{t}{m_{shi} - tm_{shi} + t} \mathbf{m}_{spec} \otimes \mathbf{s}_{spec}$$

(4.11)

More physically-based terms can be added to the basic specular equation. Blinn uses microfacets (tiny angled surfaces to simulate roughness, treated statistically) to include a term for self-shadowing and masking of the surface [37, 121, 156, 367]. That is, as light comes in or the surface is viewed at a shallow angle, the bumpiness of the surface itself can block light from getting to the eye. Other physically-based factors, such as the Fresnel reflectance, can also be included in the specular equation [29, 174]. Two papers from SIGGRAPH 99 describe more elaborate BRDF models [174, 393].

An example of a simple function that is considerably different from the standard model is:

$$\mathbf{i}_{spec} = \lceil (\mathbf{n} \cdot \mathbf{h}) - t \rceil \mathbf{m}_{spec} \otimes \mathbf{s}_{spec}$$

(4.12)

where t is some threshold value. That is, if $\mathbf{n} \cdot \mathbf{h}$ is greater than t, use 1, else use 0 as the multiplier. This equation gives a specular highlight that gives the appearance of an area light reflected on a mirror surface. In this case, t affects the apparent size of the light being reflected. The light reflection gives a uniformly bright spot. This sort of function is more useful when doing per-pixel shading (since Gouraud shading will not show the sharp fall-off to 0) but is currently unsupported by most APIs and graphics hardware. However, as will be discussed in Section 5.7.4, we can use environment mapping to give similar, arbitrarily complex specular effects.

4.3.3 Ambient Component

In our simple lighting model lights shine directly on surfaces, but nothing else does. In contrast, in the real world light emanating from a light source might bounce off a wall and then reach an object. The light from the wall would not be accounted for in either the diffuse or the specular component. (Radiosity [59, 121, 333] is a technique that would take some of those kinds of light interactions into account; approximating radiosity lighting with simple point lights is discussed by Walter et al. [365].) To attempt to simulate this indirect lighting, the lighting model includes the ambient term which is usually just some combination of material and light constants, as shown in Equation 4.13.

$$\mathbf{i}_{amb} = \mathbf{m}_{amb} \otimes \mathbf{s}_{amb} \qquad (4.13)$$

Adding this constant term means that an object will receive some minimum amount of color, even if not directly illuminated. In this way surfaces facing away from a light will not appear entirely black.

OpenGL is the only API we know of that supports an ambient value per light. Most APIs (including OpenGL) support a global ambient value, as will be seen in the next section.

Using an ambient term as the only method of illuminating surfaces that face away from all lights is often found to be unacceptable. Such areas are all given the same color, and the three-dimensional effect disappears. One solution is to make sure objects all receive at least a little direct illumination by strategically placing lights in a scene. Another common technique (used in VRML browsers, for example) is to use a *headlight* [362], which is a point light attached to the viewer's location. As the viewer moves, so does the light, and the light provides all surfaces with varying degrees of brightness.

4.3.4   Lighting Equation

In this section, the total lighting equation will be put together step by step. This equation determines how light sources interact with the material parameters of an object, and thus, it also (partly) determines the colors of the pixels that a particular object occupies on the screen.

This lighting model is a *local lighting model*, which means that the lighting depends only on light from light sources, not light from other surfaces. From the preceding sections, it could probably be guessed that the lighting is determined by the ambient, diffuse, and specular components. In fact, the total lighting intensity, called $\mathbf{i}_{tot}$, is the sum of those components, as shown in Equation 4.14 and illustrated in Figure 4.11.

$$\mathbf{i}_{tot} = \mathbf{i}_{amb} + \mathbf{i}_{diff} + \mathbf{i}_{spec} \qquad (4.14)$$

The ways in which the lighting varies with varying material parameters are shown in Plate III (following p. 194).

Now, light intensity in the real world is inversely proportional to the square of the distance from the light source, and this kind of attenuation has not been taken into account yet. This attenuation holds only for point light sources, and only the diffuse and specular component are affected by it. To give us some

Figure 4.11. The basic lighting equation is illustrated for a teapot by adding (from the left) the ambient, the diffuse, and the specular components. The resulting lighting is shown at the right. *(Tea cup model is reused courtesy of Joachim Helenklaken)*

more parameters to play with, the following formula is often used to control attenuation by distance.

$$d = \frac{1}{s_c + s_l\|\mathbf{s}_{pos} - \mathbf{p}\| + s_q\|\mathbf{s}_{pos} - \mathbf{p}\|^2} \qquad (4.15)$$

Here, $\|\mathbf{s}_{pos} - \mathbf{p}\|$ is the distance from the light source position, $\mathbf{s}_{pos}$, to the point $\mathbf{p}$ that is to be shaded; s_c is a term that controls *constant* attenuation; s_l controls *linear* attenuation; and s_q controls *quadratic* attenuation. For physically correct distance attenuation, set $s_c = 0$, $s_l = 0$, and $s_q = 1$. Equation 4.16 modifies Equation 4.14 in order to take the distance attenuation into account.

$$\mathbf{i}_{tot} = \mathbf{i}_{amb} + d(\mathbf{i}_{diff} + \mathbf{i}_{spec}) \qquad (4.16)$$

Figure 4.2 shows how a spot light illuminates the scene in a different way. A factor denoted c_{spot} is used to represent this effect. If the vertex that is about to be shaded is outside the spot light cone, then $c_{spot} = 0$, which means that the light rays from the spot light does not reach that vertex. If the vertex is inside the cone, then the following formula is used:

$$c_{spot} = \max(-\mathbf{l} \cdot \mathbf{s}_{dir}, 0)^{s_{exp}} \qquad (4.17)$$

Here, $\mathbf{l}$ is the light vector, $\mathbf{s}_{dir}$ is the direction of the spot light (i.e., a vector that points from the light source position along the center line of the spot light cone), and s_{exp} is an exponentiation factor used to control the fall-off from the center of the spot light. All vectors are assumed to be normalized. If the light source is not a spot light, then $c_{spot} = 1$. The modified lighting equation is shown below.

$$\mathbf{i}_{tot} = c_{spot}(\mathbf{i}_{amb} + d(\mathbf{i}_{diff} + \mathbf{i}_{spec})) \qquad (4.18)$$

Spot lights in Direct3D are specified differently, with an inner and outer cone angle. Light is the same intensity up to the border of the inner cone's area, falling off to darkness at the edge of the outer cone. The way the light falls off from the inner to outer cone is typically linear, but can be modified.

As discussed in Section 4.2, the material has an emissive parameter called m_{emi}. This is another ad-hoc parameter, and it describes how much light a surface emits. Note that other surfaces are not affected by this light emission; it is essentially a method for adding a solid color to a surface without having the lighting affect it.

In OpenGL, Direct3D, and most other APIs, there is also a global ambient light source parameter, a_{glob}, that approximates a constant background light coming from everywhere. It is componentwise multiplied with the ambient material parameter, m_{amb}. The incorporation of these parameters into the lighting equation is shown in Equation 4.19, and as can be seen, the new parameters are simply added to the original lighting equation.

$$i_{tot} = \mathbf{a}_{glob} \otimes \mathbf{m}_{amb} + \mathbf{m}_{emi} + c_{spot}(\mathbf{i}_{amb} + d(\mathbf{i}_{diff} + \mathbf{i}_{spec})) \qquad (4.19)$$

This equation applies only when *one* light source is used. Say that there are n light sources, each identified by an index k (superscript). The lighting equation for multiple light sources is shown in Equation 4.20.

$$\begin{aligned}
i_{tot} = \ & \mathbf{a}_{glob} \otimes \mathbf{m}_{amb} + \mathbf{m}_{emi} + \sum_{k=1}^{n} c_{spot}^{k}(\mathbf{i}_{amb}^{k} + d^{k}(\mathbf{i}_{diff}^{k} + \mathbf{i}_{spec}^{k})) \\
= \ & \mathbf{a}_{glob} \otimes \mathbf{m}_{amb} + \mathbf{m}_{emi} + \\
& + \sum_{k=1}^{n} \max(-\mathbf{l}^{k} \cdot \mathbf{s}_{dir}^{k}, 0)^{s_{exp}^{k}} \Big(\mathbf{m}_{amb} \otimes \mathbf{s}_{amb}^{k} + \\
& + \frac{\max((\mathbf{n} \cdot \mathbf{l}^{k}), 0)\mathbf{m}_{diff} \otimes \mathbf{s}_{diff}^{k} + \max((\mathbf{n} \cdot \mathbf{h}^{k}), 0)^{m_{shi}}\mathbf{m}_{spec} \otimes \mathbf{s}_{spec}^{k}}{s_{c}^{k} + s_{l}^{k}||\mathbf{s}_{pos}^{k} - \mathbf{p}|| + s_{q}^{k}||\mathbf{s}_{pos}^{k} - \mathbf{p}||^{2}} \Big)
\end{aligned}$$
$$(4.20)$$

Lighting computations usually take more time with an increasing number of light sources. Also, the sum of light source intensity contributions may be greater than 1, and the resulting lighting color is usually clamped to $[0, 1]$ when rendered. However, clamping overflow can result in color shifts. To avoid this problem, some systems scale overflowing color by the largest component. There are also even more elaborate systems, such as limiting how much any given component (diffuse, specular, etc.) can contribute to the total color.

EXAMPLE: CLAMPING VERSUS SCALING Due to lighting and materials that were too bright, a bright orange of $(2.5, 1.5, 0.5)$ is computed. It will turn into yellow,

$(1.0, 1.0, 0.5)$, when clamped to the range $[0, 1]$. By instead scaling the original color by $1/2.5$, we can change the color displayed to $(1.0, 0.6, 0.2)$, maintaining the original orange hue and saturation. □

Overflows often cause the loss of geometric detail, as the entire overflow area takes on the same color. Having the same color results in the visual effect of flatness. A similar problem when using bump mapping [38] is that bumpy surfaces with too much light will lose their bumps, as the darker and brighter areas will all have the same shade. The best solution to these sorts of problems is simply to try to avoid lighting situations that are too bright.

4.4   Aliasing and Antialiasing

In computer graphics our goal is to determine pixel values that will most accurately depict our underlying representation of the scene. The naive approach is to view the scene through a grid, find what is in the center of each grid cell, and display its computed color.

However, this approach is too simplistic. Imagine a large black triangle moving slowly across the screen's grid, a white background. As a screen grid cell is covered by the triangle, the pixel value representing this cell should drop in intensity. What actually happens is that the moment the grid cell's center is covered, the pixel color immediately goes from white to black. See the leftmost column of Figure 4.12. Shades of gray showing the coverage of the grid cell by the triangle would be preferable.

This, in fact, is precisely how most hardware-accelerated real-time rendering takes place by default. Polygons show up in pixels as either there or not there. Lines drawn have a similar problem. The edges have a jagged look because of this, and so this visual artifact is called "the jaggies." More formally, this problem is called *aliasing*, and efforts to avoid it are called *antialiasing* techniques.[2]

The subject of sampling theory and digital filtering is large enough to fill a book [130, 293, 380]. So we will focus on the basics of the problem, how it affects real-time rendering, and what can be done to alleviate it. Specifically, in this section we will provide and in-depth discussion of polygon edge aliasing. Two other common problem areas are texture aliasing and line aliasing. Texture antialiasing is discussed in Section 5.2.2. Line antialiasing is in some ways the

---

[2]Another way to view this problem is that the jaggies are not actually due to aliasing—it is only that the edges are "forced" into the grid formed by the pixels [367, 369].

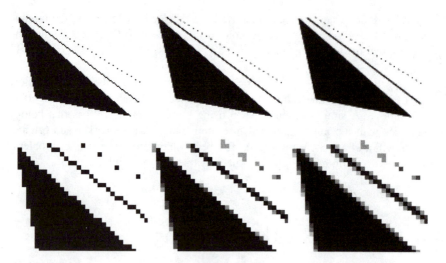

Figure 4.12. The upper row shows three images with different levels of antialiasing of a triangle, a line, and some points. The lower row images are magnifications of the upper row. The leftmost column uses only one sample per pixel, which means that no antialiasing is used. The middle column images were rendered with four samples per pixel, and the right column used eight samples per pixel. All images were rendered using InfiniteReality graphics [262].

easiest to tackle, and some hardware directly supports it. One method is to treat the line as a quadrilateral one pixel wide that is blended with its background; another is to consider it an infinitely thin, transparent, glowing object; a third is to render the line as an antialiased texture [245]. For a thorough treatment of the problem and some solutions, as well as source code on the web, see Nelson's two articles [268, 269].

In the black triangle example, one problem is sampling. A single sample is taken at the center of each pixel's grid cell, so the best that can be done at each pixel is to choose whether or not to display the triangle. By using more samples per screen grid cell and blending these in some fashion, an average pixel color can be computed.[3] Such methods are called *supersampling* techniques.

There are three ways to implement higher sampling rates. Conceptually simplest is to render the scene at a higher resolution and then combine the neighboring samples to create an image. For example, say an image of 500×400 pixels is desired. If you render an image of 1000×800 to an off-screen area and then average each 2×2 area on the screen, the desired image is generated

---

[3]Here we differentiate a pixel, which consists of an RGB color triplet to be displayed, from a screen grid cell, which is a geometric area on the screen centered around a pixel's location. See Smith's memo [337] to understand why this is important.

with 4 samples per pixel. This sampling scheme is available on at least one hardware accelerator, NVIDIA's RIVA TNT, but is considerably slower than per-pixel sampling.

A related method is the *accumulation buffer* [147]. Instead of one large off-screen buffer, this method uses a buffer that has the same resolution as (and more bit depth than) the desired image. To obtain a 2×2 sampling of a scene, 4 images are generated, with the view moved half a pixel in the screen x- or y- direction as needed. Essentially, each image generated is for a different sample position within the grid cell. These images are summed up in the accumulation buffer. After rendering, the image is averaged (in our case, divided by 4) and sent to the display. Accumulation buffers are a part of OpenGL and some hardware systems support their use [7, 379]. They can also be used for such effects as *motion blur* (where a moving object appears blurry) and *depth of field* (where objects not at the camera focus appear blurry). However, the additional costs of having to rerender the scene a few times per frame and move the result to the screen makes this algorithm costly for real-time rendering systems.

A third algorithm that is used to increase the sampling rate per pixel is Carpenter's *A*-buffer [51], sometimes called *multisampling*. This algorithm is commonly used in software for generating high-quality renderings, but at non-interactive speeds. Supersampling is used, but instead of rendering at a higher resolution or using multiple passes, a polygon's approximate coverage of each grid cell is calculated.

Each polygon rendered creates a *coverage mask* for each screen grid cell it fully or partially covers. See Figure 4.13 for an example of a coverage mask. The shade for the polygon associated with this coverage mask is (typically) computed as its shade at the center of the grid cell. The z-depth is also computed at the center.[4] The mask, shade, and z-depth make up a *fragment*.

A screen grid cell can have any number of fragments. As they collect, fragments are resolved as possible. For example, if a fragment is opaque and entirely covers a grid cell, then any fragment that has a larger z-depth can be discarded. More generally, if one or more opaque fragments partially cover a grid cell, any fragment that has a greater z-depth and is fully overlapped by the union of these fragments' coverage masks can be discarded. Because of this discarding mechanism, fragments are usually sorted by z-depth.

Once all polygons have been sent to the *A*-buffer, the color stored in the pixel is computed. This is done by determining how much of the mask of each fragment is visible, and then multiplying this percentage by the fragment's color and summing the results. See Figure 4.12 for an example of multisampling hardware in use. Transparency effects (see Section 4.5) are also folded in at this time.

---

[4]Some systems compute a pair of depths, a minimum and maximum.

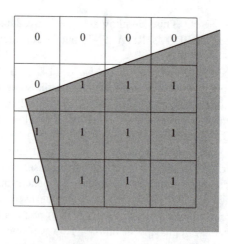

Figure 4.13. The corner of a polygon partially covers a single screen grid cell associated with a pixel. The grid cell is shown subdivided into a 4 × 4 subgrid and those cells that are considered covered are marked by a 1. The 16-bit mask for this cell, read from left to right and top to bottom, is 0000 0111 1111 0111.

Though this sounds like an involved procedure, many of the mechanisms for rendering a triangle into a Z-buffer can be reused to implement the A-buffer in hardware [379]. Storage requirements are certainly much lower than for the high-resolution technique, and the procedure requires far fewer passes than the accumulation buffer technique. The overall processing power necessary is less than in either previous method, as shading and z-depth computations are done only once for each pixel that a polygon covers. See Schilling [314] and Winner [379] for more on hardware implementations of this algorithm.

While all of these methods result in better approximations of how each polygon covers a grid cell, they have some limitations. One limit is simply the size of the coverage mask. Even at 8 × 8 (64 bits), aliasing can still be visible for edges that are nearly horizontal or vertical. This is because with such edges there are effectively 9 levels of coverage (i.e., 0 bits, 8 bits, ... , 64 bits) which are used the most, versus 65 levels for an arbitrary edge.

Another limit is that a *box filter* is often used for simplicity in combining the samples. Box filtering means adding up the samples in a grid cell without regard for position, and with samples in one cell having no effect on the color of other, neighboring pixels. This is one of the worst filters to use, but it will be with us for a long time because of its simplicity. Probably the most important things to realize here are that a pixel is not a little square [337], and that samples outside the grid cell centered around the pixel can (and should) influence the pixel's color. Other filters that allow samples to affect more than one pixel are used for higher-quality reconstruction of a scene [380].

A final factor that leads to poor antialiasing is a lack of gamma correction. This problem is discussed in Section 4.7.

Another sampling-related approach to avoiding aliasing is to distribute the samples randomly over the pixel. This is called *stochastic sampling*, and the reason it works better is that the randomization tends to replace the aliasing effects with noise, to which the human visual system is much more forgiving [116]. The most common kind of stochastic sampling is *jittering*, which works as follows. Assume that n samples are to be used for a pixel. Divide the pixel area into n regions of equal area, and place each sample at a random location in one of these regions. The final pixel color is computed by some averaged mean of the samples. Unfortunately, stochastic techniques currently are not practicable in real-time systems.

Because supersampling schemes are expensive to support in hardware, other methods have been devised that rely on more application-stage support. For example, Direct3D [83] supports two methods, edge and full-scene antialiasing. In edge antialiasing, two passes are needed. The first pass is just a standard draw. In the second pass the edges of objects are redrawn as lines that are blurred. The problem with edge antialiasing is that either all edges are redrawn, an expensive proposition, or the application must identify likely edges to redraw. Typically, we want to redraw only edges along the silhouettes of objects or at the places where materials differ considerably.

In full-scene antialiasing, multisampling schemes can be used if available. However, some hardware requires that the polygons be sorted from back to front (i.e., farthest to closest in the view) and rendered in this order. The idea here is that the hardware antialiases the polygon edges on the fly, and the back-to-front order is needed so that the blended pixel color is computed correctly. This blending takes place through a process called *compositing*, which is explained in the next section. This method of antialiasing allows rendering with only one pass through the data, but the expenses associated with sorting the scene can be considerable.

4.5 Transparency, Alpha, and Compositing

Transparency effects in real-time rendering systems are relatively simplistic and limited. Effects normally unavailable include the bending of light (refraction), attenuation of light due to the thickness of the transparent object, and reflectivity and transmission changes due to the viewing angle, to name a few. That said, a little transparency is better than none at all, and real-time systems do provide the ability to render a surface as semi-transparent, blending its color with the object behind it. It turns out that this simple form of transparency is in fact a powerful tool for a variety of techniques (see Chapter 6).

One simple method for giving the illusion of transparency is called *screen-door transparency*. The idea is to render the transparent polygon with a checkerboard fill pattern. That is, every other pixel of the polygon is rendered, thereby leaving the object behind it partially visible. Usually the pixels on the screen are close enough together that the checkerboard pattern itself is not visible. The problems with this technique include:

- A transparent object can be only 50% transparent. Patterns other than a checkerboard could be used in theory, but in practice such patterns are usually visible.

- Only one transparent object can be convincingly rendered on one area of the screen. For example, if a transparent red object and transparent green object are rendered atop a blue object, only two of the three colors can appear on the checkerboard pattern.

That said, one advantage of this technique is its simplicity. Transparent objects can be rendered at any time, in any order, and no special hardware (beyond fill pattern support) is needed.

What is necessary for more general and flexible transparency effects is the ability to blend the transparent object's color with the color of the object beyond it. For this the concept of *alpha blending* is needed [88, 290]. When an object is rendered on the screen, an RGB color and a Z-buffer depth are associated with each pixel. Another component, called alpha (α), can also be stored. Alpha is a value describing the degree of opacity of an object for a given pixel. An alpha of 1.0 means the object is opaque and entirely covers the pixel's area of interest, 0.0 means the pixel is not obscured at all.

To make an object transparent, it is rendered on top of the existing scene with an alpha less than 1.0. Each pixel covered by the object will receive a resulting RGBα (also called RGBA) from the rendering pipeline. Blending this value coming out of the pipeline with the original pixel color is done using the **over** operator, as follows:

$$\mathbf{c}_o = \alpha \mathbf{c}_s + (1 - \alpha)\mathbf{c}_d \qquad (4.21)$$

where $\mathbf{c}_s$ is the color of the transparent object (called the *source*), $\mathbf{c}_d$ is the pixel color before blending (called the *destination*), and $\mathbf{c}_o$ is the resulting color due to placing the transparent object **over** the existing scene. In the case of the rendering pipeline sending in c_s and α, the pixel's original color c_d gets replaced by the result c_o. If the incoming RGBα is, in fact, opaque ($\alpha = 1.0$), the equation simplifies to the full replacement of pixel's color by the object's color.

To render transparent objects properly into a scene usually requires sorting. First the opaque objects are rendered, then the transparent objects are blended on top of them in back-to-front order. Blending in arbitrary order can produce serious artifacts, because the blending equation is order-dependent. If the hardware supports it, it is best to use Z-buffer testing but no replacement (i.e., when an object is found to be closer, it is rendered, but it does not change the z-depth values). In this way if the sort order is slightly off, at least the transparent objects will not block each other.

One method that requires no sorting entails simplifying Equation 4.21 to:

$$c_o = \alpha c_s + c_d \tag{4.22}$$

Draw order can then be arbitrary, as the alphas of the transparent objects do not affect the destination. This does not look natural, as the opaque surfaces simply have color added to them instead of appearing filtered through the use of blending [245].

There are a number of other blending operators besides **over** [290], but these are not commonly used in real-time applications. The **over** operator can also be used for antialiasing edges. As discussed in the previous section, multisampling can be used to find the approximate percentage of a pixel covered by the edge of a polygon. Instead of storing a coverage mask showing the area covered by the object, an alpha can be stored in its place. In fact, a variety of algorithms can generate alpha values that approximate the coverage of an edge, line, or point.

As an example, say an opaque polygon is found to cover 30% of a screen grid cell. It would then have an alpha of 0.3. This alpha value is then used to blend the object's edge with the scene, using the **over** operator. While this alpha is just an approximation of the area an edge covers, this interpretation works fairly well in practice if generated properly. An example of a poor way to generate alphas is to create them for every polygon edge. Say two adjacent polygons fully cover a pixel, with each covering 50% of it. If each polygon generates an alpha value for its edge, the two alphas would combine to cover only 75% of the pixel, allowing 25% of the background to show through. This sort of error is avoided by using coverage masks or by blurring the edges outwards, as discussed in the previous section.

EXAMPLE: BLENDING A teapot is rendered onto a background using antialiasing techniques. Say at some pixel the shade of the surface is a beige, $(0.8, 0.7, 0.1)$, the background is a light blue, $(0.7, 0.7, 0.9)$, and the surface is found to cover

0.6 of the pixel. The blend of these two colors is:

$$0.6(0.8, 0.7, 0.1) + (1 - 0.6)(0.7, 0.7, 0.9)$$

which gives a color of $(0.76, 0.7, 0.42)$. □

To summarize, the alpha value can represent transparency, edge coverage, or both (if one multiplies the two alphas together). For real-time work, the objects to be rendered with transparency or antialiased edges generally need to be processed in back-to-front order after the rest of the scene has been rendered. This is necessary because as each object is processed, it sets the Z-buffer to its own values where it is visible. This way, if any objects beyond this object are processed later, they will have no effect on these pixels.

The **over** operator turns out to be useful for blending together photographs or renderings of various objects. This process is called *compositing*. In such cases the alpha value at each pixel is stored along with the RGB color value for the object. The alpha channel is sometimes called the *matte*, and shows the shape of the object.[5] See Figure 5.15 on page 124 for an example. This RGBα image can then be used to blend it with other such *elements* or against a background.

There are two ways to store the RGBα values generated. These are called *premultiplied* versus *unmultiplied* (or sometimes, *non-premultiplied*) alphas, also known as *associated* versus *unassociated* alphas. Unmultiplied alpha is simple to explain: the alpha value is kept separate from the shade of a polygon. However, note that the final color we see at a pixel is not the shade of the polygon, it is the shade multiplied by alpha, blended with the background. Say the background is black. A red polygon covering a part of a screen grid cell will make the pixel only partially red. If we want to save this image and its alphas for later use in compositing it with other elements, we would save the RGB values at the pixels as well as the alpha values. Such an RGBα value is called premultiplied, as the alpha has been factored in.

EXAMPLE: ALPHA TYPES Render a teapot for later use as an image to be composited. At some pixel the shade of the surface is a beige, $(0.8, 0.7, 0.1)$ and the surface is found to effectively cover 0.6 of the pixel. The product of these two is $(0.48, 0.42, 0.06)$. The unmultiplied RGBα is simply $(0.8, 0.7, 0.1, 0.4)$; the premultiplied RGBα is $(0.48, 0.42, 0.06, 0.4)$. If the teapot were viewed against a black background, the premultiplied RGB component $(0.48, 0.42, 0.06)$, would be what is displayed, as it would be the surface's computed shade multiplied by the amount of pixel coverage. □

---

[5] For a good summary of terminology used in compositing, see Smith and Blinn's article [338].

A useful consequence of storing premultiplied RGBα values is that the properly antialiased image can be viewed by simply ignoring the alpha value and displaying the RGB values. In unmultiplied RGBα only the computed shade at each pixel is stored in the color channels, so the color must be multiplied by the stored alpha value to see the effect of pixel coverage and transparency.

One advantage of premultiplied alphas is that the **over** Equation, 4.21, simplifies to:

$$\mathbf{c}_o = \mathbf{c}_s + \mathbf{c}_d(1 - \alpha) \qquad (4.23)$$

since $\mathbf{c}_s$ already contains the alpha value. This is not important for the rendering pipeline, where alpha values are generated on the fly, but it is helpful for simplifying manipulation of images with precomputed alpha values. As importantly, premultiplied alphas allow cleaner theoretical treatment [338].

In the world of synthetic imagery, as well as the world of film production, the premultiplied alpha is the norm. For some two-dimensional applications, an unassociated alpha is used to mask a photograph without affecting the underlying image's data. Image file formats that support alpha include PNG (unassociated alpha only) and TIFF (both types) [265].

A concept related to the alpha channel is *chroma-keying*. This is a term from video production, in which actors are filmed against a blue, yellow, or (increasingly) green screen and blended with a background. In the film industry this process is called *blue-screen matting*. The idea here is that a particular color is designated to be considered transparent; where it is detected, the background is displayed. This allows objects to be given a shape by using just RGB colors—no alpha needs to be stored. The drawback of this scheme is that the object is either entirely opaque or transparent at any pixel, i.e., alpha is effectively only 1.0 or 0.0. As an example, the GIF format allows one color (actually, one palette entry; see Section 12.1.2) to be designated as transparent. An extension to basic chroma-keying is *chroma-ranging* [122], which is simply specifying a range of colors to treat as transparent. By modifying the chroma-range on the fly, one can make various parts of objects using it appear and disappear.

4.6 Fog

For real-time computer graphics, *fog* is a simple atmospheric effect that can be added to the final image. Fog can be used for several purposes. First, it increases the level of realism for outdoor scenes. Second, since the fog effect increases with the distance from the viewer, it helps the viewer of a scene to determine how far away objects are located. Third, if used properly, it helps to provide smoother culling of objects by the far plane. If the fog is set up so that objects located near the far plane are not visible due to thick fog, then objects that go out of the view frustum through the far plane seem to fade away into the fog. Without fog, a popping effect is experienced as the object is clipped by the far plane. Fourth, fog is often implemented in hardware, so it can be used with little or no additional cost. Examples of images rendered with fog are shown in Figure 4.14.

The color of the fog is denoted c_f (which the user selects), and the *fog factor* is called $f \in [0, 1]$, which decreases with the distance from the viewer. Assume that the color of a shaded surface is c_s, then the final color of the pixel, c_p, is determined by

$$c_p = f c_s + (1 - f)c_f \tag{4.24}$$

Note that f is somewhat non-intuitive in this presentation; as f decreases, the effect of the fog increases. This is how OpenGL and Direct3D present the equation, but Glide uses an f' factor which is equal to $(1 - f)$. The main advantage of the approach presented here is that the various equations used to generate f are simplified. These equations follow.

Linear fog has a fog factor that decreases linearly with the depth from the viewer. For this purpose, there are two user-defined scalars, z_{start} and z_{end}, that determine where the fog is to start and end (i.e., become fully foggy) along the viewer's z-axis. If z_p is the z-value (depth from the viewer) of the pixel where fog is to be computed, then the linear fog factor is

$$f = \frac{z_{end} - z_p}{z_{end} - z_{start}} \tag{4.25}$$

There are also two sorts of fog that falls off exponentially, as shown in Equations 4.26 and 4.27. These are called *exponential fog*:

$$f = e^{-d_f z_p} \tag{4.26}$$

Figure 4.14. The left image shows a scene rendered without fog and the right image shows the same scene rendered with linear fog. *(The duck model is reused courtesy of Jens Larsson.)*

and *squared exponential fog*:

$$f = e^{-(d_f z_p)^2} \tag{4.27}$$

The scalar d_f is a parameter that is used to control the density of the fog. After the fog factor, f, has been computed, it is clamped to $[0, 1]$, and Equation 4.24 is applied to calculate the final value of the pixel. Examples of what the fog fall-off curves look like for linear fog and for the two exponential fog factors appear in Figure 4.15.

Tables are sometimes used in implementing these fog functions in hardware accelerators. That is, for each depth, a fog factor f is computed and stored in advance. When the fog factor at a given depth is needed, the two depths that bracket it are found in the table and the fog factors are used to linearly interpolate the value. Any values can be put into the fog table, not just those in the equations above. This allows interesting rendering styles in which the fog effect appears only at certain depths.

In theory that is all there is to the fog effect: a depth changes the color. However, there are a few simplifying assumptions that are used in some real-time systems that can affect the quality of the output. It is worth discussing each in turn.

First, fog can be applied on a vertex level or a pixel level [83]. Applying it on the vertex level means that the fog effect is computed as part of the illumination equation and interpolated across the polygon using Gouraud shading. Pixel-level fog is computed using the depth stored at each pixel. All other factors being equal, pixel-level fog gives a better result.

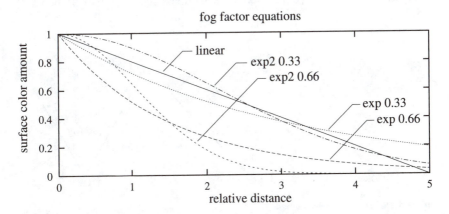

Figure 4.15. Curves for fog fall-off: linear, exponential, and squared-exponential, using various densities.

The fog-factor equations use a value along the viewer's z-axis to compute their effect. In traditional software rendering pipelines and many graphics accelerators, the z-values are computed in a non-linear fashion (see Section 12.1.3). Using these z-values directly in the fog-factor equations gives results that do not follow the actual intent of the equations. For this reason, newer graphics hardware supports *eye-relative depth* for correctly computing the depth. This is accomplished by undoing the effect of the perspective transformation so that the depth values change in a linear fashion.

A simplifying assumption is that the distance along the viewing axis is used as the depth for computing the fog effect. This assumption is made because this distance has already been computed by the rendering pipeline and so costs little to reuse. A more accurate way to compute fog is to use the true distance from the viewer to the object. This is called *radial fog, range-based fog,* or *Euclidean distance fog* [173]. Figure 4.16 shows what happens when radial fog is not used.

The highest-quality fog is generated by using pixel-level radial fog. As of this writing, this type of fog is not available on any commercial hardware accelerator [83].

Other types of fog effects are certainly possible. For example, Legakis [227] introduced a method for producing images with fog in multiple layers, where the density depends on the height from the ground, and is computed via look-up tables. Heidrich et al. [173] show how layered fog can be implemented so as to perform all computations in hardware.

A word of warning about fog in general: fog as normally implemented can become difficult to use in conjunction with multipass rendering (see Section 5.4) [187].

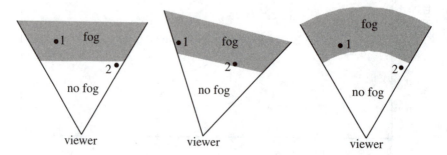

Figure 4.16. Use of z-depth vs. radial fog. On the left is one view of two objects, using view-axis-based fog. In the middle, the view has simply been rotated, but in the rotation the fog has been made to encompass object 2. On the right, we see the effect of radial fog, which will not vary when rotated about the viewer.

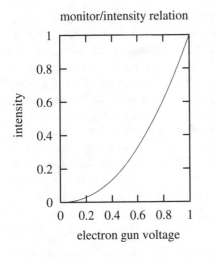
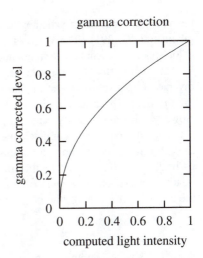

Figure 4.17. On the left is the normalized relation of voltage to intensity for an electron gun in a CRT. On the right is the gamma correction curve needed to convert a computed intensity value to the displayed pixel value. The two curves multiplied together give a linear relationship.

4.7 Gamma Correction

Once the pixel values have been computed, we need to display them on a monitor. There is a physical relationship between the voltage input to an electron gun in a cathode-ray tube (CRT) monitor and the light output by the screen. This relationship is a power function:

$$I = a(V + \epsilon)^\gamma \tag{4.28}$$

where V is the input voltage, a and γ (gamma) are constant for each monitor, ϵ is the black level (brightness) setting for the monitor, and I is the intensity generated [162, 291]. The gamma value for a particular CRT ranges from about 2.3 to 2.6.[6] See the left side of Figure 4.17. Values considerably different from this range are often claimed, but the largest source of error in gamma computation is caused by poor black level (brightness) settings [291]. While 2.5 is usually given as a good average monitor value, there is also a perceptual effect that is often factored into this equation. This is the *surround effect*, which depends on the viewing environment (assumed to be dark for television viewing, for example). The net effect is that a composite gamma of 2.2 is used by NTSC,

---

[6]Liquid-crystal displays (LCDs) have a different voltage/luminance response curve, typically S-shaped.

the color TV encoding scheme; Rec. 709 for HDTV uses a value of $1/0.45$ (about 2.222) [291]. The value of 2.2 has been proposed as part of a standard color space for computer systems and the Internet, called *sRGB* [343].

It turns out that, by coincidence, the CRT response curve nearly matches the inverse of light sensitivity of the human eye [291]. This has the effect of endowing the CRT with a near-optimal set of luminance values for displaying images. However, this nonlinearity causes a problem within the field of computer graphics. Lighting equations compute intensity values that have a linear relationship to each other. For example, a computed value of 0.5 is expected to appear half as bright as 1.0. To ensure that the computed values are perceived correctly relative to each other, *gamma correction* is necessary. At its simplest, assuming the black level ϵ is zero, the computed color component c_i is converted by:

$$c = c_i^{1/\gamma} \tag{4.29}$$

for display by the CRT (see Figure 4.17). For example, with a gamma of 2.2 and $c_i = 0.5$, the gamma-corrected c is 0.73. So, if the electron gun level is set at 0.73, an intensity level of 0.5 is displayed. Computed colors need to be boosted by this equation to be perceived properly with respect to one another when displayed on a CRT monitor.

This is the basic idea behind gamma correction; see Poynton's book and web site [291] for a thorough treatment of the subject. In practical terms, gamma correction is important to real-time graphics in a few areas:

- Cross-platform compatibility

- Color fidelity, consistency, and interpolation

- Dithering

- Line and edge antialiasing quality

- Alpha blending and compositing

- Texturing

Cross-platform compatibility affects all images displayed, not just scene renderings. SGI and Apple Macintosh computers each have their own gamma correction mechanisms built into their machines, though each has its own, different, gamma power value [291]. Their CRT monitors all have a gamma of around 2.5. What this means is that, if gamma correction is ignored, models authored and rendered on, say, an SGI machine will display differently when moved to a Macintosh or a PC. This problem instantly affects any images or VRML models made available on a web server, since currently there is no standard gamma value for web browsers [343]. Some sites have employed the strategy of attempting to detect the platform of the client requesting information and serving up images or models tailored for it.

Even if an application is limited to platforms using the same gamma mechanism, there are still problems with failing to perform gamma correction. One is color fidelity: the appearance of a color will differ from its true hue. Another problem is color consistency: without correction, intensity controls will not work as expected. If a light or material color is changed from $(0.5, 0.5, 0.5)$ to $(1.0, 1.0, 1.0)$, the user will expect it to appear twice as bright, but it will not. A third problem is color interpolation: a surface that goes from dark to light will not appear to increase linearly in brightness across its surface. Again, without gamma correction, the midtones will appear too dark.

Lack of gamma correction also adversely affects *dithering* algorithms. In dithering, two colors are displayed close together and the eye combines them and perceives a blend of the two. Without accounting for gamma, the dithered color can be perceptibly different from the color that is to be represented. Similarly, using screen-door transparency will result in a different perceived color from the blended transparency color (see Section 4.5).

In the long term, dithering problems will fade as graphics hardware continues to move toward 24-bit color displays (see Section 12.1.2). However, as the use of line and edge antialiasing in real-time rendering increases, gamma's effect on the quality of these techniques will be more noticeable. For example, say a polygon edge covers four screen grid cells (Figure 4.18). The polygon is white; the background is black. Left to right, the cells are covered $\frac{1}{8}$, $\frac{3}{8}$, $\frac{5}{8}$, and $\frac{7}{8}$. So if we are using a box filter, we want the pixels to appear as 0.125, 0.375, 0.625, and 0.875. If the system has a gamma of 2.2, we need to send values of 0.389, 0.640, 0.808, and 0.941 to the electron guns. Failing to do so will mean that the perceived brightness will not increase linearly. Sending 0.125 to the guns, for example, will result in a perceived relative brightness of only 0.010; 0.875 will be affected somewhat less and will be perceived as 0.745.

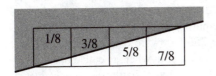

Figure 4.18. On the left, four pixels covered by the edge of a white polygon on a black (shown as gray) background, with true area coverage shown. If gamma correction is not done, the edge will be perceived similarly to the figure on the right, as the midtones are darkened.

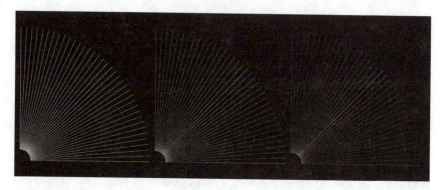

Figure 4.19. On the left, the set of antialiased lines are gamma-corrected; in the middle, the set is partially corrected; on the right, there is no gamma correction. *(Courtesy of Scott R. Nelson.)*

This non-linearity causes an artifact called *roping*, because the edge looks somewhat like a twisted rope [268]. Figure 4.19 shows this effect.

Similarly, alpha blending and compositing should be done in a linear space and the final result should be gamma-corrected. This can lead to difficulties, as pixel values stored in the color buffer are likely to be gamma-corrected. Bits of accuracy are lost as values are transferred from one computational space to another.

Texturing is another area where problems can occur. Images used as textures are normally stored in gamma-corrected form for some system. When using textures in a synthesized scene, care must be taken to gamma-correct the texture a sum total of only one time.

There are a number of solutions if gamma correction is determined to be necessary. More graphics hardware is including gamma correction as a step in the pipeline. Unfortunately, one solution on inexpensive hardware is to take 8-bit color component values generated by the rendering equation and use a look-up table to convert these to their gamma-corrected equivalent. Converting from 8-bits in linear space to 8-bits in gamma-corrected space loses precision. For example, while input color $\frac{0}{255}$ maps to output color $\frac{0}{255}$, input color $\frac{1}{255}$ maps to $\frac{21}{255}$, so output levels 1 to 20 never get used with this scheme; more precision on the input side is needed to access these output levels. For a gamma of 2.2, using such a table causes only about 184 of the 256 hardware output levels (72%) to get used. Unfortunately, this has the effect of causing what are called *banding* or *contouring* artifacts, as nearby colors jump to different hardware color values.[7]

---

[7]Contouring artifacts among the darker shades are possible even when gamma correction is done properly and 24 bits of color are used. Dithering can be used to avoid these artifacts. The point here is that 8 → 8 gamma correction will give more serious contouring artifacts.

A better solution, implemented in some hardware, is to compute the pixel value at some higher precision and use a larger look-up table to convert (e.g., using 12 bits, the look-up table has 2^{12}, or 4096, entries). This is discussed in depth by Blinn [40].

However, if the presence of gamma-correction hardware cannot be guaranteed, other solutions must be explored. About the only practical real-time solution is to attempt to perform gamma correction earlier on in the pipeline. For example, we could gamma-correct the illumination value computed at the vertex, then Gouraud shade from there. This solution partially solves the cross-platform problem, though it does not address the other rendering problems detailed previously. It is also difficult if not impossible to use with multipass rendering methods (see Section 5.4).

Another approach taken by many applications is to ignore the gamma correction problem entirely and not do anything about it. Until gamma correction support is near universal, this is sometimes the only solution. Other than cross-platform issues, the main effect of doing nothing is lowering quality in some mostly minor and insignificant ways. But, even if you find yourself in this position, it is important to know what problems are caused by a lack of gamma correction.

A final warning: some software applications (e.g., games) include a control for "gamma correction" to modify the contrast or brightness of the scene. By now it should be clear that this control is not actually performing gamma correction, but rather is a method of responding to varying monitor settings and user preferences. Gamma correction is not a user preference; it is something that can be designed into an application to allow cross-platform consistency and to improve image fidelity and rendering algorithm quality.

Further Reading and Resources

A thorough treatment of lighting, lights, materials, color, and signal processing can be found in Glassner's two-volume work *Principles of Digital Image Synthesis* [120, 121]. Hall's book [156] also gives a comprehensive treatment of lighting models, shading techniques, and color science.

Wolberg's book [380] is an exhaustive guide to sampling and filtering for computer graphics. Blinn's *Dirty Pixels* book [44] includes some excellent introductory articles on filtering and antialiasing, as well as articles on alpha, compositing, and gamma correction. A good quick read which helps correct the misunderstanding that a pixel is a little square is Smith's article on the topic [337], available on the web.

Poynton's *A Technical Introduction to Digital Video* [291] gives solid coverage of gamma correction in various media, as well as other color-related topics.

On this book's website (`http://www.realtimerendering.com/`) are pointers to Java applets that let you see the effects of the various lighting model components, as well as links to other web resources.

Chapter 5
Texturing

"All it takes is for the rendered image to look right."
–Jim Blinn

A surface's texture is its look and feel—just think of the texture of an oil painting. In computer graphics, texturing is a process that takes a surface and modifies its appearance at each location using some image, function, or other dataset. As an example, instead of precisely representing the geometry of a brick wall, a color image of a brick wall is applied to a single polygon. When the polygon is viewed, the color image appears where the polygon is located. Unless the viewer gets close to the wall, the lack of geometric detail (e.g., the fact that the image of bricks and mortar forms a smooth surface) will not be noticeable. Huge modeling, memory, and speed savings are obtained by combining images and surfaces in this way. Color image texturing also provides a way to use photographic images and animations on surfaces.

However, some textured brick walls can be unconvincing for reasons other than lack of geometry. For example, if the bricks are supposed to be shiny, whereas the mortar of course is not, the viewer will notice that the shininess is the same for both materials. To produce a more convincing experience, a specular highlighting image texture can also be applied to the surface. Instead of changing the surface's color, this sort of texture changes the wall's shininess depending on location on the surface. Now the bricks have a color from the color image texture and a shininess from this new texture.

Once the shiny texture has been applied, however, the viewer may notice that now all the bricks are shiny and the mortar is not, but each brick face appears to be flat. This does not look right, as bricks normally have some irregularity to their surfaces. By applying bump mapping, the surface normals of the bricks may be varied so that when they are rendered they do not appear to be perfectly flat. This sort of texture wobbles the direction of the polygon's original surface normal for purposes of computing lighting.

These are just three examples of the types of problems that can be solved with textures. In this chapter texturing techniques are covered in detail. First a general framework of the texturing process is presented. Next, we focus on using images to texture surfaces, since this is the most popular form of texturing used in real-time work. The various techniques for improving the appearance of image textures are detailed, and then methods of getting textures to affect the surface are explained.

5.1   Generalized Texturing

Texturing, at its simplest, is a technique for efficiently modeling the surface's properties. One way to approach texturing is to think about what happens for a single sample taken at a vertex of a polygon. As seen in the previous chapter, the color is computed by taking into account the lighting and the material, as well as the viewer's position. If present, transparency also affects the sample, and then the effect of fog is calculated. Texturing works by modifying the values used in the lighting equation. The way these values are changed is normally based on the position on the surface. So, for the brick wall example, the color at any point on the surface was replaced by a corresponding color in the image of a brick wall, based on the surface location. The specular highlight texture modified the shininess value, and the bump texture changed the direction of the normal, so each of these changed the result of the lighting equation.

Texturing can be described by a generalized texture pipeline. Much terminology will be introduced in a moment, but take heart: each piece of the pipeline will be described in detail. This full texturing process is not performed by most current real-time rendering systems, though as time goes by more parts of the pipeline will be incorporated. Once we have presented the entire process we will examine the various simplifications and limitations of real-time texturing.

A location in space is the starting point for the texturing process. This location can be in world space, but is more often in the model's frame of reference, so that as the model moves, the texture moves along with it. Using Kershaw's terminology [203], this point in space then has a *projector* function applied to it to obtain a set of numbers, called parameter-space values, that will be used for accessing the texture. This process is called *mapping*, which leads to the phrase *texture mapping*.[1] Before these new values may be used to access the texture, one or more *corresponder* functions can be used to transform the parameter-space values to texture space. These texture-space values are used to obtain

---

[1] Sometimes the texture image itself is called the texture map, though this is not strictly correct.

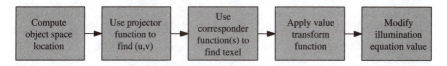

Figure 5.1. Generalized texture pipeline.

values from the texture, e.g., they may be array indices into an image texture to retrieve a pixel. The retrieved values are then potentially transformed yet again by a *value transform* function, and finally these new values are used to modify some property of the surface, such as the material or shading normal. Figure 5.1 shows this process in detail for the application of a single texture. The reason for the complexity of the pipeline is that each step provides the user with a useful control.

Using this pipeline, this is what happens when a polygon has a brick wall texture and a sample is generated on its surface (see Figure 5.2). The (x, y, z) position in the object's local frame of reference is found; say it is $(-2.3, 7.1, 88.2)$. A projector function is then applied to this position. Just as a map of the world is a projection of a three-dimensional object into two dimensions, the projector function here typically changes the (x, y, z) vector into a two-element vector (u, v). The projector function used for this example is an orthographic projection (see Section 2.3.3), acting essentially like a slide projector shining the brick wall image onto the polygon's surface. To return to the wall, a point on its plane could be transformed into a pair of values ranging from 0 to 1. Say the values obtained are $(0.32, 0.29)$. These parameter-space values are to be used to find what the color of the image is at this location. The resolution of our brick texture is, say, 256×256, so the corresponder function multiplies the (u, v) by 256 each, giving $(81.92, 74.24)$. Dropping the fractions, pixel $(81, 74)$ is found in the brick wall image, and is of color $(0.9, 0.8, 0.7)$. The original brick wall image is too dark, so a value transform function that multiplies the color by 1.1 is then applied, giving a color of $(0.99, 0.88, 0.77)$. This color modifies the surface properties by directly replacing the surface's original diffuse color, which is then used in the illumination equation.

The first step in the texture process is obtaining the surface's location and projecting it into parameter space. Projector functions include spherical, cylindrical, box, and planar projections [33, 203]. Other projector functions are not projections at all, but are an implicit part of surface formation; for example, spline surfaces have a natural set of (u, v) values as part of their definition. Non-interactive renderers often call the projector functions as part of the rendering process itself. In real-time work projector functions are usually applied at the modeling stage, and the results of the projection are stored at the vertices. This

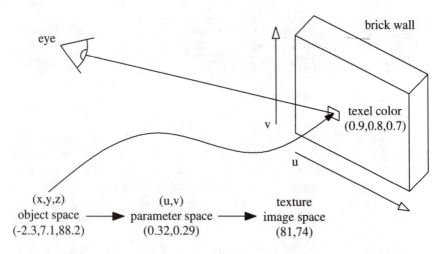

Figure 5.2. Pipeline for a brick wall.

is not always the case; for example, OpenGL's glTexGen routine provides a few different projector functions. Some methods, such as environment mapping (see Section 5.7.3), have specialized projector functions that are evaluated on the fly.

The typical method for using projector functions in real-time systems is by applying (u, v) texture coordinates at each vertex during modeling. These values are sometimes presented as a three-element vector, (u, v, w). Other systems use up to four coordinates, designated (s, t, r, q) [275]; q is used as the fourth value in a homogeneous coordinate (see Section A.4) and can be used for spot lighting effects [321]. To allow each separate texture map to have its own input parameters during a rendering pass, APIs allow multiple pairs of (u, v) values (see Section 5.5 on multitexturing). However the designation is accomplished, the idea is the same: these parameter values are interpolated across the surface and used to retrieve texture values. Before being interpolated, however, these parameter values are transformed by corresponder functions.

Corresponder functions convert parameter-space values to texture-space values. They provide flexibility in applying textures to surfaces. One corresponder is an optional matrix transformation. The use of a matrix is supported explicitly in OpenGL, and is simple enough to support at the application stage under any API. This transform is useful for the sorts of procedures which transforms normally do well at: it can translate, rotate, scale, and so on, the texture on the surface.[2]

---

[2]As discussed in Section 3.1.5, the order of transforms matters. Surprisingly, the order of transforms for textures must be the reverse of the order one would expect. This is because texture

Another class of corresponder functions controls the way an image is applied. We know that an image will appear on the surface where (u, v) are in the $[0, 1)$ range.[3] But what happens outside of this range? Corresponder functions determine the behavior.[4] Common corresponder functions are:

- **wrap**, **repeat**, or **tile** - The image repeats itself across the surface; algorithmically, the integer part of the parameter value is dropped. This function is useful for having an image of a material repeatedly cover a surface, and is often the default.

- **mirror** - The image repeats itself across the surface, but is mirrored (flipped) on every other repetition. For example, the image appears normally going from 0 to 1, then is reversed between 1 and 2, then is normal between 2 and 3, then is reversed, etc. This provides some continuity along the edges of the texture.

- **clamp** - Values outside the range $[0, 1)$ are clamped to this range. This results in the repetition of the edges of the image texture. Some APIs [122, 275] allow one parameter to be clamped while the other repeats.

- **border** - Parameter values outside $[0, 1)$ are rendered with a separately defined border color. This function is good for rendering decals onto surfaces, for example. Note that the **clamp** method can produce the same sort of effect if the border of the image texture itself is already the color you wish the rendered border to be. The border mode is useful in that it requires no such preprocessing of the image, and the border color can be modified independently.

See Figure 5.3.

For real-time work, the last corresponder is implicit, and is derived from the image's size. A texture is normally applied within the range $[0, 1)$ for u and v. As shown in the brick wall example, by multiplying parameter values in this range by the resolution of the image, one may obtain the pixel location. The pixels in the texture are often called *texels*, to differentiate them from the pixels on the screen. The advantage of being able to specify (u, v) values in a range of

---

transforms actually affect the space that determines where the image is seen. The image itself is not an object being transformed; the space defining the image's location is being changed.

[3]The notation "$[0, 1)$" means from 0 to 1, including 0 but not 1. A bracket '[' means include the number, parenthesis ')' means do not include the number in the range.

[4]In Direct3D the corresponder function is called the "texture addressing mode." Confusingly, Direct3D also has a feature called "texture wrapping," which is used with Blinn environment mapping. See Section 5.7.3

Figure 5.3. Image texture wrap, mirror, clamp, and border functions in action.

$[0, 1)$ is that image textures with different resolutions can be swapped in without having to change the values stored at the vertices of the model.

In theory, more than one corresponder function could be applied in a series (e.g., a corresponder could select a portion of the texture image, and then a border corresponder could be applied to it [203]).

The set of corresponder functions uses parameter-space values to produce texture coordinates. For image textures, the texture coordinates are used to retrieve texel information from the image. This process is dealt with extensively in Section 5.2. Two-dimensional images constitute the vast majority of texture use in real-time work, but there are other texture functions. A direct extension of image textures is three-dimensional image data which is accessed by (u, v, w) (or (s, t, r)) values. For example, medical imaging data can be generated as a three-dimensional grid; by moving a polygon through this grid, one may view two-dimensional slices of this data.

Covering an arbitrary three-dimensional surface cleanly with a two-dimensional image is often difficult or impossible [33]. As the texture is applied to some solid object, the image is stretched or compressed in places to fit the surface. Obvious mismatches may be visible as different pieces of the texture meet. A solid cone is a good example of both of these problems: the image bunches up at the tip, while the texture on the flat face of the cone does not match with the texture on the sides.

The advantage of three-dimensional textures is that they avoid the distortion and seam problems that two-dimensional texture mappings can have. A three-dimensional texture can act as a material such as wood or marble, and the model may be textured as if it were carved from this material. The texture can also be used to modify other properties, for example changing (u, v) coordinates in order to creating warping effects [245].

Three-dimensional textures can be synthesized by a variety of techniques. One of the most common is using one or more noise functions to generate values [92]. Because of the cost of evaluating the noise function, sometimes the lattice points in the three-dimensional array are precomputed and used to interpolate texture values. There are also methods of using the accumulation buffer or color buffer blending to generate these arrays [245]. However, such arrays can be large to store and often lack sufficient detail. An alternative is to evaluate the noise function on the fly. This is normally a computationally expensive endeavor, but Barad et al. [21, 22] show how the MMX architecture can be used to speed evaluation and make it practicable.

Two-dimensional texture functions can also be used to generate textures, but here the major advantages are some storage savings (and bandwidth savings from not having to send down the corresponding image texture) and the fact that such textures have essentially infinite resolution and potentially no repeatability.

It is also worth noting that one-dimensional texture images and functions have their uses. For example, these include contour lines [149, 275] and coloration determined by altitude (e.g., the lowlands are green, the mountain peaks are white).

The texture is accessed and a set of values is retrieved from it. The most straightforward data to return is an RGB triplet which is used to replace or modify the surface color; similarly, a single gray-scale value could be returned. Another type of data to return is RGBα, as described in Section 4.5. The α (alpha) value is normally the opacity of the color, which determines the extent to which the color may affect the pixel. There are certainly other types of data that can be stored in image textures, as will be seen when bump-mapping is discussed in detail (Section 5.7.4).

Once the texture values have been retrieved, they may be used directly or further transformed, and then used to modify one or more surface attributes. The modified surface attribute may then also be modified by some other operation. Recall, however, that almost all real-time systems use Gouraud shading, meaning that only certain values are interpolated across a surface. We cannot modify much beyond the RGB result of the lighting equation, since this equation was already evaluated once per vertex and we interpolate the results. Most real-time systems let us pick one of a number of methods for modifying the surface. The methods, called *combine functions* or *texture blending operations*, for gluing an image texture onto a surface include:

- **replace** - Simply replace the original surface color with the texture color. Note that this removes any lighting computed for the surface, unless the texture itself includes it.

- **modulate** - Multiply the surface color by the texture color. If the surface material is originally white, then the lighting applied to it will modify the color texture, giving a shaded, textured surface.

These two are the most common methods for simple color texture mapping. Using **replace** for texturing in an illuminated environment is sometimes called using a *glow texture*, since the texture's color always appears the same, regardless of changing light conditions. There are other property modifiers, which will be discussed as other texture techniques are introduced.

Revisiting the brick wall texture example, here is what happens in a typical real-time system. A modeler sets the (u, v) parameter values once in advance for the wall model vertices. The texture is read into the renderer, and the wall polygons are sent down the rendering pipeline. A white material is used in computing the illumination at each vertex. This color and (u, v) values are interpolated across the surface. At each pixel the proper brick image's texel is retrieved and modulated (multiplied) by the illumination color and displayed. In our original example this texture was multiplied by 1.1 at this point to make it brighter; in practice this color boost would probably be performed on the texture itself in the modeling stage. In the end, a lit, textured brick wall is displayed.

5.2 Image Texturing

In image texturing a two-dimensional image is effectively glued onto the surface of a polygon and rendered. We have walked through the process with respect to the polygon; now we will address the issues surrounding the image itself and its application to the surface. For the rest of this chapter the image texture will be referred to simply as the texture. In addition, when we refer to a pixel's cell here, we mean the screen grid cell surrounding that pixel. As mentioned in Section 4.4, a pixel is actually a displayed color value which can (and should, for better quality) be affected by samples outside of its grid cell.

The texture image size used in hardware accelerators is restricted to $2^m \times 2^n$ texels, or sometimes even $2^m \times 2^m$ square, where m and n are non-negative integers. Some graphics accelerators have an upper limit on texture size.

Assume that we have an image of size 256×256 pixels and that we want to use it as a texture on a square. As long as the projected square on the screen is roughly the same size as the texture, the texture on the square looks almost like the original image. But what happens if the projected square covers 10 times as many pixels as the original image contains (called *magnification*), or if the projected square covers only a fraction of the pixels (*minification*)? The answer is that it depends on what kind of filtering methods you use for these two separate cases.

Figure 5.4. Texture magnification. Here, a texture of size 32×64 was applied to a rectangle, which was viewed very closely (with respect to texture size). Therefore, the texture had to be magnified. On the left, the nearest neighbor filter is used, which simply selects the nearest texel to each pixel. Bilinear interpolation is used on the rectangle on the right. Here, each pixel is computed from a bilinear interpolation of the closest four neighbor texels.

5.2.1   Magnification

In Figure 5.4, a texture of size 32×64 texels is textured onto a rectangle, and the rectangle is viewed rather closely with respect to the texture size, so the underlying graphics system had to magnify the texture. The most common filtering techniques for magnification are *nearest neighbor* and *bilinear interpolation*.[5]

---

[5]There is also *cubic convolution*, which uses the weighted sum of a 4×4 array of texels, but it is currently not commonly available.

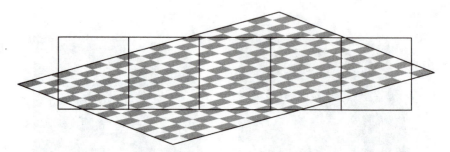

Figure 5.5. A view of a checkerboard-textured polygon through a row of pixel cells, showing how a number of texels affect each pixel.

In the left part of Figure 5.4, the nearest neighbor method was used, and the characteristic of this magnification technique is that the individual texels may become apparent. This effect is called *pixelation*. This is because this method takes the value of the nearest texel to each pixel center when magnifying, resulting in a blocky appearance. While the quality of this method is sometimes poor, it requires only one texel to be fetched per pixel.

In the right part of the same figure, bilinear interpolation (sometimes called *linear interpolation*) is used. For each pixel, this kind of filtering finds the four neighboring texels and linearly interpolates in two dimensions to find a blended value for the pixel. The result is blurrier, and much of the jaggedness from using the nearest neighbor method has disappeared.[6] Which filter is best typically depends on the desired result. The nearest neighbor can give a crisper feel when little magnification is occurring, but bilinear interpolation is usually a safer (though sometimes slower) choice in most situations.

5.2.2 Minification

When a texture is minimized, several texels may cover a pixel's cell, as shown in Figure 5.5. To get a correct color value for each pixel, you should integrate the effect of the texels influencing the pixel. However, it is difficult to determine precisely the exact influence of all texels near a particular pixel, and it is effectively impossible to do so perfectly in real-time.

Because of this limitation, a number of different methods are used in real-time work. One method is to use the nearest neighbor, which works exactly

---

[6]Looking at these images with eyes squinted has approximately the same effect as a low-pass filter, and reveals the face a bit more.

as the corresponding magnification filter does, i.e., it selects the texel closest to the center of the pixel's cell. This filter may cause severe aliasing problems. In Figure 5.6, nearest neighbor is used in the top figure. Towards the horizon, artifacts appear because only one of the many texels influencing a pixel is chosen to represent the surface. Such artifacts are even more noticeable as the surface moves with respect to the viewer, and are one manifestation of what is called *temporal aliasing*.

Another filter often available is bilinear interpolation, again working exactly as in the magnification filter. This filter is only slightly better than the nearest neighbor approach for minification. It blends four texels instead of using just one, but when a pixel is influenced by more than four texels, the filter soon fails and produces aliasing.

There are a few algorithms that are used to solve the problem for real-time rendering. Before delving into these, some filtering and sampling theory (beyond that presented in Section 4.4) is useful.

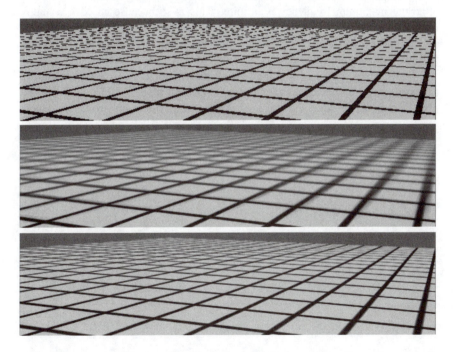

Figure 5.6. The top image was rendered with point sampling (nearest neighbor), the center with mipmapping, and the bottom with summed area tables.

Sampling and Filtering

The generation of an image is the process of sampling a three-dimensional scene in order to obtain color values for each pixel in the image. The rendering of images is inherently a sampling task, since the output device consists of an array of discrete pixels. Whenever sampling is done, aliasing may occur. This is an unwanted artifact, and we need to battle aliasing in order to generate pleasing images. Aliasing occurs when a signal is being sampled at too low a frequency. The sampled signal then appears to be a signal of lower frequency than the original. This is illustrated in Figure 5.7. For a signal to be sampled properly (i.e., so that it is possible to reconstruct the original signal from the samples), the sampling frequency has to be at least twice the maximum frequency of the signal to be sampled. This sampling frequency is called the *Nyquist rate* [293, 380] or *Nyquist limit* [369]. These concepts extend naturally to two dimensions as well, and so can be used when handling two-dimensional images.

If we knew in advance the maximum frequency in the three-dimensional scene we were about to view, then we would also know what sampling frequency would suffice in order to render an image without aliasing artifacts. However, often the maximum frequency is infinite. This is so because an edge contains infinite frequencies (because at an edge the intensity changes abruptly), and edges appear very often in computer-generated imagery. Even if the frequency is finite, the sampling rate per pixel might still have to be extremely high.

As discussed in Section 4.4, one antialiasing method is to use supersampling to distribute a number of samples evenly over each pixel cell. The color of the pixel is then some weighted mean of the samples. Note, however, that super-

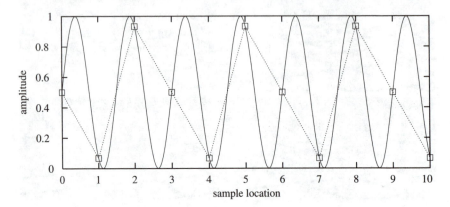

Figure 5.7. The solid line is the original signal. Sampling this signal at too low a rate gives a reconstructed signal (the dotted line) that has a frequency half that of the original.

sampling only increases the sampling rate, and thus can never eliminate— only reduce—aliasing.

Another solution to edge aliasing is filtering the edges, blurring them so that the high frequencies are eliminated or reduced. This same approach is used in solving texture aliasing. The goal is to gather the effects of the texels near the pixel, which is effectively equivalent to blurring the texture to eliminate high frequencies. The signal frequency of a texture depends upon how closely spaced its texels are on the screen. Due to the Nyquist limit, we need to make sure that the texture's signal frequency is no greater than half the sample frequency. In other words, we want to make sure that, along any one dimension, there is at most one texel for every two pixels. This is the theory, at least; in practice, systems tend to default to having one texel per pixel. The basic intent of texture antialiasing algorithms is the same: to preprocess the texture and create data structures that will allow quick approximation of the effect of a set of texels on a pixel.

Mipmapping

The most popular method of antialiasing for textures is called *mipmapping* [375]. It is implemented in some form on even the most modest graphics accelerators now produced. "Mip" stands for *multum in parvo*, Latin for "many things in a small place"—a good name for a process in which the original texture is filtered down repeatedly into smaller images.

When the mipmapping minimization filter is used, the original texture is augmented with a set of smaller versions of the texture before the actual rendering takes place. The texture (level zero) is downsampled to a quarter of the original area, with each new texel value typically computed as the average of the four neighbor texels. The new, level-one texture is called a *subtexture* of the original texture. The reduction is performed recursively until one or both of the dimensions of the texture equals 1 texel. This process is illustrated in Figure 5.8.

Two important elements in forming mipmaps are good filtering and gamma correction. The common way to form a mipmap level is to take each 2×2 set of pixels and average them to get the mip value. This is fraught with peril: the filter used is then a box filter, one of the worst filters possible. It is better to use a Gaussian or similar filter, and it is not all that complicated to code. By ignoring gamma correction, the overall perceived brightness of the mipmap level will be different than the original texture: as you get farther away from something and the uncorrected mipmaps kick in, the object will look darker.

The basic process of accessing this structure while texturing is straightforward. A screen pixel encloses an area on the texture itself. When the pixel's area is projected onto the texture (Figure 5.9), it covers a number of texels. There are two common measures used to compute a coordinate called d (which OpenGL calls λ, and which is also known as the level of detail). One is to use the longer

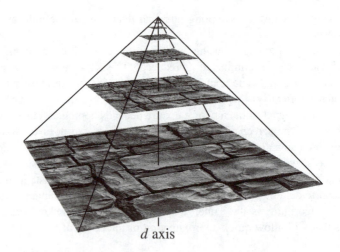

d axis

Figure 5.8. A mipmap is formed by taking the original image (level 0), at the base of the pyramid, and averaging each 2×2 area into a texel value on the next level up. The vertical axis is the third texture coordinate, d. In this figure, d is not linear; it is a measure of which two texture levels a sample uses for interpolation.

edge of the quadrilateral formed by the pixel's cell to approximate the pixel's coverage [375]; the other is to use as a measure the largest absolute value of the four differentials $\partial u/\partial x$, $\partial v/\partial x$, $\partial u/\partial y$, and $\partial v/\partial y$ [207]. Each differential is a measure of the amount of change in the texture coordinate with respect to a screen axis. For example, $\partial u/\partial x$ is the amount of change in the u texture value along the x-screen-axis for one pixel. Because mipmapping is now standard in hardware, the precise computations are not covered in depth here. See Williams's original article [375] or Flavell's presentation [107] for more about these equations. McCormack et al. [244] discuss the introduction of aliasing by the largest absolute value method, and they present an alternate formula.

The intent of computing the coordinate d is to determine where to sample along the mipmap's pyramid axis (see Figure 5.8). The goal is a pixel-to-texel ratio of at least 1:1 and preferably 2:1 [1], in order to achieve the Nyquist rate. The important principle here is that as the pixel cell comes to include more texels, a smaller, blurrier version of the texture is accessed. The (u, v, d) triplet is used to access the mipmap. The value d is analogous to a texture level, but instead of an integer value, d has the fractional value of the distance between levels. The texture level above and the level below the d location are sampled. The (u, v) location is used to retrieve a bilinearly interpolated sample from each of these two texture levels. The resulting sample is then linearly interpolated, depending on the distance from each texture level to d. This entire process is called trilinear interpolation and is performed per pixel.[7] Some hardware performs weaker versions of this algorithm, e.g., per-polygon, nearest neighbor, bilinear interpolation on the closest texture level, dithered per-pixel between two bilinear samples, or other combinations. Because trilinear interpolation uses two mipmap accesses (versus bilinear, where a single subtexture is accessed), it is twice as expensive to perform on some hardware.

One user control on the d coordinate is the *level of detail bias (LOD bias)* [122]. This is a value added to d, and so it affects the relative perceived sharpness of a texture. If we move further up the pyramid to start (increasing d), the texture will look blurrier. A good LOD bias for any given texture will vary with the image type and with the way it is used. For example, images that are somewhat blurry to begin with could use a negative bias, while poorly filtered (aliased) synthetic images used for texturing could use a positive bias. When a textured surface is moving, it often requires a higher bias to avoid temporal aliasing problems.

The result of mipmapping is that, instead of trying to sum all the texels which affect a pixel individually, precombined sets of texels are accessed and interpolated. This process takes a fixed amount of time, no matter what the level of minification. However, mipmapping has a number of flaws [107]. A major one is *overblurring*. Imagine a pixel cell that covers a large number of texels in the u direction and only a few in the v direction. This case commonly occurs when a viewer looks along a textured surface nearly edge-on. The effect of

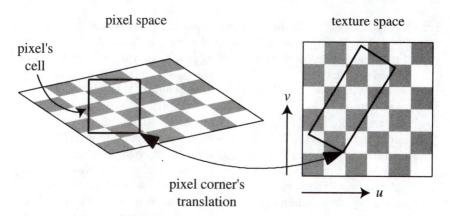

Figure 5.9. On the left is a square pixel cell and its view of a texture. On the right is the projection of the pixel cell onto the texture itself.

[7]Mipmapping and filtering in general can also be applied to three-dimensional image textures, in which case an additional level of interpolation is used.

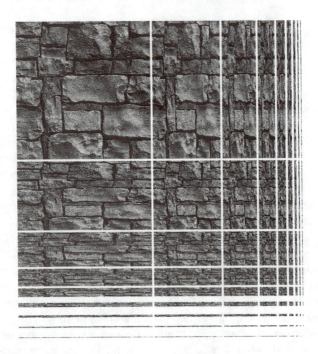

Figure 5.10. The ripmap structure. Note that the images along the diagonal from the upper left to the lower right are the mipmap subtextures.

accessing the mipmap is that square areas on the texture are retrieved; retrieving rectangular areas is not possible. To avoid aliasing, we choose the largest measure of the approximate coverage of the pixel cell on the texture. This results in the retrieved sample often being relatively blurry. This effect can be seen in the mipmap image in Figure 5.6. The lines moving into the distance on the right show overblurring.

There are a number of techniques to avoid some or all of this overblurring. One method is the *ripmap*. The idea is to extend the mipmap to include down-sampled rectangular areas as subtextures that can be accessed. Figure 5.10 shows the ripmap subtexture array. Four coordinates are used to access this structure: the usual two (u, v) values to access each subtexture, and two for a location in the ripmap array; these indicate the four subtextures among which to interpolate. These last two coordinates are computed using the pixel cell's u and v extents on the texture: the more texels included along an axis, the more downsampled the map that is used [245].

Another method is the *summed-area table* [73]. To use this method one first creates an array that is the size of the texture but contains more bits of precision for the color stored (e.g., 16 bits or more for each of red, green, and blue). At each location in this array, one must compute and store the sum of all the corresponding texture's texels in the rectangle formed by this location and texel $(0,0)$ (the origin). During texturing, the pixel cell's projection onto the texture is bound by a rectangle. The summed-area table is then accessed to determine the average color of this rectangle, which is passed back as the texture's color for the pixel. The average is computed using the texture coordinates of the rectangle shown in Figure 5.11. This is done using the formula given in Equation 5.1.

$$\mathbf{c} = \frac{\mathbf{s}[x_{ur}, y_{ur}] - \mathbf{s}[x_{ur}, y_{ll}] - \mathbf{s}[x_{ll}, y_{ur}] + \mathbf{s}[x_{ll}, y_{ll}])}{(x_{ur} - x_{ll})(y_{ur} - y_{ll})} \qquad (5.1)$$

Here, x and y are the texel coordinates of the rectangle and $\mathbf{s}[x, y]$ is the summed-area value for that texel. This equation works by taking the sum of the entire area from the upper right corner to the origin, then subtracting off areas A and B by subtracting the neighboring corners' contributions. Area C has been subtracted twice, so it is added back in by the lower left corner.

The results of using a summed-area table are shown in Figure 5.6. The lines going to the horizon are sharper near the right edge, but the diagonally crossing lines in the middle are still overblurred. Similar problems occur with the ripmap scheme. The problem is that when a texture is viewed along its diagonal, a large rectangle is generated with many of the texels situated nowhere near the pixel being added in. For example, imagine a long, thin rectangle

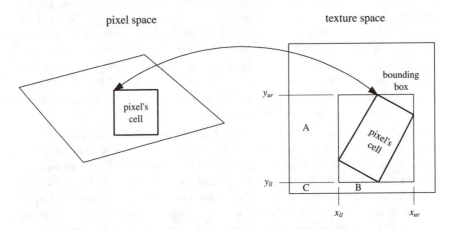

Figure 5.11. The pixel cell is back-projected onto the texture, bound by a rectangle, and the four corners of the rectangle are used to access the summed-area table.

pixel space   texture space

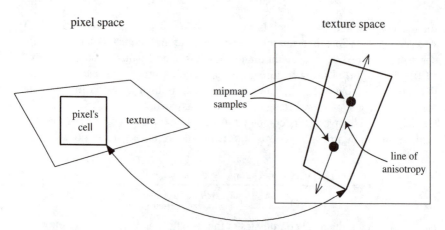

Figure 5.12. Talisman anisotropic filtering. The back-projection of the pixel cell creates a quadri-lateral. A line of anisotropy is formed parallel to the longer sides.

representing the pixel cell's back-projection lying diagonally across the entire texture in Figure 5.11. The whole texture rectangle's average will be returned, rather than just the average within the pixel cell.

Ripmaps and summed-area tables are examples of what are called *anisotropic filtering* algorithms [164]. Such algorithms are schemes that can retrieve texel values over areas which are not square. However, they are able to do this most effectively in primarily horizontal and vertical directions. Ripmaps were used in high-end Hewlett-Packard graphics accelerators in the early 1990s. To our knowledge, summed-area tables have not been implemented in any specialized hardware. Both schemes are memory intensive. While a mipmap's subtextures take only an additional third of the memory of the original texture, a ripmap's take an additional three times as much as the original. Summed-area tables take at least two times as much memory for textures of size 256×256 or less, with more precision needed for larger textures. Texture memory is a relatively precious commodity, not to be squandered.

A relatively new solution to the problem uses multiple sampling of the mipmap structure to obtain a better result. This anisotropic filtering algorithm is a part of the Talisman architecture [354], and is explained in depth by Barkans [28]. A similar system is presented by McCormack et al. [394]. The basic idea is that the pixel cell is back-projected, and this quadrilateral (quad) on the texture is then sampled a number of times, and the samples are combined. As noted above, each mipmap sample has a location and a squarish area associated with it. Instead of using a single mipmap sample to approximate this quad's coverage, the algorithm uses a number of squares to cover the quad. The shorter side of

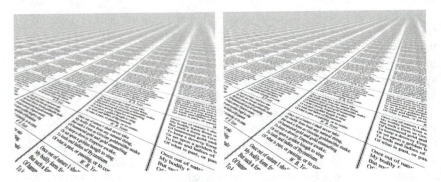

Figure 5.13. Mipmap versus anisotropic filtering of text. Trilinear mipmapping has been done on the left, 2:1 anisotropic filtering on the right, both at 640 × 480 resolution. *(Example pictures generated by software. Courtesy of NVIDIA Inc.)*

the quad is used to determine d (unlike in mipmapping, where the longer side is often used); this makes the averaged area smaller (and so less blurred) for each mipmap sample. The quad's longer side is used to create a *line of anisotropy* parallel to the longer side and through the middle of the quad. When the amount of anisotropy is between 1:1 and 2:1, two samples are taken along this line (see Figure 5.12). At higher ratios of anisotropy more samples are taken along the axis, with the two end-point samples weighted half as much as the rest of the samples.

This scheme allows the line of anisotropy to run in any direction, and so does not have the limitations that ripmaps and summed-area tables had. It also requires no more texture memory than mipmaps do, since it uses the mipmap algorithm to do its sampling. For example, a graphics accelerator can have a dual-pipe architecture that allows it to obtain and combine two mipmap samples in parallel, thus allowing it to perform anisotropic filtering up to a ratio of 2:1. We expect more parallelism to appear in chip sets as time goes on, thereby increasing the anisotropic ratio that can be used. An example of anisotropic filtering is shown in Figure 5.13.

Other minification filters are possible [164], but the mipmapping scheme and its variants are the ones that have made it into graphics hardware.

5.3   Texture Caching and Compression

A complex application may require a considerable number of textures. The amount of fast texture memory varies from system to system, but the general rule is that it is never enough. There are various techniques for *texture caching*, where a balance is sought between speed and minimizing the number of textures (or parts of textures) in memory at one time. For example, for textured polygons that are initially far away, the application may load only the smaller subtextures in a mipmap, since these are the only levels that will be accessed [1]. Each system has its own texture management tools and its own performance characteristics (e.g., 256×256 textures are optimized on some machines [83]). Some general advice is to keep the textures small—no larger than is necessary to avoid magnification problems—and to try to keep polygons grouped by their use of texture. Even if all textures are always in memory, such precautions may improve the processor's cache performance. Another method, called *tiling* or *mosaicing*, involves combining a few smaller (non-repeating) textures into a single larger texture image in order to speed access [83, 245]. However, if mipmapping is used then care must be taken to avoid having the images bleed into each other at higher subtexture levels.

For flight simulators and geographical information systems, the image datasets can be huge. The traditional approach is to break these images into smaller tiles that hardware can handle. Tanner et al. [262, 347] present an improved data structure called the *clipmap*. The idea is that the entire dataset is treated as a mipmap, but only a small part of the lower levels of the mipmap is required for any particular view. For example, if the viewer is flying above terrain and looking off into the distance, a large amount of the entire texture may be seen. However, the texture level 0 image is needed for only a small portion of this picture. Since minification will take place, a different portion of the level 1 image is needed further out, level 2 beyond that, and so on. By clipping the mipmap structure by the view, one can identify which parts of the mipmap are needed. An example of this technique is shown in Plate VIII (following p. 194).

One solution that directly attacks the memory problem is fixed-rate texture compression. By having hardware decode compressed textures on the fly, a texture can require less texture memory. Another benefit is a reduction in the bandwidth cost of transferring textures. There are a variety of image compression methods [248, 265], but it is costly to implement decoding for these in hardware. S3 came up with a scheme call S3 Texture Compression (S3TC) [304], which was chosen as a standard for DirectX 6.0. It has the advantages of creating a compressed image which is fixed in size, has independently encoded pieces, and is simple (and therefore fast) to decode. Given a particular image type and resolution, we know in advance how much space is needed for the compressed version. This is useful for texture caching, as we know that any image of the given resolution can reuse this image's memory. Each compressed part of the image can be dealt with independently from the others; there are no shared look-up tables or other dependencies, which simplifies decoding.

The image compression scheme is relatively simple. First the image is broken up into 4×4 pixel blocks, called *tiles*. For opaque images (i.e., those with no alpha channel), each 16-pixel block is encoded by storing two colors and 16 2-bit values. The two colors are represented by 16 bits (5 bits red, 6 green, 5 blue) and are chosen to bound the color range of the pixel block. Given these two colors, the encoding and decoding processes derive two other colors that are evenly spaced between them. This gives four colors to choose from, and so for each pixel a 2-bit value is stored as a selection of one of these four colors. Thus, a 16-pixel block is represented by a total of 64 bits, or an average of 4 bits per pixel. Given that an image is often originally stored with 16 or 24 bits per pixel, the scheme results in a 4:1 or 6:1 texture compression ratio. Similar schemes are used for images with 1-bit or 8-bit alpha channels [242, 304].

The main drawback of the compression scheme is that it is *lossy*. That is, the original image cannot always be retrieved from the compressed version. Only 4 different color values are used to represent 16 pixels, so if a tile has more than 4 colors in it there will be some loss. In practice, the compression scheme gives generally acceptable image fidelity. It offers the advantage of using higher-resolution compressed textures in place of uncompressed textures, for the same cost in memory.

5.4 Multipass Rendering

In computer graphics theory, all illumination equation factors are evaluated at once and a sample color is generated. In practice, the various parts of the lighting equation can be evaluated in separate passes, with each successive pass modifying the previous results. This technique is called *multipass rendering* [82, 262].

Hardware accelerators are able to significantly improve performance over software renderers for various operations; however, they do not have the flexibility to provide arbitrarily complex lighting models in a single pass. As a simple example, consider the diffuse and specular parts of the lighting equation. Say you wish to have the diffuse color modulated (multiplied) by a texture, but do not want the specular highlight to be modified by the texture. This is possible using two passes. In the first pass, you would compute and interpolate the diffuse illumination contribution and modulate it by the texture. You would then compute and interpolate the specular part and render the scene again, this time without the texture. The result would then be added to the existing diffusely lit, textured image. Since diffuse and specular components can be treated independently (see Equation 4.14 in chapter 4), it is perfectly acceptable to compute the lighting in this way.

In addition to the texture operations **replace** and **modulate** discussed on page 105, two other combine functions are commonly used in multipass rendering:

- **add** - Add the surface color and the texture color. There are also methods which subtract a bias of 0.5 in order to bring the result back within a useful range. Subtracting the texture color is also a possible function.

- **blend** - As explained in Section 4.5, two color values can be blended by an alpha value. This alpha value can come from a variety of sources: from vertices (in which each vertex is given an alpha value and the alpha is interpolated across the surface), from the image texture itself, from a constant alpha set externally, or from previous computations.

As will be seen, the alpha channel can be used for a variety of effects beyond transparency and antialiasing.

In multipass rendering the same geometry is often reused in each pass. If the transformation stage (and possibly the lighting stage) will yield identical results, it is a waste to have to recompute these results on each pass (and, as importantly, to resend the vertex data on each pass). Direct3D has support for *vertex buffers* and OpenGL for *vertex arrays*, which allow the intermediate results to be computed once and reused.

Some care has to be taken with multipass rendering when it is used with other effects, such as fog. If fog is enabled normally, multiple passes can result in fogging's being applied a number of times. Various blend modes can be used to apply fog properly [122, 187].

Multipass rendering is useful when one wants to enable a rendering system to work on a variety of hardware. For example, the game *Quake III* uses 10 passes. From Hook's notes [70]:

- (passes 1-4: accumulate bump map)

- pass 5: diffuse lighting

- pass 6: base texture (with specular component)

- (pass 7: specular lighting)

- (pass 8: emissive lighting)

- (pass 9: volumetric/atmospheric effects)

- (pass 10: screen flashes)

On the fastest machine up to 10 passes are done to render a single frame. However, if the graphics accelerator[8] cannot maintain a reasonable frame rate, various passes (those in parentheses) can be eliminated. For example, removing the bump-mapping passes reduces the model to 6 passes. The quality of the image is lower, but the real-time experience is maintained. The rendering system is said to be *scalable* if it has this ability to work in some reduced form on various platforms.

5.5   Multitexturing

Obviously, the more passes a renderer must take, the lower its overall performance. To reduce the number of passes, some graphics accelerators support *multitexturing*, in which two or more textures are accessed during the same pass [83, 322]. To combine the results of these texture accesses, a *texture blending cascade* (a pipeline) is defined that is made up of a series of *texture stages* [83], also called texture units [322]. The first texture stage combines two texture (or interpolated vertex) values, typically RGB and perhaps α (alpha), and this result is then passed on to the next texture stage. Second and successive stages then blend another texture's or interpolant's values with the previous result. This is illustrated in Figure 5.14. Another way to think of this process is that the texture units form a series like a pipeline. The triangle's interpolated vertex values enter the pipeline. Then, each texture in turn is applied to the set of values. The final output set is applied to the stored values (RGB and possibly α) in the frame buffer [322].

In addition to saving rendering passes, multitexturing actually allows more complex shading models than does the application of a single texture per pass. For example, say you want to use a lighting model with expression $AB + CD$, where each variable represents a different color texture's value. This expression is impossible to evaluate without multitexturing. A multipass algorithm could combine AB in two passes and add C in the next, but it could not fold D in because C would already have been added to AB. There is no place to keep C separate from AB, since only one color can be stored in the color buffer. With multitexturing, the first pass could compute AB. Then the second pass would compute CD and add this result to the AB in the color buffer [255].

As will be seen in the example at the end of Section 5.7.3, multitexturing can also help avoid the allocation of an alpha channel in the frame buffer.

---

[8]*Quake III* requires an accelerator.

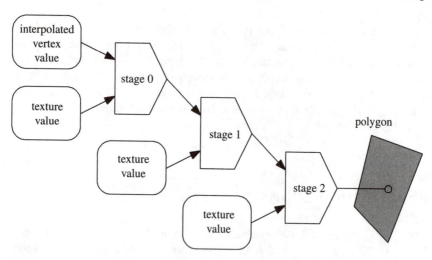

Figure 5.14. The result from a texture is combined with an interpolated value in stage 0, and the result of that combination is then combined with another texture in stage 1. This result of that combination is combined with yet another texture in stage 2 and then applied to the polygon.

5.6 Texture Animation

The image applied to a surface does not have to be static. For example, a video source can be used as a texture that changes from frame to frame.

The texture coordinates need not be static, either. In fact, for environment mapping, they usually change with each frame because of the way they are computed (see section 5.7.3). The application designer can also explicitly change the texture coordinates from frame to frame. Imagine that a waterfall has been modeled and that it has been textured with an image that looks like falling water. Say the v coordinate is the direction of flow. To make the water move, one must subtract an amount from the v coordinates on each successive frame. Subtraction from the texture coordinates has the effect of making the texture itself appear to move forward.

More elaborate effects can be created by modifying the texture coordinates. Linear transformations such as zoom, rotation, and shearing are possible [245]. Image warping and morphing transforms are also possible [380], as are generalized projections [149].

By using texture blending techniques, one can realize other animated effects. For example, by starting with a marble texture and fading in a flesh texture, one can make a statue come to life [254].

5.7 Texturing Methods

With the basic theory in place, we will now cover various other forms of texturing beyond gluing simple color images onto surfaces. The rest of this chapter will discuss the use of alpha blending in texturing, reflections via environment mapping, and rough surface simulation using bump mapping, among others. Chapter 6, on special effects, will also frequently draw upon texturing methods.

5.7.1 Alpha Mapping

The alpha value can be used for many interesting effects. One texture-related effect is decaling. As an example, say you wish to put a picture of a flower on a teapot. You do not want the whole picture, but just the parts where the flower is present. By assigning an alpha of 0 to a texel you make it transparent so that it has no effect. So, by properly setting the decal texture's alpha, you can replace or blend the underlying surface with the decal. Typically, a clamp or border corresponder function is used with a transparent border to apply the decal just once to the surface.

Another application of alpha is in making cutouts. Say you make a decal image of a tree, but you do not want the background of this image to affect the scene at all. That is, if an alpha is found to be fully transparent, then the textured surface itself does not affect that pixel. In this way you can render an object with a complex silhouette using a single polygon.

In the case of the tree, if you rotate the viewer around it, the illusion fails since the tree has no thickness. One answer is to copy this tree polygon and rotate it 90 degrees along the trunk. The two polygons form an inexpensive three-dimensional tree, and the illusion is fairly effective when viewed from ground level. See Figure 5.15. In Section 6.2.2, we discuss a method called billboarding, which is used to reduce such rendering to a single polygon.

Providing this texture effect means a slight extension of the rendering pipeline. Before testing and replacing the Z-buffer value, there needs to be a test of the alpha value. If alpha is 0, then nothing further is done for the pixel. If this additional test is not done, the tree's background color will not affect the pixel's color, but will potentially affect the z-value, which can lead to rendering errors.

Combining alpha blending and texture animation can produce convincing special effects, such as flickering torches, plant growth, explosions, atmospheric effects, etc.

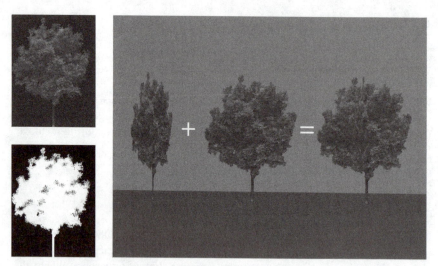

Figure 5.15. On the left, the tree texture map and the 1-bit alpha channel map below it. On the right, the tree rendered on a single polygon; by adding a second copy of the polygon rotated 90 degrees we form an inexpensive three-dimensional tree.

5.7.2   Light Mapping

In section 4.3 Phong shading was presented. This technique yields more precise lighting evaluation by computing the illumination at each pixel. But since Gouraud shading is the norm in graphics hardware, short of meshing surfaces finely in order to capture the lighting's effect more finely, it appears that general Phong shading is not possible. However, for static lighting in an environment, the diffuse component on any surface remains the same from any angle. Because of this view-independence, the contribution of light to a surface could be captured in a texture structure attached to a surface. An elaborate version of this concept was first implemented by Arvo [15] and later by Heckbert [165] in order to capture global illumination information, i.e., light bouncing around the environment.

Carmack realized that this sort of method could be applied to real-time work in lieu of using lighting equations during rendering [1]. By using a separate, precomputed texture that captured the lighting contributions, and multiplying it with the underlying surface, one could achieve Phong-like shading (see Plate IV, following p. 194). As Hook points out, this technique is more accurately termed "dark mapping," because the original surface actually decreases in intensity [187]. To make light mapping a bit easier to use and to maintain brightness,

Direct3D provides texture blending operations which boost the output intensity by a factor of two or four. Values above 1.0 are clamped to 1.0. An example is shown in Plate V (following p. 194). While multiplying the two textures has a physical meaning associated with it, for a different look another lighting model could be used, such as adding or blending the two textures together.

The light texture can simply be multiplied by the surface's material texture during the modeling stage, and the single resulting texture can be used. However, a number of advantages accrue by using light mapping in a separate stage. First, the light texture can generally be low-resolution. In many cases lighting changes slowly across a surface, so the texture representing the light can be quite small compared to the surface. Minimal processing is needed to modify or swap such light textures on the fly. Lighting situations can be reused with a variety of environments, and color textures can be tiled and have different lighting on each tile (see Plate V, following p. 194). Using texture coordinate animation techniques (Section 5.6), light textures can be made to move on walls–e.g., a moving spot light effect can be created. Also, light maps can be recalculated on the fly for dynamic (changing) lighting. In summary, the flexibility of using separate light textures often outweighs the cost of a separate pass. With multitexturing support, even this cost disappears.

Using textures to represent shadows is related to the idea of light mapping. See Section 6.6.1 for more about this method.

An interesting extension to image texture light maps is three-dimensional texture light maps, where actual beams of light are stored throughout the volume [245]. Though memory-intensive (as are all three-dimensional textures), this method has the advantage that the light is actually there in space. Moving the texture around moves the light's effect in a simple and natural way. Projective textures [245, 321] are also related to light maps, providing a more flexible method of creating lighting such as that made by a slide projector.

5.7.3 Gloss Mapping

Image light maps are typically used on diffuse surfaces, and so are sometimes called diffuse light maps. The specular component can also be affected by light mapping, but here the effect is sometimes a little more involved.

The specular component is computed using the eye direction and the light direction. In real-time work it is typically calculated at polygon vertices and interpolated. Just as a texture can be used to modulate the diffuse lighting on a surface to produce a brick wall effect, so can a different texture produce varying specularity. Such a texture is typically a monochrome (gray-scale) texture, where 1.0 means the full specular component is to be used, and 0.0 means none is used.

This technique is called *gloss mapping* [255]. The pear in Plate IX (following p. 194) shows this effect.

It is important to realize that for Gouraud-shaded objects the underlying specular component is still computed only on a per-vertex basis and interpolated. For example, imagine a brick wall where the bricks are shiny and the mortar is not. This shininess would form a gloss texture where the bricks are white and the mortar is black. Applying this texture to a single polygon with the brick wall texture will change the specular component's contribution. So if the light source is, say, a spot light, its effect will not be captured. For example, if we situated a spot light so as to give the effect shown in Plate IV (following p. 194), the light's computed intensity at the corners of the textured polygon would be zero, and it would therefore provide no specular highlighting at all across the surface.

To account for effects such as spot lights and cones of influence, the specular highlight component of the lighting equation can be replaced with a *specular light map*. This is simply a light map that portrays the spot-light or cone effect desired. A diffuse light map directly modulates a surface texture. A specular light map modulates the computed highlight contribution, and this result modulates the gloss map. In the brick wall example, the specular highlight is computed without the effect of spot lighting or cones, and so it will no longer be zero. This interpolated highlight color is multiplied by the specular light map, giving a spot-light effect to the specular contribution. Finally the gloss map is multiplied into this result, and the bricks appear shiny while the mortar does not. This whole process computes the specular contribution.

The diffuse calculations could also use a light map, but this light map is likely to have a different texture than the specular light map. This is because the diffuse light map includes both the spot-light effect and the fall-off in intensity due to the diffuse surface's angle to the light. To summarize in an equation:

$$\mathbf{o} = \mathbf{m}_{diff} \otimes \mathbf{t}_{diff} + (\mathbf{i}_{spec} \otimes \mathbf{m}_{spec}) t_{gloss} \qquad (5.2)$$

where $\mathbf{m}_{diff}$ is the diffuse light map, $\mathbf{t}_{diff}$ is the diffuse texture map, $\mathbf{i}_{spec}$ is the interpolated highlight color, $\mathbf{m}_{spec}$ is the specular spot-light effect light map, and t_{gloss} is the single-value gloss texture. This is just one possible lighting equation. For example, the light maps could have a single intensity value instead of a color. They could be replaced by interpolated diffuse lighting in the diffuse term and be left out entirely of the specular term. The interpolated specular color could be replaced by an interpolated intensity value. Lighting equations can always be changed or extended in order to create a desired effect or to increase speed.

While often convincing, this procedure has some limitations. Specular highlights are often blurry and animate poorly, as they are captured only at each vertex instead of at each pixel. In the brick wall example, if the brightest part of the highlight fell in the middle of the wall, it would not be captured by interpolation from the corners. It would be much better to have the lights' contributions per pixel, or better yet the contributions of the lights and all objects reflecting light. These contributions could then be modulated by the gloss texture. To create such reflections we can use environment mapping, the next topic.

5.7.4 Environment Mapping

Environment mapping (EM), also called reflection mapping, is a simple yet powerful method of generating approximations of reflections in curved surfaces. This technique was introduced by Blinn and Newell [36]. All EM methods start with a ray from the viewer to a point on the reflector. This ray is then reflected with respect to the normal at that point. Instead of finding the intersection with the closest surface, as ray tracing does [116], EM uses the direction of the reflection vector as an index to an image containing the environment. This is conceptualized in Figure 5.16.

The environment mapping approximation assumes that the objects and lights being reflected with EM are far away, and that the reflector will not reflect itself. If these assumptions hold, then the environment around the reflector can

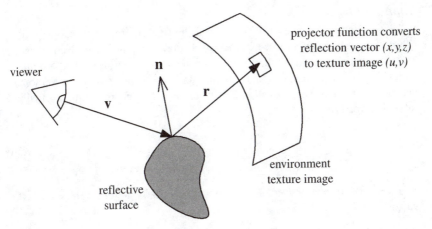

Figure 5.16. Environment mapping. The viewer sees an object, and the reflection vector **r** is computed from **v** and **n**. The reflection vector accesses the environment's representation. The access information is computed by using some projector function to convert the reflection vector's (x, y, z) to (typically) a (u, v) value, which is used to retrieve texture data.

be treated as a two-dimensional projection surrounding it.

The steps of an EM algorithm are:

- Generate a two-dimensional image of the environment (this is the environment map).

- For each pixel that contains a reflective object, compute the normal at the location on the surface of the object (if per-pixel EM is not available, then the normal is computed at triangle vertices).

- Compute the reflection vector from the view vector and the normal.

- Use the reflection vector to compute an index into the environment map that represents the objects in the reflection direction.

- Use the texel data from the environment map to color the current pixel.

There are a variety of projector functions that map the reflection vector into one or more textures. Blinn and Newell's algorithm and Greene's cubic environment mapping technique are classic mapping methods, and so are covered first. However, these two methods are only just beginning to see support in commercial hardware. The sphere map technique is presented next. It is the projector function most commonly used for EM in graphics accelerators. Finally, a new method from Heidrich and Seidel is explained, as it shows great promise for future hardware support.

Blinn and Newell's Method

In 1976, Blinn and Newell [36] developed the first environment mapping algorithm. For each environment-mapped pixel, they compute the reflection vector and then transform it into spherical coordinates (ρ, ϕ). Here ϕ, called longitude, varies from 0 to 2π radians, and ρ, called latitude, varies from 0 to π radians. (ρ, ϕ) is computed from Equation 5.3, where $\mathbf{r} = (r_x, r_y, r_z)$ is the normalized reflection vector.

$$
\rho = \arccos(-r_z)
$$
$$
\phi = \begin{cases} \arccos(r_x/\sin\rho) & \text{if } r_y \geq 0 \\ 2\pi - \arccos(r_x/\sin\rho) & \text{otherwise} \end{cases} \quad (5.3)
$$

The viewer's reflection vector is computed similarly to the light's reflection vector (see Section 4.3.2):

$$
\mathbf{r} = 2(\mathbf{n} \cdot \mathbf{v})\mathbf{n} - \mathbf{v} \quad (5.4)
$$

where $\mathbf{v}$ is the normalized vector from the eye to the surface location, and $\mathbf{n}$ is the surface normal at that location.

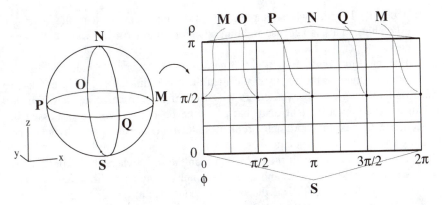

Figure 5.17. Illustration of Blinn and Newell's environment map. The sphere on the left is unfolded into the rectangle (the environment map) on the right. The key points **N, S, M, O, P**, and **Q**, mentioned in the text, are also shown.

The spherical coordinates (ρ, ϕ) are then transformed to the range $[0, 1)$ and used as (u, v) coordinates to access the environment texture, producing a reflection color. Since the reflection vector is transformed into spherical coordinates, the environment texture is an image of an "unfolded" sphere. Essentially, the texture covers a sphere that surrounds the reflection point. This projector function is sometimes called a latitude-longitude mapping, since v corresponds to latitude and u to longitude. This mapping is shown in Figure 5.17.

Some key points are displayed in this table:

name	coordinate	angles
N (north pole)	$(0, 0, 1)$	$\rho = \pi, \phi$ is undefined
S (south pole)	$(0, 0, -1)$	$\rho = 0, \phi$ is undefined
M	$(1, 0, 0)$	$\rho = \pi/2, \phi = 0$
O	$(0, 1, 0)$	$\rho = \pi/2, \phi = \pi/2$
P	$(-1, 0, 0)$	$\rho = \pi/2, \phi = \pi$
Q	$(0, -1, 0)$	$\rho = \pi/2, \phi = 3\pi/2$

Although easy to implement, this method has some disadvantages. First, there is a border at $\phi = 0$, and second, the map converges at the poles. An image used in environment mapping must match at the seam along its vertical edges (i.e., must tile seamlessly) and should avoid distortion problems near each horizontal edge.

This method computes an index into the environment map for each visible point on the objects that should have reflections. Its computations are therefore on a per-pixel basis, which implies that it is not normally feasible for real-time graphics. This is because lighting equations are normally evaluated at the vertices, not per pixel.

For real-time work, Equation 5.3 can be used to compute indices into the environment map at the vertices, and then these coordinates can be interpolated across the triangle. However, errors will occur if the vertices of a triangle have indices to the environment map that cross the poles. As will be discussed in Section 9.2.1, texture coordinate problems at the poles are difficult to avoid when using triangles for interpolation.

Errors can also occur if the endpoints span the seam where the vertical edges of the environment textures meet. For example, imagine a short line that has one u coordinate at 0.97 and the other u coordinate at 0.02. An error results if we interpolate from 0.97 to 0.02 without paying attention to the seam, as the interpolation would travel through 0.96 on down. Interpolation should go up to 0.98, 0.99, then wrap to 0.0, 0.01, 0.02. One solution to this problem is to find the absolute value of the difference between the coordinates ($0.95 = 0.97 - 0.02$ for the example). If this value is greater than 0.5, then 1.0 is added to the smaller coordinate and the texture is repeated. For the example, the range would then be 0.97 to 1.02. Some APIs have direct support to avoid seam problems. For example, Direct3D supports what they call "texture wrapping" (not to be confused with their "wrap texture address mode"; see Section 5.1).

Cubic Environment Mapping

In 1986, Greene [140] introduced another EM technique. His environment map is obtained by placing the camera in the center of the environment and then projecting the environment onto the sides of a cube positioned with its center at the camera's location. The images of the cube are then used as the environment map. In practice, the scene is rendered six times (one for each cube face) with the camera at the center of the cube, looking at each cube face with a 90-degree view angle.

This type of environment map is shown in Figure 5.18. In Figure 5.19 is a typical cubic environment map.

Greene's method is used in many photorealistic systems today, and we expect to see it in real-time rendering APIs. Its strength is that environment maps can be generated by the system itself relatively easily (vs. Blinn and Newell's method, which uses a spherical projection), and could even be generated on the fly. It also has more uniform sampling characteristics. Blinn and Newell's method has an excessive number of texels near the poles as compared to the equator.

The direction of the normalized reflection vector determines which face of the cube to use. The reflection vector coordinate with the largest magnitude selects the corresponding face (e.g., the vector $(-0.2, 0.5, -0.84)$ selects the $-Z$ face).

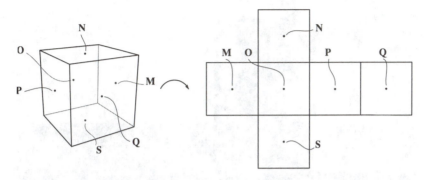

Figure 5.18. Illustration of Greene's environment map, with key points shown. The cube on the left is unfolded into the environment map on the right.

The remaining two coordinates are divided by the absolute value of the largest magnitude coordinate, i.e., 0.84. They now range from -1 to 1, and are simply remapped to $[0, 1]$ in order to compute the texture coordinates (e.g., the coordinates $(-0.2, 0.5)$ are mapped to $((-0.2/0.84 + 1)/2, (0.5/0.84 + 1)/2) \approx (0.38, 0.80)$. In the same manner as Blinn and Newell's method, this technique is per-pixel based. If two vertices are found to be on different cube faces, it is difficult to interpolate correctly between them. One method is to subdivide the problematic polygon along the cube edge [149]. Another method that can help with smaller polygons is to make the environment map faces larger than 90 degrees in view angle, then see if any face fully contains the polygon.

Voorhies and Foran [361] have developed a possible hardware solution for Greene's EM method, but as of this writing it has not been implemented in any commercial hardware.

A high-performance real-time graphics system called *PixelFlow* [259] has shaders that can be programmed to perform Greene's environment mapping method in real-time.

Sphere Mapping

First mentioned by Williams [375], this is the standard projector function used on SGI machines, and so is supported by OpenGL. It is also supported indirectly in Direct3D, since it involves accessing a single texture. A texture representing a circle is used for the environment texture (see Plate VII, following p. 194). The image is derived from the appearance of the environment as viewed orthographically in a perfectly reflective sphere, so this texture is called a sphere map. Sphere map textures can be generated using ray tracing or by warping the images generated for a cubic environment map [245].

Figure 5.19. A typical cubic environment map. *(Courtesy of Ned Greene/NYIT)*

The sphere map has a basis (see Appendix A) which is the frame of reference in which the texture was generated. That is, the image is viewed along some axis $-\mathbf{e}$ in world space, with $\mathbf{u}$ as the up vector for the image and $\mathbf{h}$ going horizontally to the right (and all are normalized). This gives a basis matrix:

$$\begin{pmatrix} h_x & h_y & h_z & 0 \\ u_x & u_y & u_z & 0 \\ -e_x & -e_y & -e_z & 0 \\ 0 & 0 & 0 & 1 \end{pmatrix} \tag{5.5}$$

To access the sphere map, first transform the surface normal, $\mathbf{n}$, and the vector from the current eye position to the vertex $\mathbf{e}$, using this matrix. This yields $\mathbf{n}'$ and $\mathbf{e}'$ in the sphere map's space. The reflection vector is then computed to access the sphere map texture:

$$\mathbf{r} = 2(\mathbf{n}' \cdot \mathbf{e}')\mathbf{n}' - \mathbf{e}' \tag{5.6}$$

with **r** being the resulting reflection vector, in the sphere map's space. From the reflection vector the parameter-space values are calculated as follows:

$$m = \sqrt{r_x^2 + r_y^2 + (r_z + 1)^2} \qquad (5.7)$$

$$u = \frac{r_x}{2m} + 0.5 \qquad (5.8)$$

$$v = \frac{r_y}{2m} + 0.5 \qquad (5.9)$$

The value m is computed in part by adding 1 to r_z, which effectively brings the hemisphere behind the reflective sphere to the front. The texture coordinates are normalized by dividing by m, then remapped from the range $[-1, 1]$ to $[0, 1]$ by the rest of the formulae.

Sphere mapping is an improvement over Blinn and Newell's method in a number of ways. The simplicity of implementing its projector function in hardware is its great strength. There is no texture seam to interpolate across and only one singularity, located around the edge of the sphere map. However, moving between two points on the sphere map is not a linear affair. As in Blinn and Newell's method, linear interpolation on the texture is just an approximation, and errors become more serious as the viewer leaves the view axis used to generate the sphere map texture. To improve quality, sphere maps can be regenerated from cubic maps on the fly [245]. If mipmapping is used, then the entire mipmap has to be generated, too. Note that OpenGL support for sphere mapping is in view space by default, so even if the view changes direction, the same mapping gets used. In other words, if you were to look at a reflective sphere and then move elsewhere and look at the same sphere, the reflection would not change but be represented by the same sphere map. A slower but more accurate approach is to compute the EM texture coordinates in the application stage for each frame.

See Plate VI (following p. 194) for an example of environment mapping done with sphere maps.

Paraboloid Mapping

Heidrich and Seidel [171, 174] propose using two environment textures, in what we call here paraboloid mapping. The idea is similar to that of sphere mapping, but instead of generating the texture by recording the reflection of the environment off a sphere, two paraboloids are used. Each paraboloid creates a circular texture similar to a sphere map, with each covering an environment hemisphere. See Figure 5.20.

As with sphere mapping, the reflection ray is computed with Equation 5.6 in the map's basis, choosing one of the two textures as the front-facing texture. The sign of the z-component of the reflection vector is used to decide which

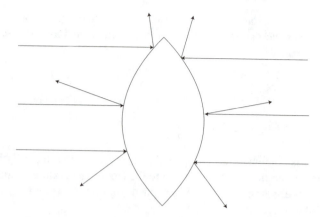

Figure 5.20. Two paraboloid mirrors that capture an environment using diametrically opposite views.

texture to access. Then the access function is simply:

$$u = \frac{r_x}{2(1 + r_z)} + 0.5 \tag{5.10}$$

$$v = \frac{r_y}{2(1 + r_z)} + 0.5 \tag{5.11}$$

for the front image, and the same with sign reversals for r_z for the back image.

The authors present an OpenGL implementation for this method. The problem of interpolating across the seam between the two textures is handled by accessing both paraboloid textures. If a sample is not on one texture it is black, and each sample will be on one and only one of the textures. Summing the results (one of which is always zero) gives the environment's contribution.

This method is superior to the sphere map scheme in that it has no singularity. Also, the paraboloid has more uniform texel sampling of the environment compared to the sphere map and even the cubical map. The paraboloid map's uniformity means that it is generally good from any view and so does not need to be regenerated. In contrast, to maintain image quality, some applications regenerate the sphere map when the viewer moves. Paraboloid mapping is a possible future candidate for hardware implementation.

Extensions and Limitations

It is worth pointing out an important use of EM techniques: specular reflections and refractions [254, 375]. As discussed in Section 4.3, Gouraud shading can miss highlights (reflections of lights) because a light's effect is assessed only at the vertices. Environment mapping can solve this problem by representing the lights in the texture. By doing so, we can simulate highlighting on a per-pixel basis (see Plate VI, following p. 194). Furthermore, to simulate a different degree of roughness, the environment's representation in the texture can be modified. By blurring the texture, we can present a rougher-appearing surface. In theory, such blurring should be done in a non-linear fashion; that is, different parts of the texture should be blurred differently. In practice, the eye tends to be fairly forgiving, because the general effect of the reflection is usually more important than the exact reflection itself.

Other advantages to using environment mapping instead of specular high-lighting include speed and versatility. The speed of accessing the environment map is constant, regardless of how many lights are represented in the texture. Environment mapping is also flexible, as reflected light sources can be linear or area lights, and more than just lights can be represented in the texture. That said, the limitations are that generating and storing EM textures can be costly in time, effort, and resources. Such textures are also often limited to a certain volume of space. For example, if the reflective object moves from one room to another, it is extremely difficult to transition smoothly from one environment texture to another. Methods such as Greene's cubic EM allows on-the-fly regeneration of environment textures, but this is a costly process.

Another potential stumbling block of EM is worth mentioning. Flat surfaces usually do not work well when environment mapping is used. The problem with a flat surface is that the rays that reflect off of it usually do not vary by more than a few degrees. This results in a small part of the EM texture's being mapped onto a relatively large surface. Normally, the individual texels of the texture become visible, unless bilinear interpolation is used; even then, the results do not look good, as a small part of the texture is extremely magnified. We have also been assuming that perspective projection is being used. If orthographic viewing is used, the situation is much worse for flat surfaces. In this case, all the reflection vectors are the same, and so the surface will get a constant color from some single texel. Other real-time techniques such as planar reflections (Section 6.5.1) may be of more use for flat surfaces.

EXAMPLE: DIFFUSE, GLOSS, AND ENVIRONMENT MAPPING Various texturing effects can be combined. One example is using environment mapping with gloss and diffuse color texturing [255]. The pear shown in Plate IX (following p. 194) is rendered using this lighting model, which looks like this:

$$\mathbf{o} = \mathbf{t}_{diff} \otimes \mathbf{i}_{diff} + t_{gloss}\mathbf{e}_{spec} \qquad (5.12)$$

where $\mathbf{t}_{diff}$ is the RGB texture, $\mathbf{i}_{diff}$ the interpolated diffuse lighting, t_{gloss} the monochrome gloss texture, and $\mathbf{e}_{spec}$ the environment map's specular color.

This model can be computed in two passes. The first texture applied to the pear is the specular highlight texture, e_{spec}. Doing so gives a black pear with a bright white highlight. The second texture is set up so that the RGB values are the diffuse texture, t_{diff}, and the alpha value is actually the gloss intensity, t_{gloss}.

To clarify: the alpha channel is not used in the traditional way here; it does not affect the opacity of the RGB values. In the second rendering pass, this texture is applied to the surface. The RGB values are multiplied by the diffuse illumination interpolated from the vertices, i_{diff}. The shading mode is set so that blending is done by multiplying the second texture's alpha value (the gloss) by the previous color (the specular environment map result from the first pass, now in the frame buffer). This product is added to the first term, the illuminated RGB texture. Essentially, the alpha channel is used as a parallel data stream, computing the effect of gloss mapping on the specular highlight while the RGB texture is multiplied by the diffuse lighting.

Using multitexturing here eliminates the need to allocate a separate alpha channel in the frame buffer. Without multitexturing, the algorithm would have to be restructured, and the t_{gloss} alpha value from the second texture would have to be stored in the frame buffer's alpha channel so that it could modulate the specular environment map in a later pass.   □

5.7.5   Bump Mapping

Introduced by Blinn in 1978 [38], *bump mapping* is a technique that makes a surface appear uneven in some manner: bumpy, wrinkled, wavy, etc. The basic idea is that, instead of changing the color components in the illumination equation, we modify the surface normal by accessing a texture. The geometric normal of the surface remains the same; we merely modify the normal used in the lighting equation. This operation has no physical equivalent; we perform changes on the surface normal, but the surface itself remains smooth in the geometric sense. Just as having a normal per vertex gives the illusion that the surface is smooth between polygons, modifying the normal per pixel changes the perception of the polygon surface itself.

There are two basic methods of modifying the normal with a bump map. One bump texturing technique uses two signed values, b_u and b_v, at each point. These two values correspond to the amount along the **u** and **v** image axes by which to vary the normal. That is, these texture values, which typically are bilinearly interpolated, are used to scale two vectors that are perpendicular to the normal. These two vectors are added to the normal to change its direction.

These two values essentially represent how steep the surface is and which way it faces at the point. See Figure 5.21.

The second method uses a *height field* to modify the surface normal's direction. That is, each monochrome texture value represents a height, so white is a high area and black a low one (or vice versa; a signed value is used to scale or negate the values in bump maps in still-image rendering systems). The height field is used to derive u and v signed values similar to those used in the first method. This is done by taking the differences between neighboring columns to get the slopes for u, and between neighboring rows for v [317]. Figure 5.22 shows an example.

Per-pixel bump mapping is extremely convincing, and offers an inexpensive way to add the effect of geometric detail. One place the illusion breaks down is around the silhouettes of objects. At these edges the viewer notices that there are no real bumps but just smooth outlines. Also note that mipmapping does not work with bump textures, as it has the effect of making the texture slopes disappear. Another artifact of using bump mapping is that shadows are not produced by the bumps, which can look unrealistic.

In classical bump mapping, the normal is varied per pixel and used in an illumination equation, which is beyond the capabilities of almost all real-time systems. However, there are a number of techniques that can be used for real-time bump mapping.

One algorithm that is conceptually simple is the dot product method. Instead of storing heights or slopes, the actual new normals for the surface are stored as

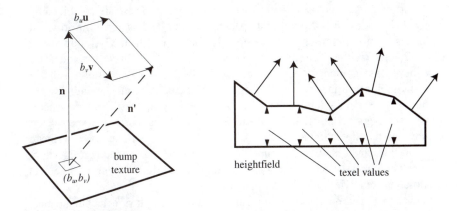

Figure 5.21. On the left, a normal vector **n** is modified in the **u** and **v** directions by the (b_u, b_v) values taken from the bump texture, giving **n'** (which is unnormalized). On the right, a height field and its effect on shading normals is shown.

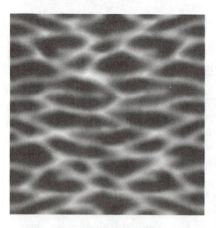 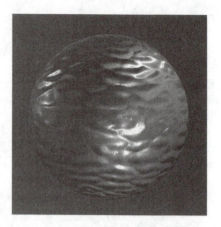

Figure 5.22. A wavy height field bump image and its use on a sphere, rendered with per-pixel illumination.

(x, y, z) vectors in a *normal map* [61]. To compute the effect of a light source, the positional light source's location is first transformed to the surface's basis (similarly to Equation 5.5). The surface's basis is formed by its geometric normal and the **u** and **v** axes of the texture. With the light now oriented with respect to the surface, the vector from each vertex to the light is computed in this basis and then normalized. The coordinates of each vertex's normal are interpolated across the surface. In other words, instead of a color or depth value, a vector to the light is interpolated.[9] The bump texture, which consists of normals, is then combined with the interpolated light vector at each pixel. These are combined by taking their dot product, which is a special texture-blending function provided for precisely this purpose. An example is shown in Plate XI (following p. 194). Computing the dot product of the normal and the light vector is exactly how the diffuse component is calculated (see Section 4.3.1), so this results in a bumpy-looking surface that will change appearance as it moves with respect to the light. For directional lights the technique is simpler still, as the vector from the polygon to the light is constant. Direct3D supports this specialized texture-blending operation as D3DTOP_DOTPRODUCT3, but that does not mean there is widespread hardware support for it. For this reason, another algorithm is more popular, as it uses commonly available capabilities, though at the cost of additional rendering passes.

This other method for Gouraud bump mapping employs a technique borrowed from two-dimensional image processing. Called *embossing* [317], it is

---

[9]The light vector that is interpolated will actually become shorter than a length of 1, but the error from this is usually unnoticeable.

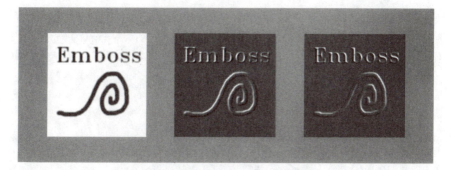

Figure 5.23. Embossing. The original image is on the left; the center shows the image embossed as if lit from the upper left; the right shows it as if lit from the upper right.

a way to give a chiselled look to an image. To obtain an embossed effect, the height field image is copied, shifted slightly, and subtracted from its original. See Figure 5.23.

This same embossing technique can be used with three-dimensional surfaces. The basic algorithm is as follows [245]:

1. Render the surface with the height field applied as a diffuse monochrome texture.

2. Shift all the vertex (u, v) coordinates in the direction of the light.

3. Render this surface with the height field again applied as a diffuse texture, subtracting from the first-pass result. This gives the emboss effect.

4. Render the surface again with no height field, simply illuminated and Gouraud-shaded. Add this shaded image to the result.

The involved part of the procedure is determining how much to shift the vertex (u, v) values in step 2. What we need to do is add to these vertex values the light's direction relative to the surface. This process is shown in Figure 5.24.

To find the light's direction relative to the surface, we need to form a coordinate system at the vertex and transform the light into this system. First retrieve the normal n at the vertex. Then find a surface vector t that follows one of the two texture coordinate axes u or v; t is tangent to (i.e., travels along) the surface. Finally create a third vector b, the binormal, which is mutually perpendicular to n and t and runs in the direction of the other texture coordinate axis (the one not used when forming t). This is done by simply computing the cross product:

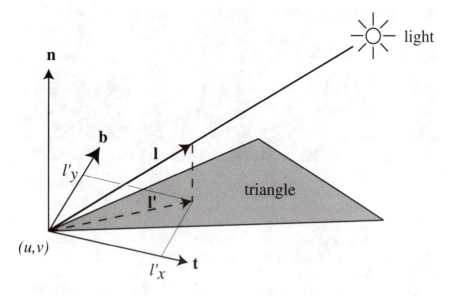

Figure 5.24. The light's direction **l** is cast upon the triangle's plane, and the resulting vector **l′** is added to the vertex's texture coordinates.

$\mathbf{b} = \mathbf{n} \times \mathbf{t}$. Normalize all these vectors and form a basis matrix:

$$\begin{pmatrix} t_x & t_y & t_z & 0 \\ b_x & b_y & b_z & 0 \\ n_x & n_y & n_z & 0 \\ 0 & 0 & 0 & 1 \end{pmatrix} \qquad (5.13)$$

This matrix is used to transform **l**, the normalized vector from the vertex to the light. Note that for curved surfaces and for flat surfaces where the light vector noticeably changes, this basis matrix creation and shift computation must be performed separately at each vertex. The resulting vector **l′** gives the direction in which to shift (u, v). For example, if **t** follows the **u** axis, then l'_x is multiplied by some value and added to texture coordinate u, and l'_y is multiplied by the same value and added to v.[10]

The value used to multiply l'_x and l'_y varies depending on the height field's characteristics and the effect desired. A good start is to resize the vector **l′** to be the width of a texel. That is, normalize l' and divide by r, where r is the bump texture's resolution [245].

---

[10]In practice, the vector **n** does not affect the calculations, and so it does not have to be placed in the basis matrix 5.13. All that is actually needed is the upper left 2×3 matrix.

When the light is nearly directly over the surface, it is often worthwhile to make the bumps have less of an effect. This is done by shifting less when the light is overhead, which occurs when the length of l' is small. To normalize l' we normally divide it by its length. If the length is found to be less than, say, $\frac{1}{16}$, then divide l' by $\frac{1}{16}$ (i.e., multiply it by 16) instead [160]. This softens the effect of a large change in the direction of l'_x and l'_y as a light passes overhead during animation.

A little more needs to be said about the blending operations in practice. The second pass's subtraction operation can bring the range of values from $[0, 1]$ to $[-1, 1]$. Since negative values cannot be stored by an unsigned byte, something else must be done. One solution is part of the following example.

EXAMPLE: EMBOSS BUMP MAPPING STAGES The goal is to bump-map a lit, diffuse, color-textured surface. One texture is used, and is set up so that the RGB channels have the color texture, and the alpha channel contains the bump height field. The alpha channel will not be used for transparency; it is just a place where the height field can be stored. In the first stage, the color texture is multiplied with the interpolated diffuse illumination computed per vertex. At the same time, the height-field data is placed in the alpha in the texture stage. Each texture stage can store and pass on RGB and alpha to the next stage.

In the second stage, the shifted texture coordinates are used. The RGB channels (containing the diffusely lit texture from the first stage) are left untouched, but the height-field alpha value is inverted (i.e., $a' = 1 - a$), then added signed to the original height-field value with a bias of -0.5. This puts the embossed effect into the alpha component of the second stage:

$$o = d + (1 - s) - 0.5$$
$$o = d - s + 0.5$$

(5.14)

where d is the destination (the first-pass height-field value rendered) and s is the source (the new value being subtracted). This gives a height field value that in fact could span the range $[-0.5, 1.5]$, but the values are clamped to $[0, 1]$. For most height-field textures the values outside $[0, 1]$ are rare and unimportant.

Finally, the shading mode is set such that after these two texture stages are performed the final alpha result (the emboss effect) is used to multiply the color result. The emboss effect modulates the diffusely lit texture and produces bump mapping [255].   □

More about the emboss bump mapping method, as well as an extension to perform specular bump mapping, can be found in the Advanced OpenGL course notes [245]. An image made with emboss bump mapping is shown in Figure 5.25.

There are other methods that can be used for Gouraud-shaded bump mapping. For example, one method is to perturb (u, v) environment-mapping coordinates by u and v differentials found in the bump texture. This gives the effect of wobbling the reflection vector, thereby wobbling the look of the reflective surface. A 2×2 matrix is also needed in order to rotate and scale the differentials before they are added [83]. This technique is a little tricky to control and can be expensive to implement in hardware.[11] Its advantage is that it requires only one additional pass and can support any number of lights, since it uses an environment map. Figure 5.25 shows an image made using this technique, as does Plate XII (following p. 194).

Hardware-supported bump mapping is an active area of research. Miller et al. [249] discuss ways of combining current hardware with table lookups and parameter caching to increase performance and functionality. Ernst et al. [96], Schilling et al. [315], Peercy et al. [285], and Ikedo & Ma [196] all propose new schemes for bump mapping and hardware support. Ernst et al. [97] give a summary of many different bump mapping techniques and propose their own Gouraud-based method. Heidrich et al. [173, 174] show how normal maps can be combined with spherical and paraboloid environment maps.

Figure 5.25. On the left is an example of bump mapping via embossing. On the right is an image created using environment-mapped bump mapping, along with a color texture. The illusion of bumpiness is created by using an environment map for the lighting and having the surface bump map vary how this environment map is accessed. *(Image on left courtesy of 3dfx Interactive, Inc. Image on right courtesy of Microsoft Inc.)*

---

[11] The Matrox G400 is the first chip we know of that supports this technique.

5.7.6 Other Texturing Techniques

This chapter has covered some of the uses of texturing. There are many others potentially useful in real-time work, including:

- Detail textures, which are used in, for example, flight simulators to add visual detail to highly magnified ground textures [245].

- Cutaway views, in which some layers of an object are peeled away [245].

- Antialiased lines and text rendered as rectangles with smooth edges by using alpha-blended transparency [149].

- Cylinder mapping, a form of environment mapping which reflects horizontal tube lights, useful in curved body visualization and anomaly detection [277].

- Realistic shading, done by using a variety of techniques to access one or more environment maps in order to approximate the reflective characteristics of the material. [172, 174].

- Volume rendering, by rendering a set of image texture slices with alpha values in back-to-front order and blending these [149, 245]. See Section 6.8.

- Line integral convolution, a technique for visualizing vector fields [173].

Undoubtedly, there are more applications of textures that remain to be discovered.

Further Reading and Resources

Heckbert has written a good survey of texture mapping [163] and a more in-depth report on the topic [164]; both are available on the web, and the URLs appear in this book's bibliography. Wolberg's book [380] is another good work on image textures, particularly in the areas of sampling and filtering. Watt's books [367, 368, 369] and Rogers' *Procedural Elements* book [300] are general texts on computer graphics which have good coverage of texturing.

The SIGGRAPH OpenGL Advanced Techniques course notes [245] have extensive coverage of texturing algorithms and are available on the web. While RenderMan is meant for high-quality still images, the *RenderMan Companion* [357] has some good material on texture mapping and on procedural textures.

For extensive coverage of three-dimensional procedural textures, see *Texturing and Modeling: A Procedural Approach* [92].

Visit this book's website, `http://www.realtimerendering.com/`, for other resources.

Chapter 6
Special Effects

"All that glitters has a high refractive index."
–Anonymous

"Special effects" is a relative term in computer graphics. In the film and television industry, today's new cool effect eventually becomes just another tool in the toolbox. Convincing hair and cloth are currently a hot property, done well at the high end, but will become mainstream for still-image rendering (though not real-time yet) as the technology moves into commercial products. Image morphing techniques that were unique and exciting just a decade ago are now a standard part of children's shows. Once upon a time, Gouraud shading, or even simple fill shading, was special.

The field of real-time rendering in many ways recapitulates the evolution of computer graphics for still images. As processors get faster, algorithms that once took minutes now take fractions of a second. Graphics accelerators help perform operations that are widely used, such as filling triangles. However, because the new factor of dedicated graphics hardware is added to the mix, new ways of performing old algorithms arise. Multipass rendering (see Section 5.4) is a prime example. In traditional computer graphics, the lighting equation is resolved at each pixel in a single pass, either by Gouraud interpolation or per-pixel shading. Software real-time rendering engines use this approach. Because graphics accelerators provide some basic operations that are extremely fast, an elaborate lighting equation can be broken into separate pieces which hardware can handle and combine in a few passes, in less time than a single software pass can be completed.

Special effects work for real-time rendering depends upon both classic computer graphics techniques and using available hardware acceleration to its best effect. Algorithms leverage the existing triangle fill, filtered texturing, and transparency support. As new capabilities become available in hardware, new special effects become possible, or more general, or at least faster. A good example of a capability that is becoming standard is the stencil buffer. The stencil buffer is

145

a special buffer that is not displayed (just as the Z-buffer is not displayed). Instead, it is normally used to mask off areas of the screen and make them unwritable. Primitives are written to the stencil buffer, and the places where these primitives appear in the buffer become the only areas of the screen where succeeding objects will be displayed. As will be seen in this chapter, techniques such as creating true reflections and shadows can be performed more rapidly when a stencil buffer is available in hardware. There are many other operations that can be aided by a stencil buffer, such as capping objects cut by an arbitrary clipping plane [245] and visualizing models formed directly by adding and subtracting solids [245, 373].

6.1   The Rendering Spectrum

Up to this point in the book we have focused on showing three-dimensional objects on the screen by representing them with polygons. This is not the only way to get an object to the screen, nor is it always the most appropriate one. The goal of rendering is to portray an object on the screen; how we attain that goal is our own decision. There is no correct way to render a scene. Each rendering method is an approximation of reality, at least if photo-realism is the goal.

Polygons have the advantage of representing the object in a reasonable fashion from any view. As the camera moves, the representation of the object does not have to change. However, to improve quality we may wish to substitute a more highly detailed model as the viewer gets closer to the object. Conversely, we may wish to use a simplified form of the model if it is off in the distance. These are called level-of-detail techniques (see Section 7.3). Their main purpose is to make the scene display faster.

However, other techniques can come into play as an object recedes from the viewer. Speed can be gained by using images instead of polygons to represent the object. It is less expensive to represent an object with a single image which can be sent quickly to the screen. Algorithms that use images to portray objects are a part of *image-based rendering*. One way to represent the continuum of rendering techniques comes from Lengyel [229] and shown in Figure 6.1. Within the field of real-time rendering, global illumination techniques such as radiosity and ray tracing are not feasible except on extremely high-end machines (or for simple demonstration programs). Such techniques will undoubtedly move into the realm of real time as processor speeds increase. Currently, these algorithms' main contribution to real-time rendering is in precomputing data such as vertex colors, light maps, environment maps, etc.

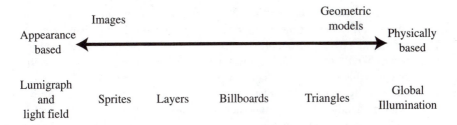

Figure 6.1. The rendering spectrum *(after Lengyel [229]).*

6.2 Image-Based Rendering

One of the simplest image-based rendering primitives is the sprite. A sprite is an image that moves around on the screen. A mouse cursor is a sprite, for example. The sprite does not have to have a rectangular shape, since various pixels can be rendered as transparent. For simple sprites there is a one-to-one mapping with pixels on the screen. Each pixel stored in the sprite will be put in a pixel on the screen. Various acceleration schemes exist for sprites, such as precompiling them into a list of individual spans of pixels and so eliminating the need to test for transparency at each pixel [58].

The idea of a sprite can be extended in many ways. Sprites can be trivially zoomed at integer zoom factors, for example, if the object represented by the sprite is to appear to approach the viewer. A 10×10-pixel sprite can be turned into a 20×20 or 30×30 sprite by simple replication. Transitions between zoom levels can be lessened by adding sprites at other resolutions. Such techniques preserve the simplicity that sprites offer for changing pixels directly on the screen.

Animation can be generated by displaying a succession of different sprites. The video stream creates a time series of sprites which are merged with the scene. Another use for a set of sprites is interactive object representation. As the viewer sees an object from different angles, different sprites can be used to represent it. The illusion is fairly weak, however, because of the jump when switching from one sprite to another.

A sprite can also be treated as an image texture on a polygon, with the image's alpha channel providing full or partial transparency. With the use of texturing acceleration hardware, such techniques incur little more cost than direct copying of pixels. Images applied to polygons can be kept facing the viewer using various billboard strategies (see Section 6.2.2).

One way to think of a scene is as a series of layers. For example, in Plate XIII (following p. 194), the tailgate is in front of the chicken, which is in front of the truck's cab, which is in front of the road and trees. From a large number of views this layering holds true. Each sprite layer has a depth associated with it. By rendering in a back-to-front order, we can build up the scene without need for a Z-buffer, thereby saving time and resources. Camera zooms simply make the object larger, which is simple to handle with the same sprite. Moving the camera in or out actually changes the relative coverage of foreground and background, which can be handled by changing each sprite layer's coverage independently. As the viewer moves perpendicularly to the direction of view, the layers can be moved relative to their depths.

However, as the view changes, the appearance of the object changes. For example, viewing a cube straight-on results in a square. As the view moves, the square appears as a warped quadrilateral. In the same way, a sprite representing an object can also be warped as its relation to the view changes. The rectangle containing the sprite still appears on a layer with a single z-depth, but the screen (x, y) coordinates of the rectangle change. Note that as the view changes, however, new faces of the cube become visible, invalidating the sprite. At such times the sprite layer is regenerated. Determining when to warp and when to regenerate is one of the more difficult aspects of image-based rendering. In addition to surface features appearing and disappearing, specular highlights and shadows add to the challenge.

This layer and image warping process is the basis of the Talisman architecture [28, 354]. Objects are rendered into sprite layers, which are then composited on the screen. The idea is that each sprite layer can be formed and then reused for a number of frames. Warping and redisplaying an image is considerably simpler than resending an object's whole set of polygons for each frame. Each layer is managed independently. For example, in Plate XIII (following p. 194), the chicken may be regenerated frequently because it moves or the view changes. The cab of the truck needs less frequent regeneration, because its angle to the camera is not changing as much in this scene. Performing warping and determining when to regenerate a layer's image is discussed in depth by Lengyel and Snyder [228]. One interesting efficiency technique is performing multipass rendering to generate the sprite, and using lower-resolution passes, which are then bilinearly magnified (see Section 5.2.1) and combined. Another possiblility is to create separate shadow and reflection sprite layers for later compositing.

Interpenetrating objects such as the wing and the tailgate are treated as one sprite. This is done because the wing has feathers both in front of and behind the tailgate. This means that each time the wing moves, the entire layer has to be regenerated. One way of avoiding this full regeneration is to split the wing into one component that is fully in front of the tailgate and one that is fully behind it. Another method was introduced by Snyder and Lengyel [341];

this method resolves some occlusion cycles (where object A partially covers B, which partially covers C, which in turn partially covers A) by using layers and compositing operations.

Pure image-layer rendering depends on fast, high-quality image warping, filtering, and compositing. Image-based techniques can also be combined with polygon-based rendering. Section 7.2 deals extensively with impostors, nailboards, and other ways of using images to take the place of polygonal content.

At the far end of the image-based rendering spectrum are image-based techniques such as QuickTime VR and the Lumigraph. In the Quicktime VR system [54], a 360° panoramic image, normally of a real scene, surrounds the viewer as a cylindrical image. As the camera's orientation changes, the proper part of the image is retrieved, warped, and displayed. Though limited to a single location, this technique has an immersive quality compared to a static scene, because the viewer's head can turn and tilt. Such scenes can serve as backdrops, and polygonal objects can be rendered in front of them. This technology is practical today, and is particularly good for capturing a sense of the space in a building, on a street, or in another location, be it real or synthetic. See Figure 6.2. QuickTime VR's run-time engine is a specialized renderer optimized for cylindrical environment mapping. This allows it to achieve an order-of-magnitude gain in performance over software polygon renderers handling the same texture map placed on a cylinder.

The Lumigraph [134] and light-field rendering [230] techniques are related to QuickTime VR. However, instead of viewing much of an environment from a single location, a single object is viewed from a set of viewpoints. Given a new viewpoint, these techniques perform an interpolation process between stored views in order to create the new view. This is a more complex problem, with a much higher data requirement (tens of megabytes for even small image sets), than those solved by QuickTime VR. The concept is akin to holography, where a two-dimensional array of views captures the object. The tantalizing aspect of the Lumigraph and light-field rendering is the ability to capture a real object and be able to redisplay it from any angle. Any real object, regardless of surface complexity, can be displayed at a nearly constant rate [336]. As with the global illumination end of the rendering spectrum, these techniques currently have limited use in real-time rendering, but they demarcate what is possible in the field of computer graphics as a whole[1].

To return to the realm of the mundane, what follows are a number of commonly used special-effects techniques that have image-based elements to them.

---

[1]Recent research by Oliveira and Bishop [273] shows how some objects can be stored in a compact, image-based form and displayed at interactive rates on a PC.

Figure 6.2. A panorama of the Mission Dolores, used by QuickTime VR to display a wide range of views, with three views below generated from it. Note how the views themselves are undistorted. *(Courtesy of Ken Turkowski.)*

6.2.1   Lens Flare and Bloom

Lens flare is a phenomenon that is caused by the lens of the eye or camera when directed at bright light. It consists of a halo and a ciliary corona. The halo appears because the lens material refracts light of different wavelengths by different amounts, as a prism does. The halo looks like a ring around the light, with its outside edge tinged with red, and its inside with violet. The ciliary corona comes from density fluctuations in the lens, and appears as rays radiating from a point, which may extend beyond the halo [342]. Camera lenses can also create secondary effects when parts of the lens reflect or refract light internally. For example, hexagonal patterns can appear due to the camera's diaphragm blades. Bloom is caused by scattering in the lens and other parts of the eye, creating a glow around the light and dimming contrast elsewhere in the scene. In video production, the video camera captures an image by converting photons to charge using a charge-coupled device (CCD). Bloom occurs in a video camera when a charge site in the CCD gets saturated and overflows into neighboring sites. As a class, halos, coronae, and bloom are called glare effects.

In practice, what this means is that we associate these effects with brightness. Once thought of as relatively rare image artifacts, they are now routinely added digitally to real photos to enhance their effect. There are limits to the light intensity produced by the computer monitor, so to give the impression of increased brightness in a scene, these glare effects are explicitly rendered. The lens flare effect is now something of a cliché due to its common use. Nonetheless, when skillfully employed, it can give strong visual cues to the viewer; see Plate XIV (following p. 194).

Figure 6.3 shows a typical lens flare. It is produced by using a set of textures for the glare effects. Each texture is applied to a square that is made to face the viewer (i.e., is placed perpendicular to the view direction). The texture is treated as an alpha map which determines how much of the square to blend into the scene. Because it is the square itself which is being displayed, the square can be given a color (typically a pure red, green, or blue) for prismatic effects for the ciliary corona. These colored, textured squares are blended using an additive effect to get other colors. Furthermore, by animating the ciliary corona, we create a sparkle effect [204].

Figure 6.3. A lens flare and its constituent textures. On the right, a halo and a bloom are shown above, and two sparkle textures below. *(Images from a Microsoft DirectX6 SDK program.)*

6.2.2 Billboarding

Lens flares have the quadrilateral drawn facing the viewer. Orienting the polygon based on the view direction is called *billboarding*, and the polygon is called a *billboard* [245]. As the view changes, the orientation of the polygon changes. Billboarding, combined with alpha texturing and animation, can be used to represent many phenomena that do not have solid surfaces. Smoke, fire, explosions, vapor trails, and clouds are just a few of the objects that can be represented by these techniques [83, 245]—see Plates XII and XV (following p. 194). Effects such as energy beams and shields are also possible. A few popular forms of billboards are described in this section.

Screen-Aligned Billboard

The first form of billboarding is the one we used for lens flares. We term this a *screen-aligned billboard*. In this case, the desired surface normal is the negation of the view direction. The view direction is a constant vector v_{dir} that the camera looks down, in world space. So the first goal is to align the billboard's normal n with the negative of this vector. In other words, we want to rotate the billboard from its current facing direction n to face to $-v_{dir}$, that is, toward the viewer. This is done by using vector-vector rotation, described in Section 3.3.2 from page 50 on. One way to conceptualize this solution is that the cross product of the two vectors forms an axis, and the billboard is rotated around this axis until it reaches its new position. The polygon's original up-direction u is rotated by the same transform to create u', which is used in the next step.

Now that the billboard is facing forward, it needs to be rotated around the v_{dir} axis until its top aligns with the view's top.[2] To perform this rotation the polygon's current up-vector u' is needed, along with v_{up}, the up-direction for the viewer (the screen's $+y$-axis), which is perpendicular to v_{dir}. Another vector-vector rotation matrix is formed using u' and v_{up}. At this point, u' is also perpendicular to v_{dir}, since the polygon is perpendicular to it and u' lies in the polygon's plane. Because of this perpendicular relation, the axis of rotation is already known to be v_{dir}, so all that is needed for this second matrix is the amount we must rotate in order to align u' with v_{up}. The two matrices that have been formed are concatenated to create a single transformation. To summarize: first rotate n to align with $-v_{dir}$ (and rotate u to create u'), then rotate u' to align with v_{up}.

The technique just described gives a way to visualize the solution in steps, which we will build upon in the next section. However, a faster, more direct

---

[2] For lens flare billboards this is not all that important, in fact, because of the textures involved; rotating a halo around an axis changes nothing, for example. However, it is relevant for other billboards of this type, so we present it here.

way to compute this transform is possible. First we form an orthonormal basis, which we use in an orthogonal matrix: $\mathbf{M} = (\mathbf{n} \quad \mathbf{u} \quad \mathbf{n} \times \mathbf{u})$. The transpose of this matrix aligns $\mathbf{n}$ with the x-axis, $\mathbf{u}$ with the y-axis, and $\mathbf{n} \times \mathbf{u}$ with the z-axis. We then create another matrix: $\mathbf{N} = (-\mathbf{v}_{dir} \quad \mathbf{v}_{up} \quad -\mathbf{v}_{dir} \times \mathbf{v}_{up})$. This matrix aligns the x-axis with $-\mathbf{v}_{dir}$, the y-axis with $\mathbf{v}_{up}$, and the z-axis with $\mathbf{v}_{dir} \times \mathbf{v}_{up}$. The billboard matrix is then $\mathbf{NM}^T$. If the original polygon starts facing along the x-axis and with its up-vector along the y-axis, then $\mathbf{M}$ is the identity matrix and so only $\mathbf{N}$ needs to be created. See Section A.3.2 for more information on change of bases.

Many graphics operations, such as computing specular highlights or performing culling, depend on creating a vector from the eye to the object. For billboards, forming this vector is unnecessary, since what is needed is to have the images project similarly onto the screen. Only the single vector along the viewer's z-axis, $\mathbf{v}_{dir}$, is needed. For screen-aligned billboards this is the right answer, as these billboards must be parallel to the image plane. Essentially, $\mathbf{v}_{dir}$ is the normal of the view plane. If $\mathbf{v}_{dir}$ were varied by the object's location, the billboards would become skewed compared to the image plane and so would be warped when projected onto it.

What this means is that this same rotation matrix can be used for all billboards of this type in the scene. So, for the lens flare effect, each square would typically start centered at the origin. Each would then be rotated to the correct straight-on orientation for the current view, then translated to its final three-dimensional position. Such billboards are useful for many purposes, such as ensuring that text is always displayed upright (hence the name "billboard").

World-Aligned Billboard

Another type of billboard uses a slightly different up-vector for the second transformation. The polygon still faces the viewer, but instead of aligning $\mathbf{u}'$ with the view's up-vector, it aligns with the world's up-vector, $\mathbf{w}_{up}$ (typically the $+y$- or $+z$-world-axis), insofar as this is possible. We term this a *world-aligned billboard*, sometimes known as an *object-aligned billboard* [69]. The effect is that if the viewer rotates along the view axis (i.e., tilts his head), the billboards change their orientation as seen on the screen. To begin, the first transformation aligning $\mathbf{n}$ with $-\mathbf{v}_{dir}$ is the same as above. For the second transformation we need to project the $\mathbf{w}_{up}$-vector onto the plane perpendicular to $-\mathbf{v}_{dir}$, since we will rotate around $\mathbf{v}_{dir}$ in order to keep the polygon facing the viewer. One way is to use two cross products:

$$
\begin{aligned}
\mathbf{r} &= \mathbf{w}_{up} \times \mathbf{v}_{dir} \\
\mathbf{t}_{up} &= \mathbf{v}_{dir} \times \mathbf{r}
\end{aligned}
\tag{6.1}
$$

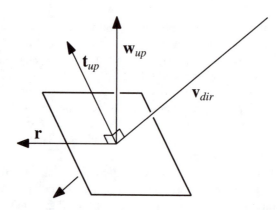

Figure 6.4. The rectangular polygon faces back up along $\mathbf{v}_{dir}$ after the first billboard rotation. To align the polygon by rotating along $\mathbf{v}_{dir}$, the $\mathbf{w}_{up}$ direction needs to be cast upon the polygon to form $\mathbf{t}_{up}$. To do this, we form the vector $\mathbf{r}$, which is in the polygon's plane and perpendicular to both $\mathbf{w}_{up}$ and $\mathbf{v}_{dir}$. Then we form $\mathbf{t}_{up}$, perpendicular to $\mathbf{v}_{dir}$ and $\mathbf{r}$.

The vector-vector rotation matrix is then formed to align $\mathbf{u}'$ with $\mathbf{t}_{up}$. This process is shown in Figure 6.4. There is a chance that $\mathbf{w}_{up}$ and $\mathbf{v}_{dir}$ are parallel (the view is looking straight up or straight down), in which case this rotation could just be ignored or an arbitrary world direction chosen instead of $\mathbf{w}_{up}$. Again a single concatenated rotation matrix can be used on all the billboards, which are then translated into their positions. If $\mathbf{w}_{up}$ changes, this matrix does have to be recomputed.

Axial Billboard

The last common type is called *axial billboarding*. In this scheme the textured object does not normally face straight-on toward the viewer. Instead, it is allowed to rotate around some fixed world-space axis and align itself so as to face the viewer as much as possible within this range. Typically this billboarding technique is used for displaying trees. Instead of representing a tree with a solid surface, or even with a pair of tree outlines as described in Section 5.7.1, a world-up-axis $\mathbf{w}_{up}$ is fixed along the trunk of the tree. The tree faces the viewer as the viewer moves, as shown in Figure 6.5.

The rotation matrix for this form of billboarding turns out to be simpler to compute than the first two. Only one rotation is needed, and we already know the predefined axis of rotation. Given the view direction $\mathbf{v}_{dir}$, we first need to project this vector onto the plane perpendicular to $\mathbf{w}_{up}$. This is done in a manner similar to that used in the previous billboarding technique, this time

Figure 6.5. As the viewer moves around the scene, the tree billboard rotates to face forward.

adjusting $\mathbf{v}_{dir}$:

$$\mathbf{s} = \mathbf{v}_{dir} \times \mathbf{w}_{up}$$
$$\mathbf{t}_{dir} = \mathbf{w}_{up} \times \mathbf{s} \tag{6.2}$$

This ensures that both this new vector $\mathbf{t}_{dir}$ and the billboard's normal $\mathbf{n}$ will be perpendicular to $\mathbf{w}_{up}$. Then all that is needed is to perform a vector-vector rotation around $\mathbf{w}_{up}$ by the angle between $\mathbf{n}$ and $\mathbf{t}_{dir}$. Once this rotation matrix is formed, we take a tree polygon with its trunk at the origin (translated there first, if need be), rotate it, then translate it to its position.

Note that the same rotation transform can be formed once and used for all the trees, even in perspective. As with screen-aligned billboards, we normally want these axial billboards to be cast as flat as possible onto the screen.

A problem with the axial billboarding technique is that if the viewer flies over the trees and looks straight down, the illusion is ruined, as the trees will look like the cutouts they are. If necessary, adding a circular, horizontal, cross-section texture of the tree (which needs no billboarding) can help eliminate the problem.

6.2.3 Full-Screen Billboarding

A screen-aligned billboard that covers the entire view can be used for a few different effects. One effect is changing the look of an environment by placing the billboard in front of everything else in the scene. For example, to give the feel (if not the real effect) of viewing a scene through night goggles, alpha-blend a green billboard on top of the entire scene [187]. This is expensive in that the entire screen must be filled, but from a programming standpoint, it is simpler than modifying the materials of all the objects in the scene. A flash effect can be created by making this foreground billboard increase in brightness and having its opacity value increase over time, then decrease. An example is shown in Plate XV (following p. 194), where the scene is red due to a flash of light.

Note that Z-buffering can be disabled in order to accelerate processing during the rendering of a full-screen billboard.

Billboards can also be placed behind everything in a scene, to simulate an environment. If the viewer changes direction, the texture on this billboard should be moved accordingly. For example, imagine a sky background for a driving simulator. As the driver turns left, the billboard continues to fill the background. However, if there are clouds in this sky background, they will not move, making the experience unconvincing. By setting the texture to repeat and uniformly modifying the u coordinates at the corners (i.e., adding the same value to each u coordinate), we can make the sky appear to rotate along with the view change. This is a form of texture animation (see Section 5.6).

6.2.4   Particle Systems

A particle system is a set of separate small objects that are set into motion using some algorithm. Applications include simulating fire, smoke, explosions, water flows, trees, whirling galaxies, and other phenomena. Particle systems are not a form of rendering, but rather a method of animation. The idea is that there are controls for creating, moving, changing, and deleting particles during their lifetimes. Figure 6.6 shows a typical particle system, a firework display.

Animation techniques are beyond the scope of this book, and there are many articles on the subject of generating and controlling particle systems [220, 245, 296, 297, 367, 368]. What is relevant here is the way the particles are represented. Representations even simpler than billboards are common—namely, points and lines. Each particle can simply be a single point rendered on the screen. Another simple technique is to represent a particle by a line segment drawn from the particle's previous location to its current location. An example is shown in Figure 6.7.

 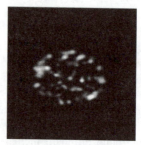 

Figure 6.6. Firework using a single screen-aligned, alpha-textured billboard varied in size and shade over time *(from a DirectX6 demonstration program, Microsoft)*.

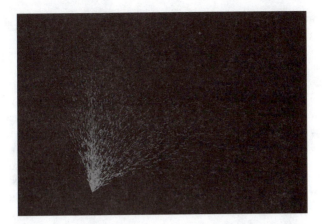

Figure 6.7. Particle system. Each of the 4000 particles in this system is a short line segment which changes intensity over time. *(Courtesy of Jeff Lander.)*

For a static camera, motion blurred particles systems can easily be rendered by altering the way we clear the screen. Instead of clearing both the color buffer and the Z-buffer, clear only the Z-buffer, and draw a rectangle filled with $RGBA = (0, 0, 0, alpha)$ that covers the entire window. Alpha will control the speed of the decay of the motion blur trail.

6.2.5 Fixed-View Effects

The viewer is not always moving. For example, for some applications, the view is fixed to one location and orientation, and the environment does not move. This is common in computer games, and also useful for training software and other situations where the user is meant to be limited to certain options. In such situations, the scene itself can be photographed, drawn, or computed in advance. To make this static part of the world more convincing, one can use a depth map associated with it. For example, a still image of a set of jumping fences might be generated using ray tracing, with a z-depth stored per pixel. As a horse (polygonal or image-based) moves through this environment, its depth will be compared to the depth of the stored image. If it passes behind a fence, the fence will appear in front of the horse. The color rectangle and z-depths from the fence image must be sent to the screen as the horse moves through each frame. However, note that only the rectangle where the horse was needs to be repaired, since the rest of the static scene is exactly the same for every frame.

In theory, each pixel in a QuickTime VR image could also have a depth value associated with it, which would allow it to occlude objects as they move in the environment. Capturing such depth information from a real scene is currently an expensive operation, though simple enough to save for a synthetic rendering. This combination would offer some sense of viewpoint control while also allowing partial and full occlusion of objects by the static world.

A concept related to the static scene is *golden thread* or *adaptive refinement* rendering [32]. In this scheme, the idea is that while the viewer is not moving, the computer can produce a better and better image as time goes on. Static objects in the scene can be made to look more realistic. Such higher-quality renderings can either be swapped in abruptly or blended in over a series of frames. This technique is particularly useful in CAD and visualization applications. There are many different types of refinement that could be done. One possibility is to use an accumulation buffer to do antialiasing (see Section 4.4) and show various accumulated images along the way. Another possibility is to perform slower per-pixel shading off screen and then fade-in this improved image. Multithreading or some interrupt mechanism is useful in avoiding locking out the user from interaction while adaptive refinement progresses, since a refinement may take considerable time.

6.3   Motion Blur

In a movie, motion blur comes from the movement of an object across the screen during a frame. For example, if an object moves from left to right, it would be more realistic for it to be represented by an object blurred horizontally on the screen. Motion blur is also a subjective process, however. If the camera is tracking an object, the object does not blur—the background does. Often motion blur is added to computer graphics images for the same reason lens flares are added: to give a psychological cue to the user. The blur itself may be overemphasized to add to the feeling of motion. See Plate XVI (following p. 194) for an example.

There are a number of approaches to producing motion blur in computer rendering. One straightforward but limited method is to model and render the blur itself. In fact, this is the rationale for drawing lines to represent particles (see Section 6.2.4). This concept can be extended. Imagine a sword slicing in front of the viewer. Before and behind the blade two polygons are added along its edge. These polygons use an alpha opacity per vertex, so that where a polygon meets the sword it is fully opaque, and at the outer edge of the polygon the alpha is fully transparent. This is a simplification, but the idea is that the model has transparency to it in the direction of movement, simulating blur.

One way to create blur is to average a series of images using the accumulation buffer [147]. The object is moved to some set of the positions it occupies during the frame and is rendered into the accumulation buffer. The final result gives a blurred image. However, for real-time rendering such a process is normally counterproductive (unless there is a good deal of extra processing power available), because it lowers the frame rate. If what is desired is the suggestion of movement instead of pure realism, the accumulation buffer can be used in a clever way that is not as costly. Imagine that eight frames of a model in motion have been generated and stored in the accumulation buffer, then displayed. On the ninth frame, the model is rendered again and accumulated, but also at this time the first frame is rendered again and subtracted from the accumulation buffer. The buffer now has eight frames of a blurred model, frames 2 through 9. On the next frame we add in frame 10 and subtract frame 2, giving the eight frames 3 through 10. In this way only two renderings per frame are needed to continue to obtain the blur effect [245].

6.4 Depth of Field

Within the field of photography there is a range where objects are in focus. Objects outside of this range are blurry, the further outside the blurrier. To simulate this effect, the accumulation buffer can be used [147]. See Figure 6.8. By varying the view and keeping the point of focus fixed, objects will be rendered blurrier relative to their distance from this focal point.

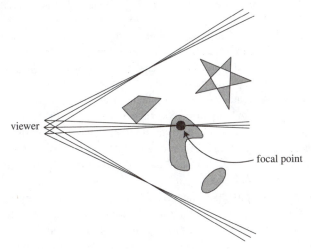

Figure 6.8. Depth of field. The viewer's location is moved a small amount, keeping the view direction pointing at the focal point, and the images are accumulated.

Figure 6.9. The left image was rendered without shadow and reflections, and so it is hard to see where the object is truly located. The right image was rendered with both shadow and reflections, and the spatial relationships are easier to estimate. *(Car model is reused courtesy of Nya Perspektiv Design AB.)*

For layer-based rendering systems, depth-of-field effects can be created by blurring a particular layer using image processing techniques [341].

6.5   Reflections

Reflections and shadows are actually part of the general lighting equation, called the *rendering equation* [200]. However, for most real-time graphics systems, these effects usually do not appear. Both of these effects contribute greatly to increasing the realism in a rendered image, but they have another important task as well. Reflections and shadows are used by the viewer as cues to determine spatial relationships between objects. This is shown in Figure 6.9. For a cost, both reflections and shadows can be added to an image. Reflections are the focus of this section, and shadow generation is treated in the next.

Reflections in surfaces are an important ingredient for realistic computer graphics and for the inspection of the quality of surfaces. We call the object that is a reflecting surface a *reflector*, and the geometry that is, potentially, reflected in the reflector, *reflected geometry*.

Environment mapping (see Section 5.7.3) gives a rough approximation of reflections. One of its major limitations is that objects near the reflector cannot be accurately reflected. The reflections in the map are valid for only one point in space, not over a surface. That said, this method can also be used to give limited recursive reflections [82, 245]. For example, say there are two reflectors in a scene, neither with an environment map at this point. If a cubic environment map is generated for one of these, the other reflector will show up in it as non-reflective, since it has no environment map yet. To produce recursive reflections, generate a cubic environment map of the scene for the first reflector (possibly generating a sphere map from it) and attach it to the reflector. For a second reflector in the scene, generate a cubic environment map of the scene from its vantage point. In this second environment map the first reflector shows up as reflective, since it now has a map of its own. This recursive process can be extended indefinitely; for example, the first reflector could now have its environment map regenerated with the second reflector now visible with its reflections, which include the first object. This technique can either be applied before real-time rendering begins (for statics scenes) or, if the processing power is available, on the fly (for dynamic scenes).

Ray tracing [116] offers a solution in which the reflection ray is emitted from a reflector and recursively traced through a scene, generating a color contribution for each pixel. Ray tracing is still too computationally intensive for real-time applications.[3] However, we can render in real time special cases and approximations of reflections. In this section, planar reflections will be presented, along with methods for handling curved reflectors and rendering frosted glass.

6.5.1   Planar Reflections

Planar reflection, by which we mean reflection off a flat surface such as a mirror, is a special case of reflection off of arbitrary surfaces. As often occurs with special cases, planar reflections are easier to implement and execute more rapidly than general reflections.

An ideal reflector follows the *law of reflection*, which states that the angle of incidence is equal to the angle of reflection. That is, the angle between the incident ray and the normal is equal to the angle between the reflected ray and the normal. This is depicted in Figure 6.10, which illustrates a simple object which is reflected in a plane. The figure also shows an "image" of the reflected object. Due to the law of reflection, the reflected image of the object is simply the object itself physically reflected through the plane. That is, instead of following the reflected ray, we could follow the incident ray through the reflector and hit the same point but on the reflected object. The conclusion that can be drawn from this principle is that a reflection can be rendered by creating a copy of the object, transforming it into the reflected position, and rendering it from there. To achieve correct lighting, light sources have to be reflected in the plane as well [258, 272], with respect to both position and direction.

---

[3]This will someday change; see Chapter 13.

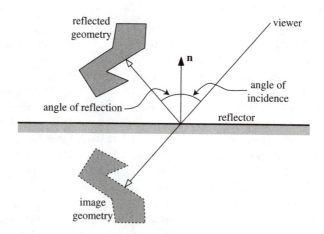

Figure 6.10. Reflection in a plane, showing angle of incidence and reflection, the reflected geometry, and the reflector.

If for a moment we assume that the reflector has a normal, $\mathbf{n} = (0,1,0)$, and that it goes through the origin, then the matrix that reflects in this plane is simply this mirror scaling matrix: $\mathbf{S}(1,-1,1)$. For the general case we derive the reflection matrix $\mathbf{M}$ given the normal of the reflector $\mathbf{n}$ and some point $\mathbf{p}$ on the reflector plane. Since we know how to reflect in the plane $y = 0$, the idea is to transform the plane into $y = 0$, then perform the simple scaling, and finally transform back. The concatenation of these matrices yields $\mathbf{M}$.

First, we have to translate the plane so that it passes through the origin, which is done with a translation matrix: $\mathbf{T}(-\mathbf{p})$. Then the normal of the reflector plane, $\mathbf{n}$, is rotated so that it becomes parallel to the y-axis: $(0,1,0)$. This can be done with a rotation from $\mathbf{n}$ to $(0,1,0)$ using $\mathbf{R}(\mathbf{n},(0,1,0))$ (see Section 3.3.2). The concatenation of these operations is called $\mathbf{F}$:

$$\mathbf{F} = \mathbf{R}(\mathbf{n},(0,1,0))\mathbf{T}(-\mathbf{p}) \tag{6.3}$$

After that, the reflector plane has become aligned with the plane $y = 0$, and then scaling, $\mathbf{S}(1,-1,1)$, is performed; finally, we transform back with $\mathbf{F}^{-1}$. Thus $\mathbf{M}$ is constructed as in Equation 6.4.

$$\mathbf{M} = \mathbf{F}^{-1}\,\mathbf{S}(1,-1,1)^T)\,\mathbf{F} \tag{6.4}$$

Note that this matrix has to be recomputed if the position or orientation of the reflector surface changes.

The scene is rendered by first drawing the objects to be reflected (transformed by $\mathbf{M}$), followed by drawing the rest of the scene with the reflector included. An example of this process is shown in Figure 6.11, and the results appear in Plate I (following p. 194). The reflector has to be partially transparent if the reflection is to be visible. As such, the transparency acts like a kind of reflectivity factor; the reflector appears more reflective with increasing transparency, and less reflective with decreasing transparency.

However, sometimes the reflections can be rendered incorrectly, as in the left part of Figure 6.12. This happens because the reflected geometry can appear at places where there is no reflector geometry. In other words, the viewer will figure out the trick, seeing that the reflected objects are actually real. The correct image can be generated with the use of the *stencil buffer* (see page 145).

To solve the problem, the reflector is rendered into the stencil buffer, with the stencil parameters set so that we can write to the screen only where the reflector is present. Then the reflected geometry is rendered with stenciling turned on. In this way, the reflected geometry is rendered only where the stencil buffer is set. Drawing one image atop another, when both occupy the same space, is called *decaling*.

Another problem that occurs with planar reflections is due to face culling (see Section 7.1.1). If backface culling is turned on and we scale an object with

Figure 6.11. The floor reflection for Plate I (following p. 194) is created by rendering much of the model again mirrored beneath the castle's floor. The floor is later rendered semitransparently (blended) so that both it and the reflection are seen. *(Courtesy of Agata and Andrzej Wojaczek (agand@clo.com), Advanced Graphics Applications Inc.)*

Figure 6.12. The left image shows an incorrectly rendered reflection against three mirrored squares. The right image was rendered with the use of the stencil buffer to mask out the part where there is visible reflector geometry, which yields a correct reflection.

a reflection matrix, then backface culling will appear to be turned off and front-face culling will appear to be turned on. Two possible solutions are to turn off face culling (with the likelihood of slower rendering) or switch from backface to frontface culling.

Objects that are on the far side of the reflector plane should not be reflected. This problem can be solved by using the reflector's plane equation. Put each triangle's vertices into this plane equation in turn; if the value is negative, the vertex is beyond the reflector plane. Discard all triangles that are on the opposite side from the viewpoint. However, triangles that intersect the plane then need to be clipped, which generates new polygons. One way to avoid having to add code for this clipping procedure is to use an *arbitrary clipping plane*, if one is available. All graphics APIs allow for clipping against the view frustum, of course. But some APIs (e.g., OpenGL) also allow the user to define additional planes that clip primitives sent against them.

Place the clipping plane so that it coincides with the plane of the reflector [157]. Using such a clipping plane when rendering the reflected objects can cull away all reflected geometry that is on the same side as the viewpoint.

If clipping planes are available, a simple and faster form of planar reflection can be used. Instead of using a mirror reflection transform on all the objects being reflected, simply reflect the viewer's position and orientation through the mirror to the opposite side of the reflector. Use the clipping plane to remove all objects on the far side of the mirror and render the scene. What appears is the reflection image. Then use the original view to blend in the reflector and render the normal scene, as before. The advantage of moving the viewer is that none of the geometry has to be manipulated in any way before being sent down to form the reflection [157, 245, 272].

Other algorithms can be combined with the planar reflection technique. For example, the reflection image can be treated as a texture, which can then be applied to the reflecting surface. Using this technique allows warping effects to be used as well, in order to make the reflector's surface appear wavy. This can be done by applying the texture to a regular grid of polygons on the reflector. However, instead of using a uniformly spaced set of (u, v) parameter-space values, these values are modified slightly (e.g., by adding in a noise function) [245]. This distorts the reflected image and thereby creates the illusion of the reflector's waviness. In theory, such two-dimensional warping techniques could be applied to the entire scene's image, allowing for underwater effects or other distortions. The scene is rendered, and the generated image is then used as a texture on a warping grid filling the screen. While currently computationally expensive, as hardware capabilities increase, such techniques will become more common.

Planar reflections for real-time rendering have also been treated by Diefenbach and Badler [82], Möller [258], and in the SIGGRAPH course on advanced OpenGL [245].

6.5.2   Glossy Effects

A number of significant global illumination effects and lighting models are presented by Diefenbach and Badler [82]. We will discuss two here, glossy reflection and refraction. The previous section presented methods that produce sharp reflections. A simple way to enhance the illusion that the reflector is truly a mirror is to fog the reflected objects seen in it. An example is shown in Plate X (following p. 194). This effect is created by having the object fade to black as the distance from the reflector increases. Something interesting to note about the plate's image is that each reflected object has been given its own rate of extinction. The eraser is made to fade away quickly relative to its distance from the reflector, while the pear can fade more slowly since it is relatively tall. Note that this technique does not use hardware fogging here. The distance from the reflector must be computed in the application stage and used to diminish the object's color with distance.

The accumulation and stencil buffers can be used together to produce the effects of fuzzy reflection and frosted glass. The stencil buffer creates the window into the effect, and the accumulation buffer captures the effect from jittering the position of the object. Fogging to black is used for the reflection, fogging to white for the refraction. Examples of these techniques are shown in Plate XVII (following p. 194).

Bastos et al. [29] use image-based techniques combined with signal processing to create glossy reflections. They also use a more elaborate model of how a surface reflects. While their method is more complex, it avoids having to perform multiple accumulation buffer passes. See their paper for details.

6.5.3 Reflections from Curved Reflectors

Ray tracing is the traditional solution for producing reflections. A reflection ray starts from the viewed location and picks up and adds in the color in the reflection direction. This process is extremely expensive for real-time rendering, as it involves per-pixel shading and finding the closest intersection for each ray [116]. It is possible to trace rays only from the reflector's vertices into the environment and add in the color found. This technique is a more elaborate form of the specular highlight contribution in the lighting equation. Tracing rays only from the vertices can significantly reduce the amount of computation, but suffers from typical Gouraud-shading artifacts. Sharp reflections will usually not be captured, though this could be considered an advantage, as the reflections will look blurry.

Ofek and Rappoport [272] present a technique for sharp, true reflections from convex and concave reflectors which can be considerably faster. Their observation is that in a convex reflector (e.g., a sphere), the reflected object is distorted by the surface but otherwise unchanged. That is, each reflected vertex is reflected by only one point on the reflector (unlike what can happen with a concave reflector). The curved reflector can be treated like a window into a mirror world, in a similar manner to the planar reflector.

Given a vertex of an object to be reflected, we would like to find where on the reflector this point is located. By finding the locations of all the vertices in a reflected object on the reflector, we create a virtual object. We draw the polygons of this virtual object and blend the results with the reflector, as with the planar reflector method. Just as the planar reflector creates a mirror object, the curved surface creates a virtual object which is rendered.

The transformation from a curved surface is considerably more complex than a planar reflection. There is rarely a direct equation for creating virtual objects. Ofek and Rappoport use an *explosion map* to accelerate the process. The idea is to subdivide a reflector's surface and associate each triangle with some part of the map. The explosion map is similar to the sphere map (see Section 5.7.3). Instead of mapping an environment to a circular texture, the curved surface's triangulated surface is exploded onto the map and its location is recorded in the texels.

The explosion takes place along the reflection rays generated by the viewer looking at the surface, cast onto a sphere. Given a reflected vertex location, the explosion map is accessed and computations are performed in order to find the virtual vertex quickly. This algorithm can also be extended to concave reflectors. The full description of this method is fairly involved, and the interested reader should see the original paper [272]. This method currently runs in real time for various relatively simple scenes; as processor power increases, wider use of this technique is likely.

6.6 Shadows

Shadows are important elements in creating a realistic image and in providing the user with visual cues about object placement. A review of many different shadow algorithms is found in the survey published by Woo et al. [382] and in Watt and Watt's book [367]. Here we will present the most important real-time algorithms. The first section handles the special case of shadows cast on planar surfaces, and the second section covers more general shadow algorithms, i.e., casting shadows onto arbitrary surfaces.

6.6.1 Planar Shadows

A simple case of shadowing occurs when objects cast shadows on planar surfaces. Two kinds of algorithms for planar shadows are presented in this section. The terminology used here is illustrated in Figure 6.13, where *occluders* are objects that cast shadows onto *receivers*. Point light sources generate only fully shadowed regions, sometimes called *hard shadows*. If area light sources are used, then soft shadows are produced. Each shadow can have a fully shadowed region, called the *umbra*, and a partially shadowed region, called the *penumbra*.

That is, at least, how it works in the real world. As we will see, *soft shadows* (i.e., with penumbrae) can be simulated by the *shadow map* algorithm. We will also present other methods that generate more physically accurate soft shadows. Soft shadows are generally preferable, if they are possible, because the soft edges let the viewer know that the shadow is indeed a shadow. Hard-edged shadows can sometimes be misinterpreted as actual geometric features, such as a crease in a surface.

More important than having a penumbra is having any shadow at all. Without some shadow as a visual cue, scenes are often unconvincing and more difficult to perceive. As Wanger shows [366], it is usually better to have an inaccurate shadow than none at all, as the eye is fairly forgiving about the shape of the

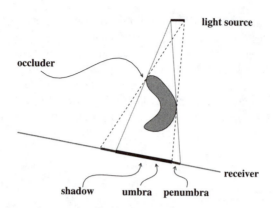

Figure 6.13. Shadow terminology: light source, occluder, receiver, shadow, umbra, and penumbra.

shadow. For example, a blurred black circle applied as a texture on the floor can anchor a person to the ground. A simple rectangular shape with per-vertex alpha transparency around the edges, perhaps a total of 10 triangles, is often all that is needed for a car's soft shadow.

In the following sections we will go beyond these simple-modeled shadows and present methods that compute shadows automatically from the occluders in a scene.

Projection Shadows

In this scheme, the three-dimensional object is rendered a second time in order to create a shadow. A matrix can be derived that projects the vertices of an object onto a plane [39, 351]. Consider the situation in Figure 6.14, where the light source is located at l, the vertex to be projected is at $\mathbf{v}$, and the projected vertex is at $\mathbf{p}$. We will derive the projection matrix for the special case where the shadowed plane is $y = 0$, then this result will be generalized to work with any plane.

We start by deriving the projection for the x-coordinate. From the similar triangles in the left part of Figure 6.14, the following equation is obtained.

$$\frac{p_x - l_x}{v_x - l_x} = \frac{l_y}{l_y - v_y}$$

$$\Longleftrightarrow \tag{6.5}$$

$$p_x = \frac{l_y v_x - l_x v_y}{l_y - v_y}$$

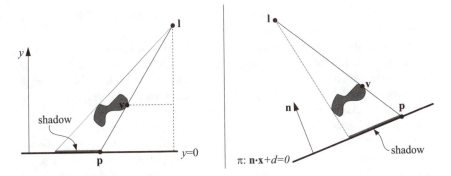

Figure 6.14. Left: A light source, located at l, casts a shadow onto the plane $y = 0$. The vertex **v** is projected onto the plane. The projected point is called **p**. The similar triangles are used for the derivation of the projection matrix. Right: The notation of the left part of this figure is used here. The shadow is being cast onto a plane, $\pi : \mathbf{n} \cdot \mathbf{x} + d = 0$.

The z-coordinate is obtained in the same way: $p_z = (l_y v_z - l_z v_y)/(l_y - v_y)$, while the y-coordinate is zero. Now these equations can be converted into the projection matrix **M** below.

$$\mathbf{M} = \begin{pmatrix} l_y & -l_x & 0 & 0 \\ 0 & 0 & 0 & 0 \\ 0 & -l_z & l_y & 0 \\ 0 & -1 & 0 & l_y \end{pmatrix} \tag{6.6}$$

It is easy to verify that $\mathbf{Mv} = \mathbf{p}$, which means that **M** is indeed the projection matrix.

In the general case, the plane onto which the shadows should be cast is not the plane $y = 0$, but instead $\pi : \mathbf{n} \cdot \mathbf{x} + d = 0$. This case is depicted in the right part of Figure 6.14. The goal is again to find a matrix that projects **v** down to **p**. To this end, the ray emanating at l, which goes through **v**, is intersected by the plane π. This yields the projected point **p**:

$$\mathbf{p} = 1 - \frac{d + \mathbf{n} \cdot \mathbf{l}}{\mathbf{n} \cdot (\mathbf{v} - \mathbf{l})}(\mathbf{v} - \mathbf{l}) \tag{6.7}$$

This equation can also be converted into projection matrix, shown in Equation 6.8, which satisfies $\mathbf{Mv} = \mathbf{p}$.

$$\mathbf{M} = \begin{pmatrix} \mathbf{n} \cdot \mathbf{l} + d - l_x n_x & -l_x n_y & -l_x n_z & -l_x d \\ -l_y n_x & \mathbf{n} \cdot \mathbf{l} + d - l_y n_y & -l_y n_z & -l_y d \\ -l_z n_x & -l_z n_y & \mathbf{n} \cdot \mathbf{l} + d - l_z n_z & -l_z d \\ -n_x & -n_y & -n_z & \mathbf{n} \cdot \mathbf{l} \end{pmatrix} \tag{6.8}$$

As expected, this matrix turns into the matrix in Equation 6.6 if the plane is $y = 0$ (that is, $\mathbf{n} = (0 \ \ 1 \ \ 0)^T$ and $d = 0$).

To render the shadow, simply apply this matrix to the objects that should cast shadows on the plane π, and render this projected object with a dark color and no illumination. In practice, you have to take measures to avoid allowing the projected polygons to be rendered beneath the surface receiving them. One method is to add some bias to the plane we project upon so that the shadow polygons are always rendered in front of the surface. Getting this bias just right is often tricky: too much and the shadows start to cover the objects and so break the illusion; too little and the ground plane pokes through the shadows due to precision error. As the angle of the surface normal away from the viewer increases, the bias must also increase.

A better method is to draw the ground plane first, then draw the projected polygons with the Z-buffer off, then render the rest of the geometry as usual. The projected polygons are then always drawn on top of the ground plane as no depth comparisons are made. The only flaw with this scheme is the one we ran into with reflections: the projected shadows can fall outside of our plane.

To solve this problem, we can use a stencil buffer. Draw the receiver to the screen and to the stencil buffer; then with the Z-buffer off, draw the projected polygons, only where the receiver was drawn; then render the rest of the scene normally.

A disadvantage of the projection method, in addition to its limitation to planar surfaces, is that the shadow has to be rendered for each frame, even though the shadow may not change. Since shadows are view-independent (their shapes do not change with different viewpoints), an idea that works well in practice is to render the shadow into a texture which is then rendered as a textured rectangle. The shadow texture would only be recomputed when the shadow changes, that is, when the light source or any shadow-casting or -receiving object moves. To increase the lifetime of a shadow texture, the shadow information can be stored in the alpha component of a texture [258]. Such a texture is rendered on top of the receiver using blending so that pixels in shadow are darkened and pixels not in shadow are left unchanged. This is a technique commonly used in games; the texture is precomputed, and a textured quadrilateral is then moved and rotated to follow the movements of a shadow-casting object. The use of modulation is the same as light mapping (see Section 5.7.2), with synthetic objects forming the map on the fly.

Another method to improve performance is to use simplified versions of the models for generating the shadow projections (see Section 9.4).

The matrices in Equations 6.6 and 6.8 do not always generate the desired results. For example, if the light source is below the topmost point on the object,

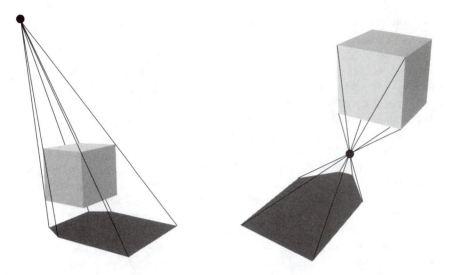

Figure 6.15. At the left, a correct shadow is shown, while in the figure on the right, an anti-shadow appears, since the light source is below the topmost vertex of the object.

then an *anti-shadow* [39] is generated, since each vertex is projected through the point of the light source. Correct shadows and anti-shadows are shown in Figure 6.15.

A similar rendering error as that found with planar reflections can occur for this kind of shadow generation. For reflections, errors occur when objects located on the opposite side of the reflector plane are not dealt with properly. In the case of shadow generation, errors occur when we use a shadow-casting object that is on the far side of the receiving plane. This is because an object beyond the shadow receiver does not cast a shadow. Shadows generated in this manner are called *false shadows*. This problem can be solved in the same manner as for planar reflections, i.e., with a clipping plane located at the shadow receiver that culls away all geometry beyond the receiver.

Soft Shadows

Projective shadows can also be made soft, by using a variety of techniques. Here we describe an algorithm from Heckbert and Herf [167, 181] that produces soft shadows. The algorithm's goal is to generate a texture on a ground plane that shows a soft shadow.[4] We then describe a different method by Gooch et al. [132].

---

[4]Basic hard shadows can also be generated using this technique.

Soft shadows appear whenever a light source extends in space, i.e., has an area. One way to approximate the effect of an area light is to sample it by using a number of point lights placed on its surface. For each of these point light sources, an image is rendered and added to the accumulation buffer. The average of these images is then an image with soft shadows. Note that, in theory, any algorithm that generates hard shadows can be used along with this accumulation technique to produce penumbrae. In practice, doing so may be difficult because of memory constraints or other factors.

Heckbert and Herf use a frustum-based method to produce their shadows. For each point light source, the occluders inside the pyramid formed by the point light source and the receiver parallelogram are transformed into a parallelepiped, with the matrix, $\mathbf{M}$, below. The parallelepiped lies in unit-screen space, which means from $(x, y) = (0, 0)$ to $(1, 1)$, and with $z = 1$ at the receiver, and $z = \infty$ at the light source. Essentially, the light is viewing the receiver, and a perspective projection is performed. Following the notation from Heckbert and Herf, the point light source is located at $\mathbf{a}$, and the receiver parallelogram has one vertex at $\mathbf{b}$, and the edge vectors $\mathbf{e}_x$ and $\mathbf{e}_y$. This is illustrated in Figure 6.16.

$$\mathbf{M} = \begin{pmatrix} q_u n_{ux} & q_u n_{uy} & q_u n_{uz} & -q_u \mathbf{n}_u \cdot \mathbf{b} \\ q_v n_{vx} & q_v n_{vy} & q_v n_{vz} & -q_v \mathbf{n}_v \cdot \mathbf{b} \\ 0 & 0 & 0 & 1 \\ q_w n_{wx} & q_w n_{wy} & q_w n_{wz} & -q_w \mathbf{n}_w \cdot \mathbf{a} \end{pmatrix} \tag{6.9}$$

$$\begin{aligned} \mathbf{e}_w &= \mathbf{b} - \mathbf{a} \\ \mathbf{n}_u &= \mathbf{e}_w \times \mathbf{e}_y & q_u &= 1/\mathbf{n}_u \cdot \mathbf{e}_x \\ \mathbf{n}_v &= \mathbf{e}_x \times \mathbf{e}_w & q_v &= 1/\mathbf{n}_v \cdot \mathbf{e}_y \\ \mathbf{n}_w &= \mathbf{e}_y \times \mathbf{e}_x & q_w &= 1/\mathbf{n}_w \cdot \mathbf{e}_w \end{aligned} \tag{6.10}$$

The matrix $\mathbf{M}$ of Equation 6.9 is not a projection matrix as were the matrices used in the previous section on planar projection shadows. Here, the transformation is from three dimensions to three dimensions (vs. from three to two). What is ingenious about this transformation is that by using the third dimension for clipping (using the near and far planes), we can avoid both anti-shadows and incorrectly generated shadows due to objects behind the receiver (false shadows).

The pyramid in Figure 6.16 is transformed by $\mathbf{M}$ into a parallelepiped. To simplify implementation, we should use either a perspective or an orthographic projection call from a graphics API so that clipping, etc., is done correctly. Since the matrix $\mathbf{M}$ transforms the pyramid to a parallelepiped, we can use an orthographic matrix after using $\mathbf{M}$. So the final projection matrix, $\mathbf{P}$, that should be used is $\mathbf{P} = \mathbf{P}_o \mathbf{M}$, where $\mathbf{P}_o$ is an orthographic projection matrix. To get the

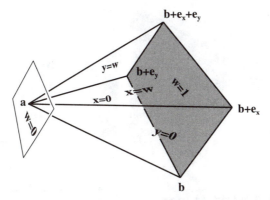

Figure 6.16. A pyramid is formed by a point, **a**, on the light source, and a parallelogram, i.e., the shadow receiver, which has one vertex at **b**, and the edge vectors e_x and e_y. Illustration after Heckbert and Herf [167].

correct three-dimensional clip, the clipping planes should be set to $n = 1$ (near) and $f = \infty$ (far) (in $\mathbf{P}_o$— see Section 3.5.1 for the effect on $\mathbf{P}_o$ of the near and far values). If $\mathbf{P}$ is used as the projection matrix in the rendering pipeline, then every polygon outside the pyramid will be culled away, and thus only the correct occluders will generate shadows on the receiver.

Let us examine what happens to points that are located behind the light source **a**, or behind the receiver. Such points should not contribute to the shadows. The mapping from the pyramid into the parallelepiped is shown in Figure 6.17. The occluders that produce shadows must be located in the gray volume, and a point **d** located behind the light source (that is, $w < 0$), will be transformed into a negative z-value, and thus not contribute to the shadow. Likewise, a point **c**, located behind the receiver ($w > 1$), will be mapped into $0 < z < 1$, and will also not contribute to any shadow. As promised, the three-dimensional clip avoids anti-shadows and false shadows.

A shadow texture for the receiver is generated in the following way. For each sample on the light source, the receiver is first rendered by using this sample as a point light source. To get better quality, increase the resolution of the texture being generated. Also, we can subdivide the receiver finely in order to simulate Phong shading on the receiver if true Phong shading is not available. Then the projection matrix is used to render all objects inside the pyramid. Since these objects should generate shadows, they are drawn in black (and so Z-buffering, texturing, and lighting can be turned off). All of these images are averaged into the accumulation buffer to produce a shadow texture.

The shadow is rendered as a textured parallelogram, which can be done very efficiently. The shadow texture has to be recomputed each time the objects or

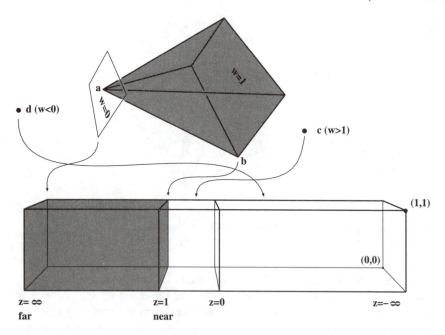

Figure 6.17. The pyramid is being mapped, using M, into a parallelepiped, with near and far planes as shown.

the light source move. If the shadow texture must be recomputed, then the bottleneck is the downloading of the texture into texture memory [167].

Another method from Gooch et al. [132] is to approximate the effect of a spherical light source in order to gain speed. A problem with the sampled area light method is that it tends to look like what it is: a number of overlapping point light sources. Instead of varying the location of samples on the light's surface, the receiving plane's location is moved up and down and the projections cast upon it are averaged. See Figure 6.18.

This method has the advantage that the shadows created are concentric, which generally looks better and so requires fewer samples. Also, we can eliminate the need to project and render the occluder multiple times. A single shadow projection can be used to generate a texture of the shadow. This texture could be copied into texture memory and then remapped correctly to accumulate the other samples. Figure 6.19 shows the result.

A problem with this method is that if the object touches the receiver then the shadow will not be modeled correctly. Darkness will appear to leak out from under the object. This problem can be overcome by rendering and averaging

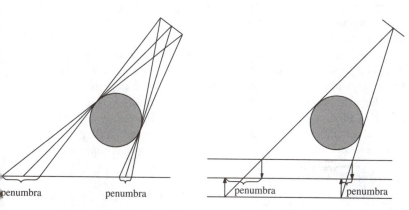

ure 6.18. Soft shadowing. On the left a number of point samples are distributed over the
ace of the light, with the hard shadow silhouette lines drawn. On the right a stack of planes
ture a penumbra.

y the lower planes. The resulting shadow is less realistic, but does not have
disturbing shadow creep effect.

This method can also overstate the umbra region, since the projected shadow
l always be larger than the object. In reality, if an area light is larger than an
ect, the object can have a smaller or nonexistent umbra region.

6.2 Shadows on Curved Surfaces

e way to extend the idea of planar shadow to curved surfaces is to use a gen-
ted shadow image as a projective texture [245, 271, 321]. Think of shadows

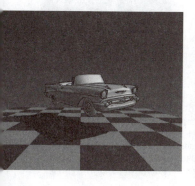

e 6.19. A non-photorealistic car with a hard projected shadow and with a soft shadow formed
concentric projections. *(Courtesy of Bruce Gooch, University of Utah.)*

from the light's point of view (literally). Whatever the light sees is illuminated; what it does not see is in shadow. So say an image of an occluder is made from the light's point of view and a texture is generated. This texture can then be projected onto the surfaces that are to receive the shadow. Essentially, each vertex on the receivers has a (u, v) texture coordinate computed for it and has the texture applied to it. When rendered, the shadow texture modulates the receiver surfaces. This idea is an extension of the light map concept discussed in Section 5.7.2. One method from Nguyen [271] is shown in Figure 6.20.

A drawback of this method is that the designer must identify which objects are occluders and which are their receivers. In this section, two algorithms are presented that generate correct shadows without the need for such intervention.

Shadow Volumes

Presented by Heidmann in 1991 [170], a method based on Crow's *shadow volumes* [72] can cast shadows onto arbitrary objects by clever use of the stencil buffer.

To begin, imagine a point and a triangle. Extending the lines from a point through the vertices of a triangle to infinity yields an infinite pyramid. The part under the triangle, i.e., the part that does not include the point, is a truncated infinite pyramid, and the upper part is simply a pyramid. This is illustrated in Figure 6.21. Now imagine that the point is actually a point light source. Then, any part of an object that is inside the volume of the truncated pyramid (under the triangle) is in shadow. This volume is called a shadow volume.

Say we view some scene and follow a ray through a pixel until the ray hits the object to be displayed on screen. While the ray is on its way to this object, we increment a counter each time it crosses a face of the shadow volume that is front-facing (i.e., facing towards the viewer). Thus, the counter is incremented

Figure 6.20. Shadow projection. On the left is the scene from the light's view. In the middle is the occluding object rendered as a shadow texture. On the right, the texture coordinates have been determined for the stairs and the shadow texture has been applied. *(Courtesy of Hubert Nguyen.)*

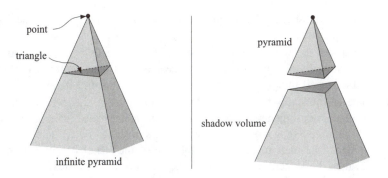

Figure 6.21. Left: The lines from a point light are extended through the vertices of a triangle to form an infinite pyramid. Right: The upper part is a pyramid, and the lower part is an infinite truncated pyramid, also called the shadow volume. All geometry that is inside the shadow volume is in shadow.

each time the ray goes into shadow. In the same manner, we decrement the same counter each time the ray crosses a back-facing face of the truncated pyramid. The ray is then going out of a shadow. Finally, the ray hits the object that is to be displayed at that pixel. If the counter is greater than zero, then that pixel is in shadow; otherwise it is not. This principle also works when there is more than one triangle that casts shadows.

Doing this geometrically is tedious and time consuming. But there is a much smarter solution [170]: the stencil buffer can do the counting for us. First, the stencil buffer is cleared. Second, the whole scene is drawn into the frame buffer with only ambient and emission components used, in order to get these lighting components in the color buffer and the depth information into the Z-buffer. Third, Z-buffering and writing to the color buffer are turned off, and then the front-facing polygons of the shadow volumes are drawn. During this process, the stencil operation is set to increment the values in the stencil buffer wherever a polygon is drawn. Similarly, the values in the stencil buffer are decremented when the back-facing polygons of the shadow volumes are drawn. Incrementing and decrementing are done only when the pixels of the rendered shadow-volume face are visible. Finally, the whole scene is rendered again, this time with only the diffuse and the specular components of the materials active, and displayed only where the value in the stencil buffer is 0. A 0 value indicates that the ray has gone into shadow as many times as it has gone out of a shadow volume—i.e., this location is illuminated by the light.

In practice, the quadrilaterals making up the shadow volume must be of finite length. If a bounding volume is available for the entire scene, then the length of the maximum extension of that bounding volume can be used to limit the size of the quadrilaterals.

Note that this method has to be adjusted if the viewer is inside the shadow volume. In this case, a value of 0 does not mean a point is in the light. For this condition the stencil buffer should be cleared to $+1$ (instead of 0).

In some architectures the stencil values are unsigned (i.e., never negative), which would cause problems for a viewer placed inside a shadow volume. Drawing a back-facing polygon would decrement values in stencil buffer below 0, and the result would be undefined. If the resolution of the stencil buffer is from 0 to $2^n - 1$, then the stencil buffer may be cleared with $2^{(n-1)}$ instead of with 0. In the final pass of the algorithm, the stencil buffer should be compared to 128 instead of 0.

Instead of computing the polygons of the shadow volumes geometrically, Haeberli [170] suggests that the scene should be drawn from the point of view of the light source that casts shadows. Then a height field is created by reading the values of the Z-buffer, and the values are used to set the height in a triangle mesh (with as many vertices as there are pixels). This height field is then an approximation of the exact shadow volume. This technique is valuable, especially for more complex scenes, but as with all sampling techniques, aliasing may occur.

An example of the shadows that the shadow volume algorithm generates is shown in Figure 6.22. Though the teapot shown in the figure does not cast a shadow, in practice this particular shadow could be generated rapidly. Since the teapot casts a shadow onto a plane, a projective shadow could be used instead

Figure 6.22. Shadow volumes. On the left, a square with cutouts casts a shadow on various objects. On the right, the various faces of the shadow volume are shown. Note that the teapot does not have a shadow volume, and so casts no shadows. *(Courtesy of Mark Kilgard, NVIDIA Inc.)*

of a shadow volume. Different shadow techniques can be used as appropriate, thereby saving time overall.

There are some limitations to the shadow volume technique. Good subpixel addressing is critical for the algorithm to work correctly [245]. Another area of concern is the explosion in the number of polygons rendered. Each triangle and each light create a total of four additional polygons which must be rendered into the stencil buffer. Three of these, the sides of the shadow volume, must be trimmed against the scene's extents (e.g., a bounding box containing all objects). To cut down on the number of polygons, the silhouette edges of the object could be found. A silhouette edge is an edge of the object where one polygon faces towards the light and the other faces away from it. Shadow volumes must be generated from only these edges, but finding such edges is computationally expensive.

A portal-based world (see Section 7.1.3) can use cells and portals for creating shadows rapidly for dynamic lights [356]. Shadows are generated as seen from the position of the light. Initially there is an infinite view frustum (everything is visible), so all polygons in the same sector (cell) as the light are illuminated. When traversing a portal to another sector, the view frustum is clipped to that portal and then the algorithm simply recurses into that other sector (but with a smaller frustum). When a polygon is visible, this results in a coplanar light-patch. This is a polygon that is coplanar with the original polygon and describes where the light hits the polygon. In this system portals are limited to a convex shape, so generating these coplanar polygons is a rapid process. This method is something like the inverse of shadow volumes, as the volume of light is tracked through the environment.

During rendering, the coplanar polygons can be used in various ways. One way is to render each coplanar polygon immediately after its associated polygon, using a blend operation. Another is to make a copy of the polygon's light map, containing the effect of any static lights. Each coplanar polygon is rendered to this map, thereby lighting it. The workload is minimized by performing this light map creation and rendering only when the associated polygon is potentially visible and has changed. This second approach has the advantage of folding all static and dynamic lights into one light map, at the cost of having to keep a copy of the original (static-only) light map.

Shadow Map

In 1978, Williams [374] proposed that a common Z-buffer-based renderer could be used to generate shadows quickly on arbitrary objects. The idea is to render the scene, using the Z-buffer algorithm, with respect to the position and direction of the light source that should cast shadows. For each pixel in the Z-buffer, the z-depth now contains the distance to the object closest to the light source. We

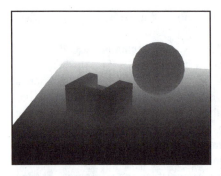 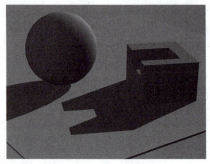

Figure 6.23. Shadow mapping. On the left is the view of the scene from the light's perspective, with white being further away. On the right is the scene rendered with this shadow map.

call the entire contents of the Z-buffer the *shadow map*. To use the shadow map the scene is rendered a second time, but this time with respect to the viewer. Now, as each drawing primitive is being rendered, its location is compared to the shadow map; if a rendered point is farther away from the light source than the value in the shadow map, then that point is in shadow; otherwise it is not. See Figure 6.23.

This technique can be implemented by exploiting texture mapping hardware [173, 321]. The shadow map is generated as described above. Then the scene is rendered from the viewer using only ambient lighting, in order to resolve visibility. A shadow testing step is then performed, which compares the z-value in the Z-buffer with the z-value (which is transformed from the coordinate system of the light source into the coordinate system of the viewer) in the shadow map. An additional value, α_p, for each pixel, p, in the frame buffer is set according to the outcome of this comparison. If the two z-values are (almost) equal, then $\alpha_p = 1$, indicating that the pixel is not in shadow. Otherwise, $\alpha = 0$, which indicates that the pixel is in shadow. Finally, the whole scene is rendered using the whole lighting equation. The final color of each pixel is the color from the ambient pass plus the color from the full rendering pass multiplied by α_p. This means that when $\alpha_p = 0$, the pixel color is taken from the ambient rendering pass, and when $\alpha = 1$, then the pixel color is that of a normal rendering pass.

Note that, when the shadow map is generated, only Z-buffering is required; that is, lighting, texturing, and the writing of color values into the color buffer can be turned off. Also, the shadow map can be used in several frames as long as neither the light source nor the objects move. The viewer is allowed to move, since shadows are view-independent.

Advantages of this method are that general-purpose graphics hardware can be used to render arbitrary shadows, and that the complexity is linear. That is, if the number of rendering primitives is increased so that the total rendering time doubles, then the shadow map algorithm is expected to generate shadows in twice the time. One disadvantage is that the quality of the shadows depends on the resolution (in pixels) of the shadow map, and also on the numerical precision of the Z-buffer. Also, since the shadow map is sampled during the comparison, the shadow map algorithm is susceptible to aliasing problems, especially close to shadow edges. A common problem is *self-shadow aliasing*, in which a polygon is incorrectly considered to shadow itself because of the imprecision inherent in this point sampling method. That is, samples generated for the light are generally not exactly at the same locations as the screen samples. When the light's stored depth value is compared to the viewed surface's depth, the light's value may be slightly lower than the surface's, resulting in this error. Such errors are shown in Figure 6.24.

One method to help renderers avoid (but not always eliminate) these problems is to introduce a bias factor [298, 383]. Another helpful method is to make sure the light frustum's near plane is as far away from the light as possible and the far plane is as close as possible. Doing so increases the effective precision of the Z-buffer.

An extension of the shadow map technique using bilinear interpolation can provide pseudo-soft shadows, though currently not normally in real-time. This extension can also help ameliorate resolution problems that cause shadows to look blocky when a single light sample covers many screen pixels. The solution is related to texture magnification (see Section 5.2.1). Instead of a single sample being taken off the shadow map, a set of samples is taken [298]. For example, the

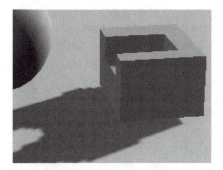 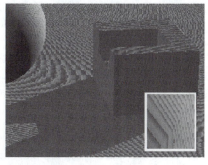

Figure 6.24. Shadow mapping problems. On the left, the bias is set too high, so the shadow creeps out from under the block object. The shadow map resolution is also too low, so the texels of the map appear in the shadow, giving it a blocky appearance. On the right there is no bias, so the surface erroneously shadows itself, in this case producing a Moiré pattern. The inset shows a zoom of part of the sphere's surface.

four texel depths closest to the sample's location on the light map could be used. The technique would not blend depths themselves, but rather the results of their comparisons with the surface's depth. That is, the surface's depth is compared to the four texel depths, and the point is then determined to be in light or shadow for each shadow map sample. These results are then bilinearly interpolated to calculate how much the light actually contributes to the surface location. This filtering results in an artificially soft shadow. Such shadows all have more or less the same-sized penumbrae, and these penumbrae change depending on the shadow map's resolution and other factors. Still, a little penumbra and smoothing is better than none at all.

Woo [383] proposes a method of avoiding many biasing problems by creating an intermediate surface. This method is a part of the original Talisman architecture [354]. Instead of keeping just the closest depth value, the two closest values are tracked in separate buffers. When the tracking is complete, these two buffers are averaged into one, which is then used as the shadow map. For a solid object, this technique usually creates a shadowing surface which passes through the middle of the surface. For example, a sphere would create a circle passing through its center and facing the light. However, this technique can also have problems. See Figure 6.25. In practice, the problems seen at j and k are relatively rare and not that noticeable, especially when using bilinear interpolation [385]. By creating an intermediate surface we can eliminate most biasing and self-shadowing problems.

Hourcade [190] introduced a more limited form of shadow mapping which also solves the biasing problem and lends itself to hardware implementation. Another way to conceptualize the problem is as the identification of what is seen by the light at a location, instead of computation of the depth. For example, if a pencil is seen at a particular location and in the shadow map it says the pencil is also seen by the light, then the pencil is illuminated. An image rendered using this technique is shown in Plate X (following p. 194).

This method has the advantage that no bias at all is necessary; only IDs are stored, not depths. However, shadowing due to resolution limits of the shadow map can occur where polygon edges are shared. That is, a location near an edge may access the shadow map and find an ID of an adjoining polygon, resulting in a shadow near the edge. For this reason IDs are assigned to entire objects instead of individual polygons. This helps, but it also means that an object with a single ID cannot cast a shadow on itself, since the occluding part will have the same ID as the receiver. Sharing IDs also fails to solve the problem of improper shadowing where separate objects touch. Magnification filtering can help here: if any of the four texels on the shadow map matches the ID, the surface is considered illuminated.

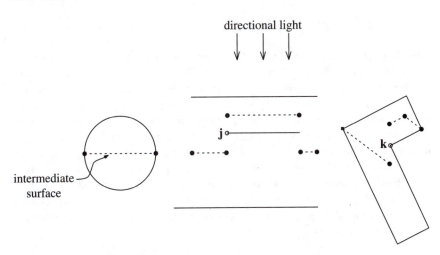

Figure 6.25. Woo's shadow mapping method. A directional light comes from directly above. The depths from each of the two surfaces closest to the light are combined to give an intermediate surface which is stored in the shadow map. This surface is shown as a dashed line. The two sets of surfaces on the right have problems due to sampling limitations. At location **j** the point may be found to be in light if the closest shadow texel sampled is to the left of it, since this intermediate surface is farther from the light. Similarly, point **k** may be considered to be in light because the intermediate surface to its left is below it.

A limitation of all of these shadow map methods is that the light is assumed to view the scene from somewhere outside of it, something like a spot light. This is because the light looks at the scene through a single frustum. Positional lights inside a scene can be represented by a six-view cube, similar to Greene's environment mapping view (see Section 5.7.3). However, getting the shadows to join properly along the seams of the cube is problematic, because factors such as bias can sometimes be different along such edges than they are on the rest of the surface. Using the same near and far planes for each cube face view helps.

6.7 Lines

Lines are perhaps the least special special effect. However, they are important in fields such as CAD for seeing the underlying model facets and discerning the object's shape. They are also useful in highlighting a selected object and in areas such as technical illustration. In addition, some of the techniques involved are applicable to other problems. We cover a few useful techniques here; more are covered in [245]. Antialiased lines are discussed in Section 4.4.

6.7.1   Edge Highlighting

Edge highlighting is a fixed-view technique (see Section 6.2.5). To highlight an object, we draw its edges in a different color, without having to redraw the surface itself. This is an extremely fast form of highlighting, since no polygons are rendered. For example, imagine a blue polygon with gray edges. As the cursor passes over the polygon we highlight it by drawing the edges in red, then drawing gray edges again when the cursor leaves. Since the view is not moving, the blue polygon never has to be redrawn; only the red highlight edges are drawn on top of the existing image. The idea is that the original gray edges were drawn properly, so that when a red edge is drawn using the same geometric description, it should perfectly replace the gray edge. This technique works well for highlighting objects in a two-dimensional drawing or when only edges are being drawn.

6.7.2   Polygon Edge Rendering

Correctly rendering edges on top of filled polygons is more difficult than it first appears. If a line is at exactly the same location as a polygon, how do we ensure that the line is always rendered in front? One simple solution is to render all lines with a bias [182, 245]. That is, each line is rendered slightly closer than it should truly be, so that it will be above the surface. This works most of the time, but there are exceptions. For example, the right side of Figure 6.11 on page 163 demonstrates some flaws of this method. As polygons become edge-on to the view, they tend to obscure some of the drawn edges due to imprecision. Also, if the bias is too large, parts of edges that should be hidden appear, spoiling the effect.

One method for producing high-quality edges uses multiple passes [182], as follows:

1. Render the filled polygon, with Z-buffer depth comparison on, Z-buffer replacement off, and the color buffer on.

2. Render the polygon edges normally (everything on).

3. Render the filled polygon again, with the Z-buffer fully on but the color buffer off.

The first step properly draws the filled polygon on the screen but does not modify the Z-buffer values. This allows the edges to draw on top of the filled polygon, since there are filled-area z-depths that could cover the edges. The final step then fills in the depths for the filled area so that the Z-buffer is in synch again with what is displayed.

This technique usually looks good but does not work well with the edge highlighting technique (unlike the bias method, which works fine with it). When the three-step algorithm is used to draw the original image, each edge is properly drawn on top of the filled region. But the edge's z-depth values are sometimes overwritten by the filled polygon's z-depth values during the third step. In other words, the edge's color may be drawn properly, but the depth values where the edge is drawn might actually be those of the filled polygon. In this case, when a highlight edge is drawn to replace the original edge, it will not appear wherever the filled polygon was in front of the original edge. In our example the highlights will be displayed in a broken-up manner, with the edge partially the original grey and partially red.

To solve this, Herrell et al. [182] present a scheme that uses a modified one-bit stencil buffer. The steps are:

1. Render the filled polygon normally, also marking its location in the stencil buffer.

2. Render the polygon edges. If a pixel is not marked in the stencil buffer, perform a normal depth compare and replace. If a pixel is marked, do not compare; instead, always replace the stored z-depth with the edge's value.

3. Clear the stencil buffer for the next pass (possibly by redrawing the filled polygon).

The method works by forcing the edge's depth values into the Z-buffer. Now when an edge is redrawn as a highlight, it will have exactly the same depth values as those that are stored and so will be drawn correctly. Step 2 of this algorithm can be performed as two separate passes using a standard stencil buffer; see [182, 245].

6.7.3 Hidden-Line Rendering

In normal wireframe drawing, all edges of a model are visible. Hidden-line rendering treats the model as solid and so draws only the visible lines. The obvious way to perform this operation is simply to render the polygons with a solid fill color the same as the background's and also render the edges. The polygons then paint over the hidden lines.

A potentially faster method is to draw all the filled polygons to the Z-buffer but not the color buffer, then draw the edges normally [245]. This second method avoids unnecessary color fills. Lines can also be drawn as partially obscured instead of fully hidden, appearing, for instance, in light gray instead of not being drawn at all. To do this, first draw all the edges in the obscured fashion desired, then proceed as before, drawing the filled polygons to the Z-buffer only and then drawing the edges again.

Figure 6.26 shows results for some of the different line rendering methods discussed here.

6.7.4   Haloing

When two lines cross, a common convention is to erase a part of the more distant line, making the ordering obvious. In computer graphics this can be relatively easily accomplished by drawing each line twice. This method erases the overlap by drawing over it in the background color. Assume the lines are black and the background white. For each line, first draw a thick version in the background color, then draw the line itself normally. A bias or other method will have to be used to ensure that the thin black line lies atop the thick white background line.

As with hidden-line rendering, this technique can be made more efficient by first drawing all the white halo lines only to the Z-buffer, then drawing the lines normally [245].

A potential problem with haloing is that lines near each other can get obscured unnecessarily by one line's halo. For example, in Figure 6.26, if the haloing lines extend all the way to the corners, then near the corners the closer lines may halo the lines further away. Because haloing is a technical illustration convention and not a physical phenomenon it is difficult to automate perfectly.

6.8   Height-Field and Volume Rendering

These techniques are entire rendering methods rather than special effects. We will discuss them briefly here, as it is important at least to know of their existence.

A height-field, as discussed in Section 5.7.4 on bump mapping, is an image that contains a set of gray-scale values representing heights.[5] A second image containing a color for each texel is also often used. In bump mapping, the

---

[5]In practice, 8 bits of gray-scale may not be sufficient. A 16- or 24-bit representation is then used, although such height fields will not display as gray-scale images.

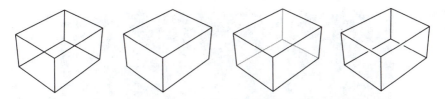

Figure 6.26. Four line rendering styles. From left to right: wireframe, hidden-line, obscured-line, and haloed line.

height-field image was used to create the illusion of bumpiness by perturbing the surface normals. Height fields can also be used as a description of true geometry. One way to render a height field is to convert it to polygons. Each texel fully describes an xyz coordinate, so the height field is treated as a quadrilateral mesh. Section 9.2.1 discusses some techniques for turning these quadrilaterals into triangles.

However, there are other ways of rendering height fields. LaMothe [219] describes a technique in which the height field is rendered by contour following. The idea is first to find the closest point in the height field for each pixel at the bottom edge of the screen. From this closest point we derive the vertical column of pixels above it by walking the height field. This vertical column of pixels forms a plane that cuts through the height field. If we ignore the actual height component, the plane intersects the height field to form a straight line through the height-field texture. By walking along this line, we may retrieve the various terrain heights and colors. The height at each texel encountered is used to determine whether and how much to travel up the vertical screen column and shade with the color of the texel. This method renders the height field from front to back, touching each pixel only once. See Figure 6.27.

Height-field data can be thought of as a form of *voxel* representation. "Voxel" is short for "volumetric pixel," and each voxel represents a regular volume of space. For example, creating clinical diagnostic images (such as CT or MRI) of a person's head may create a data set of $256 \times 256 \times 256$ voxels, each location holding one or more values. Voxel rendering can be used to show a solid model, or to make various materials (e.g., the skin and skull) partially or fully transparent. Cutting planes can be used to show only parts of the model.

There are a wide variety of voxel rendering techniques. Lacroute and Levoy [217] present a method of treating the voxel data as a set of two-dimensional image slices, then shearing and warping these and compositing the resulting images. A method that renders a surface or volume in a significantly different fashion is that of *splatting* [224, 372]. Each voxel is treated as a volume of space that is represented by an alpha-blended circular object that drops off in

Figure 6.27. A height field rendered using a voxel-based approach *(from a program by André LaMothe.)*

opacity at its fringe. The idea is that a surface or volume can be represented by screen-aligned geometry or sprites which, when rendered together, form a surface. Implicit surface techniques that form polygonal surfaces from voxel samples are also commonly used [46].

Another method makes direct use of the texturing and compositing capabilities of graphics hardware by rendering slices directly as textured quadrilaterals [245]. OpenGL Volumizer is an API for volume rendering which implements some of its rendering styles using this technique, depending on the hardware platform and desired appearance [278]. In Volumizer the data representation is isolated from the implementation details of the renderer. The library renders volumetric tetrahedra, with their appearance described by the state and attributes associated with these volumetric primitives. The tetrahedra are the exact volumetric analogs of triangles in the more familiar surface-based methods for three-dimensional graphics. See Figure 6.28.

Further Reading and Resources

For a good overview of image-based rendering research, see Lengyel's article [229], also available on the web.

Coelho and Hawash [58] use sprite display and heavily optimize it on various processors (MMX, Pentium II) using DirectX and other methods.

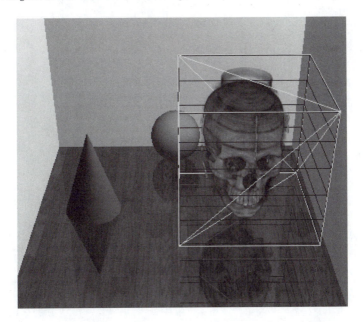

Figure 6.28. Volume visualization mixed with traditional three-dimensional techniques, done with OpenGL Volumizer. Note the reflection of the voxel-based skull in the floor. *(Courtesy of Robert Grzeszczuk, SGI.)*

A primary source used in this chapter is the SIGGRAPH Advanced OpenGL course notes [245]. Various journal articles present new algorithms, but these course notes deal with the nitty-gritty details of actually making those algorithms work.

This book's website at `http://www.realtimerendering.com/` has pointers to a number of worthwhile tutorials, demonstration programs, and code related to special effects.

Chapter 7
Speed-Up Techniques

"Now here, you see, it takes all the running you can do to keep in the same place. If you want to get somewhere else, you must run at least twice as fast as that!"
 —Lewis Carroll

One of the great myths concerning computers is that one day we will have enough processing power. Even in a relatively simple application like word processing, we find that additional power can be applied to all sorts of things, such as on-the-fly spell and grammar checking, more elaborate graphic presentation, antialiased text display, automated voice recognition and dictation, etc.

In real-time rendering we have at least three performance goals: more frames per second, higher resolution, and more (and more realistic) objects in the scene. A speed of 60–72 frames per second is generally considered enough, and perhaps 1600×1200 is enough resolution for a while, but there is no real upper limit on scene complexity. The rendering of a Boeing-777 would include $132,500$ unique parts and over $3,000,000$ fasteners, which would yield a polygonal model with over $500,000,000$ polygons [71]. Our conclusion: speed-up techniques and acceleration schemes will always be needed.

In this chapter, a smörgåsbord of algorithms for speeding up computer graphics rendering will be presented and explained. We start with *culling techniques*, followed by *impostor algorithms* and *level-of-detail techniques*. Finally, *triangle fan, strip,* and *polygon mesh techniques* are discussed.

7.1 Culling Techniques

To *cull* can mean to "select from a flock," and in the context of computer graphics this is exactly what *culling techniques* do. The flock is the whole scene that we want to render, and the selection is limited to those portions of the scene that are not considered to contribute to the final image. The rest of the scene is sent through the rendering pipeline. The actual culling can theoretically take place at any stage of the rendering pipeline. For culling algorithms that are implemented in hardware, we can typically only enable/disable or set some parameters for the culling function. For full control, the programmer can implement the algorithm in the application stage (on the CPU). Culling is often achieved by using geometric calculations but is in no way limited to these. For example, an algorithm may also use the contents of the frame buffer.

In this section we treat backface and clustered culling, hierarchical view-frustum culling, portal culling, detail culling, and occlusion culling.

7.1.1 Backface and Clustered Culling

Imagine that you are looking at an opaque sphere—approximately half of the sphere will not be visible.[1] The obvious conclusion from this observation is that what is invisible need not be rendered since it does not contribute to the image.

All *back-facing* polygons that are part of an opaque object can be culled away from further processing. A consistently oriented polygon (see Section 9.3) is back-facing if the projected polygon is oriented in, say, a counter-clockwise fashion in screen space. This test can be implemented by computing the normal of the projected polygon in two-dimensional screen space: $\mathbf{n} = (\mathbf{v}_1 - \mathbf{v}_0) \times (\mathbf{v}_2 - \mathbf{v}_0)$. This normal will either be $(0, 0, a)$ or $(0, 0, -a)$, where $a > 0$. If the negative z-axis is pointing into the screen, the first result indicates a front-facing polygon. This test can also be formulated as a computation of the signed area of the polygon (see Section A.5.4). Either culling method can be implemented immediately after the screen-mapping procedure has taken place (in the geometry stage). Culling decreases the load on the rasterizer since we do not have to scan convert the back-facing polygons. But the load on the geometry stage increases because the backface computations are done there.

Another way to determine whether a polygon is back-facing is the following. Create a vector from an arbitrary point on the plane in which the polygon lies (one of the vertices is the simplest choice) to the viewer's position[2]. Compute the dot product of this vector and the polygon's normal. A negative dot product means that the angle between the two vectors is greater than $\pi/2$ radians, so the polygon is not facing the viewer. This test can be performed after the view transform (into eye space) has taken place, which is a bit earlier in the geometry

---

[1]For orthographic viewing about 50% is not visible. For perspective viewing the percentage of backfaces increases to more than 50% as the viewer moves closer to the object.

[2]For orthographic projections, the vector to the eye position is replaced with the negative view direction, which is constant for the scene.

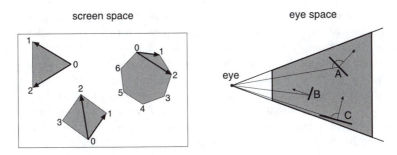

Figure 7.1. Two different tests for determining whether a polygon is back-facing. The left figure shows how the test is done in screen space. The triangle and the quadrilateral are front-facing, while the seven-sided polygon is back-facing and can be omitted from rasterization. The right figure shows how the backface test is done in eye space. Polygon A is back-facing, while B and C are front-facing.

stage than with the other method. Both of these culling techniques are illustrated in Figure 7.1.

In the article "Backface Culling Snags" [43], Blinn points out that these two tests are geometrically the same. Both compute the dot product between the normal and the vector from a point on the polygon to the eye. In the test that is done in screen space, the eye has been transformed to $(0, 0, \infty)$, and the dot product is thus only the z-component of the polygon vector in screen-space. In theory, what differentiates these tests is the space where the tests are computed—nothing else. In practice, the screen space test is often safer, because edge-on polygons that appear to face slightly forward in eye space can become slightly backward in screen-space. This happens because the eye-space coordinates get rounded off to screen-space integer pixel or subpixel coordinates.

Backface culling is normally controlled with a few functions that either enable backface or frontface culling or disable all culling. Note also that the objects need not be closed (solid) in order to take advantage of backface culling. It suffices to know that only one side of a polygon will be seen. This is often the case for buildings, where wall polygons are visible only from one side. Also, be aware that a mirroring transform (i.e., a negative scaling operation) turns back-facing polygons into front-facing ones and vice versa [43] (see Section 3.1.3).

While backface culling is a simple technique for avoiding the rasterizing of many polygons without due cause, it would be even faster if the CPU could decide with a single test if a whole set of polygons should be sent through the entire pipeline or not. Such techniques are called *clustered culling* algorithms. Hoff [185] presents a method for static models in which the space of the normals of an object is divided into small frustums which are called clusters. The frustums emanate from the center of a cube and extend to uniformly subdivided squares on the sides of the cube. In a preprocessing stage each polygon is put into the cluster where its normal lies. Thus each cluster holds a set of polygons with similar normals. When a frame is rendered, the clusters that are back-facing for a certain object are first determined. These are then used to select the clusters of polygons that should be rendered. Standard backface culling can eliminate the rasterization step for back-facing polygons, but this takes place rather late in the pipeline. The clustered culling approach is normally imple-mented in the application stage and thus avoids sending primitives through the pipeline early on.

Kumar et al. [216] take another approach whereby they partition the polygons into a set of clusters, and then hierarchically reorganize each cluster into a tree of subclusters. Each cluster is then divided into a FrontRegion, a BackRegion, and a MixedRegion. The FrontRegion and BackRegion are defined by the intersection of the halfplanes of the polygons in these regions. If the viewer is in the FrontRegion (BackRegion) of a cluster, then all polygons in that cluster (that is, all the polygons in the subtree of that cluster) are front-facing (back-facing). Otherwise, the polygons may be facing either way. At run time, the tree is traversed for each cluster, and the traversal may be pruned when all polygons in a (sub)cluster can be determined to be either front-facing or back-facing, or when a leaf has been reached. This scheme also exploits frame-to-frame coherency in order to track the region where the viewer lies.

A generalization of clustered culling from polygons to spline surfaces, called *backpatch culling*, has been presented by Kumar and Manocha [215]. A different approach to clustered culling is taken by Carter and Johannsen [52].

7.1.2   Hierarchical View-Frustum Culling

A *bounding volume* (BV) is a volume that encloses a set of objects. A BV does not contribute visually to the rendered image; instead it is usually used to speed up computations and rendering, as we will see. Moreover, for a complex scene, BVs are often organized in a bounding volume hierarchy. The essential data structure that is used to hold this hierarchy is often a *directed acyclic graph* (DAG) [68], which is a kind of tree. The term *acyclic* means that it must not contain any loops or cycles. By *directed*, we mean that as two nodes are connected by an edge, they are also connected in a certain order, e.g., from parent to child. A DAG has a *root*, the topmost node which has no parent, *internal nodes*, which have children (the root is usually an internal node), and *leaves*, which have no children. A leaf holds actual geometry to be rendered. An internal

Plate I. Castle model, viewable in real time, containing 40,760 polygons. The lighting is precomputed using radiosity, with the larger surfaces' lighting contributions captured as light-map textures. The floor reflection is created by mirroring polygons through the floor's plane and blending them with the floor polygon. The chandelier and some other elements are replaced with sets of textured polygons. *(Courtesy of Agata and Andrzej Wojaczek (agand@clo.com), Advanced Graphics Applications Inc.)*

Plate II. Car with shadows, reflections in the water puddle, and environment mapping. *(Car model is reused courtesy of Nya Perspektiv Design AB.)*

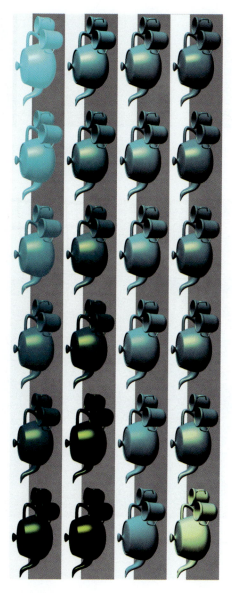

Plate III. Tea for two. If you hold the book sideways, the first row varies the ambient contribution, the second varies diffuse, the third varies specular, and the fourth varies shininess. *(Tea cup model is reused courtesy of Joachim Helenklaken.)*

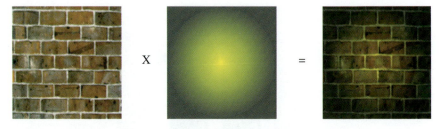

Plate IV. Light mapping. The wall texture on the left is multiplied by the light map in the middle to yield the texture on the right. *(Courtesy of J.L. Mitchell, M. Tatro, and I. Bullard.)*

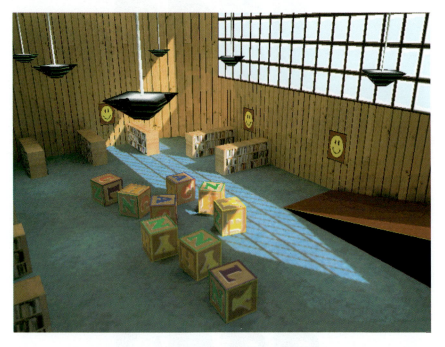

Plate V. High-resolution light maps yield sharp, detailed illumination effects. *(Courtesy of Brian Yen, Any Channel Inc.)*

Plate VI. Specular highlighting. Per-vertex specular is shown on the left, environment mapping of just the lights in the middle, and environment mapping of the entire surrounding scene on the right. *(Courtesy of J.L. Mitchell, M. Tatro, and I. Bullard.)*

Plate VII. A typical image texture used for spherical environment mapping. *(Courtesy of Paul Haeberli, SGI.)*

Plate VIII. High-resolution terrain mapping accessing a huge image database. Rendered with clipmapping to reduce the amount of data needed at one time. *(Courtesy of Aechelon Technology, Inc., 1999. C-Nova/C-Radiant Image Generator by Aechelon Technology Inc., based on SGI hardware.)*

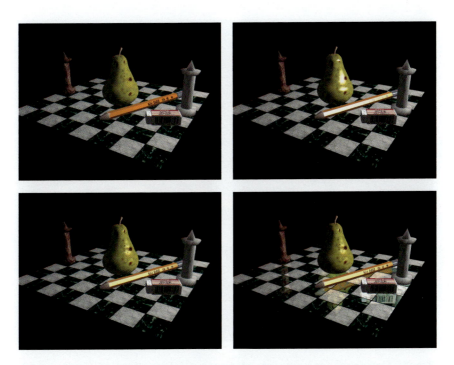

Plate IX. Upper left: diffuse textured objects. Upper right: adding a specular environment map. Lower left: adding a gloss texture to modulate the specular reflection. Lower right: adding planar reflection. *(Courtesy of J.L. Mitchell and E. Hart, ATI Technologies Inc.)*

Plate X. Shadows and fogged reflections. Shadows are added using Hourcade's algorithm, and the reflections are diminished using fog as their distance from the plane increases. *(Courtesy of J.L. Mitchell and E. Hart, ATI Technologies Inc.)*

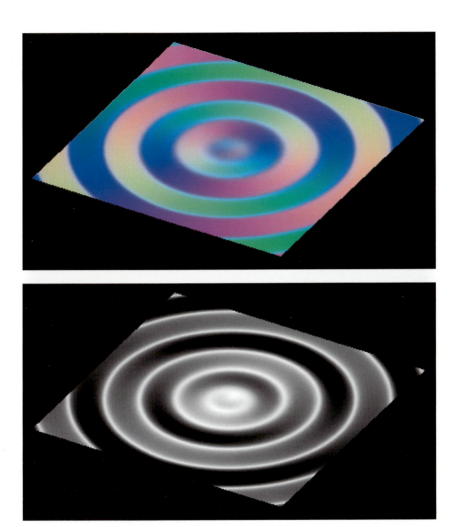

Plate XI. Bump mapping with a normal map. At the top is the surface normal map. Each color channel is actually a surface normal coordinate. The red channel is the x-coordinate, with the x-axis going from upper left to right across the surface. Green is y, and blue is z, with the plane facing up along the $+z$-axis. Each color [0,255] maps to a normal coordinate [-1,1]. At the bottom is the image produced using the normal map. *(Example pictures generated by software. Courtesy of NVIDIA Inc.)*

Plates XII. Environment-mapped bump mapping is used to make the water reflect the sky and the forest. In the foreground a sprite flies by and generates alpha-blended billboarded sprites. *(Courtesy of Digital Illusions and Matrox Graphics Inc.)*

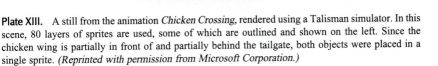

Plate XIII. A still from the animation *Chicken Crossing,* rendered using a Talisman simulator. In this scene, 80 layers of sprites are used, some of which are outlined and shown on the left. Since the chicken wing is partially in front of and partially behind the tailgate, both objects were placed in a single sprite. *(Reprinted with permission from Microsoft Corporation.)*

Plate XIV. Various glare effects, making it clear that it is nighttime. *(Courtesy of Digital Illusions CE AB.)*

Plate XV. Special effects from "Shogo: Mobile Armored Division." Screen-aligned billboarding with alpha-blended textures gives the explosion trails and smoke. The animated fire textured onto a polygon provides realism. A transparent sphere shows a shock wave effect. *(Courtesy of Monolith Productions Inc.)*

Plate XVI. Motion blur created using the accumulation buffer.

Plate XVII. Fuzzy reflections and refractions, created by using the accumulation and stencil buffers along with fog. Window design by Elsa Schmid. *(Courtesy of Paul Diefenbach.)*

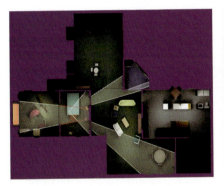

Plate XVIII. Portal culling. The left image is an overhead view of the Brooks House. The right image is a view from the master bedroom. Cull boxes for portals are in white and those for mirrors are in red. *(Courtesy of David Luebke and Chris George, UNC-Chapel Hill.)*

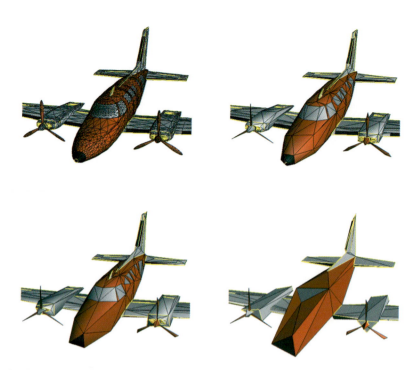

Plate XIX. Mesh simplification. Upper left shows the original mesh of 13,546 faces, upper right is simplified to 1,000 faces, lower left to 500 faces, lower right to 150 faces. *(Courtesy of Hugues Hoppe, Microsoft Research.)*

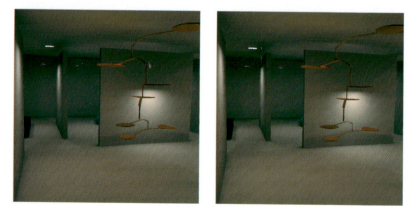

Plate XX. Simplification of radiosity solution. Left is a rendering of the original mesh (150,983 faces), right is the simplified mesh (10,000 faces). *(Courtesy of Hugues Hoppe, Microsoft Research.)*

node stores pointers to its children and possibly a transform that is applied to all its children. Both leaves and internal nodes can be enclosed by BVs. The most common BVs are spheres, axis-aligned bounding boxes (AABBs), and oriented bounding boxes (OBBs). These are described in more detail in Chapter 10. In the context of computer graphics, this hierarchy is often called a *scene graph*. An example of a scene graph is shown in Figure 7.2.

As seen in Section 2.3.4, only primitives that are totally or partially inside the view frustum need to be rendered. One way to speed up the rendering process is to compare the BV of each object to the view frustum. If the BV is outside the frustum, then the geometry it encloses can be omitted from rendering. Since these computations are done within the CPU, this means that the geometry inside the BV does not need to go through the geometry and the rasterizer stages in the pipeline. If instead the BV is inside or intersecting the frustum, then the contents of that BV may be visible and must be sent through the rendering pipeline. See Section 10.11 for methods of testing for intersection between various bounding volumes and the view frustum.

When a scene graph is available, this kind of culling can be applied hierarchically [56] with a pre-order traversal [68] from the root of the scene graph. Each node with a BV is tested against the frustum. If the BV of any type of node is outside the frustum, then that node is not processed further. The tree is pruned, since the BV's subtree is outside the view.

If the BV intersects the frustum, then traversal continues and its children are tested. When a leaf node is found to intersect, its contents (i.e., its geometry)

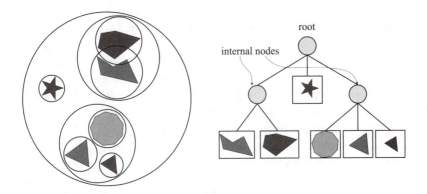

Figure 7.2. The left part shows a simple scene with six objects, each enclosed by a bounding sphere. The bounding spheres are then grouped together into larger bounding spheres until all objects are enclosed by the largest sphere. The right part shows the scene graph that is used to represent the object hierarchy on the left. The BV of the root encloses all objects in the scene.

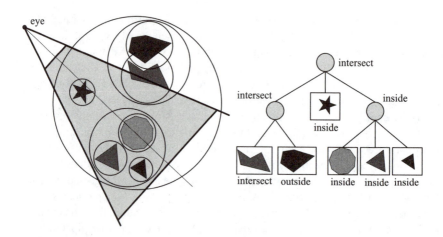

Figure 7.3. A set of geometry and its bounding volumes (spheres) are shown on the left. This scene is rendered with view-frustum culling from the point of the eye. The scene graph is shown on the right. The BV of the root intersects the frustum, and the traversal continues with testing its children's BVs. The BV of the left subtree intersects, and one of that subtree's children intersects (and thus is rendered), and the BV of the other child is outside and therefore is not sent through the pipeline. The BV of the middle subtree of the root is totally inside and is rendered immediately. The BV of the right subtree of the root is also fully inside, and the entire subtree can therefore be rendered without further tests.

is sent through the pipeline. The primitives of the leaf are not guaranteed to be inside the view frustum. Clipping (see Section 2.3.4) takes care of ensuring that only primitives inside the view frustum are being rendered.

If the BV is fully inside the frustum, its contents must all be inside the frustum. Traversal continues, but no further frustum testing is needed for the rest of such a subtree. A leaf node that is fully inside the frustum can be rendered with clipping turned off, which sometimes improves performance. An example of view-frustum culling is shown in Figure 7.3.

View-frustum culling operates in the application stage (CPU), which means that both the geometry and the rasterizer stages can benefit enormously. For large scenes or certain camera views, only a fraction of the scene might be visible, and it is only this fraction that needs to be sent through the rendering pipeline. View-frustum culling techniques exploit the spatial coherence in a scene, since objects which are located near each other can be enclosed in a BV, and nearby BVs may be clustered hierarchically. In such cases a large gain in speed can be expected. Recall also that clipping can be disabled for the BVs (and objects inside them) that are totally inside the frustum. Furthermore, if a BV intersects the frustum, then clipping can be disabled for those other frustum sides which the BV is fully inside [35]. The gains from this scheme will only appear if the underlying hardware or software supports it.

Most scene-graph-based APIs such as Direct3D retained mode [83], IRIS Performer [93, 301], and Cosmo3D [69] have view-frustum culling operating as a default. Software such as Optimizer [277] and Fahrenheit [103] include the idea of *spatialization*, in which the user's scene graph is augmented with a separate scene graph created for faster culling and picking. The leaf nodes, where most object data is located, are shared, so the expense of an additional set of internal nodes is minimal.

View-frustum culling can also be used to cull away other things than bounding volumes. For example, portals that are outside the view frustum can also be culled. Portal culling is treated in Section 7.1.3.

Other approaches that are used for view-frustum culling include octrees (see page 206) and binary space partitioning (BSP) trees [307]. These methods are not flexible enough when it comes to rendering dynamic scenes. That is, it takes too long to update the corresponding data structures when an object stored in the structure moves. But for static scenes these methods can perform better.

BSP trees have two noticeably different variants in computer graphics, which we call axis-aligned and polygon-aligned. An axis-aligned BSP tree is created as follows. A set of objects is bound by an axis-aligned bounding box (AABB). One axis of the box is chosen, and a perpendicular plane is generated that divides the set into two subsets. Some schemes fix this partitioning plane so that it divides the box exactly in half; others allow the plane to vary in position. Objects intersecting the plane either are stored at this level, become members of both subsets, or are truly split by the plane into two separate objects.[3] Each subset is now in a smaller box, and this plane splitting procedure is repeated, subdividing each AABB recursively until some criterion is fulfilled to halt the process. See Figure 7.4. The bounding boxes formed can be used in view-frustum culling; if a box is outside the frustum, its contents can be ignored.

However, there is another common type of BSP tree, the polygon-aligned form [1, 110, 111, 133]. In this scheme, a polygon is chosen as the divider, splitting space into two halves. That is, at the root a polygon is selected. The plane in which the polygon lies is used to divide the rest of the polygons in the scene into two sets. Any polygon that is intersected by the dividing plane is broken into two separate pieces along the intersection line. Now in each half-space of the dividing plane another polygon is chosen as a divider, which divides only the polygons in its half-space. This is done recursively until all

---

[3]BSP trees that use object splitting have similar properties to the polygon-plane BSP tree described in the next paragraph.

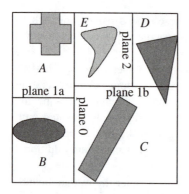
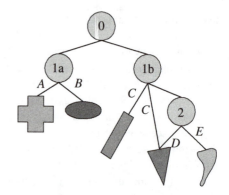

Figure 7.4. Axis-aligned BSP tree. In this example, the space partitions are allowed to be anywhere along the axis, not just at its midpoint. The spatial volumes formed are labeled A through E. In the tree on the right, note that the triangle is placed inside two boxes, C and D, because it overlaps both.

polygons are in the BSP tree. Creating an efficient polygon-aligned BSP tree is a time-consuming process, and such trees are normally computed once and stored for reuse. This type of BSP tree is shown in Figure 7.5.

This second type of BSP tree has some useful properties. One is that, for a given view, the structure can be traversed from back to front. Determine on which side of the root plane the camera is located (a simple point/plane comparison). The polygon set on the far side of this plane is then beyond the near side's set. Now with the far side's set, take the next level's dividing plane and determine

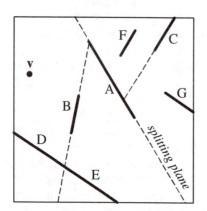
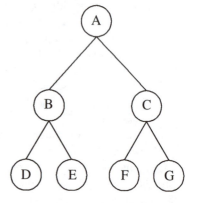

Figure 7.5. Polygon-aligned BSP tree. Polygons A through G are shown from above. Space is first split by polygon A, then each half-space is split separately by B and C. The splitting plane formed by polygon B intersects the polygon in the lower left corner, splitting it into separate polygons D and E. The BSP tree formed is shown on the right.

which side the camera is on. This subset is again beyond the nearer subset. By continuing recursively, this process establishes a strict back-to-front order, and a *painter's algorithm* can be used to render the scene. The painter's algorithm does not need a Z-buffer; if all objects are drawn in a back-to-front order, each closer object is drawn in front of whatever is behind it, and so no z-depth comparisons are required.

For example, consider what is seen by a viewer v in Figure 7.5. Regardless of the viewing direction and frustum, v is to the left of the splitting plane formed by A. So C, F, and G are further away than B, D, and E. Comparing v to the splitting plane of C, we find G to be on the opposite side of this plane, so it is displayed first. A test of B's plane determines that E should be displayed before D. The back-to-front order is then G, C, F, A, E, B, D.

Front-to-back rendering can be used to increase display speed. The basic idea here is that when a pixel is covered by a primitive, that pixel never needs to be drawn again. However, it saves no time to test each pixel to see if it has already been rendered. Instead, speed is gained by efficiently keeping track of which *pixel spans* have been rendered. A pixel span is a set of pixels drawn next to each other in a row. As each span is generated, it is tested against previously drawn spans. If visible, it is rendered and its extents are added to and merged with this set of visible spans. Gordon and Chen [133] describe this process in detail, and show how performance is increased by a factor of two to four or more.

Both types of BSP trees are sometimes referred to as k-d trees [307]. The k refers to the number of dimensions being subdivided. So a k-d tree with $k=2$ means that two dimensions are divided by splitting planes. A third dimension can exist, but the tree structure does not use or subdivide the third axis. With $k=3$, a splitting plane can affect any axis in three dimensions.

To return to view-frustum culling, BSP trees are simple to use for this operation. If the box containing the scene is visible, then the root node's splitting plane is tested. If the plane intersects the frustum (i.e., if two corners on the frustum are found to be on opposite sides of the plane, see Section 10.7), then both branches of the BSP tree are traversed. However, if the view-frustum is fully on one side of the plane, then whatever is on the other side of the plane is culled from the scene.

For view-frustum culling there is a simple technique for exploiting frame-to-frame coherency.[4] If a BV is found to be outside a certain plane of the frustum in one frame, then (assuming that the viewer does not move too quickly) it will probably be outside that plane the next frame too. So if a BV was outside a certain plane, then an index to this plane is stored (cached) with the BV. In the

---

[4]This is also called temporal coherency.

next frame in which this BV is encountered during traversal, the cached plane is tested first, and on average a speed-up can be expected [18].

If the viewer is constrained only to rotation around one axis (at a time) or to translation, which is quite common in some games, then this can also be exploited for faster frustum culling. When a BV is found to be outside a plane of the frustum, then the distance from that plane to the BV is stored with the BV. Now, if the BV only, say, translates, then the distance to the BV can be updated quickly by knowing how much the viewer has translated. This can provide a generous speed-up in comparison to a naive view-frustum culler [18].

7.1.3 Portal Culling

For architectural models, there is a set of algorithms that go under the name of *portal culling*. The first of these were introduced by Airey [2, 3] in 1990. The rationale for all portal-culling algorithms is that walls often act as large occluders in such cases. Such occluders can be exploited in a variety of ways to find the *potentially visible set* (PVS) for a set of viewpoints. A PVS is created by taking the entire scene to be rendered from a given set of viewpoints and then excluding those parts of the scene that in some way are determined *not* to contribute to the final image. This means that an algorithm discards some of the geometry in the scene that is guaranteed not to be visible. Portal culling is similar to frustum culling in that the workload for the geometry and the rasterizer stages may be decreased by using these algorithms.

Portal-culling methods preprocess the scene in some way, either automatically or by hand. The scene is divided into *cells* which usually correspond to rooms and hallways in a building. The doors and windows that connects adjacent rooms are called *portals*. Every object in a cell and the walls of the cell are stored in a data structure that is associated with the cell. In this structure we also store information on adjacent cells and the portals that connect them.

Airey et al. [2, 3] impose a BSP tree on the scene, and align the partitioning planes of the tree with the walls. This structure gives the set of cells. They then use two different techniques, one based on point sampling and the other on shadow volumes [72], to compute the PVS for each cell. Point sampling is not dependable, however, and shadow volumes can overestimate the PVS for a cell, thereby causing a loss of efficiency.

Teller and Séquin [349] present a portal and cell culling method for the two-dimensional case, which was later extended by Teller in his Ph.D. thesis [350]. One of their contributions was to create algorithms for determining smaller, more efficient PVSs. Their algorithm starts with a preprocessing phase in which the scene is subdivided into cells, and portals are identified. This structure is stored in an axis-aligned BSP tree, and the occluders and portals are in this case limited to being axis-aligned rectangles (which architectural models normally have, in the form of walls, floors, and ceilings).

Next, a data structure is built that stores the *cell-to-cell visibility*. If a straight line (sightline) can be found starting from one point in a cell and ending at one point in another cell without intersecting any geometry, then those cells are visible from each other. Cell-to-object visibility is computed for each object in each cell. If there is a sightline from a cell to an object in another cell, then the object is visible from the cell. The preprocessing can take several hours for this method, and it is thus only applicable to static scenes.

The rendering of a scene, preprocessed using this algorithm, starts by locating the cell where the viewer is located. Then the cells which the viewer can see from that position are identified (eye-to-cell visibility), followed by identification of potentially visible objects in the visible cells (cell-to-object visibility). After this step, the identified portions of the scene are rendered by culling against the view frustum.

For a densely occluded architectural scene, this algorithm was able to cull away about 99% of the geometry with a speed-up of over 100 times. For details on this algorithm, consult Teller's Ph.D. thesis [350].

Luebke and Georges [238] use a simple method which requires only a small amount of preprocessing. The only information that is needed is the data structure associated with each cell, as described above. Rendering such a scene is accomplished through the following steps:

1. Locate the cell V, where the viewer (eye) is positioned.

2. Initialize a two-dimensional bounding box P to the rectangle of the screen.

3. Render the geometry of the cell V with view-frustum culling on for the frustum that emanates from the viewer and goes through the rectangle P (initially the whole screen).

4. Recurse on portals of the cells neighboring V. For each portal of the current cell, project the portal onto the screen and find the two-dimensional axis-aligned bounding box (BB) of that projection. Compute the intersection of P and the BB of the portal (which is done with a few comparisons).

5. For each intersection: if it is empty, then the cell that is connected via that portal is invisible from the current point of view, and that cell can be omitted from further processing. If the intersection is non-empty, then

the contents of that neighbor cell can be culled against the frustum that emanates from the viewer and goes though the (rectangular) intersection.

6. If the intersection was non-empty, then the neighboring cells of that neighbor may be visible and so we recurse to Step 3 with P being the intersection BB. Each object may be tagged when it has been rendered in order to avoid rendering objects more than once.

This algorithm can be seen as a refinement process of view-frustum culling, where the frustum is diminished with each visible portal. Portals that are outside the view frustum are discarded. This is illustrated in Figure 7.6 with an example. The viewer or eye is located in cell E and therefore rendered together with its contents. The neighboring cells are C, D, and F. The original frustum cannot see the portals to cells C and D and are therefore omitted from further processing. Cell F is visible, and the view frustum is therefore diminished so that it goes through the portal that connects to F. The contents of F are then rendered with that diminished frustum. Then, the neighboring cells of F are examined—G is not visible from the diminished frustum and so is omitted, while H is visible. Again the frustum is diminished with the portal of H, and thereafter the contents of H are rendered. H does not have any neighbors that have not been visited, and the rendering is complete.

See Plate XVIII (following p. 194) for another view of the use of portals. This form of portal culling can also be used to trim content for planar reflections (see Section 6.5). The left image of the plate shows a building viewed from the top; the white lines indicate the way in which the frustum is diminished with each

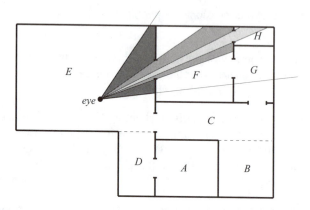

Figure 7.6. Portal culling: cells are enumerated from A to H, and portals are openings that connect the cells. Only geometry seen through the portals is rendered.

portal. The red lines are created by reflecting the frustum at a mirror. The actual view is shown in the image on the right side of the same plate, where the white rectangles are the portals and the mirror is red. Note that it is only the objects inside any of the frustums that are rendered. This method has been implemented for the Nintendo 64 and in IRIS Performer.

There are many other uses for portals [356]. For example, a different rendering engine (with different rendering modes, etc.) can be used when a portal is traversed. This means that one rendering mode may be used in the current cell, but when another cell is visible through a portal, a different mode may be used for the contents of the cell seen through the portal. Mirror reflections can be created by transforming the viewer when the contents of a cell seen through a portal are about to be rendered. That is, if the viewer looks at a portal, then the viewer's position and direction can be reflected in the plane of that portal (see Section 6.5.1). Other transformations can be used to create other effects, such as simple refractions. Portals can also be "one-way." For example, assume that you walk from cell A to cell B through a portal. If the portal is one-way, then we cannot go back from B to A—instead we may turn around and see another cell C. This is perfectly suited for creating a difficult maze [356].

7.1.4 Detail Culling

Detail culling is a technique that sacrifices quality for speed. The rationale for detail culling is that small details in the scene contribute little or nothing to the rendered images when the viewer is in motion. When the viewer stops, detail culling is usually disabled. Consider an object with a bounding volume, and project this BV onto the projection plane. The area of the projection is then estimated in pixels, and if the number of pixels is below a user-defined threshold, the object is omitted from further processing. For this reason, detail culling is sometimes called *screen-size culling* [84]. Detail culling can also be done hierarchically on a scene graph. The geometry and rasterizer stages both gain from this algorithm.

Here we will show how the number of pixels can be estimated for spheres with perspective viewing. The estimation is based on the fact that the size of the projection of an object diminishes with the distance from the viewer along the view direction. This is shown in Figure 7.7, which illustrates how the size of the projection is halved if the distance from the viewer is doubled.

We define a sphere by its center point $\mathbf{c}$ and a radius r. The viewer is located at $\mathbf{v}$ looking along the normalized direction vector $\mathbf{d}$. The distance from the view direction is simply the projection of the sphere's center onto the view vector: $\mathbf{d} \cdot (\mathbf{c} - \mathbf{v})$. We also assume that the distance from the viewer to the

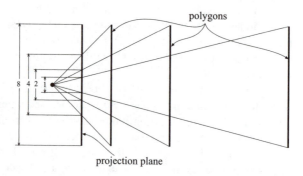

Figure 7.7. This illustration shows how the size of the projection of objects is halved when the distance is doubled.

near plane of the view frustum is n. The near plane is used in the estimation so that an object that is located on the near plane returns its original size. The estimation of the radius of the projected sphere is then:

$$p = \frac{nr}{\mathbf{d} \cdot (\mathbf{c} - \mathbf{v})} \tag{7.1}$$

The area of the projection is then πp^2. The user typically defines a value (say two pixels) that represents a threshold for the maximum size of a projected object that will be discarded by detail culling. The estimated area is then compared to this threshold. If it is smaller, then the object inside the bounding volume is not considered to contribute to the image and thus is not rendered; otherwise it is rendered.

7.1.5 Occlusion Culling

As we have seen, visibility may be solved via a hardware construction called the Z-buffer (see Section 2.4). Even though it may solve visibility correctly, the Z-buffer is not a very smart mechanism in all respects. For example, it has the following implications. Imagine that the viewer is looking along a line where 10 spheres are placed. This is illustrated in Figure 7.8. An image rendered from this viewpoint will show but one sphere, even though all 10 spheres will be scan-converted and compared to the Z-buffer and then potentially written to the color buffer and Z-buffer. The simple conclusion in this case is that nine spheres will be drawn unnecessarily. This uninteresting scene is not that likely

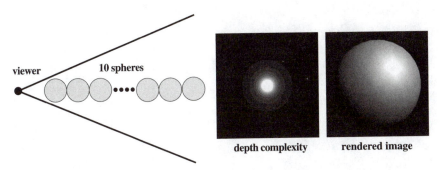

Figure 7.8. An illustration of how occlusion culling can be useful. Ten spheres are placed in a line, and the viewer is looking along this line (left). The depth complexity image in the middle shows that some pixels are written to several times, even though the final image (on the right) only shows one sphere.

to be found in reality, but it describes (from its viewpoint) a densely populated model. These sorts of configurations are found in such real scenes as a rain forest, an engine, a city, and the inside of a skyscraper.

Thus it seems plausible that an algorithmic approach to avoid this kind of inefficiency may pay off in terms of speed. Such approaches go under the name of *occlusion culling algorithms*, since they try to cull away (avoid drawing) objects that are occluded, that is, inside the view frustum but not visible in the final image. The optimal occlusion culling algorithm would select only the objects that are visible. In a sense, the Z-buffer selects and renders only those objects which are visible, but not before all objects are sent through the pipeline. The idea behind efficient occlusion culling algorithms is to perform some simple tests early on and so avoid sending data through much of the pipeline.

Pseudocode for a general occlusion culling algorithm is shown in Figure 7.9, where the function isOccluded, often called the *visibility test*, checks whether an object is occluded. G is the set of geometrical objects to be rendered; O_R is the occlusion representation. Depending on the particular algorithm, O_R represents some kind of occlusion information. O_R is set to be empty at the beginning. After that all objects (which passed the view-frustum culling test) are processed.

Consider a particular object. First we test whether the object is occluded with respect to the occlusion representation O_R. If it is occluded, then it is not processed further, since we then know that it will not contribute to the image. If the object is determined not to be occluded, then that object has to be rendered, since it probably contributes to the image (at that point in the rendering). Finally O_R is updated with that object.

```
1:    OcclusionCullingAlgorithm(G)
2:    O_R =empty
3:    for each object g ∈ G
4:        if(isOccluded(g,O_R))
5:            Skip(g)
6:        else
7:            Render(g)
8:            Update(O_R, g)
9:        end
10:   end
```

Figure 7.9. Pseudocode for a general occlusion culling algorithm. G contains all the objects in the scene, and O_R is the occlusion representation *(after Zhang [391])*.

For some algorithms, it is expensive to update the occlusion representation, so this is only done once (before the actual rendering starts) with the objects that are believed to be good occluders. This set is then updated from frame to frame.

A number of occlusion algorithms will be scrutinized in this section.

Hierarchical Z-Buffering and the Hierarchical Visibility Algorithm

One approach to occlusion culling is the *hierarchical visibility* (HV) algorithm [141]. This algorithm maintains the scene model in an octree, and a frame's Z-buffer as an image pyramid, which we call a Z-pyramid. The octree enables hierarchical culling of occluded regions of the scene, and the Z-pyramid enables hierarchical Z-buffering of individual primitives and bounding volumes. The Z-pyramid is thus the occlusion representation of this algorithm. Examples of these data structures are shown in Figure 7.10.

Any method can be employed for organizing scene primitives in an octree, although Greene et al. [141] recommend a specific algorithm that avoids assigning small primitives to large octree nodes. In general, an octree is constructed by enclosing the entire scene in a minimal axis-aligned box. The rest of the procedure is recursive in nature, and starts by checking whether the box contains fewer than a threshold number of primitives. If it does, the algorithm binds the primitives to the box and then terminates the recursion. Otherwise, it subdivides the box along its main axes using three planes, thereby forming eight boxes (hence the name octree). Each new box is tested and possibly subdivided again into $2 \times 2 \times 2$ smaller boxes. This process continues until each box contains fewer than the threshold number of primitives, or until the recursion has reached a specified deepest level [306, 307]. This is illustrated in two dimensions, where

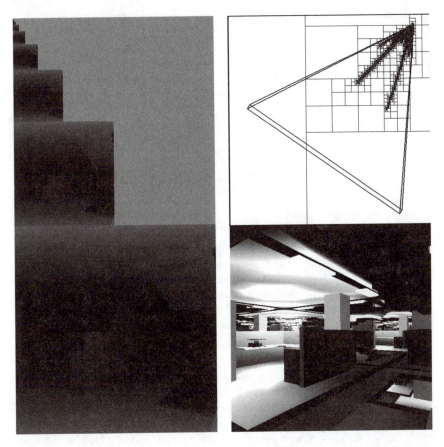

Figure 7.10. Example of occlusion culling with the hierarchical visibility algorithm [144], showing a complex scene (lower right) with the corresponding Z-pyramid (on the left), and octree subdivision (upper right). By traversing the octree from front to back and culling occluded octree nodes as they are encountered, this algorithm only visits visible octree nodes and their children (the nodes portrayed at the upper right) and only renders the polygons in visible boxes. In this example, culling of occluded octree nodes reduces the depth complexity of the polygons that need to be rendered from 84 to 2.5. *(Courtesy of Ned Greene/Apple Computer.)*

the data structure is called a *quadtree*, in Figure 7.11. The construction of an octree takes too much time to be done at runtime, so this method is best suited for static models.

Once the octree has been created, each frame is rendered in approximately front-to-back order by calling the procedure `ProcessOctreeNode` (outlined in Figure 7.12) with the root node of the octree. Octree nodes that are outside

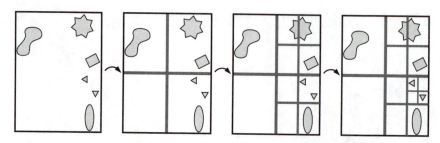

Figure 7.11. The construction of a quadtree (which is the two-dimensional version of an octree). The construction starts from the left by enclosing all objects in a bounding box. Then the boxes are recursively divided into four equal-sized boxes until each box (in this case) is empty or contains one object.

the view frustum are culled away. The first step determines whether the node's bounding box[5] is visible with respect to the Z-pyramid, using a procedure that will be described later. If the node is occluded, we do not need to process the contents of that box further, since its contents do not contribute to the final image. Otherwise, we render the primitives associated with the node into the Z-pyramid (tileInto in the pseudocode) and then process each of the node's children (if it has any) in front-to-back order using this same recursive procedure. When recursion finishes, all visible primitives have been *tiled* into the Z-pyramid, and a standard Z-buffer image of the scene has been created.

The HV algorithm performs occlusion culling very efficiently because it only traverses visible octree nodes and their children, and it only renders the primitives in visible nodes. This can save much of the work in scenes that are densely occluded. For example, in the scene pictured in Figure 7.10, more than 99% of on-screen polygons are inside occluded octree nodes, which are therefore culled by the Z-pyramid [144].

Now we will describe how the Z-pyramid is maintained and how it is used to accelerate culling. The finest (highest-resolution) level of the Z-pyramid is simply a standard Z-buffer. At all other levels, each z-value is the farthest z in the corresponding 2×2 window of the adjacent finer level. Therefore each z-value represents the farthest z for a square region of the screen. To maintain a Z-pyramid, whenever a z-value is overwritten in the Z-buffer it is propagated through the coarser levels of the Z-pyramid. This is done recursively until the top of the image pyramid is reached, where only one z-value remains (this is illustrated in Figure 7.13).

Next, we describe how hierarchical culling of octree nodes is done. To determine whether a node is visible, the front faces of its bounding box are tested

---

[5]In this case, a node's bounding box is a box in the octree.

```
1:    ProcessOctreeNode(OctreeNode N)
2:    if(isOccluded(N_BV, Z_P)) then return;
3:    for each primitive p ∈ N
4:        tileInto(p, Z_P)
5:    end
6:    for each child node C ∈ N in front-to-back order
7:        ProcessOctreeNode(C)
8:    end
```

Figure 7.12. Pseudocode for the hierarchical visibility algorithm. To render a frame this procedure is called with the root node of the octree. N_{BV} is the bounding volume of the octree node N, and Z_P is the Z-pyramid that is the occlusion representation of this algorithm. The operation tileInto renders a primitive p into the Z-pyramid, Z_P, and this also updates the entire Z-pyramid.

against the Z-pyramid. The node is occluded if all of its front faces are occluded by the Z-pyramid. To establish whether an individual face is occluded, we begin at the coarsest Z-pyramid cell that encloses the face's screen projection. The face's nearest depth within the cell (z_{near}) is then compared to the Z-pyramid value, and if z_{near} is farther, the face is known to be occluded. For densely occluded scenes, this procedure often culls an occluded face with a single depth comparison. When this initial test fails to cull a face, its visibility can be definitively established by recursively traversing from the initial Z-pyramid cell down to finer levels in the Z-pyramid. Additional depth comparisons at the encountered child cells must be performed. If this subdivision procedure does not ultimately find a visible sample on the face, the face is occluded. In scenes where the bounding boxes of octree nodes overlap deeply on the screen, this hierarchical procedure can establish visibility much more efficiently than can conventional Z-buffering. For example, in the scene pictured in Figure 7.10, hierarchical culling of octree nodes with the Z-pyramid generates roughly one hundred times fewer depth comparisons than visibility testing with conventional Z-buffering.

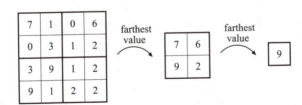

Figure 7.13. On the left, a 4×4 piece of the Z-buffer is shown. The numerical values are the actual z-values. This is downsampled to a 2×2 region where each value is the farthest (largest) of the four 2×2 regions on the left. Finally, the farthest value of the remaining four z-values is computed. These three maps compose an image pyramid which is called the hierarchical Z-buffer.

As we have seen, the original HV algorithm [141] used a Z-pyramid only for occlusion tests and employed traditional Z-buffer scan conversion to render the polygons in visible octree nodes. Subsequently, a more efficient method, called *hierarchical polygon tiling* [145], was developed. This algorithm adapts the basic screen subdivision procedure described above to polygon "tiling," that is, finding the visible samples on a polygon. When tiling a polygon into the Z-pyramid, it must be determined, at each level of subdivision where the polygon is compared to a Z-pyramid cell, whether the polygon overlaps the cell and if so, whether the polygon is occluded by the cell. Overlap tests are accelerated with coverage masks that indicate which subcells within a Z-pyramid cell are covered by the polygon, and occlusion tests are performed by comparing the polygon's nearest z-value within the cell to the Z-pyramid value. This procedure for hierarchical Z-buffering is very efficient, because it only traverses regions of the screen where a polygon is visible or nearly visible.

Hierarchical polygon tiling can be performed even more efficiently if the polygons in a scene are organized into a BSP tree (see page 197) or an "octree of BSP trees" [145]. The reason is that this enables traversing polygons in strict front-to-back order, which eliminates the need to maintain depth information. Rather, the only occlusion information required is whether or not each image sample has been written, and this information can be maintained in an image pyramid of coverage masks called a *coverage pyramid*. This is the data structure maintained by hierarchical polygon tiling with coverage masks [145], which is similar to hierarchical Z-buffering except that occlusion tests are performed with coverage-mask operations instead of depth comparisons, which accelerates tiling considerably.

The HV algorithm implemented with hierarchical tiling may well be the most efficient method known for software rendering of complex scenes composed of polygons, but it is not fast enough for real-time rendering of complex scenes on today's microprocessors. To enable real-time rendering, Greene et al. [141] suggest modifying hardware Z-buffer pipelines to support HV, which requires substituting a Z-pyramid for the Z-buffer, and including a fast feedback path to report visibility of bounding volumes. It is likely that these modifications would extend the domain of real-time rendering to much more complex scenes, such as the scene in Figure 7.10.

In the absence of this kind of hardware support, the HV algorithm can be accelerated on systems having conventional Z-buffer hardware by exploiting frame-to-frame coherency [141]. The idea is that octree nodes that were visible in one frame tend to be visible in the next. With this variation, the first frame of an animation sequence is generated with the standard HV algorithm, except that after completing the frame, a list of octree nodes that were visible in that frame (the visible node list) is created by testing nodes for visibility against the Z-pyramid. Subsequent frames are generated with the following two-pass algorithm. In the first rendering pass, primitives associated with nodes on the visible node list are rendered by Z-buffer hardware. Then, the Z-buffer of the partially rendered scene is read back from the hardware, and a Z-pyramid is built from this Z-buffer. In the second rendering pass, the standard HV algorithm is run in software, traversing the octree from front to back but skipping nodes which have already been rendered. This second pass fills in any missing parts of the scene. The final step in processing a frame is to update the visible node list. Typically, this variation of the HV algorithm runs considerably faster than the all-software version, because nearly all visible polygons are rendered with Z-buffer hardware.

Greene and Kass [143] have developed an extension to hierarchical Z-buffering which renders antialiased scenes with error bounds. Another interesting algorithm for occlusion culling is the visibility skeleton developed by Durand et al. [89, 90].

The HOM algorithm

The *hierarchical occlusion map* (HOM) algorithm [390] is another way of enabling hierarchical image-space culling (such as the hierarchical Z-buffering algorithm on page 206). However, the HOM algorithm can be used on systems that have graphics hardware but not a hardware Z-pyramid, and it can also handle dynamic scenes. The HOM algorithm is described in detail in Zhang's Ph.D. thesis [391].

We start by describing how the function isOccluded works. This function, used in the pseudocode in Figure 7.9, is a key part of the algorithm. This occlusion test takes place after the view transform (see Section 2.3.1), so the viewer is located at the origin looking down the negative z-axis, with the x-axis going to the right, and the y-axis going upwards. The test is then divided into two parts: a one-dimensional *depth test* in the z-direction and a two-dimensional *overlap test* in the xy plane, i.e., whereby the image gets projected. The overlap test supports approximate visibility culling, where objects that "shine through" small holes in the occluders can be culled away using an opacity threshold parameter.

For both tests, a set of potentially good occluders is identified before the scene is rendered, and the occlusion representation is built from these. This step is followed by the rendering of the scene, where the occluders are rendered without an occlusion test. Then the rest of the scene is processed by having each object tested against the occlusion representation. If the object occluded by the occluder representation, it is not rendered.

For the two-dimensional overlap test, the occluders are first rendered into the color buffer with a white color on a black background. Therefore, texturing, lighting, and Z-buffering can be turned off. An advantage of this operation is that a number of small occluders can be combined into a large occluder. The rendered image, which is called an *occlusion map*, is read back into the main memory of the computer. For simplicity, we assume that this image has the resolution of $2^n \times 2^n$ pixels. It is used as the base for the occlusion representation. Then a *hierarchy of occlusion maps* (HOM), i.e., an image pyramid of occlusion maps, is created by averaging over 2×2-pixel blocks to form an image of $2^{n-1} \times 2^{n-1}$ pixels. This is done recursively until a minimum size is reached (for example 4×4 pixels). The highest-resolution level of the HOM is numbered 0, with increasing numbers having decreasing resolution. The gray-scale values in the HOM are said to be the *opacity* of the pixels. A high opacity value (near white) for a pixel at a level above 0 means that most of the pixels it represents are covered by the HOM.

The creation of the HOM can be implemented either on the CPU or by texture mapping, with bilinear interpolation used as a minification filter. For large image sizes, the texture filtering approach was found to be faster, and for small image sizes, the CPU was faster. Of course, this varies with CPUs and graphics hardware. For a 1024×1024 image, Zhang et al. [390] used a 256×256 image as the base for the HOM. An example of a HOM is shown in Figure 7.14.

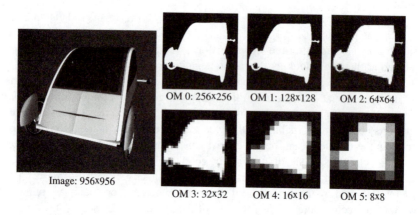

Figure 7.14. On the left is an image of 956×956 pixels. Since this covers many pixels on the screen and is rather close to the viewer, it is a good candidate for an occluder. Its HOM is created by rendering this object in white against a black background in 256×256 pixels, an image which is called occlusion map 0. This image is subsampled into 128×128 pixels by averaging over 2×2 pixels. This is done recursively down to 8×8 pixels. *(Model is reused courtesy of Nya Perspektiv Design AB.)*

The overlap test against the HOM starts by projecting the bounding volume of the object to be tested onto the screen.[6] This projection is then bounded by a rectangle, which then covers more pixels than the object enclosed in the bounding volume. So this test is a *conservative test*, meaning that even if the test results show that the object is not occluded, it may still be so. This rectangle is then compared against the HOM for overlap. The overlap test starts at the level in which the size of the pixel in the HOM is approximately the size of the rectangle. If all pixels in the rectangle are opaque (which means fully white for non-approximate culling), then the rectangle is occluded in the xy plane and the object is said to pass the test. On the other hand, if a pixel is not opaque, then the test for that pixel continues recursively to the subpixels in the HOM which are covered by the rectangle, meaning that the resolution of the occlusion maps increases with each test.

For approximate visibility culling, the pixels in the HOM are not compared to full opacity, i.e., white, but rather against an opacity threshold value, a gray-scale value. The lower the threshold value, the more approximate the culling. The advantage here is that if a pixel is not fully opaque (white) but still higher than the threshold, then the overlap test can terminate earlier. The penalty is that some object may be omitted from rendering even though it is (partially) visible. The opacity values are not constant from one level to another in the HOM, as shown in the following example.

EXAMPLE: COMPUTATION OF OPACITY THRESHOLD VALUES Assume the rendered image is 1024×1024 pixels and that the lowest level in the HOM (i.e., the one with the largest resolution) has a resolution of 128×128 pixels. A pixel in this level-zero occlusion map corresponds to an 8×8-pixel region in the rendered image. Also assume that a 2×2 region of black pixels in an 8×8 region can pass as a negligible hole. This would give an opacity value $O = 1 - 2^2/8^2 = 0.9375$. The next level in the HOM would then have a 64×64 resolution, and a pixel at this level would correspond to 16×16 pixels in the rendered image. So the opacity threshold at this level would be $O = 1 - 2^2/16^2 \approx 0.984$. ☐

We will now derive a recursive formula for computing the opacity values of the different levels in the HOM. The opacity of the level with the highest resolution in the HOM is $O_0 = 1 - \frac{n}{m}$, where n is equal to the number of black pixels that can be considered a negligible hole, and m is the number of pixels in the rendered image represented by one pixel in this occlusion map ($m = 8 \times 8$ in the example above). The next level in the HOM has a threshold of $O_1 = 1 - \frac{n}{4m} = 1 - \frac{1-O_0}{4} = \frac{3+O_0}{4}$. This reasoning can be generalized to the

---

[6]Zhang et al. [390] used oriented bounding boxes.

formula in Equation 7.2 for the kth level in the HOM.

$$O_{k+1} = \frac{(3 + O_k)}{4} \tag{7.2}$$

For more details on this topic, consult Zhang's Ph.D. thesis [391].

For the one-dimensional z-depth test, we must be able to determine whether an object is behind the selected occluders. Zhang [391] describes a number of methods, and we choose to describe the *depth estimation buffer*, which provides reasonable estimation and does not require a Z-buffer. It is implemented as a software Z-buffer that divides the screen into a number of rectangular regions that are rather large in relation to the pixel size. The selected occluders are inserted into this buffer. For each region the farthest z-value is stored. This is in contrast to a normal Z-buffer, which stores the nearest z-value at each pixel. An estimation is used to obtain a far value for an occluder quickly. The z-value of the farthest vertex of the bounding box is used to estimate the farthest z-value of an occluder. An example of a depth estimation buffer is shown in Figure 7.15. The depth estimation buffer is built for each frame. During rendering, to test whether an object passes the depth test (i.e., whether it is behind the occluders) the z-value of the nearest vertex of its bounding box is computed. This value is compared against the z-values of all regions in the depth estimation buffer that the bounding box rectangle covers in screen space. If the near value of the bounding box is larger than the stored z-depth in all regions, then the object passes the depth test, and is thus occluded in the depth direction. A resolution of 64×64 regions in the depth estimation buffer was used by Zhang et al. [390].

For an object to be occluded, it must thus first pass the overlap test; i.e., the rectangle of the projected bounding volume of the object must pass the HOM

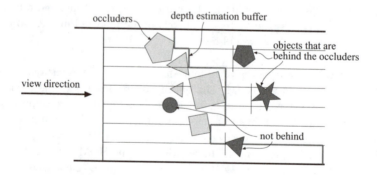

Figure 7.15. Illustration of the depth estimation buffer. Illustration after Zhang [391].

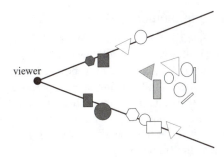

Figure 7.16. Scenario where the occluder selection for the HOM algorithm may be unsuccessful. The algorithm may select the dark gray objects as occluders, but when the light gray objects (which also are good occluders) are considered, the occluder count budget may have already been reached.

test. Then it must pass the depth test, i.e., it must be behind the occluders. If an object passes both tests, the object is occluded and is not rendered.

Before the algorithm starts, an occluder database is built, where a few criteria are used to exclude certain objects [391]. First, small objects do not work well in the occluder database, since they usually cover a small portion of the image unless the viewer is very close to them. Second, objects with a high polygon count are also avoided, as these may negatively affect the performance of the rendering of the occlusion map. Third, objects with large or ill-shaped bounding boxes (e.g., a bounding box for a skinny polygon) should be avoided, as they may cause the depth estimation buffer to be too conservative. Finally, redundant objects are avoided: for example, a clock on a wall does not contribute as much to occlusion as the wall itself.

At runtime, occluders are selected from the database. To avoid allowing the creation of the HOM to become a bottleneck, there is a limit to the number of occluders that can be selected. These are selected with respect to their distance from the viewer and to their size. Only objects inside the view frustum are selected. A case when this does not work well is shown in Figure 7.16. The number of occluders can vary during runtime using an adaptive scheme. If the portion of the scene that is culled away is low, then this number may be increased. On the other hand, if a high portion is culled away but the frame rate is low, then this number may be decreased [390]. Another technique that can be used here is to render simplified versions of the occluders. This works well as long as the occluders cover approximately the same pixels as they did before [391].

For extremely dense scenes, i.e., those with high depth complexity, the HOM algorithm was able to cull away between about 50% and 95% of the scene, with a speed-up of up to six times in some cases.

VISUALIZE fx's Hardware Implementation

Hewlett-Packard has implemented occlusion culling in the VISUALIZE fx graphics hardware [320]. The algorithm works as follows. When an object is about to be rendered, each pixel covered by its bounding box is scan-converted and tested against the contents of the Z-buffer using special-purpose hardware. If all of these pixels are further away from the viewer than the contents already in the frame buffer, then the object is guaranteed to be obscured, and it is thus not necessary to process the model inside the bounding box. Otherwise, the model is processed and rendered into the frame buffer.

This means that if a complex object is obscured, then instead of drawing the whole object, only a bounding box (consisting of at most three quadrilaterals) is scan-converted (but not drawn into the frame buffer). In this case, we gain performance by avoiding sending the complex object through the rendering pipeline. Otherwise, the bounding box is scan-converted and the object is drawn, and we actually lose a bit of performance.

Note also, that as for most occlusion culling algorithms, the performance is dependent on the order in which objects are drawn. As an example, consider a car with a motor inside it. If the hood of the car is drawn first, then the motor will (probably) be culled away. On the other hand, if the motor is drawn first, then the hood of the car will not be culled. Therefore, performance can be improved by techniques such as rough front-to-back sorting of the objects by their approximate distance from the viewer and rendering in this order.

With such techniques, performance has been reported to be between 25% and 100% faster than rendering that does not use any occlusion culling [320].

Shadow Culling

Here we describe briefly the work by Coorg and Teller [66, 67] and Hudson et al. [193]. These algorithms are quite similar, and the main idea is to select a small set of large occluders and discard the objects behind the occluders, i.e., objects that are *shadowed* by an occluder with respect to a certain viewpoint. This is done with some geometric calculations. The basic tests are shown in Figure 7.17, where the objects are represented by bounding boxes. Coorg and Teller [67] make use of *separating planes* and *supporting planes*. A separating plane is formed by an edge of an occluder polygon and a vertex of the bounding box (BB), and in such a way that the objects are on different sides of the plane. A supporting plane is constructed in a similar way except that the occluder and the BB should be located on the same side of the plane. An object is occluded if the viewer is inside all of the supporting planes, which means that the object is in shadow with respect to the viewer and the occluder. Coorg and Teller also describe a way of using several polygons that share edges as an aggregate

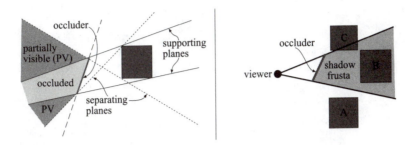

Figure 7.17. The left figure shows how Coorg and Teller's algorithm detects whether an object (the box) is occluded by a large polygon. If the viewer is in the region marked "occluded," then the object is occluded. The right figure shows how Hudson et al. detect occlusion —objects fully in shadow are occluded.

occluder, and also an efficient way of computing the separating/supporting planes using preprocessing and runtime table look-ups.

Hudson et al. [193] use an algorithm that culls away AABBs or OBBs in much the same way as we have done for a view-frustum algorithm, but the frustum does not have a far plane and may have more than four side planes, i.e., more than a left, right, bottom, and top plane. The near plane is the plane in which the occluder lies. See Sections 7.1.2 and 10.11 for more information on view-frustum culling.

To select a good occluder, Coorg and Teller [67] use the following metric, which estimates the solid angle[7] that a polygon subtends:

$$g = -\frac{a(\mathbf{n} \cdot \mathbf{v})}{\mathbf{d} \cdot \mathbf{d}} \tag{7.3}$$

Here, a is the area of the polygon, $\mathbf{n}$ is the normal of the polygon, $\mathbf{v}$ is the view direction vector, and $\mathbf{d}$ is the vector from the viewpoint to the center of the polygon. Both $\mathbf{v}$ and $\mathbf{n}$ are assumed to be normalized. The geometry involved is shown in Figure 7.18. The higher the value of g, the better the occluder is to use. The solid angle approximation estimates the "usefulness" of an occluder because: *a)* the larger the area, the larger the value; *b)* the value is inversely proportional to the distance to the occluder; and *c)* the maximum value is reached when the viewer looks at a polygon "head-on," and the value decreases with an increasing angle between the polygon normal and the view direction [67].

---

[7]The solid angle is the two-dimensional angle concept extended to three dimensions [121]. In two dimensions, an angle of 2π radians covers the whole unit circle. If we extend this to three dimensions, the solid angle would cover the whole area of the unit sphere (4π steradians).

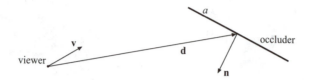

Figure 7.18. The geometry involved in the estimation of the solid angle.

Hudson et al. use the same formula but also test with random sampling to determine whether a selected occluder is good in practice. They do this by choosing a number of random viewpoints and counting the number of objects occluded by the selected occluder. They also exploit coherence in that they assume that an occluder that was good (or bad) for one frame is probably good (or bad) the next frame too. The algorithm stores the objects that were culled by an occluder for each frame. Hudson et al. found that using about eight occluders was reasonable for their algorithm.

Both of these algorithms use a hierarchical data structure to represent the scene. Coorg and Teller use a k-d tree, and Hudson et al. use a bounding volume hierarchy of AABBs. At runtime the algorithms first perform view-frustum culling, and then identify good occluders. After that, the remaining objects are culled against the occluders.

Coorg and Teller's [67] preprocessing phase used very few seconds, and the speed-up was approximately 2 to 5 times, depending on the architecture. Hudson et al. [193] note a speed-up of 55%, on average. Remember, though, that these tests were done on different platforms and for different scenes.

7.2 Impostors

Impostors[8] are a kind of rendering primitive that exploits frame-to-frame coherence efficiently if the viewer and the objects move slowly. More specifically, an impostor is an image of a complex object that is texture-mapped onto a rectangle.[9] The image is opaque where the object is present; everywhere else it is totally transparent. The use of an impostor is visualized in Figure 7.19.

---

[8]Impostors are sometimes called *sprites*.

[9]Maciel and Shirley [239] identify several different types of impostors, including the one used in this chapter, but, since the time they introduced the impostor, its definition has narrowed to the one we use here.

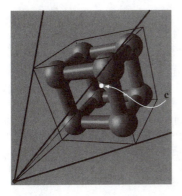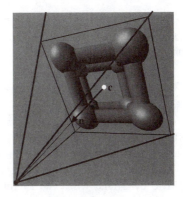

Figure 7.19. At the left an impostor is created of the object in the bounding box. The view direction is toward the center, c, of the bounding box, and an image is rendered and used as an impostor texture. This is shown on the right, where the texture is applied to a quadrilateral. The center of the impostor is equal to the center of the bounding box, and the normal (emanating from the center) points directly toward the viewpoint.

To be of any use, an impostor should be faster to draw than the object it represents, and it should closely resemble the object. Also of importance is that an impostor should be reused for several viewpoints located close together. This is usually the case because the movement of the projected image of an object diminishes with an increased distance from the viewer. This means that slowly moving objects that are located far from the viewer are candidates for this method. Another reason to use impostors is that objects located close to the viewer tend to expose the same side to the viewer as their images move [309].

An impostor of an object is created by initializing the alpha channel of the frame buffer to $\alpha = 0.0$ (i.e., fully transparent). The object is then drawn into the frame buffer, and the alpha channel is set to opaque ($\alpha = 1.0$) where the object is present. The pixels that are not written to retain their transparency. Before rendering the object to create the impostor image, the viewer is oriented so that it looks at the center of the bounding box of the object, and the impostor polygon is chosen so as to point directly towards the viewpoint (at the left in Figure 7.19). The size of the impostor is the smallest rectangle of the projected bounding box of the object. The impostor image is then read back into the texture memory and used as a texture on the polygon. Note also that the impostor texture is of the format RGBα. The rendering of the impostor starts with placing the impostor polygon at the center of the bounding box, and orienting the polygon so its normal points directly to the viewer (see the image on the right in Figure 7.19). This is therefore a kind of billboard (see Section 6.2.2).

The resolution of the texture need not exceed the screen resolution and so can be computed by Equation 7.4 [309]. This is the same sort of equation that was used for detail culling in Section 7.1.4.

$$texres = screenres\frac{objsize}{distance} \tag{7.4}$$

One limit to the usefulness of an impostor is its resolution. If a distant impostor comes closer, the individual pixels of the texture may become obvious, and so the illusion breaks down. The angles β_{scr}, which represents the angle of a pixel, and β_{tex}, which represents the angle of a texel of the impostor, can be used to determine when the lifetime of an impostor has expired. This is illustrated in Figure 7.20. When $\beta_{tex} > \beta_{scr}$, there is a possibility that the texels will be clearly visible, and so the impostor has to be regenerated from the current position of both the viewer and the object. In this way, the impostor texture adapts to the screen resolution.

We must also test whether the impostors are valid from the current point of view. Here we present Schaufler's method [309, 310]. The first observation is that when only the view direction changes, the impostors need not be updated. The reason is that even though the projection plane changes as the viewer rotates, the projection itself does not. Rather, it is the sampling of the object that may change. Another way to think of this is that the set of rays from the viewer which hit the object is the same no matter what plane we project to. This is why we can assume that the impostor will still be a good approximation under rotations of the view direction.

So we need only consider regenerating an impostor in cases where the viewer moves. Here we will look at the two extreme cases, which are shown in Figure 7.21. The left case in this figure shows how to compute an error angle called β_{trans} which increases as the viewer moves sideways (parallel to the plane of the impostor). The error angle is computed by considering how the extreme points

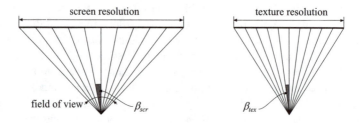

Figure 7.20. The angle of a screen pixel is computed as $\beta_{scr} = fov/screenres$, and the angle for the texture is computed similarly.

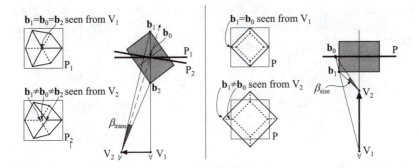

Figure 7.21. The left part illustrates the overestimate of the error angle β_{trans}, and the right part shows the overestimate of β_{size}. When any of these angles becomes greater than β_{scr}, the impostor needs to be regenerated *(after Schaufler [309])*.

on a bounding box create an angle when the viewer moves. When the viewer has moved sufficiently far, the impostor will become invalid because $\beta_{trans} > \beta_{scr}$.

The right case in Figure 7.21 shows the extreme case when the viewer moves toward the impostor. This angle is computed by considering how extreme points on the bounding box project onto the impostor plane when the viewer moves toward the impostor. Both angles β_{trans} and β_{size} can be computed with, for example, the law of cosines (see Section B.2). This is a different test than that for β_{tex}, as it measures the amount of change in perspective effect.

In conclusion, an impostor needs to be regenerated every time β_{tex}, β_{trans}, or β_{size} is greater than β_{scr}.

7.2.1 Nailboards

If impostors are augmented with a depth buffer of the same size as the impostor texture, we get a related rendering primitive called a *nailboard* [312]. The nailboard texture image is an RGB image augmented with a Δ parameter for each pixel, thus forming an RGBΔ texture. The Δ stores the depth deviation from the nailboard polygon to the correct depth of the geometry that the nailboard represents.

Because nailboards contain localized depth information, they are superior to impostors because they can help avoid visibility problems. This is especially evident when the nailboard polygon penetrates nearby geometry. Such a case is shown in Figure 7.22. If impostors are used, closely located objects must be grouped together and treated as one [312].

When a nailboard is rendered, the depth of the nailboard polygon is used as an offset for the Δ-values. For impostors, a single-bit α-value was used at

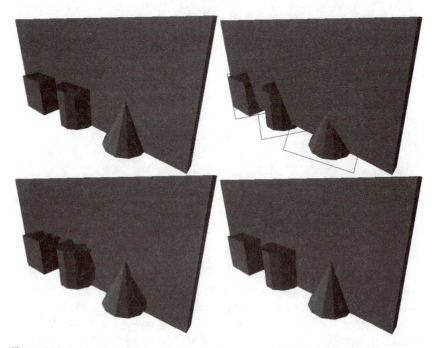

Figure 7.22. The upper left image shows a simple scene rendered with geometry. The upper right image shows what happens if impostors are created and used for the cube, the cylinder, and the cone. The bottom image shows the result when nailboards are used. The nailboard in the left image uses two bits for depth deviation, while the one on the right uses eight bits. *(Images courtesy of Gernot Schaufler.)*

each pixel for transparency. Nailboards do not need to have a separate alpha value, since one of the Δ-values can be used to represent full transparency. Since depth-difference values are stored in the Δ-components, a small number of bits can be used to store these. Typically, eight to 16 bits suffice. Schaufler also derives a method for transforming between different spaces and so obtains correct depths in the depth buffer [312].

Shade et al. [324] also describe a nailboard primitive, as well as a new primitive called a *layered depth image*, which has several depths per pixel. The reason for multiple depths is to avoid the gaps that are created due to de-occlusion (i.e. where hidden areas become visible) during the warping.

7.2.2 Hierarchical Image Caching

Hierarchical image caching is an algorithm that uses impostors arranged in a hierarchy for better performance. This technique was invented independently by Schaufler and Stürzlinger [310] and Shade et al. [323]. The basic idea is to partition the scene into a hierarchy of boxes and create an impostor for each box, and also to hierarchically create impostors for the parents in the partitioning. The impostors are then updated hierarchically. We describe these algorithms briefly in this section.

The scene is partitioned by a BSP tree[10] where the dividing planes are parallel to the main axes in order to form axis-aligned boxes. The algorithms are not restricted to the use of axis-aligned boxes—that choice merely simplifies the processing. The use of an axis-aligned BSP tree has the advantage of facilitating rendering in a roughly back-to-front order, which is required for the proper rendering of transparent objects (see Section 4.5). The algorithms try to construct a partitioning that generates nearly cubic boxes. It is also important when forming the tree to make it balanced, which means that we want approximately the same number of primitives in each pair of boxes. Another goal is to minimize the number of dividing-plane/object intersections [323]. A simple approach to generating the tree is to enclose the whole scene in a box and then recursively subdivide that box into subboxes along its longest axis [310]. The primitives are stored in all the leaf boxes that they overlap. Recursion ends either when a user-defined maximum depth of the tree is reached or when the number of primitives in a box is below a user-defined threshold. If this number is too small, then the relative overhead to generate the impostor becomes large and the method inefficient. Shade et al. [323] describe a greedy algorithm for making the subdivision. Both methods may have problems when a primitive is inside two boxes and is represented by two impostors. Cracks may then be visible. Note that the scene partition tree can also be used for view-frustum culling (see Section 7.1.2).

For each box, an impostor is generated for a certain point of view using the method in Section 7.2. General clipping planes can be used to clip the primitives against the faces of the box. This generation starts at the leaves, and the impostors propagate upward in the hierarchy toward the root of the scene partition in order to generate impostors for the parents of the leaves, and so forth on up. The impostor of a parent box is generally created by rendering the impostors of its children. Rerendering an impostor is only done when one or more of its children's impostors become invalid due to movement—either the texels become visible, which makes the impostor invalid, or the viewer moves into a location where the error of the approximation becomes too large. So, for small movements of the viewer, a large impostor can in some cases be used to render a large portion of the scene, and considerable speed-up may be achieved. Also, when one must rerender an impostor for a parent node, performance may

---

[10]This is referred to as a k-d tree in [310], but it is essentially the same thing.

still be improved if only some of its children have been rerendered and the old impostors for the others can be reused.

The rendering of a scene using hierarchical image caching is divided into two steps. First, the geometry outside the view frustum is culled using view-frustum culling (and their allocated texture memory is released for others to use), and the impostors that have become invalid are rendered and propagated toward the root of the hierarchy. The second step is to render the impostors of the hierarchy that are inside the view frustum. This is done by traversing the tree from back to front in order to avoid transparency problems.

For an extremely large outdoor scene, Shade et al. [323] reported a speed-up factor of about 12. The speed-up could be increased by allowing a larger error in the impostor approximation. The first frame in their rendering, which then included the creation of impostors for all boxes in the scene, took twice as much time as rendering the geometry only.

Normally, the hierarchical image cache only works for static scenes, since the subdivision of the scene takes significant time. However, if a nailboard primitive is available, then dynamic objects can be rendered with nailboards in order to avoid visibility and penetration problems. The static part of the scene could be rendered with the hierarchical image caching method [312].

7.2.3   Related Work

Sillion et al. [334] describe a more sophisticated impostor technique suited for urban scenery. Distant geometry is replaced with a texture that is mapped onto a mesh that coarsely follows the geometry it approximates. Decoret et al. [80] present a taxonomy of rendering errors that may occur when impostors are used, and they also introduce a new impostor, called *multi-mesh impostor* (MMI). The MMI addresses the different errors by using several meshes per impostor, and by using both pre-generated and dynamically updated impostor images. Schaufler [311] also describes a constant-frame-rate algorithm for impostors, which is similar to Funkhouser and Séquin's work [113] presented in Section 7.3.4. Rafferty et al. [294] present a technique that replaces the geometry seen through a portal with an impostor. They also use image warping for longer lifetimes of the impostors, as does Schaufler [313].

7.3   Levels of Detail

The basic idea of *levels of detail* or *LODs* is to use simpler versions of an object as it gets farther from the viewer. For example, consider a detailed car that may consist of, say, 10,000 triangles. This representation can be used when the viewer is close to the car. When the object is farther away, say covering only 10×5 pixels, we probably do not need all 10,000 triangles. Instead we can use a simplified model that has only, say, 100 triangles. Due to the distance, the simplified version looks approximately the same as the more detailed version. Some objects, such as spheres and spline surfaces, have a level of detail as part of their rendering description. The underlying geometry is curved, and a separate LOD control determines how it is tessellated into displayable polygons. Here we describe some common methods for using LODs.

7.3.1 Discrete Geometry LODs

In the simplest type of LOD, the different representations are simply models of the same object containing different numbers of primitives. A more detailed LOD has a higher number of primitives. An example of three LODs of an object is shown in Figure 7.23. This figure also shows the different LODs at different distances from the viewer. Typically, the different LODs of an object are associated with different ranges. The most detailed LOD has a range from zero to some user-defined value r_1, which means that this LOD is visible when the distance to the object is less than r_1. The next LOD has a range from r_1 to r_2 where $r_2 > r_1$. If the distance to the object is greater than or equal to r_1 and less than r_2, then this LOD is used, and so on. Therefore, the term *range-based LODs* is sometimes used. Examples of LOD ranges are illustrated

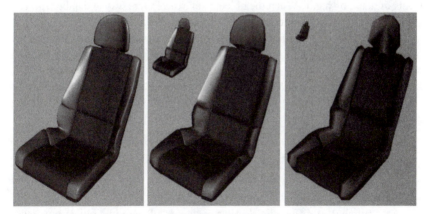

Figure 7.23. Here we show three different levels of detail for a car chair. The two pictures in the upper left corner of the middle and right images show the two chairs farther away from the viewer; still, these simplified models seem to approximate the chair fairly well from these distances. Note also how the shading degenerates as fewer triangles are used. *(Model is reused courtesy of Nya Perspektiv Design AB.)*

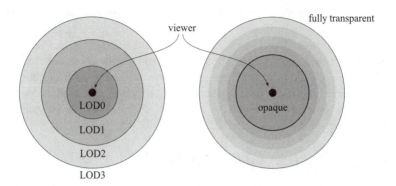

Figure 7.24. The left part of this illustration shows how range-based LODs work. When the object is in the darkest gray area, the LOD with the finest detail is rendered. When the object moves away and goes into the next zone, LOD1 is rendered instead. The right part shows how alpha LODs work. Inside the dark gray circle, the object is rendered as it usually is. However, when it goes outside that circle, the transparency increases continuously until the object is outside the biggest circle; at that point, the object is not visible any longer.

in Figure 7.24. When an object is rendered using LODs, the distance to the object is first computed and then the appropriate LOD is selected.

The simplification methods discussed in Section 9.4 can be used to generate the desired number of LODs. Another approach is to make models with different levels of detail by hand. When the object is extremely far away, it can be replaced by a box with the average color of the object on its side.

A problem here is that *popping* may occur when switching detail level. That is, when moving from one zone to another, an abrupt model substitution is often noticeable and distracting. Blending can be used to avoid this problem [93]. Even though this usually looks much better and greatly reduces the popping effect, during the transition two LODs have to be rendered and blended, which costs time.

7.3.2   Alpha LODs

A simple method that avoids popping altogether is to use alpha LODs. These do not use a number of differently detailed instances of the same object but rather only one instance per object. As the distance to the object increases the overall transparency of the object is increased (α is decreased), and the object finally disappears when it reaches full transparency ($\alpha = 0.0$). See Figure 7.24. This happens when the object is further away from the viewer than a user-defined invisibility threshold. There is also a user-defined distance that determines when an object shall start to be more and more transparent. When the invisibility threshold has been reached, the object need not be sent through the rendering pipeline at all as long as the distance remains above a threshold distance. When an object has been invisible and its distance falls below the invisibility distance, then it decreases its transparency and starts to be visible again.

The advantage of this technique is that it is experienced as much more continuous than the method in the previous section and so avoids popping. Also, since the object finally disappears altogether and need not be rendered, a significant speed-up can be expected. The disadvantage is that the object totally disappears. An example of alpha LODs is shown in Figure 7.25.

7.3.3 Geomorph LODs

The process of mesh simplification can be used to create various LOD models from a single complex object. Algorithms for performing this simplification are discussed in Section 9.4. One approach is to create a set of discrete LODs and use

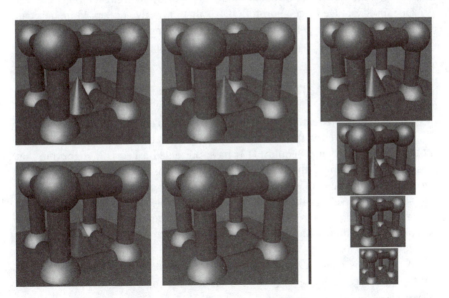

Figure 7.25. The cone in the middle is rendered using an alpha LOD. The transparency of the cone is increased when the distance to it increases, and it finally disappears. The images on the left are shown from the same distance for viewing purposes, while the images to the right of the line are shown at different sizes.

these as discussed previously. However, edge collapse methods [115, 188, 247] have an interesting property that allows another way of making a transition between LODs.

A model has two fewer polygons after an edge collapse operation is performed. What happens in an edge collapse is that an edge is shrunk until its two endpoints meet and it disappears. If this process is animated, a smooth transition occurs between the original model and its slightly simplified version. For each edge collapse a single vertex is joined with another. Over a series of edge collapses, a set of vertices move to join other vertices.

Geomorph LODs [188] are a set of models created by simplification. However, instead of using blending to transition from one model to the next, the vertices of one model move to the other model's vertex locations. Instead of moving each vertex by itself, one after another in a series, all the vertices can be moved at the same time. The simplification process gives a mapping from each vertex of the more complex model onto the simpler model. That is, we know where each vertex must move in order to get the next level of detail. Unlike blending, this method requires only a single model during the transition, although the vertices have to be interpolated to their new positions. When the transition is complete, the new level-of-detail model is used to represent the object.

One disadvantage of geomorph LODs is that only edge-collapsed models can be used for a set of neighboring representations. Simplification does not always yield pleasing simpler models, and visually disturbing artifacts can arise.

7.3.4 LOD Management

It is often a desirable feature of a rendering system to have a constant frame rate. This can be achieved if the objects in a scene are represented by, for example, LODs. Funkhouser and Séquin [113] have presented a heuristic algorithm that adapts the selection of the level of detail for all visible objects in a scene to meet the requirement of constant frame rate. This algorithm is *predictive* in the sense that it selects the detail level of the visible objects based on desired frame rate and on which objects are visible. Such an algorithm contrasts with a *reactive* algorithm, which bases its selection on the time it took to render the previous frame.

An object is called O and is rendered at a level of detail called L, which gives (O, L) for each object.[11] Two heuristics are then defined. One heuristic

---

[11] Funkhouser and Séquin have a parameter called R that represents the rendering algorithm which was used to render an object. By rendering algorithm they mean that we can change from flat-shaded to Gouraud-shaded, texture mapping, etc. Here we ignore that parameter and assume that it is part of the level of detail L. For example, we can represent an object that is textured (versus untextured)

estimates the cost of rendering an object at a certain level of detail: $Cost(O, L)$. Another estimates the benefit of an object rendered at a certain level of detail: $Benefit(O, L)$. The benefit function estimates the contribution to the image of an object at a certain LOD.

Assume the objects inside or intersecting the view frustum are called S. The main idea behind the algorithm is then to optimize the selection of the LODs for the objects S using the heuristically chosen functions. More specifically we want to maximize:

$$\sum_S Benefit(O, L) \qquad (7.5)$$

under the constraint:

$$\sum_S Cost(O, L) \leq TargetFrameTime \qquad (7.6)$$

In other words, we want to select for the objects the level of detail that gives us "the best image" within the desired frame rate. Next we describe how the cost and benefit functions can be estimated, and then we present an optimization algorithm for the above equations.

The cost function should estimate how long it takes to render an object (O, L). This function is dependent on several factors such as which graphics hardware is used, the number of polygons, which features are used during rendering, state changes, etc. If it is assumed that the application stage (i.e., the CPU) can never be a bottleneck, then a simple model can be used. In this case, the CPU is always able to feed the geometry stage at such a pace that the rest of the pipeline always has work to do. The cost of the geometry stage is divided into two parts: $Poly(O, L)$ and $Vert(O, L)$, and the whole stage is a linear combination of these. The cost of the rasterizer stage is assumed proportional to the number of pixels an object covers: $Pix(O, L)$. The cost function is then the maximum value of those stages' costs [113], i.e., the cost of the bottleneck of the pipeline:

$$Cost(O, L) = \max(c_1 Poly(O, L) + c_2 Vert(O, l), \ c_3 Pix(O, L)) \qquad (7.7)$$

The coefficients c_1, c_2, and c_3 are then determined empirically by rendering a number of objects at different sizes and levels of detail. The coefficients are then computed using a best-fitting-line algorithm.

The benefit function estimates how well an object contributes to the image. This is very complex because it includes factors such as visibility, size, colors,

---

as two levels of detail for the object.

textures, human perception, and more. However, using a heuristic, it is possible to get good results. To simplify, the benefit function is dependent on several factors that are easier to compute. The main factor is the screen size of the object—the rationale here is that the larger the screen projection of the object, the greater the contribution it makes to the benefit. We call this factor $Size(O)$. The next factor is called $Accuracy(O, L)$, which should capture the relative accuracy of a certain LOD of an object. This function is shown in Equation 7.8.

$$Accuracy(O, L) = 1 - Error = 1 - \frac{BaseError}{Samples(L)^m} \qquad (7.8)$$

The error is assumed to decrease with an increasing number of samples. The samples depend on the rendering algorithm. For flat shading the key figure is the number of polygons, and for Gouraud shading it is the number of vertices. The exponent m depends on the rendering algorithm: $m = 1$ for flat shading and $m = 2$ for Gouraud shading, which makes the error smaller for Gouraud shading and the value of the accuracy function higher. The accuracy function may have to be adjusted to the hardware and algorithms used. For example, if Phong (per-pixel) shading is used,[12] the $Samples()$ function should be proportional to the number of pixels that the object covers. The $BaseError$ is set to 0.5 [113]. Consider a curved surface approximated by a flat polygon. This would yield $Accuracy(O, L) = 1 - 0.5/1 = 0.5$, which is a rather low accuracy but much better than not rendering the polygon at all, in which case the accuracy function would be zero.[13]

The benefit function also depends on the importance of the object. For example, a wall in a room must be considered significantly more important than a clock on the wall. This function can be set by the user. Funkhouser and Séquin also add functions for focus, motion, and hysteresis. The focus function has a higher value for objects near the center of the screen than those near the border. More specifically, the benefit is reduced by an amount proportional to the distance from the center of the screen. Objects moving with high speed are considered to contribute less than slowly moving objects. Therefore the benefit is reduced by an amount proportional to the ratio of the speed of the object on the screen to the size of the average polygon of the object. Finally, if an object is changing its LOD, the hysteresis function lowers the benefit because of potential popping effects. So the benefit function is reduced by an amount proportional to the difference between the LOD number of an object in the current frame and

---

[12]As is the case for ray tracing.

[13]To get $Accuracy(O, L) = 0$ when not rendering an object at all, the $Samples(L)$ could be set to 0.5.

its LOD number in the previous frame. To sum up, the benefit function is:

$$Benefit(O, L) = Size(O) * Accuracy(O, L) * Importance(O) * \\ Focus(O) * Motion(O) * Hysteresis(O, L) \tag{7.9}$$

The benefit is thus estimated with an ad hoc function and it may have to be changed for a particular configuration of algorithms, hardware, and more.

Finally, we will discuss how to choose the level of detail for the objects in a scene. First we note the following: for some viewpoints a scene may be too complex to be able to keep up with the desired frame rate. To solve this, we can define a LOD for each object at its lowest detail level, which is simply an object with no primitives—i.e., we avoid rendering the object [113]. Using this trick, we only render the most important objects and skip the unimportant ones.

To select the "best" LODs for a scene, Equation 7.5 has to be optimized under the constraint shown in Equation 7.6. This is an NP-complete problem, which means that to solve it correctly the only thing to do is to test *all* different combinations and select the best. This is clearly infeasible for any kind of algorithm. A simpler, more feasible approach is to use a greedy algorithm that tries to maximize the $Value = Benefit(O, L)/Cost(O, L)$ for each object. This algorithm treats all the objects inside the view frustum and chooses to render the objects in descending order, i.e., the one with the highest value first. If an object has the same value for more than one LOD, then the LOD with the highest benefit is selected and rendered. This approach gives the most "bang for the buck" [113]. For n objects inside the view frustum the algorithm runs in $O(n \log n)$ time, and it produces a solution that is at least half as good as the best [113, 114]. Funkhouser and Séquin also exploit frame-to-frame coherence for speeding up the sorting of the values.

In Figure 7.26 three images are shown from the same point of view. These were rendered with different target frame times. More information about LOD management and the combination of LOD management and portal culling can be found in Funkhouser's Ph.D. thesis [114].

7.4   Triangle Strips, Fans, and Meshes

An extremely common way to increase graphics performance is to send fewer than three vertices per triangle to the graphics pipeline. The benefits of this are quite obvious: fewer points and normals need to be transformed, fewer line clips need to be performed, less lighting needs to be computed, etc. However, if the bottleneck of an application is the fillrate (i.e., the number of pixels that can be filled per second), little or no performance gain is to be expected from such savings. Two popular methods of using less data, namely triangle strips and triangle fans, will be described below, along with methods for converting a triangle mesh into triangle strips.

7.4.1   Strips

Now, how would it be possible to describe a triangle with less than three vertices (except when the triangle degenerates to a line or a point)? The secret is not to describe one triangle at a time, but instead to give a sequence of connected

Figure 7.26. Here an image was rendered with different target frame rates. The target frame rate for the top row was 10 Hz, for the middle row 20 Hz, and for the bottom row 50 Hz. The left column shows the actual images of the scene; the middle column shows the LODs—darker gray means a more detailed LOD; and the right column shows the pixel difference between the images on the left and the images rendered with the highest LODs available. The algorithm described in the text selected lower and lower LODs in order to be able to render the scene in the target frame rate. *(Courtesy of Thomas Funkhouser and Carlo Séquin.)*

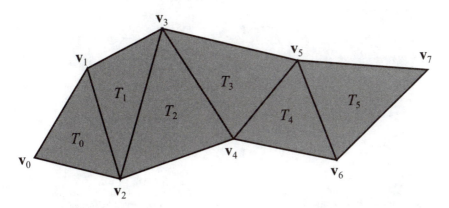

Figure 7.27. A sequence of triangles that can be represented as one triangle strip. After sending vertices $\mathbf{v}_0$, $\mathbf{v}_1$, and $\mathbf{v}_2$ for triangle T_0, it suffices to send one vertex per triangle and reuse the previous two vertices from the previous triangle in the triangle strip. Triangle T_i ($i > 0$) sends only vertex $\mathbf{v}_{i+2}$.

triangles. Consider Figure 7.27, in which a number of connected triangles is shown. If these are treated as a triangle strip, then a more compact way of sending them to the rendering pipeline is possible. It is accomplished as follows. For the first triangle (denoted T_0), all three vertices (denoted $\mathbf{v}_0$, $\mathbf{v}_1$, and $\mathbf{v}_2$) are sent (in that order), but for subsequent triangles in this strip, only one vertex has to be sent since the other two have already been sent with the previous triangle. For example, after sending triangle T_0, only vertex $\mathbf{v}_3$ is sent, and the vertices $\mathbf{v}_1$ and $\mathbf{v}_2$ from triangle T_0 are used to form triangle T_1. For triangle T_2, only vertex $\mathbf{v}_4$ is sent, and so on through the rest of the strip.

A triangle strip of n vertices is defined as an ordered vertex list

$$\{\mathbf{v}_0, \mathbf{v}_1, \ldots, \mathbf{v}_{n-1}\},$$

with a structure imposed upon it indicating that triangle i is

$$\triangle \mathbf{v}_i \mathbf{v}_{i+1} \mathbf{v}_{i+2}, \tag{7.10}$$

where $0 \leq i < n - 2$. This implies that a triangle strip of n vertices has $n - 2$ triangles; we call it a triangle strip of length $n - 2$. In order to create longer, and thus more efficient, triangles strips, a *swap*, which swaps the order of the two latest vertices, can be used if the API supports it. Triangle strips with swaps are called *generalized triangle strips* [81]. In Iris GL [198], there is an actual command for doing a swap, but in OpenGL [275], Direct3D, and most other APIs, a swap command must be implemented by resending a vertex, and thus there is

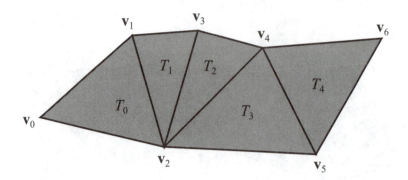

Figure 7.28. We would have to send $(\mathbf{v}_0, \mathbf{v}_1, \mathbf{v}_2, \mathbf{v}_3, \mathbf{v}_2, \mathbf{v}_4, \mathbf{v}_5, \mathbf{v}_6)$ to the graphics pipeline, to use these triangles as a strip. As can be seen, a swap has been implemented by including $\mathbf{v}_2$ twice in the list.

a penalty of one vertex per swap.[14] Since starting a new triangle strip costs two vertices, accepting the penalty imposed by a swap is still better than restarting. A triangle strip wanting to send the vertices $(\mathbf{v}_0, \mathbf{v}_1, \mathbf{v}_2, \mathbf{v}_3, swap, \mathbf{v}_4, \mathbf{v}_5, \mathbf{v}_6)$ could be implemented as: $(\mathbf{v}_0, \mathbf{v}_1, \mathbf{v}_2, \mathbf{v}_3, \mathbf{v}_2, \mathbf{v}_4, \mathbf{v}_5, \mathbf{v}_6)$, where the swap has been implemented by resending vertex $\mathbf{v}_2$. This is shown in Figure 7.28.

If a triangle strip consists of m triangles, then three vertices are sent for the first one, followed by one more (ignoring swaps) for each of the remaining $m-1$ triangles. This means that the average number of vertices, v_a, sent for a triangle strip of length m can be expressed as:

$$v_a = \frac{3 + (m-1)}{m} = 1 + \frac{2}{m} \qquad (7.11)$$

As can easily be seen, $v_a \to 1$ as $m \to \infty$. This might not seem to have much relevance for real-world cases, but consider a more reasonable value. If $m = 10$, then $v_a = 1.2$, which means that, on average, only 1.2 vertices are sent per triangle. The attractiveness of triangle strips stems from this fact. Depending on where the bottleneck is located in the rendering pipeline, there is a potential for saving two-thirds of the time spent rendering without triangle strips.[15] The speed-up is due to avoiding redundant operations, such as lighting calculations, clipping, matrix transformations, etc.

Before we examine how to decompose an arbitrary triangle mesh into triangle strips, we will take a glance at a similar concept—namely, triangle fans.

---

[14]This implementation of a swap results in a triangle with no area.
[15]This also holds for triangle fans.

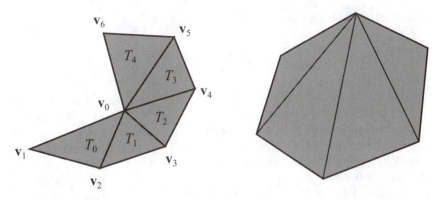

Figure 7.29. The left figure illustrates the concept of a triangle fan. Triangle T_0 sends vertices $\mathbf{v}_0$ (the center vertex), $\mathbf{v}_1$, and $\mathbf{v}_2$. The subsequent triangles, T_i ($i > 0$), send only vertex $\mathbf{v}_{i+2}$. The right figure shows a convex polygon, which can always be turned into one triangle fan.

7.4.2 Fans

Take a look at Figure 7.29, which shows a triangle fan, another kind of set of connected triangles. If we wish to render these triangles, we are in exactly the same beneficial situation as we were for triangle strips, because of the triangle-fan construction primitive supported by most low-level graphics APIs. Notice that a general convex polygon is easily converted into one triangle fan.[16] The vertex shared by all triangles is called the *center vertex* and is vertex 0 in the figure. For the starting triangle 0, send vertices 0, 1, and 2 (in that order), which is a similar start-up phase as that used for triangle strips. For subsequent triangles, the center vertex (number 0) is always used together with the previously sent vertex and the vertex currently being sent. Triangle 1 is therefore easily formed merely by sending vertex 3, thereby forming a triangle defined by vertices 0 (always included), 2 (the previously sent vertex), and 3 (the newly sent vertex, which is sent to create triangle 1). Further on, triangle 2 is constructed by sending vertex 4. Subsequent triangles are formed in the same manner.

A triangle fan of n vertices is defined as an ordered vertex list

$$\{\mathbf{v}_0, \mathbf{v}_1, \ldots, \mathbf{v}_{n-1}\}$$

(where $\mathbf{v}_0$ is called the center vertex), with a structure imposed upon the list

---

[16]Convexity testing is discussed and code is given by Schorn and Fisher [319].

indicating that triangle i is

$$\triangle \mathbf{v}_0 \mathbf{v}_{i+1} \mathbf{v}_{i+2} \qquad\qquad (7.12)$$

where $0 \leq i < n - 2$.

The analysis of the average number of vertices for a triangle fan of length m (i.e., consisting of m triangles), also denoted v_a, is the same as for triangle strips (see Equation 7.11), since they have the same start-up phase and then send only one vertex per new triangle. Similarly, when $m \to \infty$, v_a for triangle fans naturally also tends toward one vertex per triangle. For $m = 5$ (it is harder to find fans than strips, and so we use a smaller value of m than we might for strips), $v_a = 1.4$, which is still much better than 3. As for triangle strips, the start-up cost for the first triangle (always costing three vertices) is amortized over the subsequent triangles.

Any triangle fan can be converted into a triangle strip (which will contain many swaps), but not vice versa.

7.4.3 Creating Strips

Now, given an arbitrary triangle mesh, how can it be decomposed efficiently into triangle strips and fans? With luck, your graphics library provides a function or a class for doing this. Examples are the function pfdMeshGSet from Performer [93] and the class opTriStripper from Optimizer [277], which both perform well in terms of creation time and the average length of the triangle strips. A visualization of the triangle strips of a model is shown in Figure 7.30.

Obtaining optimal triangle strips has been shown to be an NP-complete problem [101], and therefore we have to be satisfied with heuristic methods that come close to the lower bound on the number of strips. Here, two methods for constructing triangle strips from polygonal models are presented.[17] The first one, called *the SGI algorithm* [6], is important for understanding the second method, called STRIPE [99, 100].

Both of these methods start by creating an adjacency data structure for the polygon set; i.e., for each edge belonging to a polygon, a reference to its neighbor polygon is stored. The number of neighbors of a polygon is called its *degree* and is an integer between zero and the number of vertices of the polygon.

Euler's theorem for *connected planar graphs* [31], which is shown in Equation 7.13, helps in determining the average number of vertices that have to be

---

[17]An algorithm for creating both strips and fans has been presented by Xiang et al. [388]. Its creation of strips is reported to be faster than those of STRIPE and the SGI algorithm. STRIPE generated less strips but used more vertices.

sent to the pipeline.

$$n_v - n_e + n_f = 2 \qquad (7.13)$$

where n_v is the number of vertices, n_e is the number of edges, and n_f is the number of faces in the graph. Since every edge has two faces (in a connected graph), and every face has at least three edges (exactly three for triangles), $2n_e \geq 3n_f$ holds. Inserting this fact into Euler's theorem and simplifying yields $n_f \leq 2n_v - 4$. If all faces are triangles, then $2n_e = 3n_f \Rightarrow n_f = 2n_v - 4$. All in all, this means that the number of triangles is less than or equal to twice the number of vertices in a triangulation, and since the average number of vertices per triangle in a strip approaches one, every vertex has to be sent at least twice (on average).

The SGI Algorithm

This algorithm works only for fully triangulated models, meaning that if a model contains polygons with more than three vertices, then these polygons have to be triangulated before being fed into the triangle strip creation code.

Greedy algorithms are optimization methods that make choices that are locally optimal (they choose what looks best at the moment) [68]; the SGI algorithm is greedy, in the sense that the next triangle in the triangle strip it chooses always has the lowest degree (lowest number of neighbors). More specifically, it starts by choosing an arbitrary triangle of lowest degree (greater than zero), and

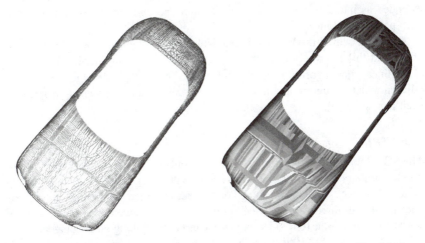

Figure 7.30. The left image shows some surfaces of a car in wireframe mode. The right image shows the same model, but here each triangle strip has been randomly colored. *(Model is reused courtesy of Nya Perspektiv Design AB.)*

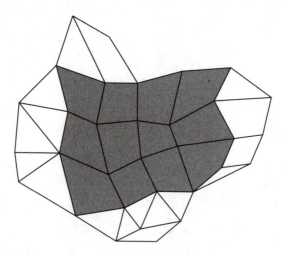

Figure 7.31. A patch is a rectangular region of quads. The largest patch in this polygon set is marked in grey. The STRIPE algorithm then turns the largest patch into a triangle strip, and finally extends the start and the end of the triangle strip as much as possible.

then continues in the manner described. If there should be a tie—that is, if there is more than one triangle with the (same) lowest degree—then the algorithm looks at the neighbors' neighbors (degrees). If again there is no unambiguous way to make a selection, a triangle is arbitrarily selected. Finally, the strip is extended as much as possible in both its start and end directions, making each strip potentially longer.

The idea behind this method is that isolated triangles will not make any strip at all, and this is exactly what the SGI algorithm tends to minimize.

A linear time algorithm can be implemented by using hash tables to store the adjacency data structure and a priority queue for finding the starting triangle of each new strip [6].

The STRIPE Algorithm

The SGI algorithm is a local method—i.e., it only checks its neighbors or neighbors' neighbors for each triangle selection. STRIPE gains efficiency by acting on a global level. It takes advantage of the fact that models often have polygons with more than three vertices. Such polygons can be triangulated in a variety of ways; for example, a four-sided polygon can be split along either diagonal.

Evans et al. [99, 100] note that typical polyhedral models contain many quadrilateral faces (quads), and that these are often connected in large regions. The idea is that such regions are easy to turn into long triangle strips. Therefore,

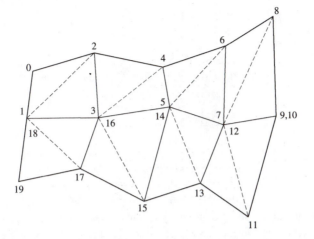

Figure 7.32. A 2 × 4 quad mesh patch is turned into one triangle strip at a cost of three swaps per turn. Each quad is triangulated in order to allow a long triangle strip to be formed. For clarity, vertex doubling is used to show the process of turning the corner and joining the upper row of quads with the lower. In order to use doubling, vertex 9 is sent twice, appearing as 9 and 10 in the figure. Two empty triangles are generated: triangles 8-9-10 and 9-10-11 have no area.

the algorithm starts by trying to find large *patches*, which are rectangular regions made of quads. This is called *patchification*, and in Figure 7.31 a typical patch is shown. Each of these regions is then turned into a strip, which is extended as far as possible in both directions. The extension is accomplished using a technique quite similar to the SGI algorithm, with the exception that polygons can be triangulated intelligently to obtain longer strips. Only patches larger than a certain cutoff size are converted into triangle strips (setting this cut-off to five was found experimentally to give the best result [100]). To convert a patch into a triangle strip, the algorithm turns each row of the patch into a triangle strip and then connects the next row by turning the corner. It costs three swaps at each turn of a patch, or alternatively it costs two extra vertices if one vertex is doubled instead. The doubling method is illustrated in Figure 7.32. Because turns are expensive, the "walk" direction on the patch is chosen to minimize the number of turns, which means that walking is done along the longest side of the patch. Some of the results of the relevant research of Evans et al. [99, 100] are that:

- There is practically no need to develop better algorithms, since the results of the current algorithms are close to the theoretical lower bound.[18]

---

[18]The theoretical lower bound for n triangles is $n + 2$ vertices.

- The STRIPE algorithm is between 10% and 30% better than the SGI algorithm.

- STRIPE gets its better performance more from reducing the number of swaps than from reducing the number of strips.

7.4.4   Polygon Meshes

Triangle fans and strips are popular acceleration primitives, but there is support for polygon meshes within both Direct3D and OpenGL. The trend is for graphics accelerators to take advantage of meshes as much as possible, for reasons detailed in Section 8.4. Essentially, it is more efficient to transform a vertex only once. Strips and fans allow some data sharing, but meshes allow full sharing.

Polygon meshes consist of a list of vertices and a set of outlines. Each vertex contains a position and other additional data, such as diffuse and specular colors, shading normal, texture coordinates, and an edge draw flag. Each outline has a list of integer indices. Each index is a number from 0 to $n - 1$, where n is the number of vertices, and so points to a vertex in the list. Forming such lists and outlines from a set of unconnected polygons is discussed in depth in Section 9.3.

Further Reading and Resources

The Inventor Mentor [371] discusses the way scene graphs operate. For an in-depth treatment of a wide range of tree structures and their precise definitions, see Samet's books [306, 307]. Abrash's book [1] offers a thorough treatment of the use of polygon-based BSP trees and their application in games such as Doom and Quake. A number of different optimizations (and their combination) of view-frustum culling are presented by Assarsson and Möller [18].

The combination of different speed-up techniques is non-trivial. Aliaga et al. [8, 9, 10] have successfully combined several algorithms for extremely large scenes.

The source code for STRIPE is available online. See reference [100] or visit this book's website at http://www.realtimerendering.com/.

Chapter 8
Pipeline Optimization

"We should forget about small efficiencies, say about 97% of the time: premature optimization is the root of all evil."
–Donald Knuth

As we saw in Chapter 2, the process of rendering an image is based on a pipelined architecture with three conceptual stages— *application*, *geometry*, and *rasterizer*. Due to this architecture, one of these stages will *always* be the bottleneck, the slowest stage in the pipeline. This obviously implies that the bottleneck stage sets the limit for the throughput, i.e., the total rendering performance, and so is a prime candidate for *optimization*.

Optimizing the performance of the rendering pipeline resembles the process of optimizing a pipelined processor (CPU) [180], in that it consists mainly of two steps. First, the bottleneck of the pipeline is located. Second, that stage is optimized in some way, and after that, step one is repeated if the performance goals have not been met. Note that the bottleneck may or may not be located at the same place after the optimization step. It is a good idea to put only enough effort into optimizing the bottleneck stage so that the bottleneck moves to another stage. Several other stages may have to be optimized before this stage becomes the bottleneck again. This is why effort should not be wasted on over-optimizing a stage.

Another way to capitalize on the pipelined construction is to recognize that when the slowest stage cannot be optimized further, the other stages can be made to work just as much as the slowest stage. This will not change performance, since the speed of the slowest stage will not be altered. For example, say that the bottleneck is in the application stage, which takes 50 milliseconds (ms), while the others each take 25 ms. This means that without changing the speed of the rendering pipeline (50 ms equals 20 frames per second), the geometry and the rasterizer stages could also do their work in 50 ms. For example, we could use a more sophisticated lighting model or increase the level of realism with shadows and reflections (assuming that this does not increase the workload on the application stage).

Pipeline optimization is a process in which we first maximize the rendering speed, then allow the stages that are not bottlenecks to consume as much time as the bottleneck. When reading this chapter, the dictum

KNOW YOUR ARCHITECTURE

should constantly be in the back of your mind, since optimization techniques vary greatly for different architectures. Note also that the division of the pipeline into the three stages— application, geometry, and rasterizing—is a conceptual division. Depending on the architecture, the true pipeline stages may look different. For example, the application and geometry stages are sometimes both performed by a single CPU, and so should be treated as one stage when optimizing.

8.1   Locating the Bottleneck

The process of optimization can be very time consuming, and so it is often infeasible to optimize every stage in the graphics pipeline. If every stage is optimized, then a boost in performance is guaranteed, but with a cost of the programmer's time and possibly with a potentially unnecessary trade-off in rendering quality. Another drawback of optimizing everything is that we will not learn which stages in the pipeline are not bottleneck stages. These stages can be exploited to create higher-quality rendering without affecting overall performance.

The first step in optimizing a pipeline is to locate the bottleneck. This is not easily done simply by timing the process, since if you clock the time from the start of rendering until the image has been rendered, you will be looking at the time it takes for the data to pass through the *entire* pipeline. It is more reasonable to check the time at one location in the code (for example, after a screen clear), and stop timing the next time that location is executed. This way, however, you will only obtain information on how long the bottleneck stage takes to execute, not on where the bottleneck is located. Recall that the total time of rendering an image is the time of the bottleneck stage.[1] Another approach would be to clock the individual stages, but that is often difficult since the rasterizer stage and sometimes the geometry stage are implemented in dedicated graphics hardware.

We have to take other approaches to locate the bottleneck. One way of doing this is to set up a number of tests, where each test only affects one stage at a time. If the total rendering time is affected, i.e., lowered, then the bottleneck has been found. A related way of testing a stage is to reduce the workload

---

[1]This is not always quite true, as there may be overhead associated with communications between stages.

on the other stages without reducing the workload on the stage being tested. If performance does not change, then the bottleneck is the stage where the workload was not altered. What follows is a set of tests that use these methods to find the bottleneck.

8.1.1   Testing the Application Stage

If the platform being used is supplied with a utility for measuring the workload on the processor(s), then that utility can be used to see if your program uses 100% (or near that) of the CPU processing power.[2] If that is the case, then your program is *CPU-limited*. When the geometry stage is performed by the CPU, this method does not work. Intel has a tool called *VTune* [363] which can analyze where the time is spent in the application or in a driver (geometry processing). Intel's *IPEAK: Graphics Performance Toolkit* [197] is a software package designed specifically for pipeline load analysis and graphics hardware accelerator measurement, and it is invaluable in writing drivers [255].

Another smarter way to test for CPU limits is to send down data that causes the other stages to do little or no work. For some APIs this can be accomplished by simply using a null driver (a driver that accepts calls but does nothing) instead of a real driver. Another method that works for some architectures is to substitute API calls. In OpenGL this can be done by replacing all `glVertex3fv` and `glNormal3fv` calls with `glColor3fv` calls [202]. This does not change the workload on the CPU at all—it sends as much data as it did before, but the workload on both the geometry and the rasterizer stages is greatly reduced. The geometry stage has no lighting to compute, no clipping to perform, no screen mapping to do, nor any vertices or normals to transform. The rasterizer stage does not receive any vertices from the geometry stage, so it does not get any primitives to render. How should this test be interpreted? If performance does not improve, then the program is definitely CPU-limited, since the geometry and rasterizer stages do not have any tasks to perform other than receiving and sending data.

8.1.2   Testing the Geometry Stage

The geometry stage is the most difficult stage to test. This is because if the workload on this stage is changed, then the workload on one or both of the other stages is often changed as well. One parameter that only affects the workload

---

[2]For Unix systems, there are usually programs called `top` or `osview` that show the process workload on the CPU(s). For Windows NT there is the Task Manager.

on the geometry stage is the type and number of light sources. If all light sources in the scene are disabled or removed and the performance goes up, then the bottleneck is located in the geometry stage, and the program is said to be *transform-limited* or *transform-bounded*. Another test is to increase the number of light sources to the maximum,[3] and to set the light source type to the most expensive one, i.e., spot lights. If the performance remains intact with these changes, then the bottleneck is *not* located in the geometry stage.

Another strategy is to test both the application and rasterizer stages for the bottleneck, and if neither of these is the bottleneck, then the geometry stage must be.

8.1.3   Testing the Rasterizer Stage

The rasterizer stage is the easiest and fastest to test: simply decrease the resolution of the window where the images are being rendered. This does not affect the application stage nor the geometry stage, but does affect the workload on the rasterizer stage, since the result is that it has to *fill* fewer pixels. Should the total rendering performance increase with a decrease of the rendering resolution, then the graphics pipeline is said to be *fill-limited* or *fill-bounded*—the bottleneck is in the rasterizer stage.

Other tests would be to turn off texturing, fog, blending, and depth buffering if those features have a performance penalty on the graphics hardware. Again, if the total rendering time decreases, then the rasterizer stage is the bottleneck.

8.2   Optimization

Once a bottleneck has been located, we want to optimize that stage to boost the performance. Optimizing techniques for the application, geometry, and rasterizer stages are presented next. Some of these optimizations trade off quality for speed, and some are just clever tricks for making the execution of a certain stage faster.

8.2.1   Application Stage

The application stage is optimized by making the code and the memory accesses of the program faster. Detailed code optimization is out of the scope of this book, and optimization techniques usually differ from one CPU manufacturer to another. The best approach is to consult the CPU manual of the computer that is used. However, here we will give some general optimization techniques that apply to most CPUs.

---

[3]There is usually a maximum number of light sources allowed in a scene.

First, turn *on* the optimization flags for the compiler. There are usually a number of different flags, and you will have to check which of these apply to your code. This may help quite a bit in some cases, but fast code cannot be created entirely by the compiler—for that, human optimization is needed, together with knowledge about the CPU architecture. For code optimization it is crucial to locate the place in the code where most of the time is spent. A good code profiler is key in finding these code hot spots. Optimization efforts should be made in these places.

The basic rule of optimization is to try a variety of tactics: reexamine algorithms, assumptions, and code syntax, trying as many variants as possible. CPU architecture and compiler performance often limit the user's ability to form an intuition about how to write the fastest code, so question your assumptions and keep an open mind. For example, Booth [47] shows a piece of code in which a seemingly useless array access actually feeds the cache and speeds the overall routine by 25%.[4]

Below we present tricks and methods for writing fast code, and then we address memory issues. These considerations apply to most pipelined CPUs with a memory hierarchy and a cache at the topmost level. The rules are constantly changing, though, so it helps to know your target architecture well (and to keep in mind that it will change someday, so some optimizations made now may eventually become useless or counterproductive). For example, `float`-to-`long` conversion is slow on Pentiums due to compliance with the C ANSI standard. A custom assembly language routine can save significant time (while sacrificing ANSI compliance) [22].

Code Issues

The list that follows gives some tricks for writing fast code.

- Avoid using division as much as possible. Such instructions usually take four to 39 times longer to execute than most of the other instructions. For example, take normalizing a three-dimensional vector. Conceptually, this is done by dividing all elements in the vector by the length of the vector. Instead of dividing three times, it is faster to compute $1/l$, where l is the length of the vector, and then multiply all elements by this factor.

- Unroll small loops in order to get rid of the loop overhead. However, this makes the code bigger and thus may degrade cache performance. Also, branch prediction usually works very well on loops.

---

[4]A cache is a small fast-memory area that exists because there is usually much coherence in a program. That is, nearby locations in memory tend to be accessed one after another, and code is often accessed sequentially.

- Conditional branches are often expensive, though most processors have branch prediction, which means as long as the branches can be consistently predicted the cost can be low. However, a mispredicted branch may be very expensive on some architectures.

- Math functions such as sin, cos, tan, exp, arcsin, etc. are expensive and should be used with care.

- Use inline code for small functions that are frequently called.

- Lower floating-point precision when reasonable. For example, on an Intel Pentium, floating-point division normally takes 39 cycles at 80 bits of precision, but only 19 cycles at 32 bits (however, at any precision, division by a power of 2 takes around 8 cycles) [47]. When choosing `float` instead of `double`, remember to attach an `f` at the end of constants, otherwise they and whole expressions will be cast to `double`. So `float x=2.42f;` is faster than `float x=2.42;`.

- Lower precision is also better, since less data is then sent down the graphics pipeline.

- Try different ways of coding the same algorithm. Predecrementing (`--cnt`) instead of postdecrementing (`cnt--`) can generate less code on some compilers, as can using indexing and avoiding pointer increments, e.g., doing `p[n] = q[n];` instead of `*p++ = *q++;` [47]. Hecker [169] shows how a surprisingly large amount of time was saved by testing variants of a simple matrix multiplier.

- Use `const` whenever possible, as the compiler may use it as a hint for optimization.

- Virtual methods, dynamic casting, and sending structs by value have some efficiency penalties.

Memory Issues

Dealing with writing fast code with respect to the memory hierarchy is becoming more and more important on the various CPU architectures. Below is a list of pointers that should be kept in consideration when programming.

- Assume nothing when it comes to the system memory routines (or anything else, for that matter). For example, Abrash [1] notes that the `memcpy()` routine he was using was found months later to not be optimized. It was performing slow byte-by-byte copies instead of copying four-byte chunks. See Libes' book [231] for tips on optimizing such routines.

- Memory that is accessed sequentially in the code should also be stored sequentially in the memory. For example, when rendering a triangle mesh, store texture coordinate #0, normal #0, color #0, vertex #0, texture coordinate #1, normal #1, etc., sequentially in memory.

- Try to exploit the cache(s) of the architecture. A bad access pattern in the memory may ruin the entire performance of the code.

- Cache prefetching [13]: for good code performance, it is vital that the code that is going to be executed and the memory that is going to be accessed next is in the cache. The penalty for not having these blocks in the cache when needed can degrade performance enormously. Some architectures have special a *prefetch* instruction that fetches a block of memory into the cache before it is being accessed.[5] On those architectures there are also compilers that automatically generate these instructions. For those that do not have a such a compiler or architecture, *garbage instructions* [47] can be used to feed a sequence of the memory into the cache.

- Avoid pointer indirection,[6] jumps, and function calls, as these may eliminate the advantages of having a cache on the CPU [344]. These problems can easily decrease the performance of the cache. Note also that a large program implies a small probability that the function that is about to be called is in the cache and thus stalls the processing [344].

- The functions `malloc()` and `free()` may be slow on some systems, so it is often better to allocate a big pool of memory at start-up, and then use your own allocation and free routines for handling the memory of that pool. The normal `malloc()` and `free()` can then be used only when necessary [183]. For multiprocessor systems this is even more important, since a call to these functions may end up in a mutual exclusion lock [344].

Another way to make the application stage run faster is to change to a machine with more processors, and then parallelize the code. Since the penalties for cache misses are greater for a multi-processor system, it is important to adapt the code to the memory system for such architectures.

---

[5]For SPARC processors there is `prefetch`, and for PowerPC it is called `dcbt` (data cache block touch).

[6]You get pointer indirection when you follow a pointer to another pointer and so on (typical for linked lists and tree structures). McVoy and Staelin [246] show a code example that follows a linked list through pointers. This causes cache misses for instructions both before and after, and their example stalls the CPU more than 100 times longer than it takes to follow the pointer (if the cache could provide the address of the pointer).

8.2.2 Geometry Stage

The geometry stage is responsible for transforms, lighting, clipping, projection, and screen mapping. Transforms and lighting are processes that can be optimized relatively easily; the rest are difficult or impossible to optimize.

Transforms

If a model is transformed into a static location, then such a transform can be avoided by *flattening* the transform. This means that instead of transforming the model each time it is rendered, the vertices and the normals are transformed once as a preprocess before the rendering starts. These transformations could involve translations, rotations, scalings, etc.

Connected Primitives

Connected primitives such as triangle strips and fans, quadrilateral (quad) strips, and polylines reduce the amount of data processed per primitive. Transform, lighting, projection, clipping, and screen-mapping operations may all gain from these savings. Triangle strips, fans, and meshes also are discussed in Section 7.4. Quad strips are similar to triangle strips in that adjacent primitives share an edge. For the first quad, all four vertices are sent. After that, only two vertices are needed for each additional quad. This results in $2 + 2n$ vertices being processed instead of $4n$. Polylines (also known as *line strips*) and quad strips are similar to triangle strips in that they exploit the fact that fewer vertices need to be sent through the pipeline if the primitives are connected. For a set of lines that are connected (i.e., where the last vertex of the previous line is connected with the first vertex of the next line), it suffices to send both vertices of the first line and then continue by sending the second vertex of each remaining line. This gives $1 + n$ vertices to process instead of $2n$.

Requiring less processing improves the performance of the geometry stage. Since fewer vertices are sent, this also accelerates the application stage a bit.

Lighting

Lighting computations can be optimized in several ways. First, the types of light sources being used should be considered. Is lighting needed for all polygons? Sometimes a model only requires texturing, or texturing with colors at the vertices, or simply colors at the vertices. For example, a large background polygon might look bad when lit by positional light sources, because its vertices are far away from the lights. It might be better simply not to light the background polygon at all. If light sources must be used, then directional light sources are faster than point lights, which in turn are faster than spot lights. Directional lights are faster because the pipeline does not need to compute and normalize the vector from the vertex to the light source position. Instead, the light direction is used. Spot lights are more expensive than point lights because with spot lights the pipeline needs to test whether vertices are inside the light cone and also to compute the exponential fall-off from the center of the light cone. Note also that a gray-scale light source can be faster than a colored light source. The number of light sources also influences the performance of the geometry stage. Some graphics accelerators are optimized for lighting calculations with only one light source. More light sources obviously means less speed.

Second, in some APIs, a *non-local viewer* can be used. This feature does not affect the view itself; it is a simplification that affects only the specular highlight computation and environment mapping calculations. The idea is to treat the camera as if it were at infinity, but only for these lighting computations. Normally, the vector from the eye to the vertex being illuminated is computed and normalized—a costly per-vertex computation. With a non-local viewer, this vector is approximated with the constant vector $(0, 0, -1)$ in eye-coordinates.[7] When used along with directional lights, it means that such values as h (see Section 4.3.2) can be computed just once for each scene. Using this feature causes a slight shift in the locations of specular highlights, but such shifts are not usually detectable.[8] One situation in which the shift is noticeable is when a flat surface is shiny and receives a bright highlight (i.e., when the light reflects toward the eye). In this case, a disturbing "flash" (sudden brightness) appears as the surface passes through this orientation, since all reflection vectors are the same. Direct3D offers a variation on the non-local viewer concept, using *parallel-point lights*. The idea is that the point light establishes a single direction vector from it to the center of a vertex mesh. This direction is then used for all vertices of the mesh, and the light is therefore parallel. This simplifies lighting computations.

Third, the normals of a model must be normalized when calculating the lighting. For a model that will *not* be scaled in any way during rendering, those normals should be normalized as a preprocess (with all scalings accounted for). This could be done in two ways. The model may be transformed as before, and the normals may be scaled (as a preprocess) in such a way that they are normalized after all transforms have been applied to the model. Or this optimization could be thought of as part of the flattening: simply flatten the transforms for the model, and after that has been done, normalize the normals. The graphics API needs to be told that the normals are already normalized so

---

[7]Or $(0, 0, 1)$, if the viewer is looking along the positive z-axis.

[8]This feature is worth avoiding when previewing a scene which will be sent to a high-quality renderer, as the shift will often be noticeable between images.

that the graphics engine does not waste time normalizing them. For uniform scaling, some implementations avoid scaling the normals.

Fourth, use the fact that flat shading is faster than Gouraud shading, since for flat shading the lighting is computed only once per polygon, instead of once per vertex as in Gouraud shading. This may not be faster for polygon meshes, where the lighting calculations at the vertices are shared by the triangles.

Fifth, if lighting is computed for both sides of a polygon and is not needed, then turn this feature off.

Sixth, materials with a specular component set to $(0, 0, 0)$ can avoid the rather expensive highlight calculations in the lighting equation (see Section 4.20). This is especially useful if the lighting computations are done with the CPU.

Finally, if light sources are static with respect to geometry, and the polygonal data is attached to a material without specular parameters, then the diffuse and ambient lighting can be precomputed and stored as colors at the vertices. For greater realism, simple shadows can be captured by direct visibility tests between lights and vertices, and then combined with the ambient and diffuse lighting (the diffuse lighting is set to zero if the object is in shadow). The result is that lighting computations can be turned off for those objects, and so they are often called *preshaded* or *prelit*. Radiosity [59, 333] is a rendering method that computes the diffuse global illumination in a scene by letting the photons bounce around until an energy equilibrium is reached. See Plate XX, following page 194. Such illumination can also be precomputed and stored as colors at the vertices or as light maps (see Section 5.7.2). Plate I (following p. 194) shows what can be done with this technique. Specular (view-dependent) contributions can be added in, though care must be taken to avoid having highlights appear in areas which are in shadow.

8.2.3   Rasterizer Stage

The rasterizer stage can be optimized in a variety of ways. For closed (solid) objects and for objects that will never show their back faces (for example, the back side of a wall in a room), backface culling should be turned on (see Section 7.1.1). For a closed object this reduces the number of triangles to be rasterized by approximately 50%. Remember that even though backface culling may help eliminate the unnecessary processing of primitives, it comes with a cost of computing whether the primitive is facing away from the viewer. For example, if all polygons are front-facing, then the backface culling calculations will actually slow down the geometry stage.

Another technique that does not degrade the rendering quality is to turn off Z-buffering at certain times. For example, after the frame buffer has been cleared, any background image can be drawn without the need for depth testing.

Algorithms such as polygon-aligned BSP trees (see Section 7.1.2) have the advantage of never needing to use the Z-buffer. Local BSP trees can also be used, which are then merged in real time during rendering [267].

If there is some geometry that tends to cover a large portion of the screen and thus occludes other objects, then there is a gain in drawing it first. This is because the occluded objects that are drawn later will not write to the Z-buffer. Also, more complex fill operations such as blending and texturing are also avoided for these occluded objects [93].

If none of these methods helps, a trade-off between speed and quality can be made. All features that have a speed penalty can be turned off. Depending on the platform, examples of such features might include expensive texture filtering (bilinear vs. mipmapping, and point vs. trilinear for mipmapping), fog, blending, line drawing and multisampling (antialiasing).

Decreasing the resolution of the window where the images are rendered is a common method of improving performance at the cost of quality. On the InfiniteReality graphics system [50, 262], *dynamic video resizing* can be used to lower the load on the rasterizer subsystem. This works by decreasing the actual image being rendered. When the generated image is to be displayed, the smaller image is enlarged to the desired size using a linear interpolation filter. There is also hardware support (called pipeline instrumentation) for measuring the workload on different stages in the pipeline, so that the size of the rendering window can be dynamically changed as the workload on the different stages of the pipeline changes. The pipeline instrumentation features are of great help in generating accurate timings and simplifying the task of optimization.

For fast line drawing with OpenGL, it is particularly important to disable Gouraud shading if that feature is not being used [245].

To understand the behavior of a program, and especially the load on the rasterizer, it is useful to visualize the depth complexity, which is the number of times a pixel is touched. One simple method of generating a depth complexity image is to use a call like OpenGL's glBlendFunc(GL_ONE, GL_ONE) [87], with Z-buffering disabled. First the image is cleared to black. All objects in the scene are then rendered with the color $(0, 0, 1)$. The effect of the blend function setting is that for each primitive rendered, the values of the written pixels will increase by $(0, 0, 1)$. However, note that if the resolution is lower than eight bits per channel, you may have to use another color, such as, for example $(0, 0, 32)$. The image at the right in Figure 8.1 was rendered with this technique. A pixel with a depth complexity of 0 is then black and a pixel of depth complexity 255 is full blue $(0, 0, 255)$. Depending on the depth complexity, you may want to use the other color channels (red and green) for drawing, in order to be able to see and interpret the depth visualization. You can also draw the primitives in

Figure 8.1. The image on the left shows a model of a three wheeler, and its depth complexity is visualized on the right—the brighter the pixel the more times the pixel has been overwritten. *(The three wheeler model is reused courtesy of Nya Perspektiv Design AB.)*

wireframe, which creates an image that includes information about where the vertices and edges of the primitives clump.

A two-pass approach can be used to count the number of pixels that pass or fail the Z-buffer depth tests [87]. In the first pass, enable Z-buffering and use the method above to count the pixels that have passed the depth test. To count the number of pixels that fail the depth test, increment the stencil buffer upon depth buffer failure. Alternately, render with Z-buffering off to obtain the depth complexity, and then subtract the first-pass results.

These methods can serve to determine the average, minimum, and maximum depth complexity in a scene, the number of pixel per primitive (assuming that the number of primitives that have made it to the scene is known), and the number of pixels that pass versus fail the depth tests. These numbers are useful for understanding the behavior of a real-time graphics application and determining where further optimization may be worthwhile.

8.2.4 Overall Optimization

Here we list some tricks and methods for increasing overall performance.

- Reduce the total number of drawing primitives that have to pass through the (entire) pipeline. This can be done by simplifying the models (see Section 9.4) or by using culling techniques (Section 7.1).

- Choose as low a precision as is possible (without rendering artifacts) on vertices, normal, colors, and texture coordinates. There is sometimes a choice between short, single, and double floating-point precision. Lower precision implies less memory, which means that the data can move more quickly through the pipeline.

- Preprocess the models for rendering in your particular context. As an example, some hardware renders only points, lines, triangles, and quadrilaterals, and some renders only triangles. If self-intersecting and concave polygons are not usually rendered correctly, it is up to the user to see to it that the system can render the data (see Section 9.2).

- Turn off features not in use. Features that are enabled but not in use, i.e., those that have no visible effect on the rendered images, may degrade performance. For example, depth buffering, blending, fog, and texturing can be turned off if a background (non-textured, non-transparent) quadrilateral is the first primitive to be drawn after a frame buffer clear.

- Minimize state changes by grouping objects with a similar rendering state (texture, material, lighting, transparency, etc.). When changing the state, there is usually a need to wholly or partially flush the pipeline. Changes in material parameters, especially shininess, can be very expensive [245]. For k-ary trees (scene graphs), where $k > 2$, leaf nodes with a shared material could be grouped for better performance. However, there are exceptions to this rule of thumb—for some graphics hardware a state change costs less than rendering a triangle [70]. Rendering polygons with a shared texture minimizes texture cache thrashing [253]. A way to minimize texture binding changes is to put several texture images into one large texture and recompute the texture coordinates for the objects involved (see Section 5.3). A disadvantage here is that textures tend to bleed when mipmapping is used.

- Set up primitives in group sizes that are optimized for your architecture. For example, the RealityEngine [7, 202] has an optimized path through the pipeline if the primitives consist of a multiple of three vertices, and the best performance is achieved for 12 vertices (which equals 10 triangles in a triangle strip). For other architectures, like SIMD[9], it is more beneficial to send many vertices at a time, since the SIMD may have significant set-up and tear-down overhead [376]. This kind of loop overhead has to be checked from system to system.

- Make sure (if possible) that all textures reside in the texture memory so that swapping is avoided.

---

[9]Single Instruction Multiple Data.

- Separate two-dimensional from three-dimensional operations, as switching between these may have a significant overhead.

- Call `glGet()` during the set-up phase and avoid it during runtime.

- Make sure to take advantage of the fact that some graphics hardware is optimized for clearing the depth and color buffers simultaneously. Also, Bigos presents a trick for avoiding buffer clears [34].

- Frame buffer reads are usually expensive and are best avoided.

- Use *display lists* (or *retained mode*, as vs. *immediate mode*) for static models if your architecture gains from them. A display list (DL) [275] stores a series of graphics API calls, typically for objects that have an unchanging shape and material. A DL is rendered by being invoked during scene traversal. The contents of the DL are stored in a chunk of consecutive memory, making for better access patterns. A DL acts as a kind of compiled command sequence which may be optimized at runtime for the current hardware configuration. Sometimes a cache for DLs is available, which may eliminate the need to send data through some parts of the pipeline. If a display list is made too small, the overhead involved makes it inefficient to use. The main drawback of DLs is data expansion [245]: in addition to all the original data, information for each command and for each list must also be stored.

A piece of general advice is that *less is more*, meaning that the less data that goes from the application to the graphics accelerator, the faster it will run.

8.3   Balancing the Graphics Pipeline

To be able to see the potential effects of pipeline optimization, it is important to measure the total rendering time per frame with double buffering disabled, i.e., in single-buffer mode. This is because with double buffering turned on, swapping of the buffers only occurs in synchronization with the frequency of the monitor. As an example, consider a monitor with an update frequency of 72 Hz. This means that it takes $t = 1/72 = 0.01389$ s $= 13.89$ ms for the electron beam of the monitor to scan and display the entire screen. Using double buffering means that the update rate of the rendered images must be a multiple of t. If your rendering takes 20 ms (50 Hz) in single-buffer mode, then that rate will be reduced to $20 < 2*13.89$ (36 Hz) in double-buffer mode. This means that the graphics pipeline in this example is idle for $2 * 13.89 - 20 = 7.78$ ms for each frame. This sounds bad, but it can actually be exploited to your advantage, which is the purpose of balancing the pipeline. The idle time can be used for higher-quality rendering.

First of all, additional work can be done by the bottleneck stage as long as we do not cross over into the next multiple of the monitor update time t (e.g., in our previous example, we do not go from 36 Hz to 24 Hz). In the previous example, features could be added until the rendering of a frame takes slightly less than $2 * 13.89$ ms. This will not alter the performance (in double-buffer mode), but if it is exploited correctly, the quality will improve.

Second, at this point of the optimization process, we have maximized the use of the bottleneck stage, but the other stages use less time to complete their tasks. In the same spirit as above, the stages that are *not* bottleneck stages can be made to work harder with no degradation of performance (as long as this extra work does not negatively affect the performance of the bottleneck stage). This is illustrated in Figure 8.2.

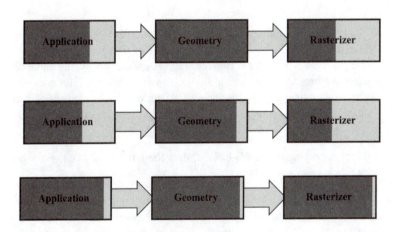

Figure 8.2. Balancing the graphics pipeline. The usage of a stage is illustrated by the dark gray rectangle—the more dark gray area there is, the less idle time a stage has. In the topmost illustration we show a system that uses only single buffering. One stage, which in this case is the geometry stage, uses 100% of its processing power. The application stage uses approximately 75%, and the rasterizer uses about 50% of the available time. The middle row shows a situation with double buffering enabled. This means that the rendering has to be synchronized with the update rate of the monitor, and so the idle time for all stages increases (if the rendering time is not perfectly synchronized with the update rate). The bottom row shows the pipeline after balancing. Here, the idle time at all the stages has been exploited, with no effect on frame rate.

Here are some ideas for using the idle time of both the bottleneck and the non-bottleneck stages:

- Increase the number of triangles (affects all stages).

- Use more lights and more expensive light source types (affects the geometry stage).

- Compute more realistic animations, implement more accurate collision detection, use more sophisticated speed-up techniques (see Chapter 7), and perform other similar tasks, if the application stage is idle.

- Use more expensive texture filtering, fog, blending, etc., if the rasterizer stage is idle.

- Immediately after a screen clear, do *not* fill the graphics pipeline with more graphics commands. Since the graphics hardware is already busy with clearing the frame buffer (which can take significant amount of time), it is better to do application-(CPU-) related work after sending a clear.

- As long as the number of filled pixels does not change, a fill-limited application can easily increase the number of polygons without affecting the performance of the rasterizer stage. In other words, the same object can be represented by more triangles. On the other hand, for a transform-limited application, the number of triangles can be decreased without affecting the number of pixels to be filled, in order to speed up the geometry stage. This is illustrated in Figure 8.3.

- If the rendering is not fill-limited, then the window where the images are drawn can be enlarged.

Most (if not all) pipelines have FIFO (first-in-first-out) queues [5, 7]. See Figure 8.4 for an example. The idea is that FIFOs can be queued up with jobs for the geometry and rasterizer stages. That is, one stage can continue to do its work even if a stage further down the pipeline is not ready for its results; instead, the results are saved so that the next stage can process them when it is ready. Such buffering helps to smooth out the balancing of the pipeline and make small bottlenecks invisible [57].

However, when a FIFO is filled, stages may be *starved* or *blocked*. A stage gets starved when, for example, the application stage is performing some computations (such as collision detection) that take a significant amount of time and the FIFOs before the geometry and the rasterizer stages are empty. In this

Figure 8.3. A large square is subdivided into a large number of triangles on the left, and into two triangles on the right. A transform-limited application can decrease the number of triangles without decreasing the number of filled pixels, in order to reduce the workload on the geometry stage. On the other hand, a fill-limited application can increase the number of triangles (which would result in better shading, as seen in Figure 4.4 in Section 4.3) without degrading performance, as long as the number of filled pixels remains constant.

case, both the geometry and the rasterizer stages are starved because they do not have anything to do. Stage blocking takes place, for example, when the rasterizer is filling a huge polygon. At the same time, the geometry stage can fill the FIFO to the rasterizer with tasks. At this point the geometry stage is blocked, since it can no longer fill the FIFO.

The location of the bottleneck may vary over time within a single frame. This fact should definitely be considered during optimization. As an example, consider a geometrically detailed human drawn against a large polygon acting as the sky. If the human is drawn first, then the pipeline becomes transform-limited, and the rasterizer will be idle. If the drawing order is reversed, the polygon goes through the pipeline to occupy the rasterizer, and then the geometry stage can process the human. The latter order is preferable, since both the geometry stage and the rasterizer stage are not idle. Blocking may occur, but at least there will be more time when both stages are active.

Figure 8.4. The rendering pipeline with FIFO queues. Some architectures are constructed like this, some do not have the first FIFO, and some do not have any FIFOs at all. The FIFOs are used to queue jobs for the subsequent stage.

Another element to consider in load balancing the pipeline is that the load may vary over time between frames. The time it takes to render a frame can be measured. If the measured time is less than a user-defined minimum threshold, then the workload (i.e., scene contents and realism) can be increased. If it goes beyond a user-defined maximum threshold, then the workload should be diminished. These maximum and minimum thresholds should be chosen with some slack, so that the workload is changed before the frame rate is affected. This technique helps to guarantee a user-defined frame rate. Another method that can help is triple buffering (see Section 12.1.4).

8.4 Host and Accelerator

In some situations an even broader view of optimization can be taken. If you have control over the machine configuration used for rendering, then you may be able to apply a thing called money directly to the problem. If the bottleneck is in, say, the application stage, then you can buy a faster processor (or save money by buying a cheaper graphics accelerator). Beyond such changes, it is worth understanding that the border between the CPU host and its graphics hardware support can be modified to some extent. Changing this border's location can increase overall performance by changing where the bottleneck is found.

Graphics hardware exists for the express purpose of accelerating various operations such as texturing and rasterization. Software on the host is slower for some operations, but has the advantage of flexibility. Consider what consequences are faced if lighting, transforming, and clipping are computed with the CPU instead of with a geometry accelerator. The graphics hardware is often poor at sharing per-vertex calculations. Connected primitives alleviate this problem to some extent [254], but not as much as is desired. For example, assume that a triangular mesh is built from a 10×10 grid of vertices. This results in 100 vertices and 162 triangles. If each of these sends three vertices, this would result in 486 floating-point numbers sent through the pipeline. The conclusion is that if lighting is calculated using the CPU (where the calculations are performed once per vertex and then shared), then lighting needs to be computed at only 100 vertices, instead of 486—the graphics card does 4.86 times more lighting calculations. If we are sending triangle strips to the hardware, say 9 strips with 18 triangles each, this cost is reduced to 180 vertices where lighting should be computed—that is still 1.8 times as many computations as doing it on the CPU. That means that the geometry accelerator still needs to be 1.8 times as fast as the CPU on lighting computations.

If lighting is computed by the CPU, then one might contend that we need to send down an additional three floating-point numbers (assuming a color is represented by three floats). This is not true, since we do not need to compute the lighting, which means that we do not need to send the normals. Also, if the colors can be sent as three unsigned bytes, then the gain from using the CPU for lighting is even greater. Clipping and transforming can gain in a similar way, since the CPU can share clipping operations between adjacent triangles and only need to transform each vertex once. This sharing also eliminates the need to send triangles from outside the view frustum through the pipeline. This line of reasoning is used in the design of the display architecture for 3D Studio MAX [49].

With some game cards, acceleration is only available for rasterization and texturing and everything else is done with the CPU. A consequence of this is that the geometric complexity is kept low—few polygons are used, and texturing techniques are used extensively in order to hide the low polygon count. However, APIs and hardware have recently evolved to provide support for treating sets of vertices as units, transforming them all just once. For example, in DirectX6.0 [83], the vertex data can be sent separately from the commands that connect vertices into drawing primitives, and thus the vertices need only be sent once through the pipeline. The primitive is called a *vertex buffer*. OpenGL supports a similar construction called a *vertex array* [245, 275].

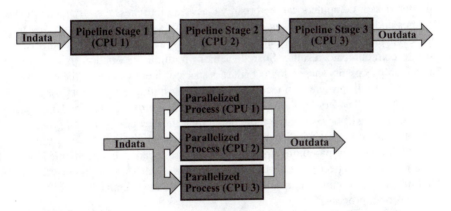

Figure 8.5. Two different ways of utilizing multiple processors. At the top we show how three processors (CPUs) are used in a *multiprocessor pipeline*, and at the bottom we show *parallel* execution on three CPUs. One of the differences between these two implementations is that lower latency can be achieved if the configuration at the bottom is used. On the other hand, it may be easier to use a multiprocessor pipeline. The ideal speed-up for both of these configurations is linear, i.e., using n CPUs would give a speed-up of n times.

For visualizing an object consisting of many small triangles, say, an airplane for design inspection, the situation is quite different. A Boeing-777 may consist of over 500 million triangles [71]. In this case, the geometric complexity is incredibly high and the triangles are often concentrated in a small volume, unlike the triangles in a game, which are spread out. Clearly, rasterization is not the bottleneck. In such cases, hardware rasterization is helpful nonetheless, since that stage can work in parallel with the geometry processing. Software's flexibility means that techniques such as those presented in Chapter 7 can be selectively tested and applied to the problem.

While more and more tasks will move into hardware over the years to come, this tension between the host's flexibility and the accelerator's additional speed will continue indefinitely. Other elements in the mix include parallelism and graphics-specific CPU commands. Hardware designers choose to encode algorithms that give the most additional functionality to the most users at the least cost in gates. Software writers also drive the process, since an algorithm that becomes standard practice in software is a likely candidate for inclusion in hardware. However, there is no known perfect architecture for all rendering situations, so there will always be a need for flexibility in software.

8.5   Multiprocessing

Multiprocessor computers can be broadly classified into *message-passing* architectures and *shared memory multiprocessors*. In message-passing designs, each processor has its own memory area, and messages are sent between the processors to communicate results. Shared memory multiprocessors are just as they sound; all processors share a logical address space of memory among themselves.

Here we will present two methods for utilizing multiple processors for real-time graphics. The first method—*multiprocessor pipelining*, also called temporal parallelism —will be covered in more detail than the second— *parallel processing*, also called spatial parallelism. These two methods are illustrated in Figure 8.5. Multiprocessor pipelining and parallel processing can also be combined, but little research has been done in this area. For this discussion we assume that a multiprocessor computer is available, but do not go into details about different types of multiprocessors.

8.5.1   Multiprocessor Pipelining

As we have seen, pipelining is a method for speeding up execution by dividing a job into certain pipeline stages which are executed in parallel. The result from one pipeline stage is passed on to the next. The ideal speed-up is n times for n pipeline stages, and the slowest stage (the bottleneck) determines the actual speed-up. Up to this point, we have seen pipelining used to run the application, geometry processing, and rasterization in parallel for a single-CPU system. This technique can also be used when multiple processors are available on the host, and is in these cases called *multiprocess pipelining* or *software pipelining*.

Since the rasterizer is always implemented in hardware, this stage cannot be pipelined further with the use of additional processors on the host.[10] The application stage can always use extra processors, while the geometry stage can use them if that stage is not implemented in hardware. For simplicity, it is assumed that the geometry stage is implemented in hardware. However, multiprocessing is not limited in any way to such an architecture—geometry processing could be done in a pipelined fashion on the host CPUs too.

So this leaves the application stage to be pipelined. Therefore, the application stage is divided into three stages [301]: APP, CULL, and DRAW. This is very coarse-grained pipelining, which means that each stage is relatively long. The APP stage is the first stage in the pipeline and therefore controls the others. It is in this stage that the application programmer can put in additional code that does, for example, collision detection. This stage also updates the viewpoint. The CULL stage can perform:

- Traversal and hierarchical view-frustum culling on a scene graph (see Section 7.1.2).

- Level of detail selection (see Section 7.3).

- State sorting—geometry with similar state is sorted into bins in order to minimize state changes. For example, all transparent objects are sorted into one bin, and these objects are also sorted in a rough back-to-front order for correct rendering.

- Finally (and always performed), generation of a simple list of all objects that should be rendered.

The DRAW stage takes the list from the CULL stage and issues all graphics calls in this list. This means that it does not traverse anything, it only feeds the geometry stage, which in turn feeds the rasterizer stage. Figure 8.6 shows some examples of how this pipeline can be used. If one processor is available, then all three stages are run on that CPU. If two CPUs are available, then APP and CULL can be executed on one CPU and DRAW on the other. Another configuration

---

[10]However, if there are multiple rasterizer units then each CPU could feed its own rasterizer.

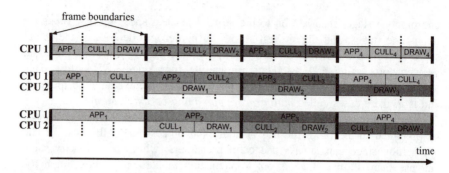

Figure 8.6. Different configurations for a multiprocessor pipeline. The thick lines represent synchronization between the stages, and the subscripts represent the frame number. At the top a single CPU pipeline is shown. In the middle and at the bottom are shown two different pipeline subdivisions using two CPUs. The middle has one pipeline stage for **APP** and **CULL** and one pipeline stage for **DRAW**. This is a suitable subdivision if **DRAW** has much more work to do than the others. At the bottom, **APP** has one pipeline stage and the other two have another. This is suitable if **APP** has more much more work than the others. Note that the bottom two configurations have more time for the **APP**, **CULL**, and **DRAW** stages.

would be to execute **APP** on one processor and **CULL** and **DRAW** on the other. Which is the best depends on the workloads for the different stages. Finally, if the host has three CPUs, then each stage can be executed on a separate CPU. This possibility is shown in Figure 8.7.

The advantage of this technique is that the throughput, i.e., the rendering speed, increases. The downside is that, compared to parallel processing, the latency is greater. Latency is the time it takes from the polling of the user's actions to the final image. This should not be confused with frame rate, which is the number of frames displayed per second. For example, say the user is using a head-mounted display. The determination of the head's position may take 50 milliseconds to reach the CPU, then it takes 15 milliseconds to render the frame. The latency is then 65 milliseconds from initial input to display. Even though the frame rate is 66.7 Hz (1/0.015 seconds), interactivity will feel sluggish because of the delay in sending the position changes to the CPU. Ignoring any delay due to user interaction (which is a constant under both systems), multiprocessing has more latency because it uses a pipeline. As is discussed in detail in the next section, parallel processing breaks up the frame's work into pieces that are run concurrently.

In comparison to using a single CPU on the host, multiprocessor pipelining gives a higher frame rate and the latency is about the same or a little greater due to the cost of synchronization. Note that the latency increases with the number of stages in the pipeline and that for a well-balanced application the speed-up is n times for n CPUs.

One technique for reducing the latency is to update the viewpoint and other latency-critical parameters at the end of the APP stage [301]. This reduces the latency by (approximately) one frame. Another way to reduce latency is to execute CULL and DRAW overlapped. This means that the result from CULL is sent over to DRAW as soon as anything is ready for rendering. For this to work, there has to be some buffering, typically a FIFO, between those stages. The stages are stalled on empty and full conditions; i.e., when the buffer is full, then CULL has to stall, and when the buffer is empty, DRAW has to stall. The disadvantage is that techniques such as state sorting cannot be used to the same extent, since primitives have to be rendered as soon as they have been processed by CULL. This latency reduction technique is visualized in Figure 8.7.

The pipeline in this figure uses a maximum of three CPUs, and the stages have certain tasks. However, this technique is in no way limited to this configuration—rather, you can use any number of CPUs and divide the work in any way you want. The key is to make a smart division of the entire job to be done so that the pipeline tends to be balanced. For example, multiprocessor pipelining has been used to speed up the occlusion culling algorithm in Section 7.1.5 using a different pipeline stage division than the one presented here [391]. Multiprocessor pipelining has also been used by Funkhouser [114] to speed up LOD management (see Section 7.3.4) and portal cullling (Section 7.1.3).

The multiprocessor pipelining technique requires a minimum of synchronization in that it need only synchronize when switching frames. In all kinds of multiprocessing systems there are many factors to consider when it comes to data sharing, data exclusion, multibuffering, and more. Details on these topics can be found in Rohlf and Helman's paper [301].

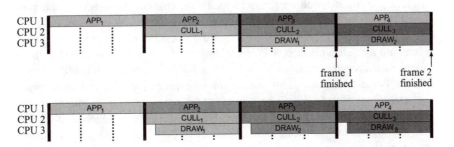

Figure 8.7. At the top, a three-stage pipeline is shown. In comparison to the configurations in Figure 8.6, this configuration has more time for each pipeline stage. The bottom illustration shows a way to reduce the latency: the CULL and the DRAW are overlapped with FIFO buffering in between.

8.5.2   Parallel Processing

The most apparent disadvantage of using a multiprocessor pipeline technique is that the latency tends to get longer. For some applications, such as flight simulators, fast games, etc., this is not acceptable.[11]

If multiple processors are available, one can try to parallelize the code instead, which may result in shorter latency. To do this, the program must possess the characteristics of *parallelism*. This means that, for a program with no or a small amount of parallelism, there is no gain in parallelizing the program—a parallel version may even become slower due to the overhead involved in extra synchronization, etc. However, many programs and algorithms do have a large amount of parallelism and can therefore benefit.

There are several different methods for parallelizing an algorithm. Assume that n processors are available. Using static assignment [75], the total work package is divided into n work packages. Each processor then takes care of a work package, and all processors execute their work packages in parallel. When all processors have completed their work packages, it may be necessary to merge the results from the processors. For this to work, the workload must be highly predictable. When that is not the case, dynamic assignment algorithms that adapt to different workloads may be used [75]. These use one or more work pools. When jobs are generated, they are put into the work pools. CPUs can then fetch one or more jobs from the queue when they have finished their current job. Care must be taken so that only one CPU can fetch a particular job, and so that the overhead in maintaining the queue does not damage performance. Larger jobs mean that the overhead for maintaining the queue becomes less of a problem, but, on the other hand, if the jobs are too big, then performance may degrade due to imbalance in the system—i.e., one or more CPUs may starve.

As for the multiprocessor pipeline, the ideal speed-up for a parallel program running on n processors would be n times. This is called *linear speed-up*. Even though linear speed-up rarely happens, the results can sometimes be very close to it.

In Figure 8.5 on page 259, both a multiprocessor pipeline and a parallel processing system with three CPUs are shown. Temporarily assume that these should do the same amount of work for each frame and that both configurations achieve linear speed-up. This means that the execution will run three times faster in comparison to serial execution (i.e., on a single CPU). Furthermore, we assume that the total amount of work per frame takes 30 ms, which would mean that the maximum frame rate on a single CPU would be $1/0.03 \approx 33$ frames per second.

---

[11]When moving the viewpoint, you usually want instant (next-frame) response, but when the latency is long this will not happen, which gives the application an unresponsive feel.

The multiprocessor pipeline would (ideally) divide the work into three equal-sized work packages and let each of the CPUs be responsible for one work packages. Each work package should then take 10 ms to complete. If we follow the work flow through the pipeline, we will see that the first CPU in the pipeline does work for 10 ms (i.e., one-third of the job) and then sends it on to the next CPU. The first CPU then starts working on the first part of the next frame. When a frame is finally finished it has taken 30 ms for it to complete, but since the work has been done in parallel in the pipeline, one frame will be finished every 10 ms. So the latency is 30 ms., and the speed-up is a factor of three (30/10).

Now, a parallel version of the same program would also divide the jobs into three work packages, but these three packages will execute at the same time on the three CPUs. This means that the latency will be 10 ms., and the work for one frame will also take 10 ms. The conclusion is that the latency is much shorter when using parallel processing than when using a multiprocessor pipeline.

Parallel processing is a huge topic in itself. See the *Further Reading and Resources* section that follows for references to work on parallel processing.

Further Reading and Resources

The *Graphics Gems* series includes a number of optimized algorithms for various graphics operations. See this book's website for links to many other performance tuning tricks and procedures at http://www.realtimerendering.com/.

Kempf and Hartman's manual [202] deals with OpenGL for a set of SGI systems and discusses ways to optimize code for their architectures.

Optimizing graphics code for the Intel processors is treated extensively in Michael Abrash's *Black Book* [1]. Rick Booth's book *Inner Loops* [47] focuses entirely on optimization for the Pentium and 486. The program *VTune* [58, 363] facilitates much of the work of determining how various assembly language instructions interact. IPEAK:GPT [197] is indispensable for accelerator driver writers and others.

For more information on compiler optimization techniques, consult the books by Muchnick [264] and Appel [13]. Issues that arise in the design of a parallel graphics API are treated by Igehy et al. [195].

See the book *Parallel Computer Architecture: A Hardware/Software Approach* [75] for more information on parallel programming. OpenMP is an API for shared memory parallel programming that may be of interest; see http://www.openmp.org.

Chapter 9
Polygonal Techniques

"Where there is matter, there is geometry."
–Johannes Kepler

Up to this point we have assumed that the model we rendered is available in exactly the format we need and with just the right amount of detail. In reality we are rarely so lucky. Various modelers have their own particular quirks and limitations, giving rise to ambiguities and errors within the data set and so within renderings. This chapter will discuss a variety of problems that are encountered within polygonal data sets, along with some of the fixes and workarounds for these problems.

The overarching goals for polygonal representation (or any other representation, for that matter) in computer graphics are visual accuracy and speed. "Accuracy" is a term that depends upon the context; for a machine part it may mean that the model displayed falls within some tolerance range, while for an aircraft simulation game what is important is the overall impression. Note that the way a model is used is a key differentiator. An engineer wants to control and position a part in real-time and wants every bevel and chamfer on the machine part visible at every moment. Compare this to a game where, if the frame rate is high enough, minor errors or inaccuracies in a given frame are allowable, since they will often disappear in the next frame. In real-time graphics work, it is important to know what the boundaries are to the problem being solved, since these determine what sorts of techniques can be applied.

The main topics covered in this chapter are *tessellation, consolidation,* and *simplification.* Polygons can arrive in many different forms, and may have to be split into more tractable primitives, such as triangles or quadrilaterals; this process is called tessellation. Consolidation is our term for the process which encompasses merging and linking polygonal data as well as deriving new data such as normals for surface shading. Simplification is taking such linked data and attempting to remove unnecessary or insignificant features within it. Tessellation ensures that data is displayable and displayed correctly; consolidation further improves data display and can improve speed by allowing computations to be shared; and simplification can provide even more speed by removing unneeded polygons.

9.1   Sources of Three-Dimensional Data

There are a number of ways models can be created. Objects can be generated by directly typing in the data, by writing programs that create such data (called *procedural modeling*), by using modeling programs, by transforming data found in other forms into surfaces or volumes, by using three-dimensional scanners which also gather depth information, or by some combination of these techniques. Our focus will be on polygonal data generated by these methods. One common thread of almost all of these techniques is that they can represent their models in polygonal form. Knowing what data sources will be used in an application is important in determining what sort of data can be expected, and so in knowing what techniques need to be applied to it.

In the modeling world, there are two main types of modelers, solid-based and surface-based. Solid-based modelers are usually seen in the area of computer aided design (CAD), and often emphasize modeling tools that correspond to actual machining processes, such as cutting, drilling, etc. Internally, they will have a computational engine which rigorously manipulates the underlying topological boundaries of the objects. What concerns us is that for display and analysis purposes such modelers have *faceters*. A faceter is software that turns the internal model representation into polygons which can then be displayed. For example, a model that appears as a sphere internally may be represented by a center point and a radius, and the faceter could turn it into any number of triangles or quadrilaterals in order to represent it. Sometimes the best speed-up is the simplest: turning down the visual accuracy required when the faceter is employed can increase speed and save storage space by generating fewer polygons.

An important consideration within CAD work is whether the faceter being used is designed for graphical rendering. There are faceters for finite element analysis (FEM), which tend to split the surface into equal-area triangles; such tessellations are strong candidates for consolidation and simplification, as they contain much graphically useless data while containing no vertex normals. Similarly, some faceters produce sets of triangles which are ideal for creating actual sample objects using stereolithography but which lack vertex normals and are often ill-suited for fast graphical display.

Surface-based modelers do not have a built-in concept of solidity; instead, all objects are thought of in terms of their surfaces. Like solid modelers, they may use internal representations and faceters to display objects such as spline surfaces. They may also allow direct manipulation of surfaces, such as adding or deleting polygons or vertices. This sort of tool can be important in keeping the polygon count low.

There are other types of modelers, such as implicit surface (including "blobby") creation systems [46], which work with concepts such as blends, weights, and fields. These modelers can create impressive organic effects by generating surfaces that are defined by the solution to some equation $f(x, y, z) = 0$. Polygonalization techniques are then used to create sets of polygons for display.

Data can also be generated from satellite imagery, by various medical scanning devices (in which image slices are generated and recombined), by three-dimensional scanners (in which a quadrilateral mesh of surface data points and sometimes their associated colors are captured), and by image registration techniques (in which two or more photos of an object are compared and depth information is derived). Such data sets are strong candidates for simplification techniques, as the data is often sampled at regular intervals, and many samples have a negligible effect on the visual perception of the data.

There are many other ways in which polygonal data is generated for surface representation. The key is to understand how that data was created and for what purpose. Often the data is not generated specifically for graphical display, or even if it is, various assumptions made by the designers about the renderer may no longer hold. There are many different three-dimensional data file formats in existence [265, 302], and translating between any two is usually not a lossless operation. Understanding what sorts of limitations and problems may be encountered is a major theme of the rest of this chapter.

9.2 Tessellation

Tessellation is the process of splitting a polygon into a set of polygons. This process can be undertaken for a variety of reasons. The most common is that many graphics APIs and hardware are optimized for triangles. Triangles are almost like atoms, in that (almost) any surface can be made out of them and rendered. Splitting a complex polygon into triangles is called triangulation. There are other reasons to tessellate polygons: the renderer may only handle convex polygons (such tessellation is called convex partitioning); or the surface may need to be subdivided (meshed) in order to catch shadows and reflected light using radiosity techniques [59, 333]. Figure 9.1 shows examples of these different types of tessellation. Non-graphical reasons for tessellation include a

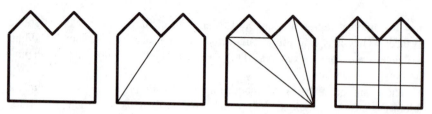

Figure 9.1. Various types of tessellation. The leftmost polygon is not tessellated, the next is partitioned into convex regions, the next is triangulated, and the rightmost is uniformly meshed.

requirement for separate small areas on a surface or a requirement for triangles to have angles at their vertices larger than some minimum angle.

Tessellation algorithms are an area of computational geometry which has been well explored and documented [266, 280]. That said, writing a robust and general tessellator is a difficult undertaking. Various subtle bugs, pathological cases, and precision problems make a fool-proof tessellator surprisingly tricky to create. In the "Further Reading and Resources" section at the end of this chapter we give some pointers to existing code.

One of the first processes a surface tessellator normally needs to perform is to determine how best to project a three-dimensional polygon into two dimensions. This is done to simplify the problem and so simplify the algorithms needed. One method is to determine which one of the xyz coordinates to discard in order to leave just two; this is equivalent to projecting the polygon onto one of three planes, the xy, the yz, or the xz. The best plane is usually the one in which the polygon has the largest projected area (this same technique is used in Section 10.6 for point-in-polygon testing). This plane can be determined by computing the area directly or by simply throwing away the coordinates corresponding to the coordinate of greatest magnitude in the polygon's normal. For example, given the polygon normal $(-5, 2, 4)$ we would throw away the x coordinates because -5 has the greatest magnitude. If using this plane leads to self-intersection (in which a polygon's edge crosses itself), we may consider casting upon the plane of the polygon itself.

The area and polygon normal test are not always equivalent, depending on the way in which the normal is computed and whether the polygon is flat. Some modelers create polygon facets which can be badly warped. A common case of this problem is the warped quadrilateral which is viewed nearly edge-on; this may form what is referred to as an *hourglass* or a *bowtie* quadrilateral. Figure 9.2 shows a bowtie quadrilateral. Casting onto the xy, xz, or yz plane that gives the largest projected area will eliminate most, but not all, self-intersection problems. If self-intersection is a possibility, then a laborious comparison among

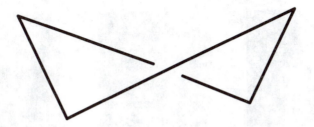

Figure 9.2. Warped quadrilateral viewed edge-on, forming a bowtie or hourglass figure.

the polygon's edges is called for. See Section 10.12 for efficient methods for performing this test.

Partitioning a polygon into convex regions can be more space- and speed-efficient than triangulating it. This is because convex polygons can easily be represented by fans of triangles, as discussed in Section 7.4. Code for a robust convexity test is given by Schorn and Fisher [319]. Note that some concave polygons can be treated as fans (such polygons are called star-shaped), but detecting these requires more work [280, 292].

Polygons are not always made of a single outline. Figure 9.3 shows a polygon made of three outlines (also called loops or contours). Such descriptions can always be converted to a single-outline polygon by carefully generating join edges between loops. This conversion process can also be reversed in order to retrieve the separate loops.

9.2.1 Shading Problems

Often data will arrive as quadrilateral meshes and must be converted into triangles for display, both to avoid bowtie problems and to provide proper input to the renderer. Once in a great while, a quadrilateral will be concave, in which case

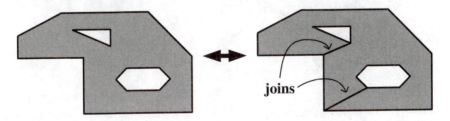

Figure 9.3. A polygon with three outlines converted to a single-outline polygon

Figure 9.4. The left figure is rendered as a quadrilateral; the middle is two triangles with upper-right and lower-left corners connected; the right shows what happens when the other diagonal is used. The middle figure is better visually than the right one.

there is only one way to triangulate it (without adding new vertices); otherwise, we may choose one of the two diagonals in order to split it. Spending a little time picking the better diagonal can sometimes give significantly better visual results.

There are a few different ways to determine how to split a quadrilateral. The basic idea is to minimize differences. For a flat quadrilateral with no additional data at the vertices, it is often best to choose the shortest diagonal. For radiosity solutions or prelit quadrilaterals (see Section 8.2.2) that have a diffuse color per vertex, choose the diagonal which has the smaller difference between the colors [2]. An example of this technique is shown in Figure 9.4. For terrain height fields there are a number of possibilities, depending on the effect desired:

Figure 9.5. On the left is a height field mesh with each quadrilateral split along the same diagonal (the view looks along these diagonals—note how visible these are). On the right, the split is made using the diagonal whose corners are closer in height, and so breaks up the pattern formed.

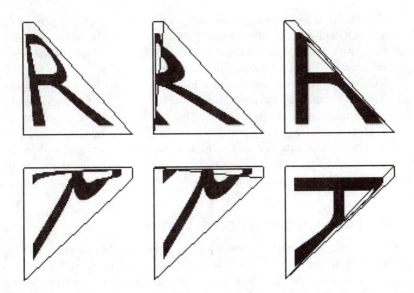

Figure 9.6. The top left shows the intent of the designer, a distorted quadrilateral with a square texture map of an "R." The two images on the right show the two triangulations and how they differ. The bottom row rotates all of the polygons; the Gouraud-interpolated quadrilateral changes its appearance.

use the diagonal that gives the largest angle between the two triangles [245]; connect the diagonal that gives triangles closest in size; connect the two vertices closest in height; or even connect the two most different in height. Any of these is normally preferable to simple consistent diagonal connections; see Figure 9.5.

There are cases where triangles cannot properly capture the intent of the designer. If a texture is applied to a warped quadrilateral, neither triangulation preserves the intent; that said, neither does pure Gouraud shading using the untessellated quadrilateral (i.e., interpolating from the left to the right edge of the quadrilateral itself). Figure 9.6 shows the problem. What is needed is either fine meshing of the surface, or a different texture-coordinate interpolation scheme, or a warping and reapplication of the texturing image itself to get the proper rendering.

This problem arises because the image being applied to the surface is to be warped when displayed. However, it is an inherent limitation of triangle texturing that it cannot warp any part of an image on a single triangle. Two texture coordinates can establish a direction and magnitude, but it takes four coordinates to define a warped mapping. A triangle has only three texture coordinates, so it is impossible to create such a mapping without additional information. Woo et al. [384] discuss this problem further.

Figure 9.6 also shows why rendering using only triangles is usually better than Gouraud interpolation across the original polygon: the quadrilateral's rendering is not rotation-invariant. Warped quadrilaterals' shading will shift around when animated; triangles' shading and textures at least do not move.

While texture distortion sounds like a pathological case, it actually happens with a common primitive: the cone. When a texture is applied to the cone and the cone is triangulated, this sort of distortion is encountered at the tip of the cone [155]. One solution to this problem is meshing each quadrilateral and then splitting these smaller quadrilaterals. This ameliorates the problem but does not fully solve it. Another solution is to correct this problem during modeling by distorting the texture and projecting it onto the cone along the cone's axis.

9.2.2   Edge Cracking and T-Vertices

A problem worth mentioning is *edge cracking*. Some modelers produce NURBS (Non-Uniform Rational B-Splines) [104, 287], a powerful primitive for describing curved surfaces. Spline surfaces are usually generated into meshes for rendering. This tessellation is done by stepping along the spline curves defining the surface and so computing vertex locations and normals.

When we use a simple stepping method, problems can occur where spline surfaces meet. At the shared edge, the points for both surfaces need to coincide. Sometimes this may happen, due to the nature of the model, but often the points generated for one spline curve will not match those generated by its neighbor. This effect is called edge cracking, and it can lead to disturbing visual artifacts as the viewer peeks through the surface. Even if the viewer cannot see through the cracks, the seam is often visible because of differences in the way the shading is interpolated.

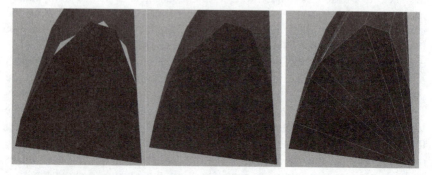

Figure 9.7. The left figure shows cracking where the two surfaces meet. The middle shows the cracking fixed by matching up edge points. The right shows the corrected mesh.

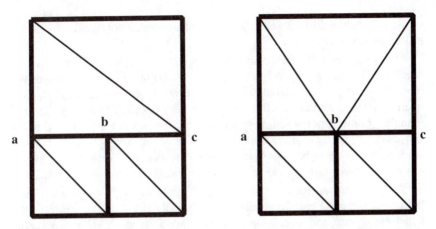

Figure 9.8. On the left, the polygon on the top did not share vertex **b** when it was triangulated, which can lead to rendering problems along the edge **ac**. On the right, vertex **b** (called a T-vertex) is now shared by the top polygon, affecting its tessellation and avoiding problems.

The process of fixing these cracks is called *edge stitching*. The goal is to make sure that all vertices along the shared edge are shared by both spline surfaces so that no cracks appear. See Figure 9.7

A related problem encountered when joining flat surfaces is that of T-vertices. This sort of problem can appear when radiosity solutions are used [30], but it will also occur when model surfaces meet but do not share all vertices. Even though the edges should theoretically meet perfectly, if the renderer does not have enough precision in representing vertex locations on the screen, then cracks can appear. One way to ameliorate this problem is to use graphics hardware with subpixel addressing [223]. However, this solution does not avoid shading artifacts that can appear. The problem can be totally eliminated by finding such edges (often a difficult procedure) and making sure to share vertices with all bordering faces. Figure 9.8 shows the problem. Cignoni et al. [55] describe a way to avoid creating degenerate (zero-area) triangles when triangulating convex polygons with T-vertices.

9.3 Consolidation

Once polygons have passed through any tessellation algorithms needed, we are left with a set of polygons to render. We may have opportunities for greater efficiency and problems with the quality of the data set. To address these concerns, it is useful to find and adjust the links between polygons; we call this phase *consolidation*.

One source of efficiency comes from forming polygon meshes from sets of separate polygons. A *polygon mesh* consists of a set of vertices and polygon outlines. Most vertices are shared among two or more polygons; for example, each interior vertex in a triangulated quadrilateral mesh is shared by an average of six triangles. Forming polygonal meshes makes for fewer necessary transformations and more efficient clipping, while also saving on memory. Triangle fans and strips as speed-up techniques were discussed in depth in Section 7.4. Meshes can be even more efficient, as they allow more data sharing (see Section 7.4.4).

API and hardware support for polygonal meshes is a growing trend. Vertex buffers in Direct3D and vertex arrays in OpenGL allow sets of vertices to be transformed once and stored for reuse. Furthermore, the transformed vertices can also be lit and clipped once and these results stored, if desired. Once the vertices are processed in this way, the results are accessed by using indices into the vertex array. Some access techniques allow for the transform results to be stored and reused directly on the graphics accelerator. This results in additional savings, as each vertex is sent down to the accelerator just once.

Another opportunity for improved efficiency is in the area of backface culling. This topic is discussed in depth in Section 7.1; what is important here is that a model has to be found to be solid, also known as *manifold* or *closed*. Solid, in this context, means that none of the backfaces should ever be visible from the outside. If this is the case, then backface culling is possible. Solidity is also important in stereolithography, the process of taking a computer-generated model and using lasers to solidify a polymer mixture with which to make an actual prototype; models without solidity can cause errors.

One quality-related problem is face orientation. Some model data comes in oriented properly, with surface normals either explicitly or implicitly pointing in the correct directions. For example, in CAD work the standard is that the vertices in the polygon outline proceed in a counter-clockwise direction when the front face is viewed. This is called a right-handed orientation (which is independent of the left-handed or right-handed viewing or modeling orientation used): think of the fingers of your right hand wrapping around the polygon's vertices in counter-clockwise order. Your thumb then points in the direction of the polygon's normal.

Other model data has no orientation or surface normals provided with it. In this case, steps must be taken to ensure that the polygon orientations are consistent, and are also pointing outwards. This consistency is important for backface culling (we need to know which are the back faces) and for vertex normal smoothing. Some polygon meshes form curved surfaces, but the polygon vertices do not have normal vectors, so they cannot be rendered with the illusion of curvature. See Figure 9.9.

Finally, many model formats do not provide surface boundary information. That is, for display and manipulation purposes, you may wish to highlight a single surface made of a set of polygons, in which case you may want to change the color of the boundary of that surface. Figure 9.9 shows surfaces with such boundaries displayed.

These are the problems; now to the solution. What follows is an algorithm that takes a set of arbitrary polygons with no known orientation and no stored normals and forms polygonal meshes with properly oriented polygons with vertex normals as desired. It also determines the solidity of the various meshes formed. Here is the overall approach; detailed explanation of each step will follow:

1. Form edge-face structures for all polygons and sort these.

2. Find groups of polygons that touch each other; determine solidity.

3. For each group, flip faces to gain consistency.

4. Determine what the inside of the mesh is, and flip all faces if needed.

5. Find smoothing groups and compute vertex normals.

6. Find boundaries.

7. Create polygonal meshes.

Not all of these steps have to be performed for all data; some can be skipped if the data is already present or the result is not needed.

Figure 9.9. The object on the left does not have normals per vertex; the one on the right does.

The first step is to form a list of all edges in the entire set of polygons, with each edge referring back to the face (polygon) with which it is associated. Each edge is stored with the first vertex stored before the second vertex, using sorting order. One vertex comes before another in sorting order if its x-coordinate value is smaller. If the x-coordinates are equal, then the y-value is used; if these match, then z is used. For example, vertex $(-3, 5, 2)$ comes before vertex $(-3, 6, -8)$; the -3's match, but $5 < 6$.

If the coordinates are identical,[1] then the edge has no length and could be discarded if the rest of the vertex data is the same; as a counterexample, at the tip of a cone, the vertex is shared but there are many vertex normals, so these are considered separate vertices.

Once this edge list is formed, it can be sorted by comparing vertex pairs, a similar manner to the comparison of the vertices themselves. If we place the vertices that form an edge in order (i.e., first vertex less than or equal to second vertex), sorting the whole list has the effect of putting identical edges next to each other on the list. A full sort is not the only way to find matching edges and is actually more than is needed; hashing is another way to find these matches [119]. In practice, system routines such as qsort are fairly efficient and may be sufficient.

A continuous group consists of polygons which are connected by edges. With all matching edges found, continuous groups of polygons can be formed and connectivity among polygons established. Note that a single data set can have a number of continuous groups. For example, a teapot can have two groups, the pot and the lid.

We now want to ensure orientation consistency, i.e., we want all polygons to have counter-clockwise outlines. For each continuous group of polygons, choose an arbitrary starting polygon. Check each of its neighboring polygons and determine whether the orientation is consistent. Orientation checking is simple: if the direction of traversal for the edge is the same for both polygons, then the neighboring polygon must be flipped. See Figure 9.10. Each polygon in a group should be checked only once for orientation. This is important because pathological forms such as Möbius strips can create internally inconsistent results.

A group can be determined to be a solid (manifold) using the easy method of noting whether all its edges are shared by an even number of polygons. Such a group may actually form separate objects if any edges share four or more polygons—e.g., if two cubes touch at one edge, that edge is part of four polygons.

Although all the faces are properly oriented at this point, they could all be oriented inward. In most cases we want them outward. The test for whether all

---

[1] In practice, data sometimes comes in with vertices extremely close but not identical. See Glassner [119] for one method of merging these vertices.

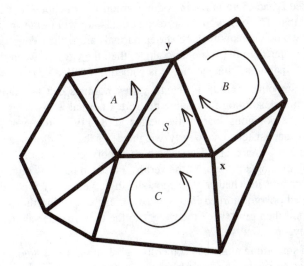

Figure 9.10. A starting polygon S is chosen and its neighbors are checked. Because the vertices in the edge shared by S and B are traversed in the same order (from **x** to **y**), the outline for B needs to be reversed.

surface normals should be flipped is to take the signed volume of the group and check the sign; if it is negative, reverse the normals.

The way to get the signed volume is as follows. First get the center point of the group's bounding box. Then compute the signed volume of each volume formed by joining the center point to each polygon (e.g., for a triangle polygon and a point, a tetrahedron is formed). The volume is equal to one-third the distance of the center point from the polygon's plane times the polygon's area. The $1/3$ term can be dropped, since we only need the sign of the volume. The calculation of the area of a triangle is given in Appendix A.

This method is not fool-proof. If the object is not solid but simply a surface description, it is definitely possible for the orientation still to be incorrect. Human intervention is needed in such cases. Even solids can be oriented incorrectly in special cases. For example, if the object is a room, the user wants its normals to face inward toward the camera.

Once the orientation is consistent, vertex normals can be generated by *smoothing techniques*. Smoothing information is something that the model's format may provide by specifying smoothing groups for the polygons, or by providing a smoothing angle. Smoothing group values are used to explicitly define which polygons in a group belong together to make up a curved surface. A smoothing angle is used when there is no smoothing group information. In this case, it is determined that if two polygons' surface normals are within the specified angle, then these two polygons will share vertex normals along their edges. If the angle formed is greater than the smoothing angle, then the edge between the polygons will be kept visible, so this technique is sometimes called *edge preservation*.

Once a smoothing group is found, vertex normals can be computed. The standard textbook solution for finding the vertex normal is to average the surface normals of the polygons sharing the vertex [118, 119]. However, this method can lead to inconsistent and poorly weighted results. Thürmer and Wüthrich [353] present a better method, in which each polygon normal's contribution is weighted by the angle it forms at the vertex. For example, this improved method gives the same result whether a polygon sharing a vertex is tessellated or not. If the tessellated polygon turned into, say, two triangles sharing the vertex, the old method would then give twice the weight to the two triangles as it would to the original polygon.

Using a smoothing angle can sometimes give an improper amount of smoothing, rounding edges which should be sharp or vice versa. However, even smoothing groups can have their own problems. Imagine the curved surface of a cone made of polygons. All the polygons are in the same smoothing group. But at the tip of the cone there should actually be many normals. Simply smoothing gives the peculiar result that the tip has one normal pointing directly out. The cone tip is a singularity; either the faceter has to provide the vertex normals or the modeler sometimes cuts off the very tip, thereby providing vertices to receive these normals properly.

Once smoothing is done, boundaries for highlighting or for a vector representation of the surface can be found. This is done by identifying all edges that have polygons in different smoothing groups, or that have an odd number of neighboring polygons. These are then the boundaries of each curved surface.

The polygons are now properly oriented, smoothed, etc. The next step is to form the meshes themselves, which are typically stored as lists of shared vertices and outlines indexing them. Eliminating duplicate vertices can be done by sorting or hashing in a fashion similar to that used with edges and so finding matches.

One question is whether to merge separate surfaces into one polygon mesh. Each separate surface (almost always) has the property that a vertex has one and only one vertex normal and texture coordinate. For example, the corner of a cube is a single vertex, but this vertex is usually treated as three separate vertices with three separate vertex normals on three separate squares. Hoppe [189] discusses memory-efficient ways to share vertex-face information while retaining surface-surface connectivity.

An additional step that could be performed at this time is tessellation. None of the previous steps depends on having triangles, so tessellation, if needed, could be delayed until the very end.

9.4 Simplification

Another sort of operation can be performed on a set of polygons. *Mesh simplification*, also known as *data reduction* or *decimation*, is the process of taking a complex model and reducing its complexity. This can be done for a variety of reasons. In Section 7.3 we discuss level-of-detail (LOD) techniques, in which an object is represented with models that vary in complexity. Model data may also appear in some form with more tessellation than is necessary for a reasonable representation. Figure 9.11 gives a sense of how the number of stored triangles can be reduced by data reduction techniques.

The main advantage of a simplified model is that it is quicker to render, since it has fewer faces and vertices.[2] The most common method of reducing the polygon count is to use an *edge collapse* operation. In this operation, an edge is removed by moving its two vertices to one spot. See Figure 9.12 for an example of this operation in action. For a solid model, an edge collapse removes a total of two triangles, three edges, and one vertex. So a closed model with 3000 triangles would have 1500 edge collapses applied to it to reduce it to zero faces.

In Figure 9.12, u was collapsed into the location of v, but v could have been collapsed into u. A simplification system limited to just these two possibilities is using a *subset placement* strategy. Melax [247] uses this strategy in his run-time simplification system. An advantage of this strategy is that, if we limit the possibilities, we may implicitly encode the choice actually made [115, 188]. Such strategies are faster because fewer possibilities need to be examined, but they also yield lower-quality approximations because a smaller solution space is examined.

By using an *optimal placement* strategy, we examine a wider range of possibilities. Instead of collapsing one vertex into another, both vertices for an edge are contracted to a new location. Hoppe [188] examines the case in which u and v both move to some location on the edge; he notes that in order to improve compression the search can be limited to checking the midpoint. Garland and

---

[2]A rule of thumb is that a triangulated polygon mesh with n vertices has about $2n$ faces and $3n$ edges. This rule can be derived using Euler's theorem that $f - e + v = 2$ for a solid's surface—see Section 7.4.3.

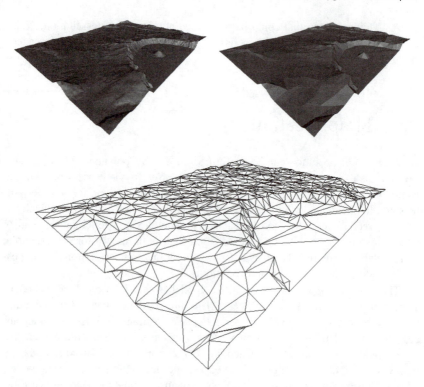

Figure 9.11. On the left is a height field of Crater Lake rendered with 200,000 triangles. The right figure shows this model simplified down to 1000 triangles. The underlying simplified mesh is shown below. *(Courtesy of Michael Garland.)*

Heckbert [115] solve a quadratic equation to find an optimal position (which may be located off of the edge). Another strategy is to limit the new placement point to the edge. The advantage of optimal placement strategies is that they tend to give higher-quality meshes. The disadvantages are extra processing, code, and memory for recording this wider range of possible placements.

To determine the best point placement, we perform an analysis on the local neighborhood. This locality is an important and useful feature for a number of reasons. If the cost of an edge collapse depends on just a few local variables (e.g., edge length and face normals near the edge), the cost function is easy to compute, and each collapse affects only a few of its neighbors. For example, say a model has 3000 possible edge collapses which are computed at the start. The edge collapse with the lowest cost-function value is performed. Because it affects only a few nearby triangles and their edges, only those edge collapse possibilities

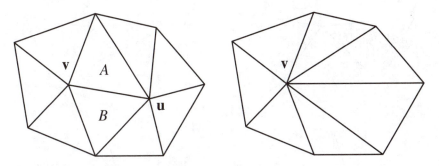

Figure 9.12. On the left is the figure before the **uv** edge collapse occurs; the right figure shows point **u** collapsed into point **v**, thereby removing triangles A and B and edge **uv**.

whose cost functions are affected by these changes need to be recomputed (say 10 instead of 3000), and the list requires only a minor bit of resorting. Because an edge-collapse affects only a few other edge-collapse cost values, a good choice for maintaining this list of cost values is a heap or other priority queue [335].

The collapse operation itself is simply an edit of the model's database; see Hoppe [189] and Melax [247] for suggestions about data structures and methods. Each edge collapse is analyzed with a cost function, and the one with the smallest cost value is performed next. An open research problem is finding the best cost function under various conditions [115, 189, 237, 247]. Depending on the problem being solved, the cost function may trade off among speed, quality, robustness, and simplicity. It may also be tailored to maintain surface boundaries, material locations, lighting effect, texture placement, volume, or other constraints.

Some edge collapses must be avoided regardless of cost; see the example in Figure 9.13. These can be detected by checking whether a neighboring polygon flips its normal direction from a collapse.

We will present Garland and Heckbert's basic cost function [115] in order to give a sense of how such functions work. To begin with, for a given vertex there is a set of triangles that share it, and each triangle has a plane equation associated with it. The cost function for moving a vertex is the sum of the squared distances between each of the planes and the new location. More formally:

$$c(\mathbf{v}) = \sum_{i=1}^{m} (\mathbf{n}_i \cdot \mathbf{v} + d_i)^2$$

is the cost function for new location $\mathbf{v}$ and m planes, where $\mathbf{n}$ is the plane's normal and d its offset from the origin.

An example of two possible contractions for the same edge is shown in Figure 9.14. Say the cube is two units long. The cost function for collapsing **e**

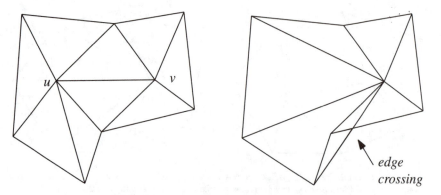

edge crossing

Figure 9.13. Example of a bad collapse. On the left is a mesh before collapsing vertex u into v. On the right is the mesh after the collapse, showing how edges now cross.

into **c** (**e** → **c**) will be 0, because the point **e** does not move off of the planes it shares when it goes to **e**. The cost function for **c** → **e** will be 1, because **c** moves away from the plane of the right face of the cube by a squared distance of 1. Because it has a lower cost, the **e** → **c** collapse would be done before **c** → **e**.

As Garland and Heckbert point out, this function can be modified in various ways. For example, one addition is to weight the values by the areas of the triangles associated with each plane. Another type of extension is to use a cost function based on maintaining other surface features. For example, the boundary curves of a model are important in portraying it, so these should be made less likely to be modified (see Plate XIX, following p. 194). Other surface features worth preserving are locations where there are material changes, texture map

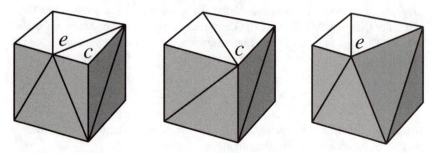

Figure 9.14. The left figure shows a cube with an extra point along one edge. The middle figure shows what happens if this point **e** is collapsed to corner **c**. The right figure shows **c** collapsed to **e**.

edges, and color-per-vertex changes. Radiosity solutions use color per vertex to record the illumination on a meshed surface and so are excellent candidates for reduction techniques [188]. See Plate XX, following page 194, for an example. The underlying mesh is shown in Figure 9.15.

The data produced by the simplification process has some other interesting features. One is reversibility: by storing the edge collapses, we can start with the simplified model and reconstruct the complex model from it. This characteristic is useful for network transmission of models, in that the edge-collapsed version of the database can be sent in an efficiently compressed form and progressively built up and displayed as the model is received [188, 348].

Edge-collapse simplification can produce a large number of level-of-detail (LOD) models (see Section 7.3) from a single complex model. A problem found in using LOD models is that the transition can sometimes be seen if one model instantly replaces another between one frame and the next [113]. This problem is called "popping." One solution is to use alpha blending (see Section 4.5) to cross-fade between model representations. Another solution is using *geomorphs* [188] to increase or decrease the level of detail. Since we know how the vertices in the more complex model map to the simple model, it is possible to create a smooth transition. See Section 7.3.3 for more details.

Polygon reduction techniques can be useful, but they are not a panacea. A talented model maker can create low-polygon-count objects which are better in quality than those generated by automated procedures. One reason this is true is that most reduction techniques know nothing about visually important elements,

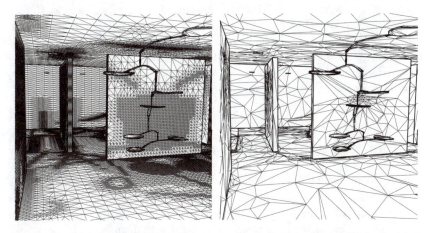

Figure 9.15. Simplification of radiosity solution. Left is the original mesh (150,983 faces), right is simplified mesh (10,000 faces). *(Courtesy of Hugues Hoppe, Microsoft Research.)*

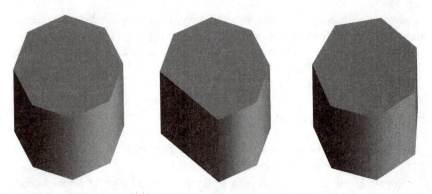

Figure 9.16. Symmetry problem. The cylinder on the left has 10 flat faces (including top and bottom). The middle cylinder has 9 flat faces after 1 face is eliminated by reduction. The right cylinder has 9 flat faces after being regenerated by the modeler's faceter.

underlying topology, or symmetry. For example, as Melax [247] points out, facial features such as the eyes and mouth are usually more important than other parts of a model of a human. The problem of maintaining symmetry is shown in Figure 9.16.

Research into mesh simplification and alternate model descriptions is an active and wide-ranging field. For example, there are also algorithms to convert surface features into bump maps [61]. Impostors [239], described in Section 7.2, are another form of alternate rendering of the same model. Kajiya [199] presents a hierarchy of scale showing how surface lighting models overlap texture mapping methods, which in turn overlap geometric details. Work such as Cook's [64] in shading languages blurs the distinction and unifies these different scales. Sprites and layered depth images can replace geometry in scenes (see Sections 6.2 and 7.2). Knowing when and how best to switch from one set of modeling and rendering techniques to another in order to maximize frame rate and quality is still an art and an open area for exploration.

Further Reading and Resources

New polygonal techniques appear all the time. Check this book's website http://www.realtimerendering.com/for the latest information. Also check the reference listing in this book of the resources discussed below, as most of the resources here also have websites associated with them.

A recent paper on tessellation by Held [179] gives a thorough overview of previous work, important issues, and a reliable, fast, and easy-to-implement algorithm. O'Rourke [280] has a good overview of tessellation algorithms. Narkhede and Manocha [266] have code available for their tessellator. The OpenGL Utility Library [275] includes a robust tessellator; this standalone utility library can be used even if you do not use OpenGL itself.

For translating three-dimensional file formats, the best book is Rule's *3D Graphics File Formats: A Programmer's Reference* [302], which includes a file translator with source code. Murray and VanRyper's *Encyclopedia of Graphics File Formats* [265] includes some information on three-dimensional file format layout.

For more on determining polygon properties such as convexity and area, see Farin and Hansford's *The Geometry Toolbox* [105]. Schorn and Fisher's convexity test code [319] is robust and fast, and available on the web.

Packages such as Optimizer [277] and Fahrenheit [103] have spline edge stitching built into them, as well as simplification algorithms. For more on NURBS and splines in general, see Farin's *Curves and Surfaces for Computer Aided Geometric Design—A Practical Guide* [104] and Piegl and Tiller's *The NURBS Book* [287].

Heckbert and Garland have a paper surveying the field of polygonal simplification [168], as does Erikson [95]. Garland also distributes source code for his simplification algorithm [115].

Chapter 10
Intersection Test Methods

"I'll sit and see if that small sailing cloud
Will hit or miss the moon."
–Robert Frost

Intersection testing is often used in computer graphics. We may wish to click the mouse on an object, or to determine whether two objects collide, or to make sure we maintain a constant height for our viewer as we navigate a building. All of these operations can be performed with intersection tests. Given its importance, intersection testing is an operation that will remain in the application stage of the pipeline for the foreseeable future. In this chapter we cover the most common ray/object and object/object intersection tests.

In interactive computer graphics applications it is often desirable to let the user select a certain object by *picking* (clicking) on it with the mouse or any other input device. Naturally, the performance of such an operation needs to be high. There are two hardware-accelerated picking methods worth mentioning. Some graphics APIs have support for defining a tiny *pick window*, into which they then render the scene. Often such picking systems will be associated with a scene graph mechanism, so that the polygons can be identified individually or as collections making up a single object. Such picking systems return the closest object(s) that overlap the pick window. This sort of system usually has the added advantage of being able to pick on lines and vertices in addition to surfaces.

Another method of picking was first presented by Hanrahan and Haeberli [159]. To support picking, the scene is rendered into the Z-buffer with lighting off and with each polygon having a unique color value which is used as an identifier. The image formed is stored off-screen and is then used for extremely rapid picking. When the user clicks on a pixel, the color identifier is looked up in this image and the polygon is immediately identified. The major disadvantage of this method is that the entire scene must be rendered in a separate pass to support this sort of picking. This method was originally presented in the context of a three-dimensional paint system; in this sort of application the amount of picking per view is extremely high.

Intersection testing offers some benefits these picking methods do not. Comparing a ray against a triangle is normally faster than sending the triangle to hardware, clipping against a pick window, then inquiring whether the triangle was picked. The location, normal vector, texture coordinates, and other surface data can be computed precisely by intersection testing methods. Such methods are also independent of hardware support (or lack thereof).

The picking problem can be solved efficiently by using the bounding volume hierarchy imposed by the scene graph. First, we compute the ray from the camera's position through the pixel which the user picked. Then, we recursively test whether this ray hits the bounding volume of the scene graph. If at any time the ray misses a bounding volume (BV), then that subtree can be discarded from further tests, since the ray will not hit any of its contents. However, if the ray hits a BV, its children's BVs must be tested as well. Finally, the recursion may end in a leaf which contains geometry, in which case the ray must be tested against each primitive in the geometry node.

As we have seen in Section 7.1.2, view-frustum culling is a means for efficiently discarding geometry that is outside the view frustum. Tests that decide whether a bounding volume is totally outside, totally inside, or partially inside a frustum must be available for this method.

In collision detection algorithms (see Chapter 11), which are also built upon hierarchies, the system must decide whether or not two primitive objects collide. These primitive objects include triangles, spheres, axis-aligned bounding boxes (AABBs), oriented bounding boxes (OBBs), and discrete oriented polytopes (k-DOPs).

In all of these cases, we have encountered a certain class of problems that require *intersection tests*. An intersection test determines whether two objects, A and B, intersect, which may mean that A is totally inside B (or vice versa), that the boundaries of A and B intersect, or that they are totally disjoint. However, sometimes more information may be needed, such as the exact intersection point(s), the distance(s) to the intersection point(s), etc. In this chapter a set of fast intersection test methods are identified and studied thoroughly. We not only present the basic algorithms, but also give advice on how to construct new and efficient intersection test methods. Naturally, the methods presented in this chapter are also of use in non-real-time computer graphics applications. For example, the algorithms presented in Sections 10.3 through 10.6 can be used in ray tracing and global illumination programs.

The chapter begins with some useful definitions followed by a list of rules of thumb for constructing intersection test methods. Then, the cookbook of intersection test methods is presented.

10.1   Definitions

This section introduces notation and definitions useful for this entire chapter.

A ray, $\mathbf{r}(t)$, is defined by an origin point, $\mathbf{o}$, and a direction vector, $\mathbf{d}$ (which, for convenience, is usually normalized, so $||\mathbf{d}|| = 1$). Its mathematical formula is shown in Equation 10.1, and an illustration of a ray is shown in Figure 10.1.

$$\mathbf{r}(t) = \mathbf{o} + t\mathbf{d} \qquad (10.1)$$

The scalar t is a variable that is used to generate different points on the ray, where t-values of less than 0 are said to lie behind the ray origin, and the positive t-values are said to lie in front of it. Also, since the ray direction is normalized, a t-value generates a point on the ray that is situated t distance units from the ray origin.

In practice, we often store a current distance l, which is the maximum distance we want to search along the ray. For example, while picking, we usually want the closest intersection along the ray; objects beyond this intersection can be safely rejected. The distance l starts at ∞. As objects are successfully intersected, l is updated with the intersection distance. In the ray/object intersection tests we will be discussing, we will normally not include l in the discussion. If you wish to use l, all you have to do is perform the normal ray/object test, then check l against the intersection distance computed and take the appropriate action.

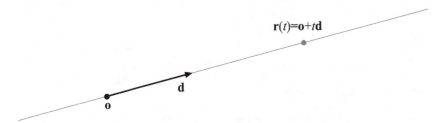

Figure 10.1. A simple ray and its parameters: $\mathbf{o}$ (the ray origin), $\mathbf{d}$ (the ray direction), and t, which generates different points on the ray, $\mathbf{r}(t) = \mathbf{o} + t\mathbf{d}$.

When talking about surfaces, we distinguish *implicit* surfaces from *explicit* surfaces. An implicit surface is defined by Equation 10.2.

$$f(\mathbf{p}) = f((p_x \quad p_y \quad p_z)^T) = 0 \tag{10.2}$$

Here, $\mathbf{p}$ is any point on the surface. This means that if you have a point that lies on the surface and you plug this point into f, then the result will be 0. Otherwise the result from f will be non-zero. An example of an implicit surface is $p_x^2 + p_y^2 + p_z^2 = r^2$, which describes a sphere located at the origin with radius r. It is easily seen that this can be rewritten as $f(\mathbf{p}) = p_x^2 + p_y^2 + p_z^2 - r^2 = 0$, which means that it is indeed implicit. Modeling and rendering with a wide variety of implicit surface types is well covered in Bloomenthal et al. [46].

An explicit surface, on the other hand, is defined by a vector function $\mathbf{f}$ and some parameters (ρ, ϕ)[1], rather than a point on the surface. Those (valid) parameters yield points, $\mathbf{p}$, on the surface. Equation 10.3 below shows the general idea.

$$\mathbf{p} = \begin{pmatrix} p_x \\ p_y \\ p_z \end{pmatrix} = \mathbf{f}(\rho, \phi) = \begin{pmatrix} f_x(\rho, \phi) \\ f_y(\rho, \phi) \\ f_z(\rho, \phi) \end{pmatrix} \tag{10.3}$$

An example of an explicit surface is again the sphere, this time expressed in spherical coordinates, where ρ is called latitude and ϕ longitude, as shown in Equation 10.4.

$$\mathbf{f}(\rho, \phi) = \begin{pmatrix} r \sin \rho \cos \phi \\ r \sin \rho \sin \phi \\ r \cos \rho \end{pmatrix} \tag{10.4}$$

As another example, a triangle, $\triangle \mathbf{v}_0 \mathbf{v}_1 \mathbf{v}_2$, can be described in explicit form like this: $\mathbf{t}(u, v) = (1 - u - v)\mathbf{v}_0 + u\mathbf{v}_1 + v\mathbf{v}_2$, where $u \geq 0$, $v \geq 0$ and $u + v \leq 1$ must hold.

Finally, we shall give definitions of three bounding volumes, namely the AABB, the OBB, and the k-DOP, used extensively in this and the next chapter.

Definition. An *axis-aligned bounding box*[2] (also called *rectangular box*), AABB for short, is a box whose faces have normals that coincide with the standard basis axes. For example, an AABB called A is described by two extreme points called $\mathbf{a}^{min}$ and $\mathbf{a}^{max}$, where $\mathbf{a}_i^{min} \leq \mathbf{a}_i^{max}$, $\forall i \in \{x, y, z\}$. $\square$

---

[1]The number of parameters is not limited to two, but can be in theory be any number; however, two is the most common.

[2]In fact, neither the AABB nor OBB needs to be used as a BV, but can act as a pure geometric box. However, these names are widely accepted.

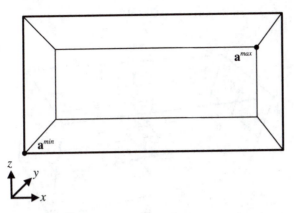

Figure 10.2. A three-dimensional AABB, called A, with its extreme points, $\mathbf{a}^{min}$ and $\mathbf{a}^{max}$, and the axes of the standard basis.

Figure 10.2 contains an illustration of a three-dimensional AABB together with notation.

Definition. An *oriented bounding box*, OBB for short, is a box whose faces have normals that are all pairwise orthogonal—i.e., it is an AABB that is arbitrarily rotated. An OBB, called, for example, B, can be described by the center point of the box, called $\mathbf{b}^c$, and three normalized vectors that describe the side directions of the box. These vectors are called $\mathbf{b}^u$, $\mathbf{b}^v$, and $\mathbf{b}^w$, and their respective positive half-lengths are called h_u^B, h_v^B, and h_w^B. $\square$

A three-dimensional OBB and its notation are depicted in Figure 10.3.

Definition. A k-DOP (*discrete oriented polytope*) is defined by $k/2$ (where k is even) normalized normals (orientations), $\mathbf{n}_i$, $1 \leq i \leq k/2$, and with each $\mathbf{n}_i$ two associated scalar values d_i^{min} and d_i^{max}, where $d_i^{min} < d_i^{max}$. Each triple ($\mathbf{n}_i$, d_i^{min}, d_i^{max}) describes a slab, S_i, which is the volume between the two planes, $\pi_i^{min} : \mathbf{n}_i \cdot \mathbf{x} + d_i^{min} = 0$ and $\pi_i^{max} : \mathbf{n}_i \cdot \mathbf{x} + d_i^{max} = 0$, and where the intersection of all slabs, $\cap_{1 \leq l \leq k/2} S_l$, is the actual k-DOP volume. $\square$

Figure 10.4 depicts an 8-DOP in two dimensions.

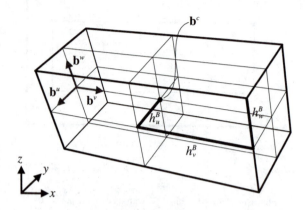

Figure 10.3. A three-dimensional OBB, called B, with its center point, $\mathbf{b}^c$, and its normalized, positively oriented side vectors, called $\mathbf{b}^u$, $\mathbf{b}^v$, and $\mathbf{b}^w$. The half-lengths of the sides are called h_u^B, h_v^B, and h_w^B.

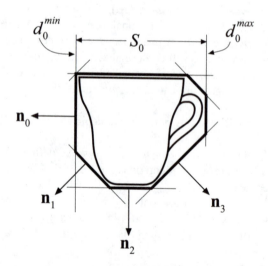

Figure 10.4. An example of a two-dimensional 8-DOP for a cup of tea, with all normals, $\mathbf{n}_i$, shown along with the zero'th slab, S_0, and the "size" of the slab: d_0^{min} and d_0^{max}.

10.2   Rules of Thumb

Before we begin studying the specific intersection methods, here are some rules of thumb that can lead to faster, more robust, and more exact intersection tests. These should be kept in mind when designing, inventing, and implementing an intersection routine:

- Perform computations and comparisons that might trivially *reject* or *accept* various types of intersections to obtain an early escape from further computations.

- If possible, *exploit* the result(s) from the previous test(s), should these fail.

- If more than one rejection or acceptance test is used, then try changing their internal order (if possible), since speed-up may result.

- Postpone expensive calculations (especially trigonometric functions, square roots, and divisions) until they are truly needed (see Section 10.5 for an example of delaying an expensive division).

- The intersection problem can often be simplified considerably by *reducing the dimension* of the problem (for example, from three dimensions to two dimensions or even to one dimension). See Section 10.6 for an example.

- If a single ray or object is being compared to many other objects at a time, look for precalculations which can be done only once before the testing begins.

- Make it a habit always to do *timing comparisons* on your computer, and use real data and testing situations for the timings.

- Finally, try making your code *robust* (meaning that it will work for all special cases and that it will be insensitive to as many floating point precision errors as possible) and make yourself aware of any limitations in it.

10.3   Ray/Sphere Intersection

Let us start with a mathematically simple intersection test—namely, that between a ray and a sphere. As we will see later, the straightforward mathematical solution can be made much faster if we begin thinking in terms of the geometry involved.

10.3.1   Mathematical Solution

A sphere can be defined by a center point, $\mathbf{c}$, and a radius, r. A more compact implicit formula (compared to the one previously introduced) for the sphere is then

$$f(\mathbf{p}) = ||\mathbf{p} - \mathbf{c}|| - r = 0 \qquad (10.5)$$

where $\mathbf{p}$ is any point on the sphere's surface. To solve for the intersections between a ray and a sphere, the ray $\mathbf{r}(t)$ simply replaces $\mathbf{p}$ in Equation 10.5 to yield

$$f(\mathbf{r}(t)) = ||\mathbf{r}(t) - \mathbf{c}|| - r = 0 \qquad (10.6)$$

Equation (10.6) is easily simplified:

$$||\mathbf{r}(t) - \mathbf{c}|| - r = 0$$
$$\Longleftrightarrow$$
$$||\mathbf{o} + t\mathbf{d} - \mathbf{c}|| = r$$
$$\Longleftrightarrow$$
$$(\mathbf{o} + t\mathbf{d} - \mathbf{c}) \cdot (\mathbf{o} + t\mathbf{d} - \mathbf{c}) = r^2 \qquad (10.7)$$
$$\Longleftrightarrow$$
$$t^2(\mathbf{d} \cdot \mathbf{d}) + 2t(\mathbf{d} \cdot (\mathbf{o} - \mathbf{c})) + (\mathbf{o} - \mathbf{c}) \cdot (\mathbf{o} - \mathbf{c}) - r^2 = 0$$
$$\Longleftrightarrow$$
$$t^2 + 2t(\mathbf{d} \cdot (\mathbf{o} - \mathbf{c})) + (\mathbf{o} - \mathbf{c}) \cdot (\mathbf{o} - \mathbf{c}) - r^2 = 0$$

The last step comes from the fact that $\mathbf{d}$ is assumed to be normalized, i.e., $\mathbf{d} \cdot \mathbf{d} = ||\mathbf{d}||^2 = 1$. Not surprisingly, the resulting equation is an equation of the second order, which means that if the ray intersects the sphere, it does so at two points (see Figure 10.5). If the solutions to the equation are imaginary, then the ray misses the sphere. If not, the two solutions t_1 and t_2 can be inserted into the ray equation to compute the intersection points on the sphere.

The resulting Equation 10.7, can be written as

$$t^2 + 2tb + c = 0 \qquad (10.8)$$

where $b = \mathbf{d} \cdot (\mathbf{o} - \mathbf{c})$ and $c = (\mathbf{o} - \mathbf{c}) \cdot (\mathbf{o} - \mathbf{c}) - r^2$. The solutions of the second-order equation are shown below:

$$t = -b \pm \sqrt{b^2 - c} \qquad (10.9)$$

Note that if $b^2 - c < 0$, then the ray misses the sphere and the intersection can be rejected and calculations avoided (e.g., the square root and some additions).

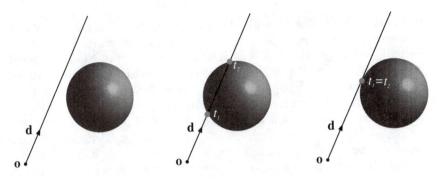

Figure 10.5. The left image shows a ray that misses a sphere and consequently $b^2 - c < 0$. The middle image shows a ray that intersects a sphere at two points ($b^2 - c > 0$) determined by the scalars t_1 and t_2. The right image illustrates the case where $b^2 - c = 0$, which means that the two intersection points coincide.

If this test is passed, both $t_0 = -b - \sqrt{b^2 - c}$ and $t_1 = -b + \sqrt{b^2 - c}$ can be computed. To find the smallest positive value of t_0 and t_1, an additional comparison needs to be executed.

If these computations are instead viewed from a geometric point of view, then better rejection tests can be discovered. The next subsection describes such a routine.

For the other quadrics, e.g., the cylinder, ellipsoid, cone, and hyperboloid, the mathematical solutions to their intersection problems are almost as straightforward as for the sphere. Sometimes, however, it is necessary to bound a surface (for example, usually you do not want a cylinder to be infinite and caps must be added to its ends), and this might add a bit of complexity to the code.

10.3.2 Optimized Solution

A common technique for optimizing intersection tests is to make some simple calculations early on that can determine whether the ray totally misses the object. Such a test is called a *rejection test*, and if the test fails, the intersection is said to be *rejected*.

For the sphere/ray intersection problem [151], we begin by observing that intersections behind the ray origin are considered uninteresting (this is normally the case in picking, etc.). Therefore, a vector $l = c - o$, which is the vector from the ray origin to the center of the sphere, is computed. All notation that is used is depicted in Figure 10.6. Also, the squared length of this vector is computed, $l^2 = l \cdot l$. Now if $l^2 < r^2$, this implies that the ray origin is inside the sphere, which in turn means that the ray is guaranteed to hit the sphere and we can exit if we only want to detect whether or not the ray hits the sphere; otherwise we proceed. Next, the projection of l onto d is computed: $d = l \cdot d$. Now, here comes the first rejection test: if $d < 0$ and the ray origin is outside the sphere, then the sphere is behind the ray origin and we can reject the intersection. Otherwise, the squared distance from the sphere center to the projection is computed using the Pythagorean theorem (Equation B.6): $m^2 = l^2 - d^2$. The second rejection test is even simpler than the first: if $m^2 > r^2$ the ray will definitely miss the sphere and the rest of the calculations can safely be omitted. If the sphere and ray pass this last test, then the ray is guaranteed to hit the sphere and we can exit if that was all we were interested in finding out.

To find the real intersection points, a little more work has to be done. First, the squared distance $q^2 = r^2 - m^2$ (see Figure 10.6) is calculated.[4] Since $m^2 <= r^2$, q^2 is greater than or equal to zero, and this means that $q = \sqrt{q^2}$ can be computed. Finally, the distances to the intersections are $t = d \pm q$, whose solution is quite similar to that of the second-order equation obtained in the previous mathematical solution section. If we are interested in only the first, positive intersection point, then we should use $t_1 = d - q$ for the case where the ray origin is outside the sphere and $t_2 = d + q$ when the ray origin is inside. The true intersection point(s) are found by inserting the t-value(s) into the ray equation (Equation 10.1).

Pseudocode for the optimized version is shown in the box below. The routine returns a boolean value which is REJECT if the ray misses the sphere and INTERSECT otherwise. If the ray intersects the sphere, then the distance, t,

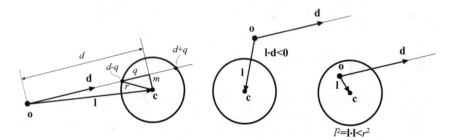

Figure 10.6. The notation for the geometry of the optimized ray/sphere intersection. In the left figure, the ray intersects the sphere in two points, where the distances are $t = d \pm q$ along the ray. The middle case demonstrates a rejection made when the sphere is behind the ray origin. Finally, at the right, the ray origin is inside the sphere, in which case the ray always hits the sphere.

---

[4]Note that the scalar r^2 is quite often stored within the data structure of the sphere in order to gain further efficiency.

from the ray origin to the intersection point along with the intersection point, **p**, are also returned.

	RaySphereIntersect$(\mathbf{o}, \mathbf{d}, \mathbf{c}, r)$ returns $(\{\text{REJECT}, \text{INTERSECT}\}, t, \mathbf{p})$
1 :	$\mathbf{l} = \mathbf{c} - \mathbf{o}$
2 :	$d = \mathbf{l} \cdot \mathbf{d}$
3 :	$l^2 = \mathbf{l} \cdot \mathbf{l}$
4 :	if$(d < 0$ and $l^2 > r^2)$ return $(\text{REJECT}, 0, \mathbf{0})$;
5 :	$m^2 = l^2 - d^2$
6 :	if$(m^2 > r^2)$ return $(\text{REJECT}, 0, \mathbf{0})$;
7 :	$q = \sqrt{r^2 - m^2}$
8 :	if$(l^2 > r^2)$ $t = d - q$
9 :	else $t = d + q$
10 :	return $(\text{INTERSECT}, t, \mathbf{o} + t\mathbf{d})$;

Note that after line 3, we can test whether **p** is inside the sphere and, if all we want to know is whether the ray and sphere intersect, the routine can terminate if they do so. Also, after line 6, the ray is guaranteed to hit the sphere. If we do an operation count (counting adds, multiplies, compares, etc.), we find that the geometric solution, *when followed to completion,* is approximately equivalent to the algebraic solution presented earlier. The important difference is that the rejection tests are done much earlier in the process, making the overall cost of this algorithm lower on average.

Optimized geometric algorithms exist for computing the intersection between a ray and some other quadrics. For example, there are methods for the cylinder [77, 178, 325] and the cone [178, 326].

10.4 Ray/Box Intersection

Two methods for determining whether a ray intersects a box are given below. The first handles both AABBs and OBBs. The second may be faster on some architectures, but can only deal with the simpler AABB. Here we use the definitions and notation of the BVs from Section 10.1.

10.4.1 Slabs Method

One scheme for ray/AABB intersection is presented by Haines [151]. This algorithm is based on Kay and Kajiya's slab method [201], which in turn is inspired by the Cyrus-Beck line clipping algorithm [78].

We extend this scheme to handle the more general OBB volume. It returns the closest positive t-value (i.e., the distance from the ray origin **o** to the point of intersection, if any exists). Optimizations for the AABB will be treated after we present the general case. The problem is approached by computing all t-values for the ray and all planes belonging to the faces of the OBB. The box is considered to be a set of three slabs[5], as illustrated in two dimensions in the left part of Figure 10.7. For each slab, there is a minimum and a maximum t-value, and these are called t_i^{min} and t_i^{max}, $\forall i \in \{u, v, w\}$. The next step is to compute the variables in Equation 10.10.

$$t^{min} = \max(t_u^{min}, t_v^{min}, t_w^{min})$$

$$t^{max} = \min(t_u^{max}, t_v^{max}, t_w^{max}) \tag{10.10}$$

Now, the clever test: if $t^{min} \leq t^{max}$, then the ray intersects the box; otherwise it misses. The reader should convince himself of this by inspecting the illustration on the right side of Figure 10.7.

Pseudocode for the ray/OBB intersection test, between an OBB (called A) and a ray (described by Equation 10.1) follows below. The code returns a boolean indicating whether or not the ray intersects the OBB (INTERSECT or

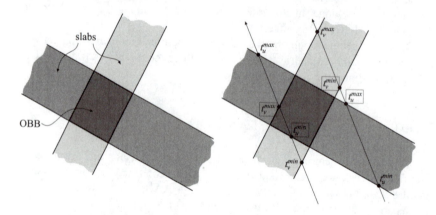

Figure 10.7. The left figure shows a two-dimensional OBB (oriented bounding box) formed by two slabs, while the right shows two rays that are tested for intersection with the OBB. All t-values are shown, and they are subscripted with v for the light gray slab and with u for the other. The extreme t-values are marked with boxes. The left ray hits the OBB since $t^{min} < t^{max}$, and the right ray misses since $t^{max} < t^{min}$.

---

[5]A slab is simply two parallel planes, which are grouped for faster computations.

REJECT), and the distance to the intersection point (if it exists). Recall that $\mathbf{a}^c$ is the center of the box, and $\mathbf{a}^u$, $\mathbf{a}^v$, and $\mathbf{a}^w$ are its half-length vectors. Recall that a^c is the center of the box, and a^u, a^v, and a^w are the normalized side directions of the box; h_u, h_v, and h_w are the positive halflengths (from the center to a box face).

```
RayOBBIntersect(o, d, A)
returns ({REJECT, INTERSECT}, t);
 1 :   t^min = -∞
 2 :   t^max = ∞
 3 :   p = a^c - o
 4 :   for each i ∈ {u, v, w}
 5 :       e = a^i · p
 6 :       f = a^i · d
 7 :       if(|f| > ε)
 8 :           t₁ = (e + h_i)/f
 9 :           t₂ = (e - h_i)/f
10 :           if(t₁ > t₂) swap(t₁, t₂);
11 :           if(t₁ > t^min) t^min = t₁
12 :           if(t₂ < t^max) t^max = t₂
13 :           if(t^min > t^max) return (REJECT, 0);
14 :           if(t^max < 0) return (REJECT, 0);
15 :       else if(- e - h_i > 0 or - e + h_i < 0) return (REJECT, 0);
16 :   if(t^min > 0) return (INTERSECT, t^min);
17 :   else return (INTERSECT, t^max);
```

Line 7 checks whether the ray direction is parallel to the normal direction of the current plane, in which case no reasonable intersections can occur. Lines 8 and 9 show a division by f; in practice, it is usually faster to compute $1/f$ and multiply by this value, since division is often expensive. Line 10 ensures that the minimum of t_1 and t_2 is stored in t_1, and consequently the maximum of these is stored in t_2. In practice, the swap does not have to be made; instead lines 11 and 12 can be repeated for the branch, and t_1 and t_2 can change positions there. Should line 13 return, then the ray misses the box, and similarly, if line 14 returns, then the box is behind the ray origin. Line 15 is executed if the ray is parallel to the slab; it tests if the ray is outside the slab. If so, then the ray misses the box and the test terminates. For even faster code, Haines discusses a way of unwrapping the loop and thereby avoiding some code [151].

There is an additional test not shown in the pseudocode that is worth adding in actual code. As mentioned when we defined the ray, we usually want to find the closest object. So after line 15, we could also test whether $t^{min} > l$, where

l is the current ray length. If this test is passed, the intersection is rejected. This test could be deferred until after the entire ray/OBB test has been completed, but it is usually more efficient to try for an early rejection inside the loop.

There are other optimizations for the special case of an OBB that is an AABB. Lines 5 and 6 change to $e = p_i$ and $f = d_i$, which makes the test faster. In practice, the $\mathbf{a}^{min}$ and $\mathbf{a}^{max}$ corners of the AABB are used on lines 8 and 9, and the addition may be avoided.

A generalization of the slabs method can be used to compute the intersection of a ray with any convex polyhedron [152].

10.4.2 Woo's Method

Woo [381] introduced some smart optimizations for finding the intersection between a ray and an AABB. Given a ray and an AABB, B, the idea is to identify three candidate planes out of the six planes composing the AABB. For each pair of parallel planes, the back-facing plane can be omitted from further consideration. After finding these three planes, we compute the intersection distances (t-values) between the ray and the planes. The largest of these distances corresponds to a potential hit. This is illustrated in Figure 10.8. Finally, if a potential hit is found, the actual intersection point is computed, and if it is located on the corresponding face of B, then it is a real hit.

Whether the slabs method or Woo's method is faster is an open question. We believe the methods are comparable in performance, with each strongly affected by the way it is used, the processor architecture, and its implementation.

Source code for Woo's method is available on the web [381].

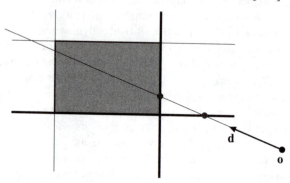

Figure 10.8. Woo's method for computing the intersection between a ray and an AABB. The candidate planes, which are front-facing and marked with fat lines, are intersected with the ray, and their intersection points are marked with grey dots. Because the leftmost intersection point is farthest from the ray origin, it is selected as a (potential) point of intersection.

10.5 Ray/Triangle Intersection

In real-time graphics libraries and APIs, triangle geometry is usually stored as a set of vertices with associated normals, and each triangle is defined by three such vertices. The normal of the plane in which the triangle lies is often not stored, in which case it must be computed if needed. There exist a lot of different ray/triangle intersection tests, and the majority of them first compute the intersection point between the ray and the triangle plane. Thereafter, the intersection point and the triangle vertices are projected on the axis-aligned plane (xy, yz, or xz) where the area of the triangle is maximized. By doing that, we reduce the problem to two dimensions, and we need only decide whether the (2D) point is inside the (2D) triangle. Several such methods exist, and they have been reviewed and compared by Haines [153].

Here, the focus will be on an algorithm that does not presume that normals are precomputed. For triangle meshes, this can amount to significant memory savings. This algorithm, along with optimizations, was discussed by Möller and Trumbore [256], and their presentation is used here.[6]

The ray from Equation 10.1 is used to test for intersection with a triangle defined by three vertices, $\mathbf{v}_1$, $\mathbf{v}_2$, and $\mathbf{v}_3$—i.e., $\triangle \mathbf{v}_1 \mathbf{v}_2 \mathbf{v}_3$.

10.5.1 Intersection Algorithm

A point, $\mathbf{t}(u, v)$, on a triangle is given by the explicit formula

$$\mathbf{t}(u, v) = (1 - u - v)\mathbf{v}_0 + u\mathbf{v}_1 + v\mathbf{v}_2 \tag{10.11}$$

where (u, v) are the *barycentric coordinates*, which must fulfill $u \geq 0$, $v \geq 0$, and $u + v \leq 1$. Note that (u, v) can be used for texture mapping, normal interpolation, color interpolation, etc. That is, u and v are the amounts by which to weight each vertex's contribution to a particular location, with $(1 - u - v)$ being the third weight.

Computing the intersection between the ray, $\mathbf{r}(t)$, and the triangle, $\mathbf{t}(u, v)$, is equivalent to $\mathbf{r}(t) = \mathbf{t}(u, v)$, which yields:

$$\mathbf{o} + t\mathbf{d} = (1 - u - v)\mathbf{v}_0 + u\mathbf{v}_1 + v\mathbf{v}_2 \tag{10.12}$$

Rearranging the terms gives:

$$\begin{pmatrix} -\mathbf{d} & \mathbf{v}_1 - \mathbf{v}_0 & \mathbf{v}_2 - \mathbf{v}_0 \end{pmatrix} \begin{pmatrix} t \\ u \\ v \end{pmatrix} = \mathbf{o} - \mathbf{v}_0 \tag{10.13}$$

---

[6]With permission from the *journal of graphics tools*, A.K. Peters Ltd.

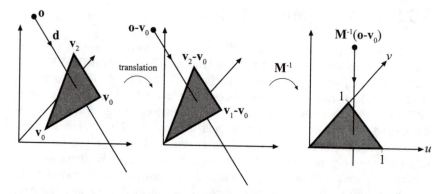

Figure 10.9. Translation and change of base of the ray origin.

This means the barycentric coordinates (u, v) and the distance, t, from the ray origin to the intersection point can be found by solving the linear system of equations above.

The above can be thought of geometrically as translating the triangle to the origin and transforming it to a unit triangle in y and z with the ray direction aligned with x. This is illustrated in Figure 10.9 (where $\mathbf{M} = (-\mathbf{d} \quad \mathbf{v}_1 - \mathbf{v}_0 \quad \mathbf{v}_2 - \mathbf{v}_0)$ is the matrix in Equation 10.13).

Arenberg [14] describes an algorithm that is similar to the one above. He also constructs a 3×3 matrix but uses the normal of the triangle instead of the ray direction $\mathbf{d}$. This method requires storing the normal for each triangle or computing each normal on the fly.

Denoting $\mathbf{e}_1 = \mathbf{v}_1 - \mathbf{v}_0$, $\mathbf{e}_2 = \mathbf{v}_2 - \mathbf{v}_0$, and $\mathbf{s} = \mathbf{o} - \mathbf{v}_0$, the solution to Equation 10.13 is obtained by using Cramer's rule:

$$\begin{pmatrix} t \\ u \\ v \end{pmatrix} = \frac{1}{\det(-\mathbf{d}, \mathbf{e}_1, \mathbf{e}_2)} \begin{pmatrix} \det(\mathbf{s}, \mathbf{e}_1, \mathbf{e}_2) \\ \det(-\mathbf{d}, \mathbf{s}, \mathbf{e}_2) \\ \det(-\mathbf{d}, \mathbf{e}_1, \mathbf{s}) \end{pmatrix} \qquad (10.14)$$

From linear algebra, we know that $\det(\mathbf{a}, \mathbf{b}, \mathbf{c}) = |\mathbf{a} \ \mathbf{b} \ \mathbf{c}| = -(\mathbf{a} \times \mathbf{c}) \cdot \mathbf{b} = -(\mathbf{c} \times \mathbf{b}) \cdot \mathbf{a}$. Equation 10.14 can therefore be rewritten as

$$\begin{pmatrix} t \\ u \\ v \end{pmatrix} = \frac{1}{(\mathbf{d} \times \mathbf{e}_2) \cdot \mathbf{e}_1} \begin{pmatrix} (\mathbf{s} \times \mathbf{e}_1) \cdot \mathbf{e}_2 \\ (\mathbf{d} \times \mathbf{e}_2) \cdot \mathbf{s} \\ (\mathbf{s} \times \mathbf{e}_1) \cdot \mathbf{d} \end{pmatrix} = \frac{1}{\mathbf{p} \cdot \mathbf{e}_1} \begin{pmatrix} \mathbf{q} \cdot \mathbf{e}_2 \\ \mathbf{p} \cdot \mathbf{s} \\ \mathbf{q} \cdot \mathbf{d} \end{pmatrix} \qquad (10.15)$$

where $\mathbf{p} = \mathbf{d} \times \mathbf{e}_2$ and $\mathbf{q} = \mathbf{s} \times \mathbf{e}_1$. These factors can be used to speed up the computations.

10.5.2   Implementation

The algorithm is summarized in the pseudocode below. Besides returning whether or not the ray intersects the triangle, the algorithm also returns the above described triple (u, v, t). The code does not cull back-facing triangles.

RayTriIntersect$(\mathbf{o}, \mathbf{d}, \mathbf{v}_0, \mathbf{v}_1, \mathbf{v}_2)$
returns $(\{\text{REJECT}, \text{INTERSECT}\}, \mathbf{u}, \mathbf{v}, \mathbf{t})$;

1 : $\mathbf{e}_1 = \mathbf{v}_1 - \mathbf{v}_0$
2 : $\mathbf{e}_2 = \mathbf{v}_2 - \mathbf{v}_0$
3 : $\mathbf{p} = \mathbf{d} \times \mathbf{e}_2$
4 : $a = \mathbf{e}_1 \cdot \mathbf{p}$
5 :   if$(a > -\epsilon$ and $a < \epsilon)$ return $(\text{REJECT}, 0, 0, 0)$;
6 : $f = 1/a$
7 : $\mathbf{s} = \mathbf{o} - \mathbf{v}_0$
8 : $u = f(\mathbf{s} \cdot \mathbf{p})$
9 :   if$(u < 0.0$ or $u > 1.0)$ return $(\text{REJECT}, 0, 0, 0)$;
10 : $\mathbf{q} = \mathbf{s} \times \mathbf{e}_1$
11 : $v = f(\mathbf{d} \cdot \mathbf{q})$
12 : if$(v < 0.0$ or $u + v > 1.0)$ return $(\text{REJECT}, 0, 0, 0)$;
13 : $t = f(\mathbf{e}_2 \cdot \mathbf{q})$
14 : return $(\text{INTERSECT}, u, v, t)$;

A few lines may require some explanation. Line 4 computes a, which is the determinant of the matrix $\mathbf{M}$. This is followed by a test that avoids determinants close to zero (ϵ is a very small number, which is set by the user, and with a properly adjusted value of ϵ, this algorithm is extremely stable[7]). In line 9, the value of u is compared to an edge of the triangle ($u = 0$), and also to a line parallel to that edge but passing through the opposite point of the triangle ($u = 1$). Although not actually testing an edge of the triangle, this second test efficiently rules out many intersection points without further calculation.

C-code for this algorithm, including both culling and non-culling versions, is available on the web [256]. The C-code has two branches: one that efficiently culls all back-facing triangles, and one that performs intersection tests on two-sided triangles. All computations are delayed until they are required. For example, the value of v is not computed until the value of u is found to be within the allowable range (this can be seen in the pseudocode as well).

The one-sided intersection routine eliminates all triangles where the value of the determinant is negative. This procedure allows the routine's only division operation to be delayed until an intersection has been confirmed.

---

[7] For floating point precision $\epsilon = 1.0^{-5}$ works fine.

The investigation in the *journal of graphics tools* [256] also showed that this method is the fastest ray/triangle intersection routine that does not need to store the normal of the triangle plane, and that it is comparable in speed to Badouel's method [19], which also computes barycentric coordinates (and so makes the comparison fair).

10.6 Ray/Polygon Intersection

Even though triangles are the most common rendering primitive, a routine that computes the intersection between a ray and a polygon is useful to have. A polygon of n vertices is defined by an ordered vertex list $\{\mathbf{v}_0, \mathbf{v}_1, \ldots, \mathbf{v}_{n-1}\}$, where vertex $\mathbf{v}_i$ forms an edge with $\mathbf{v}_{i+1}$ for $0 \leq i < n-1$ and the polygon is closed by the edge from $\mathbf{v}_{n-1}$ to $\mathbf{v}_0$. The plane of the polygon[8] is denoted $\pi_p : \mathbf{n}_p \cdot \mathbf{x} + d_p$.

We first compute the intersection between the ray (Equation 10.1) and π_p, which is easily done by replacing the $\mathbf{x}$ by the ray. The solution is presented below.

$$\mathbf{n}_p \cdot (\mathbf{o} + t\mathbf{d}) + d_p = 0$$
$$\Longleftrightarrow$$
$$t = \frac{-d_p - \mathbf{n}_p \cdot \mathbf{o}}{\mathbf{n}_p \cdot \mathbf{d}} \qquad (10.16)$$

If the denominator $|\mathbf{n}_p \cdot \mathbf{d}| < \epsilon$, where ϵ is a very small number, then the ray is considered parallel to the polygon plane and no intersection occurs.[9] Otherwise, the intersection point, $\mathbf{p}$, between the ray and the polygon plane is computed: $\mathbf{p} = \mathbf{o} + t\mathbf{d}$, where the t-value is that from Equation 10.16. Thereafter, the problem of deciding whether $\mathbf{p}$ is inside the polygon is reduced from three to two dimensions. This is done by projecting all vertices and $\mathbf{p}$ to one of the xy-, xz-, or yz-planes where the area of the projected polygon is maximized. In other words, the coordinate component that corresponds to $\max(n_{p,x}, n_{p,y}, n_{p,z})$ can be skipped and the others kept as two-dimensional coordinates. Note that this information could be precomputed and stored within the polygon. The topology of the polygon and the intersection point is conserved during this projection (assuming the polygon is indeed flat; see Section 9.2 for more on this topic). The projection procedure is shown in Figure 10.10. A two-dimensional bounding

---

[8]This plane can be computed from the vertices on the fly or stored with the polygon, whichever is most convenient. It is sometimes called the supporting plane of the polygon.

[9]We ignore the case where the ray is in the polygon's plane.

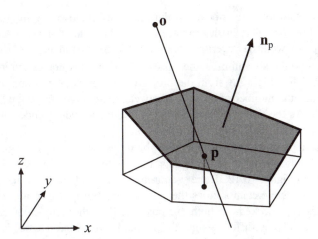

Figure 10.10. Orthographic projection of polygon vertices and intersection point **p** onto the xy-plane, where the area of the projected polygon is maximized. This is another example of using dimension reduction to obtain simpler calculations.

box (in the above mentioned plane) for the polygon is also sometimes profitable. That is, first compute the intersection with the polygon plane and then project to two dimensions and test against the two-dimensional bounding box. If the point is outside the box, then reject and return; otherwise continue with the full polygon test. This was found to be a better approach than using a three-dimensional bounding box for a polygon [386].

Now, what remains is to determine whether the two-dimensional ray/plane intersection point **p** is contained in the two-dimensional polygon. Here we will review just one of the more useful algorithms—the "crossings" test. Haines [153] provides an extensive survey of two-dimensional point-in-polygon strategies. More recently, Walker [364] has presented a method for rapid testing of polygons with more than 10 vertices. Also, Nishita et al. [270] discuss point inclusion testing for shapes with curved edges. A more formal treatment can be found in the computational geometry literature [280, 292].

10.6.1 The Crossings Test

The crossings test is based on the *Jordan Curve Theorem*, which says that a point is inside a polygon if a ray from this point in an arbitrary direction crosses an odd number of polygon edges. This test is also known as the parity or the even-odd test. This condition does not mean that all areas enclosed by the polygon are considered inside. This is shown in Figure 10.11. These enclosed areas could be included as well, however; see Haines [153] for treatment.

The crossings algorithm is the fastest test that does not use preprocessing. It works by shooting a ray from the projection of the point **p** along the positive x-axis. Then the number of crossings between the polygon edges and this ray is computed. As the *Jordan Curve Theorem* proves, an odd number of crossings indicates that the point is inside the polygon.

The test point **p** can also be thought of as being at the origin, and the (translated) edges may be tested against the positive x-axis instead. This option is depicted in Figure 10.12. If the y-coordinates of a polygon edge have the same sign, then that edge cannot cross the x-axis. Otherwise, it can, and then the x-coordinates are checked. If both are positive, then the number of crossings is incremented. If they differ in sign, the x-coordinate of the intersection between the edge and the x-axis must be computed, and if it is positive, the number of crossings is again incremented.

Problems might occur when the test ray intersects a vertex, since two crossings might be detected. This problem is solved by setting the vertex infinitesimally above the ray, which in practice is done by interpreting the vertices with $y \geq 0$ as lying above the x-axis (the ray). The code becomes simpler and speedier, and no vertices will be intersected [151].

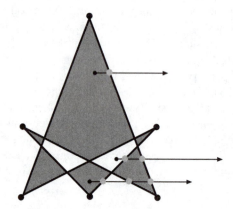

Figure 10.11. A general polygon that is self-intersecting and concave, yet all of its enclosed areas are not considered inside (only grey areas are inside). Vertices are marked with large, black dots. Three points being tested are shown, along with their test rays. According to the Jordan Curve Theorem, a point is inside if the number of crossings with the edges of the polygon is odd. Therefore, the uppermost and the bottommost points are inside (one and three crossings, respectively), while the middle point crosses two edges and is thus outside the polygon.

The pseudocode for an efficient form of the crossings test is given. It was inspired by work by Joseph Samosky [308] and Mark Haigh-Hutchinson, and the code is available on the web [153]. Two-dimensional test point t and polygon P with vertices $\mathbf{v}_0$ through $\mathbf{v}_{n-1}$ are compared.

```
        bool PointInPolygon(t, P)
        returns ({TRUE, FALSE});
1:      bool inside = FALSE
2:      e_0 = v_{n-1}
3:      e_1 = v_0
4:      bool y_0 = (e_{0y} ≥ t_y)
5:      for i = 1 to n
6:          bool y_1 = (e_{1y} ≥ t_y)
7:          if(y_0 ≠ y_1)
8:              if((e_{1y} - t_y)(e_{0x} - e_{1x}) ≥ (e_{1x} - t_x)(e_{0y} - e_{1y}) = y_1)
9:                  inside = ¬inside
10:         y_0 = y_1
11:         e_0 = e_1
12:         e_1 = v_i
13:     return inside;
```

Line 4 checks whether the y-value of the last vertex in the polygon is greater than or equal to the y-value of the test point t, and stores the result in the boolean y_0. In other words, it tests whether the first endpoint of the first edge we will test is above or below the x-axis. Line 7 tests whether the endpoints e_0 and e_1 are on different sides of the x-axis formed by the test point. If so, then line 8 tests whether the x-intercept is positive. Actually, it is a bit trickier than that: to avoid the divide normally needed for computing the intercept we perform a sign-cancelling operation here. By inverting *inside*, line 9 records that a crossing took place. Lines 10 to 12 move on to the next vertex.

In the pseudocode we do not perform a test to see whether both endpoints have positive x-coordinates. Although this is how we presented the algorithm, code based on the pseudocode above often runs faster without this test. This is because we avoid the division needed to compute the x-intercept value, since all we want to know is whether the intercept is to the left or right of the test point. When you are optimizing this routine, we recommend trying both variants and seeing which is faster in practice.

The advantages of the crossings test is that it is relatively fast and robust, and requires no additional information or preprocessing for the polygon. A disadvantage of this method is that it does not yield anything beyond the indication

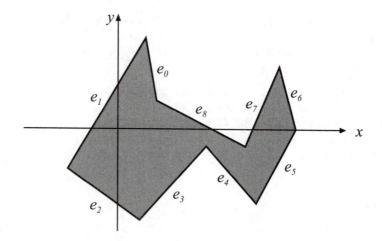

Figure 10.12. The polygon has been translated by $-\mathbf{p}$ ($\mathbf{p}$ is the point to be tested for containment in the polygon), and so the number of crossings with the positive x-axis determines whether $\mathbf{p}$ is inside the polygon. Edges e_0, e_2, e_3, and e_4 cannot cross the x-axis, since they each have both vertices on one side of the x-axis. The intersection between edge e_1 and the x-axis must be computed (but it will not yield a crossing, since the intersection has a negative x-component. Edges e_7 and e_8 will each increase the number of crossings, since the vertices of these edges have positive x-components and one negative and one positive y-component. Finally, the edges e_5 and e_6 share a vertex where $y = 0$ and $x > 0$, and they will together increase the number of crossings by one.

of whether a point is inside or outside the polygon. Other methods [153] can also compute barycentric coordinates which can be used to interpolate additional information about the test point.

10.7   Plane/Box Intersection Detection

One way to determine whether a box intersects a plane, $\pi : \mathbf{n} \cdot \mathbf{x} + d = 0$, is to insert all the vertices of the box into the plane equation. If both a positive and a negative result (or a zero) is obtained, then vertices are located on both sides of (or on) the plane, and therefore an intersection has been detected. But there are smarter, faster ways to do this test, which are presented in the next two sections, one for the AABB, and one for the OBB.

The idea behind both methods is that only two points need to be inserted into the plane equation. These points are the ones that form a diagonal of the box, where the diagonal passes through the center of the box and is more aligned to the normal, $\mathbf{n}$, of the plane than are the other pairs of points that form diagonals.

10.7.1 AABB

Given an AABB, B, defined by $\mathbf{b}^{min}$ and $\mathbf{b}^{max}$, four different diagonals can be constructed. These all pass through the center of B and have endpoints at the vertices of B. For this AABB/plane intersection test, first find out which of the box diagonals is most aligned with the plane normal, $\mathbf{n}$. After the most aligned diagonal is found, the diagonal's two AABB vertices, called $\mathbf{v}^{min}$ and $\mathbf{v}^{max}$, are inserted into the plane equation π. This equation tests which side of the plane each endpoint is on. If the signs of the results differ, or at least one of them is zero, then B intersects π. This is illustrated in Figure 10.13. This test can be improved upon by noting that if $\mathbf{v}^{min}$ is in the positive half-space of the plane (see Section 1.2.1), then $\mathbf{v}^{max}$ will also be in the positive half-space [186]. In this case, the $\mathbf{v}^{max}$ point need not be tested against the plane—we already know that the AABB does not intersect the plane. The complete test is shown in the pseudocode that follows.

```
        bool PlaneAABBIntersect(B, π)
        returns({OVERLAP, DISJOINT});
 1 :    for each i ∈ {x, y, z}
 2 :        if(nᵢ ≥ 0)
 3 :            vᵢᵐⁱⁿ = bᵢᵐⁱⁿ
 4 :            vᵢᵐᵃˣ = bᵢᵐᵃˣ
 5 :        else
 6 :            vᵢᵐⁱⁿ = bᵢᵐᵃˣ
 7 :            vᵢᵐᵃˣ = bᵢᵐⁱⁿ
 8 :    if((n · vᵐⁱⁿ + d) > 0) return (DISJOINT);
 9 :    if((n · vᵐᵃˣ + d) ≥ 0) return (OVERLAP);
 10 :   return (DISJOINT);
```

If the eight vertices of the AABB are saved in an array, then another method can be used to directly identify $\mathbf{v}^{min}$ and $\mathbf{v}^{max}$ [18]. The sign bits of the normal components are stored in a three-bit mask. For example, a normal of $(-1, 0.5, 1)$ would give a bitmask of 100; $(1, 1, -1)$ would give 001; and $(0, -1, -0.5)$ would give 011. If this mask is interpreted as a number, then it can used as an index into the array of AABB vertices in order to fetch $\mathbf{v}^{max}$ (assuming that they are ordered so that the maximum vertex is located at position 000, the minimum vertex at 111, and so on). The $\mathbf{v}^{min}$ vertex index is found by inverting the three bits in this maximum-vertex mask. If a plane is being tested against a number of boxes, index creation can be done once for the plane [154]. In other words, given a plane's orientation, the same indexed corners are always tested against it, regardless of the boxes' dimensions.

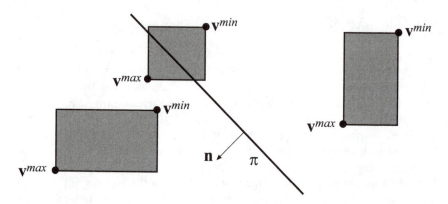

Figure 10.13. Here the $\mathbf{v}^{min}$ and $\mathbf{v}^{max}$ vertices are shown for three AABBs (in two dimensions) for a given plane. If the pair of these vertices are on the same side of the plane, then the AABB does not intersect the plane; otherwise, it does. Note that if $\mathbf{v}^{min}$ is tested against the plane first and is found to be on the same side as the plane normal, then we can immediately reject the intersection.

10.7.2   OBB

With a small change, the test from the previous section can be used to test a plane against an OBB. The trick lies in knowing how to identify the two points, $\mathbf{v}^{min}$ and $\mathbf{v}^{max}$. When that has been done, the same test as for AABBs can be used. To identify these two points, we transform the normal of the plane so that it lies in the coordinate system of the OBB. This is done as follows (see Section A.3.2 about base changing) [186].

$$\mathbf{n}' = (\mathbf{b}^u \cdot \mathbf{n}, \quad \mathbf{b}^v \cdot \mathbf{n}, \quad \mathbf{b}^w \cdot \mathbf{n})^T \tag{10.17}$$

So when finding the points $\mathbf{v}^{min}$ and $\mathbf{v}^{max}$, the transformed normal $\mathbf{n}'$ is used instead of $\mathbf{n}$. The rest of the test is the same as for AABBs.

Another way to test an OBB against a plane is to project the axes of the OBB onto the normal of the plane as shown in Figure 10.14 [136]. Half the length of the projection, called r, is computed by:

$$r = |h_u^B \mathbf{n} \cdot \mathbf{b}^u| + |h_v^B \mathbf{n} \cdot \mathbf{b}^v| + |h_w^B \mathbf{n} \cdot \mathbf{b}^w| \tag{10.18}$$

If the absolute value of the distance from the center of the OBB to the plane is larger than r, then the plane and the OBB do not intersect. So if $|\mathbf{b}^c \cdot \mathbf{n} + d| > r$, then they do not intersect; otherwise they do.

This method can also be applied to the AABB case by setting $\mathbf{b}^u = (1, 0, 0)$, $\mathbf{b}^v = (0, 1, 0)$, and $\mathbf{b}^w = (0, 0, 1)$ and simplifying.

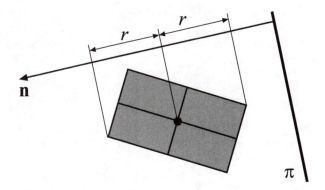

Figure 10.14. The extents of the OBB are projected onto the normal of the plane. Half the "size" of the OBB along the normal's direction is denoted r. If the distance from the center of the OBB to the plane is greater than r, then they do not intersect.

10.8   Triangle/Triangle Intersection

Since graphics hardware uses the triangle as its most important (and optimized) drawing primitive, it is only natural to perform collision detection tests on this kind of data as well. So, at the deepest levels of a collision detection algorithm lies a routine that determines whether or not two triangles intersect. More often than not, we are only concerned about whether they intersect at all, and not interested in an exact intersection.

Two of the fastest methods for this task will be studied. These are comparable in terms of speed. We have included both because the solutions are fundamentally different, and a great deal about intersection routines and rejection tests may be learned by studying them.

The problem is: given two triangles, $T_1 = \triangle u_0 u_1 u_2$ and $T_2 = \triangle v_0 v_1 v_2$ (which lie in the planes π_1 and π_2, respectively), determine whether or not they intersect.

The first method of solving this problem is here called *the interval overlap method* and was introduced by Möller [257], whose presentation is followed closely here.[10] The second, which is algorithmically simpler than the interval overlap test, comes from the ERIT package [178].

---

[10]Reused with permission from the *journal of graphics tools*, A.K. Peters Ltd.

10.8.1   Interval Overlap Method

First, the plane equation $\pi_2 : \mathbf{n}_2 \cdot \mathbf{x} + d_2 = 0$ (where $\mathbf{x}$ is any point on the plane) is computed:

$$\mathbf{n}_2 = (\mathbf{v}_1 - \mathbf{v}_0) \times (\mathbf{v}_2 - \mathbf{v}_0)$$
$$d_2 = -\mathbf{n}_2 \cdot \mathbf{v}_0 \tag{10.19}$$

Then the signed distances from the vertices of T_1 to π_2 (multiplied by a constant $\|\mathbf{n}_2\|^2$) are computed by simply inserting the vertices into the plane equation:

$$d_{\mathbf{u}_i} = \mathbf{n}_2 \cdot \mathbf{u}_i + d_2, \quad i = 0, 1, 2 \tag{10.20}$$

Now, if all $d_{\mathbf{u}_i} \neq 0$, $i = 0, 1$, and 2 (that is, no point is on the plane), and all have the same sign, then T_1 lies on one side of π_2 and the overlap is rejected. The same test is done for T_2 and π_1. These two early rejection tests allow us to avoid many computations for some triangle pairs.

If all $d_{\mathbf{u}_i} = 0$ for $i = 0, 1$, and 2, then the triangles are co-planar and this case is handled separately and discussed later. If not, the intersection of π_1 and π_2 is a line, $\mathbf{l} = \mathbf{o} + t\mathbf{d}$, where $\mathbf{d} = \mathbf{n}_1 \times \mathbf{n}_2$ is the direction of the line and $\mathbf{o}$ is some point on it. Note that due to our previous calculations and rejections, both triangles are guaranteed to intersect $\mathbf{l}$. These intersections form intervals on $\mathbf{l}$, and if these intervals overlap, the triangles overlap as well. A similar interval test is used in a different context by Laidlaw et al. [218]. Two situations that can occur are depicted in Figure 10.15.

Now, assume that we want to compute a scalar interval (on $\mathbf{l}$) that represents the intersection between T_1 and $\mathbf{l}$, and that, for example, $\mathbf{u}_0$ and $\mathbf{u}_2$ lie on the

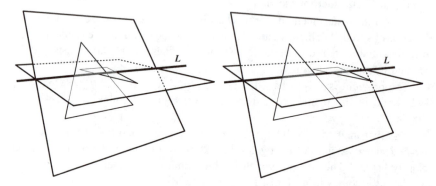

Figure 10.15. Triangles and the planes in which they lie. Intersection intervals are marked in gray in both figures. Left: the intervals along the line L overlap as well as the triangles. Right: there is no intersection; the intervals do not overlap.

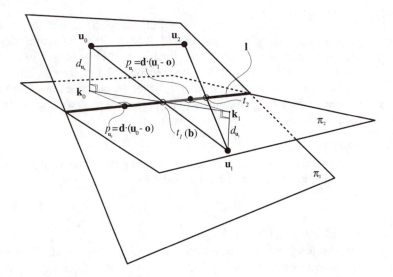

Figure 10.16. The geometrical situation. Points $\mathbf{u}_i$ are the vertices of T_1; π_1 and π_2 are the planes in which T_1 and T_2 lie; $d_{\mathbf{u}_i}$ are the signed distances from $\mathbf{u}_i$ to π_2; $\mathbf{k}_i$ are the projections of $\mathbf{u}_i$ onto π_2; and $p_{\mathbf{u}_i}$ are the projections of $\mathbf{u}_i$ onto l, which is the line of intersection.

same side of π_2 and that $\mathbf{u}_1$ lies on the other side (if not, you have already rejected it). To find scalar values that represent the intersection between the edges $\mathbf{u}_0\mathbf{u}_1$ and $\mathbf{u}_1\mathbf{u}_2$ and l, the vertices are first projected onto l:

$$p_{\mathbf{u}_i} = \mathbf{d} \cdot (\mathbf{u}_i - \mathbf{o}) \tag{10.21}$$

The geometrical situation is shown in Figure 10.16. Next, we want to use the intersection point, called $\mathbf{b}$, between the line $\mathbf{l} = \mathbf{o} + t\mathbf{d}$ and the edge $\mathbf{u}_0\mathbf{u}_1$. We call the t-value at the intersection point t_1. If we let $\mathbf{k}_i$ denote the projection of $\mathbf{u}_i$ onto π_2, we see that the triangles $\triangle\mathbf{u}_0\mathbf{b}\mathbf{k}_0$ and $\triangle\mathbf{u}_1\mathbf{b}\mathbf{k}_1$ are similar. This is also shown in Figure 10.16. Using the similar triangles, t_1 can be computed as below.

$$t_1 = p_{\mathbf{u}_0} + (p_{\mathbf{u}_1} - p_{\mathbf{u}_0})\frac{d_{\mathbf{u}_0}}{d_{\mathbf{u}_0} - d_{\mathbf{u}_1}} \tag{10.22}$$

Similar calculations are done to compute t_2, which represents the intersection between the line l and the edge $\mathbf{u}_1\mathbf{u}_2$. Together, t_1 and t_2 represent an interval on the line l where the triangle T_1 intersects l. Using similar techniques, an interval can be computed for the other triangle, T_2, as well. If these intervals overlap, the triangles intersect.

If the triangles are co-planar, they are projected onto the axis-aligned plane where the areas of the triangles are maximized. Then a simple two-dimensional triangle-triangle overlap test is performed. First, test all closed edges of T_1 for intersection with the edges of T_2. If any intersection is found, then the triangles intersect. Otherwise, we must test whether T_1 is totally contained in T_2 or vice versa. This can be done by performing a point-in-triangle test (see Section 10.5) for one vertex of T_1 against T_2 and vice versa.

Optimizations

Since the intervals can be translated without altering the result of the interval overlap test, Equation 10.21 can be simplified into:

$$p_{\mathbf{u}_i} = \mathbf{d} \cdot \mathbf{u}_i, \quad i = 0, 1, 2 \tag{10.23}$$

Therefore **o** does not need to be computed.

Also, the result of the overlap test does not change if we project l onto the coordinate axis with which it is most closely aligned, and so Equation 10.23 can be simplified further:

$$p_{\mathbf{u}_i} = \begin{cases} u_{ix}, & \text{if } |d_x| = \max(|d_x|, |d_y|, |d_z|) \\ u_{iy}, & \text{if } |d_y| = \max(|d_x|, |d_y|, |d_z|) \\ u_{iz}, & \text{if } |d_z| = \max(|d_x|, |d_y|, |d_z|) \end{cases}, \quad i = 0, 1, 2 \tag{10.24}$$

Here, u_{0x} means the x-component of $\mathbf{u}_0$, and so on. Note that the same computations are done for the vertices of the other triangle. The same principle was used by Mirtich [250] in order to get a numerically stable simplification of an integral over a polygon's area.

Implementation

To summarize, the steps of the algorithm are as follows (complete C code is available on the web [256]):

1. Compute the plane equation of Triangle 2.

2. Trivially reject if all points of Triangle 1 are on same side.

3. Compute the plane equation of Triangle 1.

4. Trivially reject if all points of Triangle 2 are on same side.

5. Compute intersection line and project onto largest axis.

6. Compute intervals for each triangle.

7. Intersect the intervals.

Note that after step 2, there is enough information to test immediately whether the triangles are co-planar, but because this is a rare occurrence, the test is deferred until after several more frequently hit rejection tests have been performed.

Robustness problems may arise when the triangles are nearly co-planar or when an edge is nearly co-planar to the other triangle (especially when the edge is close to an edge of the other triangle). To handle these cases in a reasonable way, the source code provides a constant, EPSILON (ϵ), which the user defines. As a result, if any $|d_{\mathbf{u}_i}| < \epsilon$, they are reset so that $d_{\mathbf{u}_i} = 0$. Geometrically, this means that if a point is "close enough" to the other triangle's plane, it is considered to be on the plane. The same is done for the points of the other triangle as well. The source code does not handle degenerate triangles (i.e., lines and points). To do so, those cases should be detected first and then handled as special cases.

10.8.2 ERIT's Method

The triangle/triangle intersection test found in ERIT [178] is outlined here.

1. Compute $\pi_2 : \mathbf{n}_2 \cdot \mathbf{x} + d_2$, the plane in which T_2 lies.

2. Trivially reject if all points of T_1 are on the same side of π_2 (also store the signed distances, $d_{\mathbf{u}_i}$, as in the previous algorithm).

3. Compute the intersection between π_2 and T_1, which clearly is a line segment that is co-planar with π_2. This situation is illustrated in Figure 10.17.

4. If this line segment intersects or is totally contained in T_2, then T_1 and T_2 intersect; otherwise, they do not.

Step 1 and 2 are the same as for the interval overlap method. Step 3, on the other hand, requires computation of two points, $\mathbf{p}$ and $\mathbf{q}$, in π_2 representing the line of intersection. Since we have the signed distances from the points of T_1 to π_2 (from step 2), $\mathbf{p}$ and $\mathbf{q}$ can be computed by first finding points of T_1 that lie on different sides of π_2 (i.e., they have different signs on their $d_{\mathbf{u}_i}$). When such a pair, say with index i_1 and i_2, has been found, the intersection point $\mathbf{p}$ is

$$\mathbf{p} = \mathbf{u}_{i_1} + \frac{d_{\mathbf{u}_{i_1}}}{d_{\mathbf{u}_{i_1}} - d_{\mathbf{u}_{i_2}}} (\mathbf{u}_{i_2} - \mathbf{u}_{i_1}). \tag{10.25}$$

The point $\mathbf{q}$ is computed similarly, with another pair of indices found in the same manner. Step 4 is accomplished by first projecting T_2, $\mathbf{p}$, and $\mathbf{q}$ onto the

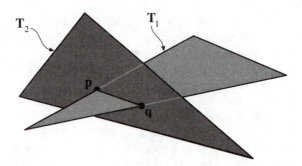

Figure 10.17. This figure depicts the way in which the ERIT method determines whether two triangles intersect. The intersection points, p and q, between triangle T_2 and triangle T_1 are computed. If the line between p and q is totally contained in T_2 or if it intersects the edges of T_2, then the triangles intersect. They are disjoint otherwise. Illustration after Held [178].

coordinate plane ($x = 0$, $y = 0$, or $z = 0$) where the area of T_2 is maximized, exactly as was done for the ray/polygon intersection methods in Section 10.6. Both points of the projected line must be tested against each *half-plane* formed by each triangle edge of T_2. Essentially, the line formed by the edge of the triangle divides the plane into two sides. If both points are outside the edge, the triangles do not intersect. After testing the line segment **pq** against all three edges, we have enough information to decide whether any of the points on **pq** is inside T_2. If that is the case, then the triangles intersect; otherwise, each edge of T_2 must be tested for intersection with the line segment formed by the two points, which can be done using the methods presented in Section 10.12. Finding intersection at any time implies that the triangles intersect; otherwise, the triangles are disjoint. This last test concludes the intersection method.

10.8.3   Performance Comparison

The interval overlap method and the method from ERIT were found to be much faster than the brute-force method[11], which took between 1.3 and 1.6 times longer to execute in comparison to the two methods detailed here [257]. On a PentiumPro, ERIT's method was found to be faster, and on Ultra-30 and on Indigo-2 the two were comparable in speed [178].

---

[11] Here, each closed edge of each triangle is tested for intersection with the other triangle and if, at any time, an intersection occurs, then the triangles intersect.

10.9 Cube/Polygon Intersection

This section presents an algorithm for determining whether a polygon intersects an axis-aligned unit cube (i.e., a cube all of whose edges have a length of one, and which is centered at the origin). Such a test can be used to build voxel-spaces, cull cubes against polyhedral volumes (e.g., view frustums) that consist of polygonal faces, or test polygons against canonical view volumes (see Section 3.5) and potentially eliminate the need for calls to clipping and lighting routines, etc.

Several intersection methods can be found in the Graphics Gems series, the first one presented by Voorhies in 1992 [360] and the second by Greene [142], which solve this problem for convex polygons. Finally, Green and Hatch [139] expanded on the gem by Voorhies, which handled only triangles. Their method is able to test an arbitrary polygon against a cube and is more robust and efficient than the earlier ones. Because of these characteristics, attention will be focused on Green and Hatch's algorithm. Code is available on the web for Voorhies's [360] and Green and Hatch's [139] algorithms.

10.9.1 General Algorithm

The construction of this procedure is efficient since it commences with some simple rejection and acceptance tests and then proceeds to more costly ones:

1. Test whether any of the polygon's vertices are inside the cube. If so, return INTERSECT. Simultaneously test whether the whole polygon is outside any of the six planes formed by the cube's faces, then the 12 formed using the cube's edges, then the eight formed using the cube's corners. If the polygon is outside any of these planes, then return DISJOINT.

2. Test polygon edges for intersection with the cube. If any edge intersects the cube, return INTERSECT.

3. Test whether the interior of the polygon intersects the cube. If so, return INTERSECT.

4. Else return DISJOINT.

We will examine each step in turn.

Step 1: Trivial accept and reject conditions are examined. If any vertex is found to be inside the cube, this means an intersection must occur and so testing can end. If all vertices are found to lie on one side of any cube face's plane,

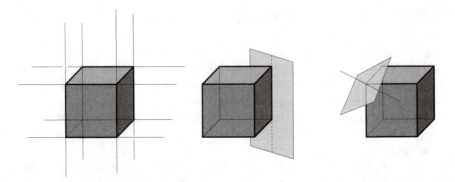

Figure 10.18. The planes used for trivial rejections in the cube/polygon intersection test. The left figure shows the six planes of the cube, which are used first in the test. The middle figure shows one of the 12 bevel planes that is formed on an edge and has a normal that coincides with the vector from the center of the cube to the center of the edge. The rightmost figure depicts one of the eight corner planes formed by a corner and with a normal that coincides with the vector from the center of the cube to the corner.

the polygon must be outside the cube. If no classification can be made using this test, rejection testing continues by checking vertices against the 12 planes (called bevel planes) adjacent to the cube edges, followed by checking the eight planes (called corner planes) adjacent to the cube corners. Examples of these test planes are depicted in Figure 10.18. For these bevel and corner planes, if a vertex is found to be outside one of them, then it must be inside the diagonally opposite (and parallel) plane. For example, a point outside the upper left edge plane must be inside the lower right edge plane. Also, as soon as a plane is found to have a point inside of it, that plane cannot trivially reject the polygon and so can be ignored in further rejection testing. Once all planes have at least one point inside of them, the trivial reject test can end, since it has failed. Note that the bevel and corner plane tests are not required for the algorithm to work, but Green found that these tests improved overall efficiency.

Step 2: Step 2 is solved by recasting the intersection test into a different problem space. The following two tests are equivalent: i) intersecting a line segment with a cube and ii) testing whether the center of the cube is inside the convex solid[12] generated by sweeping the cube from the start point of the line segment to the end point. Such a solid is shown in Figure 10.19. Testing whether a point is inside a convex solid is equivalent to testing whether this point lies on the "right" side of all the planes of the solid, so our test becomes (at most) 12 half-plane tests (since the swept solid has 12 faces). Also, since these 12 planes

---

[12]Green and Hatch [139] point out that the solid is called a skewed rhombic dodecahedron.

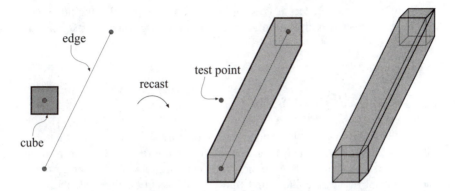

Figure 10.19. A two-dimensional example of recasting an intersection test between a square and an edge. In the middle figure, the center of the square (test point) is tested for intersection with the convex, six-sided polygon created by sweeping the square along the edge. In this case, the square does not intersect the edge, since the test point is outside the swept polygon. In three dimensions (shown at the right), the volume formed by sweeping the cube is also convex and consists of 12 faces.

come in pairs with common normals, we can exploit this knowledge to speed up the test further.

Step 3: The last test determines whether the interior of the polygon intersects the cube (note that at this point, none of the edges nor any of the vertices intersects the cube). See Figure 10.20 for an example. Voorhies [360] showed that to do this test, it is sufficient to check whether any of the four diagonals of the cube intersects the interior of the polygon. However, this test was further optimized by Green and Hatch [139], who noticed that only the cube diagonal that is most closely aligned to the polygon normal needs to be tested against the polygon (this test is presented in Section 10.7, but it can be optimized further for the special case of a cube).

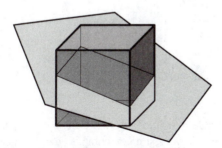

Figure 10.20. A polygon whose interior and nothing else intersects a cube. This is the last and most expensive test in the cube/polygon intersection test.

If any intersection occurs it is with this diagonal. After selecting this diagonal, it is intersected with the polygon using any of the routines described in Section 10.6.

10.10   BV/BV Intersection Tests

A closed volume that totally contains a set of objects is (in most situations) called a *bounding volume* (BV) for this set. The purpose of a BV is to provide simpler intersection tests and make more efficient rejections. For example, to test whether or not two cars collide, first find their BVs and then test whether they overlap. If they do not, then the cars are guaranteed not to collide (which we assume is the most common case). We then have avoided testing each primitive of one car against each primitive of the other, thereby saving computation.

Bounding volume hierarchies are often part of the foundation of collision detection algorithms (see Chapter 11). Four bounding volumes that are commonly used for this purpose are the sphere, the *axis-aligned bounding box* (AABB), the *discrete oriented polytope* (k-DOP), and the *oriented bounding box* (OBB). A fundamental operation is to test whether or not two bounding volumes overlap. Methods of testing overlap for the AABB, the k-DOP, and the OBB are presented in the following sections.

AABBs, OBBs, and k-DOPs are all convex polyhedra, for which a general theorem on intersection testing holds [142, 135].

Theorem. (*Separating Axis Theorem*) For any two arbitrary, convex, disjoint polyhedra, A and B, there exists a separating axis where the projections of the polyhedra, which form intervals on the axis, are also disjoint. If A and B are disjoint, then they can be separated by an axis that is orthogonal (i.e., by a plane that is parallel) to either

1. a face of A, or

2. a face of B, or

3. an edge from each polyhedron.

$\square$

This theorem is used in deriving the fast OBB/OBB overlap test in Section 10.10.4.

For spheres, the test is very simple: compute the distance between the two spheres' centers and then trivially reject if this distance is greater than the sum of the two spheres' radii. Otherwise, they intersect.

 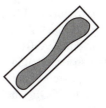

Figure 10.21. The efficiency of a bounding volume can be estimated by the "empty" volume; the more empty space, the worse the fit. A sphere (left), an AABB (middle), and an OBB (right) are shown for an object, where the OBB clearly has less empty space than the others.

The reason for using more complex BVs than the sphere and the AABB is, of course, that more complex BVs have better fits in most cases. This is illustrated in Figure 10.21.

10.10.1 Sphere/Box Intersection

An algorithm for testing whether a sphere and an AABB intersect was first presented by Arvo [16] and is surprisingly simple. The idea is to find the point on the AABB that is closest to the sphere's center, $\mathbf{c}$. One-dimensional tests are used, one for each of the three axes of the AABB. The sphere's center coordinate for an axis is tested against the bounds of the AABB. If it is outside the bounds, the distance between the sphere and the box along this axis (a subtraction) is computed and squared. After we have done this along the three axes, the sum of these squared distances is compared to the squared radius, r^2, of the sphere. If the sum is less than the squared radius, the closest point is inside the sphere, and the box overlaps.

```
      bool SphereAABB_intersect(c, r, A)
      returns({OVERLAP, DISJOINT});
1 :   d = 0
2 :   for each i ∈ {x, y, z}
3 :       if(c_i < a_i^min)
4 :           d = d + (c_i − a_i^min)²;
5 :       else if(c_i > a_i^max)
6 :           d = d + (c_i − a_i^max)²;
7 :   if(d > r²)
8 :       return (DISJOINT);
9 :   return (OVERLAP);
```

As Arvo shows, this algorithm can be modified to handle hollow boxes and spheres, as well as axis-aligned ellipsoids.

For sphere/OBB intersection, first transform the sphere's center into the OBB's space. That is, use the OBB's normalized axes as the basis for transforming the sphere's center. Now this center point is expressed in terms of the OBB's axes, so the OBB can be treated as an AABB. The sphere/AABB algorithm is then used to test for intersection.

10.10.2   AABB/AABB Intersection

An AABB is, as its name implies, a box whose faces are aligned with the main axis directions. Therefore, two points are sufficient to describe such a volume. Here we use the definition of the AABB presented in Section 10.1.

Due to their simplicity, AABBs are still commonly employed both in naive collision detection algorithms and as bounding volumes for the nodes in a scene graph. The test for intersection between two AABBs, A and B, is trivial and is summarized below.

> bool **AABB_intersect**(A, B)
> returns($\{$OVERLAP, DISJOINT$\}$);
> 1 :   for each $i \in \{x, y, z\}$
> 2 :   if$(a_i^{min} > b_i^{max}$ or $b_i^{min} > a_i^{max})$
> 3 :   return (DISJOINT);
> 4 :   return (OVERLAP);

Lines 1 and 2 loop over all three standard axis directions x, y, and z.

10.10.3 k-DOP/k-DOP Intersection

The bounding volume called a *discrete orientation polytope* or k-DOP was named by Klosowski et al. [209]. A k-DOP is a convex polytope[12] whose faces are determined by a small, fixed set of k normals, where the outward half-space of the normals is not considered part of the BV. Kay and Kajiya were the first to introduce this kind of BV, and they used them in the context of ray tracing. Also, they called two oppositely oriented normals a bounding *slab* and used them to keep the intersection cost down. This technique is used for the k-DOPs for the same reason. As a result the intersection test consists of only $k/2$ interval overlap tests. Klosowski et al. [209] have shown that, for

---

[12]A (convex) polytope is the convex hull of a finite set of points (see Section A.5.3).

moderate values of k ($k = 18$ is used in Section 11.4), the overlap test for two k-DOPs is an order of a magnitude faster than the test for two OBBs. In Figure 10.4 a simple two-dimensional k-DOP is depicted. Note that the AABB is a special case of a 6-DOP where the normals are the positive and negative main axis directions. Also note that as k increases, the BV increasingly resembles the convex hull, which is the tightest-fitting convex BV.

The intersection test that follows is trivial and also extremely fast, as has been mentioned before. If two k-DOPs, A and B (superscripted with indices A and B), are to be tested for intersection, then test all pairs of slabs (S_i^A, S_i^B) for overlap; $s_i = S_i^A \cap S_i^B$ is a one-dimensional interval overlap test, which is solved with ease.[14] If at any time $s_i = 0$, then the BVs are disjoint and the test is terminated. Otherwise, the slab overlap tests continues. If and only if all $s_i \neq 0$, $1 \leq i \leq k/2$, then the BVs intersect. Here is the pseudocode for the k-DOP/k-DOP overlap test.

$$
\begin{aligned}
&\textbf{kDOP\_intersect}(d_1^{A,max}, \ldots, d_{k/2}^{A,max}, \\
&\quad d_1^{A,max}, \ldots, d_{k/2}^{A,max}, d_1^{B,max}, \ldots, d_{k/2}^{B,max}, \\
&\quad d_1^{B,max}, \ldots, d_{k/2}^{B,max}) \\
&\texttt{returns}(\{\texttt{OVERLAP}, \texttt{DISJOINT}\});
\end{aligned}
$$

```
1 :  for each i ∈ {1,...,k/2}
2 :     if(d_i^{B,min} > d_i^{A,max} or d_i^{A,min} > d_i^{B,max})
3 :        return (DISJOINT);
4 :  return (OVERLAP);
```

Note that only k scalar values need to be stored with each instance of the k-DOP (the normals, $\mathbf{n}_i$, are stored once for all k-DOPs since they are static). If the k-DOPs are translated by $\mathbf{t}^A$ and $\mathbf{t}^B$, respectively, the test gets a tiny bit more complicated. Project $\mathbf{t}^A$ onto the normals, $\mathbf{n}_i$, e.g., $p_i^A = \mathbf{t}^A \cdot \mathbf{n}_i$ (note that this is independent of any k-DOP in particular and therefore needs to be computed only once for each $\mathbf{t}^A$ or $\mathbf{t}^B$) and add p_i^A to $d_i^{A,min}$ and $d_i^{A,max}$ in the if-statement above. The same is done for $\mathbf{t}^B$. More on k-DOPs and their use can be found in Section 11.4.

10.10.4 OBB/OBB Intersection

In this section a fast routine [135, 137] will be derived for testing whether two OBBs, A and B, overlap. The algorithm uses the *separating axis theorem*, and

---

[14]This is indeed an example of dimension reduction as the rules of thumb recommended. Here a three-dimensional slab test is simplified into a one-dimensional interval overlap test.

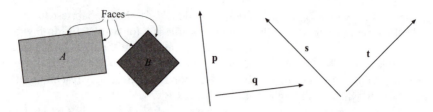

Figure 10.22. To determine whether two OBBs A and B overlap, the separating axis theorem can be used. Here it is shown in two dimensions. The separating axes should be orthogonal to the faces of A and B. The axes **p** and **q** are orthogonal to the faces of A, and **s** and **t** are orthogonal to the faces of B. The OBBs are then projected onto the axes. If both projections overlap on all axes then the OBBs overlap; otherwise they do not. So it is sufficient to find one axis that separates the projections in order to know that the OBBs do not overlap. In this example, the **q** axis is the only axis that separates the projections.

is about an order of magnitude faster than previous methods, which use closest features or linear programming. The definition of the OBB may be found in Section 10.1.

The test is done in the coordinate system formed by A's center and axes. This means that the origin is $\mathbf{a}^c$ and that the main axes in this coordinate system are $\mathbf{a}^u$, $\mathbf{a}^v$, and $\mathbf{a}^w$. Moreover, B is assumed to be located relative to A, with a translation $\mathbf{t}$ and a rotation (matrix) $\mathbf{R}$.

According to the separating axis theorem, it is sufficient to find one axis that separates A and B to be sure that they are disjoint (do not overlap). Fifteen axes have to be tested: three from the faces of A, three from the faces of B, and $3 \cdot 3 = 9$ from combinations of edges from A and B. This is shown in two dimensions in Figure 10.22. As a consequence of the orthonormality of the matrix $\mathbf{A} = (\mathbf{a}^u \ \mathbf{a}^v \ \mathbf{a}^w)$, the potential separating axes that should be orthogonal to the faces of A are simply the axes $\mathbf{a}^u$, $\mathbf{a}^v$, and $\mathbf{a}^w$. The same holds for B. The remaining nine potential axes, formed by one edge each from both A and B, are then $\mathbf{c}^{ij} = \mathbf{a}^i \times \mathbf{b}^j$, $\forall i \in \{u, v, w\}$ and $\forall j \in \{u, v, w\}$.

Assume that a potential separating axis is denoted as $\mathbf{l}$, and adopt the notation from Figure 10.23. The "radii", r_A and r_B, of the OBBs on the axis, $\mathbf{l}$, are obtained by simple projections, as expressed in Equation 10.26. Remember that h_i^A and h_i^B are always positive, and so their absolute value does not need to be computed.

$$r_A = \sum_{i \in \{u,v,w\}} h_i^A |\mathbf{a}^i \cdot \mathbf{l}|$$

$$r_B = \sum_{i \in \{u,v,w\}} h_i^B |\mathbf{b}^i \cdot \mathbf{l}| \tag{10.26}$$

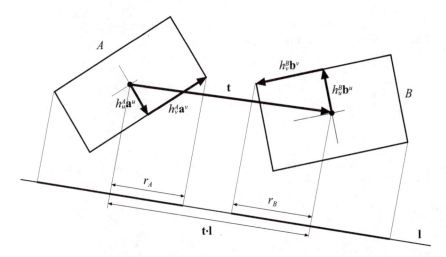

Figure 10.23. The separating axis theorem illustrated. The two OBBs, A and B, are disjoint, since the projections of their "radii" on the axis determined by l are not overlapping. Illustration after Gottschalk et al. [135].

If and only if l is a separating axis, then the intervals on the axis should be disjoint. That is, the following should hold:

$$|\mathbf{t} \cdot \mathbf{l}| > r_A + r_B \qquad (10.27)$$

Derivations and simplifications of Equation 10.27 for three cases follow—one for an edge of A, one for an edge of B, and one for a combination of edges from A and B.

First, let $\mathbf{l} = \mathbf{a}^u$. This gives the expression below.

$$|\mathbf{t} \cdot \mathbf{l}| = |\mathbf{t} \cdot \mathbf{a}^u| = |t_x| \qquad (10.28)$$

The last step comes from the fact that we are operating in the coordinate system of A, and thus $\mathbf{a}^u = (1 \ 0 \ 0)^T$. In Equation 10.29, the expressions for r_A and r_B are simplified.

$$r_A = \sum_{i \in \{u,v,w\}} h_i^A |\mathbf{a}^i \cdot \mathbf{l}| = \sum_{i \in \{u,v,w\}} h_i^A |\mathbf{a}^i \cdot \mathbf{a}^u| = h_u^A$$

$$(10.29)$$

$$r_B = \sum_{i \in \{u,v,w\}} h_i^B |\mathbf{b}^i \cdot \mathbf{l}| = \sum_{i \in \{u,v,w\}} h_i^B |\mathbf{b}^i \cdot \mathbf{a}^u| =$$

$$= h_u^B |b_x^u| + h_v^B |b_x^v| + h_w^B |b_x^w| = h_u^B |r_{00}| + h_v^B |r_{01}| + h_w^B |r_{02}|$$

The resulting equation for r_A comes from the orthonormality of $\mathbf{A}$, and in the last step in the derivation of r_B, note that

$$\mathbf{R} = \begin{pmatrix} r_{00} & r_{01} & r_{02} \\ r_{10} & r_{11} & r_{12} \\ r_{20} & r_{21} & r_{22} \end{pmatrix} = (\mathbf{b}^u \quad \mathbf{b}^v \quad \mathbf{b}^w) \tag{10.30}$$

since $\mathbf{R}$ is the relative rotation matrix. The disjointedness test for the axis $\mathbf{l} = \mathbf{a}^u$ becomes

$$|t_x| > h_u^A + h_u^B|r_{00}| + h_v^B|r_{01}| + h_w^B|r_{02}| \tag{10.31}$$

and if this expression is true, then A and B are disjoint. Similar test expressions are derived in the same manner for $\mathbf{l} = \mathbf{a}^v$ and $\mathbf{l} = \mathbf{a}^w$.

Second, let $\mathbf{l} = \mathbf{b}^u$, for which the derivation follows.

$$|\mathbf{t} \cdot \mathbf{l}| = |\mathbf{t} \cdot \mathbf{b}^u| = |t_x b_x^u + t_y b_y^u + t_z b_z^u| = |t_x r_{00} + t_y r_{10} + t_z r_{20}|$$

$$r_A = \sum_{i \in \{u,v,w\}} h_i^A |\mathbf{a}^i \cdot \mathbf{l}| = \sum_{i \in \{u,v,w\}} h_i^A |\mathbf{a}^i \cdot \mathbf{b}^u| =$$
$$= h_u^A |b_x^u| + h_v^A |b_y^u| + h_w^A |b_z^u| = h_u^A |r_{00}| + h_v^A |r_{10}| + h_w^A |r_{20}| \tag{10.32}$$

$$r_B = \sum_{i \in \{u,v,w\}} h_i^B |\mathbf{b}^i \cdot \mathbf{l}| = \sum_{i \in \{u,v,w\}} h_i^B |\mathbf{b}^i \cdot \mathbf{b}^u| = h_u^B$$

This leads to the disjointedness test in Equation 10.33 for $\mathbf{l} = \mathbf{b}^u$.

$$|t_x r_{00} + t_y r_{10} + t_z r_{20}| > h_u^A |r_{00}| + h_v^A |r_{10}| + h_w^A |r_{20}| + h_u^B \tag{10.33}$$

Again, for the remaining axes, $\mathbf{b}^v$ and $\mathbf{b}^w$, similar test are derived in the above manner.

Finally, the separating axis could be a combination of an edge from each OBB. Therefore, the axis is chosen as $\mathbf{l} = \mathbf{a}^u \times \mathbf{b}^v$. This gives:

$$
|\mathbf{t} \cdot \mathbf{l}| = |\mathbf{t} \cdot (\mathbf{a}^u \times \mathbf{b}^v)| = |\mathbf{t} \cdot (0 \quad -b_z^v \quad b_y^v)^T| =
$$
$$
= |t_z b_y^v - t_y b_z^v| = |t_z r_{11} - t_y r_{21}|
$$

$$
\begin{aligned}
r_A &= \sum_{i \in \{u,v,w\}} h_i^A |\mathbf{a}^i \cdot \mathbf{l}| = \sum_{i \in \{u,v,w\}} h_i^A |\mathbf{a}^i \cdot (\mathbf{a}^u \times \mathbf{b}^v)| = \\
&= \sum_{i \in \{u,v,w\}} h_i^A |\mathbf{b}^v \cdot (\mathbf{a}^u \times \mathbf{a}^i)| = h_v^A |\mathbf{b}^v \cdot \mathbf{a}^w| + h_w^A |\mathbf{b}^v \cdot \mathbf{a}^v| = \\
&= h_v^A |b_z^v| + h_w^A |b_y^v| = h_v^A |r_{21}| + h_w^A |r_{11}|
\end{aligned} \tag{10.34}
$$

$$
\begin{aligned}
r_B &= \sum_{i \in \{u,v,w\}} h_i^B |\mathbf{b}^i \cdot \mathbf{l}| = \sum_{i \in \{u,v,w\}} h_i^B |\mathbf{b}^i \cdot (\mathbf{a}^u \times \mathbf{b}^v)| = \\
&= \sum_{i \in \{u,v,w\}} h_i^B |\mathbf{a}^u \cdot (\mathbf{b}^i \times \mathbf{b}^v)| = h_u^B |\mathbf{a}^u \cdot \mathbf{b}^w| + h_w^B |\mathbf{a}^u \cdot \mathbf{b}^u| = \\
&= h_u^B |b_x^w| + h_w^B |b_x^u| = h_u^B |r_{02}| + h_w^B |r_{00}|
\end{aligned}
$$

The resulting test becomes:

$$
|t_z r_{11} - t_y r_{21}| > h_v^A |r_{21}| + h_w^A |r_{11}| + h_u^B |r_{02}| + h_w^B |r_{00}| \tag{10.35}
$$

Disjointedness tests for the remaining axes, formed by $\mathbf{c}^{ij} = \mathbf{a}^i \times \mathbf{b}^j$, $\forall i \in \{u,v,w\}$ and $\forall j \in \{u,v,w\}$, are derived analogously.

Once again, if any of these 15 tests is positive, the OBBs are disjoint ($A \cap B = \emptyset$). The maximum number of operations (reported to be around 180, or 240 if the transform of B into A's coordinate system is included) [137], occurs when the OBBs overlap ($A \cap B \neq \emptyset$). However, in most cases the routine may terminate earlier because a separating axis has been found. Gottschalk et al. [135] point out that the absolute values of the elements of $\mathbf{R}$ are used four times and could therefore be computed once and reused for more rapid code.

Note that testing the axes in different orders has an impact on performance. To get a good average result for two OBBs, A and B, one should first test the three axes $\mathbf{a}^u$, $\mathbf{a}^v$, and $\mathbf{a}^w$. The main reasons for this are that they are orthogonal and thus reject the overlap faster, and that they are the simplest tests [303]. After these have been tested, the axes of B could be tested, followed by the axes formed from the axes of A and B.

10.11   View Frustrum Intersection

As has been seen in Section 7.1.2, hierarchical view-frustum culling is essential
for rapid rendering of the scene graph. One of the few operations called during
bounding-volume-hierarchy (scene-graph) cull traversal is the intersection test
between the view frustum and a bounding volume. These operations are thus
critical to fast execution. Ideally, they should determine whether the BV is
totally inside (inclusion), or totally outside (exclusion), or whether it intersects
the frustum.

To review, a view frustum is a pyramid that is truncated by a near and a
far plane (which are parallel), making the volume finite. In fact, it becomes
a polyhedron. This is shown in Figure 10.24, where the names of the six
planes, *near, far, left, right, top,* and *bottom* also are marked. The view frustum
volume defines the parts of the scene that should be visible and thus rendered
(in perspective for a pyramidal frustum).

The most common bounding volumes used for internal nodes in a hierarchy
(e.g., a scene graph) and for enclosing geometry are spheres, AABBs, and OBBs.
Therefore frustum/sphere and frustum/AABB/OBB tests will be discussed and
derived here.

To see why we need the three return results outside/inside/intersect, we will
examine what happens when traversing the scene graph. If a BV is found to
be totally outside the view frustum, then that BV's subtree will not be traversed
further and none of its geometry will be rendered. On the other hand, if the BV
is totally inside, then no more frustum/BV tests need to be computed for that
subtree and every renderable leaf will be drawn. For a partially visible BV, i.e.,
one that intersects the frustum, the BV's contents are then tested in turn against
the frustum. If the BV is for a leaf, then that leaf must be rendered.

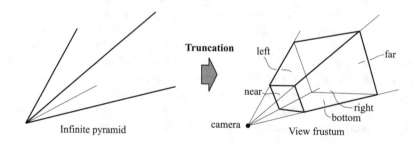

Figure 10.24. The illustration on the left is an infinite pyramid, which then is cropped by the
parallel near and far planes in order to construct a view frustum. The names of the other planes are
also shown, and the position of the camera is at the apex of the pyramid.

The complete test is called an *exclusion/inclusion/intersection test.* Sometimes the third state, intersection, may be considered too costly to compute. In this case, the BV is classified as "probably-inside." We call such a simplified algorithm an *exclusion/inclusion test.* If a BV cannot be excluded successfully, there are two choices. One is to treat the "probably-inside" state as an inclusion, meaning that everything inside the BV is rendered. This is often inefficient, as no further culling is performed. The other choice is to test each node in the subtree in turn for exclusion. This testing can often be performed at no cost, as much of the subtree may indeed be inside the frustum. Because neither choice is particularly good, some attempt at quickly differentiating between intersection and inclusion is often worthwhile, even if the test is imperfect.

It is important to realize that the quick classification tests do not have to be perfect for scene-graph culling. For differentiating exclusion from inclusion, all that is required is that the test err on the side of inclusion. That is, objects which should actually be excluded can erroneously be included. Such mistakes simply cost extra time. On the other hand, objects that should be included should never be quickly classified as excluded by the tests, otherwise rendering errors will occur. With inclusion versus intersection, either type of incorrect classification is usually legal. If a fully included BV is classified as intersecting, time is wasted testing its subtree for intersection. If an intersected BV is considered fully inside, time is wasted by rendering all objects, some of which may have been culled. However, there is an advantage to a strong inclusion test, one which always correctly classifies a BV as being fully inside the frustum. In this case, clipping can be turned off when the BV's objects are rendered, often leading to a performance gain.

Before we introduce the tests between a frustum and a sphere, AABB, or OBB, we shall describe an intersection test method between a frustum and a general object. This test is illustrated in Figure 10.25. The idea is to transform the test from a BV/frustum test to a point/volume test. Here we describe how this can be done. First, a point relative to the bounding volume (BV) is selected. Then the BV is moved along the outside of the frustum, as closely as possible to it without overlapping. During this movement, the point relative to the BV is traced, and its trace forms a new volume (a polygon with thick edges in Figure 10.25). The fact that the BV was moved as close as possible to the frustum means that if the point relative to the BV (in its original position) lies inside the traced-out volume, then the BV intersects or is inside the frustum. So instead of testing the BV for intersection against a frustum, the point relative to the BV is tested against another new volume, which is traced out by the point. In the same way, the BV can be moved on the inside of the frustum and as close as possible to the frustum. This will trace out a new, smaller frustum with planes parallel to the original frustum [18]. If the point relative to the object is inside

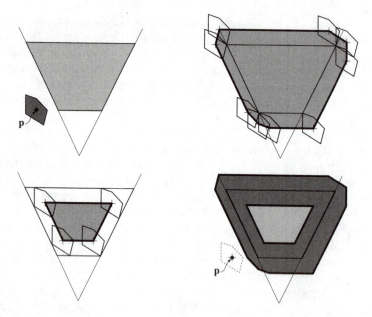

Figure 10.25. The upper left image shows a frustum (light grey) and a general bounding volume (dark gray), where a point **p** relative to the object has been selected. By tracing the point **p** where the object moves on the outside (upper right) and on the inside (lower left) of the frustum, as close as possible to the frustum, the frustum/BV can be reformulated into testing the point **p** against an outer and an inner volume. This is shown on the lower right. If the point **p** is outside the dark gray volume, then the BV is outside the frustum. The BV intersects the frustum if **p** is inside the dark gray area, and the BV is inside the frustum if **p** is inside the light gray area.

this new volume, then the BV is inside the frustum. This technique is used to derive tests in the subsequent sections. Note that the creation of the new volumes is independent of the position of the actual BV—it is only dependent on the position of the point relative to the BV. This means that a BV with an arbitrary position can be tested against the same volumes.

10.11.1   Frustum/Sphere Intersection

A frustum for an orthographic view is a box, so the overlap test in this case becomes a sphere/OBB intersection and can be solved using the algorithm presented in Section 10.10.1. To further test whether the sphere is entirely inside the box, we treat the box as hollow when we are finding the closest point. For a full presentation of this modified algorithm, along with code, see Arvo [16].

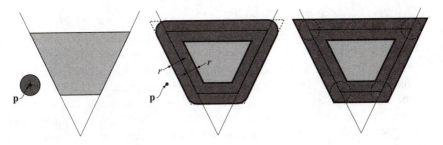

Figure 10.26. At the left, a frustum and a sphere are shown. The exact frustum/sphere test can be formulated as testing p against the dark and light gray volumes in the middle figure. At the right is a reasonable approximation of the volumes in the middle.

Following the method for deriving a frustum/BV test, we select the origin of the sphere as the point **p** to trace. This is shown in Figure 10.26. If the sphere, with radius r, is moved along the inside and along the outside of the frustum and as close to the frustum as possible, then the trace of **p** gives us the volumes that are needed to reformulate the frustum/sphere test. The actual volumes are shown in the middle segment of Figure 10.26. As before, if **p** is outside the dark gray volume, then the sphere is outside the frustum. If **p** is inside the dark gray area, then the sphere is inside the frustum. In this way the exact test can be done. However, for the sake of efficiency we use the approximation that appears on the right side of Figure 10.26. Here, the dark gray volume has been extended so as to avoid the more complicated computations that the rounded corners would require. Note that the outer volume consists of the planes of the frustum moved r distance units outwards in the direction of the frustum plane normal, and that the inner volume can be created by moving the planes of the frustum r distance units inwards in the direction of the frustum plane normals.

Assume that the plane equations of the frustum are such that the positive half-space is located outside of the frustum. Then, an actual implementation would loop over the six planes of the frustum, and for each frustum plane, compute the signed distance from the sphere's center to the plane. This is done by inserting the sphere center into the plane equation. If the distance is greater than the radius r, then the sphere is outside the frustum. If the distances to all six planes are less than $-r$, then the sphere is inside the frustum; otherwise the sphere intersects it.[15] To make the test more accurate it is possible to add extra planes for testing if the sphere is outside, in a method similar to that used by Green

---

[15]More correctly, we *say* that the sphere intersects the frustum, but the sphere center may be located in the kind of rounded corners that appear in the middle of Figure 10.26. This would mean that the sphere is outside the frustum but we report it to be inside.

and Hatch (see Section 10.9.1). However, for the purposes of quickly culling out scene-graph nodes, occasional false hits simply cause unnecessary testing, not algorithm failure, and this additional testing may cost more time overall.

Most frustums are symmetric around the view direction, meaning that the left plane is the right plane reflected around the view direction. This also holds for the bottom and top planes. To reduce the number of planes that must be tested for a symmetric frustum, an *octant test* can be added to the previous view-frustum test [18]. For this test, the frustum is divided into eight octants, much as an octree is subdivided (see Figure 10.27). When that has been done, we only need to test against the three outer planes of the octant. This means that we can actually halve the number of planes that need to be tested. While it was found that this test did not improve the performance of a frustum/sphere test, since the sphere/plane test is already so fast, it could be extended and used for arbitrary objects (see the right side of Figure 10.27). As will be seen in the next sections, this test can be used to speed up the frustum tests for AABBs and OBBs.

The full exclusion/inclusion/intersection test is commonly used; for example, Direct3D includes a `ComputeSphereVisibility` call. Bishop et al. [35] discuss the following clever optimizations for using sphere culling in a game engine. If a BV is found to be fully inside a certain frustum plane, then its children are also inside this plane. This means that this plane test can be omitted for all children, which can result in faster overall testing. They also note that

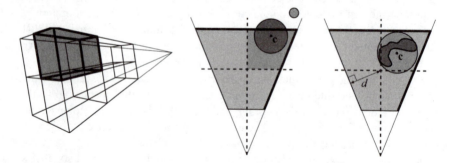

Figure 10.27. The left figure shows how a three-dimensional frustum is divided into eight octants. The other figure shows a two-dimensional example, where the sphere center **c** is in the upper right octant. The only planes that then need to be considered are the right and the far planes (thick black lines). Note that the small sphere is in the same octant as the large sphere. This technique works fine for arbitrary objects also, but the following condition must hold: the minimum distance, called d, from the frustum center to the frustum planes must be larger than the radius of a tight bounding sphere around the object. If that condition is fulfilled, then the bounding sphere can be used to find the octant.

this test elimination can speed up the clipping process itself, since fewer frustum sides need to be clipped against. For example, if by the time an object is to be rendered it is found that four clipping planes cannot affect it, then the object needs to be checked against only two clipping planes.

10.11.2 Frustum/Box Intersection

If the view's projection is orthographic (i.e., the frustum has a box shape), testing can be done using OBB/OBB intersection testing (see Section 10.10.4). For general frustum/box intersection testing there is a simple exclusion/inclusion test. This test is similar to the frustum/sphere test in that the OBB or AABB bounding box is checked against the six view-frustum planes. If all corner points of the bounding box are outside of one such plane, the bounding box is guaranteed to be outside the frustum. However, instead of checking all corner points (in the worst case) with each plane equation, we can use the smarter test presented in Section 10.7. This algorithm states that only one bounding box corner needs to be tested against a particular plane. The bounding box diagonal that most closely aligns with the plane's normal is used. For checking whether the box is outside a particular plane, test the diagonal endpoint closer in; if it is outside, the box is fully outside, and testing is done. If it survives all tests, then the box is considered inside or intersecting.

As with the frustum/sphere algorithm, this test suffers from classifying as inside boxes that are actually fully outside. An exclusion/inclusion approach that does not have this problem is to use the *separating axis theorem* (found in Section 10.10) to derive an intersection routine. Alternatively, an exact frustum/box test could be derived using the method presented in Figure 10.25, and then approximated with six inner and outer planes as we did for the frustum/sphere test (Section 10.11.1).

To determine whether the box is fully inside the frustum, test it against each frustum plane. The endpoint at the other end of the diagonal used for outside testing is now checked. If this point is found to be inside the frustum plane, the bounding box is fully inside this plane. As with the sphere, if the box is found to be inside all six frustum planes, the box is fully inside the frustum. This procedure is illustrated in Figure 10.28. The techniques discussed by Bishop for optimizing testing and clipping of bounding spheres apply here as well.

Since the plane/box test is more expensive than the plane/sphere test, there is often a gain in using the octant test from Section 10.11.1. This test would immediately discard three of the six frustum planes [18].

10.12   Line/Line Intersection Tests

In this section both two- and three-dimensional line/line intersection tests will be
derived and examined. Rays (of infinite length) and line segments (finite length)
will be intersected, and methods that are both fast and elegant will be described.

10.12.1   Two Dimensions

First Method

From a theoretical viewpoint, this first method of computing the intersection
between a pair of two-dimensional lines is really beautiful. Consider two lines,
$\mathbf{r}_1(s) = \mathbf{o}_1 + s\mathbf{d}_1$ and $\mathbf{r}_2(t) = \mathbf{o}_2 + t\mathbf{d}_2$. Since $\mathbf{a} \cdot \mathbf{a}^\perp = 0$ (the perp dot
product [184] from Section 1.2.1), the intersection calculations between $\mathbf{r}_1(s)$
and $\mathbf{r}_2(t)$ becomes elegant and simple. Note that all vectors are two-dimensional
in this subsection.

$$1: \qquad \mathbf{r}_1(s) = \mathbf{r}_2(t)$$
$$\Longleftrightarrow$$
$$2: \qquad \mathbf{o}_1 + s\mathbf{d}_1 = \mathbf{o}_2 + t\mathbf{d}_2$$
$$\Longleftrightarrow$$
$$3: \quad \begin{cases} s\mathbf{d}_1 \cdot \mathbf{d}_2^\perp = (\mathbf{o}_2 - \mathbf{o}_1) \cdot \mathbf{d}_2^\perp \\ t\mathbf{d}_2 \cdot \mathbf{d}_1^\perp = (\mathbf{o}_1 - \mathbf{o}_2) \cdot \mathbf{d}_1^\perp \end{cases} \qquad (10.36)$$
$$\Longleftrightarrow$$
$$4: \quad \begin{cases} s = \dfrac{(\mathbf{o}_2 - \mathbf{o}_1) \cdot \mathbf{d}_2^\perp}{\mathbf{d}_1 \cdot \mathbf{d}_2^\perp} \\[2mm] t = \dfrac{(\mathbf{o}_1 - \mathbf{o}_2) \cdot \mathbf{d}_1^\perp}{\mathbf{d}_2 \cdot \mathbf{d}_1^\perp} \end{cases}$$

If $\mathbf{d}_1 \cdot \mathbf{d}_2^\perp = 0$, then the lines are parallel and no intersection occurs. For lines
of infinite length, all values of s and t are valid, but for line segments (with
normalized directions), say of length l_1 and l_2 (starting at $s = 0$ and $t = 0$
and ending at $s = l_1$ and $t = l_2$), we have a valid intersection if and only if
$0 \le s \le l_1$ and $0 \le t \le l_2$. Or, if you set $\mathbf{o}_1 = \mathbf{p}_1$ and $\mathbf{d}_1 = \mathbf{p}_2 - \mathbf{p}_1$ (meaning
that the line segment starts at $\mathbf{p}_1$ and ends at $\mathbf{p}_2$) and do likewise for $\mathbf{r}_2$ with
start and end points $\mathbf{q}_1$ and $\mathbf{q}_2$, then a valid intersection occurs if and only if
$0 \le s \le 1$ and $0 \le t \le 1$. The point of intersection is obtained either by
plugging s into $\mathbf{r}_1$ or by plugging t into $\mathbf{r}_2$.

Second Method

Antonio [12] describes another way of deciding whether two line segments (i.e.,
of finite length) intersect by doing more compares and by avoiding the expensive

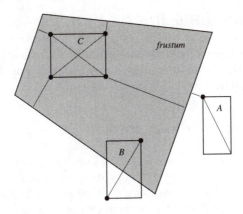

Figure 10.28. Box A is outside the frustum because its closest approaching point is outside a frustum plane. Box B intersects because it is inside three frustum planes and its test diagonal crosses the fourth frustum plane. Box C is fully inside because each frustum plane encloses each corresponding closest endpoint.

calculations (divisions) in the formulae above. This method is therefore very fast. The notation from above is used again, i.e., the first line segment goes from $\mathbf{p}_1$ to $\mathbf{p}_2$ and the second from $\mathbf{q}_1$ to $\mathbf{q}_2$. This means $\mathbf{r}_1(s) = \mathbf{p}_1 + s(\mathbf{p}_2 - \mathbf{p}_1)$ and $\mathbf{r}_2(t) = \mathbf{q}_1 + t(\mathbf{q}_2 - \mathbf{q}_1)$. The result from Equation 10.36 is used to obtain a solution to $\mathbf{r}_1(s) = \mathbf{r}_2(t)$:

$$
\begin{cases}
s = \dfrac{-\mathbf{c} \cdot \mathbf{a}^{\perp}}{\mathbf{b} \cdot \mathbf{a}^{\perp}} = \dfrac{\mathbf{c} \cdot \mathbf{a}^{\perp}}{\mathbf{a} \cdot \mathbf{b}^{\perp}} = \dfrac{d}{f} \\[4mm]
t = \dfrac{\mathbf{c} \cdot \mathbf{b}^{\perp}}{\mathbf{a} \cdot \mathbf{b}^{\perp}} = \dfrac{e}{f}
\end{cases}
\tag{10.37}
$$

In Equation 10.37, $\mathbf{a} = \mathbf{q}_2 - \mathbf{q}_1$, $\mathbf{b} = \mathbf{p}_2 - \mathbf{p}_1$, $\mathbf{c} = \mathbf{p}_1 - \mathbf{q}_1$, $d = \mathbf{c} \cdot \mathbf{a}^{\perp}$, $e = \mathbf{c} \cdot \mathbf{b}^{\perp}$, and $f = \mathbf{a} \cdot \mathbf{b}^{\perp}$. The simplification step for the factor s comes from the fact that $\mathbf{a}^{\perp} \cdot \mathbf{b} = -\mathbf{b}^{\perp} \cdot \mathbf{a}$ and $\mathbf{a} \cdot \mathbf{b}^{\perp} = \mathbf{b}^{\perp} \cdot \mathbf{a}$. If $\mathbf{a} \cdot \mathbf{b}^{\perp} = 0$, then the lines are collinear. Antonio [12] observes that the denominators for both s and t are the same, and that, since s and t are not needed explicitly, the division operation can be omitted. Set $s = d/f$ and $t = e/f$. To test if $0 \leq s \leq 1$ the following code is used:

```
1 : if(f > 0)
2 :    if(d < 0 or d > f) return NO_INTERSECTION;
3 : else
4 :    if(d > 0 or d < f) return NO_INTERSECTION;
```

After this test, it is guaranteed that $0 \leq s \leq 1$. The same is then done for $t = e/f$ (by replacing d by e in the code above. If the routine has not returned after this test, the line segments do intersect, since the t-value is then also valid.

Code for an integer version of this routine is available on the web [12], and is easily converted for use with floating point numbers.

10.12.2   Three Dimensions

Say we want to compute in three dimensions the intersection between two lines (defined by rays, Equation 10.1). The rays are again called $\mathbf{r}_1(s) = \mathbf{o}_1 + s\mathbf{d}_1$ and $\mathbf{r}_2(t) = \mathbf{o}_2 + t\mathbf{d}_2$, with no limitation on the value of t. The three-dimensional counterpart of the perp dot product is in this case the cross product, since $\mathbf{a} \times \mathbf{a} = 0$ $(\mathbf{a} \cdot \mathbf{a}^{\perp})$, and therefore the derivation of the three-dimensional version is very similar to that of the two-dimensional version. The intersection between those rays is derived below.

$$1: \qquad\qquad \mathbf{r}_1(s) = \mathbf{r}_2(t)$$
$$\Longleftrightarrow$$
$$2: \qquad\qquad \mathbf{o}_1 + s\mathbf{d}_1 = \mathbf{o}_2 + t\mathbf{d}_2$$
$$\Longleftrightarrow$$
$$3: \qquad \begin{cases} s\mathbf{d}_1 \times \mathbf{d}_2 = (\mathbf{o}_2 - \mathbf{o}_1) \times \mathbf{d}_2 \\ t\mathbf{d}_2 \times \mathbf{d}_1 = (\mathbf{o}_1 - \mathbf{o}_2) \times \mathbf{d}_1 \end{cases}$$
$$\Longleftrightarrow$$
$$4: \quad \begin{cases} s(\mathbf{d}_1 \times \mathbf{d}_2) \cdot (\mathbf{d}_1 \times \mathbf{d}_2) = ((\mathbf{o}_2 - \mathbf{o}_1) \times \mathbf{d}_2) \cdot (\mathbf{d}_1 \times \mathbf{d}_2) \\ t(\mathbf{d}_2 \times \mathbf{d}_1) \cdot (\mathbf{d}_2 \times \mathbf{d}_1) = ((\mathbf{o}_1 - \mathbf{o}_2) \times \mathbf{d}_1) \cdot (\mathbf{d}_2 \times \mathbf{d}_1) \end{cases} \qquad (10.38)$$
$$\Longleftrightarrow$$
$$5: \qquad \begin{cases} s = \dfrac{|\mathbf{o}_2 - \mathbf{o}_1 \quad \mathbf{d}_2 \quad \mathbf{d}_1 \times \mathbf{d}_2|}{||\mathbf{d}_1 \times \mathbf{d}_2||^2} \\[4mm] t = \dfrac{|\mathbf{o}_2 - \mathbf{o}_1 \quad \mathbf{d}_1 \quad \mathbf{d}_1 \times \mathbf{d}_2|}{||\mathbf{d}_1 \times \mathbf{d}_2||^2} \end{cases}$$

Step 3 comes from subtracting $\mathbf{o}_1$ $(\mathbf{o}_2)$ from both sides and then crossing with $\mathbf{d}_2$ $(\mathbf{d}_1)$, and step 4 is obtained by dotting with $\mathbf{d}_1 \times \mathbf{d}_2$ $(\mathbf{d}_2 \times \mathbf{d}_1)$. Finally, step 5, the solution, is found by rewriting the right sides as determinants (and changing some signs in the bottom equation) and then by dividing by the term located to the right of s (t).

Goldman [124] notes that if the denominator $||\mathbf{d}_1 \times \mathbf{d}_2||^2$ equals 0, then the lines are parallel. He also observes that if the lines are skew (i.e., they do not share a common plane), then the s and t parameters represent the points of closest approach.

If the rays are to be treated like line segments, with length l_1 and l_2 (assuming the direction vectors $\mathbf{d}_1$ and $\mathbf{d}_2$ are normalized), then check whether $0 \leq s \leq 1$ holds. If not, then the intersection is rejected. Otherwise, t is computed and tested against the interval 0 to l_2; if it is outside, the line segments do not intersect; otherwise they do.

10.13 Intersection Between Three Planes

Given three planes, each described by a normalized normal vector, $\mathbf{n}_i$, and an arbitrary point on the plane, $\mathbf{p}_i$, $i = 1, 2$, and 3, the unique point, $\mathbf{p}$, of intersection between those planes is given by Equation 10.39 [123]. Note that the denominator, the determinant of the three plane normals, is zero if two or more planes are parallel.

$$\mathbf{p} = \frac{(\mathbf{p}_1 \cdot \mathbf{n}_1)(\mathbf{n}_2 \times \mathbf{n}_3) + (\mathbf{p}_2 \cdot \mathbf{n}_2)(\mathbf{n}_3 \times \mathbf{n}_1) + (\mathbf{p}_3 \cdot \mathbf{n}_3)(\mathbf{n}_1 \times \mathbf{n}_2)}{|\mathbf{n}_1 \ \mathbf{n}_2 \ \mathbf{n}_3|} \quad (10.39)$$

This formula can be used to compute the corners of a BV consisting of a set of planes. An example is a k-DOP, which consists of k plane equations. Equation 10.39 can calculate the corners of the polytope if it is fed with the right planes.

If, as is usual, the planes are given in implicit form, i.e., $\pi_i : \mathbf{n}_i \cdot \mathbf{x} + d_i = 0$, then we need to find the points $\mathbf{p}_i$ in order to be able to use the equation. Any arbitrary point on the plane can be chosen. We compute the point closest to the origin, since those calculations are inexpensive. Given a ray from the origin pointing along the plane's normal, intersect this with the plane to get the point closest to the origin:

$$\left. \begin{array}{l} \mathbf{r}_i(t) = t\mathbf{n}_i \\ \mathbf{n}_i \cdot \mathbf{x} + d_i = 0 \end{array} \right\} \Rightarrow$$

$$\mathbf{n}_i \cdot \mathbf{r}_i(t) + d_i = 0$$
$$\Longleftrightarrow$$
$$t\mathbf{n}_i \cdot \mathbf{n}_i + d_i = 0 \quad (10.40)$$
$$\Longleftrightarrow$$
$$t = -d_i$$
$$\Rightarrow$$
$$\mathbf{p}_i = \mathbf{r}_i(-d_i) = -d_i\mathbf{n}_i$$

This result should not come as a surprise, since d_i in the plane equation simply holds the perpendicular, negative distance from the origin to the plane (the normal must be of unit length if this is to be true).

Further Reading and Resources

The Geometry Toolbox [105] is a good source for two-dimensional intersection routines and many other geometric manipulations useful in computer graphics. An overview of ray/object intersections is found in *An Introduction to Ray Tracing* [116]. The *Graphics Gems* series includes many different kinds of intersection routines, and reusable code is available on the web. Held [178] covers the ERIT package of intersection routines, which include many ray/object and object/object tests. Check our website, http://www.realtimerendering. com/, for the location of the code.

Chapter 11
Collision Detection

"To knock a thing down, especially if it is cocked at an arrogant angle, is a deep delight to the blood."
–George Santayana

Collision detection (CD) is a fundamental and important ingredient in many computer graphics and virtual reality (VR) applications. Areas where CD plays a vital role include virtual manufacturing, CAD/CAM, computer animation, physically-based modeling, games, flight and vehicle simulators, robotics, path and motion planning, assembly, and almost all VR simulations. Due to its huge number of uses, CD has been and still is the topic of extensive research.

Collision detection is part of what is often referred to as *interference detection*, which can be divided into three major parts: *collision detection, collision determination*, and *collision response*. The first two parts are usually algorithmically related, and they are dealt with in this chapter. Collision detection detects whether two objects collide, while collision determination finds the actual intersections between a pair of objects; finally, collision response, which is application-dependent, determines what actions should be taken in response to the collision of two objects. Collision response has been treated by a number of researchers, including Moore and Wilhelms [263], Hahn [150], and Baraff [23].

In Section 11.1 we discuss simple and extremely fast collision detection techniques. The main idea is to approximate a complex object using a set of lines. These lines are then tested for intersection with the primitives of the environment. This technique is often used in games. However, all objects cannot always be approximated with lines, and some applications may require more accurate tests.

Imagine, for example, that we want to determine whether a three-dimensional hand collides with (grabs) a three-dimensional cup of tea, where both objects are represented by triangles. How can this be done efficiently? Certainly, each triangle of the hand can be tested for intersection with each triangle of the cup of tea using the triangle/triangle intersection tests from Section 10.8. But in the

341

case where the two objects are far from each other, an algorithm should report this quickly, which would be impossible with such exhaustive testing. Even when the objects are close together, exhaustive testing is not efficient. There is a need for algorithms that handle these cases rapidly.

Section 11.2 deals with a general, hierarchical bounding volume collision detection algorithm. Then, two particular implementations with different design choices are presented in Sections 11.3 and 11.4. The systems that will be studied have the following features, where the first four are desirable for most CD systems and the last is more of a restriction.

1. They achieve interactive rates with models consisting of a large number of polygons, both when the models are far from each other and when they are in close proximity.

2. They handle *polygon soups*, i.e., general polygon models with no restrictions such as convexity or the availability of adjacency information.

3. The models can undergo rigid-body motion, i.e., rotation plus translation.

4. They provide efficient bounding volume (BV) fitting, in that they try to create a small BV for a set of geometry. Small BVs improve the performance of algorithms that determine whether there are collisions between two objects. The creation of the BVs should also be fast.

5. The methods are *static*, meaning that collision detection only occurs at discrete times. This restriction can cause unwanted quantum effects to appear [35].[1]

Since a scenario may contain tens or hundreds of moving objects, a good CD system must be able to cope with such situations as well. If the scenario contains n moving objects and m static objects, then a naive method would perform

$$nm + \binom{n}{2} \tag{11.1}$$

object tests for each frame. The first term corresponds to testing the number of static objects against the dynamic (moving) objects, and the last term corresponds

---

[1]In physics, quantum mechanics predicts that electrons tunnel through barriers that are otherwise impenetrable, a prediction which is borne out by experiments. In a static collision detection system, this could mean, for example, that a ball that is on one side of a door at time t might move to the other side at $t + \Delta t$ (i.e., the next frame), and even though a collision should have been detected between the ball and the door, a static algorithm cannot cope with this. Thus it is called a quantum effect even though it has nothing to do with quantum mechanics. A *dynamic*, as opposed to static, method deals with exactly this problem; the penalty is degradation in performance.

to testing the dynamic objects against each other. The naive approach quickly becomes expensive as m and n rise. This situation calls for smarter methods, which are the subject of Section 11.5. Such a method typically uses an algorithm that first detects all potential object-to-object collisions, which are then resolved using one of the algorithms from Section 11.3 or 11.4.

Finally, it must be pointed out that performance evaluations are extremely difficult in the case of CD, since the algorithms are sensitive to the actual collision scenarios, and there is no algorithm that performs best in all cases [135].

11.1 Collision Detection with Rays

In this section, we will present a fast technique which works very well under certain circumstances. Imagine that a car drives upward on an inclined road and that we want to use the information about the road (i.e., the primitives of which the road is built) in order to steer the car upward. This could of course be done by testing all primitives of all car wheels against all primitives of the road, using the techniques from Section 11.2. However, for games and some other applications, this kind of detailed collision detection is not always needed. Instead, we can approximate a moving object with a set of *rays*. In the case of the car, we can put one ray at each of the four wheels (see Figure 11.1). This approximation works well in practice, as long as we can assume that the four wheels are the only places of the car that will be in contact with the environment. Assume that the car is standing on a plane at the beginning, and that we place each ray at a wheel so that each origin lies at the place where the wheel is in contact with the environment. The rays at the wheels are then intersection-tested against the environment. If the distance from a ray origin to the environment is zero, then that wheel is exactly on the ground. If the distance is greater than zero

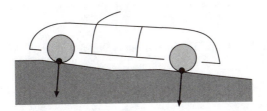

Figure 11.1. Instead of computing the collision between the entire car and the environment (the road), we place a ray at each wheel. These rays are then tested for intersection against the environment.

then that wheel has no contact with the environment, and a negative distance means that the wheel has merged "into" the environment. The application can use these distances for computing a collision response—a negative distance would move the car (at that wheel) upward, while a positive distance would move the car downward (unless the car is flying though the air for a short while).

To speed up the intersection testing, we can use the same technique we always use to speed things up in computer graphics—a *hierarchical representation*. The environment can be represented by a BSP tree (which is the same as a k-d tree). BSP trees are presented in Section 7.1.2, where they were used for view-frustum culling algorithms. BSP trees can also be used to speed up intersection testing. Depending on what primitives are used in the environment, different ray-object intersection test methods are needed (see Chapter 10). A BSP tree is not the only representation that can be used to find intersection quickly—any representation for speeding up intersection testing can be used. Ray tracing [116] books cover such algorithms in depth.

Unlike standard ray tracing, where we need the closest object in front of the ray, what is actually desired is the intersection point furthest back along the ray, which can have a negative distance. To avoid having to treat the ray as searching in two directions, the test ray's origin is essentially moved back until it is outside the bounding box surrounding the environment, and is then tested against the environment. In practice, this just means that, instead of a ray starting at a distance 0, it starts at a negative distance that lets it begin outside the box.

11.2 General Hierarchical Collision Detection

This section will present some general ideas and methods that are used in collision detection algorithms for detecting collisions between two given models. These algorithms have the five features previously listed. Common denominators of these algorithms are:

- They build a representation of each model hierarchically using bounding volumes.

- The high-level code for a collision query is similar, regardless of the kind of BV being used.[2]

- A simple cost function can be used to trim, evaluate, and compare performance.

These points are treated in the following three subsections.

---

[2]However, BV-BV overlap tests and primitive-primitive overlap tests are different depending on what BVs and primitives are used.

11.2.1 Hierarchy Building

Initially, a model is represented by a number of primitives, which in our case are polygon soups, where all polygons with more than three vertices are decomposed into triangles (see Section 9.2). Then, since each model should be represented as a hierarchy of some kind of bounding volumes, methods must be developed that build such hierarchies with the desired properties. A hierarchy that is commonly used in the case of collision detection algorithms is a data structure called a k-ary tree, where each node may at most have k children. Many algorithms have used the simplest instance of the k-ary tree, namely the binary tree, where $k = 2$. At each internal node, there is a BV that encloses all of its children in its volume, and at each leaf there are one or more primitives (which in our case are triangles). The bounding volume of an arbitrary node (either an internal node or a leaf), A, is denoted A_{BV}, and the set of children belonging to A is denoted A_c.

There are three ways to build a hierarchy, namely via a *bottom-up* method, an *incremental tree-insertion*, or a *top-down* approach. In order to create efficient, tight structures, typically the areas or the volumes of the BVs are minimized wherever possible [26, 128, 209, 274]. The first of these methods, bottom-up, starts by combining a number of primitives and finding a BV for them. Then this BV is grouped with one or more BVs constructed in a similar way, thus yielding a new, larger parent BV. This is repeated until only one BV exists, which then becomes the root of the hierarchy. Barequet et al. present BOXTREE [26], a data structure for performing ray tracing and collision detection, where the tree is built from the bottom up.

The incremental tree-insertion method starts with an empty tree. Then all other primitives and their BVs are added one at a time to this tree. This is illustrated in Figure 11.2. To make an efficient tree, an insertion point in the

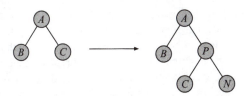

Figure 11.2. On the left a binary tree with three nodes is shown. We assume that only one primitive is stored at each leaf. Now we wish to insert a new node, named N. This node has a bounding volume (BV) and a primitive which that BV encloses. Therefore, the node will be inserted as a leaf node. In this example, say we find that the total tree volume is smaller if we insert N at the node called C (rather than at B). Then a new parent node P is created that encloses both C and the new node N.

tree must be found. This point should be selected so that the total tree volume increase is minimized. A simple method for doing this is to descend to the child that gives a smaller increase in the tree. This kind of algorithm typically takes $O(n \log n)$ time. For more sophisticated methods, see Omohundro [274]. Little is known about incremental tree-insertion in the context of collision detection, but it has been used with good results in ray tracing [128] and in intersection queries [274], so it probably works well for collision detection, too.

The top-down approach, which is used by the majority of hierarchy construction algorithms, starts by finding a BV for all primitives of the model, which then acts as the root of the tree. Then a divide-and-conquer strategy is applied, where the BV is first split into k or fewer parts. For each such part, all included primitives are found, and then a BV is created in the same manner as for the root, i.e., the hierarchy is created recursively. It is most common to find some axis along which the primitives should be split, and then to find a good split point on this axis. Note that a potential advantage of the top-down approach is that a hierarchy can be created lazily, i.e., on an as-needed basis. This means that we only construct the hierarchy for those parts of the scene where it is actually needed. But since this building process is performed during runtime, whenever a part of the hierarchy is created the performance may go down significantly. This is not acceptable for applications such as games and VR with real-time requirements, but may be a great time saver for off-line calculations such as path planning, non-real-time animation, and more [136].

In the field of computer science, the literature on tree data structures is vast, and here only a few important and interesting results will be mentioned. For more information, see, for example, the book *Introduction to Algorithms* by Cormen et al. [68].

Consider a hierarchical tree that has n leaves (for a model, this could mean that it consists of n triangles and each leaf holds only one triangle). First, Klosowski et al. [209] present an analytical proof that the binary tree minimizes the work to be done when traversing a single path from the root to the worst-case leaf. Second, the total number of nodes, including internal and external nodes (leaves), of a hierarchical tree is $2n - 1$, and the height of the tree is at least $\lceil \log_k n \rceil$, where k is the maximum number of children at an internal node. Even though $k = 2$ seems to yield the best results, it should be noted that a higher k gives a tree with a lower height, which means that it takes fewer steps to traverse the tree, but it also requires more work at each node. Another advantage of the binary tree is that it is easier to compute the hierarchies for it than it is for higher values of k.

The challenge for any CD algorithm is to find tight-fitting bounding volumes and hierarchy construction methods that create balanced and efficient trees. Note that balanced trees are expected to perform best on average in all cases, since the depth of every leaf is the same (or almost the same). This means that it takes an equal amount of time to traverse the hierarchy down to any leaf (i.e., a primitive), and that the time of a collision query will not vary depending on which leaves are accessed. In this sense, a balanced tree is optimal. However, this does not mean that it is best for all inputs. For example, if part of a model will seldom or never be queried for a collision, then those parts can be located deep in an unbalanced tree, so that the parts that are queried most often are closer to the root [136].[3]

11.2.2 Collision Testing between Hierarchies

Usually there are two different situations that the user wants to detect at different times. First, she might only be interested in whether or not the two models collide, and then the method may terminate whenever a pair of triangles has been found that overlap. Second, she might want all pairs of overlapping triangles reported. The solution to the first problem is called *collision detection*, while the solution to the second is called *collision determination*. Here, pseudocode is given that solves the first problem. The second situation can be solved with small alterations of the given code, and will be discussed later on.

A and B are two nodes in the model hierarchies, which at the first call are the roots of the models. A_{BV} and B_{BV} are used to access the BV of the appropriate node. As can be expected, the code recursively calls itself, since the model hierarchies are k-ary trees.

```
        FindFirstHitCD(A, B)
        returns ({TRUE, FALSE});
 1 :    if(not overlap(A_BV, B_BV) return FALSE;
 2 :    else if(isLeaf(A))
 3 :       if(isLeaf(B))
 4 :          for each triangle pair T_A ∈ A_c and T_B ∈ B_c
 5 :             if(overlap(T_A, T_B)) return TRUE;
 6 :       else
 7 :          for each child C_B ∈ B_c
 8 :             FindFirstHitCD(A, C_B)
 9 :    else
10 :       for each child C_A ∈ A_c
11 :          FindFirstHitCD(C_A, B)
12 :    return FALSE;
```

---

[3]In some way, this is similar to Huffman coding, where symbols that occur often are coded with a smaller number of bits than are symbols that occur more infrequently.

To find all pairs of triangles that collide, the above pseudocode is modified in the following way. The pairs of triangles that the algorithm finds are stored in a linked list, L, which begins empty. Then line 5 requires modification: if the test is passed, the program should add the triangle pair to L (instead of returning). Line 12, should return FALSE if L is empty; otherwise, it should return TRUE and the list L.

Also, note that when two internal nodes are encountered, the pseudo code (line 7) always descends to the children of B. This may not result in the same tree traversal for the calls **FindFirstHitCD**(A, B) and for **FindFirstHitCD**(B, A). To get the same execution order for these, a test could be added before the recursive calls that sees to it that the BV with the largest volume (or any other consistent feature) is descended.

To speed up the average case of the algorithm presented in the pseudocode above, *caching* can be used if we are only interested in finding out whether two objects collide [303]. If coherence is high, i.e., if objects tend to move only slightly between frames, then performance can be gained if we store in a cache the triangles that were reported to collide in the current frame. The first thing to do on the next frame is then to make a quick test using the entries in the cache to see if those parts of the objects still collide. If they do, then the code can report that the objects still collide; if not, then we can test whether the siblings of the cached triangles collide. The reason for this test is that if two triangles collided in one frame and not in the next frame, then there is a good chance that geometry nearby the cached triangles may collide, and therefore the test can proceed with the siblings (neighbors) of the cached triangles. If we still have not found a collision, the test is performed as in the pseudocode. If several objects exist in a scene and all collision pairs should be reported, then there are two ways to extend the cache. Either each pair of objects can have its own entry in the cache, or a global cache with more than one entry can be employed [303].

11.2.3   Cost Function

The function t in Equation 11.2 was first introduced (in a slightly different form, without the last term) as a framework for evaluating the performance of hierarchical BV structures in the context of speed-up techniques for ray tracing [370]. It has since then been used to evaluate the performance of CD algorithms as well [135], and it has been augmented by the last term to include a new cost specific to some systems [209, 213] that might have a significant impact on performance. This cost results from the fact that if a model is undergoing a rigid-body motion, then its BV and parts or all of its hierarchy might have to be recomputed, depending on the motion and the choice of BV.

$$t = n_v c_v + n_p c_p + n_u c_u \tag{11.2}$$

Here the parameters are

n_v : number of BV/BV overlap tests
c_v : cost for a BV/BV overlap test
n_p : number of primitive pairs tested for overlap
c_p : cost for testing whether two primitives overlap
n_u : number of BVs updated due to the model's motion
c_u : cost for updating a BV

Creating a better hierarchical decomposition of a model would result in lower values of n_v, n_p, and n_u. Creating better methods for determining whether two BVs or two triangles overlap would lower c_v and c_p. However, these are often conflicting goals, because changing the type of BV in order to use a faster overlap test usually means that we get looser-fitting volumes.

Examples of different bounding volumes that have been used in the past are spheres [191], axis-aligned bounding boxes (AABBs) [176], oriented bounding boxes (OBBs) [135, 358], k-DOPs (discrete oriented polytopes) [209, 212, 389], pie slices [26], and spherical shells [213, 214] (which provide good fits for Bézier patches). Spheres are the fastest to transform (since they do not need to be rotated), and the overlap test is also fast, but they provide quite poor fits. AABBs provide better fits and a fast overlap test, and they are a good choice if there is a large amount of axially aligned geometry in a model (as is the case in most architectural models). OBBs have much better fits but slower overlap tests. The fits of the k-DOPs are determined by the parameter k—higher values of k give better fits, slower overlap testing, and poorer transform speed.

There are obviously many parameters to fine tune in order to get good performance, which is the goal of the following two sections on the OBBTree and k-DOPTree. Both have their own strengths and weaknesses.

11.3   OBBTree

At SIGGRAPH 96, Gottschalk et al. [135] presented a paper called "OBBTree: A Hierarchical Structure for Rapid Interference Detection," which has strongly influenced further research on CD algorithms.[4] Their approach and their parameters will be treated thoroughly in this section.

---

[4]In 1981, Ballard [20] did similar work in two dimensions for computing intersections between curves, so his work was a precursor to the OBBTree.

The OBBTree was designed to perform especially well if *parallel close proximity*, where two surfaces are very close and nearly parallel, is found during collision detection. For such tests, the OBBTree performed better than the k-DOPTree [209]. These kinds of situations often occur in tolerance analysis and in virtual prototyping.

Choice of Bounding Volume

As the name of the *OBBTree* algorithm implies, the bounding volume used is the oriented bounding box, the OBB. One reason for this is that both the AABB (axis-aligned bounding box) and the sphere, which were commonly used in previous CD algorithms, provide quite poor fits in general. That is, they contain a lot of empty space compared to the geometry they are holding. The convergence of the OBB to the underlying geometry of the models was generally better than that for either AABBs or spheres. Another reason was that the authors developed a new method for determining whether two OBBs overlap. This new method is about a magnitude faster than previous methods. The speed of this test results in part from the fact that the OBBs are transformed so that one of them becomes an AABB centered around the origin. The actual transform (presented below in Section 11.3) takes 63 operations, and the OBB/OBB test may exit early due to one of the 15 axis tests. After the transformation, an exit after the first axis test takes 17 operations, and an exit after the last axis would take 180 operations.[5] OBB/OBB overlap testing is treated in Section 10.10.4.

In terms of the performance evaluation framework of Section 11.2.3, the above reasoning means that n_v and n_p are lower for OBBs than for AABBs and spheres.

Van den Bergen has suggested a simple technique for speeding up the overlap test between two OBBs [358]: simply skip the last nine axis tests that correspond to a direction perpendicular to one edge of the first OBB and one edge of the second OBB. Geometrically, this can be thought of as doing two AABB/AABB tests [136], where the first test is done in the coordinate system of the first OBB and the other is done in the coordinate system of the other. This is illustrated in Figure 11.3. The shortened OBB/OBB test (which omits the last nine axis tests) will sometimes report two disjoint OBBs as overlapping. In these cases, the recursion in the OBBTree will go deeper than necessary. The reason for using such extensive recursion is that it was found that these last nine axis tests culled away only a small proportion of the overlaps. The net result was that the average performance was improved by skipping these tests. Van den Bergen's technique has been implemented in a collision detection package called SOLID [358, 359], which also handles deformable objects.

---

[5]Extra arithmetic error testing would take nine extra operations.

Figure 11.3. At the left are two (two-dimensional) OBBs (A and B) that are to be tested for overlap with an OBB/OBB overlap test that omits the last nine axis tests. If this is interpreted geometrically, then the OBB/OBB overlap test is approximated with two AABB-AABB overlap tests. The middle illustration shows how A is bounded by an AABB in the coordinate system of B. C and B do not overlap, so the test continues on the right. Here B is enclosed with an AABB in the coordinate system of A. A and D are reported to overlap. In this case, A and B would erroneously be reported to overlap.

Hierarchy Building

The basic data structure is a binary tree with each internal node holding an OBB (see Section 10.1 for a definition) and each external (leaf) node holding only one triangle. The top-down approach developed by Gottschalk et al. for creating the hierarchy is divided into finding a tight-fitting OBB for a polygon soup and then splitting this along one axis of the OBB, which also categorizes the triangles into two groups. For each of these groups, a new OBB is computed.

It has been shown that a tight-fitting OBB enclosing an object can be found by computing (via a statistical method) an orientation of the triangles of the convex hull [135, 137].[6] Here we will present the formulae for computing a good-fit OBB. The derivation is found in Gottschalk's Ph.D. thesis [137].

First, the convex hull of an object must be computed. This can be done with, for example, the *Quickhull* algorithm [25]. This gives us, say, n triangles defined as $\triangle \mathbf{p}^k \mathbf{q}^k \mathbf{r}^k$, where $\mathbf{p}^k$, $\mathbf{q}^k$, and $\mathbf{r}^k$ are the vertices of triangle k, $0 \leq k < n$. We also denote the area of triangle k as a^k, and the total area of the convex hull as $a^H = \sum_{k=0}^{n-1} a^k$. Furthermore, the centroid of triangle i (which is the mean of the vertices) is $\mathbf{m}^i = (\mathbf{p}^i + \mathbf{q}^i + \mathbf{r}^i)/3$. The centroid of the whole convex hull, $\mathbf{m}^H$, is as in Equation 11.3, that is, the weighted mean of the triangle centroids.

$$\mathbf{m}^H = \frac{1}{a^H} \sum_{k=0}^{n-1} a^k \mathbf{m}^k \tag{11.3}$$

---

[6]The triangles of the convex hull were chosen for two reasons. The first is that this method leaves the orientation of the OBB unaffected by interior points of the objects. The second is that using triangles instead of vertices means that non-uniform sampling of the vertices of the convex hull can be avoided, as such sampling can make for bad-fitting OBBs.

With the use of these definitions, we will present a formula that computes a 3×3 covariance matrix, whose eigenvectors (see Section A.3.1 on how to compute the eigenvectors) are the direction vectors for a good-fit box.

$$\mathbf{C} = [c_{ij}] = \left[\left(\frac{1}{a^H} \sum_{k=0}^{n-1} \frac{a^k}{12} (9m_i^k m_j^k + p_i^k p_j^k + q_i^k q_j^k + r_i^k r_j^k) \right) - m_i^H m_j^H \right],$$

$$0 \leq i, j < 3 \qquad\qquad (11.4)$$

After computing $\mathbf{C}$, the eigenvectors are computed and normalized. These vectors are the direction vectors, $\mathbf{a}^u$, $\mathbf{a}^v$, and $\mathbf{a}^w$, of the OBB. We must next find the center and the half-lengths of the OBB. This is done by projecting the points of the convex hull onto the direction vectors and finding the minimum and maximum along each direction. These will determine the size and position of the box, i.e., will fully specify the OBB according to its definition (see Section 10.1).

When computing the OBB, the most demanding operation is the convex hull computation, which takes $O(n \log n)$ time, where n is the number of primitives of the object. The basis calculation takes at most linear time, and the eigenvector computation takes constant time, which means that computing an OBB for a set of n triangles takes $O(n \log n)$ time.

After we have computed an OBB for a set of triangles, the volume and the triangles should be split and formed into two new OBBs. Gottschalk et al. use a strategy that takes the longest axis of the box and splits it into two parts of the same length. An illustration of this procedure is shown in Figure 11.4. A plane that contains the center of the box and has the box axis for its normal is thus used to partition the triangles into two subgroups. A triangle that crosses this plane is assigned to the group that contains its centroid. If the longest axis cannot be subdivided (in the rare case that all centroids of all triangles are located on the dividing plane), the other axes are tried in diminishing order.

For each of the subgroups, the matrix method is used to compute (sub-) OBBs. Gottschalk et al. also point out that, if the OBB is instead split at the median center point, then balanced trees are obtained, which in a sense are optimal.

Since the computation of the convex hull takes $O(n \log n)$ and the creation of a binary tree takes $O(\log n)$, the total running time for the creation of an OBBTree is $O(n \log^2 n)$.

Handling Rigid-Body Motions

In the OBBTree hierarchy, each OBB, A, is stored together with a rigid-body transformation (a rotation matrix $\mathbf{R}$ and a translation vector $\mathbf{t}$) matrix $\mathbf{M}_A$. This matrix holds the relative orientation and position of the OBB with respect to its parent.

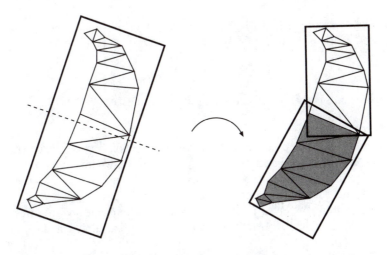

Figure 11.4. This figure shows how a set of geometry with its OBB is split along the longest axis of the OBB, at the split point marked by the dashed line. Then the geometry is partitioned into two subgroups, and an OBB is found for each of them. This procedure is repeated recursively in order to build the OBBTree.

Now, assume that we start to test two OBBs, A and B, against each other. The overlap test between A and B should then be done in the coordinate system of one of the OBBs. Let us say that we decide to do the test in A's coordinate system. In this way, A is an AABB (in its own coordinate system) centered around the origin. The idea is then to transform B into A's coordinate system. This is done with the matrix below, which first transforms B into its own position and orientation (with $\mathbf{M}_B$) and then into A's coordinate system (with the inverse of A's transform, $\mathbf{M}_A^{-1}$).

$$\mathbf{T}_{AB} = \mathbf{M}_A^{-1}\mathbf{M}_B \qquad (11.5)$$

The OBB/OBB overlap test takes as input a matrix consisting of a 3×3 rotation matrix $\mathbf{R}$ and a translation vector $\mathbf{t}$, which hold the orientation and position of B with respect to A (see Section 10.10.4), so $\mathbf{T}_{AB}$ is decomposed as below.

$$\mathbf{T}_{AB} = \left(\begin{array}{cc} \mathbf{R} & \mathbf{t} \\ \mathbf{0}^T & 0 \end{array} \right) \qquad (11.6)$$

Now, assume that A and B overlap, and that we want to descend into A's child called C. A smart technique for doing this is presented here [136]. We choose to do the test in C's coordinate system. The idea is then to transform B into A's coordinate system (with $\mathbf{T}_{AB}$) and then transform that into the coordinate system of C (using $\mathbf{M}_C^{-1}$). This is done with the following matrix, which is then used as the input to the OBB/OBB overlap test.

$$\mathbf{T}_{CB} = \mathbf{M}_C^{-1}\mathbf{T}_{AB} \qquad (11.7)$$

This procedure is then used recursively to test all OBBs.

Miscellaneous

The **FindFirstHitCD** pseudocode for collision detection between two hierarchical trees, as presented in Section 11.2.2, can be used on two trees created with the above algorithms. All that needs to be exchanged is the `overlap()` function, which should point to a routine that tests two OBBs for overlap.

All algorithms involved in OBBTree have been implemented in a free software package called *RAPID* (Robust and Accurate Polygon Interference Detection) [295].

11.4 *k*-DOPTree

A variant of hierarchical collision detection was presented as a technical sketch (a short paper) [177] at SIGGRAPH 96. In 1997, this was supplemented with a much more detailed report [209]. In the spirit of the OBBTree, we call this the k-DOPTree algorithm, since the BV used is a k-DOP. To recap, a k-DOP is the volume formed by the intersection of a set of slabs. See Section 10.1 for the full definition of a k-DOP, and Section 10.10.3 for k-DOP overlap testing.

Choice of Bounding Volume

The rationale behind choosing the k-DOP as the BV for the CD hierarchy is that it has both a faster BV/BV overlap test than the OBB and a tighter fit. The overlap test is faster because the directions of the planes of the k-DOP are fixed. Of course, this only holds in non-extreme cases, i.e., for reasonable values of k. As k grows, the k-DOP tends to resemble the convex hull, which is the tightest-fitting convex BV. The k-DOP is not always tighter than the OBB, however. For example, if a triangle is bounded by a well-aligned OBB, then we get a rectangle in three dimensions, which is a fairly good bound. For a k-DOP we can get a worse fit, since the triangle may be badly aligned with respect to the chosen directions.

For k-DOPs there is a cost for updating the BVs of the moving models. That is, n_u (the number of BVs updated due to motion) and c_u (the cost for updating a BV) affect the total cost function for performance evaluation. This was not the case for the OBB, since the motion transform is an integral part of the OBB/OBB overlap test.

What happens to n_v (the number of overlap tests performed) in comparison to the OBBTree is hard to say, since this is highly scenario-dependent. But at least the k-DOP performs better in terms of tighter-fitting BVs, i.e., having a lower n_v, than both spheres and AABBs (which are simple k-DOPs, and so any k-DOP with $k > 6$ is bound to have a tighter fit). 6-DOPs (AABBs), 14-DOPs, 18-DOPs, and 26-DOPs were tested in order to find a good compromise between the BV tightness (affecting n_v, n_p, and n_u) and the BV/BV overlap cost (c_v). It was found that $k = 18$ gave the best execution times for several different scenarios [209]. The choice of normals for $k = 18$ (and for the other k-values as well) was made with efficiency in mind. In addition to the three normals of an AABB, normals that cut off the edges of an AABB were used. The other six normals form the same sorts of planes as the bevel-edge planes described in Section 10.9.1. This selection of normals makes the projection of the vertices onto the normals (an operation involved in the creation of a k-DOP) extremely cheap. This is because only additions and subtractions need to be computed, thanks to the fact that the elements of the unnormalized normals are either zero or ± 1. An example of a two-dimensional 8-DOP is shown on the left in Figure 11.5.

Hierarchy Building

As was mentioned above, Klosowski et al. show that the binary tree is optimal in some ways, and so the k-DOPTree also uses a binary tree. The main difference between it and the OBBTree is that the leaves may contain an arbitrary number

Figure 11.5. This illustrates how the approximation method handles rotating objects. The left Figure shows an 8-DOP for a tea cup, and the middle Figure shows a rotated version of the tea cup, and a best-fit 8-DOP for the rotated object. However, this amount of computation can be costly. The approximation method transforms the initial 8-DOP in the left Figure, and a new 8-DOP for the transformed 8-DOP is found, as shown in the right Figure. The previous 8-DOP of the tea cup appears in grey.

of triangles.[7] For static models, the (maximum) number of triangles allowed was 1 per leaf, and for dynamic (moving) models it was 40 per leaf. The reason for this difference is that it is expensive to transform the k-DOPs.

The creation of the hierarchy is based on a top-down approach. To find a k-DOP for a set of triangles, the vertices of the set are simply projected onto each normal, $\mathbf{n}_i$, of the k-DOP, and the extreme values (min,max) stored in d^i_{min} and d^i_{max}. This yields the minimum k-DOP for the given parameters and for this particular triangle set.

When it comes to splitting the k-DOP into two subvolumes, four methods have been investigated [209] for the selection of one of the main axes, x, y, or z:

1. *Min Sum* selects the axis that minimizes the sum of the subvolumes.

2. *Min Max* selects the axis that minimizes the larger of the two subvolumes.

3. *Splatter* computes the variances of the projections of the centroids of the triangles onto each axis and selects the axis that yields the largest variance.

4. *Longest Side* simply selects the axis along which the BV is longest.

The most profitable method was found to be Splatter, since it performed well both when constructing the hierarchy and when detecting collisions.

Along the axis selected by the Splatter method, a point must be chosen where the k-DOP is to be split. While it is easy to imagine that the best method would be to split at the median of the centroid coordinates along the split axis, experimental results show that the mean of the centroid coordinates performed better. The depth of the k-DOPTree was usually higher when using the mean (i.e., the tree was more unbalanced), but the BVs were tighter, resulting in shorter collision detection times [175, 209]. After a split point has been determined, each triangle is put in the respective subvolume in which its centroid lies.

Updating the k-DOPTree Due to a Rigid-Body Motion

Since the orientations of the planes of the k-DOPs are fixed, a rigid-body motion of an object makes the hierarchy invalid (translations can be handled, but not rotations), and therefore it must be rebuilt or updated in some way.

Klosowski et al. [209] proposed two ways of updating the k-DOPs fairly efficiently, while maintaining the same structure of the hierarchy. The methods are called the *approximation method* and *hill climbing*. The approximation method

---

[7]The particular implementation of the OBBTree called RAPID [295] allows only one triangle per leaf, but the code could easily be extended to handle more than one.

allows the algorithm to avoid recomputing a new k-DOP for the transformed geometry from scratch by using the original k-DOP. Instead of reforming a k-DOP from the transformed vertex locations for the geometry, vertex locations at the corners of the original k-DOP are transformed and used. This results in less work if there are fewer vertices in the k-DOP than in the geometry it contains. This procedure is depicted in Figure 11.5. Note that the size of the k-DOP often grows with this technique, making for worse fits of the underlying geometry.

The hill climbing method requires additional storage, since it requires the convex hull of the geometry that the current node contains. At each frame, local updates are made to a new best-fit k-DOP for the geometry. A local update tests whether a vertex that was maximal (i.e., furthest out) along one of the k-DOP's normals is still maximal. This is done by checking the neighboring vertices recursively. If one of the neighbors is now maximal, it is selected to form the new k-DOP.

The hill climbing method is the more expensive of the two, but it also gives a tighter BV. Therefore, since the root of the tree is the most frequently visited node, the root is recomputed using the hill climbing method, and its children are recomputed using the approximation method. The results were found to be worse when the hill climbing method was used for any additional nodes.

11.5 A Multiple Objects CD System

Consider an old-style clock consisting of springs and cog-wheels. Say this clock is represented as a detailed, three-dimensional model in the computer. Now imagine that the clock's movements are to be simulated using collision detection. The spring is wound and the clock's motion is simulated as collisions are detected and responses are generated. Such a system would require collision detection between possibly hundreds of pairs of objects. The previously described algorithms only detect collisions between one pair of objects (two-body collision detection). A brute-force search of all possible collision pairs is incredibly inefficient and so is impractical under these circumstances.

Here, we will describe a two-level collision detection system [60, 192, 234] which is targeted at large-scale environments with multiple objects in motion. The first level of this system reports potential collisions among all the objects in the environment. These results are then sent to the second level, which performs exact collision detection between each pair of objects. Any of the algorithms from Sections 11.3 and 11.4 (or any other method that detects collisions between two objects, for that matter) can be used for this task.

11.5.1   The First-Level CD

In order to minimize triggerings of the second-level system (that is, to report as few potential object/object collisions as possible), each object is enclosed in a BV and some algorithm finds all BV/BV pairs that overlap.

A simple approach is to use an axis-aligned bounding box (AABB) for each object. To avoid recomputing this AABB for an object undergoing rigid-body motion, the AABB is adjusted to be a *fixed cube* large enough to contain the object in any arbitrary orientation. Dynamically sized boxes have also been investigated [60, 192], but their performance was found to be poorer.[8] The fixed cubes are used to determine rapidly which pairs of objects are totally disjoint in terms of these bounding volumes.

Instead of fixed cubes, spheres can be used. This is reasonable, since the sphere is the perfect BV with which to enclose an object at any orientation. An algorithm for spheres is presented by Kim et al [206]. Yet another approach is to use the convex hull or any other convex polyhedron, using for example the Lin-Canny algorithm [232, 233] or the V-clip [251, 252] instead of fixed cubes. In the next section we focus on fixed cubes.

Sweep-and-Prune

The fixed cubes are used in a *sweep-and-prune* technique [24, 233] which exploits the *temporal coherence* most often found in virtual environments. Temporal coherence means that objects undergo small (if any) changes in their position and orientation from frame to frame (and so it is also called *frame-to-frame coherence*).

Lin [233] points out that the overlapping bounding box problem in three dimensions can be solved in $O(n \log^2 n + k)$ time (where k is the number of pairwise overlaps), but it can be improved upon by exploiting coherence and so be reduced to $O(n + k)$.

If two AABBs overlap, then all three one-dimensional intervals (formed by start and end points of AABBs) in each main axis direction must also overlap. Here we will describe how all overlaps of a number of one-dimensional intervals can be detected efficiently when the frame-to-frame coherency is high (which is what we can expect in a reasonable application). Given that solution, the three-dimensional problem for AABBs is solved by using the one-dimensional algorithm for each of the three main axes.

Assume that n intervals are represented by s_i and e_i where $s_i < e_i$ and $0 \leq i < n$. These values are sorted in one list in increasing order. This list is then swept from start to end. When a start point s_i is encountered, the corresponding interval is put into an active interval list. When an end point is

---

[8]For long, skinny objects, dynamically sized AABBs may be faster [236].

encountered, the corresponding interval is removed from the active list. Now, if the start point of an interval is encountered while there are intervals in the active list, then the encountered interval overlaps all intervals in the list. This is shown in Figure 11.6.

This procedure would take $O(n \log n)$ to sort all the intervals, plus $O(n)$ to sweep the list and $O(k)$ to report k overlapping intervals, resulting in an $O(n \log n + k)$ algorithm. However, due to temporal coherence, the lists are not expected to change very much from frame to frame, and so a *bubble sort* or *insertion sort* [210] can be used with great efficiency after the first pass has taken place. These sorting algorithms sort nearly-sorted lists in an expected time of $O(n)$.

Insertion sort works by building up the sorted sequence incrementally. We start with the first number in the list. If we only consider this entry then the list is sorted. Next, we add the second entry. If the second entry is smaller than the first, then we change places of the first and the second entries; otherwise we leave them be. We continue to add entries, and we change the places of the entries until the list is sorted. This procedure is repeated for all objects that we want to sort, and the result is a sorted list.

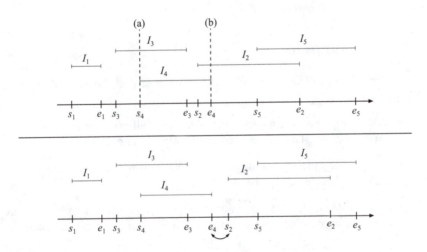

Figure 11.6. At the top, the interval I_4 is encountered (at the point marked (a)) when there is only one interval in the active list (I_3), so it is concluded that I_4 and I_3 overlap. When I_2 is encountered I_4 is still in the active list (since e_4 has not been encountered yet), and so I_4 and I_2 also overlap. When e_4 is encountered, I_4 is removed (at the point marked (b)) from the active list. At the bottom, I_2 has moved to the right, and when the insertion sort finds that s_2 and e_4 need to change places, it can also be concluded that I_2 and I_4 do not overlap any longer. Illustration after Baraff and Witkin [24].

To use temporal coherence to our advantage, we keep a boolean for each interval pair. A specific boolean is TRUE if the pair overlaps and FALSE otherwise. The values of the booleans are initialized at the first step of the algorithm when the first sorting is done. Assume that a pair of intervals were overlapping in the previous frame and so their boolean was TRUE. Now, if the start point of one interval exchanges places with the end point of the other interval, then the status of this interval pair is inverted, which in this case means that their boolean is then FALSE and they do not overlap anymore. The same goes in the other direction, i.e., if a boolean was FALSE, then it becomes TRUE when one start point changes place with one end point. This is also illustrated in Figure 11.6.

So we can create a sorted list of intervals for all three main axes and use the above algorithm to find overlapping intervals for each axis. If all three intervals for a pair overlap, their AABBs (which the intervals represent) also overlap; otherwise they do not.

Keeping track of the overlap status changes takes $O(n + e_x + e_y + e_z)$, where e_i is the number of swaps along the i-axis [233]. In the worst case, the number of swaps, in each direction, takes $O(n^2)$ time with a small constant. However, the expected time is linear, which results in an $O(n + k)$-expected-time sweep-and-prune algorithm, where, again, k is the number of pairwise overlaps. This makes for fast overlap detection of the fixed cubes.

11.5.2   Summary

The outline of the collision detection system is summarized below, and depicted in Figure 11.7.

- First, using the sweep-and-prune algorithm, all pairs of objects whose fixed cubes overlap are detected and stored in the pair list.

- Second, the object pairs are sent to exact collision detection algorithms, such as OBBTree and k-DOPTree.

- Finally, the results from collision detection are forwarded and taken care of by the application, so that action (collision response) can be taken.

Further Reading and Resources

See this book's website, http://www.realtimerendering.com/, for the latest information and free software in this rapidly evolving field. For spatial data structures other than a k-ary tree, consult Samet's books [306, 307]

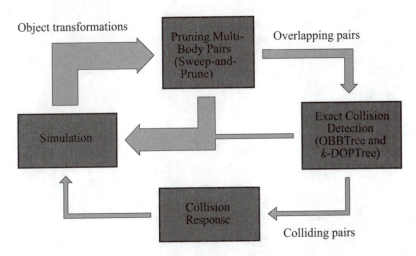

Figure 11.7. The outline of the collision detection system. The overlapping object pairs found by the sweep-and-prune technique are reported to the exact CD system, which in turn reports true collisions to a part of the system that should compute the collision response. Finally, all objects are treated by the simulation, where objects get their transforms, for example. After Cohen et al. [60].

for information on octrees, k-d trees, etc. See Naylor et al. [267] for BSP (binary space partition) algorithms. An extensive survey of collision detection algorithms was presented by Lin and Gottschalk [235] in 1998.

The OBBTree algorithm has been extended by Eberly to handle dynamic collision detection. This is described in a technical report [91] and briefly in *IEEE CG&A* [35].

Another method for transforming the k-DOPs is presented by Zachmann [389]. This resembles the approximation method in that a transformed k-DOP is enclosed in a new k-DOP which is aligned with the one that it is tested against. Konečný presents an efficient method for performing this operation using linear programming techniques [212].

Chapter 12
Graphics Hardware

"Within the next few years, there will be single-chip graphics devices more powerful and versatile than any graphics system that has ever been built, at any price."
–David Kirk, Chief Scientist, NVIDIA Inc.

Despite the fact that graphics hardware is evolving at a rapid pace, there are some general concepts and architectures that are still commonly used in its design. Our goal in this chapter is to give some sense of the various hardware elements of a graphics system and how they relate to one another. We begin by discussing the different buffers that can be a part of a real-time rendering system, how these buffers can be used, and how the contents of the color buffer is sent to the monitor. We then present an overview of graphics architecture concepts, followed by three case studies of specific graphics systems. Other parts of the book discuss various hardware elements in terms of their use with particular algorithms. Here we discuss hardware on its own terms.

12.1 Buffers and Buffering

12.1.1 A Simple Display System

In Section 2.4 we saw that the colors of the pixels are located in a color buffer. Visible primitives affect these pixels. Here we will use a simple model to describe how the contents of the color buffer end up on the monitor (or any other device). The memory of the frame buffer may be located in the same memory as the CPU uses for its tasks, in dedicated frame-buffer memory, or in a dedicated memory that is shared between buffers and textures. The color buffer is a part of the frame buffer. It is in some way connected to a *video controller*, which in turn is

363

Frame Buffer   **Output Device**
                                                                     (e.g. monitor)

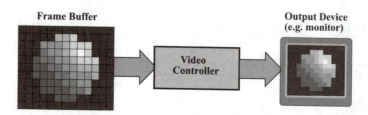

Figure 12.1. A simple display system: the color buffer is scanned by the video controller, which fetches the colors of the pixels. These colors are in turn used to control the intensities on the output device.

connected to the monitor. This is illustrated in Figure 12.1. The video controller is also called a digital-to-analog converter (DAC), since the digital pixel value is converted to an analog equivalent for the monitor. Gamma correction (see Section 4.7) should be done between the color buffer and the DAC. Because every pixel must be read for each frame and sent through gamma correction and digital-to-analog conversion, each of these systems must be able to deal with high bandwidths.

The job of the video controller is to scan through the color buffer, scan line by scan line, at the same rate as the monitor, and to do this in synchronization with the beam of the monitor. The rate is typically between 60 and 120 times per second (Hertz). During this time, the colors of the pixels in the color buffer are used to control the intensities of the monitor beam. Note that the electron beam usually moves in a left-to-right and up-to-down manner. Because of this, the beam does not contribute to the image on the screen when it moves from the right side to the left. This is called the *horizontal retrace*. Related to this is the *line rate* or *horizontal refresh rate*, the amount of time it takes to complete one entire left-right-left cycle. The *vertical retrace* is the movement of the beam from the bottom to the upper left corner, i.e., its return to position to begin the next frame. This is shown in Figure 12.2. The *vertical refresh rate* is the number of times per second the monitor performs this process. Most viewers notice flicker at rates less than 72 Hz.

EXAMPLE: MONITOR TIMING The VESA (Video Electronics Standards Association) specifies standard monitor timings. The VESA standard for a 1280×1024 resolution display at 75 Hz is an example. At 75 Hz the screen updates once every 13.33 milliseconds. The standard specifies a *frame size*, which defines the relationship between the resolution and retrace times. The frame size for a 1280×1024 resolution screen is 1688×1066. This size is related to the *pixel clock*, which is the rate at which pixels are refreshed. The pixel clock is

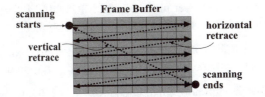

Figure 12.2. The horizontal and vertical retraces of a monitor. The color buffer shown here has five scan lines of pixels. The scanning of the lines starts at the upper left corner and proceeds one scan line at a time. At the end of a scan line it stops scanning and moves to the line below the current line. This passage is called horizontal retrace. When the bottom right corner is reached, the scanning ends and moves back to the upper left corner in order to be able to scan the next frame. This movement is called vertical retrace.

$1688 \times 1066 \times 75$ Hz, or 135 MegaHertz (MHz). This is about 7.4 nanoseconds per pixel. The *line rate*, which is the monitor's frame rate times the number of scan lines, is then $75 \times 1066 = 79,950$ lines per second. The frame size can be used to derive the vertical retrace time. Subtract 1024, the vertical resolution, from 1066, the vertical frame size, to get 42, the vertical *sync length*. So vertical retrace takes the same amount of time as drawing 42 lines on the screen. This gives $42 \times 1688 \times 7.4$ nanoseconds, or about 525 microseconds for vertical retrace to occur. $\qquad\qquad\square$

Related to this topic is interlacing. Computer monitors are typically non-interlaced, or what is commonly known as *progressive scan*. In television, the horizontal lines are interlaced, so that during one vertical refresh the odd numbered lines are drawn, and during the next one the even numbered lines are drawn. Filtering computer animation for television is non-trivial. Snyder et al. [340] discuss one way to tackle the problem. One method of achieving additional acceleration for PC graphics accelerators is to use *scanline interleave* (SLI) mode. In this scheme, two chipsets run in parallel; one handles the odd scan lines, the other the even.

12.1.2   The Color Buffer

The color buffer usually has a number of different color modes, based on the number of bytes of depth. These modes include:

- Indexed or pseudo-color: one byte per pixel, allowing 2^8 or 256 colors, chosen from a larger set by three look-up tables (LUTs).

- High color: two bytes per pixel, of which 15 or 16 bits are used for the color, giving 32,768 or 65,536 colors, respectively.

- True color or RGB color: three or four bytes per pixel, of which 24 bits are used for the color, giving $16,777,216 \approx 16.8$ million different colors.

Some systems offer the option of mixing modes, with a different mode for each window. Many other modes exist; we will discuss the modes listed above as a representative subset.

In pseudo (or indexed) color mode, a palette of up to 256 colors is chosen and used for color representation. Each color in the palette is represented by 8 bits each of red, green, and blue, meaning that the 256 colors can be chosen from a set of 16.8 million colors. For example, on the PC, a typical palette (also known as a color table or look-up table) might consist of the following:

- 20 colors reserved by the system for user interface controls.

- 6 evenly spaced levels of red, green, and blue, giving $6 \times 6 \times 6$ or 216 colors.

- 20 colors for gray-scale color support.

There is much support within different APIs for this color mode, as it used to be the main color mode supported on most machines. Much work has been done on finding ways to dither in order to give the illusion of colors not in the palette, on ways of creating optimal palettes, on ways of performing animation by changing the look-up table colors from frame to frame, and much else.

It is the high and true color modes which predominate in the field of real-time rendering at present. In the quest for speed, some hardware accelerators currently do not support the true color mode. This is because two bytes of memory per pixel may usually be accessed more quickly than three or four bytes per pixel.

The high color mode has 16 bits of color resolution to use. Typically this amount is split into at least 5 bits each for red, green, and blue. This leaves one bit, which is usually given to the green channel, resulting in a 5-6-5 division. The green channel is chosen because it has the largest luminance effect on the eye, and so requires greater precision. This division yields 32 or 64 equally spaced, fixed levels of color per channel. An alternate division is 5-5-5-1, where the single bit is not used.

With 32 or 64 levels of color, it is possible to discern differences in adjacent color levels. For example, a smoothly shaded Gouraud triangle may become shaded with contours as the color jumps from level to level across the surface; see Figure 12.3. The human visual system further increases this problem due to a perceptual phenomenon called *Mach banding* [120, 156]. This problem

Figure 12.3. As the rectangle is shaded from white to black, banding appears. Although each gray-scale bar has a solid intensity level, each can appear to be darker on the left and lighter on the right due to Mach banding.

is usually termed *banding* or *contouring* [291]. Placing a texture on a banded surface can help mask the problem. Dithering can lessen the effect, so some newer hardware has support for it. Barkans [27] discusses traditional dithering and a newer hardware scheme called Color Recovery. For many applications, high color mode can be adequate.

True color uses 24 bits of RGB[1] color, one byte per color channel. Internally, these colors may be stored as 24 or 32 bits. A 32-bit representation can be present for speed purposes, because various hardware commands are optimized for groups of four bytes (or larger). The extra 8 bits can also be used to store an alpha channel (see Section 4.5), giving the pixel an RGBA value. The 24-bit color (no alpha) representation is also called the *packed pixel format*, which can save frame buffer memory in comparison to its 32-bit, unpacked counterpart.

Using 24 bits of color is almost always acceptable for real-time rendering. It is still possible to see banding of colors, but much less likely than with only 16 bits. Gamma correction can also affect the number of color levels (see Section 4.7). Note that when using multipass techniques to increase the quality of the images, it is better to have more precision in the color buffer (i.e., eight bits per pixel). If the precision is too low, then quantization effects may be visible and annoying to the viewer.

This quantization problem is one of the main arguments for more bits per channel. For example, some high-end (e.g., SGI) machines compute color internally as 12 bits or more, since the additional bits are useful for image storage, compositing, gamma correction, image processing, etc. Only 8 bits per channel are displayed, but various banding problems are avoided by this approach.

It is often the case that an API supports higher-precision colors than the underlying hardware does. For example, in OpenGL the RGBA values can be numbers between 0.0 and 1.0, and the floating point representations of these then have essentially 24 bits of precision (i.e., the mantissa) per channel. The hardware rounds off to the nearest available color, or uses a more sophisticated technique such as dithering in order to approximate these colors.

---

[1] On Intel systems the ordering is often reversed to BGR.

In image file formats you can see a mirroring of the various color buffer architectures [265]. GIF is an indexed LUT format. TIFF and PNG support indexing and true color. Targa also has 16- and 32-bit modes. The successive versions of the Windows BMP format are practically a study of the evolution of the PC color buffer.

In any color mode, we may also think of the image as consisting of a set of color planes. For example, a true color system has 24 color planes. Some systems also support overlay planes, which are normally one to eight bits of independent color data which is stored separately. One color or bit of the overlay plane is used to denote that the pixel is transparent. This overlay plane can be drawn to in a manner similar to the color buffer. The hardware places any image in this overlay plane in front of the underlying color buffer on the monitor. The overlay plane is useful for a number of operations, such as menus and other user interface elements, primitive highlighting, cursors, heads-up displays, etc. The advantage is that such elements can be changed without affecting (and requiring the system to refresh) the underlying scene.

12.1.3 Z-buffering and W-buffering

As we saw in Section 2.4, the Z-buffer (also called the depth buffer) can be used to resolve visibility. This kind of buffer typically has between 16 and 32 bits for each pixel. For orthographic viewing, the corresponding world-space distance values are proportional to the z-value, and so the depth resolution is uniform. For example, say the world-space distance between the near and far planes is 100 meters, and the Z-buffer stores 16 bits per pixel. This means that the distance between any adjacent depth values is the same, 100 meters $/2^{16}$, i.e., about 1.5 millimeters.

However, for perspective viewing this is not the case. Instead, the distribution is non-uniform, and the resolution is finer at the lower depth values. The distribution is also highly dependent on the near and far values of the projection. Setting the near value as far out as possible without clipping gives better overall resolution in the viewed range. Bringing the far plane in as close as possible also helps, of course, but maximizing the near plane's distance is usually more critical [245]. Depth resolution is important because it helps us avoid rendering errors. For example, say you modeled a sheet of paper and placed it on a desk, ever so slightly above the desk's surface.[2] With error in the least significant

---

[2]If the paper were placed exactly at the same height as the desk, i.e,. the paper and desk were made coplanar, then there would be no right answer. Sometimes called z-fighting, this problem is due to poor modeling and cannot be resolved by better z precision.

bits of the z-depths computed for the desk and paper, the desk can poke through the paper at various spots. A higher depth precision can help eliminate such problems. Subpixel addressing, in which the position within the pixel's cell is used for the location of endpoints (vs. using the center of the pixel), also has a major effect on correct Z-buffer primitive ordering [223].

For the Z-buffer, we store the value of z/w after projection. The characteristics of the perspective transform matrix (see Section 3.5) result in greater precision for objects closer to the viewer. This is especially true when there is a large difference between the near and the far values. When the near value is close to the far value, the precision tends to be uniform over the depth. To return to the paper and desk example, this change in precision can mean that as the viewer moves farther away from the paper, the desk poke-through problem occurs more frequently.

An alternate hardware architecture is called W-buffering, or occasionally q-buffering [122]. This technique stores the w-value after the perspective transform, which is essentially the world-space depth, scaled. Here the precision of the depth value is always uniform for all depths. With W-buffering, the w-values are not linearly interpolated from the endpoints of a triangle or span, but rather a nonlinear interpolation is used. What actually occurs is that $1/w$ is interpolated across the textured surface, then inverted to get w per pixel. This value non-linearly interpolates texture coordinates across a surface, providing perspective-correct texture mapping. Briefly, if you linearly interpolate (u, v) texture coordinates across a surface, you will get incorrect-looking results when viewing a polygon in perspective.[3] An in-depth discussion of the proper way to interpolate, hyperbolic interpolation, is provided by Blinn [42, 45]. If the texture interpolation problem was solved in hardware, depth resolution uniformity could also be provided.

So which is better, W- or Z-buffering? W-buffering is usually better when there is a need for good precision for distant objects. This is the case in flight simulators [70] and in certain games. Z-buffering would be better when, for example, examining CAD models where only one model is usually examined at a time and this model is held in front of the viewer. In terms of numbers, more of the depth range gains from Z-buffering when (approximately) $n/f > 0.3$, where n is the near plane and f is the far plane. When $n/f \leq 0.3$, most of the depth range gains from W-buffering. Also, note that Z-buffering is always better when $n/f > 0.5$ [45].

---

[3]More specifically, a polygon that does not directly face the viewer. Screen-aligned billboards (see Section 6.2.2) will never encounter this problem

12.1.4   Single, Double, and Triple Buffering

In Section 2.4 we mentioned that double buffering is used in order for the viewer not to see the actual rendering of the primitives. Here we will describe single, double, and even triple buffering.

Assume that we only have a single buffer. This buffer has to be the one that is currently shown to the viewer. As polygons for a frame are drawn, we will see more and more of them as the monitor refreshes—an unconvincing effect. Even if our frame rate is equal to the monitor's update rate, single buffering has problems. If we decide to clear the buffer or draw a large polygon, then we will briefly be able to see the actual partial changes to the color buffer as the beam of the monitor passes those areas which are being drawn. Sometimes called tearing, because the image displayed looks as if it were briefly ripped in two, this is not a desirable feature for real-time graphics.[4] Single buffering is useful, however, in other contexts. For example, when a drawing area is updated very infrequently then single buffering may be sufficient. This is often the case when a small image appears in a window. That buffer is usually only redrawn when another window has covered the image and is suddenly moved so that the image should be visible. Single buffering is also useful for optimizing the pipeline (see Section 8.3).

To avoid the visibility problem, double buffering is commonly used; here, a finished image is shown in the *front buffer*, while an off-screen *back buffer* contains the scene that is currently being drawn. The back buffer and the front buffer are then swapped at an appropriate time, e.g., during vertical retrace in order to avoid tearing. Immediately after the swap, the (new) back buffer is first cleared and then rendering starts there, while the new front buffer is being shown to the user. This process is shown in Figure 12.4. The swap is sometimes implemented on the PC using a *page flipping* technique [70]. This means that the front buffer is associated with the address of a special register. This address points to the pixel at the position $(0, 0)$ which may be at the lower left or upper left corner. When buffers are swapped, the address of the register is changed to the address of the back buffer. Panning the screen is easily done by writing to the register. Another way to implement swapping on the PC is to use a technique called *BLT swapping* [70] or, simply, *blitting*. For this method there is one and only one piece of memory that is always displayed, often called the video RAM. To do a swap of the back buffer, which may reside in the host memory or in any other video memory, a piece of hardware called the BitBLT engine copies the contents of the back buffer into the front buffer.

---

[4]On some systems, like the old Amiga, you could actually test where the beam was and so avoid drawing there. Thus, some real-time graphics can work fine with single buffering.

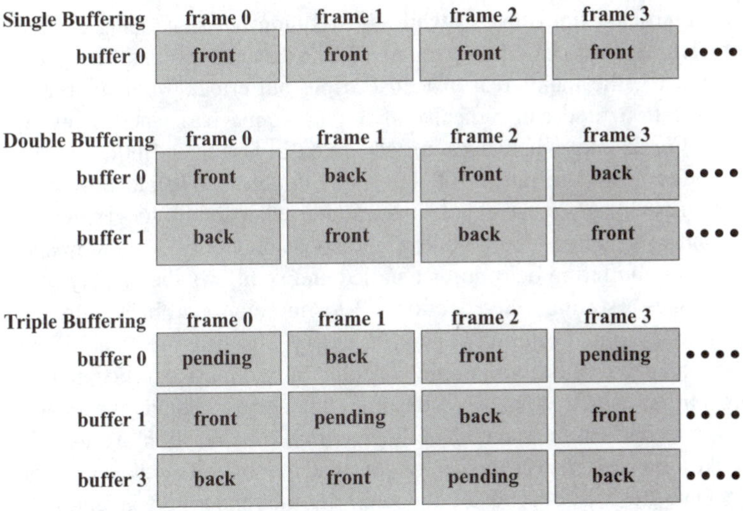

Single Buffering	frame 0	frame 1	frame 2	frame 3	
buffer 0	front	front	front	front	• • • •

Double Buffering	frame 0	frame 1	frame 2	frame 3	
buffer 0	front	back	front	back	• • • •
buffer 1	back	front	back	front	• • • •

Triple Buffering	frame 0	frame 1	frame 2	frame 3	
buffer 0	pending	back	front	pending	• • • •
buffer 1	front	pending	back	front	• • • •
buffer 3	back	front	pending	back	• • • •

Figure 12.4. For single buffering, the front buffer is always shown. For double buffering, buffer 0 is first in front and buffer 1 is in the back. Then they swap from front to back and vice versa for each frame. Triple buffering works by having a pending buffer as well. Here, a buffer is first cleared, and rendering to it is begun (pending). Second, the system continues to use the buffer for rendering until the image has been completed (back). Finally, the buffer is shown (front).

The double buffer can be augmented with a second back buffer, which we call the *pending buffer*. This is called *triple buffering* [122, 242]. The pending buffer is similar to the back buffer in that it is also off-screen, and in that it can be modified while the front buffer is being displayed. The pending buffer becomes part of a three-buffer cycle. During one frame, the pending buffer can be accessed. At the next swap, it becomes the back buffer, where the rendering is completed. Then it becomes the front buffer and is shown to the viewer. At the next swap, the buffer again turns into a pending buffer. This course of events is visualized at the bottom of Figure 12.4.

Triple buffering has a number of advantages over double buffering. First, the system can access the pending buffer while waiting for the vertical retrace. With double buffering, a swap can stall the graphics pipeline. While waiting for the vertical retrace so a swap can take place, a double-buffered construction must simply be kept waiting. This is so because the front buffer must be shown to the viewer, and the back buffer must remain unchanged because it has a finished image in it, waiting to be shown. If swapping is accomplished with blitting, triple buffering offers additional rendering time by allowing draw access to the pending buffer during this time. A related advantage is that clearing the buffer can take significant time, and so while the pending buffer is being cleared, the back buffer can be accessed in parallel. These advantages also make the load better balanced, the major reason to use triple buffering. Minor variations in image generation time can radically affect the frame rate when using double buffering. For example, if images are generated in less than 1/60th of a second and a monitor's update rate is 60 Hz, both double and triple buffering will display 60 new images a second. If images later take slightly longer than 1/60th of a second to generate, double buffering can display only 30 new images per second. Triple buffering does not get stalled and so allows the display of nearly 60 new images a second.[5] See Section 8.3 for more on load balancing.

The idea of triple buffering is good in theory, but there are some limitations and disadvantages. First, an additional color buffer must be allocated for the pending buffer, which obviously consumes memory. Second, the latency increases up to one entire frame. This means that the "reaction" to user inputs, such as key strokes, mouse moves, or joystick moves, gets delayed. This happens because these user events are ignored after the rendering begins in the back buffer. Finally, on some architectures (e.g., 3dfx's Voodoo [122]), the pending buffer cannot be used along with auxiliary buffers such as the depth or alpha-channel buffer. This means that for real-time rendering, the rendering technique cannot use Z-buffering during any part of the process in which it uses triple buffering. This can limit triple buffering to applications using rendering techniques such as sprite layers (see Section 6.2), voxel rendering (Section 6.8), or polygon-aligned BSP trees (Section 7.1.2).

Triple buffering can easily be exploited if there is direct hardware support for it, or if there is the ability to allocate your own buffers.

In theory, more than three buffers could be used. If the amount of time to compute a frame varies considerably, more buffers give more balance and an overall higher display rate, at the cost of more potential latency. To generalize, multibuffering can be thought of as a ring structure. There is a rendering pointer and a display pointer, each pointing at a different buffer. The rendering pointer leads the display pointer, moving to the next buffer when the current rendering buffer is done being computed. The only rule is that the display pointer should never be the same as the rendering pointer [86].

12.1.5   Stereo Buffers

Some hardware also has support for stereo rendering, in which two images are used in order to make objects look more three-dimensional. With two eyes, the

---

[5]Double buffering can achieve the rate of triple buffering by allowing tearing to occur. Instead of waiting for the vertical retrace, some rendering systems do swapping during *horizontal blanking*, when the electron beam is returning to the left edge of the screen.

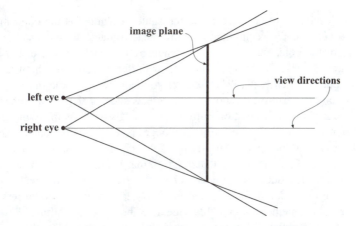

Figure 12.5. Stereo rendering. Note that the image plane is shared between the two frustums, and that the frustums are asymmetric. Such rendering would be used on, for example, a stereo monitor. Shutter glasses could use separate image planes for each eye.

visual system takes two views, and in combining them retrieves depth information. This ability is called *stereopsis* or *stereo vision* [108, 120]. The idea behind stereo vision is to render two images, one for the left eye and one for the right eye (as shown in Figure 12.5), and then use some technique that ensures that the human viewer experiences a depth in the rendered image. These two images are called the *stereo pair*. One common method for creating stereo vision is to generate two images, one in red and one in green, composite these images, then view the result with red-green glasses. In this case, only a normal single display buffer is needed, but display of color is problematic. For color images, the solution can be as simple as having two small screens, one in front of each (human) eye, in a head-mounted display. Another hardware solution is the use of shutter glasses, in which only one eye is allowed to view the screen at a time. Two different views can be displayed by rapidly alternating between eyes and synchronizing with the monitor [74].

For these latter forms of stereography, two separate display buffers are needed. When viewing is to take place in real time, double buffering is used together with stereo rendering. In this case there have to be two front and two back buffers (one set for each eye), so the color buffer memory requirement doubles.

12.1.6 Stencil and Accumulation Buffering

The stencil and accumulation buffers were first described in Section 2.4. The sizes of these buffers are important to hardware designers. The first requirement to note is that both buffers need to be the same resolution as the color buffer. This is so because the accumulation buffer must be able to add and subtract images from the color buffer, and the stencil buffer must be able to mask off certain parts of the color buffer. The stencil buffer typically has between one and eight bits for each pixel. With one bit you can create simple masking, and with more bits you can create more subtle effects such as shadow volumes (see Section 6.6.2). The accumulation buffer typically has twice as many bits as the color buffer has. So a color buffer of 24 bits per pixel (8 bits per color channel) would have 48 bits per pixel (16 bits per color channel). The reason why the accumulation buffer is normally that large is that the accuracy is better when several images are added to the accumulation buffer in order to create effects such as depth of field, antialiasing, and motion blur. Accumulation buffers with 8 bits per color channel are possible, and may be used by shifting down the images to be accumulated, but the quality will be lower due to lost bits.

12.1.7 Memory

Here we will mention a few different memory architectures that have been used for memory layout. The SGI O2 uses a fully unified memory system, which means that it can use any part of the host memory for textures and different kinds of buffers [205]. A somewhat less unified layout is to have dedicated memory on the graphics chip, which can then be used for textures and buffers in any way desired. This is the approach taken by the Neon chip [244] (see Section 12.2.2). The VISUALIZE fx architecture [320] (see Section 12.2.3) uses separate texture and buffer memory on the graphics card. The InfiniteReality [262] (see Section 12.2.4) also does this, but, due to its scalable nature, it has to replicate the texture memory across each rasterizer.

EXAMPLE: MEMORY REQUIREMENTS Assume that we have a color buffer of 1280×1024 pixels with true colors, i.e., 8 bits per color channel. This would require $1280 \times 1024 \times 3 = 3.75$ megabytes (MB). Using double buffering doubles this value to 7.5 MB. Also, assume that we have a stencil buffer of eight bits per pixel and an accumulation buffer of 48 bits per pixel. This alone would require seven bytes per pixel, which is equal to 8.75 MB. Also, let us say that the depth buffer has 24 bits per pixel. The depth buffer would then need 3.75 MB of memory. This system would therefore require $7.5 + 8.75 + 3.75 = 20$ MB of memory for these buffers. Stereo buffers would double the color buffer size, and an alpha value would add an additional one byte per pixel (1.25 MB) of memory.   □

12.2 Architecture

In this section, we will first present a general architecture for a real-time computer graphics system. We will then describe three real-world graphics systems. We avoid talking about specific performance values for bandwidth, fill rate, etc., since these numbers tend to become outdated quickly.

12.2.1 General

Generally speaking, current graphics systems are built as shown in Figure 12.6. This illustration also shows where hardware acceleration may be located.

The host is the computer system without any graphics hardware, i.e, it is a system with CPU(s), memory, buses, etc. Applications run on the host, i.e., on the CPU(s). The geometry pipeline stage may be performed on the host, or it may be hardware-accelerated, or both. Some CPUs even have support for geometry acceleration on the chip. For example, the Intel Pentium III has streaming, single-instruction/multiple-data (SIMD) extensions, called SSE, that work in parallel on short arrays of numbers. If there is separate graphics hardware geometry acceleration, then this will help to reduce the workload on the application. Finally, the rasterizer is (almost) always hardware-accelerated. The interface between the application and the graphics hardware is called a *driver*.

It is becoming more and more common to parallelize both the geometry and the rasterizer stages in order to achieve faster and higher-quality graphics. The idea is to compute multiple results simultaneously and then merge these at a later stage. In general, a parallel graphics architecture has the appearance shown in Figure 12.7. The result of the graphics database traversal is sent to a number of *geometry engines* (GEs) that work in parallel. Together these GEs do the

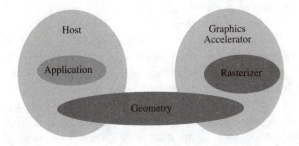

Figure 12.6. A general graphics system. The rasterizer is always hardware-accelerated, while the geometry may either be located on the host or be hardware accelerated or both. Application code runs on the host. (Illustration after Cox et al. [70].)

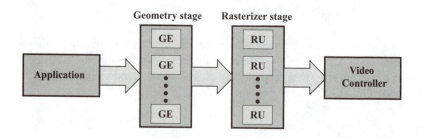

Figure 12.7. The general architecture for a high-performance, parallel computer graphics architecture. Each geometry engine (GE) processes (i.e., transforms, projects, etc.) a portion of the geometry to be rendered, and each rasterizer unit (RU) takes care of a portion of the pixel calculations.

geometry-stage work of the rendering pipeline (see Section 2.3), and forward their results to a set of *rasterizer units* (RUs), which together implement the rasterizer stage in the rendering pipeline. Most parallel systems are of the type *Sort-Middle*, which means that the primitives are sorted between the GEs and the RUs [260]. This means that the primitives are assigned arbitrarily to the GEs, and that each RU is responsible for a region of pixels on the screen. After the GEs have processed the geometry, each processed primitive is sent to the RU responsible for the region in which it lands.

All these components (host, geometry processing, and rasterization) connected together give us a multiprocessing system. For such systems there are two problems that are well-known and almost always associated with multiprocessing: *load balancing* and *communications* [70]. The programmer can affect the load balance; techniques for doing so are discussed in Chapter 8. Communications can be a problem if the bandwidth of the buses is too low. Therefore, it is of extreme importance to design a graphics system so that the bottleneck does not occur in the bus from the host to the graphics hardware.

When it comes to sending data to the graphics hardware, there are two methods—*push* and *pull*. The pull method works by writing data to the system memory. The graphics hardware can then *pull* data from those memory locations during an entire frame. The *push* method writes data to the graphics hardware. Since the push method only writes the data once, there is more memory bandwidth available for the application than with the pull method. However, when using the push method, you may need large FIFO queues on the graphics cards in order to get a balanced system. Alternately, if geometry acceleration is available, then the pull method may be better, since the CPU may not need to touch the data. The conclusion is that best method to use depends on the circumstances.

It is worth mentioning that the geometry acceleration stage may have storage for geometry or display lists.

As mentioned before, the geometry stage can be located on the host, on special geometry acceleration hardware, or on both. The special hardware can be implemented on a custom chip, fully pipelined and parallelized. This usually gives the best performance and the best cost per gate, but once it has been implemented there is not much flexibility. So another approach is to use one or more general-purpose CPUs or DSPs (digital signal processing chips) for geometry processing. This gives more flexibility, since the program that drives these can be changed relatively easily. Some CPUs also have support for geometry processing on the chip; having such a CPU on the host naturally helps performance.

The rasterizer must be implemented on custom chip(s) for the sake of speed. The first step in rasterization is *setup*, which computes various deltas and slopes from the vertex information. Such computation is needed in order to rasterize the primitive and do interpolation. Color and depth are interpolated over the primitive. If there is a texture associated with the primitive, then texture coordinates are interpolated and the texture applied. Some hardware supports interpolating two colors, allowing a separate specular color [275] to avoid the weakening of this component's effect when texturing. Interpolation is not always linear; see Section 12.1.3.

Primitive setup and interpolation produces a *fragment*, which is simply data for a pixel covered by a primitive, i.e., its depth, alpha value, color, etc. With this data, fragment processing is performed. These tests include:

- The alpha test; if alpha is 0 the fragment is not visible at all.

- The stencil test, which may mask the fragment with the contents of the stencil buffer .

- The depth test, which determines whether the fragment is visible by comparing its depth to the stored depth value.

- Fog, which can blend a fragment with a fog color.

- Alpha blending, which can blend the fragment's data with the original pixel's data.

The order of all operations in the rasterizer is highly dependent on the particular implementation. Note that some rasterizer chips support only triangles, and do not support points and lines directly—these primitives are rendered by drawing rectangles representing them. Also, some rasterizers use subpixel addressing to help avoid holes and overlaps caused by T-vertices (see Section 9.2.2) [223].

This technique also allows you to avoid having objects poke through one another, as discussed in Section 12.1.3. Subpixel addressing also helps eliminate the shifting and snapping of objects and textures as the viewer moves through a scene.

12.2.2   Case Study: Neon

In this section we will study the most complex configuration of the Neon chip from Compaq [244]. This is a single-chip architecture without geometry acceleration. The host has to do all the geometry processing and then send the transformed data to the chip. The architecture of Neon is shown in Figure 12.8. The designers of this architecture chose the single-chip construction because it is easier to design than a multiple-chip architecture. The design complexity is smaller for a single chip, and generalized logic circuits can be used by more than one function. Some data paths may be extremely fast since they are on-chip, and the two-dimensional and three-dimensional data use the same path through the chip. The Neon chip uses a unified memory architecture, which means that texture and all kinds of buffers (color, depth, stencil, and off-screen buffers) share the on-board memory, which is 128 MB for the maximum configuration. The greatest advantage here is that this memory can be allocated dynamically for different buffers and textures. No memory is wasted on features that are not used. This also means that the texture memory need not be replicated as it must in the InfiniteReality architecture (see Section 12.2.4).

The data can get to the Neon chip in two ways: either it is pushed by the host, or it is pulled by the chip using DMA (direct memory access). Since this is a rasterizer chip, the host first does the geometry processing of the data and then Neon continues from there. The interface between the host and the chip (which in this case is a PCI interface) forwards the graphics commands to the Command Parser, which is the first stop on this rasterizer.

The Command Parser decodes the graphics commands and converts the data into the internal fixed point format used by the rasterizer. This data is then sent on to the Fragment Generator (FG), as seen in Figure 12.8. The FG determines which fragments are inside the primitive (point, line, triangle, quadrilateral) by using half-plane equations bounding the primitive [288]. The FG does the setup and generates the fragments in batches of eight in order to reduce texture cache thrashing and to amortize read latencies. Visible fragments are sent on to the Texel Central.

The Texel Central (TC) is the crossbar between the memory controllers, so everything that has to be fetched or downloaded to the on-chip memory has

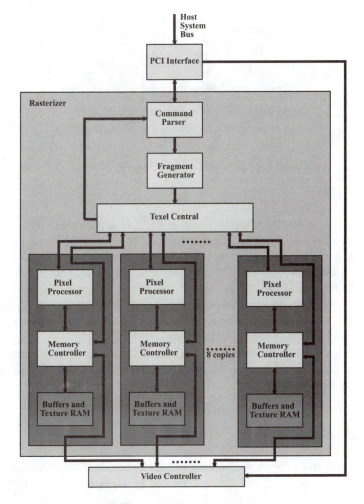

Figure 12.8. The architecture of the Neon graphics chip from Compaq.

to go through the TC. A small (256-byte) texel cache is also maintained here. McCormack et al. [244] describe several ways to improve the texel cache hit rate. The TC also takes care of perspective-correct texturing and texture filtering.

Each fragment is then sent to one of the eight Pixel Processors (PP). Each PP is responsible for a part of the frame buffer, and each fragment is sent to the PP that is responsible for the part where it belongs. To balance rendering, the Neon chip uses an interleaving pattern as shown in Figure 12.9. This pattern

0	1	2	3	4	5	6	7	0	1
2	3	4	5	6	7	0	1	2	3
4	5	6	7	0	1	2	3	4	5
6	7	0	1	2	3	4	5	6	7
0	1	2	3	4	5	6	7	0	1

Figure 12.9. The interleaving pattern used by Neon. The numbers inside the pixels (squares) represents the memory controller that owns the pixel.

is also good for texture mapping, since a 2×2 region of texels maps to four different memory controllers. The PP also handles the depth, stencil, and alpha tests, alpha blending, fogging, and dithering (if fewer than 8 bits are used for each color component). Finally, the PP sees to it that the relevant information is written to the memory controller, which writes it to the on-chip memory. This completes the rasterization of a primitive. The video controller then refreshes the display by requesting data from the memory controllers, a process which also merges pixel data with overlay plane data.

It is also worth mentioning that the Neon chip can draw antialiased points and lines, and that is has some hardware for pipeline instrumentation to help in locating bottlenecks.

12.2.3 Case Study: VISUALIZE fx

Here we will study the most complex configuration, called fx^6, from the VISUALIZE fx graphics hardware family produced by Hewlett-Packard [320]. This hardware is used on both PCs and Unix machines as a high-end graphics system. A coarse view of the architecture is shown in Figure 12.10, and as can be seen, it has geometry processing in hardware. The reason for the separate texture accelerator is that the system is also available without hardware texturing.

Next, we will briefly discuss the interface chip, the geometry board, texturing and rasterization, and the video controller of the VISUALIZE fx^6.

The Interface Chip

The host sends data to the fx^6 card, and the interface chip takes care of the data. The task of the interface chip is to direct the data to the different components of the system. The chip includes data buffering in order to make the system

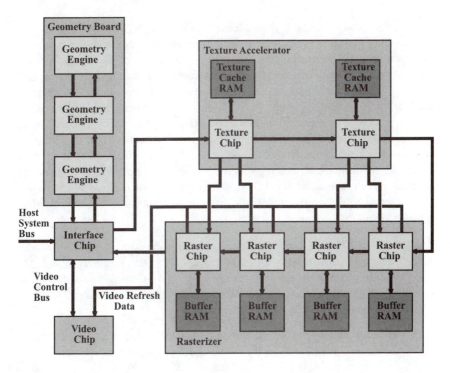

Figure 12.10. The architecture of the VISUALIZE fx[6] graphics hardware from Hewlett-Packard. Illustration after Scott et al. [320].

more balanced. The interface chip can send the data through different paths of the system depending on the type of data. If the interface chip receives three-dimensional data, then this data is sent to the geometry board for geometry processing. If the data is two-dimensional, then it is sent directly to the texture accelerator, which may filter the texture data and send it on to the rasterizer. Two-dimensional data is kept waiting at the interface chip until all three-dimensional data that already is in the geometry board has been sent to the first texture chip. There is also an unbuffered two-dimensional path which works like the buffered version but has higher priority. The reason for this is to allow texture data, etc., to be sent so that pending operations can be completed.

Geometry Board

Only three-dimensional data is sent to the geometry board. The VISUALIZE fx[6] consists of three geometry engines in a chain, but can be extended to have up to eight. The data is sent from the interface chip through all geometry engines, which select jobs from the bus in a least-busy fashion. This simply means that the geometry engine that has least data to process takes care of the data coming in on the bus. The geometry engine takes care of typical operations for this stage: model and view transform, lighting, texture computations, projection, and clipping. The texture computations may involve texture coordinate calculations, such as environment mapping, transformation by a matrix, linear generation, and projection. The geometry engines also compute the setup variables for the rasterizer. The results from the geometry engines are sent back to the interface chip on a bus that goes from the last geometry engine (located at the top in Figure 12.10) through all other geometry engines. The data from the geometry stage is sent on this bus in a FIFO (first in, first out) order. Some of the results are converted by the interface chip into fixed point numbers so that the rasterizer can use them next.

Texturing and Rasterization

After three-dimensional data has been processed by the geometry board, the interface chip sends it to the first texture chip. Two-dimensional data is sent directly to this texture chip. The texture chips have four main tasks:

- Provide storage for a texture cache which they maintain. The texture cache works much like a common CPU cache, in that it sees to it that a portion of a texture is in the cache and that this can be reused by other objects or by itself (in the next frame).

- From the setup variables that were computed by the geometry board, the texture chips compute perspective-correct texture coordinates.

- Retrieve and filter (magnify or minify) texture data.

- Pass on the filtered results to the rasterizer.

After passing through the texture chips, the data moves on to the rasterizers, which render points, lines, and triangles and do fragment processing. After the three-dimensional data has generated pixel data using the rasterizers, it is sent back to the interface chip, where it is discarded. For two-dimensional operations, the data is not always discarded. For example, when an image is to be moved on the screen, pixel data has to be read from the frame-buffer chip first. This data is then sent back to the interface chip, which sends it on another round through the texture chips and the rasterizer, but this time with another address so that the image ends up in another position.

As can be seen in the chip diagram (Figure 12.10), the rasterizers control and access the frame-buffer RAM. These memory chips contain not only the color buffer (RGBA), but also an overlay buffer, the depth buffer, and the stencil buffer. The rasterizers also send video refresh data (i.e., the pixels' colors) to the video chip (the video controller) and handle windows and overlays.

The fx chips also have support for simple occlusion culling (described in Section 7.1.5). The idea is to test whether the bounding box of a (complex) object is occluded before sending the data of the object to the geometry board.

Video Chip

To be able to send color buffer contents and other video refresh data to the video controller, there is a bus from the raster chips (which control the buffers) to the video chip (video controller). The video chip also maps pixel colors to true colors (for example, a 16-bit color is converted to 24 bits) and performs digital-to-analog conversion, video timing, and output.

12.2.4   Case Study: InfiniteReality

The maximum configuration of the InfiniteReality graphics system [50, 205, 262] from SGI will be studied here. This is a high-performance system which is highly parallelized as a *Sort-Middle* architecture with many special features. The VISUALIZE fx graphics system is similar to the InfiniteReality from a broad view, but it does not exploit parallelism as much as the Infinite Reality system does. The InfiniteReality architecture is shown in Figure 12.11.

We will study the geometry board and the raster memory board of the InfiniteReality architecture.

Geometry Board

The geometry board consists of a *host interface processor* (HIP), a *geometry distributor*, *geometry engines*, and a FIFO queue at the end. The main task of the HIP is to see to it that the rest of the graphics system has work to do. To help with this task, two different ways of supporting display lists (see page 254) are implemented. First, compiled display lists can be pulled (see Section 12.2.1) from the host memory using DMA (direct memory access). This greatly reduces the load on the host. Second, the HIP has 16 MB of memory, of which 15 MB is available as a cache for display lists. This storage is used as much as possible, but the system goes back to the pull method when the cache is full. Since the cache avoids pulling data from the host, caching is much faster. If display lists are not used, then per-vertex data can be sent from the host to the HIP.

After passing through the HIP, the data is sent to the geometry distributor. This unit passes data to the geometry engines in a least-busy fashion. This was found to be better than round-robin, since the loads of the data tend to vary from

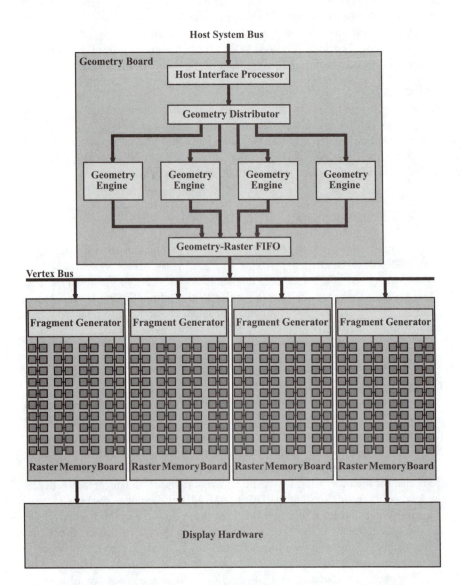

Figure 12.11. The architecture of the InfiniteReality graphics hardware from SGI. *(after Montrym et al. [262]).*

one time to another. In the geometry distributor, each graphics command is also associated with a number. This is so that the FIFO can recreate the order of the primitives as required by, for example, OpenGL [262].

The geometry engines (GEs) were implemented using a semi-custom ASIC (application-specific integrated circuit). Since all three vertices of a triangle must be processed geometrically, the heart of a GE is three floating-point cores (FPC) that execute in a SIMD (single-instruction/multiple-data) arrangement. This means that each GE can process the three coordinates of a three-dimensional vertex in parallel. Each FPC has an ALU (arithmetic logic unit), a multiplier, and a 32-word register file with two read and two write ports. The whole FPC is implemented as a four-stage pipeline. These three FPCs per GE share an on-chip memory of 2560 words (32 bits). This piece of memory holds the state of OpenGL, but is also used for scratch computations and for queuing incoming vertex data. The main idea behind this construction is to make a cost-efficient architecture with high performance. After the vertices have been processed by the FPCs, a floating-to-fixed-point conversion takes place.

The results from the GEs are then sent to the geometry-raster FIFO which merges the streams from the GEs into one stream and sees to it that the graphic commands are in the same order as they were issued. The FIFO can hold a maximum of 65,536 vertices. The merged stream is then written to the vertex bus, as shown in Figure 12.11.

To exploit the bandwidth of the vertex bus, only the screen-space vertex information is sent here. All data on this bus is broadcast to the fragment generators on the raster memory board.

Raster Memory Board

Each raster memory board has a single fragment generator, a copy of the entire texture memory, and 80 image engines which control the frame-buffer memory. The fragment generator receives and assembles vertex data from the vertex bus. Then, scan conversion is performed by evaluating the plane equations (from the setup) rather than doing interpolation over the primitives. This requires less setup but more computations per pixel [262]. The reason for this design choice was that the trend in many areas is toward many small triangles, so setup time becomes a significant part of the rasterization process. The fragment generator also calculates texel addresses, texture filtering, mipmap level of detail, color, and depth interpolation. Fog and combination with the interpolated color is also taken care of here.

Fragments are then output by the fragment generators and distributed equally among the 80 image engines on the raster memory board. To balance the workload across the image engines, each fragment generator is responsible for several vertical, two-pixel-wide lines. The scan conversion completes all pixels in such a two-pixel-wide vertical line before proceeding to the next line for every primitive. To avoid fill-rate limitations for large primitives, all image engines must be responsible for part of each vertical line that its fragment generator owns. Also, all image engines must appear equally on each horizontal line. So, for four raster memory boards with a total of 320 image engines (80 per raster memory board), the image engine tiling pattern is 320×80 pixels [262].

Display Hardware

Each image engine drives a signal to the display hardware. The display hardware can drive up to eight different display output channels, and each has a video timing generator, dynamic video resize hardware, gamma correction, and digital-to-analog conversion. It also has a 32,768 entry color index, and the color components are maintained at 12 bits per component.

Extra Features

The InfiniteReality graphics system supports drawing of the primitives with the antialiasing technique presented in Section 4.4, using four or eight samples per pixel. It also has hardware support for pipeline instrumentation, which is extremely valuable when optimizing an application. This hardware can be used to find out whether an application is fill-limited, or either transform- or CPU-limited. The InfiniteReality hardware also has dynamic video resizing hardware. This is described in Section 8.2.3. There is also hardware support for texture loading and paging. For extremely large textures, there is hardware-supported clipmapping [262, 347], which we discussed briefly in Section 5.3.

12.2.5   Other Architectures

There are many other three-dimensional graphics architectures that have been proposed and built over the years. Three of the larger-scale efforts have been Pixel-Planes, PixelFlow, and Talisman. A high-performance graphics system called PixelFlow [102, 259, 261] has been developed by the graphics group at the University of North Carolina, Chapel Hill. PixelFlow [259] is an example of the Sort-Last architecture. Talisman [28, 354] is a commercial architecture from Microsoft meant for image-based rendering algorithms. It is discussed briefly in Section 6.2.

Further Reading and Resources

Blinn offer a detailed comparison of Z-buffering and W-buffering [45].

The OpenGL Advanced Techniques course notes [245] discuss ways of creating stereo pairs, and are available on the web.

The annual *SIGGRAPH* and *SIGGRAPH/Eurographics Workshop on Graphics Hardware* conference proceedings are good sources for more information, as are *IEEE Computer Graphics and Applications* and other journals.

Check this book's website, `http://www.realtimerendering.com/`, for information on benchmarking tests and results, as well as other hardware-related links.

Chapter 13
The Future

"Prediction is difficult, especially of the future."
–Niels Bohr

"The best way to predict the future is to create it."
–Alan Kay

"I program my home computer,
beam myself into the future."
–Kraftwerk

There are two parts to the future: you and everything else. This chapter is about both of these. First there will be the obligatory predictions, some of which may even come true. More important is the second part of this chapter, which is about some places for you to go next. It is something of an extended "Further Reading and Resources" section, but also discusses ways to proceed from here—sources of information, conferences, programming tools, etc.

13.1   Everything Else

So, when will we be able to generate in real-time an animated film such as 1998's *A Bug's Life* by Pixar or *Antz* by PDI? The short answer is: decades. Generating an average frame of *A Bug's Life* (*ABL*) takes three to four hours (with up to 20 hours rare but possible) on a 330 MHz UltraSPARC, and requires about a gigabyte of geometric data alone, as of 1998 [146]. To reach a minimum real-time rate of 12 frames per second, this means a speed-up of about $150,000$ times is needed. Moore's Law gives an acceleration rate of 2 times every 1.5

years or, more usefully, about 10 times every 5 years [339]. This puts real-time *ABL* at around 26 years out, the year 2024. It might take longer to get there—Moore's Law may fail in the long run, for whatever reasons.

It may also take less time. Consumer-level (i.e., game) graphics chipsets are currently doubling in speed every six months, and are predicted to continue to do so in the near future. For whatever reasons (e.g., highly competitive market, widening user base feeding growth and research, improved algorithms and architectures), Moore's Law is currently being beaten in this area. This situation seems unlikely to continue, and the application-stage processors are still following Moore's Law, but it is an interesting phenomenon. At a six-month doubling rate, an average frame of *ABL* would be possible at real-time rates by 2007. We can always dream ...

Prediction is a game of chance, since there are many possible futures. Much easier is predicting what will not happen. Processors and accelerators will be found to be good enough as they are, graphics will become superfluous, hand-held devices will never require real-time three-dimensional graphics, etc.: these are all great predictions to bet against.

What is interesting to watch is the way in which real-time graphics is becoming the tail that wags the dog. There are many compute-intensive tasks out there, such as weather prediction, fluid flow simulation, cryptography, etc. Real-time computer graphics is a computationally expensive task that millions of people have direct contact with through computer games. Intel realizes this and aims its instruction set extensions squarely at this arena. Graphics sells games, and games sell chips.

One of the best features of real-time rendering from a marketing perspective is that graphics eats huge amounts of processing power and other resources. There are a few directions of growth. One is frame rate. Once a rate of about 72 Hz is reached, faster speeds are irrelevant to the visual system, though one could argue that latency could be improved by a rate higher than this. Another area for growth is monitor resolution. IBM's Roentgen display offers 2560×2048 resolution, with 200 dots per inch (DPI). A resolution of 1200 DPI, 36 times the Roentgen display's density, is offered by many printer companies today. A third area is bits per pixel. For color display, 24 bits is likely to hold as the maximum for a long time to come, but more bits can be used. However, all of these directions of growth have some determinable useful limits for humans.

The direction in which it is difficult to perceive any limit is scene complexity. By complexity we mean both the number of objects in a scene and the way these objects are rendered. Ignoring all other directions for growth, this single factor makes graphics a bottomless pit for processing power to fill. Depth complexity of scenes will rise, primitives will get smaller, illumination models will become more complex, and so on. Some argue that in the very long term, rendering may best be solved by some variant of ray tracing, in which huge numbers of rays sample the environment for the eye's view of each frame. And there will also be colonies on Mars, underwater cities, and personal jet packs[1].

13.2 You

So, while you and your children's children are waiting for ray tracing to take over the world, what do you do in the meantime? Program, of course: discover new algorithms, create applications, design new hardware, or whatever else you enjoy doing. In this section we cover various resources we have found to be useful in keeping on top of the field of real-time rendering.

This book does not exist in a vacuum; it draws upon a huge number of sources of information. If you are interested in a particular algorithm, track down the original sources. Journal and conference articles in computer graphics are usually not utterly mysterious. Often one of the hardest parts of learning a new topic is simply taking the first step of getting hold of an article. Here are a few ways of tracking down articles:

- Check the reference in this book. We have included web URLs whenever possible. Downloading an article is as easy as it gets.

- Search the web yourself for the title and author. It is more and more common for authors to make their work available for download. For example, over half of the papers in the *SIGGRAPH '98 Proceedings* are available on the web for free.

- Visit this book's website for links to article databases. Some are free, and some have relatively modest subscription fees considering the size of their offerings.

- Use your feet, if there is a research library nearby.

- Check your grapevine; someone else you know may have the article.

- Buy it. Some organizations sell back issues, proceedings, or the articles themselves. There are also occasionally article collections issued by the IEEE and the ACM.

---

[1] Interactive ray tracing of complex scenes is possible today. For example, a system with 60 CPUs has rendered a scene with 35 million spheres at 15 frames a second [283].

- Write to the author. Normally do this only if all else has failed, but it is worth a try. All authors want to have their works read. The main reason this is a last resort should be obvious: authors are often busy people, so it is best to avoid asking them if it is unnecessary.

There are many resources which can help you keep abreast of the field. In the area of research, the *SIGGRAPH Proceedings* is a premier venue for new ideas, but hardly the only one. Other technical gatherings, such as the various *Eurographics* conferences and workshops, the *Symposium on Interactive 3D Graphics*, and the *Graphics Interface* conference, publish a significant amount of material relevant to real-time rendering. Of course, one of the best ways to stay in touch is actually to attend these conferences. There are also many field-specific conferences, such as the Game Developers Conference (GDC).

There are a number of journals that publish technical articles, such as *IEEE Computer Graphics and Applications*, the *journal of graphics tools*, *ACM Transactions on Graphics*, and *IEEE Transactions on Visualization and Computer Graphics*, to mention a few.

If you are looking for material more tutorial in nature, consider subscribing to *Game Developer* magazine. There are usually one or two articles on some facet of real-time graphics in each issue, well illustrated and written in plain English, often with associated code and demonstration programs available for download. Another good source is Jim Blinn's column in *IEEE Computer Graphics and Applications*, which often deals with important topics not normally covered in textbooks. His columns have been collected into two worthwhile books [43, 44].

Trade magazines such as *Computer Graphics World*, *MCV USA*, and the online magazine *The WAVE Report* are good sources for news and trends.

Throughout this book we have pointed to various books related to each chapter's contents. Here we will list a few books of general interest:

- The *Graphics Gems* series. Mentioned numerous times already, these deserve your attention. A storehouse of many different algorithms, these books contain something for every programmer. The code to the books is provided free online, and is actively maintained with bug fixes. Book errata are also available online.

- Watt and Watt's *Advanced Animation and Rendering Techniques* book. A little old at this point, it nonetheless contains an impressive amount of advanced material and technical detail.

- Roger's *Procedural Elements for Computer Graphics* has much nitty-gritty detail about implementing many essential algorithms.

- Foley, van Dam, Feiner, and Hughes' *Computer Graphics—Principles and Practice* is a classic reference for the field of computer graphics. We recommend buying the third edition when it becomes available, which should be soon.

- Glassner's *Principles of Digital Image Synthesis* is a complementary volume to all the above. Instead of covering algorithms, it covers the science and mathematics behind computer graphics in great detail. Errata are available at the author's website.

We refer you one last time to our website for links to online resources at http://www.realtimerendering.com/. Some information on the web is available nowhere else, and there is a huge amount of useful material out there. We will do our best to point you to those resources which we consider the most worthwhile. Links to the resources discussed in this chapter are also available at the site.

In the past few pages you have been flooded with places to go next. Our last words of advice are to go and do it. The field of real-time computer graphics is continually evolving, and new ideas and features are appearing at an increasing rate. There are many combinations of techniques that have only begun to be explored. Even areas that seem old and well-established are worth revisiting; computer architectures change, and what worked (or did not work) a decade ago may no longer apply. What makes real-time rendering a qualitatively different field from other areas of computer graphics is that it provides different tools and has different goals. Today, hardware-accelerated texturing, filtering, alpha-blending, stencil buffering, and other operations change the relative costs of algorithms and so change our ways of doing things.

This book comes 25 years after one of the milestone papers in the field of computer graphics, "A Characterization of Ten Hidden-Surface Algorithms" by Sutherland, Sproull, and Schumacker, published in 1974 [346]. Their 55-page paper is an incredibly thorough comparison of 10 different algorithms. What is interesting is that the algorithm described as "ridiculously expensive," the brute-force technique not even dignified with a researcher's name and mentioned only in the appendices, is what is now called the Z-buffer. This eleventh hidden surface technique won out because it was easy to implement in hardware and because memory densities went up and costs went down. The research done by Sutherland et al. was perfectly valid for its time. As conditions change, so do the algorithms. It will be exciting to see what happens in the next 25 years. How we will look back on this current era of rendering technology? No one knows, and each person can potentially have a significant effect on the way the future turns out. There is no one future, no course that must occur. You create it.

Appendix A
Some Linear Algebra

BOOK I.
DEFINITIONS.
   A point is that which has no part.
   A line is a breadthless length.
   The extremities of a line are points.
   A straight line is a line which lies evenly with the points
      on itself.

–The first four definitions from *Elements* by Euclid [98]

This appendix deals with the fundamental concepts of linear algebra that are of greatest use for computer graphics. Our presentation will not be as mathematically abstract and general as these kinds of descriptions often are, but will rather concentrate on what is relevant to our context. For the inexperienced reader, it can be seen as a short introduction to the topic, and for the more experienced one it may serve as a review, if needed.

We will start with an introduction to the Euclidean spaces. This may feel abstract at first, but in the section that follows, these concepts are connected to geometry, bases, and matrices. So bite the bullet during the first section, and reap the reward in the rest of the appendix, and in many of the other chapters of this book.

If you are uncertain about the notation used in this book, take a look at Section 1.2.

A.1   The Euclidean Space

The n-dimensional real Euclidean space is denoted $\mathbb{R}^n$. A vector $\mathbf{v}$ in this space is an n-tuple, that is, an ordered list of real numbers[1]:

$$\mathbf{v} \in \mathbb{R}^n \Longleftrightarrow \mathbf{v} = \begin{pmatrix} v_0 \\ v_1 \\ \vdots \\ v_{n-1} \end{pmatrix} \text{ with } v_i \in \mathbb{R}, \ i = 0, \ldots, n-1 \qquad (\text{A.1})$$

The vector can also be presented as a row vector, but most computer graphics book use column vectors, in what is called the column-major form. We call $v_0, \ldots, v_{n-1}$ the elements, the coefficients, or the components of the vector $\mathbf{v}$. All bold lower-case letters are vectors that belong to $\mathbb{R}^n$, and italicized lower-case letters are scalars that belong to $\mathbb{R}$. For vectors in Euclidean space there exist two operators, *addition* and *multiplication by a scalar*, which work as might be expected:

$$\mathbf{u} + \mathbf{v} = \begin{pmatrix} u_0 \\ u_1 \\ \vdots \\ u_{n-1} \end{pmatrix} + \begin{pmatrix} v_0 \\ v_1 \\ \vdots \\ v_{n-1} \end{pmatrix} = \begin{pmatrix} u_0 + v_0 \\ u_1 + v_1 \\ \vdots \\ u_{n-1} + v_{n-1} \end{pmatrix} \in \mathbb{R}^n \quad \textbf{(addition)}$$

$$(\text{A.2})$$

and

$$a\mathbf{u} = \begin{pmatrix} au_0 \\ au_1 \\ \vdots \\ au_{n-1} \end{pmatrix} \in \mathbb{R}^n \qquad \textbf{(multiplication by a scalar)} \qquad (\text{A.3})$$

The $\in \mathbb{R}^n$ simply means that addition and multiplication by a scalar yields vectors of the same space. As can be seen, addition is done componentwise, and multiplication is done by multiplying all elements in the vector with the scalar a.

---

[1]Note that the subscripts start at 0 and end at $n-1$, a numbering system which follows the indexing of arrays in many programming languages, such as C and C++. This makes it easier to convert from formula to code. Some computer graphics books and linear algebra books start at 1 and end at n.

Now we will present a series of rules that hold for the Euclidean space.[2] Addition of vectors in the Euclidean space also works as might be expected:

(i) $(\mathbf{u}+\mathbf{v})+\mathbf{w}=\mathbf{u}+(\mathbf{v}+\mathbf{w})$ **(associativity)**

(ii) $\mathbf{u}+\mathbf{v}=\mathbf{v}+\mathbf{u}$ **(commutativity)**

(A.4)

There is a unique vector, called the zero vector, which is $\mathbf{0}=(0,0,\ldots,0)$ with n zeros, such that:

(iii) $\mathbf{0}+\mathbf{v}=\mathbf{v}$ **(zero identity)** (A.5)

There is also a unique vector $-\mathbf{v}=(-v_0,-v_1,\ldots,-v_{n-1})$ such that:

(iv) $\mathbf{v}+(-\mathbf{v})=\mathbf{0}$ **(additive inverse)** (A.6)

Rules for multiplication by a scalar work as follows:

(i) $(ab)\mathbf{u}=a(b\mathbf{u})$

(ii) $(a+b)\mathbf{u}=a\mathbf{u}+b\mathbf{u}$ **(distributive law)**

(iii) $a(\mathbf{u}+\mathbf{v})=a\mathbf{u}+a\mathbf{v}$ **(distributive law)**

(iv) $1\mathbf{u}=\mathbf{u}$

(A.7)

For the Euclidean space we may also compute the *dot product*[3] of two vectors $\mathbf{u}$ and $\mathbf{v}$. The dot product is denoted $\mathbf{u}\cdot\mathbf{v}$, and its definition is shown below.

$$\mathbf{u}\cdot\mathbf{v}=\sum_{i=0}^{n-1}u_iv_i \quad \textbf{(dot product)} \qquad (A.8)$$

For the dot product we have the rules:

(i) $\mathbf{u}\cdot\mathbf{u}\geq 0$, with $\mathbf{u}\cdot\mathbf{u}=0$ if and only if $\mathbf{u}=(0,0,\ldots,0)=\mathbf{0}$

(ii) $(\mathbf{u}+\mathbf{v})\cdot\mathbf{w}=\mathbf{u}\cdot\mathbf{w}+\mathbf{v}\cdot\mathbf{w}$

(iii) $(a\mathbf{u})\cdot\mathbf{v}=a(\mathbf{u}\cdot\mathbf{v})$

(iv) $\mathbf{u}\cdot\mathbf{v}=\mathbf{v}\cdot\mathbf{u}$ **(commutativity)**

(v) $\mathbf{u}\cdot\mathbf{v}=0\iff\mathbf{u}\perp\mathbf{v}$

(A.9)

---

[2] Actually, these are the definition of the Euclidean space.
[3] Also called *inner (dot) product* or *scalar product*.

The last formula means that if the dot product is zero then the vectors are orthogonal (perpendicular). The norm of a vector, denoted $||\mathbf{u}||$, is a non-negative number that can be expressed using the dot product:

$$||\mathbf{u}|| = \sqrt{\mathbf{u} \cdot \mathbf{u}} = \sqrt{\left(\sum_{i=0}^{n-1} u_i^2\right)} \quad \textbf{(norm)} \qquad \text{(A.10)}$$

The following rules hold for the norm:

$(i) \quad ||\mathbf{u}|| = 0 \iff \mathbf{u} = (0, 0, \ldots, 0) = \mathbf{0}$

$(ii) \quad ||a\mathbf{u}|| = |a|\,||\mathbf{u}||$

$(iii) \quad ||\mathbf{u} + \mathbf{v}|| \leq ||\mathbf{u}|| + ||\mathbf{v}|| \qquad \textbf{(triangle inequality)}$

$(iv) \quad |\mathbf{u} \cdot \mathbf{v}| \leq ||\mathbf{u}||\,||\mathbf{v}|| \qquad \textbf{(Cauchy–Schwartz inequality))}$

$$\text{(A.11)}$$

The next section shows how we can use the theory in this section by interpreting everything geometrically.

A.2 Geometrical Interpretation

Here we will interpret the vectors (from previous section) geometrically. For this, we first need to introduce the concepts of *linear independence* and the *basis*.[4]

If the only scalars to satisfy Equation A.12 are $v_0 = v_1 = \ldots = v_{n-1} = 0$, then the vectors, $\mathbf{u}_0, \ldots \mathbf{u}_{n-1}$, are said to be linearly independent. Otherwise, the vectors are linearly dependent.

$$v_0\mathbf{u}_0 + \cdots + v_{n-1}\mathbf{u}_{n-1} = 0 \qquad \text{(A.12)}$$

For example, the vectors $\mathbf{u}_0 = (4, 3)$ and $\mathbf{u}_1 = (-8, -6)$ are *not* linearly independent, since $v_0 = 2$ and $v_1 = -1$ (among others) satisfy Equation A.12.

If a set of n vectors, $\mathbf{u}_0, \ldots, \mathbf{u}_{n-1} \in \mathbb{R}^n$, is linearly independent and any vector $\mathbf{v} \in \mathbb{R}^n$ can be written as

$$\mathbf{v} = \sum_{i=0}^{n-1} v_i\mathbf{u}_i \qquad \text{(A.13)}$$

---

[4]Note that the concepts of linear independence and the basis can be used without any geometry.

then the vectors $\mathbf{u}_0, \ldots, \mathbf{u}_{n-1}$ are said to span the Euclidean space $\mathbb{R}^n$. If in addition, $v_0, \ldots, v_{n-1}$ are uniquely determined by $\mathbf{v}$ for all $\mathbf{v} \in \mathbb{R}^n$, then $\mathbf{u}_0, \ldots, \mathbf{u}_{n-1}$ is called a basis of $\mathbb{R}^n$. What this means is that every vector can be described uniquely by n scalars $(v_0, v_1, \ldots, v_{n-1})$ and the basis vectors $\mathbf{u}_0, \ldots, \mathbf{u}_{n-1}$. As a consequence, basis vectors can never be parallel (because they would then be linearly dependent). The dimension of the space is n, if n is the largest number of linearly independent vectors in the space.

An example of a linearly independent basis is $\mathbf{u}_0 = (4, 3)$ and $\mathbf{u}_1 = (2, 6)$. This spans the Euclidean space, as any vector can be expressed as a unique combination of these two vectors. For example, $(-5, -6)$ is described by $v_0 = -1$ and $v_1 = -0.5$ and no other combinations of v_0 and v_1.

Now, if the basis is implicit (i.e., does not need to be stated), then $\mathbf{v}$ can be described as:

$$\mathbf{v} = \begin{pmatrix} v_0 \\ v_1 \\ \vdots \\ v_{n-1} \end{pmatrix} \tag{A.14}$$

which is exactly the same vector description as in Expression A.1, and so this is the one-to-one mapping of the vectors in Section A.1 onto geometrical vectors.[5] An illustration of a three-dimensional vector is shown in Figure A.1. A vector $\mathbf{v}$ can either be interpreted as a point in space or as a directed line segment (i.e., a direction vector). All rules from Section A.1 apply in the geometrical sense, too. For example, the addition and the scaling operators from Equation A.2 are visualized in Figure A.2. A basis can also have different "handedness." A three-dimensional, right-handed basis is one in which the x-axis is along the

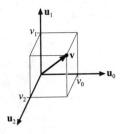

Figure A.1. A three-dimensional vector $\mathbf{v} = (v_0, v_1, v_2)$ expressed in the basis formed by $\mathbf{u}_0, \mathbf{u}_1, \mathbf{u}_2$ in $\mathbb{R}^3$. Note that this is a right-handed system.

---

[5]In mathematics this is called an isomorphism.

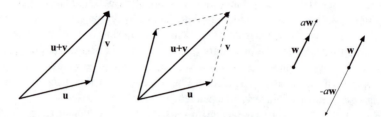

Figure A.2. Vector-vector addition is shown in the two figures on the left. They are called the head-to-tail axiom and the parallelogram rule. The two rightmost figures show scalar-vector multiplication for a positive and a negative scalar, a and $-a$, respectively.

thumb, the y-axis is along index-finger, and the z-axis is along the middle finger. If this is done with the left hand, a left-handed basis is obtained. See page 407 for a more formal definition of "handedness."

The norm of a vector (see Equation A.10) can be thought of as the length of the vector. To create a vector of unit length, i.e., of length one, the vector has to be normalized. This can be done by dividing by the length of the vector: $\mathbf{q} = \frac{1}{||\mathbf{p}||}\mathbf{p}$, where $\mathbf{q}$ is the normalized vector, which also is called a unit vector.

For $\mathbb{R}^2$ and $\mathbb{R}^3$, or two- and three-dimensional space, the dot product can also be expressed as below, which is equivalent to Expression A.8.

$$\mathbf{u} \cdot \mathbf{v} = ||\mathbf{u}||\ ||\mathbf{v}|| \cos\phi \quad \textbf{(dot product)} \qquad (A.15)$$

Here ϕ (shown at the left in Figure A.3) is the smallest angle between $\mathbf{u}$ and $\mathbf{v}$. From the sign of the dot product several conclusions can be drawn. First,

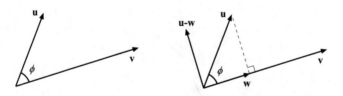

Figure A.3. The left figure shows the notation and geometric situation for the dot product. In the rightmost figure orthographic projection is shown. The vector $\mathbf{u}$ is orthogonally (perpendicularly) projected onto $\mathbf{v}$ to yield $\mathbf{w}$.

$\mathbf{u} \cdot \mathbf{v} = 0 \Leftrightarrow \mathbf{u} \perp \mathbf{v}$, i.e., $\mathbf{u}$ and $\mathbf{v}$ are orthogonal (perpendicular) if their dot product is zero. Second, if $\mathbf{u} \cdot \mathbf{v} > 0$, then it is easily seen that $0 < \phi < \frac{\pi}{2}$, and likewise if $\mathbf{u} \cdot \mathbf{v} < 0$ then $\frac{\pi}{2} < \phi \leq \pi$.

Now we will go back to the study of basis for a while, and introduce a special kind of basis that is said to be *orthonormal*. For such a basis, consisting of the basis vectors $\mathbf{u}_0, \ldots, \mathbf{u}_{n-1}$, the following must hold:

$$\mathbf{u}_i \cdot \mathbf{u}_j = \begin{cases} 0, & i \neq j \\ 1, & i = j \end{cases} \tag{A.16}$$

This means that every basis vector must have a length of one, i.e., $\|\mathbf{u}_i\| = 1$, and also that each pair of basis vectors must be orthogonal, i.e., the angle between them must be $\pi/2$ radians (90°). In this book, we will mostly use two- and three-dimensional orthonormal bases. If the basis vectors are mutually perpendicular, but not of unit length, then the basis is called *orthogonal*.

Let $\mathbf{p} = (p_0, \ldots, p_{n-1})$, then for an orthonormal basis it can also be shown that $p_i = \mathbf{p} \cdot \mathbf{u}_i$. This means that if you have a vector $\mathbf{p}$ and a basis (with the basis vectors $\mathbf{u}_0, \ldots, \mathbf{u}_{n-1}$), then you can easily get the elements of that vector in that basis by taking the dot product between the vector and each of the basis vectors. The most common basis is called the standard basis, where the basis vectors are denoted $\mathbf{e}_i$. The ith basis vector has zeroes everywhere except in position i, which holds a one. For three dimensions, this means $\mathbf{e}_0 = (1, 0, 0)^T$, $\mathbf{e}_1 = (0, 1, 0)^T$, and $\mathbf{e}_2 = (0, 0, 1)^T$. We also denote these vectors $\mathbf{e}_x$, $\mathbf{e}_y$, and $\mathbf{e}_z$, since they are what we normally call the x-, the y-, and the z-axes.

A very useful property of the dot product is that it can be used to project a vector orthogonally onto another vector. This orthogonal projection (vector), $\mathbf{w}$, of a vector $\mathbf{u}$ onto a vector $\mathbf{v}$ is depicted on the right in Figure A.3.

For arbitrary vectors $\mathbf{u}$ and $\mathbf{v}$, $\mathbf{w}$ is determined by

$$\mathbf{w} = \left(\frac{\mathbf{u} \cdot \mathbf{v}}{\|\mathbf{v}\|^2} \right) \mathbf{v} = \left(\frac{\mathbf{u} \cdot \mathbf{v}}{\mathbf{v} \cdot \mathbf{v}} \right) \mathbf{v} = t\mathbf{v}, \tag{A.17}$$

where t is a scalar. The reader is encouraged to verify that Expression A.17 is indeed correct, which is quite easily done by inspection and the use of Equation A.15. The projection also gives us an orthogonal decomposition of $\mathbf{u}$, which is divided into two parts, $\mathbf{w}$ and $(\mathbf{u} - \mathbf{w})$. It can be shown that $\mathbf{w} \perp (\mathbf{u} - \mathbf{w})$, and of course $\mathbf{u} = \mathbf{w} + (\mathbf{u} - \mathbf{w})$ holds. An additional observation is that if $\mathbf{v}$ is normalized, then the projection is $\mathbf{w} = (\mathbf{u} \cdot \mathbf{v})\mathbf{v}$. This means that $\|\mathbf{w}\| = |\mathbf{u} \cdot \mathbf{v}|$, i.e., the length of $\mathbf{w}$ is the absolute value of the dot product between $\mathbf{u}$ and $\mathbf{v}$.

Cross Product

The cross product, also called the vector product, and the previously introduced dot product are two very important operations on vectors.

Figure A.4. The geometry involved in the cross product.

The cross product in $\mathbb{R}^3$ of two vectors, **u** and **v**, denoted by $\mathbf{w} = \mathbf{u} \times \mathbf{v}$, is defined by a unique vector **w** with the following properties:

1. $||\mathbf{w}|| = ||\mathbf{u} \times \mathbf{v}|| = ||\mathbf{u}||\,||\mathbf{v}|| \sin \phi$, where ϕ is, again, the smallest angle between **u** and **v**. See Figure A.4.

2. $\mathbf{w} \perp \mathbf{u}$ and $\mathbf{w} \perp \mathbf{v}$.

3. **u**, **v**, **w** form a right-handed system.

From this definition it is deduced that $\mathbf{u} \times \mathbf{v} = \mathbf{0}$ if and only if $\mathbf{u} \parallel \mathbf{v}$ (i.e., **u** and **v** are parallel), since then $\sin \phi = 0$. The cross product also comes equipped with the following laws of calculation, among others:

$\mathbf{u} \times \mathbf{v} = -\mathbf{v} \times \mathbf{u}$ **(anti-commutativity)**

$(a\mathbf{u} + b\mathbf{v}) \times \mathbf{w} = a(\mathbf{u} \times \mathbf{w}) + b(\mathbf{v} \times \mathbf{w})$ **(linearity)**

$$\left.\begin{array}{l} (\mathbf{u} \times \mathbf{v}) \cdot \mathbf{w} = (\mathbf{v} \times \mathbf{w}) \cdot \mathbf{u} = \\ (\mathbf{w} \times \mathbf{u}) \cdot \mathbf{v} = -(\mathbf{v} \times \mathbf{u}) \cdot \mathbf{w} = \\ -(\mathbf{u} \times \mathbf{w}) \cdot \mathbf{v} = -(\mathbf{w} \times \mathbf{v}) \cdot \mathbf{u} \end{array}\right\} \quad \text{(A.18)}$$

(scalar triple product)

$\mathbf{u} \times (\mathbf{v} \times \mathbf{w}) = (\mathbf{u} \cdot \mathbf{w})\mathbf{v} - (\mathbf{u} \cdot \mathbf{v})\mathbf{w}$ **(vector triple product)**

From these laws it is obvious that the order of the operands is crucial in getting correct results from the calculations.

For three-dimensional vectors, **u** and **v**, in an orthonormal basis, the cross product is computed according to Equation A.19.

$$\mathbf{w} = \left(\begin{array}{c} w_x \\ w_y \\ w_z \end{array} \right) = \mathbf{u} \times \mathbf{v} = \left(\begin{array}{c} u_y v_z - u_z v_y \\ u_z v_x - u_x v_z \\ u_x v_y - u_y v_x \end{array} \right) \quad \text{(A.19)}$$

A method called Sarrus's scheme, which is simple to remember, can be used to derive this formula:

$$
\begin{array}{cccccc}
+ & + & + & & - & - & - \\
\searrow & \searrow & \searrow & & \swarrow & \swarrow & \swarrow \\
\mathbf{e}_x & \mathbf{e}_y & \mathbf{e}_z & \mathbf{e}_x & \mathbf{e}_y & \mathbf{e}_z \\
u_x & u_y & u_z & u_x & u_y & u_z \\
v_x & v_y & v_z & v_x & v_y & v_z
\end{array}
\qquad \text{(A.20)}
$$

To use the scheme, follow the diagonal arrows, and for each arrow generate a term by multiplying the elements along the direction of the arrow and giving the product the sign associated with that arrow. The result, shown below, is the formula presented above.

$$
\mathbf{u} \times \mathbf{v} = +\mathbf{e}_x(u_y v_z) + \mathbf{e}_y(u_z v_x) + \mathbf{e}_z(u_x v_y) - \mathbf{e}_x(u_z v_y) - \mathbf{e}_y(u_x v_z) - \mathbf{e}_z(u_y v_x)
$$

A.3   Matrices

This section presents the definitions concerning matrices and some common, useful operations on them. Even though this presentation is (mostly) for arbitrarily sized matrices, square matrices of the sizes 2×2, 3×3, and 4×4 will be used in the chapters of this book. Note that Chapter 3 deals with transforms represented by matrices.

A.3.1   Definitions and Operations

A matrix, $\mathbf{M}$, can be used as a tool for manipulating vectors and points. $\mathbf{M}$ is described by $p \times q$ scalars (complex numbers are an alternative but not relevant here), m_{ij}, $0 \leq i < p - 1$, $0 \leq j < q - 1$, ordered in a rectangular fashion (with p rows and q columns) as shown in Equation A.21.

$$
\mathbf{M} = \begin{pmatrix}
m_{00} & m_{01} & \cdots & m_{0,q-1} \\
m_{10} & m_{11} & \cdots & m_{1,q-1} \\
\vdots & \vdots & \ddots & \vdots \\
m_{p-1,0} & m_{p-1,1} & \cdots & m_{p-1,q-1}
\end{pmatrix} = [m_{ij}]
\qquad \text{(A.21)}
$$

The notation $[m_{ij}]$ will be used in the equations below and is merely a shorter way of describing a matrix. There is a special matrix called the *unit matrix*, $\mathbf{I}$,

which contains ones in the diagonal and zeros elsewhere. This is also called
the *identity matrix*. Equation A.22 shows its general appearance. This is the
matrix-form counterpart of the scalar number one.

$$
\mathbf{I} = \begin{pmatrix}
1 & 0 & 0 & \cdots & 0 & 0 \\
0 & 1 & 0 & \cdots & 0 & 0 \\
\vdots & \vdots & \vdots & \ddots & \vdots & \vdots \\
0 & 0 & 0 & \cdots & 1 & 0 \\
0 & 0 & 0 & \cdots & 0 & 1
\end{pmatrix}
\tag{A.22}
$$

Next the most ordinary operations on matrices will be reviewed.

Matrix-Matrix Addition

Adding two matrices, say $\mathbf{M}$ and $\mathbf{N}$, is only possible for equal-sized matrices
and is defined as

$$
\mathbf{M} + \mathbf{N} = [m_{ij}] + [n_{ij}] = [m_{ij} + n_{ij}]
\tag{A.23}
$$

that is, componentwise addition, very similar to vector-vector addition. The
resulting matrix is of the same size as the operands. The following operations are
valid for matrix-matrix addition: i) $(\mathbf{L}+\mathbf{M})+\mathbf{N} = \mathbf{L}+(\mathbf{M}+\mathbf{N})$, ii) $\mathbf{M}+\mathbf{N} = \mathbf{N}+\mathbf{M}$, iii) $\mathbf{M}+\mathbf{0} = \mathbf{M}$, iv) $\mathbf{M}-\mathbf{M} = \mathbf{0}$, which are all very easy to prove.

Scalar-Matrix Multiplication

A scalar a and a matrix, $\mathbf{M}$, can be multiplied to form a new matrix of the same
size as $\mathbf{M}$, which is computed by $\mathbf{T} = a\mathbf{M} = [am_{ij}]$. $\mathbf{T}$ and $\mathbf{M}$ are of the same
size, and these trivial rules apply: i) $0\mathbf{M} = \mathbf{0}$, ii) $1\mathbf{M} = \mathbf{M}$, iii) $a(b\mathbf{M}) = (ab)\mathbf{M}$, iv) $a\mathbf{0} = \mathbf{0}$, v) $(a+b)\mathbf{M} = a\mathbf{M}+b\mathbf{M}$, vi) $a(\mathbf{M}+\mathbf{N}) = a\mathbf{M}+a\mathbf{N}$.

Transpose of a Matrix

$\mathbf{M}^T$ is the notation for the transpose of $\mathbf{M} = [m_{ij}]$, and the definition is $\mathbf{M}^T = [m_{ji}]$, i.e., the columns become rows and the rows become columns. For the
transpose operator, we have: i) $(a\mathbf{M})^T = a\mathbf{M}^T$, ii) $(\mathbf{M}+\mathbf{N})^T = \mathbf{M}^T+\mathbf{N}^T$,
iii) $(\mathbf{M}^T)^T = \mathbf{M}$, iv) $(\mathbf{MN})^T = \mathbf{N}^T\mathbf{M}^T$.

Trace of a Matrix

The trace of a matrix, denoted $\operatorname{tr}(\mathbf{M})$, is simply the sum of the diagonal elements
of a square matrix, as shown below.

$$
\operatorname{tr}(\mathbf{M}) = \sum_{i=0}^{n-1} m_{ii}
\tag{A.24}
$$

Matrix-Matrix Multiplication

This operation, denoted $\mathbf{MN}$ between $\mathbf{M}$ and $\mathbf{N}$, is only defined if $\mathbf{M}$ is of size $p \times q$ and $\mathbf{N}$ is of size $q \times r$, in which case the result, $\mathbf{T}$, becomes a $p \times r$ sized matrix. Mathematically, the operation is as shown below, for the matrices named above.

$$\mathbf{T} = \mathbf{MN} = \begin{pmatrix} m_{00} & \cdots & m_{0,q-1} \\ \vdots & \ddots & \vdots \\ m_{p-1,0} & \cdots & m_{p-1,q-1} \end{pmatrix} \begin{pmatrix} n_{00} & \cdots & n_{0,r-1} \\ \vdots & \ddots & \vdots \\ n_{q-1,0} & \cdots & n_{q-1,r-1} \end{pmatrix} =$$

$$= \begin{pmatrix} \sum_{i=0}^{q-1} m_{0,i} n_{i,0} & \cdots & \sum_{i=0}^{q-1} m_{0,i} n_{i,r-1} \\ \vdots & \ddots & \vdots \\ \sum_{i=0}^{q-1} m_{p-1,i} n_{i,0} & \cdots & \sum_{i=0}^{q-1} m_{p-1,i} n_{i,r-1} \end{pmatrix}$$

$$\text{(A.25)}$$

In other words, each row of $\mathbf{M}$ and column of $\mathbf{N}$ are combined using a dot product, and the result placed in the corresponding row and column element. The elements of $\mathbf{T}$ are computed as $t_{ij} = \sum_{k=0}^{q-1} m_{i,k} n_{k,j}$, which can also be expressed as $t_{ij} = \mathbf{m}_{i,} \cdot \mathbf{n}_{,j}$, that is, using the dot product and the matrix-vector indexing from Section 1.2.1. Note also that an $n \times 1$ matrix, $\mathbf{S} = \begin{pmatrix} s_{00} & s_{10} & \cdots & s_{n-1,0} \end{pmatrix}^T$, is very similar to an n-tuple vector. If seen as such, then matrix-vector multiplication, between $\mathbf{M}$ ($p \times q$) and $\mathbf{v}$ (q-tuple), can be derived from the definition of matrix-matrix multiplication. This is shown in Equation A.26, resulting in a new vector, $\mathbf{w}$.

$$\mathbf{w} = \mathbf{Mv} = \begin{pmatrix} m_{00} & \cdots & m_{0,q-1} \\ \vdots & \ddots & \vdots \\ m_{p-1,0} & \cdots & m_{p-1,q-1} \end{pmatrix} \begin{pmatrix} v_0 \\ \vdots \\ v_{p-1} \end{pmatrix} =$$

$$= \begin{pmatrix} \sum_{k=0}^{q-1} m_{0,k} v_k \\ \vdots \\ \sum_{k=0}^{q-1} m_{p-1,k} v_k \end{pmatrix} = \begin{pmatrix} \mathbf{m}_{0,} \cdot \mathbf{v} \\ \vdots \\ \mathbf{m}_{p-1,} \cdot \mathbf{v} \end{pmatrix} = \begin{pmatrix} w_0 \\ \vdots \\ w_{p-1} \end{pmatrix}$$

$$\text{(A.26)}$$

These three rules hold for the matrix-matrix multiplication: $i)$ $(\mathbf{LM})\mathbf{N} = \mathbf{L}(\mathbf{MN})$, $ii)$ $(\mathbf{L} + \mathbf{M})\mathbf{N} = \mathbf{LN} + \mathbf{MN}$, $iii)$ $\mathbf{MI} = \mathbf{IM} = \mathbf{M}$. Also, in general $\mathbf{MN} \neq \mathbf{NM}$, if the dimensions of the matrices are the same. This means that some pairs of matrices do commute, but usually they do not.

Determinant of a Matrix

The determinant is only defined for square matrices, and in the general case, the definition is recursive or defined via permutations [226]. Here the focus will be on determinants for 2×2 and 3×3 matrices, since those are the only ones usually needed in computer graphics.

The determinant of $\mathbf{M}$, written $|\mathbf{M}|$, for these matrices appears in Equation A.27 and A.28.

$$|\mathbf{M}| = \begin{vmatrix} m_{00} & m_{01} \\ m_{10} & m_{11} \end{vmatrix} = m_{00}m_{11} - m_{01}m_{10} \qquad (A.27)$$

$$|\mathbf{M}| = \begin{vmatrix} m_{00} & m_{01} & m_{02} \\ m_{10} & m_{11} & m_{12} \\ m_{20} & m_{21} & m_{22} \end{vmatrix} = \qquad (A.28)$$

$$= m_{00}m_{11}m_{22} + m_{01}m_{12}m_{20} + m_{02}m_{10}m_{21} -$$
$$- m_{02}m_{11}m_{20} - m_{01}m_{10}m_{22} - m_{00}m_{12}m_{21}$$

In these two equations, a certain pattern can be distinguished: the positive terms are the elements multiplied in the diagonals from the top downwards to the right and the negative terms are the elements in the diagonals from the top downwards to the left, where a diagonal continues on the opposite side if an edge is crossed. Note that if the top row in $\mathbf{M}$ is replaced by $\mathbf{e}_x \ \mathbf{e}_y \ \mathbf{e}_z$, the middle row by $u_x \ u_y \ u_z$, and the bottom row by $v_x \ v_y \ v_z$, the cross product $\mathbf{u} \times \mathbf{v}$ is obtained according to Sarrus's scheme (see Section A.2 on the cross product).

Another useful way to compute the determinant for 3×3 matrices is to use the dot and the cross product as in Equation A.29, which is reminiscent of the column vector indexing introduced in Section 1.2.1.

$$|\mathbf{M}| = |\mathbf{m}_{,0} \ \mathbf{m}_{,1} \ \mathbf{m}_{,2}| = |\mathbf{m}_x \ \mathbf{m}_y \ \mathbf{m}_z| = (\mathbf{m}_x \times \mathbf{m}_y) \cdot \mathbf{m}_z \qquad (A.29)$$

The following notation is also used for determinants:

$$|\mathbf{M}| = \det(\mathbf{M}) = \det(\mathbf{m}_x, \mathbf{m}_y, \mathbf{m}_z) \qquad (A.30)$$

Observe that the scalar triple product from Equation A.18 can be applied to Equation A.29; that is, if the vectors are rotated, the determinant remains unchanged, but changing the places of two vectors will change the sign of the determinant.

If $n \times n$ is the size of $\mathbf{M}$, then the following apply to determinant calculations: $i)$ $|\mathbf{M}^{-1}| = 1/|\mathbf{M}|$, $ii)$ $|\mathbf{MN}| = |\mathbf{M}| \, |\mathbf{N}|$, $iii)$ $|a\mathbf{M}| = a^n|\mathbf{M}|$, $iv)$ $|\mathbf{M}^T| = |\mathbf{M}|$. Also, if all elements of a row (or a column) are multiplied by a scalar,

a, then $a|\mathbf{M}|$ is obtained, and if two rows (or columns) coincide (i.e., the cross product between them is zero), then $|\mathbf{M}| = 0$. The same result is obtained if any row or column is composed entirely of zeroes.

The orientation of a basis can be determined via determinants. A basis is said to form a right-handed system, also called a positively oriented basis, if its determinant is positive. The standard basis has this property, since $|\mathbf{e}_x \ \mathbf{e}_y \ \mathbf{e}_z| = (\mathbf{e}_x \times \mathbf{e}_y) \cdot \mathbf{e}_z = (0 \ 0 \ 1)^T \cdot \mathbf{e}_z = \mathbf{e}_z \cdot \mathbf{e}_z = 1 > 0$. If the determinant is negative, the basis is called negatively oriented or is said to be forming a left-handed system.

Some geometrical interpretations of the determinant are given in Section A.5.

Adjoints

The adjoint[6] is another form of a matrix that can sometimes be useful, as seen in Section 3.1.7 and below, where the inverse of a matrix is computed. We start by defining the subdeterminant (also called cofactor) $d_{ij}^{\mathbf{M}}$ of an $n \times n$ matrix $\mathbf{M}$ as the determinant that is obtained by deleting row i and column j and then taking the determinant of the resulting $(n-1) \times (n-1)$ matrix. An example of computing the subdeterminant $d_{02}^{\mathbf{M}}$ of a 3×3 matrix is shown in Equation A.31.

$$d_{02}^{\mathbf{M}} = \begin{vmatrix} m_{10} & m_{11} \\ m_{20} & m_{21} \end{vmatrix} \tag{A.31}$$

For a 3×3 matrix the adjoint is then

$$\text{adj}(\mathbf{M}) = \begin{pmatrix} d_{00} & -d_{10} & d_{20} \\ -d_{01} & d_{11} & -d_{21} \\ d_{02} & -d_{12} & d_{22} \end{pmatrix} \tag{A.32}$$

where we have left out the superscript $\mathbf{M}$ of the subdeterminants for clarity. Note the signs and the order in which the subdeterminants appear. If we want to compute the adjoint $\mathbf{A}$ of an arbitrary sized matrix $\mathbf{M}$ then the component at position (i, j) is:

$$a_{ij} = (-1)^{(i+j)} d_{ji}^{\mathbf{M}} \tag{A.33}$$

Inverse of a Matrix

The multiplicative inverse of a matrix, $\mathbf{M}$, denoted $\mathbf{M}^{-1}$, which is dealt with here, only exists for square matrices with $|\mathbf{M}| \neq 0$. If all elements of the matrix

---

[6]Sometimes the adjoint has another definition than the one presented here, i.e., the adjoint of a matrix $\mathbf{M} = [m_{ij}]$ is denoted $\mathbf{M}^* = [\overline{m_{ji}}]$, where $\overline{m_{ji}}$ is the complex conjugate.

under consideration are real scalars, then it suffices to show that $\mathbf{MN} = \mathbf{I}$ and $\mathbf{NM} = \mathbf{I}$, where then $\mathbf{N} = \mathbf{M}^{-1}$. The problem can also be stated thus: if $\mathbf{u} = \mathbf{Mv}$ and a matrix $\mathbf{N}$ exists such that $\mathbf{v} = \mathbf{Nu}$, then $\mathbf{N} = \mathbf{M}^{-1}$.

The inverse of a matrix can be computed either implicitly or explicitly. If the inverse is to be used several times, then it is more economical to compute $\mathbf{M}^{-1}$ explicitly, i.e., to get a representation of the inverse as an array of $n \times n$ real numbers. On the other hand, if only a linear system of the type $\mathbf{u} = \mathbf{Mv}$ needs to be solved (for $\mathbf{v}$), then an implicit method, like *Cramer's rule*, can be used. For a linear system of the type $\mathbf{Mv} = \mathbf{0}$, $|\mathbf{M}| = 0$ is a requirement if there is to be a solution, $\mathbf{v}$.

Using Cramer's rule to solve $\mathbf{u} = \mathbf{Mv}$ gives $\mathbf{v} = \mathbf{M}^{-1}\mathbf{u}$, but not $\mathbf{M}^{-1}$ explicitly. Equation A.34 shows the general solution for the elements of $\mathbf{v}$.

$$v_i = \frac{d_i}{|\mathbf{M}|}$$

(A.34)

$$d_i = |\mathbf{m}_{,0} \quad \mathbf{m}_{,1} \quad \ldots \quad \mathbf{m}_{,i-1} \quad \mathbf{u} \quad \mathbf{m}_{,i+1} \quad \ldots \quad \mathbf{m}_{,n-1}|$$

The terms d_i are thus computed as $|\mathbf{M}|$, but column i is replaced by $\mathbf{u}$. For a 3×3 system the solution obtained by Cramer's rule is presented below.

$$\mathbf{v} = \begin{pmatrix} v_x \\ v_y \\ v_z \end{pmatrix} = \frac{1}{|\mathbf{M}|} \begin{pmatrix} \det(\mathbf{u}, \mathbf{m}_y, \mathbf{m}_z) \\ \det(\mathbf{m}_x, \mathbf{u}, \mathbf{m}_z) \\ \det(\mathbf{m}_x, \mathbf{m}_y, \mathbf{u}) \end{pmatrix}$$

(A.35)

Many terms in this equation can be factorized using the scalar triple product rule and then reused for faster calculation. For example, this is done in Section 10.5 when computing the intersection between a ray and a triangle.

For a 2×2 matrix, $\mathbf{M}$, the explicit solution is given by Equation A.36, and as can be seen, it is very simple to implement, since $|\mathbf{M}| = m_{00}m_{11} - m_{01}m_{10}$.

$$\mathbf{M}^{-1} = \frac{1}{|\mathbf{M}|} \begin{pmatrix} m_{11} & -m_{01} \\ -m_{10} & m_{00} \end{pmatrix}$$

(A.36)

However, for larger sizes there are no such formulae, and Cramer's rule also becomes infeasible for matrices larger than 3×3, or perhaps 4×4. Gaussian elimination[7] is then the method of preference, and it can be used to solve for $\mathbf{u} = \mathbf{Mv} \Rightarrow \mathbf{v} = \mathbf{M}^{-1}\mathbf{u}$—that is, an implicit solution, as is the case for Cramer's rule. But Gaussian elimination can also be used to compute the matrix

---

[7]A discussion of Gaussian elimination is beyond the scope of this text, but can be found in virtually any book on linear algebra [225, 226].

M^{-1} explicitly. Consider the system in Equation A.37, where u and v are arbitrary vectors of the same dimension as M and I (the identity matrix).

$$Mu = Iv \qquad (A.37)$$

Performing Gaussian elimination on this system until M has been transformed into the identity matrix I means that the right side identity matrix has become the inverse M^{-1}. Thus, u and v are in fact not of any particular use; they are merely means for expressing Equation A.37 in a mathematically sound way.

For the general case, the adjoint from the previous section can be used:

$$M^{-1} = \frac{1}{|M|}\text{adj}(M) \qquad (A.38)$$

Some important rules of computation for the inverse of matrices are:
$i)$ $(M^{-1})^T = (M^T)^{-1}$, $\quad ii)$ $(MN)^{-1} = N^{-1}M^{-1}$.

Eigenvalue and Eigenvector Computation

The solution to the *eigenvalue* problem has a large range of uses. For example, one application area is the computation of tight bounding volumes (see Section 11.3). The problem is stated as follows:

$$Ax = \lambda x \qquad (A.39)$$

where λ is a scalar.[8] The matrix A has to be square (say of size $n \times n$), and $x \neq 0$, then, if x fulfills the above equation, x is said to be an *eigenvector* to A, and λ is its belonging *eigenvalue*. Rearranging the terms of Equation A.39 yields Equation A.40.

$$(\lambda I - A)x = 0 \qquad (A.40)$$

This equation has a solution if and only if $p_A(\lambda) = \det(\lambda I - A) = 0$, where the function $p_A(\lambda)$ is called the characteristic polynomial to A. The eigenvalues, $\lambda_0, \ldots, \lambda_{n_1}$, are thus solutions to $p_A(\lambda) = 0$. Focus for a while on a particular eigenvalue λ_i to A. Then x_i is its corresponding eigenvector if $(\lambda_i I - A)x_i = 0$, which means that once the eigenvalues have been found, the eigenvectors can be found via Gaussian elimination.

Some theoretical results of great use are: $i)$ $\text{tr}(A) = \sum_{i=0}^{n-1} a_{ii} = \sum_{i=0}^{n-1} \lambda_i$, $ii)$ $\det(A) = \prod_{i=0}^{n-1} \lambda_i$, $\quad iii)$ if A is real (consists of only real values) and is symmetric, i.e., $A = A^T$, then its eigenvalues are real and the different eigenvectors are orthogonal.

---

[8]We use λ (even though this is not consistent with our notation) because that is what most texts use.

Orthogonal Matrices

Here we will shed some light on the concept of an orthogonal matrix, its properties, and its characteristics. A square matrix, $\mathbf{M}$, with only real elements is orthogonal if and only if $\mathbf{M}\mathbf{M}^T = \mathbf{M}^T\mathbf{M} = \mathbf{I}$. That is, when multiplied by its transpose it yields the identity matrix.

The orthogonality of a matrix, $\mathbf{M}$, has some significant implications such as: $i)$ $|\mathbf{M}| = \pm 1$, $ii)$ $\mathbf{M}^{-1} = \mathbf{M}^T$, $iii)$ $\mathbf{M}^T$ is also orthogonal, $iv)$ $||\mathbf{M}\mathbf{u}|| = ||\mathbf{u}||$, $v)$ $\mathbf{M}\mathbf{u} \perp \mathbf{M}\mathbf{v} \Leftrightarrow \mathbf{u} \perp \mathbf{v}$, $vi)$ if $\mathbf{M}$ and $\mathbf{N}$ are orthogonal, so is $\mathbf{M}\mathbf{N}$.

The standard basis is orthonormal because the basis vectors are mutually orthogonal and of length one. Using the standard basis as a matrix, we can show that the matrix is orthogonal[9]: $\mathbf{E} = (\mathbf{e}_x \ \mathbf{e}_y \ \mathbf{e}_z) = \mathbf{I}$, and $\mathbf{I}^T\mathbf{I} = \mathbf{I}$.

To clear up some possible confusion, an orthogonal matrix is not the same as an orthogonal vector set (basis). A set of vectors may be mutually perpendicular, and so be called an orthogonal vector set. But, if these are bound together as a set of row or column vectors making a matrix, this does not automatically make the matrix orthogonal. An orthogonal matrix's transpose must be its inverse. An orthonormal vector set (basis), on the other hand, always forms an orthogonal matrix if the vectors are inserted into the matrix as a set of rows or columns. A better term for an orthogonal matrix would be an orthonormal matrix, since it is always composed of an orthonormal basis, but even mathematics is not always logical.

A.3.2   Change of Base

Assume we have a vector, $\mathbf{v}$, in the standard basis (see Section 1.2.1), described by the coordinate axes $\mathbf{e}_x$, $\mathbf{e}_y$, and $\mathbf{e}_z$. Furthermore, we have another coordinate system described by the arbitrary basis vectors $\mathbf{f}_x$, $\mathbf{f}_y$, and $\mathbf{f}_z$ (which must be non-coplanar, i.e., $|\mathbf{f}_x \ \mathbf{f}_y \ \mathbf{f}_z| \neq 0$). How can $\mathbf{v}$ be expressed uniquely in the basis described by $\mathbf{f}_x$, $\mathbf{f}_y$, and $\mathbf{f}_z$? The solution is [225]:

$$\mathbf{F}\mathbf{w} = \left(\ \mathbf{f}_x \ \ \mathbf{f}_y \ \ \mathbf{f}_z \ \right)\mathbf{w} = \mathbf{v}$$
$$\Longleftrightarrow$$
$$\mathbf{w} = \mathbf{F}^{-1}\mathbf{v} \tag{A.41}$$

where $\mathbf{w}$ is $\mathbf{v}$ expressed in the new basis, described by $\mathbf{F}$.

A special situation occurs if the matrix $\mathbf{F}$ is orthogonal, which implies that the inverse is easily obtained by $\mathbf{F}^{-1} = \mathbf{F}^T$. Therefore Equation A.41 simplifies

---

[9]Note that the basis is orthonormal, but the matrix is orthogonal, though they mean the same thing.

to Equation A.42.

$$\mathbf{w} = \mathbf{F}^T \mathbf{v} = \begin{pmatrix} \mathbf{f}_x^T \\ \mathbf{f}_y^T \\ \mathbf{f}_z^T \end{pmatrix} \mathbf{v} \qquad (A.42)$$

Orthogonal coordinate system changes are the most common ones in the context of computer graphics.

A.4 Homogeneous Notation

This section is probably the most important in this chapter, since it influences many areas of computer graphics and is almost never treated in a common linear algebra book.

A point describes a location in space, while a vector describes a direction and has no location. Using 3×3 matrices (or 2×2 for two dimensions), it is possible to perform linear transformations such as rotations, scalings, and shears on coordinates. However, translation cannot be performed using such matrices. This lack is unimportant for vectors, for which translation has no meaning, but translation is meaningful for points.

Homogeneous notation is useful for transforming both vectors and points, and includes the ability to perform translation only on points. It augments 3×3 matrices to the size of 4×4, and three-dimensional points and vectors get one more element. So a homogeneous vector is $\mathbf{p} = (p_x, p_y, p_z, p_w)^T$. As will soon be made clear, $p_w = 1$ for points, and $p_w = 0$ for vectors. For projections other values can be used for p_w (see Section 3.5).

Equation A.43 shows how a 3×3 matrix, $\mathbf{M}$, is augmented (in the simplest case) into the homogeneous form.

$$\mathbf{M}_{4 \times 4} = \begin{pmatrix} m_{00} & m_{01} & m_{02} & 0 \\ m_{10} & m_{11} & m_{12} & 0 \\ m_{20} & m_{21} & m_{22} & 0 \\ 0 & 0 & 0 & 1 \end{pmatrix} \qquad (A.43)$$

Rotation, scaling, and shear matrices can replace $\mathbf{M}$ in the equation above, and affect both vectors and points, as they should. A translation, however, uses the additional elements of the augmented matrix to obtain the goal of the foundation. A typical translation matrix, $\mathbf{T}$, which translates a point by a vector, $\mathbf{t}$, is shown in Equation A.44.

$$\mathbf{T} = \begin{pmatrix} 1 & 0 & 0 & t_x \\ 0 & 1 & 0 & t_y \\ 0 & 0 & 1 & t_z \\ 0 & 0 & 0 & 1 \end{pmatrix} \tag{A.44}$$

It is quickly verified that a vector $\mathbf{v} = (v_x \ \ v_y \ \ v_z \ \ 0)^T$ is unaffected by the $\mathbf{Tv}$ transform due to the fact that its last element is 0. If the point $\mathbf{p} = (p_x \ p_y \ p_z \ 1)^T$ is transformed as $\mathbf{Tp}$, the result is $(p_x+t_x \ \ p_y+t_y \ \ p_z+t_z \ \ 1)^T$, i.e., $\mathbf{p}$ translated by $\mathbf{t}$.

Matrix-matrix multiplications (and thus concatenations of homogeneous matrices) and matrix-vector multiplications are carried out precisely as usual, and therefore the foundation has been established as desired. In Chapter 3, many kinds of different homogeneous transforms will be introduced and thoroughly dissected.

A.5 Geometry

This section is concerned with presenting some useful geometrical techniques that are used extensively in, for example, Chapter 10.

A.5.1 Lines

Two-Dimensional Lines
For two-dimensional lines, there are two main mathematical descriptions: the implicit form, and the explicit form. The latter is parametric, and a typical equation for it is Equation A.45:

$$\mathbf{r}(t) = \mathbf{o} + t\mathbf{d} \tag{A.45}$$

Here $\mathbf{o}$ is a point on the line, $\mathbf{d}$ is the direction vector of the line, and t is a parameter which can be used to generate different points, $\mathbf{r}$, on the line.[10]

The implicit form is different in that it cannot generate points explicitly. Assume, instead, that on our line of interest, called L, any point can be described by $\mathbf{p} = (p_x, p_y) = (x, y)$, where the latter coordinate notation is used only in Equation A.46, because this is the line equation form that most people learn first.

$$ax + by + c = 0 \tag{A.46}$$

---

[10]The points are named $\mathbf{r}$ here because in other chapters the line is usually referred to as a ray.

For **p** to lie on the line L, it must fulfill the above equation. Now, if the constants a and b are combined into a vector $\mathbf{n} = (n_x, n_y) = (a, b)$, then Equation A.46 can be expressed using the dot product as

$$\mathbf{n} \cdot \mathbf{p} + c = 0. \tag{A.47}$$

A common task is, naturally, to compute the constants of a line. Looking at Figure A.5 and using its notation, we may see that one way of describing L would be $\mathbf{n} \cdot (\mathbf{p} - \mathbf{q}) = 0$, where $\mathbf{q}$ is another point on the line. Thus, $\mathbf{n}$ must be perpendicular to the line direction, i.e., $\mathbf{n} = (\mathbf{p} - \mathbf{q})^{\perp} = (-(p_y - q_y), p_x - q_x) = (a, b)$, and $c = -\mathbf{q} \cdot \mathbf{n}$. Then, given two points on L, $\mathbf{n} = (a, b)$ and c can be calculated.

Rewriting Equation A.47 as a function, $f(\mathbf{p}) = \mathbf{n} \cdot \mathbf{p} + c$, allows some very useful properties to be derived. Nothing is now assumed about **p**; it can be any point in the two-dimensional plane. First, if again $\mathbf{q} \in L$, the following holds:

1. $f(\mathbf{p}) = 0 \iff \mathbf{p} \in L$.

2. $f(\mathbf{p}) > 0 \iff \mathbf{p}$ lies on the same side of the line as the point $\mathbf{q} + \mathbf{n}$.

3. $f(\mathbf{p}) < 0 \iff \mathbf{p}$ lies on the same side of the line as the point $\mathbf{q} - \mathbf{n}$.

This test is usually called a *half-plane test* and is used in, for example, some point-in-polygon routines (see Section 10.6). Second, $f(\mathbf{p})$ happens to be a measure for the perpendicular distance from **p** to L. In fact, it turns out that the *signed distance*, f_s, is found by using Equation A.48.

$$f_s(\mathbf{p}) = \frac{f(\mathbf{p})}{\mathbf{n} \cdot \mathbf{n}} \tag{A.48}$$

If $\|\mathbf{n}\| = 1$, that is, **n** is normalized, then $f_s(\mathbf{p}) = f(\mathbf{p})$.

Three-Dimensional Lines

In three dimensions, the implicit form of a line is often expressed as the intersection between two non-parallel planes. An explicit form is shown in Equation A.49. This equation is heavily used in computing the intersection between a line (or ray) and a three-dimensional surface.

$$\mathbf{r}(t) = \mathbf{o} + t\mathbf{d} \tag{A.49}$$

This is exactly the same equation used for the two-dimensional line, except that the points and the direction vector are now three-dimensional.

The distance from a point **p** to $\mathbf{r}(t)$ can be computed by first projecting **p** onto $\mathbf{r}(t)$, using Equation A.17. Assuming **d** is normalized, this is done by computing the vector $\mathbf{w} = ((\mathbf{p} - \mathbf{o}) \cdot \mathbf{d})\mathbf{d}$. Then the sought-for distance is $\|(\mathbf{p} - \mathbf{o}) - \mathbf{w}\|$.

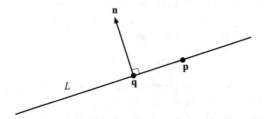

Figure A.5. Notation used for the implicit form of a two-dimensional line equation. L is the line, p and q are points on the line, and **n** is a vector perpendicular to the direction of L.

A.5.2 Planes

Since the three-dimensional plane is a natural extension of the two-dimensional line, it can be expected that the plane has similar properties as the line. In fact any hyperplane, which is the name for a plane of an arbitrary dimension, has these similar characteristics. Here, the discussion will be limited to the three-dimensional plane.

First, the plane can be described in both explicit and implicit form. Equation A.50 shows the explicit form of the three-dimensional plane.

$$\mathbf{p}(u,v) = \mathbf{o} + u\mathbf{d}_u + v\mathbf{d}_v \tag{A.50}$$

Here **o** is a point lying on the plane, $\mathbf{d}_u$ and $\mathbf{d}_v$ are direction vectors that span the plane (i.e, they are non-collinear), and u and v are parameters that generate different points on the plane. The normal of this plane is $\mathbf{d}_u \times \mathbf{d}_v$.

The implicit equation for the plane, called π, shown in Equation A.51, is identical to Equation A.47, with the exception that the plane equation is augmented with an extra dimension, and c has been renamed to d.

$$\mathbf{n} \cdot \mathbf{p} + d = 0 \tag{A.51}$$

Again, **n** is the normal of the plane, **p** is any point on the plane, and d is a constant which determines part of the position of the plane. As was shown above, the normal can be computed using two direction vectors, but it can naturally also be obtained from three non-collinear points, **u**, **v**, and **w**, lying on the plane, as $\mathbf{n} = (\mathbf{u} - \mathbf{w}) \times (\mathbf{v} - \mathbf{w})$. Given **n** and a point **q** on the plane, the constant is computed as $d = -\mathbf{n} \cdot \mathbf{q}$. The half-plane test is equally valid. By denoting $f(\mathbf{p}) = \mathbf{n} \cdot \mathbf{p} + d$, the same conclusions can be drawn as for the two-dimensional line; that is:

1. $f(\mathbf{p}) = 0 \Longleftrightarrow \mathbf{p} \in \pi$.

2. $f(\mathbf{p}) > 0 \Longleftrightarrow \mathbf{p}$ lies on the same side of the plane as the point $\mathbf{q} + \mathbf{n}$.

3. $f(\mathbf{p}) < 0 \Longleftrightarrow \mathbf{p}$ lies on the same side of the plane as the point $\mathbf{q} - \mathbf{n}$.

The signed distance from an arbitrary point $\mathbf{p}$ to π is obtained by exchanging the two-dimensional parts of Equation A.48 for their three-dimensional counterparts for the plane. Also, it is very easy to interpret the meaning of d using the signed distance formula. This requires inserting the origin, $\mathbf{0}$, into that formula; $f_s(\mathbf{0}) = d$, which means that d is the shortest (signed) distance from the origin to the plane.

A.5.3 Convex Hull

For a set of points, the *convex hull* is defined as the smallest set that satisfies the condition that the straight line between any two points in the set is totally included in the set as well. This holds for any dimension.

In two dimensions, the construction of the convex hull is intuitively illustrated by the rubberband/nail scheme. Imagine that the points are nails in a table, and that a rubber band is held in such a way that its interior includes all nails. The rubber band is then released, and now the rubber band is in fact the convex hull of the nails. This is illustrated in Figure A.6.

The convex hull has many areas of use; the construction of bounding volumes is one. The convex hull is by its definition the smallest convex volume for a set of points, and is therefore attractive for those computations. Algorithms for

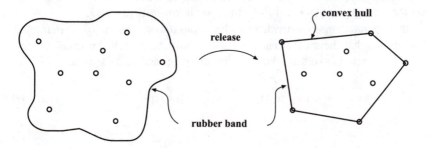

Figure A.6. The rubberband/nail scheme in action. The left figure shows the rubber band before it has been released and the right figure shows the result after. Then the rubber band is a representation of the convex hull of the nails.

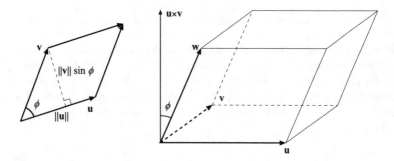

Figure A.7. Left figure: A parallelogram whose area is computed by multiplying the length of the base ($\|\mathbf{u}\|$) with the height ($\|\mathbf{v}\|\sin\phi$). Right figure: The volume of a parallelepiped is given by $(\mathbf{u} \times \mathbf{v}) \cdot \mathbf{w}$.

computing the convex hull in two and three dimensions can be found in, for example, books by de Berg et al. [31] or O'Rourke [280]. A fast algorithm, called *QuickHull*, is presented by Barber et al. [25].

A.5.4   Miscellaneous

Area Calculation

A parallelogram defined by two vectors, $\mathbf{u}$ and $\mathbf{v}$, starting at the origin, trivially has the area $\|\mathbf{u} \times \mathbf{v}\| = \|\mathbf{u}\|\,\|\mathbf{v}\|\sin\phi$, as shown in Figure A.7.

If the parallelogram is divided by a line from $\mathbf{u}$ to $\mathbf{v}$, two triangles are formed. This means that the area of each triangle is half the area of the parallelogram. So, if a triangle is given by three points, say $\mathbf{p}$, $\mathbf{q}$, and $\mathbf{r}$, its area is:

$$\text{Area}(\triangle \mathbf{pqr}) = \frac{1}{2}\|(\mathbf{p} - \mathbf{r}) \times (\mathbf{q} - \mathbf{r})\| \qquad (A.52)$$

Volume Calculation

The scalar triple product, from Equation A.18, is sometimes also called the volume formula. Three vectors, $\mathbf{u}$, $\mathbf{v}$ and $\mathbf{w}$, starting at the origin, form a solid, called a parallelepiped, whose volume is given by the equation below. The volume and the notation are depicted in Figure A.7.

$$\text{Volume}(\mathbf{u}, \mathbf{v}, \mathbf{w}) = (\mathbf{u} \times \mathbf{v}) \cdot \mathbf{w} = |\mathbf{u} \quad \mathbf{v} \quad \mathbf{w}| \qquad (A.53)$$

This is a positive value only if the vectors form a positively oriented basis. The formula intuitively explains why the determinant of three vectors is zero if the vectors do not span the entire space $\mathbb{R}^3$: in that case, the volume is zero, meaning that the vectors must lie in the same plane (or one or more of them may be the zero vector).

Further Reading and Resources

For a more thorough treatment of linear algebra, the reader is directed to, for example, the books by Lawson [225] and Lax [226]. Hutson and Pym's book [194] gives an in-depth treatment of all kinds of spaces (and more). A lighter read is Farin and Hansford's *The Geometry Toolbox* [105], which builds up a geometric understanding for transforms, eigenvalues, and much else.

The 30th edition of the *CRC Standard Mathematical Tables and Formulas* [392] is a recent major update of this classic reference. Much of the material in this appendix is included, as well as a huge amount of other mathematical knowledge.

Appendix B
Trigonometry

"Life is good for only two things, discovering mathematics and teaching mathematics."
–Siméon Poisson

This appendix is intended to be a reference to some simple laws of trigonometry as well as some more sophisticated ones. The laws of trigonometry are particularly important tools in computer graphics. One example of their usefulness is that they provide ways to simplify equations and thereby to increase speed.

B.1 Definitions

According to Figure B.1, where $\mathbf{p} = (p_x \quad p_y)^T$ is a unit vector, i.e., $\|\mathbf{p}\| = 1$, the fundamental trigonometric functions, sin, cos, and tan, are defined by Equation B.1.

> **Fundamental trigonometric functions :**
>
> $$\sin\phi = p_y$$
>
> $$\cos\phi = p_x$$
>
> $$\tan\phi = \frac{\sin\phi}{\cos\phi} = \frac{p_y}{p_x}$$

(B.1)

The sin, cos, and tan functions can be expanded into MacLaurin series as shown in Equation B.2. These are beneficial because they clarify the origins of

419

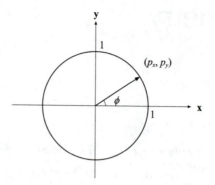

Figure B.1. The geometry for the definition of the sin, cos, and tan functions.

some of the derivatives (shown in Equation set B.4).

MacLaurin series :

$$\sin\phi = \phi - \frac{\phi^3}{3!} + \frac{\phi^5}{5!} - \frac{\phi^7}{7!} + \cdots + (-1)^n \frac{\phi^{2n+1}}{(2n+1)!} + \cdots$$

$$\cos\phi = 1 - \frac{\phi^2}{2!} + \frac{\phi^4}{4!} - \frac{\phi^6}{6!} + \cdots + (-1)^n \frac{\phi^{2n}}{(2n)!} + \cdots$$

$$\tan\phi = \phi + \frac{\phi^3}{3} + \frac{2\phi^5}{15} + \cdots + (-1)^{n-1} \frac{2^{2n}(2^{2n}-1)}{(2n)!} B_{2n}\phi^{2n-1} + \cdots$$

$$(B.2)$$

The two first series hold for $-\infty < \phi < \infty$, the last one for $-\pi/2 < \phi < \pi/2$ and B_n is the nth Bernoulli number.[1]

The inverses of the trigonometric functions, arcsin, arccos, and arctan, are defined as in Equation B.3.

---

[1]The Bernoulli numbers can be generated with a recursive formula, where $B_0 = 1$ and then for $k > 1$, $\sum_{j=0}^{k-1} \binom{k}{j} B_j = 0$.

> **Inverses of trigonometric functions:**
>
> $$p_y = \sin\phi \Leftrightarrow \phi = \arcsin p_y, \quad -1 \le p_y \le 1, \quad -\tfrac{\pi}{2} \le \phi \le \tfrac{\pi}{2}$$
>
> $$p_x = \cos\phi \Leftrightarrow \phi = \arccos p_x, \quad -1 \le p_x \le 1, \quad 0 \le \phi \le \pi$$
>
> $$\frac{p_y}{p_x} = \tan\phi \Leftrightarrow \phi = \arctan\frac{p_y}{p_x}, \quad -\infty \le \frac{p_y}{p_x} \le \infty, \quad -\tfrac{\pi}{2} \le \phi \le \tfrac{\pi}{2}$$

(B.3)

The derivatives of the trigonometric functions and their inverses are summarized below.

> **Trigonometric derivatives:**
>
> $$\frac{d\sin\phi}{d\phi} = \cos\phi$$
>
> $$\frac{d\cos\phi}{d\phi} = -\sin\phi$$
>
> $$\frac{d\tan\phi}{d\phi} = \frac{1}{\cos^2\phi} = 1 + \tan^2\phi$$
>
> $$\frac{d\arcsin t}{dt} = \frac{1}{\sqrt{1-t^2}}$$
>
> $$\frac{d\arccos t}{dt} = -\frac{1}{\sqrt{1-t^2}}$$
>
> $$\frac{d\arctan t}{dt} = \frac{1}{1+t^2}$$

(B.4)

B.2 Trigonometric Laws and Formulae

We begin with some fundamental laws about right triangles. To use the notation from Figure B.2, the following laws apply:

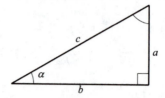

Figure B.2. A right triangle and its notation.

Right triangle laws:

$$\sin \alpha = \frac{a}{c}$$

$$\cos \alpha = \frac{b}{c}$$ (B.5)

$$\tan \alpha = \frac{\sin \alpha}{\cos \alpha} = \frac{a}{b}$$

Pythagorean relation: $c^2 = a^2 + b^2$ (B.6)

For arbitrarily angled triangles, the following well-known rules are valid, using the notation from Figure B.3.

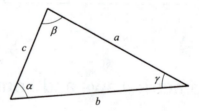

Figure B.3. An arbitrarily angled triangle and its notation.

$$\textbf{Law of sines}: \quad \frac{\sin\alpha}{a} = \frac{\sin\beta}{b} = \frac{\sin\gamma}{c}$$

$$\textbf{Law of cosines}: \quad c^2 = a^2 + b^2 - 2ab\cos\gamma \tag{B.7}$$

$$\textbf{Law of tangents}: \quad \frac{a+b}{a-b} = \frac{\tan\dfrac{\alpha+\beta}{2}}{\tan\dfrac{\alpha-\beta}{2}}$$

Named after their inventors, the following two formulae are also valid for arbitrarily angled triangles.

$$\textbf{Newton's formula}: \quad \frac{b+c}{a} = \frac{\cos\dfrac{\beta-\gamma}{2}}{\sin\dfrac{\alpha}{2}} \tag{B.8}$$

$$\textbf{Mollweide's formula}: \quad \frac{b-c}{a} = \frac{\sin\dfrac{\beta-\gamma}{2}}{\cos\dfrac{\alpha}{2}}$$

The definition of the trigonometric functions (Equation B.1) trivially gives the *trigonometric identity*:

$$\textbf{Trigonometric identity}: \quad \cos^2\phi + \sin^2\phi = 1 \tag{B.9}$$

Here follow some laws that can be exploited to simplify equations and thereby make their implementation more efficient.

Double angle relations :

$$\sin 2\phi = 2\sin\phi\cos\phi = \frac{2\tan\phi}{1+\tan^2\phi}$$

$$\cos 2\phi = \cos^2\phi - \sin^2\phi = 1 - 2\sin^2\phi = 2\cos^2\phi - 1 = \frac{1-\tan^2\phi}{1+\tan^2\phi}$$

$$\tan 2\phi = \frac{2\tan\phi}{1-\tan^2\phi}$$

$$\tag{B.10}$$

Extensions of the laws above are called the *multiple angle relations*, shown below.

Multiple angle relations :

$$\sin(n\phi) = 2\sin((n-1)\phi)\cos\phi - \sin((n-2)\phi)$$

$$\cos(n\phi) = 2\cos((n-1)\phi)\cos\phi - \cos((n-2)\phi)$$

$$\tan(n\phi) = \frac{\tan((n-1)\phi) + \tan\phi}{1 - \tan((n-1)\phi)\tan\phi}$$

(B.11)

Equations B.12 and B.13 show a collection of laws which we call the *angle sum* and *angle difference relations*.

Angle sum relations :

$$\sin(\phi + \rho) = \sin\phi\cos\rho + \cos\phi\sin\rho$$

$$\cos(\phi + \rho) = \cos\phi\cos\rho - \sin\phi\sin\rho$$

$$\tan(\phi + \rho) = \frac{\tan\phi + \tan\rho}{1 - \tan\phi\tan\rho}$$

(B.12)

Angle difference relations :

$$\sin(\phi - \rho) = \sin\phi\cos\rho - \cos\phi\sin\rho$$

$$\cos(\phi - \rho) = \cos\phi\cos\rho + \sin\phi\sin\rho$$

$$\tan(\phi - \rho) = \frac{\tan\phi - \tan\rho}{1 + \tan\phi\tan\rho}$$

(B.13)

Next follow the *product relations*.

Product relations :

$$\sin\phi\sin\rho = \frac{1}{2}(\cos(\phi-\rho) - \cos(\phi+\rho))$$

$$\cos\phi\cos\rho = \frac{1}{2}(\cos(\phi-\rho) + \cos(\phi+\rho))$$

$$\sin\phi\cos\rho = \frac{1}{2}(\sin(\phi-\rho) + \sin(\phi+\rho))$$

(B.14)

The formulae in Equations B.15 and B.16 go under the names *function sums and differences* and *half-angle relations*.

Function sums and differences :

$$\sin\phi + \sin\rho = 2\sin\frac{\phi+\rho}{2}\cos\frac{\phi-\rho}{2}$$

$$\cos\phi + \cos\rho = 2\cos\frac{\phi+\rho}{2}\cos\frac{\phi-\rho}{2}$$

$$\tan\phi + \tan\rho = \frac{\sin(\phi+\rho)}{\cos\phi\cos\rho}$$

$$\sin\phi - \sin\rho = 2\cos\frac{\phi+\rho}{2}\sin\frac{\phi-\rho}{2}$$

$$\cos\phi - \cos\rho = -2\sin\frac{\phi+\rho}{2}\sin\frac{\phi-\rho}{2}$$

$$\tan\phi - \tan\rho = \frac{\sin(\phi-\rho)}{\cos\phi\cos\rho}$$

(B.15)

Half − angle relations :

$$\sin \frac{\phi}{2} = \pm \sqrt{\frac{1 - \cos \phi}{2}}$$

$$\cos \frac{\phi}{2} = \pm \sqrt{\frac{1 + \cos \phi}{2}}$$

$$\tan \frac{\phi}{2} = \pm \sqrt{\frac{1 - \cos \phi}{1 + \cos \phi}} = \frac{1 - \cos \phi}{\sin \phi} = \frac{\sin \phi}{1 + \cos \phi}$$

(B.16)

Further Reading and Resources

The first chapter of *Graphics Gems* [117] provides other geometric relationships that are useful in computer graphics. The 30th edition of the *CRC Standard Mathematical Tables and Formulas* [392] includes the formulae in this appendix and much more.

Bibliography

[1] Abrash, Michael, *Michael Abrash's Graphics Programming Black Book, Special Edition*, The Coriolis Group, Inc., Scottsdale, Arizona, 1997.

[2] Airey, John M., John H. Rohlf, and Frederick P. Brooks Jr., "Towards Image Realism with Interactive Update Rates in Complex Virtual Building Environments," *Computer Graphics (1990 Symposium on Interactive 3D Graphics)*, vol. 24, no. 2, pp. 41–50, March 1990.

[3] Airey, John M., *Increasing Update Rates in the Building Walkthrough System with Automatic Model-Space Subdivision and Potentially Visible Set Calculations*, Ph.D. Thesis, Technical Report TR90-027, Department of Computer Science, University of North Carolina at Chapel Hill, July 1990.

[4] Akeley, K., and T. Jermoluk, "High-Performance Polygon Rendering," *Computer Graphics (SIGGRAPH '88 Proceedings)*, vol. 22, no. 4, pp. 239–246, August 1988.

[5] Akeley, Kurt, "The Silicon Graphics 4D/240GTX Superworkstation," *IEEE Computer Graphics and Applications*, vol. 9, no. 4, pp. 71–83, July 1989.

[6] Akeley, K., P. Haeberli, and D. Burns, `tomesh.c`, a C-program on the *SGI Developer's Toolbox CD*, 1990.

[7] Akeley, Kurt, "RealityEngine Graphics," *Computer Graphics (SIGGRAPH '93 Proceedings)*, pp. 109–116, August 1993.

[8] Aliaga, D., J. Cohen, H. Zhang, R. Bastos, T. Hudson, and C. Erikson, "Power Plant Walkthrough: An Integrated System for Massive Model Rendering," Technical Report TR#97-018, Computer Science Department, University of North Carolina at Chapel Hill, 1997. `ftp://ftp.cs.unc.edu/pub/publications/techreports/FILE.html`

[9] Aliaga, D., J. Cohen, A. Wilson, H. Zhang, C. Erikson, K. Hoff, T. Hudson, W. Stürzlinger, E. Baker, R. Bastos, M. Whitton, F. Brooks Jr., and D. Manocha, "A Framework for the Real-Time Walkthrough of Massive Models," Technical Report UNC TR#98-013, Computer Science Department, University of North Carolina at Chapel Hill, 1998. ftp://ftp. cs.unc.edu/pub/publications/techreports/FILE.html

[10] Aliaga, D., J. Cohen, A. Wilson, E. Baker, H. Zhang, C. Erikson, K. Hoff, T. Hudson, W. Stürzlinger, R. Bastos, M. Whitton, F. Brooks, and D. Manocha, "MMR: An Interactive Massive Model Rendering System Using Geometric and Image-Based Acceleration," *Proceedings 1999 Symposium on Interactive 3D Graphics*, pp. 199–206, April 1999.

[11] Angel, Edward, *Interactive Computer Graphics—A top-down approach with OpenGL*, Addison-Wesley, Reading, Massachusetts, 1997.

[12] Antonio, Franklin, "Faster Line Segment Intersection," in David Kirk, ed., *Graphics Gems III*, Academic Press, Inc., Boston, pp. 199–202, 1992. http://www.acm.org/tog/GraphicsGems/

[13] Appel, Andrew W., with Maia Ginsburg, *Modern Compiler Implementation in C*, Cambridge University Press, New York, 1998.

[14] Arenberg, Jeff, "Re: Ray/Triangle Intersection with Barycentric Coordinates," in Eric Haines, ed., *Ray Tracing News*, vol. 1, no. 11, November 1988. http://www.acm.org/tog/resources/RTNews/html/rtnews5b.html"#art3

[15] Arvo, James, "Backward Ray Tracing," *SIGGRAPH '86 Developments in Ray Tracing course notes*, August 1986.

[16] Arvo, James, "A Simple Method for Box-Sphere Intersection Testing," in Andrew S. Glassner, ed., *Graphics Gems*, Academic Press, Inc., Boston, pp. 335–339, 1990. http://www.acm.org/tog/GraphicsGems/

[17] Arvo, James, ed., *Graphics Gems II*, Academic Press Inc., Boston, 1991. http://www.acm.org/tog/GraphicsGems/

[18] Assarsson, Ulf, and Tomas Möller, "Optimized View Frustum Culling Algorithms," Technical Report 99-3, Department of Computer Engineering, Chalmers University of Technology, March 1999. http://www. ce.chalmers.se/staff/uffe

[19] Badouel, Didier, *An Efficient Ray-Polygon Intersection*, in *Graphics Gems*, ed. Andrew S. Glassner, Academic Press Inc., Boston, pp. 390–393, 1990. http://www.acm.org/tog/GraphicsGems/

[20] Ballard, Dana H., "Strip Trees: A Hierarchical Representation for Curves," *Graphics and Image Processing*, vol. 24, no. 5, pp. 310–321, May 1981.

[21] Barad, Haim and Mark Atkins, "Implementing Mixed Rendering," *Game Developer*, vol. 4, no. 6, pp. 34–42, September 1997.

[22] Barad, Haim, Mark Atkins, Or Gerlitz, and Daniel Goehring, "Real-Time Procedural Texturing Techniques Using MMX," http://www.gamasutra.com/features/programming/19980501/mmxtexturing_01.htm

[23] Baraff, D., "Curved Surfaces and Coherence for Non-Penetrating Rigid Body Simulation," *Computer Graphics (SIGGRAPH '90 Proceedings)*, vol. 24, no. 4, pp. 19–28, August 1990.

[24] Baraff, David, and Andrew Witkin, "Physically Based Modeling," *Course 13 notes at SIGGRAPH '98*, 1998. http://www.cs.cmu.edu/~baraff/sigcourse/

[25] Barber, C.B., D.P. Dobkin, and H. Huhdanpaa, "The Quickhull Algorithm for Convex Hull," Geometry Center Technical Report GCG53, July 1993. http://www.geom.umn.edu/software/qhull/

[26] Barequet, G., B. Chazelle, L.J. Guibas, J.S.B. Mitchell, and A. Tal, "BOX-TREE: A Hierarchical Representation for Surfaces in 3D," *Eurographics '96*, Eurographics Association, eds. J. Rossignac and F. Sillion, Blackwell Publishers, vol. 15, no. 3, pp. C-387–C-484, August 1996.

[27] Barkans, Anthony C., "Color Recovery: True-Color 8-Bit Interactive Graphics," *IEEE Computer Graphics and Applications*, vol. 17, no. 1, pp. 67–77, Jan./Feb. 1997.

[28] Barkans, Anthony C., "High-Quality Rendering Using the Talisman Architecture," in the *Proceedings of the 1997 SIGGRAPH/Eurographics Workshop on Graphics Hardware*, Los Angeles, CA, pp. 79–88, August 1997.

[29] Bastos, Rui, Kenneth Hoff, William Wynn, and Anselmo Lastra, "Increased Photorealism for Interactive Architectural Walkthroughs," *Proceedings 1999 Symposium on Interactive 3D Graphics*, pp. 183–190, April 1999.

[30] Baum, Daniel R., Stephen Mann, Kevin P. Smith, and James M. Winget, "Making Radiosity Usable: Automatic Preprocessing and Meshing Techniques for the Generation of Accurate Radiosity Solutions," *Computer Graphics (SIGGRAPH '91 Proceedings)*, vol. 25, no. 4, pp. 51–60, July 1991.

[31] de Berg, M., M. van Kreveld, M. Overmars, and O. Schwarzkopf, *Computational Geometry—Algorithms and Applications*, Springer-Verlag, Berlin, 1997.

[32] Bergman, L. D., H. Fuchs, E. Grant, and S. Spach, "Image Rendering by Adaptive Refinement," *Computer Graphics (SIGGRAPH '86 Proceedings)*, vol. 20, no. 4, pp. 29–37, August 1986.

[33] Bier, Eric A., and Kenneth R. Sloan, Jr., "Two-Part Texture Mapping," *IEEE Computer Graphics and Applications*, vol. 6, no. 9, pp. 40–53, September 1986.

[34] Bigos, Andrew, "Avoiding Buffer Clears," *journal of graphics tools*, vol. 1, no. 1, pp. 19–20, 1996.

[35] Bishop, L., D. Eberly, T. Whitted, M. Finch, and M. Shantz, "Designing a PC Game Engine," *IEEE Computer Graphics and Applications*, pp. 46–53, Jan./Feb. 1998. http://computer.org/cga/cg1998/g1toc.htm

[36] Blinn, J.F., and M.E. Newell, "Texture and reflection in computer generated images," *Communications of the ACM*, vol. 19, no. 10, pp. 542–547, October 1976.

[37] Blinn, James F., "Models of Light Reflection for Computer Synthesized Pictures," *ACM Computer Graphics (SIGGRAPH '77)*, vol. 11, no. 2, pp. 192–198, July 1977.

[38] Blinn, James, "Simulation of wrinkled surfaces," *Computer Graphics (SIGGRAPH '78 Proceedings)*, vol. 12, no. 3, pp. 286–292, August 1978.

[39] Blinn, Jim, "Me and My (Fake) Shadow," *IEEE Computer Graphics and Applications*, vol. 8, no. 1, pp. 82–86, January 1988. Also collected in [43].

[40] Blinn, Jim, "Dirty Pixels," *IEEE Computer Graphics and Applications*, vol. 9, no. 4, pp. 100–105, July 1989. Also collected in [44].

[41] Blinn, Jim, "A Trip Down the Graphics Pipeline: Line Clipping," *IEEE Computer Graphics and Applications*, vol. 11, no. 1, pp. 98–105, January 1991. Also collected in [43].

[42] Blinn, Jim, "Hyperbolic Interpolation," *IEEE Computer Graphics and Applications*, vol. 12, no. 4, pp. 89–94, July 1992. Also collected in [43].

[43] Blinn, Jim, *Jim Blinn's Corner: A Trip Down the Graphics Pipeline*, Morgan Kaufmann Publishers, Inc., San Francisco, 1996.

[44] Blinn, Jim, *Jim Blinn's Corner: Dirty Pixels*, Morgan Kaufmann Publishers, Inc., San Francisco, 1998.

[45] Blinn, Jim, "W Pleasure, W Fun," *IEEE Computer Graphics and Applications*, vol. 18, no. 3, pp. 78–82, May/June 1998.

[46] Bloomenthal, Jules, ed., *Introduction to Implicit Surfaces*, Morgan Kaufmann Publishers, Inc., San Francisco, 1997.

[47] Booth, Rick, *Inner Loops*, Addison-Wesley, Reading, Massachusetts, 1997.

[48] Bresenham, J.E., "Algorithm for Computer Control of a Digital Plotter," *IBM Systems Journal*, vol. 4, no. 1, pp. 25–30, 1965.

[49] Brittain, Don, "Don's 3D Studio MAX R2 Page" http://www.west.net/~brittain/3dsmax2.htm

[50] Burwell, John M., "Redefining High Performance Computer Image Generation," Proceedings of the IMAGE Conference, Scottsdale, Arizona, June 1996.

[51] Carpenter, Loren, "The A-buffer, an Antialiased Hidden Surface Method," *Computer Graphics (SIGGRAPH '84 Proceedings)*, vol. 18, no. 3, pp. 103–108, July 1984.

[52] Carter, Michael B., and Andreas Johannsen, "Clustered Backface Culling," *journal of graphics tools*, vol. 3, no. 1, pp. 1–14, 1998.

[53] Catmull, Edwin, "Computer Display of Curved Surfaces," *Proceedings of the IEEE Conference on Computer Graphics, Pattern Recognition and Data Structures*, Los Angeles, pp. 11–17, May 1975.

[54] Chen, S. E., "Quicktime VR - An Image-Based Approach to Virtual Environment Navigation," *Computer Graphics (SIGGRAPH '95 Proceedings)*, pp. 29–38, August 1995.

[55] Cignoni, P., C. Montani, and R. Scopigno, "Triangulating Convex Polygons Having T-Vertices," *journal of graphics tools*, vol. 1, no. 2, pp. 1–4, 1996.

[56] Clark, James H., "Hierarchical Geometric Models for Visible Surface Algorithms," *Communications of the ACM*, vol. 19, no. 10, pp. 547–554, October 1976.

[57] Clay, Sharon R., "Optimization for Real-Time Graphics Applications," Silicon Graphics Inc., February 1996. http://www.sgi.com/software/performer/presentations/tune_wp.pdf

[58] Coelho, Rohan, and Maher Hawash, *DirectX, RDX, RSZ, and MMX Technology*, Addison-Wesley, Reading, Massachusetts, 1998. Includes VTune evaluation version. New chapters 24 and 25 are available online at http://www.awl.com

[59] Cohen, M.F., and J.R. Wallace, *Radiosity and Realistic Image Synthesis*, Academic Press Professional, Boston, 1993.

[60] Cohen, Jonathan D., Ming C. Lin, Dinesh Manocha, and Madhave Ponamgi, "I-COLLIDE: An Interactive and Exact Collision Detection System for Large-Scaled Environments," *Proceedings 1995 Symposium on Interactive 3D Graphics*, pp. 189–196, 1995. http://www.cs.unc.edu/~geom/

[61] Cohen, Jonathan D., Marc Olano, and Dinesh Manocha, "Appearance-Preserving Simplification," *Computer Graphics (SIGGRAPH '98 Proceedings)*, pp. 115–122, July 1998. http://www.cs.unc.edu/~geom/APS/

[62] Cook, Robert L., and Kenneth E. Torrance, "A reflectance model for computer graphics," *Computer Graphics (SIGGRAPH '81 Proceedings)*, vol. 15, no. 3, pp. 307–316, July 1981.

[63] Cook, Robert L., and Kenneth E. Torrance, "A Reflectance Model for Computer Graphics," *ACM Transactions on Graphics*, vol. 1, no.1, pp. 7–24, January 1982.

[64] Cook, Robert L., "Shade Trees," *Computer Graphics (SIGGRAPH '84 Proceedings)*, vol. 18, no. 3, pp. 223–231, July 1984.

[65] Cook, Robert L., Loren Carpenter, and Edwin Catmull, "The Reyes Image Rendering Architecture," *Computer Graphics (SIGGRAPH '87 Proceedings)*, vol. 21, no. 4, pp. 95–102, July 1987.

[66] Coorg, S., and S. Teller, "Temporally Coherent Conservative Visibility," *Twelfth Annual ACM Symposium on Computational Geometry*, May 1996.

[67] Coorg, S., and S. Teller, "Real-Time Occlusion Culling for Models with Large Occluders," in *Proceedings 1997 Symposium on Interactive 3D Graphics*, pp. 83–90, April 1997.

[68] Cormen, T.H., C.E. Leiserson, and R. Rivest, *Introduction to Algorithms*, MIT Press, Inc., Cambridge, Massachusetts, 1990.

[69] "Cosmo3D—Programmer's Guide," Silicon Graphics Inc., 1997.

[70] Cox, Michael, David Sprague, John Danskin, Rich Ehlers, Brian Hook, Bill Lorensen, and Gary Tarolli, "Developing High-Performance Graphics Applications for the PC Platform," *Course 29 notes at SIGGRAPH '98*, 1998.

[71] Cripe, Brian and Thomas Gaskins, "The DirectModel Toolkit: Meeting the 3D Graphics Needs of Technical Applications," *Hewlett-Packard Journal*, pp. 19–27, May 1998. http://www.hp.com/hpj/98may/ma98a3.htm

[72] Crow, Franklin C., "Shadow Algorithms for Computer Graphics," *Computer Graphics (SIGGRAPH '77 Proceedings)*, vol. 11, no. 2, pp. 242–248, July 1977.

[73] Crow, Franklin C., "Summed-Area Tables for Texture Mapping," *Computer Graphics (SIGGRAPH '84 Proceedings)*, vol. 18, no. 3, pp. 207–212, July 1984.

[74] Cruz-Neira, Carolina, Daniel J. Sandin, and Thomas A. DeFanti, "Surround-screen Projection-based Virtual Reality: The Design and Implementation of the CAVE," *Computer Graphics (SIGGRAPH '93 Proceedings)*, pp. 135–142, August 1993. http://www.ee.iastate.edu/~cruz/sig93.paper.html

[75] Culler, David E., and Jaswinder Pal Singh, with Anoop Gupta, *Parallel Computer Architecture: A Hardware/Software Approach*, Morgan Kaufmann Publishers Inc., San Francisco, 1998.

[76] Cunningham, Steve, "3D Viewing and Rotation using Orthonormal Bases," in Andrew S. Glassner, ed., *Graphics Gems*, Academic Press, Inc., Boston, pp. 516–521, 1990. http://www.acm.org/tog/ GraphicsGems/

[77] Cychosz, J.M. and W.N. Waggenspack Jr., "Intersecting a Ray with a Cylinder," in Paul S. Heckbert, ed., *Graphics Gems IV*, AP Professional, Boston, pp. 356–365, 1994. http://www.acm.org/tog/ GraphicsGems/

[78] Cyrus, M., and J. Beck, "Generalized two- and three-dimensional clipping," *Computers and Graphics*, vol. 3, pp. 23–28, 1978.

[79] Dam, Erik B., Martin Koch, and Martin Lillholm, "Quaternions, Interpolation and Animation," Technical Report DIKU-TR-98/5, Department of Computer Science, University of Copenhagen, July 1998. http://ftp.diku.dk/students/myth/quat.html

[80] Decoret, Xavier, Gernot Schaufler, François Sillion, and Julie Dorsey, "Multi-layered impostors for accelerated rendering," *Proceedings of Eurographics '99*, vol. 18, no. 3, 1999.

[81] Deering, Michael, "Geometry Compression," *Computer Graphics (SIGGRAPH '95 Proceedings)*, pp. 13–20, August 1995.

[82] Diefenbach, Paul J., and Norman I. Badler, "Multi-Pass Pipeline Rendering: Realism for Dynamic Environments," *Proceedings 1997 Symposium on Interactive 3D Graphics*, pp. 59–70, April 1997. http://www.openworlds.com/employees/paul/index.html

[83] "DirectX 6.0 SDK," Microsoft, 1998. http://www.microsoft.com/directx/default.asp

[84] "DirectModel 1.0 Specification," Hewlett-Packard, September 1997.

[85] Do Carmo, Manfred P., *Differential Geometry for Curves and Surfaces*, Prentice-Hall, Inc., Englewoods Cliffs, New Jersey, 1976.

[86] Donovan, Walt, Personal communication, 1999.

[87] Dorbie, Angus, Personal communication, 1998-9.

[88] Duff, Tom, "Compositing 3-D Rendered Images," *Computer Graphics (SIGGRAPH '85 Proceedings)*, vol. 19, no. 3, pp. 41–44, July 1985.

[89] Durand, Frédo, George Drettakis, and Claude Puech, "The Visibility Skeleton: A Powerful and Efficient Multi-Purpose Global Visibility Tool," *Computer Graphics (SIGGRAPH '97 Proceedings)*, pp. 89–100, August 1997. http://w3imagis.imag.fr/Membres/Fredo.Durand/ PUBLI/siggraph97/index.htm

[90] Durand, Frédo, George Drettakis, and Claude Puech, "The 3D Visibility Complex: a unified data–structure for global visibility of scenes of polygons and smooth objects," *Canadian Conference on Computational Geometry*, pp. 153–158, August 1997.

[91] Eberly, David, "Dynamic Collision Detection using Oriented Bounding Boxes," http://www.magic-software.com/

[92] Ebert, David S., F. Kenton Musgrave, Darwyn Peachey, Ken Perlin, and Steven Worley, *Texturing and Modeling: A Procedural Approach*, second edition, AP Professional, San Diego, 1998.

[93] Eckel, George, *IRIS Performer Programmer's Guide*, Silicon Graphics Inc., 1997. http://www.sgi.com/software/performer/ manuals.html

[94] Elber, Gershon, "Line illustrations in computer graphics," *The Visual Computer*, vol. 11, no. 6, pp. 290–296, 1995.

[95] Erikson, C., "Polygonal Simplification: An Overview," Technical Report TR96-016, UNC Chapel Hill Computer Science Department, 1996. http://www.cs.unc.edu/~eriksonc/Research/ Paper/Index.html

[96] Ernst, I., D. Jackel, H. Russeler, and O. Wittig, "Hardware Supported Bump Mapping: A step towards higher quality real-time rendering," in *10th Eurographics Workshop on Graphics Hardware*, pp. 63–70, 1995.

[97] Ernst, I., H. Russeler, H. Schulz, and O. Wittig, "Gouraud Bump Mapping," *Proceedings of the 1998 Eurographics/SIGGRAPH Workshop on Graphics Hardware*, Lisbon, Portugal, pp. 47–53, August 1998.

[98] Euclid (original translation by Heiberg, with introduction and commentary by Sir Thomas L. Heath), *The Thirteen Books of EUCLID'S ELEMENTS*, Second Edition, Revised with Additions, Volume I (Books I, II), Dover Publications, Inc., New York, 1956.

[99] Evans, F., S. Skiena, and A. Varshney, "Stripe: A Software Tool For Efficient Triangle Strips," *Visual Proceedings (SIGGRAPH '96)*, p. 153, August 1996. http://www.cs.sunysb.edu/~stripe/

[100] Evans, F., S. Skiena, and A. Varshney, "Optimizing Triangle Strips for Fast Rendering," *Proceedings of the IEEE Visualization'96*, eds. Yagel, R. and G.M. Nielson, San Francisco, pp. 319–326, October 1996. http://www.cs.sunysb.edu/~stripe/

[101] Evans, F., S. Skiena, and A. Varshney, "Efficiently Generating Triangle Strips for Fast Rendering," *ACM Transactions of Graphics*, April 1997. http://www.cs.sunysb.edu/~stripe/

[102] Eyles, J., S. Molnar, J. Poulton, T. Greer, A. Lastra, N. England, and L. Westover, "PixelFlow: The Realization," in the *Proceedings of the 1997 SIGGRAPH/Eurographics Workshop on Graphics Hardware*, Los Angeles, CA, pp. 57–68, August 1997.

[103] "The Fahrenheit Project," 1997. http://www.sgi.com/fahrenheit/

[104] Farin, Gerald, *Curves and Surfaces for Computer Aided Geometric Design—A Practical Guide*, Fourth Edition (First Edition, 1988), Academic Press Inc., San Diego, 1996.

[105] Farin, Gerald E. and Dianne Hansford, *The Geometry Toolbox for Graphics and Modeling*, A.K. Peters Ltd., Boston, 1998. http://eros.cagd.eas.asu.edu/~farin/gbook/gbook.html

[106] Fisher, F., and A. Woo, "R.E versus N.H Specular Highlights," in Paul S. Heckbert, ed., *Graphics Gems IV*, Academic Press, Inc., Boston, pp. 388–400, 1994.

[107] Flavell, Andrew, "Run Time Mip-Map Filtering," *Game Developer*, vol. 5, no. 11, pp. 34–43, November 1998. http://www.gdmag.com/code.htm

[108] Foley, J.D., A. van Dam, S.K. Feiner, and J.H. Hughes, *Computer Graphics—Principles and Practice*, Second Edition, Addison-Wesley, Reading, Massachusetts, 1990.

[109] Foley, J.D., A. van Dam, S.K. Feiner, J.H. Hughes, and R.L. Philips, *Introduction to Computer Graphics*, Addison-Wesley, Reading, Massachusetts, 1994.

[110] Fuchs, H., Z.M. Kedem, and B.F. Naylor, "On Visible Surface Generation by A Priori Tree Structures," *Computer Graphics (SIGGRAPH '80 Proceedings)*, vol. 14, no. 3, pp. 124–133, July 1980.

[111] Fuchs, H., G.D. Abram, and E.D. Grant, "Near Real-Time Shaded Display of Rigid Objects," *Computer Graphics (SIGGRAPH '89 Proceedings)*, vol. 17, no. 3, pp. 65–72, July 1983.

[112] Fuchs, H., J. Poulton, J. Eyles, T. Greer, J. Goldfeather, D. Ellsworth, S. Molnar, G. Turk, B. Tebbs, and L. Israel, "Pixel-Planes 5: A Heterogeneous Multiprocessor Graphics System Using Processor-Enhanced Memories," *Computer Graphics (SIGGRAPH '89 Proceedings)*, vol. 23, no. 3, pp. 79–88, July 1989.

[113] Funkhouser, Thomas A., and Carlo H. Séquin, "Adaptive Display Algorithm for Interactive Frame Rates During Visualization of Complex Virtual Environments," *Computer Graphics (SIGGRAPH '93 Proceedings)*, pp. 247–254, August 1993. http://www.cs.princeton.edu/~funk/

[114] Funkhouser, Thomas A., *Database and Display Algorithms for Interactive Visualization of Architectural Models*, Ph.D. Thesis, University of California, Berkeley, 1993. http://www.cs.princeton.edu/~funk/

[115] Garland, Michael, and Paul S. Heckbert, "Simplifying Surfaces with Color and Texture using Quadric Error Metrics," *IEEE Visualization 98*, pp. 263–269, July 1998. http://www.cs.cmu.edu/~garland/

[116] Glassner, Andrew S., ed., *An Introduction to Ray Tracing*, Academic Press Inc., London, 1989.

[117] Glassner, Andrew S., ed., *Graphics Gems*, Academic Press Inc., 1990. http://www.acm.org/tog/GraphicsGems/

[118] Glassner, Andrew S. "Computing Surface Normals for 3D Models," Andrew S. Glassner, ed., *Graphics Gems*, Academic Press Inc., pp. 562–566, 1990.

[119] Glassner, Andrew, "Building Vertex Normals from an Unstructured Polygon List," in Paul S. Heckbert, ed., *Graphics Gems IV*, AP Professional, Boston, pp. 60–73, 1994.

[120] Glassner, Andrew S., *Principles of Digital Image Synthesis*, vol. 1, Morgan Kaufmann Publishers Inc., San Francisco, 1995.

[121] Glassner, Andrew S., *Principles of Digital Image Synthesis*, vol. 2, Morgan Kaufmann Publishers Inc., San Francisco, 1995.

[122] *Glide 3.0 Programming Guide*, 3dfx Interactive, Inc., 1998. `http://www.3dfx.com/`

[123] Goldman, Ronald, "Intersection of Three Planes," in Andrew S. Glassner, ed., *Graphics Gems*, Academic Press, Inc., pp. 305, 1990.

[124] Goldman, Ronald, "Intersection of Two Lines in Three-Space," in Andrew S. Glassner, ed., *Graphics Gems*, Academic Press, Inc., pp. 304, 1990.

[125] Goldman, Ronald, "Matrices and Transformations," in Andrew S. Glassner, ed., *Graphics Gems*, Academic Press, Inc., pp. 472–475, 1990.

[126] Goldman, Ronald, "Recovering the Data from the Transformation Matrix," in James Arvo, ed., *Graphics Gems II*, Academic Press, Inc., pp. 324–331, 1991.

[127] Goldman, Ronald, "Decomposing Linear and Affine Transformations," in David Kirk, ed., *Graphics Gems III*, Academic Press, Inc., pp. 108–116, 1992.

[128] Goldsmith, Jeffrey, and John Salmon, "Automatic Creation of Object Hierarchies for Ray Tracing," *IEEE Computer Graphics and Applications*, vol. 7, no. 5, pp. 14–20, May 1987.

[129] Golub, Gene, and Charles Van Loan, *Matrix Computations*, Third Edition, Johns Hopkins University Press, 1996.

[130] Gonzalez, Rafael C., Richard E. Woods, and Ralph C. Gonzalez, *Digital Image Processing*, Third Edition, Addison-Wesley, Reading, Massachusetts, 1992.

[131] Gooch, Amy, Bruce Gooch, Peter Shirley, and Elaine Cohen, "A Non-Photorealistic Lighting Model for Automatic Technical Illustration," *Computer Graphics (SIGGRAPH '98 Proceedings)*, pp. 447–452, July 1998. `http://www.cs.utah.edu/~gooch/SIG98/abstract.html`

[132] Gooch, Bruce, Peter-Pike J. Sloan, Amy Gooch, Peter Shirley, and Richard Riesenfeld "Interactive Technical Illustration," *Proceedings 1999 Symposium on Interactive 3D Graphics*, pp. 31–38, April 1999. `http://www.cs.utah.edu/~bgooch/ITI/`

[133] Gordon, Dan, and Shuhong Chen, "Front-to-back display of BSP trees," *IEEE Computer Graphics and Applications*, vol. 11, no. 5, pp. 79–85, September 1991.

[134] Gortler, Steven J., Radek Grzeszczuk, Richard Szeliski, and Michael F. Cohen, "The Lumigraph," *Computer Graphics (SIGGRAPH '96 Proceedings)*, pp. 43–54, August, 1996. http://www.research. microsoft.com/~cohen/

[135] Gottschalk, S., M.C. Lin, and D. Manocha, "OBBTree: A Hierarchical Structure for Rapid Interference Detection," *Computer Graphics (SIGGRAPH '96 Proceedings)*, pp. 171–180, August, 1996. http: //www.cs.unc.edu/~geom/OBB/OBBT.html

[136] Gottschalk, Stefan, Personal communication, 1999.

[137] Gottschalk, Stefan, *Collision Queries using Oriented Bounding Boxes*, Ph.D. Thesis, Department of Computer Science, University of North Carolina at Chapel Hill, 1999.

[138] Gouraud, H., "Continuous shading of curved surfaces," *IEEE Transactions on Computers*, vol. C-20, pp. 623–629, June 1971.

[139] Green, D. and D. Hatch, "Fast Polygon-Cube Intersection Testing," in Alan Paeth, ed., *Graphics Gems V*, AP Professional, Boston, pp. 375–379, 1995. http://www.acm.org/tog/GraphicsGems/

[140] Greene, Ned, "Environment Mapping and Other Applications of World Projections," *IEEE Computer Graphics and Applications*, vol. 6, no. 11, pp. 21–29, November 1986.

[141] Greene, Ned, Michael Kass, and Gavin Miller, "Hierarchical Z-Buffer Visibility," *Computer Graphics (SIGGRAPH '93 Proceedings)*, pp. 231–238, August 1993.

[142] Greene, Ned, "Detecting Intersection of a Rectangular Solid and a Convex Polyhedron," in Paul S. Heckbert, ed., *Graphics Gems IV*, AP Professional, Boston, pp. 74–82, 1994.

[143] Greene, Ned, and Michael Kass, "Error-Bounded Antialiased Rendering of Complex Environments," *Computer Graphics (SIGGRAPH '94 Proceedings)*, pp. 59–66, July 1994.

[144] Greene, Ned, *Hierarchical Rendering of Complex Environments*, Ph.D. Thesis, University of California at Santa Cruz, Report No. UCSC-CRL-95-27, June 1995.

[145] Greene, Ned, "Hierarchical Polygon Tiling with Coverage Masks," *Computer Graphics (SIGGRAPH '96 Proceedings)*, pp. 65–74, August 1996.

[146] Gritz, Larry, Personal communication, 1999.

[147] Haeberli, P., and K. Akeley, "The Accumulation Buffer: Hardware Support for High-Quality Rendering," *Computer Graphics (SIGGRAPH '90 Proceedings)*, vol. 24, no. 4, pp. 309–318, August 1990.

[148] Haeberli, Paul, "Paint By Numbers: Abstract Image Representations," *Computer Graphics (SIGGRAPH '90 Proceedings)*, vol. 24, no. 4, pp. 207–214, August 1990.

[149] Haeberli, Paul, and Mark Segal "Texture Mapping as a Fundamental Drawing Primitive," *4th Eurographics Workshop on Rendering*, pp. 259–266, 1993. http://www.sgi.com/grafica/texmap/index.html

[150] Hahn, James K., "Realistic Animation of Rigid Bodies," *Computer Graphics (SIGGRAPH '88 Proceedings)*, vol. 22, no. 4, pp. 299–308, 1988.

[151] Haines, Eric, "Essential Ray Tracing Algorithms," Chapter 2 in Andrew Glassner, ed., *An Introduction to Ray Tracing*, Academic Press Inc., London, 1989.

[152] Haines, Eric, "Fast Ray-Convex Polyhedron Intersection," in James Arvo, ed., *Graphics Gems II*, Academic Press, Inc., pp. 247–250, 1991. http://www.acm.org/tog/GraphicsGems/

[153] Haines, Eric, "Point in Polygon Strategies," in Paul S. Heckbert, ed., *Graphics Gems IV*, AP Professional, Boston, pp. 24–46, 1994. http://www.acm.org/tog/GraphicsGems/

[154] Haines, Eric, and John Wallace, "Shaft Culling for Efficient Ray-Traced Radiosity," in P. Brunet and F.W. Jansen, eds., *Photorealistic Rendering in Computer Graphics (Proceedings of the Second Eurographics Workshop on Rendering)*, Springer-Verlag, New York, pp. 122–138, 1994. http://www.acm.org/tog/editors/erich/

[155] Haines, Eric, "The Curse of the Monkey's Paw," in Eric Haines, ed., *Ray Tracing News*, vol 10, no. 2, June 1997. http://www.acm.org/tog/resources/RTNews/html/rtnv10n2.html"#art8

[156] Hall, Roy, *Illumination and Color in Computer Generated Imagery*, Springer-Verlag, New York, 1989.

[157] Hall, Tim, "A how to for using OpenGL to Render Mirrors," *comp.graphics.api.opengl* newsgroup, August 1996.

[158] Hanrahan, Pat, "A Survey of Ray-Surface Intersection Algorithms," Chapter 3 in Andrew Glassner, ed. *An Introduction to Ray Tracing*, Academic Press Inc., London, 1989.

[159] Hanrahan, P., and P. Haeberli, "Direct WYSIWYG Painting and Texturing on 3D Shapes," *Computer Graphics (SIGGRAPH '90 Proceedings)*, vol. 24, no. 4, pp. 215–223, August 1990.

[160] Hart, Evan, Personal communication, 1999.

[161] He, Xiao D., Kenneth E. Torrance, François X. Sillion, and Donald P. Greenberg, "A Comprehensive Physical Model for Light Reflection," *Computer Graphics (SIGGRAPH '91 Proceedings)*, vol. 25, no. 4, pp. 175–186, July 1991.

[162] Hearn, Donald, and M. Pauline Baker, *Computer Graphics*, Second Edition, Prentice-Hall, Inc., Englewoods Cliffs, New Jersey, 1994.

[163] Heckbert, Paul, "Survey of Texture Mapping," *IEEE Computer Graphics and Applications*, vol. 6, no. 11, pp. 56–67, November 1986. http://www.cs.cmu.edu/~ph/#papers

[164] Heckbert, Paul S., "Fundamentals of Texture Mapping and Image Warping," Report No. 516, Computer Science Division, University of California, Berkeley, June 1989. http://www.cs.cmu.edu/~ph/#papers

[165] Heckbert, Paul S., "Adaptive Radiosity Textures for Bidirectional Ray Tracing," *Computer Graphics (SIGGRAPH '90 Proceedings)*, vol. 24, no. 4, pp. 145–154, August 1990.

[166] Heckbert, Paul S., ed., *Graphics Gems IV*, AP Professional, Boston, 1994. http://www.acm.org/tog/GraphicsGems/

[167] Heckbert, Paul S., and Michael Herf, *Simulating Soft Shadows with Graphics Hardware*, Technical Report CMU-CS-97-104, Carnegie Mellon University, January 1997.

[168] Heckbert, Paul S., and Michael Garland, "Survey of Polygonal Surface Simplification Algorithms," to appear as a CMU-CS Technical Report. http://www.cs.cmu.edu/~garland/

[169] Hecker, Chris, "More Compiler Results, and What To Do About It," *Game Developer Magazine*, pp. 14–21, August/September 1996. http://www.d6.com/users/checker/misctech.htm

[170] Heidmann, Tim, "Real shadows, real time," *Iris Universe*, No. 18, pp. 23–31, Silicon Graphics Inc., November 1991.

[171] Heidrich, Wolfgang, and Hans-Peter Seidel, "View-independent Environment Maps," *Proceedings of the 1998 Eurographics/SIGGRAPH Workshop on Graphics Hardware*, Lisbon, Portugal, pp. 39–45, August 1998.

[172] Heidrich, Wolfgang, and Hans-Peter Seidel, "Efficient Rendering of Anisotropic Surfaces Using Computer Graphics Hardware," *Image and Multi-dimensional Digital Signal Processing Workshop (IMDSP)*, 1998. http://www9.informatik.uni-erlangen.de/eng/research/rendering/anisotropic/

[173] Heidrich, Wolfgang, Rüdifer Westermann, Hans-Peter Seidel, and Thomas Ertl, "Applications of Pixel Textures in Visualization and Realistic Image Synthesis," *Proceedings 1999 Symposium on Interactive 3D Graphics*, pp. 127–134, April 1999.

[174] Heidrich, Wolfgang, and Hans-Peter Seidel, "Realistic, Hardware-accelerated Shading and Lighting," *Computer Graphics (SIGGRAPH '99 Proceedings)*, pp. 171-178, August 1999. http://www.mpi-sb.mpg.de/~heidrich/

[175] Held, M., J.T. Klosowski, and J.S.B. Mitchell, "Speed Comparison of Generalized Bounding Box Hierarchies," Technical Report, Department of Applied Math, SUNY Stony Brook, 1995.

[176] Held, M., J.T. Klosowski, and J.S.B. Mitchell, "Evaluation of Collision Detection Methods for Virtual Reality Fly-Throughs," *Proceedings of the 7th Canadian Conference on Computational Geometry*, pp. 205–210, 1995.

[177] Held, M., J.T. Klosowski, and J.S.B. Mitchell, "Real-Time Collision Detection for Motion Simulation within Complex Environments," *Visual Proceedings (SIGGRAPH '96)*, p. 151, August 1996.

[178] Held, Martin, "ERIT—A Collection of Efficient and Reliable Intersection Tests," *journal of graphics tools*, vol. 2, no. 4, pp. 25–44, 1997. http://www.acm.org/jgt/papers/Held97

[179] Held, Martin, "FIST: Fast Industrial-Strength Triangulation," submitted for publication, 1998. http://www.cosy.sbg.ac.at/~held/publications.html

[180] Hennessy, John L., and David A. Patterson, *Computer Architecture—A quantitative approach*, Morgan Kaufmann Publishers, Inc., Palo Alto, California, 1990.

[181] Herf, M., and P.S. Heckbert, "Fast Soft Shadows," sketch in *Visual Proceedings (SIGGRAPH '96)*, p. 145, August 1996.

[182] Herrell, Russ, Joe Baldwin, and Chris Wilcox, "High-Quality Polygon Edging," *IEEE Computer Graphics and Applications*, vol. 15, no. 4, pp. 68–74, July 1995.

[183] Hill, Steve, "A Simple Fast Memory Allocator," in David Kirk, ed., *Graphics Gems III*, Academic Press, Inc., pp. 49–50, 1992. http://www.acm.org/tog/GraphicsGems/

[184] Hill, F.S., Jr., "The Pleasures of "Perp Dot" Products," in Paul S. Heckbert, ed., *Graphics Gems IV*, AP Professional, Boston, pp. 138–148, 1994.

[185] Hoff III, Kenneth E., "Backface Cluster Culling using Normal-Space Partitioning," 1996. http://www.cs.unc.edu/~hoff/techrep/quickbfc.html

[186] Hoff III, Kenneth E., "A Faster Overlap Test for a Plane and a Bounding Box," 1996. http://www.cs.unc.edu/~hoff/research/vfculler/boxplane.html

[187] Hook, Brian, "Multipass Rendering and the Magic of Alpha Blending," *Game Developer*, vol. 4, no. 5, pp. 12–19, August 1997.

[188] Hoppe, Hugues, "Progressive Meshes," *Computer Graphics (SIGGRAPH '96 Proceedings)*, pp. 99–108, August 1996. http://research.microsoft.com/~hoppe/

[189] Hoppe, Hugues, "Efficient Implementation of Progressive Meshes," *Computers and Graphics*, vol. 22, no. 1, pp. 27-36, 1998. http://research.microsoft.com/~hoppe/

[190] Hourcade, J.C., and A. Nicolas, "Algorithms for Antialiased Cast Shadows," *Computers and Graphics*, vol. 9, no. 3, pp. 259–265, 1985.

[191] Hubbard, Philip M., "Approximating Polyhedra with Spheres for Time-Critical Collision Detection," *ACM Transactions on Graphics*, vol. 15, no. 3, pp. 179–210, 1996.

[192] Hudson, T., M. Lin, J. Cohen, S. Gottschalk, and D. Manocha, "V-COLLIDE: Accelerated collision detection for VRML," *Proceedings of VRML '97*, Monterey, California, February 1997.

[193] Hudson, T., D. Manocha, J. Cohen, M. Lin, K. Hoff, and H. Zhang, "Accelerated Occlusion Culling using Shadow Frusta," *Thirteenth ACM Symposium on Computational Geometry*, Nice, France, June 1997.

[194] Hutson, V., and J.S. Pym, *Applications of Functional Analysis and Operator Theory*, Academic Press, London, 1980.

[195] Igehy, Homan, Gordon Stoll, and Pat Hanrahan, "The Design of a Parallel Graphics Interface," *Computer Graphics (SIGGRAPH '98 Proceedings)*, pp. 141–150, July 1998. http://graphics.stanford.edu/papers/parallel_api/

[196] Ikedo, T., and J. Ma, "The Truga001: A Scalable Rendering Processor," *IEEE Computer Graphics and Applications*, vol. 18, no. 2, pp. 59–79, March/April 1998. http://computer.org/cga/cg1998/g2toc.htm

[197] *IPEAK*, Intel Corporation, http://www.pentium.com/design/ipeak/

[198] *Iris Graphics Library Programming Guide*, Silicon Graphics Inc., 1991.

[199] Kajiya, James T., "Anisotropic Reflection Models," *Computer Graphics (SIGGRAPH '85 Proceedings)*, vol. 19, no. 3, pp. 15–21, July 1985.

[200] Kajiya, James T., "The Rendering Equation," *Computer Graphics (SIGGRAPH '86 Proceedings)*, vol. 20, no. 4, pp. 143–150, August 1986.

[201] Kay, T.L. and J.T. Kajiya, "Ray Tracing Complex Scenes," *Computer Graphics (SIGGRAPH '86 Proceedings)*, vol. 20, no. 4, pp. 269–278, August 1986.

[202] Kempf, Renate, and Jed Hartman, *OpenGL on Silicon Graphics Systems*, Silicon Graphics Inc., 1998.

[203] Kershaw, Kathleen, *A Generalized Texture-Mapping Pipeline*, M.S. Thesis, Program of Computer Graphics, Cornell University, Ithaca, New York, 1992.

[204] Kilgard, Mark, "Fast OpenGL-rendering of Lens Flares," http:// reality.sgi.com/mjk/tips/lensflare/

[205] Kilgard, Mark J., "Realizing OpenGL: Two Implementations of One Architecture," *Proceedings of the 1997 SIGGRAPH/Eurographics Workshop on Graphics Hardware*, Los Angeles, California, pp. 45–55, August 1997. http://reality.sgi.com/mjk/twoimps/twoimps.html

[206] Kim, Dong-Jin, Leonidas J. Guibas, and Sung-Yong Shin, "Fast Collision Detection Among Multiple Moving Spheres," *IEEE Transactions on Visualization and Computer Graphics*, vol. 4, no. 3., July/September 1998.

[207] Kirk, David B., and Douglas Voorhies, "The Rendering Architecture of the DN-10000VS," *Computer Graphics (SIGGRAPH '90 Proceedings)*, vol. 24, no. 4, pp. 299–307, August 1990.

[208] Kirk, David, *Graphics Gems III*, Academic Press Inc., Boston, 1992. http://www.acm.org/tog/GraphicsGems/

[209] Klosowski, J.T., M. Held, J.S.B. Mitchell, H. Sowizral, and K. Zikan, "Efficient Collision Detection Using Bounding Volume Hierarchies of k-DOPs," *IEEE Transactions on Visualization and Computer Graphics*, vol. 4, no. 1, 1998.

[210] Knuth, Donald E., *The Art of Computer Programming: Sorting and Searching*, vol. 3, Second Edition, Addison-Wesley, Reading, Massachusetts, 1998.

[211] Kochanek, Doris H.U., and Richard H. Bartels, "Interpolating Splines with Local Tension, Continuity, and Bias Control," *Computer Graphics (SIGGRAPH '84 Proceedings)*, vol. 18, pp. 33–41, July 1984.

[212] Konečný, Petr, *Bounding Volumes in Computer Graphics*, M.S. Thesis, Faculty of Informatics, Masaryk University, Brno, April 1998. http://www.fi.muni.cz/~pekon/

[213] Krishnan, S., A. Pattekar, M.C. Lin, and D. Manocha, "Spherical Shell: A Higher Order Bounding Volume for Fast Proximity Queries," *Proceedings of Third International Workshop on Algorithmic Foundations of Robotics*, pp. 122–136, 1998. http://www.cs.unc.edu/~dm/

[214] Krishnan, S., M. Gopi, M. Lin, D. Manocha, and A. Pattekar, "Rapid and Accurate Contact Determination between Spline Models using Shell-Trees," *Proceedings of Eurographics '98*, vol. 17, no. 3, pp. C315–C326, 1998. http://www.cs.unc.edu/~dm/

[215] Kumar, Subodh, and Dinesh Manocha, "Hierarchical Visibility Culling for Spline Models," *Graphics Interface 96*, Toronto, Canada, pp. 142–150, May 1996. ftp://ftp.cs.unc.edu/pub/publications/techreports/FILE.html

[216] Kumar, S., D. Manocha, B. Garrett, and M. Lin, "Hierarchical Back-Face Computation," *Proceedings of Eurographics Rendering Workshop 1996*, pp. 235–244, June 1996.

[217] Lacroute, Philippe, and Marc Levoy, "Fast Volume Rendering Using a Shear-Warp Factorization of the Viewing Transformation," *Computer Graphics (SIGGRAPH '94 Proceedings)*, pp. 451–458, July 1994. http://www-graphics.stanford.edu/papers/shear/

[218] Laidlaw, D.H., W.B. Trumbore, and J. Hughes, "Constructive Solid Geometry for Polyhedral Objects," *Computer Graphics (SIGGRAPH '86 Proceedings)*, vol. 20, no. 4, pp. 161–168, August 1986.

[219] LaMothe, André, "Real-Time Voxel Terrain Generation," *Game Developer Magazine*, vol. 4, no. 8, pp. 34–44, November 1997. http://www.gdmag.com/code.htm

[220] Lander, Jeff, "The Ocean Spray in Your Face," *Game Developer Magazine*, vol. 5, no. 7, pp. 13–19, July 1998. http://www.gdmag.com/code.htm

[221] Lansdown, John, and Simon Schofield, "Expressive Rendering: A Review of Nonphotorealistic Techniques," *IEEE Computer Graphics and Applications*, vol. 15, no. 3, pp. 29–37, May 1995. http://computer.org/cga/cg1995/g3toc.htm

[222] Lastra, Anselmo, Steven Molnar, Marc Olano, and Yulan Wang, "Real-Time Programmable Shading," *Proceedings of the 1995 Symposium on Interactive 3D Graphics*, pp. 59–66, April 1995.

[223] Lathrop, Olin, David Kirk, and Doug Voorhies, "Accurate Rendering by Subpixel Addressing," *IEEE Computer Graphics and Applications*, vol. 10, no. 5, pp. 45–53, September 1990.

[224] Laur, David, and Pat Hanrahan, "Hierarchical Splatting: A Progressive Refinement Algorithm for Volume Rendering," *Computer Graphics (SIGGRAPH '91 Proceedings)*, vol. 25, no. 4, pp. 285–288, July 1991.

[225] Lawson, Terry, *Linear Algebra*, John Wiley & Sons, Inc., New York, 1996.

[226] Lax, Peter D., *Linear Algebra*, John Wiley & Sons, Inc., New York, 1997.

[227] Legakis, Justin, "Fast Multi-Layer Fog," *Conference Abstracts and Applications (SIGGRAPH '98)*, p. 266, July 1998.

[228] Lengyel, Jed, and John Snyder "Rendering With Coherent Layers," *Computer Graphics (SIGGRAPH '97 Proceedings)*, pp. 233–242, August 1997. http://www.research.microsoft.com/~jedl/

[229] Lengyel, Jed, "The Convergence of Graphics and Vision," *Computer*, pp. 46–53, July 1998. http://www.research.microsoft.com/~jedl/

[230] Levoy, Marc, and Pat Hanrahan "Light Field Rendering," *Computer Graphics (SIGGRAPH '96 Proceedings)*, pp. 31–42, August, 1996. http://www-graphics.stanford.edu/papers/light/

[231] Libes, Don, "Obfuscated C and Other Mysteries," Wiley Books, 1996.

[232] Lin, M.C., and J. Canny, "Efficient Collision Detection for Animation," *Proceedings of the Third Eurographics Workshop on Animation and Simulation*, England, 1991.

[233] Lin, M.C., *Efficient Collision Detection for Animation and Robotics*, Ph.D. Thesis, University of California, Berkeley, 1993.

[234] Lin, M.C., D. Manocha, J. Cohen, and S. Gottschalk, "Collision Detection: Algorithms and Applications," *Proceedings of Algorithms for Robotics Motion and Manipulation*, Jean-Paul Laumond and M. Overmars, eds., A.K. Peters pp. 129–142, 1996.

[235] Lin, M.C., and S. Gottschalk, "Collision Detection between Geometric Models: A Survey," *Proceedings of IMA Conference on Mathematics of Surfaces*, 1998. http://www.cs.unc.edu/~dm/

[236] Lin, M.C., Personal communication, 1998.

[237] Lindstrom, Peter, and Greg Turk, "Fast and Memory Efficient Polygonal Simplification," *IEEE Visualization 1998*, pp. 279–286, July 1998. http://www.cc.gatech.edu/gvu/people/peter.lindstrom/

[238] Luebke, David P., and Chris Georges, "Portals and Mirrors: Simple, Fast Evaluation of Potentially Visible Sets," *Proceedings 1995 Symposium on Interactive 3D Graphics*, pp. 105–106, April 1995.

[239] Maciel, P., and P. Shirley, "Visual Navigation of Large Environments Using Textured Clusters," *Proceeding 1995 Symposium on Interactive 3D Graphics*, pp. 96–102, 1995. ftp://ftp.cs.indiana.edu/pub/shirley/interactive95.ps.Z

[240] Maillot, Patrick-Giles, "Using Quaternions for Coding 3D Transformations," in Andrew S. Glassner, ed., *Graphics Gems*, Academic Press, Inc., Boston, pp. 498–515, 1990. http://www.acm.org/tog/GraphicsGems/

[241] Markosian, Lee, Michael A. Kowalski, Samuel J. Trychin, Lubomir D. Bourdev, Daniel Goldstein, and John F. Hughes, "Real-Time Nonphotorealistic Rendering," *Computer Graphics (SIGGRAPH '97 Proceedings)*, pp. 415–420, August 1997. http://www.cs.brown.edu/research/graphics/research/npr/home.html

[242] McCabe, Dan, and John Brothers, "DirectX 6 Texture Map Compression," *Game Developer Magazine*, vol. 5, no. 8, pp. 42–46, August 1998. http://www.gdmag.com/code.htm

[243] McCloud, Scott, *Understanding Comics: The Invisible Art*, Harper Perennial, 1994.

[244] McCormack, Joel, Bob McNamara, Christopher Gianos, Larry Seiler, Norman P. Jouppi, Ken Corell, Todd Dutton, and John Zurawski, "Implementing Neon: A 256-Bit Graphics Accelerator," *IEEE Micro*, vol. 19, no. 2, March/April 1999. http://www.research.digital.com/wrl/publications/abstracts/98.1.html

[245] McReynolds, Tom, David Blythe, Brad Grantham, and Scott Nelson, "Programming with OpenGL: Advanced Techniques," *Course 17 notes at SIGGRAPH '98*, 1998. http://www.sgi.com/software/opengl/advanced98/notes/

[246] McVoy, Larry, and Carl Staelin, "lmbench: Portable tools for performance analysis," *Proceedings of the USENIX 1996 Annual Technical Conference*, San Diego, pp. 120–133, January 1996. http://www.bitmover. com/lmbench/

[247] Melax, Stan, "A Simple, Fast, and Effective Polygon Reduction Algorithm," *Game Developer*, vol. 5, no. 11, pp. 44–49, November 1998. http://www.cs.ualberta.ca/~melax/polychop/

[248] Miano, John, "The Programmer's Guide to Compressed Image Files," Addison-Wesley, Reading, Massachusetts, 1999.

[249] Miller, Gavin, Mark Halstead, and Michael Clifton, "On-the-Fly Texture Computation for Real-Time Surface Shading," *IEEE Computer Graphics and Applications*, vol. 18, no. 2, pp. 44–58, March/April 1998. http://computer.org/cga/cg1998/g2toc.htm

[250] Mirtich, Brian, "Fast and Accurate Computation of Polyhedral Mass Properties," *journal of graphics tools*, vol. 1, no. 2, pp. 31–50, 1996. http://www.acm.org/jgt/papers/Mirtich96/

[251] Mirtich, Brian, "V-Clip: Fast and Robust Polyhedral Collision Detection," Technical Report TR97-05, 1997. http://www.merl.com/projects/vclip/

[252] Mirtich, Brian, "V-Clip: fast and robust polyhedral collision detection," *ACM Transactions on Graphics*, vol. 17, no. 3, July 1998.

[253] Mitchell, Jason L., "Optimization of Direct3D Applications for Hardware Acceleration," *Gamasutra*, vol. 1, no. 12, December 5, 1997. http://www.gamasutra.com/features/programming/121297/optimizing_direct3d_01.htm

[254] Mitchell, Jason L., Michael Tatro, and Ian Bullard, "Multitexturing in DirectX 6," *Game Developer*, vol. 5, no. 9, pp. 33–37, September 1998. http://www.gamasutra.com/features/programming/19981009/multitexturing_01.htm

[255] Mitchell, Jason L., Personal communication, 1998-9.

[256] Möller, Tomas, and Ben Trumbore, "Fast, Minimum Storage Ray-Triangle Intersection," *journal of graphics tools*, vol. 2, no. 1, pp. 21–28, 1997. http://www.acm.org/jgt/papers/MollerTrumbore97/

[257] Möller, Tomas, "A Fast Triangle-Triangle Intersection Test," *journal of graphics tools*, vol. 2, no. 2, pp. 25–30, 1997. http://www.acm.org/jgt/papers/Moller97/

[258] Möller, Tomas, *Real-Time Algorithms and Intersection Test Methods for Computer Graphics*, Ph.D. Thesis, Technology, Technical Report No. 341, Department of Computer Engineering, Chalmers University of October 1998.

[259] Molnar, S., J. Eyles, and J. Poulton, "PixelFlow: High-Speed Rendering Using Image Composition," *Computer Graphics (SIGGRAPH '92 Proceedings)*, vol. 26, no. 2, pp. 231–240, July 1992.

[260] Molnar, S., M. Cox, D. Ellsworth, and H. Fuchs, "A Sorting Classification of Parallel Rendering," *IEEE Computer Graphics and Applications*, vol. 14, no. 4, pp. 23–32, July 1994.

[261] Molnar, S., "The PixelFlow Texture and Image Subsystem," in the *Proceedings of the 10th Eurographics Workshop on Graphics Hardware*, Maastricht, Netherlands, pp. 3–13, August 28–29, 1995.

[262] Montrym, J., D. Baum, D. Dignam, and C. Migdal, "InfiniteReality: A Real-Time Graphics System," *Computer Graphics (SIGGRAPH '97 Proceedings)*, pp. 293–302, August 1997.

[263] Moore, Matthew, and Jane Wilhelms, "Collision Detection and Response for Computer Animation," *Computer Graphics (SIGGRAPH '88 Proceedings)*, vol. 22, no. 4, pp. 289–298, August 1988.

[264] Muchnick, Steven, "Advanced Compiler Design and Implementation," Morgan Kaufmann Publishers, San Francisco, 1997.

[265] Murray, James D., and William VanRyper, *Encyclopedia of Graphics File Formats*, Second Edition, O'Reilly, Sebastopol, California, 1996. http://www.ora.com/centers/gff/index.htm

[266] Narkhede, Atul, and Dinesh Manocha, "Fast Polygon Triangulation Based on Seidel's Algorithm," Paeth, Alan W., ed., *Graphics Gems V*, AP Professional, Boston, pp. 394–397, 1995. Improved code at: http://www.cs.unc.edu/~dm/CODE/GEM/chapter.html

[267] Naylor, B., J. Amanatides, and W. Thibault, "Merging BSP Trees Yield Polyhedral Modeling Results," *Computer Graphics (SIGGRAPH '89 Proceedings)*, vol. 23, no. 3, pp. 115–124, July 1989.

[268] Nelson, Scott R., "Twelve characteristics of correct antialiased lines," *journal of graphics tools*, vol. 1, no. 4, pp. 1–20, 1996. http://www.acm.org/jgt/papers/Nelson96/

[269] Nelson, Scott R., "High quality hardware line antialiasing," *journal of graphics tools*, vol. 2, no. 1, pp. 29–46, 1997. http://www.acm.org/jgt/papers/Nelson97/

[270] Nishita, Tomoyuki, Thomas W. Sederberg, and Masanori Kakimoto, "Ray Tracing Trimmed Rational Surface Patches," *Computer Graphics (SIGGRAPH '90 Proceedings)*, vol. 24, no. 4, pp. 337–345, August 1990.

[271] Nguyen Hubert Huu, "Casting Shadows on Volumes," *Game Developer*, vol. 6, no. 3, pp. 44–53, March 1999.

[272] Ofek, E., and A. Rappoport, "Interactive Reflections on Curved Objects," *Computer Graphics (SIGGRAPH '98 Proceedings)*, pp. 333–342, July 1998.

[273] Oliveira, Manuel M., and Gary Bishop, "Image-Based Objects," *Proceedings 1999 Symposium on Interactive 3D Graphics*, pp. 191–198, April 1999. http://www.cs.unc.edu/~ibr/pubs.html

[274] Omohundro, Stephen M., "Five Balltree Construction Algorithms," Technical Report #89-063, International Computer Science Institute, 1989. http://www.icsi.berkeley.edu/techreports/

[275] OpenGL Architecture Review Board, J. Neider, T. Davis, and M. Woo, *OpenGL Programming Guide*, Third Edition, Addison-Wesley, Reading, Massachusetts, 1999.

[276] OpenGL Architecture Review Board, *OpenGL Reference Manual*, Third Edition, Addison-Wesley, Reading, Massachusetts, 1999.

[277] *OpenGL Optimizer Programmer's Guide: An Open API for Large-Model Visualization*, Silicon Graphics Inc., 1997. http://www.sgi.com/software/optimizer/

[278] *OpenGL Volumizer Programmer's Guide*, Silicon Graphics Inc., 1998. http://www.sgi.com/software/volumizer/tech_info.html

[279] Oren, Michael, and Shree K. Nayar, "Generalization of Lambert's Reflectance Model," *Computer Graphics (SIGGRAPH '94 Proceedings)*, pp. 239–246, July 1994. http://www.cs.columbia.edu/~oren/

[280] O'Rourke, Joseph, *Computational Geometry in C*, Second Edition, Cambridge University Press, Cambridge, 1998. `ftp://cs.smith.edu/pub/compgeom/`

[281] Paeth, Alan W., "A Fast Algorithm for General Raster Rotation," in Andrew S. Glassner, ed., *Graphics Gems*, Academic Press, Inc., Boston, pp. 179–195, 1990. `http://www.acm.org/tog/GraphicsGems/`

[282] Paeth, Alan W., ed., *Graphics Gems V*, AP Professional, Boston, 1995. `http://www.acm.org/tog/GraphicsGems/`

[283] Parker, Steven, William Martin, Peter-Pike J. Sloan, Peter Shirley, Brian Smits, Charles Hansen, "Interactive Ray Tracing," *Proceedings 1999 Symposium on Interactive 3D Graphics*, pp. 119–134, April 1999. `http://www2.cs.utah.edu/~bes/`

[284] Paul, Richard P.C., *Robot Manipulators: Mathematics, Programming, and Control*, MIT Press, Cambridge, Mass., 1981.

[285] Peercy, M., J. Airey, and B. Cabral, "Efficient Bump Mapping Hardware," *Computer Graphics (SIGGRAPH '97 Proceedings)*, pp. 303–306, August 1997.

[286] Phong, Bui Tuong, "Illumination for Computer Generated Pictures", *Communications of the ACM*, vol. 18, no. 6, pp. 311–317, June 1975.

[287] Piegl, L. and W. Tiller, *The NURBS Book*, Springer-Verlag, Berlin/Heidelberg, Second Edition, 1997.

[288] Pineda, Juan, "A Parallel Algorithm for Polygon Rasterization," *Computer Graphics (SIGGRAPH '88 Proceedings)*, vol. 22, no. 4, pp. 17–20, August 1988.

[289] Pletinckx, Daniel, "Quaternion calculus as a basic tools in computer graphics," *The Visual Computer*, vol. 5, pp. 2–13, 1989.

[290] Porter, Thomas, and Tom Duff, "Compositing digital images," *Computer Graphics (SIGGRAPH '84 Proceedings)*, vol. 18, no. 3, pp. 253–259, July 1984.

[291] Poynton, Charles, *A Technical Introduction to Digital Video*, John Wiley & Sons, Inc., New York, pp. 91–114, 1996. `http://www.inforamp.net/~poynton/Poynton-colour.html`

[292] Preparata, F.P., and M.I. Shamos, *Computational Geometry: An Introduction*, Springer-Verlag, New York, NY, 1985.

[293] Proakis, John G., and Dimitris G. Manolakis, *Digital Signal Processing—Principles, Algorithms, and Applications*, Third Edition, Macmillan Publishing Company, New York, 1996.

[294] Rafferty, Matthew, Daniel Aliaga, Voicu Popescu, and Anselmo Lastra, "Images for Accelerating Architectural Walkthroughs," *IEEE Computer Graphics and Applications*, vol. 18, no. 6, pp. 38–45, Nov./Dec. 1998.

[295] Source code for collision detection by the Research Group on Modeling, Physically-Based Simulation and Applications at the University of North Chapel Hill, *RAPID—Robust and Accurate Polygon Interference Detection*, available at http://www.cs.unc.edu/~geom/OBB/OBB.html, 1997.

[296] Reeves, William T., "Particle Systems—A Technique for Modeling a Class of Fuzzy Objects," *ACM Transactions on Graphics*, vol. 2, no. 2, pp. 91–108, April 1983.

[297] Reeves, William T., and Ricki Blau, "Approximate and Probabilistic Algorithms for Shading and Rendering Structured Particle Systems," *Computer Graphics (SIGGRAPH '85 Proceedings)*, vol. 19, no. 3, pp. 313–322, July 1985.

[298] Reeves, William T., David H. Salesin, and Robert L. Cook, "Rendering Antialiased Shadows with Depth Maps," *Computer Graphics (SIGGRAPH '87 Proceedings)*, vol. 21, no. 4, pp. 283–291, July 1987.

[299] Rogers, David F., *Mathematical Elements for Computer Graphics*, Second Edition, McGraw-Hill, New York, 1989.

[300] Rogers, David F., *Procedural Elements for Computer Graphics*, Second Edition, McGraw-Hill, New York, 1997.

[301] Rohlf, J., and J. Helman, "IRIS Performer: A High Performance Multiprocessing Toolkit for Real-Time 3D Graphics," *Computer Graphics (SIGGRAPH '94 Proceedings)*, pp. 381–394, July 1994.

[302] Rule, Keith, *3D Graphics File Formats: A Programmer's Reference*, Addison-Wesley, Reading, Massachusetts, 1996. http://www.europa.com/~keithr/

[303] Rundberg, Peter *An Optimized Collision Detection Algorithm*, M.S. Thesis, Department of Computer Engineering, Chalmers University of Technology, Gothenburg, 1999. `http://www.ce.chalmers.se/staff/biff/exjobb/`

[304] "S3TC DirectX 6.0 Standard Texture Compression," S3 Inc., 1998. `http://www.s3.com/savage3d/s3tc.htm`

[305] Saito, Takafumi, and Tokiichiro Takahashi, "Comprehensible Rendering of 3-D Shapes," *Computer Graphics (SIGGRAPH '90 Proceedings)*, vol. 24, no. 4, pp. 197–206, August 1990.

[306] Samet, Hanan, *Applications of Spatial Data Structures: Computer Graphics, Image Processing and GIS*, Addison-Wesley, Reading, Massachusetts, 1989.

[307] Samet, Hanan, *The Design and Analysis of Spatial Data Structures*, Addison-Wesley, Reading, Massachusetts, 1989.

[308] Samosky, Joseph, *SectionView: A system for interactively specifying and visualizing sections through three-dimensional medical image data*, M.S. Thesis, Department of Electrical Engineering and Computer Science, Massachusetts Institute of Technology, 1993.

[309] Schaufler, Gernot, "Dynamically Generated Impostors," *GI Workshop on "Modeling - Virtual Worlds - Distributed Graphics,"* D.W. Fellner, ed., Infix Verlag, pp. 129–135, November 1995. `http://www.gup.uni-linz.ac.at:8001/staff/schaufler/papers/`

[310] Schaufler, G., and W. Stürzlinger, "A Three Dimensional Image Cache for Virtual Reality," in *Proceedings of Eurographics '96*, pp. 227–236, 1996. `http://www.gup.uni-linz.ac.at:8001/staff/schaufler/papers/`

[311] Schaufler, Gernot, "Exploiting Frame to Frame Coherence in a Virtual Reality System," *VRAIS '96*, Santa Clara, California, pp. 95–102, April 1996. `http://www.gup.uni-linz.ac.at:8001/staff/schaufler/papers/`

[312] Schaufler, Gernot, "Nailboards: A Rendering Primitive for Image Caching in Dynamic Scenes," *Eurographics Rendering Workshop 1997*, pp. 151–162, 1997. `http://www.gup.uni-linz.ac.at:8001/staff/schaufler/papers/`

[313] Schaufler, Gernot, "Per-Object Image Warping with Layered Impostors," *Proceedings of the 9th Eurographics Workshop on Rendering '98*, Vienna, Austria, pp. 145–156, June 29–July 1 1998. http://www.gup.uni-linz.ac.at:8001/staff/schaufler/papers/

[314] Schilling, Andreas, and Wolfgang Straßer, "EXACT: Algorithm and Hardware Architecture for an Improved A-buffer," *Computer Graphics (SIGGRAPH '93 Proceedings)*, pp. 85–92, August 1993.

[315] Schilling, Andreas, G. Knittel, and Wolfgang Straßer, "Texram: A Smart Memory for Texturing," *IEEE Computer Graphics and Applications*, vol. 16, no. 3, pp. 32–41, May 1996. http://computer.org/cga/cg1996/g3toc.htm

[316] Schlag, John, "Using Geometric Constructions to Interpolate Orientations with Quaternions," in James Arvo, ed., *Graphics Gems II*, Academic Press, Inc., pp. 377–380, 1991.

[317] Schlag, John, "Fast Embossing Effects on Raster Image Data," in Paul S. Heckbert, ed., *Graphics Gems IV*, AP Professional, Boston, pp. 433–437, 1994. http://www.acm.org/tog/GraphicsGems/

[318] Schlick, Christophe, "A Fast Alternative to Phong's Specular Model," in Paul S. Heckbert, ed., *Graphics Gems IV*, AP Professional, Boston, pp. 385–387, 1994.

[319] Schorn, Peter and Frederick Fisher, "Testing the Convexity of Polygon," in Paul S. Heckbert, ed., *Graphics Gems IV*, AP Professional, Boston, pp. 7–15, 1994. http://www.acm.org/tog/GraphicsGems/

[320] Scott, N., D. Olsen, and E. Gannett, "An Overview of the VISUALIZE fx Graphics Accelerator Hardware," *Hewlett-Packard Journal*, pp. 28–34, May 1998. http://www.hp.com/hpj/98may/ma98a4.htm

[321] Segal, M., C. Korobkin, R. van Widenfelt, J. Foran, and P. Haeberli, "Fast Shadows and Lighting Effects Using Texture Mapping," *Computer Graphics (SIGGRAPH '92 Proceedings)*, vol. 26, no. 2, pp. 249–252, July 1992.

[322] Segal, Mark, and Kurt Akeley, *The OpenGL Graphics System: A Specification (Version 1.2.1)*, Editor (v1.1): Chris Frazier, Editor (v1.2): Jon Leech, March 1998. http://www.opengl.org/

[323] Shade, J., D. Lischinski, D. Salesin, T. DeRose, and J. Snyder, "Hierarchical Image Caching for Accelerated Walkthroughs of Complex Environments," *Computer Graphics (SIGGRAPH '96 Proceedings)*, pp. 75–82, August 1996. http://www.cs.washington.edu/research/grail/pub/abstracts.html#HierImageCache

[324] Shade, J., Steven Gortler, Li-Wei He, and Richard Szeliski, "Layered Depth Images," *Computer Graphics (SIGGRAPH '98 Proceedings)*, pp. 231–242, July 1998. http://www.research.microsoft.com/MSRSIGGRAPH/1998/ldi.htm

[325] Shene, Ching-Kuang, "Computing the Intersection of a Line and a Cylinder," in Paul S. Heckbert, ed., *Graphics Gems IV*, AP Professional, Boston, pp. 353–355, 1994.

[326] Shene, Ching-Kuang, "Computing the Intersection of a Line and a Cone," in Alan Paeth, ed., *Graphics Gems V*, AP Professional, Boston, pp. 227–231, 1995.

[327] Shirley, Peter, *Physically Based Lighting Calculations for Computer Graphics*, Ph.D. Thesis, University of Illinois at Urbana Champaign, December 1990.

[328] Shoemake, Ken, "Animating Rotation with Quaternion Curves," *Computer Graphics (SIGGRAPH '85 Proceedings)*, vol. 19, no. 3, pp. 245–254, July 1985.

[329] Shoemake, Ken, "Quaternions and 4×4 Matrices," in James Arvo, ed., *Graphics Gems II*, Academic Press, Inc., pp. 351–354, 1991.

[330] Shoemake, Ken, "Polar Matrix Decomposition," in Paul S. Heckbert, ed., *Graphics Gems IV*, AP Professional, Boston, pp. 207–221, 1994. http://www.acm.org/tog/GraphicsGems/

[331] Shoemake, Ken, "Euler Angle Conversion," in Paul S. Heckbert, ed., *Graphics Gems IV*, AP Professional, Boston, pp. 222–229, 1994. http://www.acm.org/tog/GraphicsGems/

[332] Shoemake, Ken, "Robust Universal Euler Angle Extraction," work in progress, 1999.

[333] Sillion, François, and Claude Puech, *Radiosity and Global Illumination*, Morgan Kaufmann Publishers, Inc., San Francisco, 1994.

[334] Sillion, François, G. Drettakis, and B. Bodelet, "Efficient Impostor Manipulation for Real-Time Visualization of Urban Scenery," *Computer Graphics Forum*, vol. 16, no. 3, pp. 207–218, 1997.

[335] Skiena, Steven, *The Algorithm Design Manual*, Springer Verlag, 1997.
http://www.cs.sunysb.edu/~algorith/

[336] Sloan, Peter-Pike, Michael F. Cohen, and Steven J. Gortler, "Time Critical
Lumigraph Rendering," *Proceedings 1997 Symposium on Interactive 3D
Graphics*, pp. 17–23, April 1997.

[337] Smith, Alvy R., "A Pixel is Not a Little Square, a Pixel is Not a Little
Square, a Pixel is Not a Little Square! (And a Voxel is Not a Little Cube),"
Technical Memo 6, Microsoft Research, July 1995. http://www.
research.microsoft.com/~Alvy/Memos/default.htm

[338] Smith, Alvy Ray, and James F. Blinn, "Blue Screen Matting," *Computer
Graphics (SIGGRAPH '96 Proceedings)*, pp. 259–268, August 1996.

[339] Smith, Alvy Ray, "The Stuff of Dreams," *Computer Graphics World*, pp.
27–29, July 1998.

[340] Snyder, John, Ronen Barzel, and Steve Gabriel, "Motion Blur on
Graphics Workstations," in David Kirk, ed., *Graphics Gems III*, Aca-
demic Press, Inc., pp. 374–382, 1992. http://www.acm.org/tog/
GraphicsGems/

[341] Snyder, John, and Jed Lengyel, "Visibility Sorting and Compositing
without Splitting for Image Layer Decompositions," *Computer Graphics (SIGGRAPH '98 Proceedings)*, pp. 219–230, July 1998. http:
//www.research.microsoft.com/~jedl/

[342] Spencer, Greg, Peter Shirley, Kurt Zimmerman, and Donald Greenberg,
"Physically-Based Glare Effects for Digital Images," *Computer Graphics
(SIGGRAPH '95 Proceedings)*, pp. 325–334, August 1995. http://
www.cs.utah.edu/~shirley/papers.html

[343] Stokes, Michael, Matthew Anderson, Srinivasan Chandrasekar, and Ri-
cardo Motta, "A Standard Default Color Space for the Internet - sRGB,"
Version 1.10, Nov. 1996. http://www.color.org/sRGB.html

[344] Stone, John, Personal communication, 1998.

[345] Strauss, Paul S., "A Realistic Lighting Model for Computer Animators," *IEEE Computer Graphics and Applications*, vol. 10, no. 6, pp. 56–64, November 1990.

[346] Sutherland, Ivan E., Robert F. Sproull, and Robert F. Schumacker, "A Characterization of Ten Hidden-Surface Algorithms," *Computing Surveys*, vol. 6, no. 1, March 1974.

[347] Tanner, Christopher C., Christopher J. Migdal, and Michael T. Jones, "The Clipmap: A Virtual Mipmap," *Computer Graphics (SIGGRAPH '98 Proceedings)*, pp. 151–158, July 1998.

[348] Taubin, Gabriel, André Guéziec, William Horn, and Francis Lazarus, "Progressive Forest Split Compression," *Computer Graphics (SIGGRAPH '98 Proceedings)*, pp. 123–132, July 1998.

[349] Teller, Seth J., and Carlo H. Séquin, "Visibility Preprocessing For Interactive Walkthroughs," *Computer Graphics (SIGGRAPH '91 Proceedings)*, vol. 25, no. 4, pp. 61–69, July 1991.

[350] Teller, Seth J., *Visibility Computations in Densely Occluded Polyhedral Environments*, Ph.D. Thesis, Department of Computer Science, University of Berkeley, 1992.

[351] Tessman, Thant, "Casting Shadows on Flat Surfaces," *Iris Universe*, pp. 16–19, Winter 1989.

[352] Thomas, Spencer W., "Decomposing a Matrix into Simple Transformations," in James Arvo, ed., *Graphics Gems II*, Academic Press, Inc., pp. 320–323, 1991. http://www.acm.org/tog/GraphicsGems/

[353] Thürmer, Grit, and Charles A. Wüthrich, "Computing Vertex Normals from Polygonal Facets," *journal of graphics tools*, vol. 3, no. 1, pp. 43–46, 1998.

[354] Torborg, J., and J.T. Kajiya, "Talisman: Commodity Realtime 3D Graphics for the PC," *Computer Graphics (SIGGRAPH '96 Proceedings)*, pp. 353–363, August 1996.

[355] Turkowski, Ken, "Properties of Surface-Normal Transformations," in Andrew Glassner, ed., *Graphics Gems*, Academic Press, Inc., pp. 539–547, 1990. http://www.worldserver.com/turk/computergraphics/index.html

[356] Tyberghein, Jorrit, Personal communication, 1999. `http://crystal.linuxgames.com`

[357] Upstill, S., *The RenderMan Companion—A Programmer's Guide to Realistic Computer Graphics*, Addison-Wesley, Reading, Massachusetts, 1990.

[358] van den Bergen, G., "Efficient Collision Detection of Complex Deformable Models Using AABB Trees," *journal of graphics tools*, vol. 2, no. 4, 1997. `http://www.acm.org/jgt/papers/vanDenBergen97`

[359] van den Bergen, G., "A Fast and Robust GJK Implementation for Collision Detection of Convex Objects," submitted for publication, 1998.

[360] Voorhies, Douglas, "Triangle-Cube Intersection," in David Kirk, ed., *Graphics Gems III*, AP Professional, Boston, pp. 236–239, 1992. `http://www.acm.org/tog/GraphicsGems/`

[361] Voorhies, D., and J. Foran, "Reflection Vector Shading Hardware," *Computer Graphics (SIGGRAPH '94 Proceedings)*, pp. 163–166, July 1994.

[362] International Standard ISO/IEC 14772-1:1997. `http://www.vrml.org/`

[363] *VTune*, Intel Corporation, `http://www.pentium.com/design/perftool/vtune/`

[364] Walker, R., and J. Snoeyink, "Using CSG Representations of Polygons for Practical Point-in-Polygon Tests," *Visual Proceedings (SIGGRAPH '97)*, p. 152, August 1997.

[365] Walter, Bruce, Gün Alppay, Eric P. F. Lafortune, Sebastian Fernandez, and Donald P. Greenberg, "Fitting Virtual Lights For Non-Diffuse Walkthroughs," *Computer Graphics (SIGGRAPH '97 Proceedings)*, pp. 45–48, August 1997. `http://www.graphics.cornell.edu/~bjw/virtlite.html`

[366] Wanger, Leonard, "The effect of shadow quality on the perception of spatial relationships in computer generated imagery," *Computer Graphics (1992 Symposium on Interactive 3D Graphics)*, vol. 25, no. 2, pp. 39–42, 1992.

[367] Watt, A., and M., Watt, *Advanced Animation and Rendering Techniques—Theory and Practice*, Addison-Wesley, Workingham, England, 1992.

[368] Watt, Alan, *3D Computer Graphics*, Addison-Wesley, Harlow, England, (First Edition, 1989) Second Edition, 1993.

[369] Watt, Alan, and Fabio Policarpo, *The Computer Image*, Addison-Wesley, Harlow, England, 1998.

[370] Weghorst, H., G. Hooper, and D. Greenberg, "Improved Computational Methods for Ray Tracing," *ACM Transactions on Graphics*, pp. 52–69, 1984.

[371] Wernecke, Josie, *The Inventor Mentor*, Addison-Wesley, Reading, Massachusetts, 1994.

[372] Westover, Lee, "Footprint Evaluation for Volume Rendering," *Computer Graphics (SIGGRAPH '90 Proceedings)*, vol. 24, no. 4, pp. 367–376, August 1990.

[373] Wiegand, T.F., "Interactive Rendering of CSG Models," *Computer Graphics Forum*, vol. 15, no. 4, pp. 249–261, 1996.

[374] Williams, Lance, "Casting Curved Shadows on Curved Surfaces," *Computer Graphics (SIGGRAPH '78 Proceedings)*, vol. 12, no. 3, pp. 270–274, August 1978.

[375] Williams, Lance, "Pyramidial Parametrics," *Computer Graphics*, vol. 7, no. 3, pp. 1–11, July 1983.

[376] Wilt, Nicholas, Personal communication, 1998.

[377] Winkenbach, Georges, and David H. Salesin, "Computer–Generated Pen–And–Ink Illustration," *Computer Graphics (SIGGRAPH '94 Proceedings)*, pp. 91–100, July 1994. http://www.cs.washington.edu/research/grail/pub/abstracts.html#PenAndInk

[378] Winkenbach, Georges, and David H. Salesin, "Rendering Parametric Surfaces in Pen and Ink," *Computer Graphics (SIGGRAPH '96 Proceedings)*, pp. 469–476, August 1996. http://www.cs.washington.edu/research/grail/pub/abstracts.html#RendParaSurfPenInk

[379] Winner, Stephanie, Mike Kelley, Brent Pease, Bill Rivard, and Alex Yen, "Hardware Accelerated Rendering of Antialiasing Using a Modified A-Buffer Algorithm," *Computer Graphics (SIGGRAPH '97 Proceedings)*, pp. 307–316, August 1997.

[380] Wolberg, George, *Digital Image Warping*, IEEE Computer Society Press, 1990.

[381] Woo, Andrew, "Fast Ray-Box Intersection," in Andrew Glassner, ed., *Graphics Gems*, Academic Press, Inc., pp. 395–396, 1990. http://www.acm.org/tog/GraphicsGems/

[382] Woo, A., P. Poulin, and A. Fournier, "A Survey of Shadow Algorithms," *IEEE Computer Graphics and Applications*, vol. 10, no. 6, pp. 13–32, November 1990.

[383] Woo, Andrew, "The Shadow Depth Map Revisited," in David Kirk, ed., *Graphics Gems III*, AP Professional, Boston, pp. 338–342, 1992. http://www.acm.org/tog/GraphicsGems/

[384] Woo, Andrew, Andrew Pearce, and Marc Ouellette, "It's Really Not a Rendering Bug, You See...," *IEEE Computer Graphics and Applications*, vol. 16, no. 5, pp. 21–25, September 1996. http://computer.org/cga/cg1996/g5toc.htm

[385] Woo, Andrew, Personal communication, 1998.

[386] Worley, Steve, and Eric Haines, "Bounding Areas for Ray/Polygon Intersection," in Eric Haines, ed., *Ray Tracing News*, vol. 6, no. 1, January 1993. http://www.acm.org/tog/resources/RTNews/html/rtnv6n1.html#art3

[387] Wyvill, Brian, "Symmetric Double Step Line Algorithm," in Andrew S. Glassner, ed., *Graphics Gems*, Academic Press, Inc., pp. 101–104, 1990. http://www.acm.org/tog/GraphicsGems/

[388] Xiang, X., M. Held, and J.S.B. Mitchell, "Fast and Effective Stripification of Polygonal Surface Models," *Proceedings 1999 Symposium on Interactive 3D Graphics*, pp. 71–78, April 1999. http://www.cosy.sbg.ac.at/~held/projects/strips/strips.html

[389] Zachmann, Gabriel, "Rapid Collision Detection by Dynamically Aligned DOP-Trees," *Proceedings of IEEE Virtual Reality Annual International Symposium—VRAIS '98*, Atlanta, Georgia, March 1998.

[390] Zhang, H., D. Manocha, T. Hudson, and K.E. Hoff III, "Visibility Culling using Hierarchical Occlusion Maps," *Computer Graphics (SIGGRAPH '97 Proceedings)*, pp. 77–88, August 1997. http://www.cs.unc.edu/~zhangh/hom.html

[391] Zhang, Hansong, *Effective Occlusion Culling for the Interactive Display of Arbitrary Models*, Ph.D. Thesis, Department of Computer Science, University of North Carolina at Chapel Hill, July 1998.

[392] Zwillinger, Dan, "CRC Standard Mathematical Tables and Formulas," 30th Edition, CRC Press, 1995. `http://freeabel.geom.umn.edu/docs/reference/CRC-formulas/`

The following references were added in a corrected printing:

[393] Cabral, Brian, Marc Olano, and Phillip Nemec, "Reflection Space Image Based Rendering," *Computer Graphics (SIGGRAPH '99 Proceedings)*, pp.165–170, August 1999.

[394] McCormack, Joel, Ronald Perry, Keith I. Farkas, and Norman P. Jouppi, "Feline: Fast Eliptical Lines for Anisotropic Texture Mapping," *Computer Graphics (SIGGRAPH '99 Proceedings)*, pp. 243–250, August 1999.

Index

A Bug's Life, 389–390
A-buffer, *see* buffer
AABB, *292–293*, 330, 349
    orthographic projection, 58
AABB/AABB intersection, *see* intersection testing
AABB/plane intersection, *see* intersection testing
AABB/ray intersection, *see* intersection testing
acceleration schemes, *see* speed-up techniques
accumulation buffer, *see* buffer
ACM Transactions on Graphics, 392
adaptive refinement, 158
adjoint, *see* matrix
affine transform, *see* transform
aliasing, *81*, 84, 85, *110*
    jaggies, 81
    polygon edge, 81
    self-shadow, 181
    shadow map, 181
    temporal, 109, 113
    texture, 109, 114
alpha, *86*, 97, 120, 121, 123
    premultiplied, 88–89
    texture, 105
    unmultiplied, 88–89
alpha blending, *86–87*, 94, 96, 123, 377
alpha channel, 19, *88*, 124, 136, 141, 147

alpha LOD, *see* levels of detail
alpha mapping, *see* texturing
alpha test, 377
ambient component, *see* lighting model
angle difference relations, *see* trigonometric formulae
angle sum relations, *see* trigonometric formulae
animation, 48, 52–57, 122, 152, 156, 392
    particle system, 156
    sprite, 147
    texture, *see* texturing
anisotropic filtering, *see* texturing, minification
anisotropic reflection, 143
anisotropic scaling, *see* transform, scaling, non-uniform
anti-shadow, *see* shadow
antialiasing, 81–85, 374
    edge, 85, 87, 94, 95
    full scene, 85
    InfiniteReality, 386
    line, 81
    texturing, 111
Antz, 389
application stage, *see* pipeline
approximate visibility culling, *see* culling
arccos, 420–421
arcsin, 420–421
arctan, 420–421
area calculation, 416

parallelogram, 416
  triangle, 416
ASIC, 385
atan2, 39
axis aligned bounding box, *see* AABB
axis-aligned BSP tree, *see* BSP tree

back buffer, *see* buffer
back plane, 58n
backface culling, *see* culling
backpatch culling, *see* culling
balanced tree, 223, 347, 352
balancing the pipeline, *see* pipeline
banding, 367
banding artifacts, 96, 367
barycentric coordinates, 303
basis, 132, 140, *398–399*, *401*
  orientation, 407
  orthogonal, 401
  orthonormal, 401, 410
  standard, 5, 41, *401*, 410
Bernoulli number, 420
BGR, 367n
bias, 170
bias factor, *see* shadow, shadow map
bilinear interpolation,
    see interpolation
billboard, 123, 147, *152–156*, 219
binary tree, *345*, 346, 352, 355
binormal, 139
BitBLT, 370
bitmask, 311
blending operations, *see* texturing
Blinn and Newell's environment
    mapping, *see* environment
    mapping
Blinn lighting equation, *see* lighting
    equation
blocking, *see* stage blocking
bloom, 151
BLT swapping, 370

blue-screen matting, 89
border, *see* texturing
bottleneck, 8, *241*, 242, 257, 376
  localization, 242–244
    application stage, 243
    geometry stage, 243–244
    rasterizer stage, 244
bottom-up, *see* collision detection
bounding volume, *194*, 290, *322*,
    323, 342
  collision detection, *see* collision
    detection
bounding volume hierarchy, 194, 218,
    290, 322
bowtie, *see* polygon
box filter, 84, 95
box/plane intersection, *see* intersec-
    tion testing
box/ray intersection, *see* intersection
    testing
box/sphere intersection, *see* intersec-
    tion testing
BSP tree, 18n, *197–199*, 200, 210
  axis-aligned, *197*, 223
  collision detection, 344
  intersection testing, 344
  polygon-aligned, *197–199*
bubble sort, *see* sort
buffer
  A-buffer, 83–84
  accumulation, *19*, 83, 105,
    373–374
    antialiasing, 158
    depth of field, 159
    glossy effects, 165
    motion blur, 158
    soft shadow, 172, 173
  back, 18, 370
  color, *17*, 363–365, *365–368*
  double, 17–18, 370–371

frame, *19*, 254, 363, 372
  front, 18, 370
  memory, 374
  pending, 371
  single, 254, 255, *370*
  stencil, *19*, 145, 373–374, 377
    glossy effects, 165
    polygon edge rendering, 185
    projection shadow, 170
    reflection, 163–164
    shadow volume, 176–178
  stereo, 372–373
  triple, 371–372
  W-buffer, 369, 386
  Z-buffer, *18*, 368–369, 386
    shadow map, 179
bump mapping, 99, 136–142
  embossing, 138–142
  height field, 137
  normal map, 138
  overflow, 81
BV, *see* bounding volume
BV/BV intersection,
       see intersection testing

C^n continuity, *see* continuity, C^n
cache, *245*, 247
  collision detection, 348
  display list, 254, 383
  hierachical image, 224
  memory, 118, 247
  texture, 117–118, 382
    Neon, 379
    thrashing, 253, 378
    VISUALIZE fx, 382
cache prefetching, 247
cache thrashing
  texture, 378
camera space, 12
canonical view volume, 14, 58

cathode-ray tube, *see* CRT
cell, *see* culling, portal
center point
  in VRML, 33
centroid, 351
change of base, *see* matrix
chroma-keying, 89
chroma-ranging, 89
ciliary corona, 150, 151
clamp, *see* texturing
clipmap, *see* texturing
clipping, 16
clipping plane, 164–165
closed model, 276
cluster, 194
clustered culling, *see* culling
code optimization, *see* optimization
code profiler, 245
cofactor, *see* matrix, subdeterminant
coherence
  frame-to-frame, 218
coherency
  frame-to-frame, 199, 210
    collision detection, 348,
      358, 360
  spatial, 196
  temporal, *see* coherency, frame-
    to-frame
collision detection, 11, 341–361
  bottom-up, 345
  bounding volume, 349
  bounding volume hierarchy,
    344, 345
  caching, 348
  cost function, 348–349
  dynamic algorithm, 342, 361
  hierarchical, 344–349
  hierarchy building, 345–347
  incremental tree-insertion,
    345–346

k-DOPTree, 354–357
multiple objects, 357–360
OBBTree, 349–354
parallel close proximity, 350
pseudocode, 347
RAPID, 354
rigid-body motion, 342, 352–354, 356–357
SOLID, 350
static algorithm, 342
sweep-and-prune, 358–360
top-down, 345, *346*
  k-DOPTree, 355–356
  OBBTree, 351–352
with rays, 343–344
collision determination, 341
collision response, 341, 344
color, 5, 66, 97
clamping, 80
overflow, 81
scaling, 80
shift, 80
color buffer, *see* buffer
color mode, 365
high color, 366–367
indexed, 365–366
true color, 366–367, 390
color planes, 368
column-major form, 32n, 396
combine functions, *see* texturing, blending operations
communication, 376
compositing, 88, 94, 97
compression, *see* texturing
Computer Graphics World, 392
concatenation, *see* transform
connected primitives, 248, 258
conservative test, 213
consolidation, *see* polygonal techniques

continuity, 54–55
  C^n, 54
  G^n, 54
contour, *see* polygon, contour
contour following, 187
contour lines, 105
contouring artifacts, 96, 367
convex hull, 324, 325, 351, 352, *415–416*
  bounding volume, 354
convex region, *see* polygon
Cook-Torrance lighting model, *see* lighting model
coordinate system
  left-handed, 57, 60
  right-handed, 57, 60, 276, 399
corona, 150, 151
corresponder function, *see* texturing
cos, 419
counter-clockwise vertex order, 28, 192, 276, 278
coverage mask
  A-buffer, *83*, 84
coverage pyramid, 210
CPU-limited, 243
Cramer's rule, 304, *see* matrix, inverse
cross product, 43n, 401–403
  notation, 4
crossings test,
  see intersection testing
CRT, 93, 94, 97, 254, *364–365*, 390
cube/polygon intersection, *see* intersection testing
cubic convolution, *see* texturing, magnification
cubic environment mapping, *see* environment mapping
culling, 191–218, 252
  approximate visibility, 211, 213

backface, 163–164, 192–193, 250
  orientation consistency, 28, 276
backpatch, 194
clustered, 193–194
detail, 203–204
frontface, 193
hierarchical Z-buffering, 206–211
hierarchical polygon tiling, 210
hierarchical view frustum, 194–200, 330
hierarchical view-frustum, 261
hierarchical visibility algorithm, 206–211
HOM algorithm, 211–215
occlusion, 204–218, 263
  representation, 205
portal, 197, *200–203*, 224, 263
  shadows, 179
shadow, 216–218
view frustum, 194–200, 330
view-frustum, 261
VISUALIZE fx, 216
curve segment, 54–55
cut-off angle, 67
cutaway views, *see* texturing
cylinder mapping, *see* environment mapping

DAC, *see* digital-to-analog converter
DAG, *see* directed acyclic graph
dark mapping, *see* texturing
data reduction, *see* simplification, 281
decaling, 123, 163
decimation, *see* simplification, 281
decomposition
  transform, *see* transform
depth buffer, *see* buffer, W-buffer and Z-buffer

depth complexity, 251n
depth estimation buffer, 214
depth of field, 83, *159–160*, 374
depth test, 214, 250, 252, 377
detail culling, *see* culling
detail texture, *see* texturing
determinant, *see* matrix
  notation, 4
diffuse component, *see* lighting model
diffuse surface, 71, 125, 126
digital-to-analog converter, *364*, 386
dimension reduction, *see* intersection testing
direct memory access, *see* DMA
directed acyclic graph, 194
directional light, *see* light source
discrete geometry LOD, *see* levels of detail
discrete oriented polytope, *see* k-DOP
display hardware
  InfiniteReality, 386
display list, 254, 377, 383
display system, 363–365
distance attenuation, *see* lighting equation
dithering, 94–96, 367
division, 245
DMA, 378, 383
Doom, 240
dot product, 43n, *397–398*, 400–401
  notation, 4
double angle relations, *see* trigonometric formulae
double buffer, *see* buffer
driver, 375
dynamic video resizing, *see* optimization, 386

edge antialiasing, *see* antialiasing
edge collapse, *see* simplification
edge cracking, *see* polygon

edge highlighting, *see* line
edge list, 278
edge stitching, *see* polygon
eigenvalue, *see* matrix
eigenvector, 352, *see* matrix
electron beam, 364
embossing, *see* bump mapping
emissive component, *see* lighting model
environment mapping, 127–136
    Blinn and Newell's method, *128–130*, 130, 133
    cubic, 130–131
    cylinder mapping, 143
    limitations of, 135
    paraboloid mapping, 133–134
    specular highlighting using, 134–135
    sphere mapping, 131–133
ERIT's method, *see* intersection testing
Euclidean space, 396–399
Euler angles, 24, *37*, 39, 49
Euler transform, *see* transform
Euler's theorem, 236
Eurographics, 392
explicit surface, *see* surfaces
explosion map, 166
eye space, *13*, 20
eye-relative depth, 92

faceter, 268
false shadow, *see* shadow
fan, *see* triangle fan
far plane, 58, 63, 330
    optimizing, 368
FIFO, *256–257*, 263, 376, 382, 383, 385
fill bounded, *see* fill limited
fill-limited, 244
filtering, 81, 84, 97, 110–111
    for television, 365

fixed-view effects, 157–158
flat shading, *see* shading
flatten transform, *see* transform
fog, *89–92*, 100, 120, 377, 385
    color, 90
    exponential, 90–91
    eye-relative, 92
    factor, 90
    glossy reflection, 165
    linear, 90
    pixel level, 91
    radial, 92
    vertex level, 91
force feedback, 11
fragment, *377*
    A-buffer, 83
    RenderMan, 69
frame buffer, *see* buffer
frame rate, 1, 262, 264, 365, 390
    constant, 224, 228–231
frame size, 364
frame-to-frame coherency, *see* coherency, 194
front buffer, *see* buffer
frontface culling, *see* culling
frosted glass, 165
frustum, 15, 330
frustum intersection, *see* intersection testing
frustum/object intersection, *see* intersection testing
full scene antialiasing, *see* antialiasing

G^n continuity, *see* continuity, G^n
Game Developer, 392
Game Developers Conference, 392
gamma correction, *93–97*, 364, 367
    alpha blending, 96
    compositing, 96

cross platform compatibility, 94
    texturing, 96
garbage instructions, 247
Gaussian elimination, *see* matrix,
    inverse
GDC, 392
generalized texturing, *see* texturing
geodesic curve, 49
geometry board
    InfiniteReality, 383–385
    VISUALIZE fx, 381–382
geometry engine, 375, 376, 382–385
geometry stage, *see* pipeline
geomorph LOD, *see* levels of detail
gimbal lock, *see* transform, Euler
glare effects, 151
global ambient, *see* lighting model
global illumination, 69, 149,
        165, 250
gloss mapping, 135
glossy effects, 165–166
golden thread, 158
Gouraud shading, *see* shading
graphics driver, 375
Graphics Gems, 392
graphics hardware, *see* hardware
Graphics Interface, 392
graphics rendering pipeline, *see* pipeline
greedy algorithm, 237

half plane test, 414
half-angle relations, *see* trigonomet-
    ric formulae
half-plane test, 413
halo, 150
haloing, *see* line
handedness, 399
    left-handed basis, 400, 407
    right-handed basis, 399, 407
hard shadow, *see* shadow

hardware
    geometry stage, 377
    InfiniteReality, 82, 251,
        383–386
    interface, 378, 380
    Neon, 378–380
    PixelFlow, 386
    rasterizer, 377
    Talisman, 116, 148, 182, 386
    VISUALIZE fx, 380–383
HDTV, 94
He's lighting model, *see* lighting model
head, 37, 39, 49
headlight, 78
height field, *see* bump mapping
height field rendering, 188
height field tessellation, 273
height-field rendering, 186
Hermite interpolation,
        see interpolation
hidden line rendering, *see* line
hierarchical Z-buffering, *see* culling
hierarchical collision detection, *see*
    collision detection
hierarchical image caching, *see*
    impostor
hierarchical occlusion map, *see* culling,
    HOM algorithm
hierarchical polygon tiling, *see* culling
hierarchical view frustum culling,
        see culling
hierarchical visibility algorithm, *see*
        culling
hierarchy building,
        see collision detection
high color mode, *see* color mode
highlight, *73–77*, 126–127,
        134–135, 249
highlighting, 183–185, 277, 280, 368
hither, 58n

homogeneous notation, 4, 23, 28, 102, *411–412*
homogenization, 28, 57
horizontal blanking, 372n
horizontal refresh rate,
    see refresh rate
horizontal retrace, *see* retrace
hourglass, *see* polygon
hyperbolic interpolation, 369

identity matrix, *see* matrix
IEEE Computer Graphics and Applications, 392
IEEE TVCG, 392
image engine, 385–386
image pyramid, 206, 209, 212
image size, *see* texturing
image texturing, *see* texturing
image-based rendering, 147–158
immediate mode, 254
implicit surface, *see* surfaces
implicit surface modeler,
    see modeler
impostor, 218–224
    hierarchical image caching, 222–224
    nailboard, 221–222, 224
in-order traversal, 195
incremental tree-insertion, *see* collision detection
indexed color mode, *see* color mode
InfiniteReality, *see* hardware
inline code, 246
inner product, *see* dot product
insertion sort, *see* sort
instance, 12
interactivity, 1
interface, *see* hardware
interference detection, 341
interlacing, 365
internal node, *see* node

interpolation, 14, 48–49, 52–57, 64, 130, 133
    bilinear, *107–109*, 113
    Hermite, 54–56
    hyperbolic, 369
    linear, 53
    trilinear, 113
intersection, *see also* collision detection
intersection testing, 289–340
    k-DOP/k-DOP, 324–325
    AABB/AABB, 324
    BV/BV, 322–329
    crossings test, 307–310
    cube/polygon, 319–322
    dimension reduction, 295
    ERIT's method, 317–318
    frustum, 330–335
    frustum/box, 335
    frustum/sphere, 332–335
    interval overlap method, 314–317
    Jordan curve theorem, 307
    line/line, 336–339
    OBB/OBB, 325–329
        shortened, 350
    octant test, 334, 335
    pick window, 289
    picking, 289–290
    plane/box, 310–312
    ray/box, 299–302
    ray/plane, 306
    ray/polygon, 306–310
    ray/sphere, 295–299
    ray/triangle, 303–306
    rejection test, 297
    rules of thumb, 295
    separating axis theorem, 322, 326, 335
    slabs method, 299–302

sphere/box, 323–324
sphere/sphere, 322
sweeping, 320
three planes, 339–340
triangle/triangle, 313–318
Woo's method, 302
interval overlap method, *see* intersection testing
inverse matrix, *see* matrix
IPEAK, 243, 265
isotropic scaling, *see* transform,
scaling, uniform

jaggies, *see* aliasing
jittering, 29, 85, 165
joint, 53–56
Jordan curve theorem, *see* intersection testing

k-ary, 253
k-ary tree, *345*
k-d tree, *199*, 218, 223n
k-DOP, *293–349*
collision detection, 354–355
k-DOPTree, *see* collision detection

Lambert's law, 71
latency, 259, *262–263*, 265, 372, 390
latitude, 128, 292
law of cosines, *see* trigonometric
formulae
law of reflection, *see* reflection
law of sines, *see* trigonometric
formulae
law of tangents, *see* trigonometric
formulae
layered depth image, 222
lazy creation, 346
LCD, 93n
leaf node, *see* node
left-handed basis, *see* handedness

left-handed coordinate system, *see*
coordinate system
length of vector, *see* vector
lens flare, 150–152
level of detail bias, *see* texturing
levels of detail, *224–231*, 261, 263
alpha, 226–227
benefit function, 229
bias, 113
cost function, 229
discrete geometry, 225–226
geomorph, 227–228
management, 228–231
popping, *226*, 227, 230, 285
range, 225
levels-of-detail
simplification, 285
light cone, 67
light field rendering, 149
light mapping, *see* texturing
light source, 13–14, *65–67*, 78–80,
248, 250
area, 135, 167, 172
directional, 65, 248, 249
drop off, 67
gray-scale, 249
multiple, 80
parallel-point, 249
parameters, 66–67
point light, 65, 248
spot light, *65*, 67, 69, 79, 125,
126, 248
lighting, 13–14, 68
two-sided, 250
lighting equation, 78–81
Blinn, 74
distance attenuation, 78–79
Phong, 73
lighting model, 69–81
ambient component, 77–78

Cook-Torrance, 70
diffuse component, 71–73
emissive component, 80
global ambient, 80
He, 70
local, 78
Oren and Nayar, 70
specular component, 73–77
lighting optimization,
    see optimization
line, 16, 183–186, 412–413
antialiasing, 94, 95
drawing, 7, 251
edge highlighting, 184
fast drawing of, 251
haloing, 186
hidden line rendering, 186
hidden-line rendering, 185
polygon edge rendering,
    184–185
polyline, 248
strip, 248
three dimensional, 413
    explicit, 413
    implicit, 413
two dimensional, 413
    explicit, 412
    implicit, 412
two-dimensional, 412
line integral convolution, 143
line rate, 365
line/line intersection, *see* intersection testing
linear algebra, 395–417
linear independence, 398–399
linear interpolation, *see* interpolation
linear speed-up, 264
load balance, 258, 372, 376
local lighting model, *see* lighting model
LOD, *see* levels of detail

longitude, 128, 292
loop, *see* polygon, loop
loop unrolling, 245
lossy compression, *see* texturing, compression
Lumigraph, 149

Möbius strips, 278
Mach banding, 69, 366, 367
magnification, *see* texturing, 182
manifold, *276*, 278
material, 67–68, 70, 75, 78, 97, 104
ambient parameter, 68
diffuse parameter, 68
emissive parameter, 68
shininess parameter, 68
specular parameter, 68
matrix, 403–411, *see also* transform
addition, 404
adjoint, 35, 407, 409
change of base, 410–411
definition, 403
determinant, 28, 406–407
eigenvalue, 409
eigenvector, 409
homogeneous form, 411
identity, 404, 409, 410
inverse, 24, 26–29, 33–37, 42, 59, *407–409*, 410
    Cramer's rule, 36, 408
    Gaussian elimination, 36, 408–409
multiplication, 405
orthogonal, 34, 36, 38, 47, *410*
rotation, 27, 37
orthographic, *see* projection
perspective, *see* projection
quaternion, 47
rigid-body, 33, 34
rotation, 26
    about an arbitrary axis, 42

from one vector to another, 50–52
scalar multiplication, 404
scaling, 28
shear, 29, 30
subdeterminant, 407
trace, 26, 47, 404
translation, 25
transpose, 24, 29, 34, *404*
notation, 4
VRML transform, 33
matte, 88
MCV USA, 392
memory allocation, 247
memory optimization,
see optimization
mesh, *see* polygon
message-passing architecture,
see multiprocessing
microfacets, 77
minification, *see* texturing
mipmapping, *see* texturing, minification
mirror, *see* texturing
mirror transform, *see* transform, reflection
model space, 12
model transform, *see* transform
modeler, *268–269*
modulate, *see* texturing, blending operations
Mollweide's formula, *see* trigonometric formulae
monitor, 93, 94, 97, 254, *364–365*, 390
Moore's Law, 389–390
mosaicing, *see* texturing, tiling
motion blur, 83, *158–159*, 374
multipass rendering, 92, 97, *119–121*, 367

multiple angle relations, *see* trigonometric formulae
multiprocessing, 260–265, 376
dynamic assignment, 264
message-passing, 260
parallel, 264–265
pipeline, 260–263
shared memory multiprocessor, 260
static assignment, 264
multisampling, 83, 85
multitexturing, *see* texturing
multum in parvo, 111

nailboard, *see* impostor
near plane, 58, 63, 204, 330
optimizing, 368
nearest neighbor, *see* texturing
negatively oriented, *see* handedness, left-handed basis
Neon, *see* hardware
Newton's formula, *see* trigonometric formulae
node, *194–196*
testing, 330
VRML, 32
noise, 165
noise function, *see* texturing
non-commutativity, 31, 43
non-local viewer, 75, *249*
non-photorealistic rendering, 71, 175
non-uniform scaling, *see* transform, scaling
norm of vector, *see* vector
normal map, *see* bump mapping
normal transform, *see* transform
normalize vector, *see* vector
normalized device coordinates, 15, 58
NPR, *see* non-photorealistic rendering

NTSC, 93
NURBS, 274, 287
Nyquist limit, *see* sampling

OBB, *293*, 330, 349
    collision detection, 350
OBB/OBB intersection, *see* intersection testing
OBB/plane intersection, *see* intersection testing
OBB/ray intersection, *see* intersection testing
OBBTree, *see* collision detection
occluder database, 215
occlusion culling, *see* culling
occlusion map, 212
occlusion representation, *see* culling
octant test, *see* intersection testing
octree, *206–207*, 210, 211, 334, 361
opacity threshold, 211, 213–214
optimal placement,
    see simplification
optimization
    application stage, 244–247
    balancing, *see* pipeline,
      balancing
    code, 244–247, 265
    dynamic video resizing, 251
    geometry stage, 248–250
    lighting, 248–250
    memory, 246–247
    money, 258
    multiprocessing,
      see multiprocessing
    overall, 252–254
    pipeline, 241–265
    pipelined processor, 241
    rasterizer stage, 250–251
    transform, 248
Oren and Nayar's lighting model,
    see lighting model

orientation, *see* polygon
oriented bounding box, *see* OBB
orthogonal basis, *see* basis
orthogonal decomposition, 401
orthogonal vector projection,
    see projection
orthogonal vectors, 398
orthographic viewing, 192n
orthonormal basis, *see* basis
outline, *see* polygon, with multiple
    outlines
over operator, 86–88
overlay planes, *368*, 380, 382

packed pixel format, 367
page flipping, 370
painter's algorithm, 199
painting effects, 71
paraboloid mapping, *see* environment
    mapping
parallel close proximity, *see* collision detection
parallel graphics, 265, 375
parallel processing,
    see multiprocessing
parallel projection, *see* projection,
    orthographic
parallelism, 117, 260, 264, 383
    spatial, 260
    temporal, 260
parameter space values,
    see texturing
particle system, 156–157
PDI, 389
pending buffer, *see* buffer
penumbra, *see* shadow
per-pixel operations, 17
per-polygon operations, *see* per-vertex
    operations
per-vertex operations, 11
perp dot product, *4–5*, 336, 338

perspective projection,
    see projection
perspective viewing, 192n, 368
Phong lighting equation, *see* light-
    ing equation
Phong shading, *see* shading
pick window,
    see intersection testing
picking, 197, 289–291, 297
pipeline, *7–21*, 241–265, 378–386
    application stage, 8, *10–11*, 241
    balancing, 254–258
    bottleneck, *see* bottleneck
    conceptual stages, 8
    flush, 253
    functional stages, 9
    gamma correction, 96–97, 364
    geometry stage, 8, *11–17*,
        241, 375
    idle time utilization, 256
    instrumentation, 251, 380, 386
    multiprocessing, *see* multipro-
        cessing
    optimization, *see* optimization
    rasterizer stage, 8, *17–19*, 241
    software, 261
    speed-up, 8
    stages, 8
    texturing, *see* texturing
pipelined
    geometry stage, 377
pitch, 37–39, 49
Pixar, 389
pixel, 17n, 82n, 84, 97
pixel span, 199
PixelFlow, 131, *see* hardware
planar reflection, *see* reflection
plane, 4, 414–415
    explicit, 414
    implicit, 414

plane/AABB intersection, *see* inter-
    section testing
plane/box intersection, *see* intersec-
    tion testing
plane/OBB intersection, *see* inter-
    section testing
plane/ray intersection, *see* intersec-
    tion testing
point, 399, 411, 412
point light, *see* light source
pointer indirection, 247
polygon
    bowtie, 270
    contour, 271
    convex region, 271
    edge cracking, 274
    edge stitching, 275
    edges for joining outlines, 271
    hourglass, 270
    loop, 271
    mesh, *240*, 250, 276
    orientation, 276
    star-shaped, 271
    T-vertex, 275, 377
    with multiple outlines, 271
polygon soup, 342, 345, 351
polygon-aligned BSP tree,
    see BSP tree
polygon/cube intersection, *see* inter-
    section testing
polygon/ray intersection, *see* inter-
    section testing
polygonal techniques, 267–287
    consolidation, 267, 275–281
    simplification,
        see simplification
    smoothing, 279–280
    tessellation, 225, 267,
        269–275, 286
    triangulation, 269, 273

polyline, 248
polytope, 324n
popping, *see* levels of detail
portal, *see* culling
portal culling, *see* culling
positively oriented, *see* handedness,
        right-handed basis
potentially visible set, 200
precision, 170, 184, 252
    color, 96, 114, 366, 367
    depth, 181, 369
    floating point, 246
    subpixel, 275
prefetch instruction, 247
prelit, 250, 272
preshaded, 250, 272
procedural modeling, 144, 268
product relations, *see* trigonometric
        formulae
progressive scan, 365
projection, 14–15, 57–63
    3D polygon to 2D, 306
    3D triangle to 2D, 303
    orthogonal vector, 401
    orthographic, 14–15, 24,
        57–60
    parallel, *see* projection, ortho-
        graphic
    perspective, 14, 15, 24, *60–63*
projective texturing, *see* texturing
projector function, *see* texturing
pseudo color mode, *see* color mode,
        indexed
pull, *376*, 378, 383
push, *376*, 378
PVS, *see* potentially visible set
Pythagorean relation, *see* trigonomet-
        ric formulae

quad strip, 248
quadrilateral mesh

shading, 271
quadtree, 207
Quake, 240
Quake III, 120
quantization, 367
quaternion, 38, 42–52
    addition, 44
    conjugate, 44
    definition, 43
    Euler transform, 49–50
    identity, 44
    imaginary units, 43
    inverse, 44
    laws of multiplication, 45
    matrix conversion, 46–48
    multiplication, 43
    norm, 44
    `slerp`, 48
    spherical linear interpolation,
        48–49, 56
    transforms, 45–52
    unit, 45
QuickTime VR, *149*, 157

radiosity, 69, 77, *250*, 269, 272
    simplification, 285
    T-vertex problem, 275
range-based fog, *see* fog
RAPID, *see* collision detection
rasterizer
    InfiniteReality, 385–386
    Neon, 378–380
    VISUALIZE fx, 382–383
rasterizer stage, *see* pipeline
rasterizer unit, 376
ray, *291*
ray tracing, 131, 157, 161
    reflection, 166
ray/object intersection, *see* intersec-
        tion testing

RealityEngine, 253
reflection, *160–167*
  anisotropic, 143
  curved, 166–167
  glossy, 165
  law of, 161
  mapping, 127
  planar, 161–165, 202
  recursive, 160
  transform, 28, 162
reflection vector, *73–75*, 249
  environment mapping, *128*, 130,
    132, 133, 135, 142
refraction, 85, 134
  glossy, 165
refresh rate
  horizontal, 364
rejection test,
  see intersection testing
rendering equation, 160
rendering pipeline, *see* pipeline
rendering spectrum, 146
rendering speed, 9, 10
rendering state, 253
RenderMan, 69, 143
repeat, *see* texturing
replace, *see* texturing,
  blending operations
retained mode, 254
retrace
  horizontal, 364
  vertical, 364, 370
RGB, 66, 105
RGB color mode, *see* color mode,
  true color
RGBA, *86*, 88, 367
  texture, 105
right triangle laws, *see* trigonometric formulae
right-handed basis, *see* handedness

right-handed coordinate system, *see*
  coordinate system
rigid-body motion
  collision detection, *see* collision
    detection
rigid-body transform, *see* transform
ripmap, *see* texturing, minification
Roentgen display, 390
roll, 37, 39, 49
root node, *see* node
roping, 96
rotation, *see* transform
rotation around a point, 27
row-major form, 32n

S3 texture compression, *see* texturing, compression
sampling, 81, 82, 97, 110–111
  Nyquist limit, *110*, 111, 112
Sarrus's scheme
  cross product, 403
  determinant, 406
scalable, 121
scalar product, *see* dot product
scaling, *see* transform
scan conversion, 17
scan line, 364
scanline interleave mode, 365
scene graph, 195, 203, 290
screen coordinates, 16
screen mapping, 16–17
screen size culling, *see* culling,
  detail
screen-door transparency,
  see transparency
second-order equation, 296
self-shadow aliasing, *see* aliasing
separating axis theorem, *see* intersection testing
separating plane, 216

setup, 17n, 377
  InfiniteReality, 385
  Neon, 378
  VISUALIZE fx, 382
SGI algorithm, *see* triangle strip
shading, 13–14, 68–69
  flat, 68
  Gouraud, 14, *68–69*
    rotation invariant, 274
  Phong, *68–69*, 77, 173
  problems, 271–274
shadow, 160, 167–183
  anti-shadow, 171
  false shadow, 171, 172
  hard, 167
  on curved surfaces, 175–183
  penumbra, *167*, 172, 182
  planar, 167–175
    soft, 171–175
  portal, 179
  projection, 168–171
  pseudo-soft, 181
  shadow map, 179–183
    bias, 182
    bias factor, 181
  soft, 167, 172
  umbra, *167*, 175
  volume, 176–179
shadow culling, *see* culling
shared memory multiprocessor, *see*
  multiprocessing
shear, *see* transform
shininess, *76*, 253
shortest arc, 49
SIGGRAPH, 391, 392
simplification, 226, 252, 267,
  281–286
  cost function, 282–285
  edge collapse, 281, 283
  level-of-details, 285

optimal placement, 281
  reversibility, 285
sin, 419
single buffer, *see* buffer
singular value decomposition, 36n
sketching, 71
slab, 293, 300n
slabs method,
  see intersection testing
slerp, *see* quaternion
SLI, 365
smoothing, *see* polygonal techniques
soft shadow, *see* shadow
software pipelining,
  see multiprocessing
solid
  volume of, 279
solid angle, 217
solid based modeler, *see* modeler
sort
  bubble sort, 359
  insertion sort, 359
  qsort, 278
Sort-Middle, *376*, 383
span, 399
spatial coherency, *see* coherency
spatial parallelism, *see* parallelism
spatial relationship, 160
spatialization, 197
special effects, 145
spectrum
  rendering, *see* rendering spectrum
specular component, *see* lighting model
specular highlight, *see* highlight
specular light map, *see* texturing
speed-up, 8, 263, 264
speed-up techniques, *191–240*, 268,
  see also optimization
culling, *see* culling

impostor, *see* impostor

levels of detail,
  see levels of detail

triangle strip, fan, mesh,
  see triangle strip, triangle
  fan, polygon mesh

sphere, 268, 330, 349

sphere formula, 292, 296

sphere mapping, *see* environment
  mapping

sphere/box intersection, *see* intersection testing

sphere/frustum intersection, *see* intersection testing

sphere/ray intersection, *see* intersection testing

sphere/sphere intersection, *see* intersection testing

spherical coordinates, 128

spherical linear interpolation,
  see quaternion

splatting, 188

spline, 54, 64
  surfaces, 274

spline surfaces, 101

splines, 287

spot exponent, 67

spot light, *see* light source

sprite, *147–148*, 218n
  layered, 147–148

sRGB, 94

stage
  blocking, 256, 263
  starving, 256, 263

standard basis, *see* basis

star-shaped polygon, *see* polygon

starving, *see* stage starving

state changes, 253, 261

state sorting, 261

stencil buffer, *see* buffer

stencil test, 377

stereo buffer, *see* buffer

stereo vision, 373

stereolithography, 268, *276*

stereopsis, 373

stitching, *see* polygon,
  edge stitching

stochastic sampling, 85

strip, *see* triangle strip

STRIPE algorithm, *see* triangle strip

subdeterminant, *see* matrix

subpixel addressing, 179, *369*, 377
  T-vertex, 275

subtexture, *see* texturing

summed-area table, *see* texturing,
  minification

supersampling, *82–83*, 111

superscalar, 11

supporting plane, 216, 306n

surface based modeler, *see* modeler

surfaces
  explicit, *292*
    sphere, 292
    triangle, 292, 303
  implicit, *292*
    sphere, 296

surround effect, 93

swap, 18, 370,
  371 *see* triangle strip

sweep-and-prune,
  see collision detection

sweeping, *see* intersection testing

synchronization
  monitor, 254, *364*, 371, 373

T-vertex, *see* polygon

Talisman, *see* hardware

tan, 419

tangent vector, 54

Taylor series, *see* trigonometric
  formulae

tearing, 370
technical illustration, 71
temporal aliasing, *see* aliasing,
        temporal
temporal coherency, *see* coherency,
        frame-to-frame
temporal parallelism, *see* parallelism
tessellation, *see* polygonal techniques
texel, 103
texture cache, *see* cache
texture memory
        InfiniteReality, 385
texture space, 100
texturing, 18, 99–144
        aliasing, *see* aliasing, texturing
        alpha mapping, 123
        animation, 122–123, 125, 156
        antialiasing, *see* antialiasing
        blending operations
                add, 120
                blend, 120
                modulate, 105
                replace, 105
        border, 103
        bump mapping,
                see bump mapping
        clamp, 103
        clipmap, *118*, 386
        compression, 118–119
                lossy, 119
                S3TC, 118–119
        corresponder function, *100*,
                102–104
        cutaway views, 143
        dark mapping, 124
        decaling, 123
        detail, 143
        distortion, 273–274, 369
        environment mapping, *see* en-
                vironment mapping

        generalized, 100–106
        gloss mapping, 125–127
        glow, 106
        image, 106–117
        image size, 106
        level of detail bias, 113
        light mapping, 124–125
        magnification, 106–108
                bilinear interpolation, 108
                cubic convolution, 107n
                nearest neighbor, 108
        minification, 106, 108–117
                anisotropic filtering, 116–117
                bilinear interpolation, 109
                level of detail, 111
                mipmapping, 111–114
                nearest neighbor, 108
                ripmap, *114*, 116
                summed-area table, 114–116
                trilinear interpolation, 113
        mirror, 103
        multitexturing, 121
        noise, 104
        one dimensional, 105
        perspective correction, 369
        pipeline, 100–101
        projective, 125
        projector function, *100*,
                101–102
        repeat, 103
        specular light map, 126
        subtexture, 111
        three dimensional, 104–105
        tiling, 118, 253
        value transform function, 101
        volume rendering, 143
three plane intersection, *see* inter-
        section testing
throughput, *10*, 241, *262*
tile, *see* texturing, repeat

tiling, *see* texturing
timing, 10, 242, 251, 295
    monitor, 364
top-down, *see* collision detection
trace of matrix, *see* matrix
trade-off
    speed vs. quality, 21, 251
transform, *see also* matrix, 411
    affine, 25
    angle preserving, 33
    concatenation of, 31–33
    constraining a, 39
    decomposition, 40
    Euler, *36–40*
        extracting parameters, 38–40
        gimbal lock, *38*, 49
    flattening the, 248, 249
    inverse, *35–36*
    length preserving, 33
    mirror, *see* transform, reflection
    model, 12–13
    normal, 34–35
    optimize, *see* optimization
    projection, *see* projection
    quaternion, *see* quaternion
    reflection, 28, 193
    rigid-body, *33–34*, 40
        collision detection, 352
    rotation, 26–27
        about an arbitrary axis,
            41–42
        from one vector to another,
            50–52
    scaling, 27–29
        anisotropic, *see* transform, scal-
          ing, non-uniform
        isotropic, *see* transform, scal-
          ing, uniform
        non-uniform, 28
        uniform, 28

shear, 29–31
translation, 25–26
view, 12–13
volume preserving, 30
VRML, 32
transform bounded, *see* transform
    limited
transform limited, 257
transform optimization,
        see optimization
transform-limited, 244
translation, *see* transform
transparency, 85–89, 165, 261
    screen-door, 86, 95
    sorting, 87
transpose
    matrix, *see* matrix
triangle fan, *235–236*, 248, 271
triangle formula, 292, 303
triangle strip, *232–234*, 248, 258
    creating, 236–240
    generalized, 233
    SGI algorithm, 237–238
    STRIPE algorithm, 238–240
    swap, 233
triangle/triangle intersection, *see* in-
    tersection testing
triangulation, *see* polygonal techniques
trigonometric formulae, 421–426
    angle difference relations, 424
    angle sum relations, 424
    double angle relations, 423
    function sums and differences,
        425
    half-angle relations, 426
    law of cosines, 423
    law of sines, 423
    law of tangents, 423
    Mollweide's formula, 423
    multiple angle relations, 424

Newton's formula, 423
product relations, 425
Pythagorean relation, 422
right triangle laws, 421
trigonometric identity, 423
trigonometric functions
    derivatives, 421
    inverses, 420
    Taylor series, 420
trigonometry, 419–426
    functions, 419–421
trilinear interpolation, *see*
    interpolation
triple buffer, *see* buffer
true color mode, *see* color mode

umbra, *see* shadow
unified memory architecture, 378
uniform scaling, *see* transform,
    scaling
unit matrix, *see* matrix, identity

value transform function,
    see texturing
vector, 396
    addition, 396, 399
    geometrical, 399, 411, 412
    length, 400
    norm, 398, 400
    notation, 4
    normalize, 400
    scalar multiplication, 396, 399
    zero, 397
vector product, *see* cross product
vertex array, 120, 259, 276
vertex buffer, 120, 259, 276
vertical refresh rate, *see* refresh rate
vertical retrace, *see* retrace
VESA, 364

video controller, 363
    Neon, 380
    VISUALIZE fx, 383
video RAM, 370
view frustum, *see* frustum
view frustum culling, *see* culling
view independent
    diffuse component, 72
view transform, *see* transform
visibility test, 205
visual appearance, 65
VISUALIZE fx, *see* hardware
    culling, *see* culling
volume
    solid, *see* solid
volume calculation
    parallelepiped-box, 416–417
volume rendering, 104, 143,
    187–188
voxel, 187
VRML transform, *see* transform
VTune, 243, 265

W-buffer, *see* buffer
WAVE Report, 392
window coordinates, 16
wireframe, 185, 187, 252
Woo's method,
    see intersection testing
world space, *12*, 14, 60
world-space, 368
wrap, *see* texturing, repeat

yaw, 37n
yon, 58n

Z-buffer, *see* buffer
z-fighting, 368n
Z-pyramid, 206, *208*
zero vector, *see* vector